Mental Health: The New Law

Mental Health: The New Law

Professor Philip Fennell
Cardiff Law School, Cardiff University

JORDANS

Published by
Jordan Publishing Limited
21 St Thomas Street
Bristol BS1 6JS

Whilst the publishers and the author have taken every care in preparing the material included in this work, any statements made as to the legal or other implications of particular transactions are made in good faith purely for general guidance and cannot be regarded as a substitute for professional advice. Consequently, no liability can be accepted for loss or expense incurred as a result of relying in particular circumstances on statements made in this work.

British Library Cataloguing-in-Publication Data

A catalogue record for this book is available from the British Library.

ISBN 978 1 84661 074 5

Reprinted September 2008, December 2009

Typeset by Letterpart Ltd, Reigate, Surrey

Printed in Great Britain by CPI Antony Rowe, Chippenham, Wiltshire

To my wife and good friend Vic,
a most remarkable woman, and to Danielle and James

PREFACE

Proposals to reform the Mental Health Act 1983 (MHA 1983) have been under discussion for almost a decade, and have culminated in the Mental Health Act 2007 (MHA 2007). Although an amending Act, the MHA 2007 is far reaching in its effects, substantially and radically amending not only the MHA 1983, but also the Mental Capacity Act 2005 (MCA 2005) and the Domestic Violence, Crime and Victims Act 2004 (DVCVA 2004). Mental health law has now attained a level of complexity unrivalled since the days prior to the Mental Health Act 1959, which swept away the tangled body of law in the Lunacy and Mental Treatment Acts, and the Mental Deficiency Acts. Between them the MHA 1983 and the MCA 2005 provide a comprehensive code of mental health legislation, each providing powers to deprive people of their liberty and treat without consent, each based on distinct eligibility criteria for compulsion, and each with its own Code of Practice.

There are currently no Government plans to provide a consolidation Act merging the provisions of the MHA 2007 with the MHA 1983. A consolidated version of the two statutes is provided in Appendix I. The amended provisions of the DVCVA 2004 are reproduced in Appendix 2. The provisions for *Bournewood* authorisations for deprivation of liberty under the new Schedules A1 and 1A to the MCA 2005 are found in Appendix 3 along with the other amendments to the MCA 2005 and to other enactments.

The Government has issued a timetable for implementation of the MHA 2007, which may be found on website of the Care Services Improvement Partnership/National Institute for Mental Health in England.[1] Some provisions are already in force, such as those relating to restriction orders in future being without limit of time, the approval of training courses for Approved Mental Health Professionals and section 26 which places civil partners alongside spouses in the hierarchy for determining the nearest relative.[2] The Government's current intention is to bring in the main changes in the MHA 2007 by October 2008, which is the proposed implementation date for the new definition of mental disorder, the new criteria for detention, and the introduction of Supervised Community Treatment. The provisions for *Bournewood* authorisations for deprivation of liberty under the new Schedules A1 and 1A to the MCA 2005 will be brought into force in April 2009. Some provisions will not be introduced until even later, such as those on

---

[1]   http://www.mhact.csip.org.uk/news/latest-news/commencement-plan.html.
[2]   The Mental Health Act 2007 (Commencement No 3) Order 2007, SI 2007/2798.

Independent Mental Health Advocates (October 2009) and age appropriate accommodation for children (April 2010).

The aim of this book is to explain the new framework of mental health legislation in a way which is accessible not only to professionals but to service users, carers, and interested lay readers.

Professor Philip Fennell
October 2007

LIST OF ABBREVIATIONS

AC	Approved Clinician
AMHP	Approved Mental Health Professional
ANH	Artificial Nutrition and Hydration
ASW	Approved Social Worker
BNF	British National Formulary
CAMHS	Child and Adolescent Mental Health Services
CCfW	Care Council for Wales
CPA	Care Programme Approach
CPS	Crown Prosecution Service
CRC	UN Convention on the Rights of the Child 1989
CSA 2000	Care Standards Act 2000
CTO	Community Treatment Order
DoH	Department of Health
ECHR	European Convention on Human Rights
ECT	Electro Convulsive Therapy
GSCC	General Social Care Council
IMCA	Independent Mental Capacity Advocate
IMHA	Independent Mental Health Advocate
JCHR	Parliamentary Joint Committee on Human Rights
LHB	Local Health Board
LSSA	Local Social Services Authority
MCA 2005	Mental Capacity Act 2005
MHA 1983	Mental Health Act 1983
MHA 2007	Mental Health Act 2007
MHAC	Mental Health Act Commission
MHRT	Mental Health Review Tribunal
NHS	National Health Service
NHSFT	National Health Service Foundation Trust
NICE	National Institute of Clinical and Public Health Excellence
NR	Nearest Relative
PCT	Primary Care Trust
PVS	Permanent Vegetative State

RC	Responsible Clinician
RMO	Responsible Medical Officer
SCT	Supervised Community Treatment
SOA 2003	Sexual Offences Act 2003
SOAD	Second Opinion Appointed Doctor

CONTENTS

TABLE OF CASES

References are to paragraph numbers.

TABLE OF STATUTES

References are to paragraph numbers.

TABLE OF STATUTORY INSTRUMENTS

References are to paragraph numbers.

TABLE OF EUROPEAN AND INTERNATIONAL LEGISLATION

References are to paragraph numbers.

Chapter 1

BACKGROUND

THE MENTAL HEALTH ACT 2007 AND THE MENTAL CAPACITY ACT 2005: TWO DIFFERENT TYPES OF MENTAL HEALTH LEGISLATION

1.1   The Mental Health Act 2007 ('MHA 2007') comes into force between now and October 2008. This was the Government's third attempt this century to introduce major reform of the Mental Health Act 1983 ('MHA 1983'). The MHA 2007 also amends the Mental Capacity Act 2005 ('MCA 2005') to introduce new procedures for deprivation of liberty, and the amendments to that Act are as significant as those to the MHA 1983. These will come into force in March 2009. The MHA 2007 also significantly amends the Domestic Violence, Crime and Victims Act 2004, increasing the rights of victims of crimes committed by mentally disordered offenders, and underlining the position of the MHA 1983 at the intersection between the health and criminal justice systems.

1.2   The MHA 2007 and the MCA 2005 are both mental health statutes in the sense that each provides authority to detain and to treat without consent, albeit in different ways and subject to different safeguards. The MCA 2005 operates on the basis of incapacity due to mental disability and best interests. Decisions about admission to hospital or treatment may be taken on a person's behalf if they lack capacity, which means 'unable to make a decision for himself in relation to the matter because of an impairment of, or disturbance in the functioning of the mind or brain'. Decisions under the Mental Capacity Act 2005 must be made in the incapacitated person's best interests. The MCA 2005 uses the term 'mental disability' meaning any 'Impairment or disturbance of the functioning of mind or brain'.

1.3   The MHA 2007 operates on the basis of mental disorder and risk to self or others. The definition of mental disorder is 'any disorder or disability of the mind'. People with mental disorder may be detained and treated without consent if their mental disorder is of a nature or degree justifying detention and detention is necessary for their health or safety or for the protection of others. There are limits to 'mental disorder' under the 2007 Act, such as that learning disability is not a mental disorder for the purposes of long-term detention, unless there is abnormally aggressive or seriously irresponsible conduct, and addiction to alcohol or drugs are not themselves to be regarded as mental disorders. However, for many mentally disordered people there will be two alternative legal frameworks under which decisions about their care and treatment may be taken out of their hands and exercised by others.

1.4   This raises the problem of the interface between these two codes, each containing as it does powers to detain and to treat without consent, and the question:

> 'When is it appropriate for someone to be given treatment without consent under the Mental Health Act, and when should the Mental Capacity Act be used?'

The interface between the two statutes is discussed in Chapter 6 in relation to deprivation of liberty and in relation to treatment without consent in Chapter 10.

MENTAL HEALTH LEGISLATION

1.5   A basic difference between psychiatry and other branches of medicine, which provides a key *raison d'etre* of mental health legislation is that, in some cases, patients need to be forced, in their own interests or for the protection of others, to accept admission to hospital or treatment without consent. That lack of consent may arise because the patient lacks capacity to consent, or because he or she refuses intervention. Mental health legislation provides authority for intervention without consent. It legitimises detentions carried out in accordance with correct procedure. It provides safeguards against arbitrary deprivation of liberty and arbitrary interference with physical integrity, in accordance with the positive obligations of states to provide effective review under Arts 5 and 8 of the European Convention on Human Rights.[1] The different functions performed by mental health legislation are discussed further below (at para **2.1** below), but a core function is to strike a fair balance between, on the one hand, individual rights to liberty and physical integrity and, on the other, society's entitlement to impose therapy without consent, whether that lack of consent arises from incapacity or refusal.

1.6   The Mental Health Act 1959 ('MHA 1959') still provides the basic framework of contemporary mental health legislation. The MHA 2007 is the fifth significant amendment to the 1959 Act which conferred discretionary powers on doctors and social workers to detain and treat compulsorily persons suffering from mental disorder where necessary for their health or safety or for the protection of others. The Mental Health Act 1959 broke with the past by abolishing 'judicial certification' prior to admission as the safeguard against wrongful detention of non-offender patients. 'Certification' by judicial personnel was replaced with 'sectioning' by mental health experts, with the patient enjoying a right to seek review of the need for detention before a Mental Health Review Tribunal ('MHRT'). 'Sectioning' meant an application

---

[1]   As laid down by the European Court of Human Rights in *Storck v Germany (App no 61603/00)* (2005) 43 EHRR 96.

made by a social worker supported by two medical recommendations presented to, and formally received by, someone acting on behalf of the managers of the receiving hospital.

1.7 The first substantial amendment was by the Mental Health (Amendment) Act 1982, consolidated with the MHA 1959 into the Mental Health Act 1983, which placed more emphasis on safeguards for patients' rights to seek review of detention and compulsory treatment, and the right to be treated in the setting which imposed the minimum necessary restrictions on freedom. The 1982 amendments were also motivated by a desire to comply with the ruling of the European Court of Human Rights in *X v United Kingdom*[2] that there had been a breach of Art 5(4) which entitles people detained on grounds of unsoundness of mind to speedy review of the lawfulness of detention before a court which must have the power to order discharge. The MHA 1983 extended the right to apply to the tribunal to patients detained under s 2 for assessment, and to offender patients subject to restriction orders. It also gave the MHRT the power to direct discharge of a restriction order patient. Previously the MHRT's role was confined to advising the Home Secretary on fitness for discharge. The MHA 1983 introduced a Mental Health Act Commission to supervise the operation of the Act and to protect the rights of detained patients. It also required that an application for detention could come only from the patient's nearest relative or an Approved Social Worker who with special training in the implementation of compulsory powers under the Act.

1.8 The MHA 1983 was further amended by the Mental Health (Patients in the Community) Act 1995 to introduce arrangements for supervised discharge of patients who had been detained under the Act. This Act effectively marked the turning of the tide away from a rights-based focus towards an approach based on risk management, public protection, and ensuring compliance with medication. The 1995 Act was a response to concern about high profile homicides committed by mentally disordered people in the community. The powers of supervised discharge introduced by the 1995 Act were rarely used, being seen as bureaucratic and ineffective in ensuring compliance.

1.9 The third significant reform illustrates the effect of the Human Rights Act 1998 ('HRA 1998') on mental health legislation. The HRA 1998 requires public authorities to act compatibly with Convention rights. A public authority includes any court or tribunal. It also includes any body or person certain of whose functions are of a public nature, which can include people exercising functions relating to detention and compulsory treatment.[3] Section 6(1) of the HRA 1998 makes it 'unlawful for a public authority to act in a way which is incompatible with a Convention right.' Under s 7(1):

---

2   *(Application 7215/75)* (1981) 4 EHRR 188, ECtHR.
3   Human Rights Act 1998, s 6(3). See also *R (on the application of Wilkinson) v Responsible Medical Officer Broadmoor Hospital* [2001] EWCA Civ 1545, CA.

'A person who claims that a public authority has acted (or proposes to act) in a way which is made unlawful by section 6(1) may—

(a)   bring proceedings against the authority under this Act in the appropriate court or tribunal, or
(b)   rely on the Convention right or rights concerned in any legal proceedings.'

The Human Rights Act has produced a significant body of case-law on the MHA 1983. In *R (on the application of H) v London North and East Region Mental Health Review Tribunal (Secretary of State for Health intervening)*,[4] the Court of Appeal granted a declaration of incompatibility under s 4 of the HRA 1998 holding that s 72 of the MHA 1983 was incompatible with the right to review under Art 5(4) of the European Convention on Human Rights ('ECHR'). Section 72 provided that a Mental Health Review Tribunal only came under a duty to discharge if satisfied that the patient was not suffering from mental disorder of a nature or degree warranting detention. The Court of Appeal held that the positioning of the burden of proof on the applicant to satisfy the tribunal of the absence of detainable mental disorder was incompatible with Art 5(4) the effect of which was that the review body had to satisfy itself that the conditions were met in order for detention to be continued. Section 10(2) allows primary legislation to be amended by ministerial order by the minister. This power was used to introduce the Mental Health Act 1983 (Remedial) Order 2001[5] which amended the MHA 1983 so that a tribunal is under a duty to discharge if it is not satisfied that the patient is suffering from mental disorder of a nature or degree justifying detention.

1.10   The fourth major change was the removal from the MHA 1983 to the Mental Capacity Act 2005 of the jurisdiction of the Court of Protection over the property and affairs of people who lack mental capacity because of mental disorder, and the extension of that jurisdiction to cover health and personal welfare decision-making.

1.11   The Mental Health Act 2007 emphasises public protection and risk management. It extends powers of compulsion, introduces compulsory community treatment orders, broadens the definition of detainable mental disorder, increases the range of different professional/occupational groups eligible to exercise powers of compulsion, and entrenches new legislative concepts of compliance with medication as a key goal of mental health legislation. Whilst the MHA 1983 represented a turn towards patients' rights, the main emphasis of the MHA 2007 is on duties of service users to accept medication, to reside in specified places, and to desist from specified conduct, and duties of professionals and Mental Health Review Tribunals in their decision-making to have regard to risk and non-compliance. There are some provisions which arguably increase detained patients' rights of self-determination, such as the prohibition on giving Electro Convulsive Therapy ('ECT') to a patient (detained or not) who retains decision-making capacity

---

[4]   [2001] 3 WLR 512, CA.
[5]   SI 2001/3712.

and refuses treatment. There are also new provisions relating to patient advocacy, and treatment of children in age appropriate environments, but overall the emphasis is on public protection and risk management.

1.12 The MHA 2007 amends the MCA 2005 to introduce a procedure to be employed to detain adults who lack mental capacity and who are not actively resisting detention. In *HL v United Kingdom*[6] the European Court of Human Rights ruled that procedural safeguards are needed where anyone lacking mental capacity is subject to control over their residence, movement, and treatment which reaches a sufficient degree and intensity to amount to a deprivation of liberty. The MHA 2007 repeals the prohibition on deprivation of liberty under the MCA 2005 and introduces two new Schedules to the MCA 2005 (1A and A1) providing a complex procedure to authorise deprivations of liberty of mentally incapacitated adults. This will allow deprivation of liberty to be authorised not just in hospital but also in a privately run residential care home.

POLICY CONTEXT: MENTAL HEALTH LAW REFORM

Mental health services

1.13 Since the 1950s there has been a marked shift of mental health care from a primarily hospital-based model to community care. Between 1954 and 2004 the total number of in-patient beds in psychiatric hospitals fell from a peak of 154,000 to 32,400.[7] During the same period the population increased from 45m to over 53m.[8] These bed reductions have led to a massive upsurge in the numbers of people with severe and enduring mental illness being looked after in the community. Although bed numbers have been decreasing, admissions of psychiatric patients to hospital run at approximately 250,000 per year. Compulsory admissions have been steadily increasing from less than 20,000 per year in the 1960s and 1970s to over 27,000 in 2005–2006. In 2005–2006 there were 27,353 admissions under powers of detention in the Mental Health Act 1983, 1,664 of which were under the offender provisions of the Act. A further 20,000 people were detained under the Act following admission as an informal patient. On 31 March 2006 there were 14,600 patients detained in hospital, of whom 12,100 were in National Health Service hospitals and 2,500 in private hospitals. If there are 32,000 psychiatric beds and at any one time 14,000 detained patients are detained, this suggests the percentage of the in-patient psychiatric population at any one time who are detained is much greater than the level of 10 per cent between the 1950s and 1990s.

---

[6]   *(Application 45508/99)* (2004) 40 EHRR 761, 81 BMLR 131, ECtHR.
[7]   L Warner *Beyond the Water Towers: The Unfinished Revolution in Mental Health Services 1985–2005* (2005), pp 37–47, especially at p 37.
[8]   National Statistics (2007).

1.14 Private sector hospitals now provide over 15 per cent of beds for detained patients. Private sector residential care homes have taken over the provision of non-hospital care for elderly people with mental illness and for adults with learning disabilities. There is no power under the Mental Health Act 1983 to detain people in residential care homes. They may be required to reside there, under guardianship, but Mental Health Act guardianship has not, until now, given the power to deprive someone of their liberty, which is the province of powers of detention. Many elderly patients who would previously have been admitted informally to long-stay NHS hospitals are now being looked after in private residential care homes. Some will be deprived of their liberty, and will require authorisations under the new power to detain people in residential care homes under Schs A1 and 1A to the Mental Capacity Act 2005 introduced by s 50 of the MHA 2007.

1.15 Direct care outside institutions, both physical and emotional, is now provided largely by informal/unpaid carers, 1.5m of whom provide over 20 hours unpaid care per week and 985,000 of whom provide over 50 hours.[9] Cost savings to the State have clearly been a major driver of policy in this area. The average annual cost of a psychiatric bed has increased from £17,500 in 1983 to £70,000 in 2005.[10] The Association of the British Pharmaceutical Industry claims that the ability of psychiatric medication to maintain people in the community has resulted in savings from reduced use of hospital beds in 2001–2002 of £7,434m.[11] The shift towards care in the community and the reduction in hospital beds has led to a desire to ensure that patients may be subject to an effective obligation to take their medication, and carers are expected to play a vital role in ensuring that patients take their medication.

Debate about mental health law reform

1.16 There are three principal drivers of mental health law and policy:

- reducing stigma and promoting social inclusion;

- management of risk to the public and to sufferers themselves; and

- protection of human rights.[12]

Since the 1990s successive governments have pursued a public safety agenda in relation to mental health services responding to concerns about homicides by mentally disordered people. These fears have had a profound impact on mental

---

[9] Commission for Social Care Inspection *The State of Social Care 2005–2006* (2006) (available at http://www.csci.org.uk/PDF/state_of_social_care.pdf).

[10] Answer by John Bowis (Minister for Health) to question from Alan Milburn, House of Commons *Hansard* Written Answers (12 February 1996, p 16) (available at http://www.mind.org.uk/News+policy+and+campaigns/Policy/MindandMA1Advocacy.html).

[11] See http://www.abpi.org.uk.

[12] House of Lords, House of Commons Joint Pre-Parliamentary Scrutiny Committee *Report on the Draft Mental Health Bill* (HL Paper 79(1), HC Paper 95(1), Session 2004–2005), paras 18–22.

health law and policy and produce tensions between the agendas of public safety and social inclusion.[13] The Government has followed its immediate predecessors in pursuing a legislative agenda of increased control over mentally disordered people in the community whilst at the same time, through the National Service Frameworks for England and Wales, promoting policies of social inclusion, combating stigma, and user and carer involvement in decisions about care.[14] Although Convention compliance has been a major issue in mental health law since the 1981 decision of the Strasbourg Court in *X v United Kingdom*, since the Human Rights Act 1998 it has become a direct issue in the courts, and has also come to be a major focus of ethical debate about law reform.

1.17 The risk management/public protection agenda has come to prominence as a result of inquiries into homicides by people who have been receiving psychiatric services. Most notable among these were the killing of Jonathan Zito by a stranger, Christopher Clunis, who suffered from schizophrenia, and the conviction in 1996 of Michael Stone, who had a personality disorder and was addicted to drugs and alcohol, for the murders of Lyn and Megan Russell. Since 1992 health authorities have had a duty to carry out an independent inquiry in any case of homicide or suicide by a mentally disordered person in their care. The inquiry into the care of Christopher Clunis[15] identified a woeful catalogue of failure to provide adequate supervision, that there had been no s 117 after-care plan, and that the authorities had failed to manage or oversee provision of health and social services for the patient. The *Report of the Independent Inquiry into the Care and Treatment of Michael Stone* carried out on behalf of the South East Coast Strategic Health Authority was completed in 2002 but not published until September 2006.[16] The Stone case has been used in support of the argument for removal of the so-called 'treatability test', the precondition of detention of people with personality disorder, that medical treatment in hospital must be likely to alleviate or prevent deterioration in the patient's condition. These and other homicide inquiries have led to a desire on the part of the Government to strengthen the powers of mental health professionals to require patients with mental illness to accept medication in the community, and to reduce the obstacles to detention of people with personality disorder who pose a risk to other people.

1.18 The MHA 2007 marks the culmination of a lengthy period of debate which began in July 1998 when then Secretary of State for Health, Frank Dobson, declared that community care had failed, and that 'a third way' in

---

13   P Fennell 'Reforming the Mental Health Act 1983: "Joined Up Compulsion"' (2001) *Journal of Mental Health Law* (Jun) 5–20.

14   Department of Health *National Service Framework for Mental Health: Modern Standards and Service Models* (2000); Welsh Assembly Government *Strategy Document for Adult Mental Health Services in Wales: Equity, Empowerment, Effectiveness, Efficiency* (2001).

15   Ritchie et al (2004) at p 106.

16   South East Coast Strategic Health Authority (2006).

mental health was necessary.[17] The third way would steer a path between reliance on putting all mentally ill people in institutions – 'out of sight – out of mind' – and community care where people with mental health problems could be 'left off the books' thereby putting themselves and other people at risk. The third way was not greatly different from the policy proclaimed by Stephen Dorrell in the last years of John Major's Conservative Government, replacing community care by a 'Spectrum of Care'.[18] Like 'Spectrum of Care', the 'third way' involves developing a range of services, from the top-security special hospitals which provide care for patients with dangerous or violent proclivities to community provision. This would include:

> 'specialist regional secure units in every NHS Region; accommodation in every locality to provide short-term round the clock nursing care and supervision; assertive outreach teams to keep tabs on people who have been discharged and make contact with people who shy away from getting help; and changes to enable carers and professionals to respond promptly and effectively to the needs of mentally ill patients in the community.'

1.19 The 'third way' included a promise of 'root and branch review' of mental health law:

> 'to reflect the opportunities and limits of modern therapies and drugs ... It will cover such possible measures as compliance orders and community treatment orders to provide a prompt and effective legal basis to ensure that patients get supervised care if they do not take their medication and their condition deteriorates.'[19]

The Secretary of State subsequently appointed a Committee chaired by Professor Genevra Richardson to consider reform of the Mental Health Act 1983. The Minister, Paul Boateng, at the Department of Health press conference launching the Richardson Committee left them in no doubt that, whilst they were at liberty to consider 'root and branch reform', they should remember the Government's key imperative was to 'make clear that non-compliance with agreed treatment plans is not an option'. From the very outset it became clear that imposing an obligation on community patients to comply with treatment, and making that obligation enforceable in some way, were to be the key goals of law reform.

The Richardson Committee

1.20 The Richardson Committee recommended a system that employed a broad definition of mental disorder, but narrower accompanying criteria for compulsion, provided for a single pathway to compulsion regardless of whether

---

[17] During the last years of the Conservative Government policy was packaged in 'point-plans' (usually ten-point plans), for the Blair Government the mantra was 'the third way'.

[18] *The Spectrum of Care – A summary of comprehensive local services for people with mental health problems* and the *NHS Patient's Charter for Mental Health Services* (NHS Executive – EL(97)1).

[19] Department of Health *Press Release 98/311* (29 July 1998).

compulsion was to be in hospital or in the community, and placed the Mental Health Tribunal at the centre of the system of safeguards, authorising compulsion, hearing applications for review of compulsion, and approving the compulsory treatment plan. Under their proposals, after 28 days compulsory assessment, tribunal authorisation would be required for compulsory treatment either in hospital or in the community. The Committee sidestepped the issue of how compulsory powers in the community would be enforced. Clear undertakings had already been given by Minister Boateng at the committee launch, that compulsory treatment in the community did not mean forcibly injecting people on their kitchen tables. The Committee did not say anything about enforcement in the event of non-compliance with medication in the community.

1.21 The Richardson Committee was concerned that the broad concept of mental disorder might lead to a potential 'net widening' effect. Because of this, and their concern to produce a non-discriminatory and principled framework for intervention in the absence of consent, the Committee recommended the introduction of strict accompanying conditions of compulsion, including a capacity test.[20] Under their proposals anyone who lacked capacity could be subject to compulsion if necessary for their own health, or safety, or for the protection of others. Anyone retaining capacity could be subject to compulsion only if there was a substantial risk of serious harm to the health or safety of the patient or to the safety of others. The Committee also proposed a further condition of compulsion that there must be positive clinical measures, which were likely to prevent deterioration or secure an improvement in the patient's condition. Without this, they said, healthcare professionals might be forced 'to engage in activities they would regard as inappropriate and possibly unethical'.[21]

1.22 Richardson attached great importance to the inclusion of principles on the face of the Act which in their view would be educative and would provide a guide as to how provisions should be interpreted. The Committee recommended that some principles should be spelt out on the face of the legislation, whilst others should be reflected in the Code of Practice.[22] They regarded the principle of non-discrimination on grounds of mental health as central to the provision of treatment and care to those suffering from mental disorder. However, they also recognised that it would not be appropriate to express the principle within the legislation itself. Instead, they endorsed the approach of giving considerable emphasis in the Code of Practice to the principle that wherever possible the principles governing mental health care should be the same as those which govern physical health.

1.23 The Committee also recommended that the legislation should state one of its main purposes as recognising and enhancing patient autonomy. They

---

[20] Department of Health *Report of the Expert Committee: Review of the Mental Health Act 1983* (1999), para 5.96.

[21] Ibid, para 5.99.

[22] Ibid, paras 2.14–2.25.

then went on to list ten principles, noting at the outset that they did not intend them to be susceptible of specific enforcement on the part of individuals. The principles advocated included the least restrictive alternative, that necessary care, treatment and support be provided both in the least invasive manner and in the least restrictive manner and environment compatible with the delivery of safe and effective care, taking account of the safety of other patients, carers and staff. The other principles recommended included that there should be a preference for informal and consensual care, reciprocity, participation, equality, respect for diversity, recognition of carers, provision of information, and effective communication.

The Mental Health Bills 2002 and 2004

1.24 In 2000, the Government issued a two-volume White Paper, *Part 1: The New Legal Framework and Part 2: High Risk Patients,*[23] following which the Department of Health ('DoH') and the Home Office together produced the Draft Mental Health Bill 2002, heralded as an example of 'joined-up government'.[24] The 2002 Bill rejected many of the Richardson Committee proposals, among them that the legislation should include a requirement to have regard to principles such as non-discrimination and proportionality. The Government published a Draft Bill based on the White Paper in 2002. The partnership between the Department of Health and the Home Office is the key to understanding the prominence of the public safety agenda in the process of reform. The 2002 Bill retained the proposal for a Tribunal authorised community treatment order, and contained special procedures for detaining so-called 'high risk patients', who had not yet committed an offence but might do so.

1.25 The Government identified the following failings in the MHA 1983:[25]

'The 1983 Act ... fails to address the challenge posed by a minority of people with mental disorder who pose a significant risk to others as a result of their disorder. It has failed properly to protect the public, patients or staff. Severely mentally ill patients have been allowed to lose contact with services once they have been discharged into the community. Such patients have been able to refuse treatment in the community. And it is the community as well as those patients which has paid a heavy price. We also need to move away from the narrow concept of treatability which applies to certain categories of mental disorder in the 1983 Act. New legislation must be clearly framed so as to allow all those who pose a significant risk of serious harm to others as a result of their mental disorder to be detained in a therapeutic environment where they can be offered care and treatment to manage their behaviour.'

---

[23] *Reforming the Mental Health Act, Part 1 The New Legal Framework and Part 2 High Risk Patients* Cm 5016–1 and Cm 5016–2 (2000).

[24] P Fennell 'Joined Up Compulsion: The White Paper on Reform of the Mental Health Act 1983' (2001) *Journal of Mental Health Law* (Jun) 5–20.

[25] Cm 5016–1 (2000), para 1.15.

The Mental Health Act 1983 is described as 'outmoded, based on treatment within hospitals, complex, confusing and lacking in explicit statements of its underlying principles'. There were two primary policy goals behind the White Papers and the 2002 Bill. The first was to introduce more effective compulsory community powers than guardianship or supervised discharge to ensure that patients in the community are subject to an effective undertaking to carry on with medication. The second was to ensure that dangerous severely personality disordered patients can be subject to detention in the mental health system. Both these policy goals have been achieved by the MHA 2007.

1.26 So widespread was the opposition to the public order ethos of the Government's proposals that an umbrella organisation was formed to oppose them, the Mental Health Alliance. The alliance included all the major stakeholders outside the Government, service user organisations, carer groups, the major mental health charities, the Royal Colleges of Psychiatry and Nursing, the British Psychological Society, UNISON, the British Association of Social Workers, the Law Society, the BMA and organisations representing children in mental health care. In broad terms the Mental Health Alliance agenda was to seek restoration of the Richardson Committee proposals, which had largely been taken up in Scotland by the Millan Committee.[26] The Millan Committee recommendations led to the Mental Health (Care and Treatment) (Scotland) Act 2003. The Scottish Act adopts a broad definition of mental disorder, and the model of tribunal authorised compulsion with a community treatment order option. It sets out principles on the face of the Act. It adopts as conditions of compulsion that the judgment of the patient in relation to decisions about the provision of medical treatment is significantly impaired by their mental disorder, and it is a condition of compulsion that medical treatment is available which would either prevent the disorder from worsening or alleviate any of the symptoms or effects of the disorder.

1.27 Meanwhile, in England the Government remained resistant to these ideas. The consultation on the 2002 Bill elicited over 2,000 responses, and the result was a resounding thumbs-down from stakeholders and from the Mental Health Alliance. The Department of Health and the Home Office rejected the evidence of the key stakeholders in their document *Improving Mental Health Law: Towards a New Mental Health Act*[27] which accompanied the Draft Mental Health Bill 2004. The 2004 Bill was introduced in substantially in the same form as the 2002 version, and was subject to strong criticism by the Joint Pre-Parliamentary Scrutiny Committee. Initially, the Government expressed determination to proceed with the 2004 Bill, but later opted to introduce an amending measure rather than a comprehensive new code.[28] One of the main

---

[26] *New Directions: Report on the Review of the Mental Health (Scotland) Act 1984* – laid before the Scottish Parliament by the Scottish Ministers (SE/2001/56, January 2001). Available at http://www.scotland.gov.uk/health/mentalhealthlaw/millan/Report/rnhs-00.asp.

[27] Department of Health and Home Office *Improving Mental Health Law: Towards a New Mental Health Act* (2004).

[28] House of Lords, House of Commons Joint Pre-Parliamentary Scrutiny Committee *Report on the Draft Mental Health Bill* (HL Paper 79(1). HC Paper 95(1), Session 2004–2005); P Fennell

reasons for this decision appears to have been concern that the Mental Health Tribunal would be unable to deal with the caseload engendered by authorising each use of long-term compulsion rather than exercising a the current review function. The Mental Health Act 2007 is an amending Act, grafted on to the basic framework of the Mental Health Act 1983, rather than a comprehensive new code.

The Mental Health Act 2007

1.28   The MHA 2007 will introduce a broader definition of mental disorder, recast the criteria for compulsion, establish new powers of Supervised Community Treatment, and will create the statutory roles of Approved Mental Health Professional ('AMHP') (to replace the Approved Social Worker ('ASW')), Responsible Clinician ('RC') (to replace the Responsible Medical Officer ('RMO')), as well as the completely new role of Independent Mental Health Advocate ('IMHA'). The MHA 2007 also makes changes in relation to nearest relatives, prompted by the ruling of the European Court of Human Rights in *JT v United Kingdom*,[29] introduces into the MCA 2005 new procedures to authorise deprivation of liberty of mentally incapacitated people to comply with the ruling in *HL v United Kingdom*,[30] and changes the process of automatic referral of patients' cases to Mental Health Review Tribunals. The MHA 2007 also provides extra safeguards in relation to Electro Convulsive Therapy ('ECT') and contains new powers (new Part 4A) to give treatment in the community. The Act puts limits on the use of ECT to treat children, and entitles children to age appropriate accommodation subject to clinical need.

1.29   If a person diagnosed with mental disorder needs hospitalisation and treatment in their own interests but also for the protection of others, and they are resisting admission, that person is likely to be detained under the MHA 1983. If a person with mental disorder needs treatment for mental disorder in their own best interests, and they lack capacity, but are not resisting treatment, their care is likely to be managed under the MCA 2005.

POLICY CONTEXT: MENTAL CAPACITY LAW REFORM

1.30   The process of mental capacity law reform effectively began in 1989 with two events. One was the House of Lords ruling in *Re F (Sterilisation: Mental Patient)*[31] enunciating the common law doctrine of medical necessity that doctors have the power and, in certain cases, the duty to give a mentally incapacitated patient treatment which is necessary in her or his best interests.

'Protection! Protection! Protection! The Government's response to the Joint Parliamentary Scrutiny Committee on the Mental Health Bill 2004' (2005) *Journal of Mental Health Law* (Nov) 1–13.

[29]   (2000) 30 EHRR CD 77, ECtHR.

[30]   *(Application 45508/99)* (2004) 40 EHRR 761, ECtHR.

[31]   [1990] 2 AC 1, HL.

The Lords ruling in *Re F (Sterilisation: Mental Patient)*[32] also established the jurisdiction of the Family Division to grant declarations in the best interests of mentally incapacitated adults. The other key event was that the Law Commission began its consideration of decision-making on behalf of mentally incapacitated adults, which culminated in proposals for a Mental Incapacity Bill. Following the recommendations of the Pre-Parliamentary Scrutiny Committee, the Bill was renamed the Mental Capacity Bill to emphasise the presumption that adult patients are capable and the principle of personal autonomy.

1.31 The Mental Capacity Act 2005 and its accompanying rules, regulations and Code of Practice provide a complete legislative framework of decision-making for mentally incapacitated adults. The common law doctrine of necessity enabling treatment without consent and restraint has been codified by ss 5 and 6 which allow a range of steps to be taken on behalf of a mentally incapacitated person by carers, health and care professionals, indeed anyone where it is reasonable for that person to take action and the action is in the patient's best interests. The jurisdiction to grant declarations and to appoint deputies will be taken over by the Court of Protection.[33] The Act recognises the binding nature of 'valid and applicable' advance decisions made by a person, who is capable, to refuse specified treatments should they lose capacity in the future. It provides for a person who is still capable to grant a lasting power of attorney to a person of their choice to take decisions about their property and affairs health and personal welfare, in the event that they become incapable in the future. It confers jurisdiction on the Court of Protection to appoint a deputy, a proxy decision maker on matters concerning property and affairs, or health and personal welfare.

'The *Bournewood* Gap'

1.32 Unlike the MHA 2007, which operates by a procedure requiring applications and supporting medical evidence on statutory forms, like the common law before it, the MCA 2005 operates by providing in ss 5 and 6 a defence in respect of acts of care and treatment done for a person where reasonable steps have been taken to assess capacity, where the person is reasonably believed to lack capacity and where the intervention is reasonably believed to be in the person's best interests. The MCA 2005 cannot currently be used to authorise deprivation of liberty. Under the Mental Health Act 1959 and the MHA 1983 it was accepted practice that patients who lacked capacity and did not resist admission to hospital should be admitted informally, without using Mental Health Act powers of detention. It was only if the incapacitated person persistently and purposefully attempted to leave hospital, or refused to go there in the first place, that powers of detention should be used. This raised the question whether a person is 'de facto detained' without the rights of review

---

[32] *Re F (Sterilisation: Mental Patient)* sub nom *F v West Berkshire Health Authority (Mental Health Act Commission intervening)* [1990] 2 AC 1, [1989] 2 All ER 545, [1989] 2 WLR 1025, [1989] 2 FLR 376, HL.

[33] MCA 2005, ss 15–19.

which attach to the legal status of detained patient, if they would be prevented from leaving if they tried to do so, such as might be the situation of an elderly patient with dementia on a locked ward.

1.33 The legality of this approach was not questioned until the late 1990s when the case of *R v Bournewood Community and Mental Health NHS Trust, ex parte L (Secretary of State for Health and others intervening)* was taken to the House of Lords, and then, as *HL v United Kingdom*,[34] to the European Court of Human Rights. In *HL v United Kingdom,* the Strasbourg Court held that HL, who lacked mental capacity because of autism, and who had been admitted informally to a hospital run by the Bournewood Trust, should have been detained using a procedure prescribed by law.

1.34 Mr L has autism and profound intellectual disability. He lacked capacity to consent or dissent to being in hospital. He had lived with his carers, the Es, for three years. One day he became agitated and disturbed at a day centre, was given valium, and was taken to the learning disability hospital run by the Bournewood Trust and kept there. His doctor instructed staff that he was to be stopped from leaving if he tried to do so. Although he never did attempt to leave the hospital, his carers, the Es, were prevented from visiting, in case he might want to go home with them. He showed symptoms of abandonment, withdrawing, becoming sad, and losing weight. He was also on higher doses of sedative medication in hospital than were ever necessary in the community. His psychiatrist admitted him under the common law doctrine of necessity, rather than using the powers of detention under the Mental Health Act 1983.

1.35 The carers challenged the common law detention on the grounds that the procedure prescribed by law under the Mental Health Act 1983 had not been followed. The Court of Appeal held that L had been detained and that his detention was unlawful because it had not been carried out in accordance with the Mental Health Act. Following this ruling L was discharged from hospital and returned to the care of Mr and Mrs E, where he has continued to make steady progress ever since. The House of Lords in *Bournewood*[35] ruled by a 3:2 majority that HL had not been detained for the purposes of the law of false imprisonment. They also ruled unanimously that, even if he had been detained, there was a power at common law to restrain and detain a mentally incapacitated person in their best interests. The common law doctrine of necessity was extended by the House of Lords to confer a power on a doctor to restrain and detain a mentally incapacitated adult if it was necessary in his or her best interests. The House of Lords decided *Bournewood* just before the Human Rights Act 1998 came into force.

1.36 An application was made on L's behalf to the Strasbourg Court, which held in *HL v United Kingdom* that, where a compliant incapacitated patient is to be deprived of his liberty, this must be done in accordance with a procedure

---

[34]   *(Application 45508/99)* (2004) 40 EHRR 761, ECtHR.
[35]   *R v Bournewood Community and Mental Health NHS Trust, ex parte L (Secretary of State for Health and others intervening)* [1998] 3 All ER 289, HL.

prescribed by law. Whatever the position under English law, the Strasbourg Court held that removal of HL to the hospital, and his retention there without access to his carers, amounted to a deprivation of liberty under the Convention, and had to be carried out in accordance with a procedure prescribed by law, as required by Art 5(1)(e) of the Convention. Moreover, he was entitled, under Art 5(4), to the opportunity, by himself, or through a proxy, to challenge the lawfulness of that detention. The Strasbourg Court refused to treat compliant incapacitated patients as on a par with capable patients who were consenting, and reaffirmed the importance of the right to liberty:

> 'The right to liberty in a democratic society is too important for a person to lose the benefit of Convention protection simply because he has given himself up to detention, especially when it is not disputed that that person is legally incapable of consenting to, or disagreeing with, the proposed action.'

The ruling in *HL v United Kingdom* came at a very late stage in the Parliamentary passage of the Mental Capacity Bill. The Mental Capacity Act 2005 currently provides that the power to restrain a person under s 6 of that Act does not authorise 'deprivations of liberty'. Various last minute amendments to the Mental Capacity Bill intended to fill 'the *Bournewood* Gap' were introduced and then abandoned. The ill-fated Mental Health Bill 2004 was beginning its Pre-Parliamentary Scrutiny. The Government felt that the problem could be addressed in a considered way by waiting for the introduction of mental health legislation, which could either provide for deprivations to take place under a Mental Health Act procedure or could introduce a new procedure by amendment of the Mental Capacity Act. Amendments have now been introduced into the Mental Capacity Act 2005 by the Mental Health Act 2007[36] to plug 'the *Bournewood* Gap' with a procedure to authorise deprivations of liberty of mentally incapacitated adults. *Bournewood* patients will be deprived of their liberty under the Mental Capacity Act rather than the Mental Health Act.

CONCLUSION

1.37 The Mental Health Act 1983 (as amended by the MHA 2007) provides for detention and treatment without consent on grounds of mental disorder and risk to self or to others. The Mental Capacity Act 2005 authorise deprivation of liberty in a hospital if the patient lacks capacity, is not resisting admission, and deprivation of liberty is necessary in her or his best interests. The MCA 2005 also authorise deprivation of liberty in a residential care home of someone who is incapable of consenting, even if they are resisting admission. Chapter 2 summarises the reforms to the Mental Health Act 1983, to the Domestic Violence, Crime and Victims Act 2004 and to the Mental

---

[36] MHA 2007, s 50. This comes into force in March 2009.

Capacity Act 2005, which have been introduced by the Mental Health Act 2007, and the functions that they are designed to perform within the mental health system.

Chapter 2

OVERVIEW OF THE MENTAL HEALTH ACT 2007

FUNCTIONS OF MENTAL HEALTH LEGISLATION

2.1 Since the Mental Health Act 1959 English and Welsh mental health legislation has performed a number of functions, and has followed the same essential framework. The basic structure of powers will endure under the Mental Health Act 2007, and the Act continues to perform the following functions:

(1) defining mental disorder;

(2) providing powers to detain and treat without consent;

(3) providing compulsory community powers;

(4) providing safeguards against arbitrary detention or unnecessary treatment (particularly upholding Convention Rights under Arts 3, 5 and 8);

(5) setting out principles for the treatment of mentally disordered people;

(6) providing powers and safeguards in relation to treating children for mental disorder;

(7) providing a framework for transfer of patients in lawful custody from one jurisdiction to another; and

(8) providing effective protection for mentally disordered people under the criminal law.

The function of providing a framework for managing property and affairs of mentally disordered people has been removed from Part 7 of the Mental Health Act 1983 and is now dealt with under the Mental Capacity Act 2005.

DEFINING 'MENTAL DISORDER'

2.2 The first function is to define the scope of the term 'mental disorder' and thereby delineate broadly the population who may be subject to detention.

Part 1 of the MHA 1983 defined 'mental disorder'. It followed the pattern of the MHA 1959 by having a general definition of mental disorder for the up to 28 day power of admission for assessment (mental illness, psychopathic disorder, arrested or incomplete development of mind and 'any other disorder or disability of mind'). A narrower, more elaborate system of subcategories applied to admission for treatment for up to six months: mental illness, and severe mental impairment (sometimes referred to as the major disorders), and mental impairment and psychopathic disorder. All of these, bar mental illness, required an association with abnormally aggressive or seriously irresponsible conduct. Someone with a learning disability or a personality disorder unaccompanied by abnormally aggressive or seriously irresponsible conduct could not be detained for treatment, but could be detained for up to 28 days' assessment.

2.3   A further drawback of the subcategories was that detention on grounds of mental impairment or psychopathic disorder could only take place if the patient was 'treatable' in the sense that medical treatment in hospital was likely to alleviate or prevent deterioration in his condition. This requirement has been construed generously by the courts. In *Reid v Secretary of State for Scotland*[1] the House of Lords held that the term was wide enough to include treatment which alleviates or prevents deterioration in the symptoms of the disorder, not the disorder itself, and that anger management classes in the structured environment of a high security hospital were likely to be preventing deterioration in the patient's mental condition. This was because they resulted in the patient being less physically aggressive, and if he were not in hospital he would probably commit criminal offences which would lead to an inevitable deterioration in his condition. As Richard Jones puts it, the interpretation in the case law of the treatability test was so broad that 'it is difficult to imagine the circumstances that would cause a patient to fail it'.[2] In *Reid v Secretary of State for Scotland*[3] Lord Hope held that the provision gives effect to the policy that people with psychopathic disorder or mental impairment 'should only be detained under compulsory powers if there is a good prospect that the treatment they will receive there will be of benefit'. His Lordship went on to hold that the term 'treatment' was 'wide enough to include treatment which alleviates or prevents deterioration of the symptoms of the mental disorder'.[4] Lord Hutton[5] held that the test could be satisfied where 'anger management in the structured setting of the State Hospital in a supervised environment resulted in the patient being less physically aggressive'. Despite the breadth of the treatability test, the Government saw it as a fault-line in the legislation which enables psychiatrists to decide that a person with psychopathic disorder who might be dangerous to others should not be detained because they are not treatable. The effect of the case-law is that a person who is being contained as a detained patient in the structured environment of a hospital may be held to be

---

[1]   [1999] 1 All ER 481, HL.
[2]   RM Jones *Mental Health Act Manual* (Sweet and Maxwell, 10th edn, 2006), p 42.
[3]   [1999] 1 All ER 481 at 493, HL.
[4]   [1999] 1 All ER 481 at 497, HL.
[5]   [1999] 1 All ER 481 at 515, HL.

treatable. Nevertheless, in the MHA 2007, in addition to adopting a general definition of mental disorder – 'any disorder or disability of the mind' – for all durations of detention, the Government has decided to replace the current treatability test with a new requirement in s 4 of the MHA 2007 that treatment is available for the patient which is 'appropriate in his case, taking into account the nature and degree of the mental disorder and all other circumstances of his case'. This is discussed further below under criteria for detention.

2.4   The MHA 2007 applies one broad definition – 'any disorder or disability of the mind' – to all types of detention whether as an offender or a non-offender patient. This new definition is modelled on the 'catch all' definition used for admission for assessment: 'any other disorder or disability of mind'. The scope of admission for assessment under s 2 is not significantly altered by the MHA 2007. A person with a learning disability unaccompanied by abnormally aggressive or seriously irresponsible conduct can still be admitted under s 2. It remains the case under the MHA 2007 that a person with a learning disability[6] can only be detained for treatment under s 3 if the disability is associated with abnormally aggressive or seriously irresponsible conduct on his part. But the term psychopathic disorder disappears from the Act. By broadening and simplifying the definition of mental disorder to 'any disorder or disability of the mind', the 2007 Act removes many of the perceived obstacles to detention of people with personality disorder. No longer is abnormally aggressive or seriously irresponsible conduct necessary before someone with a personality disorder may be detained. They may be detained for treatment if appropriate treatment including nursing and psychological treatment is available and provided detention is deemed necessary for their health or safety or for the protection of others.

2.5   The MHA 2007 also removes all exclusions other than 'dependence on alcohol or drugs' neither of which may be considered to be a disorder or disability of the mind. By removing the sexual deviancy exclusion the Government intends to bring paraphilia (and hence paedophilia) clearly within the scope of detainable mental disorders. They were concerned that the sexual deviancy exclusion enabled paedophiles to avoid detention under mental health legislation, where this might be otherwise deemed necessary on grounds of risk to others. The changes to the definition of mental disorder and the impact of the change from treatability to availability of appropriate treatment are discussed in full in Chapter 3.

---

6   Defined as a state of arrested or incomplete development of the mind which includes significant impairment of intelligence and social functioning: MHA 1983, s 1(4), as inserted by MHA 2007, s 2(3).

PROVIDING POWERS TO DETAIN AND TREAT WITHOUT CONSENT

2.6   The second function is providing a framework of powers whereby health and social care professionals may detain and treat mentally disordered people without consent. Powers to detain non-offender patients are provided in Part 2 of the Act, powers to detain offenders in Part 3. The first key task of a framework of compulsory powers is to specify which professional groups are eligible to exercise those powers, and who is eligible to provide the evidence necessary to justify detention. The second is to set the criteria for detention or compulsory powers in the community. Chapter 4 explains and discusses the statutory roles of the Approved Mental Health Professional ('AMHP') and the Responsible Clinician ('RC'). Chapter 5 deals with the role of relatives, carers, Independent Mental Health Advocates and Hospital Managers. Chapter 6 deals with powers to detain patients under Part 2 of the Mental Health Act 1983, and the power to deprive mentally incapacitated adults of their liberty under the changes introduced to the Mental Capacity Act 2005 by the MHA 2007.

Who may exercise compulsory powers? The statutory roles: Approved Mental Health Professionals, Responsible Clinicians, Nearest Relatives and Independent Mental Health Advocates

2.7   Although it was and remains possible for an application for detention or guardianship to come from the patient's nearest relative, it would normally come from a specially trained Approved Social Worker, whose role was to ensure that the necessary treatment cannot be provided without detention, to see that the section is effectively carried out, medical recommendations are obtained, and the patient is safely 'taken and conveyed' in legal custody (with police support if necessary) to the hospital. In response to concerns about poor decision-making by social workers under the MHA 1959, the MHA 1983 required an increased mandatory statutory period of training before a person could become an Approved Social Worker ('ASW') entitled to apply for a person's detention under the Act.

Approved Mental Health Professional ('AMHP')

2.8   The MHA 2007 now opens the power to apply for detention to 'Approved Mental Health Professionals' who need not be a social worker but could be a nurse, psychologist, or occupational therapist with appropriately recognised training. The Act requires an application for non-emergency admission to be supported by two medical recommendations, to the effect that the patient is suffering from mental disorder of a nature or degree warranting detention in the interests of his health or safety or for the protection of others. One of the recommending doctors must be approved under s 12 of the MHA 1983 as having special experience in the diagnosis or treatment of mental disorder. The evidential requirement of medical recommendations from doctors will remain under the 2007 Act.

Responsible Clinician

2.9   The second major professional role change affects those eligible to be the person in charge of decisions about treatment without consent and prolongation of detention, who, under every Act since 1959 has been 'the responsible medical officer' ('RMO'), who had to be a doctor. The RMO goes, to be replaced by the 'responsible clinician' ('RC') who need not be a doctor but could be a nurse, psychologist, an occupational therapist, or a social worker, provided they have undergone responsible clinician training. The MHA 1959 devolved the functions of being in charge of treatment and renewing detention from the Medical Superintendent to the RMO, but at the same time preserved the medical monopoly of power. The MHA 2007 dismantles that monopoly, by conferring the power to be in charge of treatment and detention on other professions. The legal effects of these changing professional roles will be discussed in detail in Chapter 4.

Nearest Relative

2.10   The MHA 2007 has also introduced reforms affecting the non-professional role of the 'nearest relative' who has the power to apply for compulsory admission, to seek discharge and challenge the patient's detention before a Mental Health Review Tribunal ('MHRT'). The identity of the nearest relative is determined according to a statutory list, beginning with husband or wife, father or mother, son or daughter. The 2007 Act modifies that list to recognise civil partners, as well as same or opposite sex couples living together as man and wife.[7] The rights of the nearest relative remain essentially unchanged by the 2007 Act. The Act does however introduce a new possibility for the patient to seek displacement of an unsuitable nearest relative. This is necessitated by successful challenges in the European Court of Human Rights and in the English Courts under the Human Rights Act 1998.

2.11   The nearest relative has a right under Art 8 of the European Convention on Human Rights to respect for their family life with the patient and vice versa. But the patient also has the right to respect for privacy under Art 8. In *JT v United Kingdom*[8] the applicant complained was that her nearest relative according to the statutory formula was her mother, who was living with a man who JT alleged had abused her in the past. Each time JT applied for discharge from detention to a MHRT, the tribunal rules required that her mother, as nearest relative, be informed. JT objected to her mother being given information about her life. The European Commission on Human Rights held that the absence in the MHA 1983 of any possibility for a patient to apply to

---

[7]   See *R (on the application of SSG) v Liverpool City Council* at http://www.dh.gov.uk/en/ Policyandguidance/Healthandsocialcaretopics/Mentalhealth/DH_4077674.

[8]   (2000) 30 EHRR CD 77, ECtHR.

the County Court to change her nearest relative was an interference with her right to respect for her private life under Art 8(1) of the European Convention and could not be justified under Art 8(2). A friendly settlement was reached whereby the UK Government undertook to:

(1)   enable a patient to apply to the court to replace his nearest relative where there were reasonable grounds to object to a particular individual acting in that capacity; and

(2)   prevent certain persons from acting as the nearest relative of the patient.

Subsequently, the English High Court in *R (on the application of M) v Secretary of State for Health*[9] granted a declaration of incompatibility under the Human Rights Act 1998 that the absence of a right for a patient to seek displacement of a nearest relative was incompatible with Art 8.

2.12   Under the MHA 2007 the nearest relative will retain the rights set out in the MHA 1983, and the patient will have the right to apply to the county court to displace a nearest relative on grounds of unsuitability, as necessitated by the friendly settlement in *JT v United Kingdom*. In *R (on the application of E) v Bristol City Council*[10] the Court held that in order to ensure compatibility with Art 8 the Approved Social Worker's duty to consult the nearest relative about compulsory admission 'if practicable' does not apply if the patient objects to that person being consulted as the nearest relative. This remains the law under the 2007 Act. The AMHP does not have a duty to consult the NR if the patient is capable and objects, but the NR remains the NR until displaced or until they confer their function on someone else. The Nearest Relative is discussed in Chapter 5.

Independent Mental Health Advocates

2.13   Section 30(2) introduces new ss 130A–130D placing a duty upon the Secretary of State (or Welsh Assembly) to provide advocacy services for all detained patients (except those held under ss 4, 5, 135 or 136), guardianship patients and patients subject to community treatment orders. Advocacy must include help in obtaining information about and understanding the provisions of the Act which subject him to compulsion, any conditions or restrictions, what medical treatment is being given or is proposed and why, the requirements of the Act which apply in relation to that treatment. Advocacy must also include help in obtaining information about and understanding any rights which may be exercised by or in relation to him and help by way of representation or otherwise in exercising those rights. Section 130D places a duty upon hospital managers and in certain cases responsible clinicians to provide qualifying patients with information that advocacy services are available. Advocates will have the right to meet patients in private, and to meet

---

9   [2003] EWHC 1094 (Admin).
10   [2005] EWHC 74 (Admin), [2005] MHLR 83.

professionals. They will have access to patient records only where a capable patient gives consent, or, in the case of an incapable patient, where access would not conflict with a decision of a health care attorney, a deputy, or the Court of Protection, and the person holding the records agrees that the records are relevant to the matter at issue and access is 'appropriate'. Advocacy services are discussed in Chapter 5.

The criteria for detention in hospital

Human rights

2.14 The second key aspect of a system of compulsory powers is that it sets the criteria which must be satisfied before detention may take place. Article 5(1) of the Convention on Human Rights protects against arbitrary detention. Article 5(1)(e) reflects the attitudes of the 1950s, authorising detention on grounds of unsoundness of mind, alcoholism, addiction to drugs, vagrancy, or to prevent the spread of infectious diseases, provided that detention takes place in accordance with a procedure prescribed by law. The Strasbourg Court has built additional safeguards through its jurisprudence. In 1979 in *Winterwerp v Netherlands*[11] the Court laid down three important substantive and procedural requirements for lawful detentions of persons of unsound mind:

(1) except in emergencies, the individual must reliably be shown to be suffering from a true mental disorder on the basis of objective expertise;

(2) the mental disorder must be of a kind or degree justifying confinement;

(3) those carrying out the detention must satisfy themselves at intervals that the criteria for detention continue to be met.[12]

Winterwerp also established that mere deviancy from society's norms is not to be regarded as mental disorder, and detention must be a proportionate response to the patient's circumstances.[13]

2.15 *Winterwerp* laid down two procedural requirements. First, that the objective medical evidence be presented to a competent authority. In the case of non-offender patients the competent authority is the hospital managers, with offenders it is the sentencing court. The second requirement is that the detaining authority must review the continued need for detention.

---

[11] *(Application 6301/73)* Series A, No 33, p 16, para 37, ECtHR.

[12] *Winterwerp v The Netherlands* ibid; *X v United Kingdom (Application 7215/75)* (1981) 4 EHRR 188, ECtHR; and *Van der Leer v Netherlands (Application 11509/85)* (1990) 12 EHRR 567, ECtHR.

[13] *Litwa v Poland (Application 26629/95)* (2000) 63 BMLR 199, ECtHR.

Non-offender patients

2.16 The *Winterwerp* requirements are met in the detention procedures for non-offenders under the Mental Health Acts 1983 and 2007. Admission is by administrative process, based on professional expertise and checks and balances. Only an Approved Mental Health Professional ('AMHP') (with specialised mental health training) or the patient's nearest relative may apply for detention, supported by two medical recommendations, one from a person with psychiatric expertise. The AMHP presents objective medical evidence of a true mental disorder of a kind or degree warranting detention to a competent authority, the hospital managers. The competent authority has the duty to review the detention at reasonable intervals and to discharge if the criteria are not met. An application may only be made if the treatment cannot be provided without detention, reflecting the principle of proportionality. Nothing in Art 5 or the case-law requires admission to be authorised by a court or tribunal, so the current admission procedures are Convention compliant.[14]

2.17 The criteria which must be met for detention for treatment of a non-offender patient under s 3 of the MHA 1983 will now be:

(1)   that the patient is suffering from mental disorder of a nature or degree which makes it appropriate for him to receive medical treatment in a hospital;

(2)   that it is necessary for the health or safety of the patient or for the protection of other persons that he should receive such treatment and it cannot be provided unless he is detained; and

(3)   that appropriate treatment is available to him.

The major differences introduced by the MHA 2007 are:

(1)   the removal of the subcategories of mental disorder which apply to detention for treatment under s 3; and

(2)   the replacement of the so-called 'treatability test' with the test of availability of appropriate treatment.

Appropriate treatment is available

2.18 Medical treatment for mental disorder is redefined in s 145. It includes nursing and also psychological intervention and specialist mental health habilitation, rehabilitation and care. Psychological interventions are expressly mentioned for the first time. These include psychotherapy and other interactive treatments requiring co-operation from the patient, often the main treatments used for people with personality disorders. The 'treatability test' under the

---

[14]   *HL v United Kingdom* (2004) 40 EHRR 761, ECtHR.

MHA 1983 applied to psychopathic disorder and mental impairment. The doctor had to certify that medical treatment was likely to alleviate or prevent deterioration in the patient's condition, which would be hard to do if the patient was resolutely not co-operating. This might happen if a person with a personality disorder refused to engage with cognitive behaviour therapy. Treatment might be available and appropriate but unlikely to make any difference if the patient were refusing to participate. The MHA 2007 requires only that appropriate treatment is available. Treatment must have the *purpose* of alleviating or preventing 'a worsening of the disorder or more of its symptoms or manifestations'.[15] But it need not be likely to achieve those purposes. The patient's refusal to accept treatment can no longer be an obstacle to detention, as long as the treatment is available.

2.19 The 'treatability issue' has generated massive debate for more than a decade. It is not overdramatic to say that opinion leaders within the psychiatric profession see the issue as crucial in preserving their role as doctors rather than agents of state policies of preventive detention. Service users see the issue in terms of entitlement to therapeutic intervention rather than containment. The Government perceives the treatability test as a serious fault-line in mental health legislation which gave psychiatrists discretion not to detain people with personality disorders who pose a risk to others, or to themselves.

2.20 The general definition of mental disorder means the welcome disappearance of the stigmatising term psychopathic disorder from the face of the Act. It also preserves and arguably extends the possibility to detain people with a personality disorder, who are believed to pose a risk to self or others. If violent conduct is a manifestation of their disorder, available appropriate treatment of that manifestation might include nursing supervision, as well as psychological interventions such as anger management or cognitive behaviour therapy. It could also include specialist mental health habilitation, rehabilitation and care. These changes have set the legal scene for increased use of mental health legislation to detain people who have not yet committed a crime but who have a personality disorder and pose a risk to self or to others. This will be done by removing various sources of discretionary power not to detain, such as the treatability test, and the exclusions in relation to sexual deviancy and other immoral conduct.

The Bournewood Gap: deprivation of liberty of mentally incapacitated adults

2.21 Section 50 of the MHA 2007 is intended to take the consequences of *HL v the United Kingdom*. This comes into force in March 2009. Section 50(4) repeals the provisions in the MCA 2005 prohibiting deprivations of liberty. It inserts new ss 4A, 4B and 16A into the Mental Capacity Act 2005. These provisions make it lawful to deprive a person of their liberty only if a standard or urgent authorisation (under the new Schs A1 and 1A to the 2005 Act) is in

---

[15]   MHA 1983, s 145(4), as inserted by MHA 2007, s 7(3).

force or the Court of Protection has ordered a deprivation of liberty in deciding a personal welfare matter. Standard or urgent authorisations may be sought after the person has already been deprived of his or her liberty. The procedures for *Bournewood* authorisations as they have come to be known, will authorise deprivations of liberty in hospitals and care homes. They will extend the scope of powers of detention considerably and bring into the system many patients who would hitherto have been dealt with informally. It is open to debate whether the new procedures will meet the requirements of the case-law from the Strasbourg Court and from the English Courts under the Human Rights Act 1998. It is also suggested that a more effective system might be to build on the reforms to guardianship in the 2007 Act and to use guardianship to authorise deprivation of liberty. These complex procedures are explained and discussed in Chapter 6 which deals with all the Procedures for Detention of Non-offender Patients under the Mental Health Act and the Mental Capacity Act.

Offender patients

2.22   Part 3 of the MHA 1983 provides a framework of powers to sentence to a hospital order with or without restrictions, to remand to hospital for reports or treatment, and to transfer mentally disordered prisoners from prison to hospital. The main changes flow from the definition of mental disorder – remand for treatment, sentencing and transfer powers were limited to patients suffering from various subcategories of mental disorder. These limitations have been removed by the substitution of 'any disorder or disability of mind' for references to the subcategories wherever they appeared under the 1983 Act. As is the case with non-offenders, the scope of powers to detain mentally disordered offenders is further increased by replacing the 'treatability test' with the test of 'availability of appropriate treatment'.

2.23   Section 37 enables offenders with mental disorder to be sentenced to hospital orders for six months renewable. The new wide definition of mental disorder and the test of availability of appropriate treatment apply to this power. Section 41 provides that a Crown Court judge who considers it necessary may impose restrictions on discharge. One significant change introduced by the MHA 2007 is that whilst under the MHA 1983 these restrictions could be time limited or without limit of time, henceforth they will automatically be without limit of time. The restrictions are that the patient may not be granted leave of absence or discharge from hospital, nor may he be transferred to another hospital without the leave of the Mental Health Unit in the Home Office, acting on behalf of the Home Secretary. The reforms to Part 3 of the 1983 Act are discussed in Chapter 7 which deals with mentally disordered offenders.

The criteria which must be met for compulsory powers in the community

2.24 Under the Mental Health Act 1983 there were three compulsory powers over patients in the community:

(1) extended leave under s 17;

(2) guardianship under s 7;

(3) after-care under supervision under ss 25A–25J.

Neither guardianship nor after-care under supervision are much used.[16] Section 17 leave is the most frequently used vehicle for imposing control over patients in the community. The reason for its attractiveness is its simplicity. It is granted and may be revoked on the authority of a single clinician. The ultimate sanction for non-compliance is detention, if the clinician considers continued non-compliance will make it necessary to recall the patient for the patient's health or safety or for the protection of others. The difficulty is that, in order for recall to be an effective sanction, there must be a bed available for the patient to be recalled to.

2.25 Under the MHA 1959 and the MHA 1983, s 17 leave was granted by the Responsible Medical Officer, usually a consultant psychiatrist, and this power was used to provide the equivalent of a community treatment order, by granting leave subject to a condition of compliance with medication. Under the MHA 2007, s 17 leave is granted by the responsible clinician ('RC'), who need not be a doctor. A patient may be granted leave subject to such conditions as the RC thinks necessary in the interests of the patient or for the protection of other persons. Under the 1959 and 1983 Acts this power has been exercised by the Responsible Medical Officer, under the 2007 Act it passes to the Responsible Clinician. The patient remains liable to be detained. This means that the patient is still subject to the section authorising detention, and may be returned to hospital and to detained patient status if deemed necessary by the Responsible Clinician for his or her health or safety or for the protection of others. The case-law on s 17 leave centres around the need, if this is arrangement is to be long-term, for renewal of the section authorising the patient's detention, raising questions about the lawfulness of renewing a section authorising detention when the patient is living in the community? Current case-law holds that the patient's liability to detention may be renewed

---

[16] At any time about 1,000 people are subject to Mental Health Act guardianship in England and Wales. Jonathan Bindman's *Evaluation of Supervised Discharge and Guardianship* (published by the Department of Health in 2002) found that: 'Both measures continue to be used only for a very small proportion of patients under the care of mental health services and their apparent effectiveness is likely to be a consequence of careful selection of patients.' The numbers under supervised discharge went from 160 in 1997 to 596 in 1999 (Department of Health Research Findings Register – see http://www.refer.nhs.uk/ViewRecord.asp?ID=703).

repeatedly while he or she continues to live in the community, so long as the patient needs some treatment in hospital, not necessarily as an in-patient.[17]

2.26 Chapter 4 of the MHA 2007 repeals ss 25A–25J of the MHA 1983 on after-care under supervision and replaces them with new ss 17A–17G introducing the new 'community treatment orders' or supervised community treatment ('SCT'). After-care under supervision was introduced by the Mental Health (Patients in the Community) Act 1995 in a climate of concern about homicides by people receiving treatment for mental disorder in the community, and whilst the practice of renewing detention of patient on s 17 leave was subject to challenge in the courts. After-care under supervision was limited to patients who were not offenders subject to Home Office restrictions, and who had been detained following admission for treatment for up to six months, under a hospital order or following transfer from prison. Such a patient could be placed under supervised discharge and could be subject to various requirements including residing at a specified place and attending a specified place to receive medical treatment. A patient who did not attend could be 'taken and conveyed' in custody to that place. The patient could then be held at that place while a decision was taken whether they could be given treatment under common law using reasonable force, or whether they needed to be detained under the 1983 Act.

2.27 The low use of supervised community treatment is generally attributed to the fact that, by comparison with s 17 leave, the procedural requirements are onerous, and there was a lack of clarity about what should happen when a patient is taken and conveyed to the place of treatment and still refuses the treatment. The ultimate sanction – re-detention – could be employed if the professionals went through the sectioning procedure afresh. By contrast, under s 17 re-detention by recall requires the authority of one clinician. Scarcely surprising then, that s 17 remains the favoured option. Particularly so, now that the case-law recognises the lawfulness of renewing the authority to detain a patient living in the community, as long as some of the treatment required is received in hospital, not necessarily as an in-patient. Under the MHA 2007, s 17 leave remains, but it is intended that its role will be reduced and supplanted by the community treatment order CTO under s 17A. To reinforce this policy, a responsible clinician considering granting leave for more than seven days must first consider whether the patient should be 'dealt with' under s 17A instead. Although the Government clearly sees CTOs as preferable to s 17 leave, clinicians may well continue to see s 17 leave as the preferred option. Compulsory community powers are dealt with in Chapter 8.

SAFEGUARDS

2.28 The third function of mental health legislation is to provide a system of safeguards to ensure that powers to detain or to treat compulsorily are not

---

[17] *R (on the application of DR) v Mersey Care NHS Trust* [2002] EWHC 1810 Admin.

misused, and that fundamental rights of freedom from arbitrary detention and physical integrity are not interfered with. These matters are dealt with in Parts 4, 4A and 5 of the Mental Health Act 1983. Part 5 deals with review of detention. Mental Health Review Tribunals established under the MHA 1959 fulfil the function of providing, as required by Art 5(4) of the European Convention on Human Rights, access to a court with power to review the lawfulness of detention and direct discharge if detention is not warranted. Provisions authorising treatment without consent for mental disorder, subject to a statutory second opinion, are contained in Part 4 (introduced by the Mental Health Act 1983) for in-patients, and in Part 4A (introduced by the Mental Health Act 2007) for patients on a community treatment order ('CTO').

Review of compulsory powers by hospital managers

2.29 The managers of the detaining hospital perform an important role in reviewing the need for detention. The application and reports authorising compulsory admission are forwarded to the managers, who are the detaining authority. Detention is renewed by the Responsible Clinician furnishing to the managers a report to the effect that the patient still suffers from mental disorder of a nature or degree justifying detention in the interests of his health or safety or for the protection of others. The hospital managers have a power to discharge the patient which may be exercised at any time during the patient's detention and on any grounds. The Act enables NHS trusts and PCTs (but not NHS foundation trusts) to delegate functions to committees or subcommittees whose members need not be directors of the trust. The MHA 2007 enables the power to discharge in a NHS foundation trust to be exercised by any three or more persons authorised by the board of the trust in that behalf each of whom is neither an executive director of the board nor an employee of the trust.[18] The role of the hospital managers is discussed in Chapter 5.

Mental Health Review Tribunals

2.30 Part 5 of the MHA 1983, which is amended by Chapter 5 of the Mental Health Act 2007, deals with Mental Health Review Tribunals. These were first established under the MHA 1959 to provide patients with an opportunity to seek review by a judicial body of the continued need for their detention. Article 5(4) of the European Convention on Human Rights entitles detainees to take proceedings by which the lawfulness of detention must be decided speedily by a court and release ordered if it is not lawful. In *X v United Kingdom*,[19] the Strasbourg Court held that the court must be able to review the applicability of the *Winterwerp* criteria.[20] If they are not met, the court must have the power to direct the patient's discharge. Review of the 'lawfulness' of detention must be carried out in light of domestic legal requirements, the Convention, and the principle of proportionality. Article 5(4) review is carried

---

[18] MHA 1983, s 23(6), as inserted by s 45(1) of the MHA 2007.
[19] (1981) 4 EHRR 188, ECtHR.
[20] (1981) 4 EHRR 188 at 189, ECtHR. See also *Hutchison Reid v United Kingdom* (2003) 37 EHRR 211, ECtHR.

out jointly by the High Court and by Mental Health Review Tribunals ('MHRTs'). The High Court reviews the formal legality of decisions to detain and renew detention via judicial review and habeas corpus. Review of the continued applicability of the *Winterwerp* criteria is done by MHRTs, which have the power to direct discharge.

2.31   The main reforms to the MHRT introduced by the MHA 2007 are to provide that there shall be some changes in the system of automatic references to the MHRT where a patient has not applied for review, and that there shall henceforth be one MHRT for England, and one for Wales. England and Wales will each will have a President appointed by the Lord Chancellor from among the legal chairman of MHRTs in that country.[21] The jurisdiction and functioning of the MHRTs are fully discussed in Chapter 9.

Consent to treatment and statutory second opinions

2.32   Part 4 provides a system of statutory second opinion safeguards in relation to certain treatments for mental disorder. No patient may be given psychosurgery or hormone implants to reduce male sex drive without a certificate from a panel of three people appointed by the Mental Health Act Commission that the patient is capable and has consented. Moreover, the doctor member of the panel must certify that the treatment ought to be given having regard to the likelihood that it will alleviate or prevent deterioration in the patient's condition. The new test for the second stage of this process and for the decision under ss 58 (medicines) and 58A (ECT) will be that it is appropriate for the treatment to be given. It is appropriate for treatment to be given to a patient if the treatment is appropriate in his case, taking into account the nature and degree of the mental disorder from which he is suffering and all other circumstances of his case.[22]

2.33   Under the MHA 1983, ECT or medicines for mental disorder could be given without consent to a detained patient, subject to a written statement from a Second Opinion Doctor ('SOAD') appointed by the Mental Health Act Commission ('MHAC') certifying that the treatment ought to be given. Under the MHA 2007 there will be a separate regime for medicines which remain under s 58 and may (subject to a second opinion), be given without consent to a capable patient who is refusing them. Medicines may be given if the responsible clinician certifies that the patient is capable of understanding the nature purpose and likely effects of the treatment and has consented. A patient does not become eligible to seek a second opinion for psychiatric medication given without consent until three months have elapsed since the first occasion during that period of detention when medication was administered. So for three months medicines may be given without consent under the direction of the responsible clinician. Thereafter, if they are to be given without consent, a second opinion must be obtained. It does not make any difference whether the

---

[21]   MHA 1983, s 65(1) and (1A), as inserted by MHA 2007, s 38(2).
[22]   MHA 1983, s 64(3), as inserted by MHA 2007, s 6(3).

SOAD certifies the patient to be incapable of understanding the nature purpose and likely effects of the treatment, or to be refusing it. In either case the medicine may be given subject to the test of appropriateness outlined above. ECT will in future be dealt with by a separate procedure under s 58A.

2.34 Section 35 of the MHA 2007 adds a new Part 4A to the MHA 1983 comprising ss 64A–64K. These provisions authorise 'relevant treatment' to be given to a community patient who has not been recalled to hospital. They set out the circumstances in which medication for mental disorder may be given to a community patient in the community (not necessarily in a hospital or clinic). They apply parts of the decision-making framework of the Mental Capacity Act 2005 to treatment under the Mental Health Act and authorise treatment in the community without the consent of an incapable patient:

(a) if there is consent from someone authorised under the MCA 2005 to make decisions on the patient's behalf;

(b) if the patient lacks capacity and force is not necessary to secure compliance; or

(c) if emergency treatment needs to be given, using force if necessary, to a patient who lacks capacity.

Their general intent is to clarify the circumstances in which treatment may be given in the community without consent if necessary. Parts 4 and 4A are explained in Chapter 10.

Mental Health Act Commission

2.35 The Mental Health Act Commission ('MHAC') was established by the MHA 1983.[23] The MHAC is a multidisciplinary body appointed by the Secretary of State for Health, with a general duty to oversee the use of compulsory powers under the 1983 Act. Scrutiny of admission documents remains the province of hospital managers. The jurisdiction to discharge remains with MHRTs. The MHAC has specific duties of investigating the handling of complaints made by or on behalf of detained patients. It must report biennially to Parliament, and assists the Secretary of State in preparing a Code of Practice. Commissioners visit hospitals regularly, usually with advance warning, but sometimes not, and interview patients under detention.[24] The MHAC also appoints and oversees the operation of the system of second opinions in Part 4 and now Part 4A of the Act.

2.36 The Government has already announced plans to merge the Healthcare Commission and Commission for Social Care Inspection into a new integrated body to ensure that services across the whole care pathway are safe and fit for

---

[23] The establishment of a Commission was recommended by *The Report of The Review of Rampton Hospital* Cmnd 8073 (1980), para 4.7.

[24] MHA 1983, ss 119–121.

purpose. This was announced in the Chancellor's Budget 2005 statement as part of a broad cross-Government strategy to modernise public service inspection and reduce the number of public sector inspectorates. The new body is to be established during 2009. The Government has indicated that the new regulator will inherit and continue the important role currently undertaken by the MHAC in England, and has promised that:[25]

> 'In a separate process, we will review the necessary duties and powers required by the new regulator to keep under review the operation of mental health legislation; to ensure that mental health service users are as effectively protected by the new regulator as they are now and to emphasise the importance of equality and human rights in mental health care. This will learn lessons from the effective visiting programme that commissioners have undertaken.'

The role and function of the MHAC is discussed in Chapter 10.

Victims' rights

2.37   Section 48 and Sch 6 of the Mental Health Act 2007 significantly amend Chapter 2 of Part 3 of the Domestic Violence, Crime and Victims Act 2004. These provisions entitle a victim or any person acting for a victim of a sexual or violent offence where the offender is subject to a restriction order or and restriction direction, to be notified of their right to make representations to the local probation board about whether the patient should be subject to any conditions in the event of his conditional discharge from hospital and if so what those conditions should be. Schedule 6 to the MHA 2007 extends this right to victims of sexual or violent offences where the offender is sentenced to a hospital order without restrictions, or is given a transfer direction without restrictions. In such cases the victim or representative is entitled to make representations as to what conditions he should be subject to in the event of his discharge from hospital under a community treatment order.[26] The victim or representative is entitled to receive information about any conditions that are imposed on discharge.[27] Furthermore, where the offender is subject to a hospital order without restrictions, the victim may ask to make representations or to receive information, and if they do so the probation board must notify the victim of the hospital's name and address and the hospital must be notified of the victim's address.[28] The probation board is required to forward any representations made to the person responsible for determining matters to do with discharge, ending of restrictions, conditional discharge or discharge subject to a community treatment order. The changes to the 2004 Act require responsible clinicians, Mental Health Review Tribunals, and the Secretary of State (in the case of a restricted patient) when considering whether to discharge to notify the hospital managers who must notify the local probation board, and

---

[25]   Department of Health *The future regulation of health and adult social care in England* (2006), paras 1.15–1.16.

[26]   Domestic Violence, Crime and Victims Act 2004, s 36(5).

[27]   Ibid, s 36(6)

[28]   Ibid, s 36A.

give victims the chance to make representations and information about discharge and conditions. Since the 2004 Act came into force MHRTs have been granting rights to victims to make representations in relation to discharge and conditions of discharge. The changes to the Domestic Violence, Crime and Victims Act 2004 are significant in that they require responsible clinicians of all offender patients who have committed sexual or violent offences to consider the victim's representations before discharging either conditionally or under a community treatment order. Tribunals too must consider the victim's representations. The rights of victims are discussed in Chapter 7 (powers of discharge of mentally disordered offenders) and Chapter 8 (powers to send on extended leave, to make community treatment orders, and to conditionally discharge offender patients who are subject to restrictions). They are also discussed in relation to the Mental Health Review Tribunal in Chapter 9.

PRINCIPLES AND CODES OF PRACTICE

Principles

2.38 The idea behind principles and Codes of Practice is that they should offer guidance on how the legislation is to be implemented, but that they should also promote respect for the individual human dignity of the mentally disordered person. Both the Mental Capacity Act and the Mental Health Act have fundamental principles. Each has its own statutory Code to guide professionals on using of their powers and discharging their responsibilities. The Mental Capacity Act has statutory principles set out in the Act. The Mental Health Act has principles in its Code of Practice. This prompts the question what practical differences there are in the status of principles under each regime. There has been a trend in mental health law reform to argue for the adoption of statutory principles to guide the way in which the Act is implemented. There was much debate, following Richardson, about including principles on the face of the Mental Health Act 2007, such as non-discrimination, least restrictive alternative, respect for autonomy and diversity, reciprocity and consensual care. Including principles in the Act was a key goal of the Mental Health Alliance. The Mental Health (Care and Treatment) (Scotland) Act 2003 includes principles in s 1 which professionals must have regard to. These include respect for the past and present wishes of the patient, the importance of full patient participation, minimum restriction of freedom of the patient necessary in the circumstances, encouragement of equal opportunities, and the views, needs and circumstances of the patient's carer.

2.39 The Parliamentary Joint Committee on the Draft Mental Health Bill 2004 recommended that principles should appear on the face of the Act, and that it was not appropriate to 'leave fundamental guiding principles to the Code of Practice'.[29] In the Code is where they have been left by the MHA 2007, the main victory being in securing the appearance in the statute of a list of

---

[29]   House of Lords, House of Commons Joint Pre-Parliamentary Scrutiny Committee *Report on the Draft Mental Health Bill* (HL Paper 79(1), HC Paper 95(1), Session 2004–2005), para 64.

'matters' to be reflected in the principles. Generally, the principles have been intended to promote treating mentally disordered people and their carers with respect.

MCA 2005 principles

2.40 The Mental Capacity Act 2005 sets out five statutory principles. They are:

(1) a person must be assumed to have capacity unless it is established that they lack capacity;

(2) a person is not to be treated as unable to make a decision unless all practicable steps to help him to do so have been taken without success;

(3) a person is not to be treated as unable to make a decision merely because he makes an unwise decision;

(4) an act done, or decision made, under this Act for or on behalf of a person who lacks capacity must be done, or made, in his best interests;

(5) before the act is done, or the decision is made, regard must be had to whether the purpose for which it is needed can be as effectively achieved in a way that is less restrictive of the person's rights and freedom of action.[30]

Section 1 merely says that the following principles apply. It does not say that those making decisions must have to have regard to them. Richard Jones argues that:[31]

> 'Although there is no legal duty placed on persons or bodies to apply the principles, a failure to do so could be cited in legal proceedings as evidence of unlawful conduct.'

2.41 The emphasis of the MCA 2005 and its accompanying Code is on empowerment and personal autonomy, enabling people to plan for future incapacity. This might be done by a valid and effective advance decision refusing treatment which is binding, or an advance statement requesting specific treatment which is not binding but which must be considered by doctors in determining what is in the patient's best interests. Or it might be done by appointing a treatment proxy using the lasting power of attorney. If no proxy has been appointed, interventions be carried out by others without consent in the patient's best interests, but only after reasonable steps have been taken to assess capacity, the person is reasonably believed to lack capacity. The ethos of both the 2005 Act and the Code is based on upholding dignity while protecting the best interests of vulnerable people. The power to make an advance decision refusing treatment or the power to appoint a proxy with

---

[30]   Mental Capacity Act 2005.
[31]   RM Jones *Mental Capacity Act Manual* (Sweet and Maxwell, 2005), para 9/9.

instructions to refuse it raises the question when an advance refusal of psychiatric treatment is binding, and when it may be overridden by detention and compulsory treatment under the Mental Health Act 1983. These issues are governed by ss 5, 6, 28 and 37 of the Mental Capacity Act 2005, and are discussed in full in Chapter 10 which deals with consent to treatment for mental disorder. The principles in the Mental Capacity Act 2005 reflect a presumption of autonomy, of the least restrictive alternative, and of regard for the best interests of patients.

Mental Health Act 1983

2.42 The Mental Health Act 1983 does not contain principles, but the Mental Health Act Code of Practice does. The legal status of the guidance in the Mental Health Act Code is that whilst the '[1983] Act does not impose a legal duty to comply with the Code but as it is a statutory document, failure to follow it could be referred to in legal proceedings'. Chapter One of the current Code is entitled 'Guiding Principles'. Paragraph 1.1 says that:[32]

'The detailed guidance in the Code needs to be read in the light of the following broad principles, that people to whom the Act applies (including those being assessed for possible admission should:

- Receive recognition of their basic human rights under the European Convention on Human Rights (ECHR).
- Be given respect for their qualities, abilities and diverse backgrounds as individuals and be assured that account will be taken of their age, gender, sexual orientation, social ethnic, cultural and religious background, but that general assumptions will not be made on the basis of any of those characteristics.
- Have their needs full taken into account, although it is recognised that, within available resources, it may always not be practicable to meet them in full.
- Be given any necessary treatment or care in the least controlled or segregated facilities compatible with ensuring their own health or safety or the safety of other people.
- Be treated and cared for in such a way as to promote the greatest practicable degree their self determination and personal responsibility, consistent with their own needs and wishes.
- Be discharged from detention or other powers provided by the Act as soon as it is clear their application is no longer justified.'

This list is then followed by five further principles.

2.43 First, is that patients should be treated in accordance with the Care Programme Approach ('CPA'). All service users, whether or not they have been detained, who have been in contact with the specialist psychiatric service are entitled to be dealt with under the CPA. The CPA requires a risk assessment, a

---

[32] Department of Health and Welsh Office *Mental Health Act 1983 Code of Practice* (1999), para 1.1.

needs assessment, a written care plan which will be regularly reviewed and a key worker (now known as a 'care co-ordinator'). In 1996 the CPA was extended to all patients receiving care from the specialist psychiatric services.[33] The current guidance on the CPA is *Modernising the Care Programme Approach*.[34] This provides that there are two levels of CPA, standard and enhanced. Standard CPA is for people whose mental illness is less severe or who have low risk factors or have an active informal support network. But a major reason why a patient with a severe mental illness will be found to have low risk factors is if they are receiving intensive support from their informal support network. Their needs may be great but they will be assigned to standard CPA and this will be significant because CPA is used as a rationing tool, and some social services authorities have tried to limit services to both patients and carers to those who are on enhanced CPA. People are on enhanced CPA if their mental disorder is assessed as posing a potential risk to their own safety or to that of other people. Resources follow risk. The Government is currently discussing proposals to dispense with standard CPA and introduce a new system whereby eligibility would be restricted to those currently on enhanced CPA.

2.44   The second principle emphasises the responsibility of staff to make sure that effective communication takes place between themselves and patients, and to do everything possible to overcome any barriers to communication. The third principle is patient confidentiality, that information about a patient should not be disclosed without a patient's consent, unless it is necessary to pass on information 'in the public interest, for instance where personal health or safety is at risk'. Then information should be revealed on a 'need to know' basis. The fourth principle is recognition of the rights of victims of crimes committed by mentally disordered offenders. These rights have been significantly strengthened since the Code was issued by the Domestic Violence, Crime and Victims Act 2004, and the amendments to that Act introduced by the Mental Health Act 2007. The final principle is recognition of the duty of hospital managers to give information about rights to patients and nearest relatives, and to collect information about ethnicity of all patients admitted under the Act.

Mental Health Act 2007

2.45   Section 8 of the Mental Health Act 2007 (cross-heading 'fundamental principles') puts the principles in the Code of Practice, amending s 118 which governs preparation of the Code of Practice. The amendments require the Code to include a statement of the principles which the Secretary of State thinks should 'inform decisions under this Act'.[35] The new concept of principles which 'should inform decisions' is different from the principles that professionals must have regard to. In preparing the statement of principles the

---

[33]   NHS Executive (1996).
[34]   Care Programme Approach Association *The Care Programme Approach Handbook* (Chesterfield Care Programme Approach Association, 2003).
[35]   MHA 1983, s 118(2A)–(2B), as inserted by MHA 2007, s 8.

Secretary of State must, in particular, ensure that 'each of the following matters is addressed' (the 'matters' are in the statute, the principles will be in the Code):

(a) respect for patients' past and present wishes and feelings;

(b) respect for diversity generally including, in particular, diversity of religion, culture and sexual orientation (within the meaning of s 35 of the Equality Act 2006);

(c) minimising restrictions on liberty;

(d) involvement of patients in planning, developing and delivering care and treatment appropriate to them;

(e) avoidance of unlawful discrimination;

(f) effectiveness of treatment;

(g) views of carers and other interested parties;

(h) patient well-being and safety; and

(i) public safety.

2.46 This is a good deal weaker than a statutory requirement to have regard to principles spelt out in statute, and crystallises the difference between the two statutes. Respect for human rights and confidentiality have disappeared from the list. The practical impact on patients' rights may be small, since now that the Human Rights Act 1998 is in force, all public authorities are under a legal duty to act compatibly with Convention Rights. But this is scant justification for removing the Code's emphasis to mental health professionals of the need to respect Convention rights. The principles now clearly include public safety for the first time, as well as the effectiveness of treatment, will certainly include emphasis on compliance with medication. In line with Government policy announced by ministers Dobson and Boateng in 1998, the Mental Health Act 2007 and the principles mark a shift towards seeking to impose obligations on patients to comply with medication, and on professionals to manage risk.

The legal status of the Code: seclusion, and restraint

2.47 The Code of Practice gives guidance on how the Act should be implemented. It also provides guidance on interventions which find no mention in the legislation. In October 2007 the Department of Health issued a Draft Code of Practice for England for consultation.[36] Seclusion and restraint provide an important example of interventions which potentially breach the

---

[36] See http://www.dh.gov.uk/en/Consultations/Liveconsultations/DH_079842.

right of physical integrity in Art 8. No provisions in the MHA 1983 expressly justify seclusion. It is, however, subject to guidance under the MHA Code of Practice, where it is defined as:

> 'the supervised confinement of a patient in a room, which may be locked to protect others from significant harm. Its sole aim is to contain severely disturbed behaviour which is likely to cause harm to others.'

The Code requires that seclusion should only be used as a last resort and for the shortest period possible, a reflecting common law necessity and the Convention principle of proportionality. It should never be used as a punishment or threat, as part of a treatment programme, because of shortage of staff, or where there is a risk of suicide or self harm.[37] Although there have at various points in recent history been calls to ban seclusion, it has retained its place as an accepted psychiatric practice, to the extent that the present day Code of Practice on the Mental Health Act 1983, whilst not regarding it as 'a treatment technique', describes it as falling within the broad legal definition of 'medical treatment' in s 145, a position confirmed by the Court of Appeal and the House of Lords in *R (on the application of Munjaz) v Mersey Care NHS Trust; R (on the application of S) v Airedale NHS Trust.*[38]

2.48 The applicants in these cases challenged their seclusion in breach of the MHA Code of Practice.[39] The case establishes that legal powers to seclude exist under the MHA 1983 and outlines the impact of Arts 3 and 8 of the Convention on those powers. The effects had not reached the level of severity necessary to engage the prohibition in Art 3 against inhuman or degrading treatment. However, there was a potential breach of the right to respect for private life (physical integrity) in Art 8. The European Court had already held in *Raininen v Finland*[40] that respect for privacy under Art 8(1) includes 'the physical and moral integrity of the individual, and extends to deprivations of liberty ... affording a protection in relation to conditions of detention that do not reach the level of severity required by Article 3'.

2.49 The Court of Appeal upheld both challenges to seclusion, holding that Ashworth were only entitled to depart from the Code if they had good reason to do so on the facts of the individual case, and that Airedale were not justified in keeping S in seclusion from the time when it ceased to be a necessary and proportionate response to the risk he presented to others. The Court of Appeal held that Convention rights obliged them to afford a status and weight to the Code consistent with the State's obligation to avoid ill-treatment of patients detained by or on the authority of the State. Seclusion would infringe Art 8 unless justified under Art 8(2) to protect health or the rights and freedoms of

---

[37] *Mental Health Act Code of Practice* (1998), para 19.16.

[38] [2003] EWCA Civ 1036. See now [2005] UKHL 58. Lord Bingham (at para [20]) said that medical treatment is in my opinion an expression wide enough to cover nursing and caring for a patient in seclusion, even though seclusion cannot properly form part of a treatment programme.

[39] [2003] EWCA Civ 1036.

[40] (1997) 26 EHRR 563, ECtHR.

others. Since the justifications under the MHA 1983 were very broad, the Code of Practice had an important role to play in securing that they had the necessary degree of predictability and transparency to comply with Art 8(2).

2.50 There was no appeal in the *Airedale* case, but the House of Lords overturned the Court of Appeal's ruling on the status of the Code in *Munjaz,* holding that the Code has the status of guidance which should be followed unless there was a good reason for departing from it, and that a good reason need not be because of the facts of the individual case. A good reason might be a policy reason arise from the exigencies of running a high security hospital which might justify differences in the seclusion policy, relating for example to frequency of medical review, to contend with the fact that the hospital exists to treat people who need treatment in conditions of security on grounds of their violent or dangerous proclivities.

2.51 Since 1999, the National Institute of Clinical and Public Health Excellence ('NICE') has assumed responsibility for issuing guidance on psychiatric treatment. NICE was initially set up with two functions:[41]

(1) promoting 'clinical excellence and the effective use of available resources in the National Health Service ('NHS') through the development and dissemination of guidelines for the management of certain diseases or conditions, guidance on the appropriate use of certain interventions, audit methodologies and the dissemination of these to support frontline staff and patients';

(2) advising on 'good clinical practice in the use of existing treatment options, appraising evidence on new health interventions, and advising the NHS on how they can be implemented and on how best they fit alongside the range of existing treatments. The Institute will promote the appropriate use of treatments which offer good value to patients, and will discourage the use of those that do not'.

NICE has issued a range of guidance on psychiatric treatment, including ECT, anti-psychotic medication, the use of cholinesterase inhibitor drugs in the treatment of dementia, interventions to prevent self-harm, and on the management of violence in psychiatric patients.[42] Each piece of guidance is prefaced by a standard statement that:

---

[41] National Institute of Clinical Excellence *Framework Document*, paras 3.1 and 3.2 (see further www.nice.org.uk).

[42] National Institute of Clinical Excellence *Dementia: the treatment and care of people with dementia in health and social care* (2001); *Guidance on the use of newer (atypical) antipsychotic drugs for the treatment of schizophrenia* (Technology Appraisal Guidance 43, June 2002); *Guidance on the Use of Electro Convulsive Therapy* (Technology Appraisal Guidance 59, April 2003); *Self-Harm: The Short Term Physical and Psychological Management and Secondary Prevention of Self-Harm in Primary and Secondary Care* (Clinical Guideline 16, July 2004); *Violence: The Short-Term Management of Disturbed/Violent Behaviour in In-Patient Psychiatric Settings* (Clinical Guideline 25, February 2005). All guidance available at www.nice.org.uk.

'health professionals are expected to take it fully into account when exercising their clinical judgment. The guidance does not override the individual responsibility of health professionals to make decisions appropriate to the circumstances of the individual patient, in consultation with the individual patient and or guardian or carer.'

In relation to management of violence the guidance provides that:[43]

'Failure to act in accordance with the guideline may not only be a failure to act in accordance with best practice, but in some circumstances may have legal consequences. For example, any intervention required to manage disturbed behaviour must be a reasonable and proportionate response to the risk it seeks to address.'

2.52   NICE Guidance on the management of violence in psychiatric settings refers to both seclusion and restraint. It states that: 'These interventions are *management strategies* and are *not* regarded as *primary treatment techniques*'.[44] Although legally these are 'treatments for mental disorder', in reality they are legally sanctioned treatments *of mentally disordered people*. The courts have been willing to accept that treatment designed to prevent harm to others can be in the best interests of the patient. The law on restraint and seclusion is explained in Chapter 10.

CHILDREN

2.53   Children may be detained under the Mental Health Act 1983, with parental consent, or under the Children Act 1989. The MHA 2007 introduces new provisions affecting children including a 'requirement' of age appropriate accommodation, provisions restricting the use of ECT on children under new s 58A, and new provisions governing treatment in the community of child community patients. Chapter 11 outlines the basic framework of powers of detention and compulsory treatment of children and the effect of the changes introduced by the 2007 Act.

TRANSFERRING PATIENTS SUBJECT TO COMPULSION ACROSS JURISDICTIONS

2.54   Part 6 entitled 'Removal and return of patients within the United Kingdom' introduces a new range of reciprocal arrangements enabling restricted patients, detained patients and community patients to be transferred in custody of necessary from any part of the United Kingdom, Channel Islands or the Isle of Man. Until now there has been little co-ordination between the

---

[43]   National Institute for Clinical Excellence *Violence: The Short-Term Management of Disturbed/Violent Behaviour in In-Patient Psychiatric Settings* (Clinical Guideline 25, February 2005), p 10.
[44]   Emphasis added.

different legal regimes involved. The new provisions are designed to rectify this problem, by providing a co-ordinated regime of powers to take and retake patients, to remove them from one jurisdiction and convey them in custody to another, and to ensure that they are subject to lawful compulsion when they reach their destination.

OFFENCES AGAINST MENTALLY DISORDERED PEOPLE

2.55 Mentally disordered people may need special protection from the criminal law, either because they are not in a position because of their mental disorder to complain about their treatment in an institution, or where consent is a defence to an offence, such as a sexual offence, and the victim suffers from mental disorder which renders her or him incapable of consenting, or vulnerable to undue influence. Mental health legislation must provide effective protection via the criminal law of the rights of mentally disordered people, and the Mental Health Act sets out a number of special offences in relation to mentally disordered people. The transfer provisions, together with the offences under the Mental Health Act, are discussed in Chapter 12.

CONCLUSION

2.56 We have two mental health statutes: the Mental Health Act 1983 and the Mental Capacity Act 2005. The MCA 2005 has statutory principles. Its ethos is based on the welfare and 'best interests' of the individual. It employs the paternalist power of the State as parens patriae for the individual's benefit. The lead Department has been the Lord Chancellor's Department (now the Ministry of Justice). The MHA 1983 provides for intervention on paternalist grounds in the interests of the patient's health, and also where it is necessary for the patient's safety. The significant difference is that the MHA 1983 also deploys the police power of the State where someone's mental disorder warrants their detention for treatment and detention is necessary for the protection of other people. A more overt emphasis on public protection is found in Part 3 of the MHA 1983, which provides for the sentencing of mentally disordered offenders, and transfers from prison. This means that there are two Government Departments involved in policy-making, the Department of Health, and the Home Office (now the Ministry of justice). Although the Home Office Mental Health Unit for restricted patients has now transferred to the Ministry of Justice the key goals of protecting the public and preventing re-offending remain. This goal is reflected in the inclusion of public safety and alongside patient well-being among the matters to be addressed in drawing up the principles for the Code. Although a person may be detained under the MHA 1983 in the interests of their own health or safety, the key difference from the MCA 2005 is the availability of detention for the protection of others. The Mental Health Act marks the intersection between the health system and the criminal justice system.

2.57 Little wonder then, that when the Joint Parliamentary Scrutiny Committee considered the Mental Health Bill 2004, Lord Rix and Mrs Angela Browning MP were anxious in their questions to witnesses to ensure that people with learning disabilities and people with Autism or Asperger's should not be treated as mentally disordered for the purposes of the Mental Health Act. If decisions need to be taken about admission to hospital or treatment of patients in these diagnostic groups these should be made within the statutory framework of the Mental Capacity Act 2005. This is reflected in the MHA 2007 by the exclusion of learning disability from powers of long-term detention unless there is abnormally aggressive or seriously irresponsible conduct. For people with learning disabilities and autistic spectrum disorder, being admitted and treated as a mentally disordered person under mental health legislation is to be avoided as stigmatising. There is a general perception that the Mental Capacity Act is for people with mental illness of old age, or for people with learning disability. They should only be dealt with under mental health legislation if abnormally aggressive or seriously irresponsible in their conduct. The Mental Health Act is seen by the Government as being for other groups of people with mental disorders, such as younger adults with psychotic illnesses or personality disorders, who may be articulating resistance to treatment, and, perhaps most important, who may pose a risk to others.

2.58 The Mental Health Act 2007 is a radical reform in mental health legislation for a number of reasons, but perhaps most notably for its complexity and its greater emphasis on patient obligations, particularly community obligations to accept medication and to behave in accordance with conditions. A person on a community treatment order may be obliged to accept medication and to desist from certain conduct. If they do not comply, they may be recalled to hospital. If after 72 hours they still have not accepted treatment, their community treatment order will lapse and they will resume detained patient status. Emergency treatment for mental disorder may be given without consent in the community using reasonable force if necessary, where the patient lacks capacity (or is a *Gillick* incompetent minor). Non-emergency treatment may be given if the patient is capable and consents. Treatment may be given even if there is reason to believe the patient is refusing it as long as force is not necessary. So in a non-emergency situation the patient may be told that if s/he does not consent to the treatment s/he may be recalled to hospital and held for up to 72 hours while professionals decide whether to allow the section to be reinstated. Patients who are aware of this power dynamic are likely to comply with the obligation to accept treatment without force being necessary even though there is reason to believe they are resisting treatment.

2.59 The Mental Health Act 2007 and the Mental Capacity Act 2005 are companion mental health statutes. If they are to be placed on a spectrum between health and criminal justice statutes, the Mental Capacity Act is a health and welfare statute, whereas the Mental Health Act marks the intersection between the health care system and the penal system. Between them they provide a framework for detaining mentally incapacitated patients where necessary in their best interests and mentally disordered people whether they retain capacity or not, where it is necessary for the health or safety of the patient or for the protection of others. Part 3 provides the link with the criminal justice system. The new community treatment orders are intended to provide an equivalent to conditional discharge for mentally disordered offenders sentenced to hospital orders without restrictions. The Mental Health Act offers powers to detain people adjudged to present a risk to public safety without the need to arrest them for any offence. In the chapters which follow the effect of the MHA 2007 is examined in the context of the European Convention on Human Rights and the Human Rights Act 1998. At the core of the changes introduced by the 2007 Act are the new broad definition of mental disorder and the test of availability of appropriate treatment. Chapter 3 below explains and discusses the definition of mental disorder and the conditions of compulsion.

Chapter 3

'MENTAL DISORDER' AND THE AVAILABILITY OF APPROPRIATE TREATMENT

INTRODUCTION

3.1   At the core of the changes introduced by the MHA 2007 are the new broad definition of mental disorder and the test of availability of appropriate treatment. As the Joint Parliamentary Committee put it in their scrutiny of the 2004 Bill:[1]

> 'The definition and conditions are at the heart of the Bill. Not only will vital decisions about people's lives be directly based upon them, but the remainder of the Bill depends on and is shaped by them ... Any legislation designed to deprive individuals who have committed no offence of their personal liberty and autonomy requires Parliament to go to considerable lengths to satisfy itself that the Government has got the balance right and is creating a framework in which mental health professionals can more appropriately exercise their judgment.'

The MHA 2007 widens the definition of mental disorder, the Government's intention being to create an effective legal framework within which risk to self and others may be managed.

The definition of 'mental disorder'

3.2   The MHA 2007 abolishes the four separate categories of mental disorder applicable to longer-term admission for treatment under the MHA 1983, and introduces a single simplified definition of mental disorder that applies throughout the Act. It is 'any disorder or disability of the mind.' Until the 2007 Act comes into force a person may only be detained for treatment for up to six months if classified as suffering from mental illness, psychopathic disorder, mental impairment or severe mental impairment. Once the 2007 Act is in force, a person will be able to be detained if suffering from 'any disorder or disability of the mind', regardless of whether the detention is for a short or a long period.

3.3   The new broad definition, which is basically the 'catch all' at the end of the broad definition of mental disorder in the old s 1(2), will extend the scope of powers of detention, particularly in relation to personality disorder, the

---

[1]   House of Lords, House of Commons Joint Pre-Parliamentary Scrutiny Committee *Report on the Draft Mental Health Bill* (HL Paper 79(1), HC Paper 95(1), Session 2004–2005), para 81.

group causing most concern to the Government, perceived as high risk for offending behaviour, particularly sex offences. The MHA 1983 classification of such people would be psychopathic disorder, which requires abnormally aggressive or seriously irresponsible conduct. The Government saw three major fault lines in the 1983 Act:

(i)   the definition of psychopathic disorder;

(ii)   the exclusion that no-one may be treated as mentally disordered by reason only of sexual deviancy; and

(iii)   the 'treatability' test.

They represented an unacceptable obstacle to using powers of detention under the Mental Health Act to protect society against the risk from sex offenders with personality disorders emerging from prison at the end of determinate sentences. They could not be rearrested until they committed an offence. In the Government's view, the MHA 1983 put too many obstacles in the way of detaining them on grounds of personality disorder if they were assessed as high risk for re-offending.

3.4   In 1995 Dr Jim Higgins summarised the implications of a diagnosis of psychopathy as often being that:[2]

> 'the patient is untreatable, has no proper place in a hospital and is disliked by clinical staff. It is often employed in order to reject patients for treatment and for this purpose may be deliberately applied to patients with other psychiatric disorders such as schizophrenia or hypomania.'

The Reed Committee – which examined the issue in 1994 – emphasised this point, stating that:[3]

> 'As a consequence people who might benefit from medical care were, at times, denied it and remained in prison or be left unsupported in the community. The implications for public safety were clearly matters of concern.'

3.5   The Reed committee recommended replacement of the stigmatising term 'psychopathic disorder' with 'personality disorder'. In fact neither term will appear in the statute. Personality disorder will fall within 'any disorder or disability of the mind'. The treatability test will go, as will the exclusion for sexual deviancy. The Government has invested considerably in developing services for offender patients and has established special units for Dangerous

---

[2]   'Crime and Mental Disorder: Forensic Aspects of Psychiatric Disorder' in D Chiswick and R Cope (eds) *Practical Forensic Psychiatry* (Gaskell Royal College of Psychiatrists, 1995), at pp 65–66.

[3]   Department of Health and Home Office *Report of the Department of Health and Home Office Working Group on Psychopathic Disorder* (HMSO, 1994), para 10.16v.

People with Severe Personality Disorder in Broadmoor and Rampton High Security Hospitals and Whitemoor Prison, the aim being to develop effective treatment programmes for this group.[4]

Treatability and appropriate treatment

3.6   For patients suffering from psychopathic disorder or mental impairment detention for treatment under s 3 or under a s 37 hospital order was only possible if medical treatment for mental disorder was likely to alleviate or prevent deterioration in their condition – the 'treatability' test. It could therefore be to a patient's advantage to be reclassified under the MHA 1983 from 'mental illness' or 'severe mental impairment' (which used to be known as the 'major disorders' and where it was assumed that treatment would be of benefit) to 'psychopathic disorder' or mental impairment (which used to be known as the 'minor disorders' where a treatability test applied). If not treatable, such a patient would be entitled to discharge.[5] The numerous provisions relating to reclassification under the MHA 1983 have now been rendered obsolete and these provisions are repealed by the MHA 2007.

The rejection of significantly impaired judgment as a condition of compulsion

3.7   The Richardson Committee recommended that capacity play a part in the conditions of compulsion, to the extent that a higher threshold of risk to self or others would be required to impose compulsion on a capable person. This was rejected by the Government in 2000. The Millan Committee, whose recommendations formed the basis of the Mental Health (Care and Treatment) (Scotland) Act 2003, learned from this experience of Richardson and proposed the intermediate concept of significantly impaired judgment. The Scottish Act requires as a condition of compulsion that the person's judgment *in relation to the decision to accept treatment* must be significantly impaired. The Scottish Code of Practice emphasises that it is a separate concept to incapacity, even though similar factors are taken into account, including consideration of:

> 'the extent to which the person's mental disorder might affect adversely affect their ability to believe, understand and retain information concerning their care and treatment, to make decisions based on that information, and to communicate those decisions to others.'

The question is whether judgment is significantly impaired, not whether the person lacks capacity. A person's judgment might be significantly impaired if they lacked insight into the fact that they had a mental illness, or where their ability to use information and weigh it in the balance to make a decision was impaired by a depressive illness.

---

4   The website of the DPSPD projects is http://www.dspdprogramme.gov.uk, where will be found the slogan: 'Ensuring the public is protected from some of the most dangerous people in society'.
5   *Reid v United Kingdom* (2003) 37 EHRR 9, ECtHR.

3.8   The Department of Health and the Home Office have successfully fought off attempts to install the concept of significantly impaired judgment in the MHA 2007. They were concerned that:[6]

> 'it is possible that people who are at very great risk to themselves or to others would nonetheless retain the ability to make unimpaired decisions about treatment.'

Dawson, in his excellent comparative survey of community treatment orders, suggests that the decision-making of people with less severe personality disorders would probably not be sufficiently impaired to meet the test, and that:[7]

> 'This is one principled way to exclude most persons with a personality disorder from cover by an involuntary patient regime.'

The Government's agenda is to remove all obstacles, principled or not, to mental health detention of people with personality disorder where there is risk, so it is little surprise that the significantly impaired judgment test has been rejected.

THE EUROPEAN CONVENTION ON HUMAN RIGHTS AND DETENTION ON GROUNDS OF UNSOUNDNESS OF MIND

3.9   Article 5(1) of the European Convention on Human Rights provides that no-one shall be deprived of his liberty unless the deprivation is carried out in accordance with a procedure prescribed by law and is necessary in a democratic society on one of a number of grounds. One of those grounds, set out in Art 5(1)(e), is deprivation of liberty on grounds of unsoundness of mind. In order for a non-emergency detention on grounds of unsoundness of mind to conform to the requirements of Art 5(1)(e) of the ECHR there must be reliable evidence of a true mental disorder.

Unsoundness of mind

3.10   In *Winterwerp v Netherlands* the European Court of Human Rights laid down the substantive and procedural requirements for lawful detention of persons of unsound mind. Three minimum conditions ('the *Winterwerp* criteria') must be satisfied:

---

[6]   *Government Response to the Report of the Joint Committee on the Draft Mental Health Bill* Cm 6624 (2005), response to recommendation 26, p 16.
[7]   John Dawson 'Community Treatment Orders: International Comparisons' (May 2005) *Law Foundation New Zealand*, p 100.

(1)   Except in emergency cases, the individual must reliably be shown to be of unsound mind. This has been held to entail the establishment of a true mental disorder on the basis of objective expertise.

(2)   The mental disorder must be of a kind or degree justifying compulsory confinement.

(3)   The validity of continued confinement depends on the persistence of such a mental disorder. This implies that it is for those carrying out the detention to satisfy themselves at intervals that the criteria for detention continue to be met.[8]

The court in *Winterwerp* declined to define 'unsoundness of mind' as it was a term whose meaning is constantly evolving as research in psychiatry progresses, an increasing flexibility in treatment is developing, and society's attitude to mental illness changes.[9] Although this confers broad discretion on clinicians, there are two limiting factors. There must be a true mental disorder, and it must be of a kind or degree warranting confinement.

A true mental disorder

3.11   Psychiatrists might view a true mental disorder as being one which appears in either the Diagnostic and Statistical Manual of Mental Disorders of the American Psychiatric Association (DSM-IV-R)[10] or the International Classification of Diseases of the World Health Organisation (ICD-10).[11] The DSM-IV is a 900-page reference book classifying 300 different disorders, each one containing a list of symptoms some or all of which must be present for the specific diagnosis. In the United States, a DSM IV diagnosis is the key to insurance coverage. All mental health professionals must list a diagnostic label from the DSM together with a code number in order to obtain insurance reimbursement for treatment.[12] Both DSM-IV and ICD-10 contain many conditions ranging from psychotic illnesses such as bipolar illness and schizophrenia, to depression or Alzheimer's, to personality disorders, disorders of sexual preference, and addictions ranging from addiction to alcohol and drugs to nicotine and caffeine related disorders. In psychiatry there is much greater reliance on the clinician's observation rather than scientific tests, and hence greater subjectivity in the diagnostic process.

---

[8]   *Winterwerp v Netherlands (Application 6301/73)* (1979) 2 EHRR 387, ECtHR; *X v United Kingdom (Application 7215/75)* (1981) 4 EHRR 188, 1 BMLR 98, ECtHR; and *Van der Leer v Netherlands (Application 11509/85)* (1990) 12 EHRR 567, ECtHR.

[9]   *Winterwerp v Netherlands* (1979) 2 EHRR 387, at para 37.

[10]   *Diagnostic and Statistical Manual of Mental Disorders* (American Psychiatric Association, 4th edn (DSM-IV), 1994).

[11]   World Health Organisation *Tenth Revision of the International Classification of Disease (ICD-10); Classification of Mental and Behavioural Disorders* (1992).

[12]   H Kutchins and S Kirk *Making us Crazy: DSM – The Psychiatric Bible and the Creation of Mental Disorders* (Constable London, 1997).

3.12 For these reasons, it is important to note DSM-IV's cautionary reminder that:[13]

'[I]n most situations the clinical diagnosis of a DSM-IV mental disorder is not sufficient to establish the existence for legal purposes of a 'mental disorder' ... In determining whether an individual meets a specified legal standard (e.g. for competence, criminal responsibility or disability), additional information is usually required beyond that contained in the DSM-IV diagnosis. This might include information about the individual's functional impairments ... [A]ssignment of a particular diagnosis does not imply a specific level of impairment or disability.'

Broad as the scope of DSM disorders is, the Government does not wish to be tied down by the need for a disorder to appear in its pages in order to be a true mental disorder. In the debates during the Public Bill Committee stage, the Minister of State Rosie Winterton MP said it 'cannot be said that something that is not in any classification is not a mental disorder'.[14]

Distinguishing between deviancy from society's norms and mental disorder

3.13 There is great sensitivity about the boundary between mental disorder and deviant conduct. This is due in part to the history of abuses of psychiatry, particularly in the Soviet Union, where dissidents were detained in psychiatric hospitals, their alleged illness being their dissident views and conduct. It is also due to the desire on the part of psychiatrists to be seen primarily as therapists rather than agents of social control. Decisions to detain on grounds of unsoundness of mind must be free from arbitrariness. The Strasbourg Court has held that Art 5(1)(e) cannot be taken to permit the detention of a person simply because his views deviate from the norms prevailing in a particular society.[15]

3.14 Both ICD-10 and DSM-IV are keen to emphasise the distinction between mental disorder and deviance, but offer only imprecise boundaries between the two. Each offers a clinical definition of mental disorder. In DSM-IV mental disorder is:[16]

'A clinically significant behavioural or psychological syndrome or pattern that occurs in an individual and that is associated with present distress (eg a painful symptom) or disability (ie impairment in one or more important areas of functioning) with a significantly increased risk of suffering death, pain, disability or an important loss of freedom.'

---

[13] See p xxiii.
[14] Public Bill Committee, col 16.
[15] *Winterwerp v Netherlands* (1979) 2 EHRR 387, at para 37.
[16] DSM-IV, p xxi.

DSM-IV emphasises the importance of distinguishing between mental disorder and behaviour which might be expected in legitimate response to traumatic events. To be regarded as a mental disorder the syndrome or pattern of behaviour cannot be:[17]

'[A]n expectable and culturally sanctioned response to a particular event, for example, the death of a loved one. Whatever its original cause, it must currently be considered a manifestation of a behavioural, psychological, or biological dysfunction in the individual. Neither deviant behaviour (e.g. political religious or sexual) nor conflicts that are primarily between the individual and society are mental disorders unless the deviance or conflict is a symptom of a dysfunction in the individual as described above.'

3.15 ICD-10 too lays emphasis on the concept of individual dysfunction as the means of distinguishing between deviance and mental disorder in these terms:[18]

'Disorder is used to imply the existence of a clinically recognisable set of symptoms or behaviour associated in most cases with distress and with interference with personal functions. Social deviance alone, without personal dysfunction, should not be included in mental disorder as defined here.'

The exclusions

3.16 There was an exclusion in s 1(3) of the MHA 1983 that a person should not be treated as suffering from mental disorder by reason only of promiscuity or other immoral conduct, sexual deviancy, or dependence on alcohol or drugs. The Government's concern was that people whose disorder manifested itself in sexual behaviour, and who were adjudged high risk to commit sex offences, might avoid detention under mental health legislation by availing themselves of one of the exclusions. The original Mental Health Bill 2006 removed the exclusions, except those for addiction. The House of Lords amended the Bill to provide that a person should not be considered to have a mental disorder solely on the grounds of:

(a)   his substance misuse (including dependence on alcohol or drugs);

(b)   his sexual identity or orientation;

(c)   his commission or likely commission of illegal or disorderly acts; or

(d)   his cultural, religious or political beliefs.

---

[17]   DSM-IV, p xxii.
[18]   ICD-10, 5.

This amendment was overturned in the Commons Public Bill Committee and replaced by a single provision (now s 3 of the MHA 2007) stating that dependence on alcohol or drugs is not considered to be a disorder or disability of the mind.

Dependence on alcohol or drugs

3.17 The exclusion refers to dependence and so extreme intoxication is not prevented from being a mental disorder by this provision. The Draft Code of Practice emphasises that other mental disorders relating to the use of alcohol or drugs are not excluded, and these include withdrawal state with delirium or associated psychotic disorder, organic mental disorders association with prolonged abuse of drugs or alcohol, or even severe acute intoxication (drunkenness) provided all the relevant criteria are met.[19]

3.18 Dependence on alcohol or drugs appears in the diagnostic manuals as a mental disorder. Addiction is a separate ground of detention under Art 5(1)(e). Use of alcohol or drugs is not, by itself, regarded clinically as a disorder or disability of the mind, but the Government considers that 'the effects of such use may be'.[20] The effect of the statement in s 3 of the MHA 2007 that 'dependence on alcohol or drugs is not considered to be a disorder or disability of the mind' is that:[21]

> 'no action can be taken under the 1983 Act in relation to people simply because they are dependent on alcohol or drugs (including opiates, psycho-stimulants or some solvents), even though in other contexts their dependence would be considered clinically to be a mental disorder.'

3.19 The exclusion does not mean that addicts are excluded entirely from the scope of the MHA 1983. A person may have a mental disorder which is completely unrelated to their dependence on alcohol or drugs. Excess consumption of alcohol or drugs may precipitate recognised forms of mental illness such as Korsakoff's Syndrome, drug induced psychoses, delirium consequent on withdrawal, or depression. The Explanatory Notes also point out that the exclusion does not mean that:

> '[P]eople may never be treated without consent under the 1983 Act for alcohol or drug dependence. Like treatment for any other condition which is not itself a mental disorder, treatment for dependence may be given under the 1983 Act if it forms part of treatment for a condition which is a mental disorder for the purposes of the 1983 Act.'

---

[19] DoH *Mental Health Act 1983 Draft Revised Code of Practice* (2007), para 3.9. See http://www.dh.gov.uk/en/Consultations/Liveconsultations/DH_079842.

[20] Department of Health, Ministry of Justice, Welsh Assembly Government *Mental Health Act 2007 Explanatory Notes* (2007), para 25.

[21] Ibid, para 26.

This might occur where the dependence is a consequence of the mental disorder and treatment may therefore be given under s 63 of the MHA 1983.[22]

Promiscuity, other immoral conduct, or sexual deviancy

3.20 The Government considers that deletion of the exclusion for promiscuity or 'other immoral conduct' makes no practical difference, since 'clinically ... neither by itself is regarded as a mental disorder', and 'sexual orientation (homo-, hetero- and bi-sexuality) alone is not regarded as a mental disorder'.[23] Removing the sexual deviance exclusion is intended to have an effect and the Explanatory Notes make clear what it is – to allow detention of paedophiles under the Act:[24]

> 'some disorders of sexual preference are recognised clinically as mental disorders. Some of these disorders might be considered "sexual deviance" in the terms of the current exclusion (for example paraphilias like fetishism or paedophilia). On that basis, the amendment would bring such disorders within the scope of the 1983 Act.'

3.22 The arguments which the Government intend to eliminate by this change are exemplified in the case of *R (on the application of MN) v Mental Health Review Tribunal*[25] where the patient was detained as suffering from psychopathic disorder where a necessary component is abnormally aggressive or seriously irresponsible conduct. The patient argued that the only such conduct of this nature which he had engaged in was directed towards pursuing his sexually deviant urges as a paedophile. Therefore he argued he was entitled to discharge by the Mental Health Review Tribunal ('MHRT') as the only behavioural components of his disorder were acts in pursuit of his sexually deviancy. The MHRT rejected his argument, viewing it as fallacious. Their decision was upheld by Calvert-Smith J because it had taken into account not only the sexual deviancy, but also other symptoms which stood outside the actual sexual deviancy.

3.23 The MHRT considered it wrong to exclude consideration of abnormally aggressive behaviour or seriously irresponsible behaviour in pursuit of sexual deviancy. If the conduct of a paedophile, while he is pursuing his sexual gratification, was abnormally aggressive or seriously irresponsible then such behaviour could amount to psychopathy. In other words, diagnosis of psychopathy can be based on the way a paedophile conducts his sexual assaults. The MHRT was satisfied that N's behaviours included serious manipulative lying outside his sexual pursuits, fantasies of using violence to gratify his desires and concerns that he might strangle someone to achieve his sexual desires clearly. Also N's serious lying, outside his sexual pursuits, to manipulate

---

[22] *B v Croydon Health Authority* [1995] 1 All ER 683, CA.
[23] Department of Health, Ministry of Justice, Welsh Assembly Government *Mental Health Act 2007 Explanatory Notes* (2007), para 24.
[24] Ibid.
[25] [2007] EWHC 1524 (Admin).

others cannot be discounted altogether by reason of his institutionalisation. The MHRT was satisfied that there was a seriously aggressive nature which existed as well as his sexual needs.[26] The High Court upheld their decision. These lines of argument will no longer be possible. The MHA 2007 does away with them by abolishing the sexual deviancy exclusion and the requirement that anyone who suffers from personality disorder must be abnormally aggressive or seriously irresponsible in their conduct. There would be no obstacle to detaining N under the MHA 2007 on grounds of personality disorder.

3.24 Considerable concern was expressed by the Joint Committee on Human Rights about gender identity dysphoria and transvestic fetishism, given that transexualism may be regarded as falling within the right to personal development and physical and moral integrity under Art 8.[27] The Government's response was that both conditions may be regarded as mental disorders, since 'gender dysphoria is a disorder of gender identity, not sexuality', and hence has never been excluded from the MHA 1983. Transvestic fetishism, by contrast, would be considered clinically to be an abnormality of sexual preference. The Government thinks that a court might consider transvestic fetishism 'sexual deviancy' for the purposes of the MHA 1983, and so removing that exclusion brings it within the scope of the 1983 Act.[28] However:[29]

> '15. While very different from one another, gender dysphoria and transvestic fetishism are like very many other mental disorders which are in theory covered by the 1983 Act, but which in practice would not be expected to lead to people being detained. Other examples include mild depression and anxiety, phobia of flying and various forms of sexual dysfunction.
> 16. On the other hand, if a person did meet the criteria for detention as a result of gender identity or transvestic fetishism (or any other equally unlikely disorder) and needed to be detained for their own sake or to protect others then it is right that mental health legislation should enable appropriate action to be taken. But for that to happen there would have to be wholly exceptional – and very hard to envisage – circumstances.'

3.25 The JCHR argued for express exclusions, beyond simply those for addiction, to be included in the legislation, to reflect human rights obligations:[30]

> 'Obligations under EU law have made it necessary to provide express legal protection against employment discrimination on grounds of sexual orientation or gender reassignment.[31] The European Court of Human Rights has held that

---

[26]   [2007] EWHC 1524 (Admin) at [26]–[28].
[27]   House of Lords, House of Commons Joint Committee on Human Rights *Legislative Scrutiny: Mental Health Bill: Fourth Report of Session 2006-07* (HL Paper 40, HC Paper 288), paras 14 and 15; *Legislative Scrutiny: Seventh Progress Report: Fifteenth Report of Session 2006-07* (HL Paper 555, HC Paper 112), paras 1.4–1.6.
[28]   Ibid, Seventh Progress Report, p 19.
[29]   Ibid.
[30]   Ibid, para 1.6.
[31]   Employment Equality (Sexual Orientation) Regulations 2003, SI 2003/1661; Employment

sexual identity is protected by virtue of the right to respect for private life under Article 8. Freedom of religion (Article 9), freedom of association and freedom of expression of religious, cultural or political beliefs are protected by Articles 10 and 11 of the Convention. Discrimination in the way rights (including the right to protection against arbitrary detention under Article 5) are protected on grounds of ethnicity, religious, cultural or political beliefs, age or any other status is also proscribed by Article 14 of the Convention.'

Their argument was rejected, but this summary serves as a salutary reminder to the Government and clinicians of the human rights context in which the Mental Health Act operates, and where the boundary between mental disorder and deviancy from society's norms may lie.

Clinically recognised mental disorders

3.26 The Explanatory Notes to the Bill give the following examples of 'clinically recognised mental disorders':[32]

'[M]ental illnesses such as schizophrenia, bipolar disorder, anxiety or depression, as well as personality disorders, autistic spectrum disorders and learning disabilities. Disorders or disabilities of the brain are not regarded as mental disorders unless (and only to the extent that) they give rise to a disability or disorder of the mind as well.'

If a brain injury or a brain tumour, for example, causes a mental disorder or a mental disability, or manifests itself in a disturbance of mental functioning, then there will be a disability or disorder of the mind. We now consider the examples given in the Explanatory Notes.

Bipolar disorder

3.27 Bipolar disorder (also known as 'manic depressive illness') is a form of affective (mood) disorder where the sufferer suffers oscillations in mood or affect between profound depression and elation. The elated state may be described as hypomania or mania, hypomania being a lesser degree of mania. It involves mild elevation of mood increased energy and activity. The person may be extremely talkative, over-familiar, and may show increased sexual energy. Mania is where the person's mood has been elevated out of keeping with their circumstances for at least one week and is so severe as to disrupt ordinary social and work activities more or less completely. The signs are rapid fire speech, grandiosity, and decreased need for sleep. Bipolar illness may entail manic episodes of four to five months followed by depressions of six months or more, or it may be more rapid cycling.[33] Bipolar illness may be accompanied by

---

Equality (Sexual Orientation) (Amendment) Regulations 2003, SI 2003/2827; and Sex Discrimination (Gender Reassignment) Regulations 1999, SI 1999/1102.

[32]   *Mental Health Act 2007 Explanatory Notes*, para 17.

[33]   ICD-10, categories F30–F39; Mood (Affective) Disorders, p 112.

psychotic features. The term 'psychotic' indicates the presence of hallucinations, delusions, abnormalities of behaviour, such as gross excitements and over-activity, marked psychomotor retardation, disorganised speech or disorganised or catatonic behaviour.[34]

Schizophrenia

3.28 The most common psychotic illness is schizophrenia which, together with schizotypal and other delusional disorders, is grouped in ICD-10, ss F20–F29. These disorders are characterised by 'fundamental and characteristic distortions of thinking and perception, and by inappropriate or blunted affect (mood)'.[35] The characteristic distortions of thinking and perception include hallucinations, visual and auditory, delusions, attaching grossly disproportionate importance to minor and irrelevant matters, and developing an unshakable belief in the importance of bizarre ideas. As ICD-10 evocatively describes it:[36]

> 'The disturbance involves the most basic functions that give a normal person a feeling of individuality, uniqueness and self-direction. The most intimate thoughts, feelings, and acts are often felt to be know to or shared by others, and explanatory delusions may develop, to the effect that natural or supernatural forces are at work to influence the afflicted individual's behaviour or thoughts.'

Paranoid schizophrenia is the commonest type of schizophrenia in most parts of the world. Its classic symptoms include delusions of persecution, exalted birth, special mission, bodily change or jealousy, hallucinatory voices that threaten the patient or give commands, or auditory hallucinations without verbal form. There may also be hallucinations of smell, or taste or of sexual or other bodily sensations. Schizoaffective disorders are a hybrid of schizophrenia and bipolar illness where the symptoms of both illnesses are present at the same time or within a few days of each other.

Anxiety

3.29 Both ICD-10[37] and DSM-IV[38] include stress-related and anxiety disorder. These include post traumatic stress disorder, phobic anxiety disorders (agoraphobia, social phobias, animal phobia, examination phobia), other anxiety disorders manifested in panic attacks, or disorders where patients repeatedly present physical symptoms requesting medical investigations, in spite of repeated negative findings and reassurance from doctors. It is rare for patients with anxiety disorders to be detained under mental health legislation, their affliction rarely being of a nature or degree warranting detention. Obsessive compulsive disorder can on occasion produce disabling effects to the

---

[34] ICD-10, pp 5–6; DSM-IV, p 273.
[35] ICD-10, p 86.
[36] ICD-10, pp 86–87.
[37] ICD-10, categories F40–F48.
[38] DSM-IV, p 393.

requisite nature or degree. Here obsessive thoughts enter the patient's head again and again, and this is followed by ceaseless repetition of compulsive acts or rituals of stereotyped behaviour.

Depression

3.30 Depressive disorder is where the person is profoundly depressed in mood, involving loss of interest or pleasure in nearly all activities, and may be accompanied by feelings of worthlessness or guilt which may reach delusional proportions. In severe cases there may be thoughts of suicide or self harm, or the person may be beyond communication or refusing food and fluids.

Learning disability

3.31 The term currently favoured in the United Kingdom to describe people with intellectual impairment is 'learning disability', reflecting a move away from medical models of treatment in hospitals towards an emphasis on small residential units, integrated into the community, where the skills of residents can be developed and their individuality can be better respected.

3.32 New s 1(4) of the MHA 1983 defines learning disability as:[39]

'a state of arrested or incomplete development of the mind which includes significant impairment of intelligence and social functioning.'

This broadly corresponds with the ICD-10 and DSM-IV category of 'mental retardation', defined in ICD-10 as:[40]

'A condition of arrested or incomplete development of mind especially characterised by impairment of the skills manifested during the developmental period, which contribute to the overall level of intelligence, ie cognitive, motor language and social abilities.'

For there to be a learning disability there must be a state of arrested or incomplete development of the mind, and it must include significant impairment of intelligence and social functioning.

Arrested or incomplete development of the mind

3.33 The Mental Health Act 1983 Draft Revised Code of Practice states that an adult with arrested or incomplete development of mind is one who has experienced a significant impairment of the normal process of maturation of intellectual and social development that occurs during childhood and adolescence. Hence:[41]

---

[39]   Inserted by s 2(3) of the MHA 2007.
[40]   ICD-10, categories F70–F79 at p 226. See also DSM-IV, 3.17–3.19.
[41]   Department of Health *Mental Health Act 1983 Draft Revised Code of Practice* (2007), para 37.4. See http://www.dh.gov.uk/en/Consultations/Liveconsultations/DH_079842.

'The Act embraces the general understanding that features which qualify as a learning disability are present prior to adulthood. For the purposes of the Act, learning disability does not include people whose intellectual disorder derives from accident, injury or illness occurring after they completed normal maturation (although such conditions do fall within the definition of mental disorder in the Act).'

People with learning disability will remain ineligible for long term detention or guardianship unless they have abnormally aggressive or seriously irresponsible conduct. This will not apply to people with 'acquired learning disability' since, following the Code's approach, they do not suffer from 'learning disability'. They are eligible for long term detention or guardianship, provided the other criteria are met, even if their conduct is not abnormally aggressive or seriously irresponsible.

Significant impairment of intelligence and social functioning

3.34 Diagnosis is based on a combination of arrested or incomplete development of intelligence and lack of social competence. Some IQ tests can disadvantage people whose education has been interrupted, or people from different ethnic backgrounds, and verbal tests may disadvantage people with communication problems. Standardised IQ tests, although an important indicator, do not determine the question whether a person is suffering from arrested or incomplete development of mind, or of its level of severity, and a full social assessment is required.

3.35 Whether the impairment is considered to be 'significant' is a matter for clinical judgment. The DSM-IV and ICD-10 state that the diagnosis of 'mental retardation' may be made for someone who has an IQ score of 70 or below. IQ scores are not determinative. In *Meggary v Chief Adjudications Officer*, where the issue was whether a child with autistic disorder had a 'severe impairment of intelligence and social functioning' and was therefore entitled to disability living allowance, Simon Brown LJ made clear that intelligence included insight and sagacity as well as intellectual intelligence. He said this:[42]

'In most cases, no doubt, the measurement of IQ will be the best available method of measuring intelligence. But among the dictionary definitions of intelligence one finds the reference not merely to the functions of understanding and intellect but also to the qualities of insight and sagacity. It seems to me that in the case if an autistic child those qualities may well be lacking and to the extent that they are there will be a functional impairment which overlaps both limbs of the regulation, ie both intelligence and social functioning.'

3.36 In *R v Hall* the Court of Appeal considered the meaning of the words 'severe impairment of intelligence and social functioning' in the context of an appeal against conviction for unlawful sexual intercourse with a 'defective' contrary to the Sexual Offences Act 1956. A person was a mental defective for

---

42   (1999) *The Times*, 11 November, CA.

the purposes of the 1956 Act if she suffered from 'severe impairment of intelligence and social functioning'. The Court of Appeal held that these were 'not terms of art' but 'ordinary English words', and that on a natural reading of the words 'severe impairment' was to be measured 'against the standard of normal persons', not by comparison with other people with learning disabilities.[43] The same must be true of significant impairment.

Autistic spectrum disorders

3.37 The DSM-IV category of 'Disorders Usually first Diagnosed in Infancy, Childhood or Early Adolescence' includes a category of Pervasive Developmental Disorders, which includes autistic disorder and Asperger's disorder, as well as mental retardation. The essential features of autistic disorder according to the DSM-IV are the presence of markedly abnormal or impaired development in social interaction, communication or awareness of others, leading to gross and sustained impairment in reciprocal social interaction, failure to develop peer relationships. The Draft Revised Code of Practice states that while it is possible for someone on the autistic spectrum to meet the conditions for treatment under the Mental Health Act without having any other form of mental disorder, even if it is not associated with abnormally aggressive or seriously irresponsible behaviour, this is likely to happen only very rarely.[44] The Revised Draft Code urges that assessment should take place by specialists in autistic spectrum disorders and that, where appropriate, someone who knows the service user should be present at initial assessment, provided it can be done without breaching the person's confidentiality. Knowledge of the person's early development history and usual pattern of behaviour will help prevent someone with an autistic spectrum disorder from being wrongly brought under compulsion.[45] The Code warns against construing as mental disorder warranting detention eccentricity or repetitive behaviour which might be a coping mechanism.

3.38 Asperger's Disorder entails severe and sustained impairment in social interaction and the development of restricted, repetitive patterns of behaviour interests and activities, causing clinically significant impairment in social, occupational or other areas of functioning. It is distinguished in the DSM-IV from autistic disorder, by the lack of clinically significant delays in acquisition of language, or in cognitive development or development of age-appropriate self-help skills.[46] A person with Aspergers might have a high IQ and therefore fall outside the definition of learning disability.

3.39 Although people with high measured IQ can still have these diagnoses, where the person has an IQ below 70, they may be counted as learning disabilities for the purpose of the Act, so an association of the disability with

---

[43]   (1987) 86 Cr App R 159, per Parker LJ at 162, CA.
[44]   Department of Health *Mental Health Act 1983 Draft Revised Code of Practice* (2007), para 37.16. See http://www.dh.gov.uk/en/Consultations/Liveconsultations/DH_079842
[45]   Ibid, para 37.21.
[46]   DSM-IV, p 75.

abnormally aggressive or seriously irresponsible conduct will be needed for long-term detention, a community treatment order, guardianship, a mental health disposal by a criminal court, or transfer to hospital.

The requirement that learning disability be associated with abnormally aggressive or seriously irresponsible conduct for long-term detention, guardianship or a CTO, or in relation to the offender provisions of the MHA 1983

3.40 For the most part people with learning disabilities are ineligible for detention under long-term powers of detention, under guardianship, or under the offender provisions in Part 3 of the MHA 1983 unless their learning disability was associated with abnormally aggressive or seriously irresponsible conduct. This provision was introduced in relation to learning disability in the 1983 Act. It is lifted from the definition of psychopathic disorder in the MHA 1959. Lord Rix explained to the House of Lords during the debates on the 2006 Bill that these words represented the:[47]

> 'best compromise we could then reach between the Government's position that people with a learning disability should come under the scope of the Act, and my position that people with a learning disability are not ill and should not be treated as if they were.'

This argument has worked for learning disability but not for personality disorder, which might equally be said not to be an illness. The MHA 2007 preserves the position under the MHA 1983 for people with learning disability, but it removes the requirement of abnormally aggressive or seriously irresponsible conduct if someone is to be detained on grounds of personality disorder.

3.41 Section 2 inserts new s 1(2A) and (2B) providing that for the purposes of detention for treatment (s 3), guardianship and guardianship orders (ss 7 and 37), community treatment orders (s 17A), detention under a hospital order (s 37), detention under a hospital direction (s 45A) transfer from prison (ss 47 and 48), use of remand powers and interim hospital orders (ss 35–38), and making a hospital order where it is impracticable or inappropriate to bring the offender to court (s 51) a person may not be considered to be suffering from a mental disorder simply as a result of having a learning disability, unless that disability is associated with abnormally aggressive or seriously irresponsible conduct on the part of the person concerned. This also applies to the power to renew detention, guardianship or a community treatment order (ss 20 and 20A), and to the Mental Health Review Tribunal's power of discharge (s 72). As the Explanatory Notes to the MHA 2007 put it:[48]

---

[47] *Hansard*, HL Deb, vol 687, col 662.
[48] Department of Health, Ministry of Justice, Welsh Assembly Government *Mental Health Act 2007 Explanatory Notes* (2007), para 22.

'In those cases where the 1983 Act as it stands now effectively precludes the use of detention or other compulsory measures on the basis of a learning disability which is not associated with abnormally aggressive or seriously irresponsible conduct, the same will be true of the Act as amended.'

The phrase requires the learning disability to be associated with the abnormally aggressive or seriously irresponsible conduct. Although this does not necessarily imply a cause-effect relationship, any such conduct which arises from other sources such as a physical disorder or severe toothache, is excluded.

3.42   In *R v Trent Mental Health Review Tribunal, ex parte Ryan*, Nolan LJ said that whether conduct amounts:[49]

'to seriously irresponsible or abnormally aggressive behaviour seems to me ... to raise questions other than of a purely clinical nature.'

The Mental Health Act Code of Practice states that abnormally aggressive behaviour is:[50]

'[B]ehaviour which leads to a conclusion that the actions are outside the usual range of aggressive behaviour, and which causes actual damage and/or real distress occurring recently or persistently or with excessive severity.'

Irresponsible conduct is:[51]

'[B]ehaviour which shows a lack of responsibility, a disregard of the consequences of action taken, and, where the results cause actual damage or real distress, either recently or persistently or with excessive severity.'

Such conduct on the part of the person need not be current nor have been particularly recent. The requirement will be met if the learning disability has been associated with such conduct in the past and that there is a real risk that, if treatment in hospital is discontinued, that conduct will manifest itself in the future. In *Lewis v Gibson*, Thorpe LJ said this:[52]

'To make a balanced assessment of the patient's present state some regard must be had to the past history and the future propensity. A conclusion based only on the recent past, which might represent a transient phase of quiescence, would be superficial.'

3.43   In *R (on the application of P) v Mental Health Review Tribunal (East Midlands and North East Region)*[53] the issue was whether a person could still be suffering from psychopathic disorder even though there had been no recent

---

[49]   [1992] COD 157.
[50]   Department of Health and Welsh Office *Code of Practice on the Mental Health Act 1983* (TSO, 3rd edn, 1999), para 30.5.
[51]   Ibid.
[52]   [2005] EWCA Civ 587, [2005] MHLR 309, para 31.
[53]   [2002] EWCA Civ 697, CA.

abnormally aggressive or seriously irresponsible conduct. P's index offence was at a pub in 1992. It was not in dispute that he suffered from psychopathic disorder at the time of his index offence, manslaughter of a young man whom he had ferociously assaulted. But there had been no abnormally aggressive or seriously irresponsible conduct for some years. Pill LJ said this:[54]

> 'The extent to which abnormally aggressive or seriously irresponsible conduct now occurs may throw light on whether there is psychopathic disorder, but the disorder may still exist even though there has been no such conduct for years. I have no difficulty in accepting that the tribunal were entitled to decide that a disorder which admittedly existed in 1992 still existed in 2000, even though, because of successful management of the condition, no abnormally aggressive or seriously irresponsible conduct has occurred for years.'

3.44 A number of cases have considered the issue of seriously irresponsible conduct. In *Re F (Mental Health Act: Guardianship)*,[55] the issue was whether a learning disabled 17-year-old was exhibiting seriously irresponsible conduct by wanting to return to a home where she had suffered neglect and possible sexual abuse. If her conduct was seriously irresponsible, she would be eligible for Mental Health Act guardianship. The Court of Appeal held that guardianship could not be used as she was not behaving seriously irresponsibly since the urge to return to one's home and family is 'almost universal'.

3.45 *Re F* was applied in *Newham London Borough Council v S (adult: court's jurisdiction)*,[56] Wall J held that guardianship could not be used in S's case to remove her from the care of her father who was having serious difficulty coping with her to residential care, because:[57]

> 'the only example of "seriously irresponsible conduct" on S's part was her total lack of road sense and a tendency to rush into the road without looking'.

This was not enough to satisfy the statutory test. In each case although guardianship was held not to be available, the court achieved the same effect by using its inherent jurisdiction to determine where an incapacitated person should live.

3.46 The abnormally aggressive or seriously irresponsible conduct exclusion closes off the possibility of using guardianship to rescue people with learning disabilities from abusive situations where it is the irresponsible conduct of *others* which is putting *them* at risk and they are passively enduring abuse. Jones is rightly critical of the preservation of the status quo as having little to commend it, a monument to the effectiveness of the learning disability lobby, but little else.[58] In 1989 Beverley Lewis, a young woman with a profound learning disability starved to death in her mother's living room. Beverley's

---

[54]   [2002] EWCA Civ 697 at [23]–[26].
[55]   [2000] 1 FLR 192, CA.
[56]   [2003] EWHC 1909 (Fam).
[57]   [2003] EWHC 1909 (Fam) at [11].
[58]   RM Jones *Annotations to the Mental Health Act 2007*, section 2.

mother was herself mentally ill and was severely neglecting Beverley, who was passively enduring neglect, but whose own conduct was not seriously irresponsible. Therefore, guardianship or admission for treatment under the Mental Health Act could not be used to rescue her from this fate.[59]

3.47 Nowadays an application could be made to the Court of Protection on the grounds that Beverley lacked capacity and removal was in her best interests, or, after March 2009, she could be deprived of her liberty under the Mental Capacity Act authorisation. These are cumbrous procedures by comparison with guardianship, which has a procedure which is currently in use and readily understood. Under the MHA 2007, a completed guardianship application authorises a person to be taken and conveyed to their required place of residence, to be required to reside there and grant access to professionals, to be returned there if they abscond, and to attend specified places for treatment education or training. This is capable of amounting to the complete and effective control over residence, treatment, movement of the degree and intensity required to amount to a deprivation of liberty.[60]

3.48 Removal of the abnormally aggressive or seriously irresponsible conduct requirement for guardianship in cases of learning disability would provide a means of rescue for many people with learning disabilities from abusive situations, without complex legal process, and with effective redress via the Mental Health Review Tribunal.

Personality disorders

3.49 In *Koniarska v United Kingdom*[61] the Strasbourg Court gave a strong indication that psychopathic disorder and personality disorder amount to unsoundness of mind for the purposes of Art 5(1)(e). The applicant was a juvenile suffering from psychopathic disorder which had been deemed untreatable. Her detention was found necessary as there was a danger of her injuring herself or other persons. There could thus be said to be both medical and social reasons for her detention, and the court considered the detention might have been justified under Art 5(1)(e) on grounds of unsoundness of mind. In the event no ruling on the Art 5(1)(e) point was necessary as the detention was justified under Art 5(1)(d) as it was the detention of a minor for the purposes of educational supervision. However, it is clear from this case and the later decision in *Reid v United Kingdom*[62] that personality disorder is unsoundness of mind for Convention purposes.

3.50 Under the MHA 1983 a person with a personality disorder could only be detained if they had a diagnosis of 'psychopathic disorder', meaning 'a

59 P Fennell 'Blaming the Law: Lessons from the Case' (1989) *The Guardian*, 3 November, p 38; 'Beverley Lewis – Was the Law to Blame?' (1989) 139 NLJ 1557–1558; 'Falling through the legal loopholes' (1989) *Social Work Today*, 30 November, pp 18–20.
60 *HL v United Kingdom* (2004) 40 EHRR 761, ECtHR.
61 *(Application 33670/96)* Decision of 12 October 2000, ECtHR.
62 (2003) 37 EHRR 9, ECtHR.

persistent disorder or disability of mind (whether or not including significant impairment of intelligence) which *results in* abnormally aggressive or seriously irresponsible conduct'. As the Reed Committee noted in 1994 the group labelled as 'psychopathically disordered' is 'extremely heterogeneous', covering:[63]

> 'at one end of the spectrum highly dangerous serial murderers and rapists, and at the other disturbed young women whose disorder mainly manifested itself in repeated self-harm'.

The MHA 2007 removes the requirement of abnormally aggressive or seriously irresponsible conduct requirement in cases of personality disorder.

3.51   Personality disorders are grouped together in ICD-10 categories F60-69 'Disorders of Adult Personality and Behaviour', and defined as:[64]

> 'Clinically significant conditions and behaviour patterns which tend to be persistent and are characteristic of an individual's characteristic lifestyle and mode of relating to self and others. They are deeply ingrained and enduring behaviour patterns, manifesting themselves as inflexible responses to a broad range of personal and social situations. They represent either extreme or significant deviations from the away the average individual in a given culture perceives, thinks, feels, and particularly relates to others.'

The DSM-IV gives the following diagnostic features of personality disorder in general, assuming there is no other mental disorder, substance abuse, or head trauma to explain them:[65]

> 'An enduring pattern of inner experience and behaviour that deviates markedly from the individual's culture. This is manifested in two or more of the following areas:
>
> (1)   cognition (ie ways of perceiving and intereting self, other people and events)
> (2)   affectivity (ie the range, intensity, lability and appropriateness of emotional response)
> (3)   interpersonal functioning
> (4)   impulse control.'

The enduring pattern must be inflexible and pervasive across a wide range of personal and social situations, and must lead to clinically significant distress or impairment in social, occupational or other important areas of functioning. The pattern must also be stable and of long duration and its consent must be traceable back at least to adolescence or early adulthood.

---

[63]   Department of Health and Home Office *Report of the Department of Health and Home Office Working Group on Psychopathic Disorder* (HMSO, 1994), para 10.16(iii).
[64]   ICD-10, p 200.
[65]   DSM-IV, p 633.

3.52   The DSM-IV lists ten types of personality disorder:[66]

- paranoid personality disorder is a pattern of distrust and suspiciousness interpreting others' motives as malevolent;

- schizoid personality disorder manifested in a pattern of detachment form social relationships and a restricted range of emotional expression;

- schizotypal personality disorder is a pattern of acute discomfort in close relationships, cognitive or perceptual distortions and eccentricities of behaviour;

- antisocial personality disorder is a pattern of disregard for and violation of the rights of others;

- borderline personality disorder is a pervasive pattern of instability of interpersonal relationships, self-image and affects and marked impulsiveness that begins in early adulthood, is present in a variety of contexts, and is manifested in frantic efforts to avoid real or imagined abandonment, including self-mutilation or self harm;

- histrionic personality disorder is a pattern of excessive emotionality and attention seeking;

- narcissistic personality disorder is a pattern of grandiosity, need for admiration and lack of empathy;

- avoidant personality disorder is a pattern of social inhibition feelings of inadequacy and hypersensitivity to negative evaluation;

- dependent personality disorder is a pattern of submissive and clinging behaviour relating to an excessive need to be taken care of;

- obsessive compulsive Personality disorder is a pattern of preoccupation with orderliness, perfectionism and control.

There is an eleventh category of personality disorder not otherwise specified, which covers (inter alia) the situation where a person meets the general criteria for personality disorder, but traits of several different types of personality disorder are evident.

3.53   The now legally obsolete psychopathic disorder equates broadly to the DSMIV category of Anti-Social Personality Disorder or the ICD-10 category of Dissocial Personality Disorder which usually comes to attention because of

---

[66]   DSM-IV, p 629.

a gross disparity between behaviour and the prevailing social norms and according to the ICD-10 is characterised by the following:[67]

> '(a)   callous unconcern for the feelings of others;
> (b)   gross and persistent attitude of irresponsibility and disregard for social norms, rules and obligations;
> (c)   incapacity to maintain enduring relationships, although having no difficulty in establishing them;
> (d)   very low tolerance to frustration and a low threshold for discharge of aggression, including violence;
> (e)   incapacity to experience guilt and to profit from experience, particularly punishment;
> (f)   marked proneness to blame others, or to offer plausible rationalisations, for the behaviour which has brought the individual in conflict with society.'

3.54 Psychopathic disorder required a cause effect relationship between the disorder and any abnormally aggressive or seriously irresponsible conduct. This is no longer necessary. It will in most cases be aggressive or irresponsible behaviour which will bring the individual to the attention of the psychiatric services, but it is not necessary to show that the conduct is caused by the disorder. So a patient with a diagnosis of one of the above listed personality disorders, who meets the other statutory criteria will be liable to compulsion. Removal of the term 'psychopathic disorder' and its key component of abnormally aggressive or seriously irresponsible conduct from the Act broadens considerably the scope of powers to detain people with personality disorder. One of the Government's key concerns is to ensure that sex offenders with personality disorders emerging from prison following determinate sentences will be detainable under the non-offender provisions of the MHA 1983. This is a key reason for the change to a single broad definition of 'mental disorder', coupled with the removal of the sexual deviancy exclusion (see paras **3.20–3.26** above), and the replacement of the treatability test (see paras **3.57–3.64** below).

Mental disorder of a kind or degree warranting confinement

3.55 Not only must a person be suffering from mental disorder but it must be of a kind or degree warranting confinement, reception into guardianship or a community treatment order. Determining whether mental disorder is of the relevant nature or degree warranting treatment in hospital depends on whether the relevant admission criteria (necessity for own health or safety or for the protection of others and availability of appropriate treatment) are met. The disorder must be of a nature or degree making it appropriate for the person to receive treatment in hospital. As the Explanatory Notes state, 'nature' refers to the particular mental disorder from which the patient is suffering, its chronicity, its prognosis, and the patient's previous response to receiving treatment for disorder. 'Degree' refers to the current manifestation of the patient's disorder.[68]

---

[67]   ICD-10, F60.2, p 204.

[68]   Department of Health, Ministry of Justice, Welsh Assembly Government *Mental Health Act 2007 Explanatory Notes* (2007), para 31; *R v Mental Health Review Tribunal for the South Thames Region, ex parte Smith* [1999] COD 148, QBD.

3.56 Treatment in hospital must be necessary in the interests of the person's own health or safety or for the protection of other persons. Appropriate treatment must be available. *Winterwerp* also established that detention must be a necessary and proportionate response to the patient's circumstances. Other less severe measures must have been considered and found to be insufficient to safeguard the individual or public interest, leaving no alternative to detention.[69]

REPLACING TREATABILITY WITH AVAILABILITY OF APPROPRIATE TREATMENT

3.57 The 'treatability test' under the MHA 1983 applied to psychopathic disorder and mental impairment. For detention or renewal the doctor had to certify that medical treatment was likely to alleviate or prevent deterioration in the patient's condition, which would be hard to do if the patient was resolutely not co-operating. This might happen if a person with a personality disorder refused to engage with cognitive behaviour therapy. Treatment might be available and appropriate but unlikely to make any difference if the patient refused to participate.

3.58 The MHA 2007 requires only that appropriate treatment be available regardless of whether the patient accepts it. Section 3(4) of the MHA 1983 states that:[70]

> 'references to appropriate medical treatment, in relation to a person suffering from mental disorder, are references to medical treatment which is appropriate in his case, taking into account the nature and degree of the mental disorder and all other circumstances of his case.'

'All the circumstances of the case' would require consideration of, inter alia, the patient's age, gender, cultural background, family and social circumstances, and living accommodation, as well as medical considerations.

3.59 In addition to replacing the treatability test, the MHA 2007 introduces the test of availability of appropriate treatment where it had not existed hitherto, in s 36 (remand for treatment), s 48 (transfer of unsentenced prisoners) and s 51(6) (hospital orders where it is impracticable or inappropriate to bring a detainee before the court).[71]

3.60 The Government's intention is:[72]

---

[69] *Litwa v Poland* (2001) 33 EHRR 53, (2000) 63 BMLR 199, ECtHR.
[70] Inserted by MHA 2007, s 4(3).
[71] Ibid, s 5.
[72] Joint Committee on Human Rights *Legislative Scrutiny: Mental Health Bill Fourth Report of Session 2006–07* (HL Paper 40, HC Paper 288, 4 February 2007), p 45; Appendix 1 – Letter of 17 November 2006 from The Rt Hon Rosie Winterton MP, Minister of State, Department of Health to the JCHR, para 8.

'To remove ground for argument about the efficacy or likely efficacy of a treatment which can be used to prevent detention of people who present a risk to themselves or others.'

If the 'treatability test' required clinicians to predict whether treatment would work for a particular patient, which might not always be possible, a decision might be taken not to detain under civil powers in the Mental Health Act even though the patient posed a significant risk to self or to others.[73] The second aim is to ensure that people with personality disorders are not too readily ruled out as being beyond help, and interventions should be developed to treat these afflictions, which can cause great distress to sufferers and their loved ones.

3.61   The Minister of State, Rosie Winterton, took the unusual step of writing to the Joint Committee on Human Rights prior to its scrutiny of the Mental Health Bill 2006 to explain the basis of the Government's view that the Bill was 'Convention compliant'. In relation to treatability the Government's position was based on *Reid v United Kingdom*[74] where the European Court of Human Rights said that Art 5(1)(e) imposed no requirement that detention in a mental hospital was conditional on the illness or condition being of a nature or degree amenable to medical treatment. The Court held (at para 51) that confinement under Art 5(1)(e) may be necessary not only where a person needs therapy, medication or other clinical treatment to cure or alleviate his condition, but also where the person needs control and supervision to prevent him, for example, causing harm to himself or other persons.

3.62   The Joint Committee on Human Rights noted the strongly held views of psychiatrists during the Committee stage in the House of Lords, that if the treatability test was to be abolished, it should be replaced with the test that treatment is available which is likely to be of therapeutic benefit to the patient. This was to avoid a perceived risk of psychiatrists becoming mere custodians rather than therapists, and psychiatric detention becoming perceived as preventive detention. The Committee considered that there was nothing in the European Convention on Human Rights to prevent abolition of the treatability test. They also noted Art 17(1)(iii) of Council of Europe Recommendation No (2004)10 of the Committee of Ministers to member states concerning the human rights and dignity of persons with mental disorder, which requires that detention has a 'therapeutic purpose.' This is broadly defined (in Art 2(3)) as 'including prevention, diagnosis, control, cure or treatment'.

3.63   The UK Government has reserved the right not to comply with the Council of Europe Recommendation as a whole. Nevertheless, Chris Bryant, a Labour MP, tabled an amendment to address concerns about the absence of a test of therapeutic benefit, and which has brought England and Wales into compliance with this provision of the Recommendation. Section 7(3) of the MHA 2007 inserts a new subs (4) into s 145, requiring treatment to have a 'therapeutic purpose':

---

[73]   *Hansard*, HL Deb, vol 688, col 319.
[74]   (2003) 37 EHRR 9, ECtHR.

'Any reference in this Act to medical treatment, in relation to mental disorder, shall be construed as a reference to medical treatment the purpose of which is to alleviate, or prevent a worsening of, the disorder or one or more of its symptoms or manifestations.'

As Baroness Royall put it on behalf of the Government:[75]

'"Symptoms" is intended to cover the consequences of which patients themselves complain while "manifestations" more obviously covers the evidence of the disorder as seen by other people.'

So a manifestation could be violent conduct, sex offending, or self-harming. Treatment must have the *purpose* of alleviating or preventing 'a worsening of the disorder or one or more of its symptoms or manifestations'.[76] But it need not be likely to achieve those purposes. The patient's refusal to accept treatment can no longer be an obstacle to detention, as long as the treatment is available. The Minister of State at the Department of Health, Rosie Winterton, went so far as to say that she had been informed that:[77]

'lawyers have advised their patients not to engage with treatment because if it can be proved that they are not treatable they have to be released.'

3.64 Medical treatment for mental disorder is redefined in s 145. It includes nursing and also psychological intervention and specialist mental health habilitation, rehabilitation and care. Psychological interventions are expressly mentioned for the first time. These include psychotherapy and other interactive treatments requiring co-operation from the patient, often the main treatments used for people with personality disorders.

CONCLUSION

3.65 The new single broad definition of 'mental disorder' has the potential to broaden the scope of compulsory powers. The combined effect of the changes to the definition, the removal of all exclusions save those for addiction, and the replacement of the treatability test with appropriate treatment, is to remove areas of discretion not to use compulsory powers. There will be many fewer legitimate reasons for clinicians not to use compulsory powers under the Act with relation to people with personality disorder. In addition to broadening the scope of compulsory powers, the MHA 2007 also extends the power to use them to new professional groups beyond the medical and social work professions. Chapters 4 and 5 discuss the statutory roles conferred by the MHA 2007.

---

[75] *Hansard*, HL Deb, vol 693, col 835.
[76] MHA 1983, s 145(4), as inserted by MHA 2007, s 7(3).
[77] Public Bill Committee, cols 121–122.

Chapter 4

STATUTORY POWERS AND RESPONSIBILITIES: THE POWERS AND DUTIES OF MENTAL HEALTH STAFF

OVERVIEW

4.1   This chapter deals with the statutory roles conferred by the MHA 2007 on Approved Mental Health Professionals ('AMHPs'), doctors who provide medical recommendations in support of community powers, Responsible Clinicians ('RCs') and Approved Clinicians ('ACs'). Chapter 2 (ss 9–22) of the MHA 2007 (entitled 'Professional Roles'), provides for the key roles in imposing and managing compulsory powers to be performed by a wider range of professionals than at present. It replaces the 'approved social worker' ('ASW') with the 'approved mental health professional' ('AMHP'), and the 'responsible medical officer' ('RMO') with the 'responsible clinician' ('RC').

Approved Mental Health Professionals (AMHPs)

4.2   Under Part 2 of the MHA 1983 an application for detention or guardianship may be made only by an approved social worker or the patient's nearest relative.[1] The MHA 2007 opens the role of applicant for detention to 'Approved Mental Health Professionals' who need not be social workers but could be a nurse, psychologist, or occupational therapist with appropriately recognised training.

4.3   The MHA 1983 requires an application for non-emergency admission to be made to the managers of the receiving hospital. Each application must be supported by two doctors' recommendations, to the effect that the patient is suffering from mental disorder of a nature or degree warranting detention in the interests of his health or safety or for the protection of others. One of the recommending doctors must be approved under s 12 of the MHA 1983. The AMHP also acquires the new responsibility of agreeing the appropriateness and the terms of a community treatment order ('CTO') proposed by the RC.[2]

---

[1]   MHA 1983, s 11(1).
[2]   MHA 1983, s 17A, as inserted by MHA 2007, s 32(2).

Section 12 approved doctors

4.4   A s 12 doctor is approved as having special experience in the diagnosis or treatment of mental disorder. The evidential requirement of medical recommendations from doctors for detention will remain under the MHA 2007. Once detained under the MHA 1983, a patient has been assigned a responsible medical officer to be in charge of treatment. RMOs are replaced under the 2007 Act by responsible clinicians. Where two recommendations are necessary for compulsory admission under ss 2 or 3, one must come from a s 12 approved doctor.

Approved Clinicians ('ACs') and Responsible Clinicians ('RCs')

4.5   RCs replace RMOs, and need not be medically qualified, provided they have undergone approved clinician ('AC') training. Under the 1983 Act, the RMO has been the registered medical practitioner in charge of the treatment of the patient, and has extensive powers. These include the power to send the patient on leave, and to recall from leave (s 17), the power to renew detention (s 20), the power to discharge (s 23), the power to block discharge by the nearest relative (s 25) and the power to direct the patient to accept treatment, subject to the second opinion safeguards in Part 4. In practice RMOs have usually been consultant psychiatrists.

4.6   Under the MHA 2007, RCs (who need not be a doctor as long as they are an 'Approved Clinician' ('AC')) will take over most of the functions of RMOs. As the Explanatory Notes point out 'some functions currently reserved to RMOs may be taken instead by another AC, not just the RC'.[3] Approval as an AC is not restricted to medical doctors, and may be extended to practitioners from other professions, such as nursing, psychology, occupational therapy and social work. In addition to assuming the functions of RMOs, RCs will also have the power to initiate, with the agreement of an AMHP, a Community Treatment Order.[4]

The impact of the Human Rights Act 1998

4.7   The Human Rights Act 1998 requires public authorities to act compatibly with Convention rights. A key question is whether AMHPs, doctors recommending detention, responsible clinicians, and others carrying out functions under the Mental Health Act will be 'a public authority' for the purposes of the HRA 1998. A public authority includes any body or person certain of whose functions are functions of a public nature.[5] Section 6(1) of the HRA 1998 makes it 'unlawful for a public authority to act in a way which is incompatible with a Convention right.' Under s 7(1):

---

[3]   Department of Health, Ministry of Justice, Welsh Assembly Government *Mental Health Act 2007 Explanatory Notes* (2007), para 48.

[4]   MHA 1983, s 17A, as inserted by MHA 2007, s 32(2).

[5]   HRA 1998, s 6(3).

'A person who claims that a public authority has acted (or proposes to act) in a way which is made unlawful by s 6(1) may—

(a) bring proceedings against the authority under this Act in the appropriate court or tribunal, or

(b) rely on the Convention right or rights concerned in any legal proceedings.'

In *R (on the application of Wilkinson) v Responsible Medical Officer Broadmoor Hospital*, Hale LJ said this:[6]

'Health authorities and NHS trusts and their staff are clearly public authorities. Under section 6(3), a public authority includes "a person certain of whose functions are functions of a public nature": this is apt to cover the actions of private doctors and others carrying out statutory functions under the Mental Health Act.'

Although this statement was obiter, it is a strong indication that anyone exercising statutory functions which engage the Convention rights of service users is a public authority.

4.8 The rights most likely to be engaged are the protection against arbitrary deprivation of liberty (Art 5) and the right to respect for private life (Art 8) which includes physical integrity and confidentiality. In order to comply with Art 5 an AMHP, for example, must ensure that the detention is carried out in accordance with correct procedure under the Mental Health Act, with objective medical evidence of a true mental disorder which is of a nature or degree warranting detention, and that detention is strictly necessary, ie:[7]

'that other less severe measures have been considered and found to be insufficient to safeguard the individual or public interest which might require that the person concerned be detained.'

4.9 In order to comply with Art 8 an AMHP would have to ensure that any disclosure of confidential information can be justified under Art 8(2) as being in accordance with the law and necessary in a democratic society (a proportionate response) in the interests of national security, public safety or the economic well-being of the country, for the prevention of disorder or crime, for the protection of health or morals, or for the protection of the rights and freedoms of others.

Section 139 of the Mental Health Act 1983

4.10 Section 139 of the MHA 1983 provides a defence and a procedural hurdle in respect of actions brought against people purportedly acting pursuant to the Act:[8]

---

[6]   [2001] EWCA Civ 1545 at [61].
[7]   *Litwa v Poland* (2001) 33 EHRR 53, ECtHR.
[8]   MHA 1983, s 139(1).

'No person shall be liable ... to any civil or criminal proceedings to which he would have been liable apart from this section in respect of any act purporting to be done in pursuance of this Act or any regulations or rules made under this Act, unless the act was done in bad faith or without reasonable care.'

The procedural hurdle is that leave of the High Court is required for civil proceedings and the leave of the Director of Public Prosecutions for criminal prosecutions.[9] The procedural hurdle does not apply to proceedings against the Secretary of State, the National Assembly for Wales, a Strategic Health Authority, Health Authority, Special Health Authority, or Primary Care Trust or against a National Health Service trust. Under the MHA 1959 the applicant needed to show substantial grounds for the contention of bad faith or negligence before leave could be granted. This is no longer necessary, but the defence that a person acted in good faith and with reasonable care remains under the 1983 and 2007 Acts.

4.11 Section 139 does not apply to habeas corpus or judicial review. In *R v Governor of Pentonville Prison, ex parte Azam*[10] Lord Denning MR held that if Parliament was to suspend habeas corpus express words of clear implication would be necessary. In *R v Hallstrom and another, ex parte W*, the Court of Appeal applied this principle and held that the requirement of leave does not apply to public law applications for judicial review.[11] Since then, in *R (on the application of Wilkinson) v Responsible Medical Officer Broadmoor Hospital* Brooke LJ said, obiter, that a civil claim under s 7 of the Human Rights Act 1998 would be caught by the language of s 139(1) and would require leave.[12] Hale LJ expressed herself 'inclined to agree' emphasising that: 'proceedings under s 7(1) are not confined to judicial review, and indeed it would be most surprising if they were'. Her Ladyship then went on to say that:[13]

'Section 8(1) provides that "In relation to any act (or proposed act) of a public authority which the court finds is (or would be) unlawful, it may grant such relief or remedy, or make such order, within its powers as it considers just and appropriate." In some cases, for example where delegated legislation or the policy of a public authority is in question, then the appropriate remedies will only be available in judicial review. But in others, where specific invasions of individuals' rights are in question, an ordinary action would be more appropriate.'

The position would appear to be that no leave is required for habeas corpus or judicial review, including a judicial review application under s 7. But where Convention Rights are being upheld by ordinary action under s 7 of the HRA 1998 leave may be required. Hale LJ stressed that the court had not heard

---

9   MHA 1983, s 139(2).
10 [1974] AC 18 at 31, CA.
11 [1985] 3 All ER 775, CA.
12 [2001] EWCA Civ 1545 at [54].
13 [2001] EWCA Civ 1545 at [61].

argument on this point, and there might be a case for drawing a distinction between 'ordinary actions in tort' and ordinary actions under s 7 of the HRA 1998.[14]

4.12 In *Winch v Jones*, a negligence action, the Master of the Rolls held that a plaintiff is entitled to leave if he or she can show that the case deserves further examination.[15] However, this was thrown into doubt by Farquharson LJ's subsequent statement in *James v Mayor and Burgesses of Havering* that the purpose of section was to protect professionals from actions in respect of mere error, and that a prima facie case of bad faith or lack of reasonable care should be made out before leave would be granted.[16]

THE APPROVED MENTAL HEALTH PROFESSIONAL

4.13 Section 18 of the MHA 2007 replaces the role of ASW with that of Approved Mental Health Professional (AMHP). Only an AMHP or the patient's nearest relative may make an application for detention or guardianship. AMHPs are defined in s 114(10). An AMHP who is 'acting on behalf of' local social services authority (LSSA) in England must be approved by any LSSA whose area is in England, and if 'acting on behalf' of a LSSA in Wales must be approved by any LSSA whose area is in Wales.

Approval as an AMHP

4.14 A LSSA may approve a person to act as an AMHP as long as the person is not a doctor. Doctors are specifically excluded by s 114(2). The Draft Mental Health (Approval of Persons to be Approved Mental Health Professionals) Regulations 2007 provide that only the following can be approved:

(a) a social worker registered with the General Social Care Council;

(b) a first-level nurse, registered in subpart 1 of the Nurses' Part of the Register established and kept by the Nursing and Midwifery Council, with a recordable qualification in mental health nursing;

(c) a first-level nurse, registered in subpart 1 of the Nurses' Part of the Register established and kept by the Nursing and Midwifery Council, their field of practice being learning disabilities nursing;

(d) an occupational therapist registered with the Health Professions Council;

(e) a chartered psychologist listed in the British Psychological Society's Register of Chartered Psychologists.

---

14 [2001] EWCA Civ 1545 at [61].
15 [1986] QB 296, [1985] 3 All ER 97, CA.
16 (1992) 15 BMLR 1, CA.

The LSSA must be satisfied that any candidate for approval has 'appropriate competence in dealing with persons who are suffering from mental disorder'.[17] The person must also comply with any regulations issued by the Secretary of State for Health if the authority is located in England, or the Welsh Ministers if the authority is located in Wales.[18] The regulations will set out conditions for approval, factors as to competency, and requirements for training.

4.15 Since there will be separate regulations for England and Wales, it is possible that these may contain different criteria for approval. For this reason the Explanatory notes state that:[19]

> '[A]n AMHP approved by a LSSA in England may only act on behalf of an English LSSA, and an AMHP approved by a Welsh LSSA may only act on behalf of a Welsh LSSA. This means that a Welsh LSSA cannot arrange for an English-approved AMHP to act on their behalf and vice versa. However, it does not mean that a Welsh-approved AMHP cannot make an application to admit a patient in England or convey a patient in England and vice versa. It is also possible for an AMHP with the appropriate competencies to be approved in both territories.'

Training courses for English and Welsh AMHPs from all professional backgrounds will be approved by the General Social Care Council ('GSCC') and the Care Council for Wales ('CCfW'), the statutory bodies set up to regulate the social work profession.[20]

Professional regulation of AMHPs

4.16 Part 4 of the Care Standards Act 2000 ('CSA 2000') requires the GSCC and CCfW to provide codes of practice for social care workers, which includes 'a person who engages in relevant social work'. 'Relevant social work' is defined as 'social work which is required in connection with any health, education or social services provided by any person'. To ensure that AMHPs from different professional backgrounds continue to be regulated by their own professional bodies, new s 114A(4) states that the functions of an approved mental health professional shall not be considered to be 'relevant social work' for the purposes of Part 4 of the CSA 2000. The GSCC and CCfW codes of practice will continue to apply to social workers when carrying out AMHP functions, and these bodies are given a new statutory power to lay down standards of conduct and practice expected of social workers when carrying out the functions of an approved mental health professional.[21]

---

[17] MHA 1983, s 114, as inserted by MHA 2007, s 18.
[18] MHA 1983, s 114(4)–(8), as inserted by MHA 2007, s 18.
[19] Department of Health, Ministry of Justice, Welsh Assembly Government *Mental Health Act 2007 Explanatory Notes* (2007), para 67.
[20] MHA 1983, s 114A, as inserted by MHA 2007, s 19.
[21] CSA 2000, s 62(1A), as inserted by MHA 2007, s 20.

The role of the AMHP

4.17 AMHPs take over the key function in the compulsory admission process previously performed by ASWs. Where a LSSA have reason to think that an application for admission to hospital or a guardianship application may need to be made in respect of a patient within their area, they must make arrangements for an AMHP to consider the patient's case on their behalf.[22] LSSAs are also under a duty, if so required by the nearest relative of a patient residing in their area, to direct an AMHP as soon as practicable to consider a patient's case with a view to making an application for compulsory admission.[23] The AMHP is then under a duty to make an application for compulsory admission, but only if s/he is satisfied that such an application ought to be made in repect of the patient, and is of the opinion – having regard to any wishes expressed by relatives or any other relevant circumstances – that it is necessary or proper for the application to be made by him/her.[24]

4.18 The duty on LSSAs to direct an AMHP to consider compulsory admission or guardianship is not confined to cases where the nearest relative has requested it, as it may arise from the request of someone else, who gives the LSSA reason to believe that an application may be necessary. Where the AMHP has considered a case as the result of a request by the nearest relative, and decides not to make an application for compulsory admission, s/he must inform the nearest relative of the reasons in writing.

4.19 The AMHP takes over the ASW role to:[25]

> 'arrange and co-ordinate the assessment, taking into account all factors to determine if detention in hospital is the best option for a patient or if there is a less restrictive alternative'.

Since the AMHP assumes the existing powers and duties of the ASW under the MHA 1983, the law governing the role remains broadly the same.

The personal responsibility of the AMHP

4.20 The Draft Revised MHA 1983 Code of Practice emphasises the individual professional responsibility of the AMHP and states that:[26]

> 'Although AMHPs act on behalf of a LSSA, they do so as independent professionals and must exercise their own judgment based on social and medical evidence when deciding whether to apply for a patient to be brought under the statutory powers of the Act. The role of the AMHP is to provide an independent

---

22 MHA 1983, s 13(1), as inserted by MHA 2007, Sch 2, para 5(2).
23 MHA 1983, s 13(4), as amended by MHA 2007, Sch 2, para 5(5).
24 MHA 1983, s 13(1B), as amended by MHA 2007, Sch 2, para 5(2).
25 Department of Health, Ministry of Justice, Welsh Assembly Government *Mental Health Act 2007 Explanatory Notes* (2007), para 71.
26 Department of Health *Mental Health Act 1983 Draft Revised Code of Practice* (2007), para 4.44. See http://www.dh.gov.uk/en/Consultations/Liveconsultations/DH_079842.

decision about whether there are alternatives to detention under the Act or not, bringing a social care perspective to their decision.'

The AMHP has overall responsibility for coordinating the assessment and have a professional responsibility for ensuring that the patient is taken and conveyed to hospital (see para **4.31** below) unless different policies agreements apply at local level.[27]

4.21 Whereas ASWs were employed by LSSAs, there is no longer a requirement that an AMHP be an officer (employee) of an LSSA.[28] AMHPs do, however, 'act on behalf of the LSSA'. The phrase 'acting on behalf of the LSSA' does not signify that the LSSA can direct AMHPs in their individual decision-making. New s 13(1A) retains the individual personal responsibility of the AMHP by requiring that the AMHP must be:

(a)   satisfied that such an application ought to be made in respect of the patient; and

(b)   of the opinion, having regard to any wishes expressed by relatives of the patient or any other relevant circumstances, that it is necessary or proper for the application to be made by him, he shall make the application.[29]

This is in effectively identical terms to the old s 13(1) of the MHA 1983 which, as Judge LJ in *St George's Healthcare NHS Trust v S* said:[30]

> 'makes clear that the social worker must exercise her own independent judgment on the basis of all the available material, including her interview and assessment of the patient, and personally make the appropriate decision. When doing so she is required to take account of the recommendations made by the medical practitioners.'

4.22   The intention of the phrase 'acting on behalf of the LSSA' is to make clear that an AMHP carries out their functions on behalf of the LSSA and, as Baroness Royall put it, thereby 'underline the independence of the AMHP from the trust that may employ the doctors who also examine a patient's case for admission'.[31] The original scheme of the MHA 1959 and MHA 1983 was that the applicant was employed by social services and the recommending doctors would be employed by the NHS. As the Explanatory Notes state, 'unlike with ASWs, there is no longer a requirement that an AMHP be an officer (employee) of an LSSA'.[32] There is now nothing to stop both AMHP

---

[27]   Department of Health *Mental Health Act 1983 Draft Revised Code of Practice* (2007), para 10.13. See http://www.dh.gov.uk/en/Consultations/Liveconsultations/DH_079842.

[28]   Department of Health, Ministry of Justice, Welsh Assembly Government *Mental Health Act 2007 Explanatory Notes* (2007), para 65.

[29]   Inserted by MHA 2007, Sch 2, para 5.

[30]   [1998] 3 All ER 673 at 694, CA.

[31]   *Hansard*, HL Deb, vol 688, col 681.

[32]   Department of Health, Ministry of Justice, Welsh Assembly Government *Mental Health Act 2007 Explanatory Notes* (2007), para 65.

and the doctors recommending detention being employed by the same NHS trust, but for the purposes of the application for detention, the AMHP acts not for the trust, but on behalf of the LSSA. The aim is to provide 'a mix of professional perspectives at the point in time when a decision is being made regarding a patient's detention'. Although all those involved may be employed by the NHS, 'the skills and training required of AMHPs aim to ensure that they provide an independent social perspective'.[33]

4.23   Another reason for stating that the AMHP acts on behalf of the LSSA is to ensure, in Baroness Royall's words:[34]

'that the responsibility for providing that an AMHP service is in place clearly lies with the LSSA, whether or not it chooses to enter into arrangements with another body, such as a trust, to provide the service.'

Under the original s 114 of the MHA 1983 a clear statutory duty did lie with social services to appoint a sufficient number of ASWs. The MHA 2007 repeals this provision.

The assessment

4.24   Before making an application for compulsory admission, it is the duty of the AMHP to interview the patient '*in a suitable manner*' and satisfy him/herself that detention in hospital is in 'all the circumstances of the case, the most appropriate way of providing the care and treatment which the patient needs'.[35] The Code of Practice states that the [AMHP] should offer the patient the opportunity to be interviewed privately unless there is reasons to fear physical harm, and should explain the purpose of the visit, the AMHP role and the role of other professionals.

4.25   In *Re GM (Patient: Consultation)*[36] the patient was interviewed by the ASW prior to an emergency application under s 4 for detention for up to 72 hours. During the currency of the s 4, an application for admission for treatment under s 3 was made without a fresh interview. Burton J held that a fresh interview would only be necessary for the purposes of the s 3 application if the s 4 had expired before the decision to detain under s 3 was made. The purpose of the phrase 'in a suitable manner' is to ensure that the AMHP conducts the interview so as to take account of the needs of patients with communication difficulties or whose first language is not English. The Draft Revised Mental Health Act 1983 Code of Practice provides guidance on overcoming barriers to communication.[37]

---

[33]   Department of Health, Ministry of Justice, Welsh Assembly Government *Mental Health Act 2007 Explanatory Notes* (2007), para 67.

[34]   *Hansard*, HL Deb, vol 688, col 682.

[35]   MHA 1983, s 13(2).

[36]   [2000] MHLR 41.

[37]   Department of Health *Mental Health Act 1983 Draft Revised Code of Practice* (2007), paras 2.5–2.13, 4.3 and 4.36–4.39.

4.26 'All the circumstances of the case' include the past history of the patient and his or her disorder, his or her present condition and social and family factors relevant to it; the wishes of the family; and medical opinion. In order to assess the relevant options, the AMHP will need to be informed of the availability and suitability of other ways of giving the patient the care and treatment needed, such as informal admission, day care, out-patient treatment, crisis intervention centres, community psychiatric nursing and social work support, primary health care support, support from family, friends or voluntary organisations.

4.27 The Draft Illustrative Code of Practice (at para 2.6) states that:

'In judging whether compulsory admission is appropriate, those concerned should consider not only the statutory criteria but should also take account of:

- the guiding principles;
- the patient's wishes and view of his or her own needs;
- the patient's social and family circumstances and cultural background;
- the nature of the mental disorder and its course;
- other forms of care or treatment including, where relevant, consideration of whether the patient would be willing to accept medical treatment in hospital informally or as an out-patient and of whether guardianship would be appropriate;
- the needs of the patient's family and carers and or others with whom he or she lives;
- the burden on those close to the patient of a decision to admit or not to admit under the Act.

Ordinarily only then should the applicant (in consultation with other professionals) judge whether the criteria stipulated in any of the admission sections are satisfied, and take the decision accordingly. In certain circumstances the urgency of the situation may curtail detailed consideration of all these factors.'

Informing and consulting the Nearest Relative

4.28 Section 11(3) of the MHA 1983 places an AMHP under a duty – either before or within a reasonable time after making an *application for admission for assessment* – to take all such steps as are practicable to inform the person appearing to be the nearest relative that an application is about to be or has been made, and that the nearest relative has the power (subject to the limitations in s 25) to direct the discharge of the patient.

4.29 When the AMHP is making an application for admission for treatment or for guardianship, s 11(4) requires that the nearest relative be consulted – unless it appears to the AMHP that in the circumstances such consultation is not practicable or would involve unreasonable delay. There is no duty to consult if it is not practicable. The word 'practicable' was interpreted in *R (on the application of E) v Bristol City Council*[38] to take account of the wishes,

---

[38] [2005] EWHC 74 (Admin), [2005] MHLR 83.

health and well-being of the patient. The Code of Practice had said that 'practicability' refers to the availability of the nearest relative and not to the appropriateness of informing or consulting the person concerned. Bennet J held that the Code was 'wrong' and contrary 'to common sense' on this point. Impracticability could be invoked where here it was known that the NR intensely disliked the patient, or where, as here, the patient was competent and had strongly expressed her wish that the NR not be consulted. Bennet J counselled caution before removing the important role of the NR on grounds of practicability. However, if it were likely to be detrimental to the patient or an infringement of their right to respect for private life under Art 8 of the European Convention on Human Rights.

4.30 If the nearest relative objects to an application for admission for treatment or a guardianship application, the AMHP cannot proceed with it. An unreasonable objection by a nearest relative is one of the grounds in s 29(3) on which the court may order the transfer of the powers of nearest relative to another person. An AMHP is on the list of potential applicants for such an order.

The power to 'take and convey'

4.31 Applicants for compulsory admission under Part 2, whether they are an AMHP or the nearest relative, are authorised by s 6(1) to 'take and convey', or to authorise others to take and convey the patient to hospital. Even if delegation takes place, the AMHP inherits the ultimate responsibility of the ASW 'to ensure that the patient is conveyed in a lawful and humane manner, and should give guidance to those asked to assist' and if the patient is likely to be violent or dangerous, police assistance should be requested.[39] Section 137 of the Act provides that any person who is required or authorised by the Act to be conveyed to any place, kept in custody or detained in a place of safety or at any place specified by the Secretary of State under s 42(6), shall be deemed to be in legal custody. Any person authorised under the Act to take and convey a patient to any such place has all the powers of a constable whilst so acting, including the power of arresting a person who is wilfully obstructing a police officer in the execution of his duty, and the power to use reasonable force in effecting an arrest.

The power to retake

4.32 By virtue of s 138(1)(a), where a patient escapes, the person who had the patient in legal custody – an AMHP or a constable – is empowered to retake the patient. With regard to absconding patients, AMHPs have the power under s 18 – also conferred on the police and hospital staff, to take into custody and return to hospital any patient who has absented him or herself from the hospital without leave, or who has failed to return to the hospital on the expiry

---

[39] Department of Health and Welsh Office *Code of Practice on the Mental Health Act 1983* (TSO, 1999), paras 11.4–11.7.

of the leave. This power also applies in the case of patients who have absconded from hospitals or compulsory community powers in Scotland, Northern Ireland, the Channel Islands or the Isle of Man (see Part 6 of the MHA 1983). Where an offender patient is subject to a hospital order made under Part 3 of the MHA 1983, an AMHP is one of the persons authorised under s 40(1) to take and convey the patient to hospital.

Application for a warrant to enter premises

4.33   An AMHP has the power under s 135 of the Act to lay an information on oath before a justice of the peace to the effect that there is reasonable cause to suspect that a person believed to be suffering from mental disorder:

(a)   has been or is being ill-treated, neglected, or being kept otherwise than under proper control; or

(b)   is living alone and is unable to care for him or herself.

The magistrate may then issue a warrant authorising a police officer to enter the premises (using force if necessary) accompanied by an AMHP and a doctor. If the social worker and the doctor think fit, the patient may be removed to a place of safety with a view to making an application for compulsory admission.

Duty to assess person detained under s 136

4.34   Where a constable has found a person in a public place who appears to be suffering from mental disorder and to be in immediate need of care and control, s/he may remove that person to a place of safety under s 136 if he or she considers it necessary in the interests of that person or for the protection of others. The purpose of removal is to enable the patient to be examined by a medical practitioner and assessed by an AMHP, and to enable any necessary arrangements for his or her care to be made.

Powers of entry and inspection

4.35   Section 115 is amended to empower an AMHP to enter at all reasonable times and inspect any premises other than a hospital in which a mentally disordered person is living, if he or she has reasonable grounds to believe that the person is not under proper care. Under the MHA 1983 this power could only be exercised within the area of the employing local authority. Under the new s 115 there is no geographical limitation on where the power may be exercised.[40] The AMHP may be required to produce a duly authenticated document to show that he or she is an AMHP.

---

[40]   Inserted by MHA 2007, Sch 2, para 8.

Role on making, renewal and revocation of a community treatment order

4.36 Unless an AMHP states in writing that he agrees with the responsible clinician's (RC's) opinion that the statutory criteria are met, and that it is appropriate, the RC may not make, renew or revoke a community treatment order.[41] The AMHP must also agree the conditions to be applied. The Revised Draft Code of Practice states that the AMHP may be a member of the patient's multi-disciplinary team, but this is not essential. The Code then goes on to emphasise that the need for the AMHP's agreement is seen as an important safeguard. The AMHP must reach an independent professional view:[42]

'If the AMHP does not agree that a CTO should be made, or agree to the conditions, then SCT cannot go ahead. The AMHP's decision and the reasons for it should be recorded in the patient's notes. It would not be appropriate for the responsible clinician to approach another AMHP for an alternative view.'

It is difficult to see how an AMHP who is a member of the multi-disciplinary team can be seen as bringing sufficient independence to the process to amount to a significant safeguard. Article 20(2) of Council of Europe Recommendation Rec (2004)10 of the Committee of Ministers to member states concerning the protection of the human rights and dignity of persons with mental disorder recommends that the decision to subject a person to involuntary treatment should be taken by a court or another competent body. Assuming that an order to comply with medication in the community falls within this provision, the fact remains that under the MHA 2007 a CTO may be imposed on a patient with restrictive conditions as to behaviour potentially interfering with rights under Art 8, on the authority of a RC and an AMHP without a legal requirement to seek the authority of the hospital managers or another competent body. The court or other competent body authorising involuntary treatment should, according to Art 20(2), take into account the opinion of the person concerned, and act in accordance with procedures provided by law based on the principle that the person concerned should be seen and consulted. Although the Government has reserved its right not to comply with all or part of this recommendation, this would not prevent the European Court of Human Rights from using this provision as an aid to interpretation of the scope of this procedural obligation in Art 8 regarding the right to respect for private life.

Conflicts of interest

4.37 Section 22 replaces s 12(3)–(7) of the MHA 1983, which specified when a medical practitioner may not provide a medical recommendation, because of their position either in relation to the applicant, the patient or the other recommending doctor. These provisions are replaced by a power to enable

---

[41] MHA 1983, ss 17A(4)(b), 20A(8), 17F(4)(b), as inserted by MHA 2007, s 34(2) and (3).
[42] Department of Health *Mental Health Act 1983 Draft Revised Code of Practice* (2007), para 28.11.

regulations to be made setting out when, because of a potential conflict of interest, an AMHP may not make an application for admission to hospital or guardianship; or a doctor may not provide a medical recommendation accompanying such an application.[43] The regulation making power is broader than the old provisions in s 12, as it covers conflicts of interest involving AMHPs as well as doctors. This extension is necessitated because the AMHP may now be employed in the same trust as the recommending doctors, and it will be important that regulations ensure the requisite degree of independence when the AMHP is making an application.

MEDICAL RECOMMENDATIONS AND S 12 APPROVED DOCTORS

4.38 Applications for compulsory admission for assessment under s 2 or for treatment under s 3 require two medical recommendations from doctors who are fully registered under the Medical Act 1983. One medical recommendation must be given by a practitioner approved under s 12(2) as having special experience in the diagnosis or treatment of mental disorder. Unless that practitioner has previous acquaintance with the patient, the other such recommendation must, if practicable, be given by a doctor who has such previous acquaintance. Emergency admissions for assessment for up to 72 hours under s 4 require only one medical recommendation, which should, if practicable, be given by a doctor who has previous acquaintance with the patient. As Jones points out, for s 4: 'There is no legal requirement for the recommending doctor to be approved under s 12.'[44]

4.39 The medical recommendations required for an application for admission or a guardianship application must be signed on or before the date of the application, and must be given by doctors who have personally examined the patient either together or separately. If they have examined the patient separately, not more than five days must have elapsed between the days on which the separate examinations took place.[45]

4.40 Section 6(1) provides that a duly completed application is sufficient authority for the applicant, or any person authorised by the applicant, to take the patient and convey him to the hospital within the 14 days following the date on which the patient was last examined by a doctor giving a medical recommendation. For emergency applications the period is 24 hours.

4.41 As with the AMHP, a doctor giving medical recommendations is exercising functions of a public nature in an area where Art 5 is engaged,

[43] The regulations will be made by the Secretary of State for Health in England and the Welsh Ministers in Wales: MHA 1983, s 12A, as introduced by MHA 2007, s 22.

[44] RM Jones *Mental Health Act Manual* (Sweet and Maxwell, 10th edn, 2006), p 46.

[45] MHA 1983, s 12(1).

providing the necessary objective medical evidence of a true mental disorder which is of a nature or degree warranting detention, and that detention is strictly necessary, ie:[46]

'that other less severe measures have been considered and found to be insufficient to safeguard the individual or public interest which might require that the person concerned be detained.'

The report must focus on the patient's actual current state of mental health and not past events.[47]

4.42 Jones submits that the ASW (now the AMHP) and the recommending doctors:[48]

'have assumed personal responsibility towards the patient to take reasonable care to avoid an inappropriate and/or unlawful detention. It follows that an action for negligence could be brought.'

Perhaps the most persuasive argument for this view is s 139 of the MHA 1983 which states that no-one shall be liable to any civil or criminal proceedings in respect of any act purporting to be done in pursuance of the Act unless the act was done in bad faith or without reasonable care. This clearly suggests there can be liability in negligence for acts done in pursuance of the Act. Equally persuasive is Lord Atkin's famous statement in *Everett v Griffiths* that:

'[I]t is just as it is convenient that the law should impose a duty to take reasonable care that such persons, if sane, should not suffer the unspeakable torment of having their sanity condemned and their liberty restricted; and I am glad to record my opinion, ineffectual though it may be, that for such an injury the English law provides a remedy.'

Doctors providing medical recommendations must act compatibly with Convention rights, in good faith and with reasonable care.

4.43 Interestingly, the Minister of State – Rosie Winterton – in her evidence to the Joint Committee on Human Rights would not accept that there is any 'requirement in relation to the European Court of Human Rights for doctors to decide about initial detention'. The minister stated that 'as a matter of policy:

'[W]e decided to keep doctors as making the decision because at initial detention, some patients are not known to services or have disengaged from services, so a patient's clinical needs may not be known at that point. We felt that it was practical that doctors, with their broad diagnostic skills should decide whether people should be detained.'

---

[46] *Litwa v Poland* (2001) 33 EHRR 53, ECtHR.
[47] *Varbanov v Bulgaria* [2000] MHLR 263.
[48] RM Jones *Mental Health Act Manual* (Sweet and Maxwell, 10th edn, 2006), p 87.

The Minister recorded the Government's acceptance of:[49]

> 'the case for a medical expert's opinion where someone of unsound mind is to be detained, but we do not agree that it gives authority for the proposition that a psychiatrist must provide the necessary medical expertise in each case.'

This view is difficult to square with Art 20(4) of Council of Europe Recommendation (2004)10 of the Committee of Ministers to member states concerning the protection of the human rights and dignity of persons with mental disorder that:

> 'Involuntary placement, involuntary treatment, or their extension should only take place on the basis of examination by *a doctor having the requisite competence and experience*, and in accordance with valid and reliable professional standards.'

The Government has reserved its right not to comply with all or part of this recommendation, but this would not prevent the European Court of Human Rights from using this provision as an aid to interpretation of Art 5.

4.44   As authority, the Government relies on the Commission decision in *Schuurs v the Netherlands*[50] involving complaints about the detention of the patient on the basis of a certificate by a general practitioner. The patient's complaints were about the fact that the GP did not properly examine her and that she was not allowed to make representations to the District Court that ordered her detention in hospital for six months. Her complaints did not raise any objection to the examination being carried out by a general medical practitioner rather than a psychiatrist. The Commission did not rule on this matter. The decision is therefore weak authority for the proposition that the evidence need not come from someone with psychiatric expertise. The only circumstance where an application for admission would be made on the basis of a recommendation from a GP would be the emergency procedure under s 4. Since the *Winterwerp* requirement of objective medical evidence applies 'otherwise than in emergencies'. This would not infringe Art 5.

4.45   In any event detention requires medical recommendations from doctors. Section 16 of the MHA 2007 amends s 12 of the MHA 1983 so that a registered medical practitioner who has been approved as an AC is also approved for the purposes of s 12. The Explanatory Note to the Act states that:[51]

> 'It is expected that the competencies a registered medical practitioner will require in order to be approved as an AC will be such that they will have the "special

---

[49]   House of Lords, House of Commons Joint Committee on Human Rights *Legislative Scrutiny: Seventh Progress Report: Fifteenth Report of Session 2006–2007* (HL Paper 555, HC Paper 112), para 1.9.

[50]   41 D & R 186.

[51]   *Explanatory Notes*, para 62.

experience in the diagnosis or treatment of mental disorder" required for section 12 approval. ACs who are not registered medical practitioners will not be deemed to be section 12 approved.'

The other professional eligible to be approved clinicians ('ACs') will not be eligible to provide medical recommendations for detention or guardianship.

APPROVED CLINICIANS ('ACS') AND RESPONSIBLE CLINICIANS ('RCS')

4.46 The 'responsible clinician' ('RC') is defined in s 34 of the MHA 1983 as:

(a) in the case of a patient who is liable to be detained for assessment or treatment or who is a community patient the approved clinician ('AC') with overall responsibility for the patient's case;

(b) in relation to a patient subject to guardianship, the AC authorised by the responsible local social services authority to act (either generally or in any particular case or for any particular purpose) as the RC;

(c) for a person under guardianship of someone other than a local authority, the patient has a 'nominated medical attendant', who must be a doctor and who acts as the AC for various purposes.[52]

In order to be a responsible clinician, a person must be an approved clinician.

Approved Clinicians ('ACs')

4.47 Approval is not restricted to medical practitioners, and may be extended to practitioners from other professions, such as nursing, psychology, occupational therapy and social work. Approved clinicians acquire some of the powers previously reserved to doctors. For example, s 9 of the MHA 2007 amends s 5(2) and (3) of the MHA 1983 so that an AC, in addition to a registered medical practitioner, may hold an inpatient for up to 72 hours from the time a report is furnished to the hospital managers if the AC thinks an application for admission under the Act should be made.

4.48 An AC may be authorised under s 24 by the nearest relative ('NR') to visit and examine a patient in private for the purposes of advising about exercising the NR's power of discharge, or for the purpose of a reference (s 67) or an application (s 76) to the Mental Health Review Tribunal ('MHRT'), or if authorised by the Mental Health Act Commission ('MHAC') under s 120(4). An AC is empowered to visit and examine the patient in private, and is entitled to the production of the patient's medical records. It is an offence under s 129

---

[52]   Inserted by MHA 2007, s 9(10).

wilfully to obstruct an AC in carrying out these functions, or to refuse to produce records where the AC has authority to ask for them.

4.49 An AC may give evidence in court in certain cases under Part 3. An AC may furnish a report to a criminal court following remand for reports under s 35, provide evidence to a criminal court on which the remand for reports can be extended,[53] may give evidence as to the availability of a bed for an offender patient who is to be remanded for reports or treatment or to be given a hospital order, interim hospital order, or hospital direction,[54] give evidence on the basis of which a patient transferred from prison may be remitted to prison.[55] An AC will be eligible to provide a mental condition report on the basis of which an accused person may apply for remand for reports or treatment to be terminated.[56]

4.50 In order to be eligible for approval as an AC, a person must be:

(a) a registered medical practitioner;

(b) a chartered psychologist listed in the British Psychological Society's Register of Chartered Psychologists;

(c) a first-level nurse, registered in subpart 1 of the Nurses' Part of the Register established and kept by the Nursing and Midwifery Council, with a recordable qualification in mental health or learning disabilities nursing. This means that the nurse must be a specialist practitioner or a nurse prescriber;

(d) an occupational therapist, registered with the Health Professions Council;

(e) a social worker, registered with the General Social Care Council.

The person must then demonstrate the competencies listed in Sch 2.

Understanding of the AC and RC Roles

4.51 The competencies require an AC to demonstrate a comprehensive understanding of the role of the approved clinician, including the role of the responsible clinician, legal responsibilities and key functions.

Ability to carry out an assessment

4.52 The person must demonstrate ability to identify the presence or absence of mental disorder and the severity of the disorder, to undertake a broad

---

[53] MHA 1983, s 35(5). Section 36(4) provides that extension of the period of remand for treatment under s 36 may only be done on the evidence of the RC.
[54] MHA 1983, ss 35(4), 36(3), 37(4), 38(4), 44(2) and 45A(5).
[55] MHA 1983, ss 50(1) and 53(2).
[56] MHA 1983, ss 35(8) and 36(7).

mental health assessment and formulations incorporating biological, psychological, cultural and social perspectives. The person must also demonstrate 'broad understanding' of all mental health related treatments, ie physical, psychological and social interventions. The person must show an advanced level of skills in making and taking responsibility for complex judgments and decisions, without referring to supervision in each individual case. An AC must be able to assess, manage and take responsibility for decisions relating to complexity, at all levels of clinical risk, and the safety of the patient and others within an evidence based framework for risk assessment and management. Finally, an AC must be able to assess the capacity of patients with regard to consent to treatment.

Leadership & multi-disciplinary team working

4.53 An AC must be able to effectively lead a multi-disciplinary team and assimilate and respect the (potentially diverse) views and opinions of other professionals, service users, and carers, weigh evidence appropriately, seek consensus, and make informed decisions if no consensus can be reached within the team. An AC must demonstrate respect for the opinions of others, but be 'able to reach a balanced decision from a variety of stakeholder contributions'. The person must be able to take an independent view, including the ability to take dispassionate decisions and to weigh up evidence, including the views of others, objectively. Finally they must understands the limits of their own skills and know when to delegate.

Treatment

4.54 In relation to treatment an AC must show ability to formulate and appropriately review treatment in the context of a multi-disciplinary team, and to clarify the aims of the treatment, both to the service user and carer and the team. The AC must also show a broad understanding of the different treatment approaches and their applicability to different patients.

Reciprocal recognition of approval in England and Wales

4.55 New s 142A of the MHA 1983, gives the Secretary of State, jointly with Welsh Ministers, the power to specify in regulations the circumstances in which s 12 approval in England and approval as an AC should be considered to mean approval in Wales as well, and vice versa.[57]

---

[57] Inserted by the MHA 2007, s 17.

Responsible Clinicians ('RCs')

4.56 The definition of the RC is the AC with 'overall responsibility for the patient's case'[58] RCs have a number of powers and duties under Parts 2, 3, 4, and 5 of the MHA 1983, as amended by the MHA 2007. The RC's powers are set out below.

Power to grant leave of absence to a patient who is liable to be detained (s 17)

4.57 The RC may grant either indefinite leave or leave for a specified period, subject to such conditions as he or she considers necessary in the interests of the patient or for the protection of others (see paras **8.20–8.26** below). Before granting leave of more than seven days, the RC must consider whether the patient should be dealt with under a s 17A community treatment order ('CTO') instead.[59]

Supervised Community Treatment (SCT) and the power to initiate a community treatment order (s 17A)

4.58 Section 17A(1) gives the RC the power, 'by order in writing' to 'discharge a detained patient from hospital subject to his being liable to recall in accordance with section 17E'. This is called a 'community treatment order' ('CTO') (see paras **8.27–8.36** below).[60]

Power to recall to hospital from s 17 leave or from a community treatment order (ss 17 and 17E)

4.59 A patient who is on s 17 leave from a hospital may have their leave revoked and be recalled to the hospital where they were detained if the RC considers it necessary in the interests of the patient's health or safety or for the protection of other persons. Revocation and recall are by the RC giving notice in writing 'to the patient or to the person for the time being in charge of the patient'.[61]

4.60 A community patient may be recalled to any hospital[62] if in the RC's opinion:

(a) the patient requires medical treatment in hospital for his mental disorder; and

---

[58] MHA 1983, ss 34(1), 55(1), 64(1) and 79(6), as inserted by MHA 2007, ss 9–12.
[59] MHA 1983, s 17(2A) and (2B), inserted by MHA 2007, s 33(2).
[60] MHA 1983, s 17A(3).
[61] MHA 1983, s 17(4).
[62] MHA 1983, s 17E(3) provides that: 'The hospital to which a patient is recalled need not be the responsible hospital.'

(b)   there would be a risk of harm to the health or safety of the patient or to other persons if the patient were not recalled to hospital for that purpose.

A patient may also be recalled for breach of a condition of a CTO, although this is not a necessary condition of recall (see paras **8.37–8.41** below).

Power to revoke a community treatment order (s 17F)

4.61   Recalling a patient from leave under s 17(4) automatically revokes the leave and the patient resumes detained patient status in the hospital from which they were granted leave. By contrast, recalling a community patient means that the patient may be detained in a hospital for up to 72 hours immediately following return to hospital. A separate decision under s 17F is necessary to revoke a CTO. The RC may revoke a CTO by order in writing if of the opinion that the conditions for detention under s 3(2) are satisfied in respect of the patient. An AMHP must agree with that opinion and that it is appropriate to revoke the order. If a CTO is revoked, the patient reverts to detained patient status and is treated for the purposes of renewal of detention as if they had been admitted for treatment on the date of the order being revoked (see paras **8.42** and **8.43** below).[63]

Power to renew the authority to detain patients detained under ss 3 or 37 (s 20)

4.62   The RC must examine a patient who is detained for treatment during the last two months of the current period of detention, with a view to deciding whether the authority to detain should be renewed. If it appears to the RC that the conditions of detention under s 3 are met, he or she is under a duty to furnish a report to that effect to the managers, and the act of furnishing the report has the effect of renewing the authority to detain the patient. The conditions are:

(1)   the patient is suffering from mental disorder of a nature or degree which makes it appropriate for him to receive medical treatment in a hospital; and

(2)   it is necessary for the health or safety of the patient or for the protection of other persons that he should receive such treatment *and* that it cannot be provided unless he continues to be detained; and

(3)   appropriate medical treatment is available for him.[64]

Before furnishing a report renewing the authority to detain, the RC is required to consult one or more other persons who have been professionally concerned with the patient's medical treatment), and to secure the written agreement of

---

[63]   MHA 1983, s 17G.
[64]   MHA 1983, s 20(4), as inserted by MHA 2007, s 4(4) and Sch 1, para 4.

another person who belongs to a different profession from the responsible clinician that the renewal conditions set out in subsection are satisfied.[65]

4.63 The Joint Committee on Human Rights took the view that the requirement in *Winterwerp v Netherlands*[66] of objective medical evidence of a true mental disorder, coupled with the ruling in *Varbanov v Bulgaria*[67] indicated that the opinion justifying renewal of detention should come from a medically qualified expert who has recognised skills in psychiatric diagnosis and treatment. The Government took the view that the term 'medical expertise' in *Winterwerp* was:

> 'used in the wider sense and the court was not seeking to lay down which sort of qualifications available in a national system would be acceptable and which would not.'

In light of the need to modernise the workforce, the Government's view is that *Winterwerp* must be broadly interpreted and that what is required is a person who is able to make a decision as to whether or not the person in question is of unsound mind.

4.64 The draft competencies for a person to become an AC include the ability to identify the presence and severity of mental disorder. The Government contend that such a person will have the objective medical expertise required by Art 5. It is open to argument whether the Strasbourg Court would support the Government's contention that it is for national authorities to decide which professionals possess the required expertise to perform functions under the Act. The Government argues that this comes within the 'margin of appreciation' allowed to national authorities to have when applying the ECHR. The JCHR countered that:

> 'Despite the Government's belief that the precise qualifications for providing medical expertise are a matter for the Member States, there are equally grounds for considering that the requirement of medical expertise has a minimum content in European law.'

That minimum content was suggested to be a medical qualification or a chartered clinical psychologist.[68] Although the Government has reserved its right not to comply with Council of Europe Recommendation (2004)10 on the protection of the human rights and dignity of persons with mental disorder, Art 20(4) of that recommendation represents a consensus as to the importance of medical expertise from a doctor when it states that:

---

[65] MHA 1983, s 20(5), (5A); MHA 2007 s 9(4).
[66] (1979) 2 EHRR 387, ECtHR.
[67] [2000] ECHR 31365/96, [2000] MHLR 263, ECtHR.
[68] House of Lords, House of Commons Joint Committee on Human Rights *Legislative Scrutiny: Seventh Progress Report: Fifteenth Report of Session 2006–2007* (HL Paper 555, HC Paper 112), paras 1.7–1.14.

'Involuntary placement, involuntary treatment, or their extension should only take place on the basis of examination by *a doctor having the requisite competence and experience.*'

Power to renew a community treatment order (s 20A)

4.65 Within the last two months of a community treatment order the RC must:

(1) examine the patient; and

(2) consult 'one or more other persons who have been professionally concerned with the patient's medical treatment';

(3) if there is a written statement from an AMHP agreeing that the conditions for making a CTO are met, and it is appropriate to do so, submit to the hospital managers a report renewing the CTO.

Furnishing the report has the effect of renewing the CTO for six months if it is the first renewal, and for 12 months in the case of the second or subsequent renewals.[69]

Power to discharge a patient from detention, guardianship or a community treatment order (s 23)

4.66 The RC has the power under s 23(2) to discharge a patient from detention, guardianship or SCT by order in writing. This does not apply to patients who are subject to restrictions on discharge under Part 3 of the Act. Before the decision is taken to discharge, the RC is responsible for ensuring, in consultation with the other professionals concerned, that the patient's needs for health and social care are fully assessed and the care plan addresses them. The RC is also responsible for ensuring that a proper assessment is made of risks to the patient or other people and that plans, services and support are available to manage those risks. In the case of offender patients, the circumstances of any victim and their families must be taken into account. Consideration should be given to whether a patient being discharged from detention meets the criteria for guardianship or a CTO.[70]

4.67 The Draft Illustrative Code emphasises that RCs must keep under review the appropriateness of exercising the discharge power:[71]

'If at any time, a responsible clinician concludes that the criteria which would justify renewing the patient's detention or extending the patient's CTO (as the case may be) are not met, the responsible clinician should exercise the power of discharge. It is neither necessary nor appropriate to wait until the Act requires the

---

[69] MHA 1983, s 20A, as inserted by MHA 2007, s 34(3).
[70] Draft Illustrative Code, paras 27.5–27.6.
[71] Draft Illustrative Code, para 22.10(a).

responsible clinician to examine the patient with a view to deciding whether to furnish a report under section 20 or 20A.'

In *Winterwerp v Netherlands* the Court held that the validity of continued confinement depends on the continued existence of mental disorder of a nature or degree warranting compulsion. It is part of the RC's role to keep this under review.

Power to prevent discharge by the nearest relative by issuing a 'barring certificate' to the managers of the hospital (s 25)

4.68 Where the nearest relative wishes to discharge a detained patient, 72 hours notice must be given.[72] The RC may then, within that period, forward to the managers a 'barring certificate', if he or she considers that the patient if discharged, would be likely to act in a manner dangerous to self or others.

Duty to report to the Ministry of Justice on the condition of offender patients subject to restrictions

4.69 The RC is required by s 41(6) to examine, at intervals not exceeding one year (or more frequently if required by the Minister of Justice), any patient in his or her care who is subject to a restriction order. A report must then be furnished to the Minister of Justice on the patient's condition. A similar obligation exists under s 49(3) with patients who have been transferred from prison subject to restriction directions.

Powers and duties under Parts 4 and 4A with relation to the administration of medical treatment

4.70 For the purposes of Part 4, the RC means the AC 'with overall responsibility for the case of the patient in question'.[73] Section 12 of the MHA 2007 amends Part 4 so that powers and duties previously limited to doctors may now be exercised by either the RC or an AC. For example, s 63 now provides that a patient's consent is not required for treatment for mental disorder which is not covered by the second opinion procedures in ss 57, 58 and 58A, provided 'it is given by or under the direction of the approved clinician in charge of the treatment'. The AC in charge of treatment is also responsible for signing a certificate that the patient is capable and is consenting to medicines or ECT for mental disorders, for authorising emergency treatment of detained and community patients, for assessing capacity and authorising treatment of adult and child community patients who lack capacity to consent, and for deciding that treatment of detained or recalled community patients ought not to be discontinued, pending a second opinion, because it is necessary to prevent serious suffering on the patient's part.[74]

---

[72] MHA 1983, s 23.
[73] MHA 1983, s 64(1).
[74] MHA 1983, ss 58(3)(a), 58A(3)(c), 62(1), 64G, 64D, 64F, 62(2) and 62A(5) respectively.

4.71   The Explanatory Notes clarify the reason for the frequent use in Parts 4 and 4A of the phrase 'approved clinician in charge of treatment' rather than 'responsible clinician':[75]

> 'In the majority of cases the AC in charge of the treatment will be the patient's RC, but where, for example, the RC is not qualified to make decisions about a particular treatment (e g medication if the RC is not a doctor or a nurse prescriber) then another appropriately qualified professional will be in charge of that treatment, with the RC continuing to retain overall responsibility for the patient's case.'

Parts 4 and 4A are discussed in detail in Chapter 10.

CONCLUSION

4.72   The MHA 2007 introduces significant changes to the roles of mental health staff responsible for implementing compulsory powers under the MHA 1983, widening the range of occupational groups who are eligible to implement compulsion. Chapter 5 examines the role of the nearest relative ('NR'), the Independent Mental Health Advocate ('IMHA') and the hospital managers.

---

[75]   *Explanatory Notes*, para 57.

Chapter 5

RELATIVES, INDEPENDENT MENTAL HEALTH ADVOCATES, AND HOSPITAL MANAGERS

INTRODUCTION

5.1   This chapter deals with Nearest Relatives ('NRs'), Independent Mental Health Advocates ('IMHAs'), and Hospital Managers. Chapter 3 of the Act (entitled Patient Safeguards) contains the changes in relation to NRs (ss 23–26) and introduces new entitlements to the services of an Independent Mental Health Advocate (s 30). This chapter also explains the role of the 'hospital managers' in relation to detained and community patients.

The Nearest Relative

5.2   The nearest relative of a patient exercises important functions in relation to compulsory powers under Part 2 (see para **5.6** below). The nearest relative for the purposes of the MHA 1983 is defined in s 26, which is amended to give the legal standing of a spouse to civil partners. This provision is already in force. In order to comply with the ruling of the European Court of Human Rights in *JT v United Kingdom*,[1] the MHA 2007 also introduces a new power for the patient to apply to the county court to displace the nearest relative on the grounds that the person is unsuitable to act in that capacity.

Independent Mental Health Advocates

5.3   Section 30(2) introduces new ss 130A–130D placing a duty upon the Secretary of State (or Welsh Assembly) to provide advocacy services for all detained patients (except those held under ss 4, 5, 135 or 136), guardianship patients and patients subject to community treatment orders. This provision will be brought into force in October 2009. Advocacy must include help in obtaining information about and understanding the provisions of the Act which subject him to compulsion, any conditions or restrictions, what medical treatment is being given or is proposed and why, the requirements of the Act which apply n relation to that treatment; advocacy must also include help in obtaining information about and understanding any rights which may be exercised by or in relation to him and help by way of representation or otherwise in exercising those rights.

---

[1]   (2000) 30 EHRR CD 77, [2000] 1 FLR 909.

5.4 Section 130D places a duty upon hospital managers and, in certain cases, RCs to provide qualifying patients with information that advocacy services are available. Advocates will have the right to meet patients in private, and to meet professionals. They will have access to patient records only where a capable patient gives consent, or, in the case of an incapable patient, where access would not conflict with a decision of a health care attorney, a deputy, or the Court of Protection, and the person holding the records agrees that the records are relevant to the matter at issue and access is 'appropriate'.

Hospital Managers

5.5 The hospital managers are the detaining authority for patients who are not subject to restrictions.[2] Applications for admission are addressed to the hospital managers, the managers receive the report from the Responsible Clinician which renews detention, the managers have the power to direct discharge, and the managers have duties to give information to patients about their rights under the Act. The main changes introduced by the MHA 2007 in relation to managers are:

(1)   the introduction of a duty on hospital managers to ensure that an age appropriate environment is provided to patients who are under 18;

(2)   changes in the provisions requiring the managers to refer a patient's case to a Mental Health Review Tribunal; and

(3)   introduction of a provision enabling foundation trusts to delegate their discharge power to a subcommittee in the same way as is already the case with other NHS bodies (this last provision is already in force).

THE NEAREST RELATIVE ('NR')

5.6 The MHA 2007 has introduced changes in relation to the 'nearest relative' ('NR') who has the power to apply for compulsory admission, to seek discharge and challenge the patient's detention before a Mental Health Review Tribunal ('MHRT'). The NR has various functions with relation to patients detained under Part 2 of the Act. These include the right to:

(a)   apply for compulsory admission or guardianship (s 11(1));

(b)   be consulted before any such application is made by an AMHP (s 11(3));

(c)   object to and block an application for guardianship or admission for treatment (s 11(4));

---

[2]   MHA 1983, s 11(2), which provides that every application for admission must be addressed to the managers of the hospital to which admission is sought, and s 6(2) which says that the application is sufficient authority for the managers to detain the patient in the hospital.

(d)   discharge the patient from detention or guardianship (ss 23 and 25); and

(e)   apply for a Mental Health Review Tribunal hearing to determine the patient's fitness for discharge (s 66(1)(g) and (h));

(f)   information about the patient's and nearest relative's rights (s 132(4)) and to be informed if the patient is discharged from detention (s 133). These rights are not available if the patient objects.

NRs may not exercise their rights in respect of patients subject to special restrictions under Part 3 of the MHA 1983.

5.7   The identity of the nearest relative is determined according to a statutory list, beginning with husband or wife, father or mother, son or daughter. The MHA 2007 modifies that list to recognise civil partners, as well as same or opposite sex couples living together as man and wife.[3] The rights of the nearest relative remain essentially unchanged by the MHA 2007. The Act does, however, introduce a new possibility for the patient to seek displacement of an unsuitable nearest relative. This is necessitated by successful challenges in the European Court of Human Rights and in the English Courts under the Human Rights Act 1998.

5.8   Section 26(1) as amended provides that 'relative' means any of the following persons:

(a)   husband, wife or civil partner;

(b)   son or daughter;

(c)   father or mother;

(d)   brother or sister;

(e)   grandparent;

(f)   grandchild;

(g)   uncle or aunt;

(h)   nephew or niece.

The 'nearest relative' is the person who appears first on this list and, if there is more than one relative coming into the same category, the eldest is to take priority. The definition of 'husband', 'wife' or 'civil partner' includes a person with whom the patient has been living as husband or wife or civil partner for

---

3   See *R (on the application of SSG) v Liverpool City Council* at http://www.dh.gov.uk/en/ Policyandguidance/Healthandsocialcaretopics/Mentalhealth/DH_4077674.

not less than six months, although such a person cannot take precedence over a legal spouse or civil partner unless there has been a separation or desertion. Any person who has resided with the patient for five years or more or is caring for the patient is counted as a relative.[4] A non-relative who is caring for the patient is treated as a relative by virtue of s 26(4). Where a relative is caring for a patient they will take precedence over any other relative, even a spouse. In *Re D (Mental Patient: Habeas Corpus)*[5] the Court of Appeal held that the words 'caring for' have their ordinary meaning, and that although services need not have been provided over a long period, they must be more than minimal and must have a quality of continuity.

5.9   The nearest relative of a child who is in care is determined in accordance with s 27 whereby the nearest relative will be the local authority unless the patient is married in which case it will be the spouse. If the child is subject to guardianship under s 5 of the Children Act 1989, s 28 of the MHA 1983 applies, the nearest relative will be the guardian, and no spouse can take precedence. If a child is a ward of court an application for compulsory admission requires the leave of the court, as does any application by the nearest relative to the MHRT. If the patient is ordinarily resident in the UK and the person who would be the nearest relative is ordinarily resident abroad, that person is ineligible to be nearest relative by virtue of s 26(5)(a). This exclusion does not apply in a case where the patient him or herself is ordinarily resident abroad.

5.10   Section 132(4) of the Act requires the managers of any hospital or mental nursing home where a patient is detained to take such steps as are practicable to inform the relative of the patient's rights under the Act, and of his or her powers and duties under the Act. This duty applies unless the patient has requested that the relative not be informed of the fact that the admission has taken place.

5.11   In certain circumstances a nearest relative may authorise another person to perform the functions of nearest relative under the Act. The nearest relative must give written notice of such authorisation to the person authorised and to the hospital managers or, in the case of a patient under guardianship, to the local social services authority and the guardian. The authority may be revoked at any time.[6]

Displacing the Nearest Relative

5.12   The nearest relative has a right under Art 8 of the European Convention on Human Rights to respect for their family life with the patient and vice versa. But the patient also has the right to respect for privacy under Art 8. In *JT v*

---

[4]   MHA 1983, s 26, as amended by MHA 2007, s 26.
[5]   [2000] 2 FLR 848, CA.
[6]   Draft Mental Health (Hospital, Guardianship and Consent to Treatment) Regulations, reg 21 which will allow the NR to grant or revoke in writing, including email, authority to exercise the functions of the NR.

United Kingdom[7] the applicant complained that her nearest relative according to the statutory formula was her mother, who was living with a man who JT alleged had abused her in the past. Each time JT applied for discharge from detention to a MHRT, the tribunal rules required that her mother, as nearest relative, be informed. JT objected to her mother being given information about her life. The European Commission on Human Rights held that the absence in the MHA 1983 of any possibility for a patient to apply to the County Court to change her nearest relative was an interference with her right to respect for her private life under Art 8(1) of the European Convention and could not be justified under Art 8(2). A friendly settlement was reached whereby the UK Government undertook to:

(1)   enable a patient to apply to the court to replace his nearest relative where there were reasonable grounds to object to a particular individual acting in that capacity; and

(2)   prevent certain persons from acting as the nearest relative of the patient.

Subsequently, the English High Court in *R (on the application of M) v Secretary of State for Health*[8] granted a declaration of incompatibility under the Human Rights Act 1998 that the absence of a right for a patient to seek displacement of a nearest relative was incompatible with Art 8.

5.13 Section 29 of the Act empowers a county court to make an order directing that the functions of nearest relative be exercised by another person or by the local social services authority. Section 23 of the MHA 2007 amends s 29 and introduces the possibility for the patient to seek displacement of an unsuitable nearest relative. An application for such an order may be made by the patient, any relative of the patient, any other person with whom the patient is residing (or was last residing before admitted to hospital), or by an AMHP. A relative or person residing with the patient may apply for the functions of nearest relative to be conferred on him or her personally or on any other willing person whom the court considers suitable. If the applicant is an AMHP, the effect of a successful application will be that the local social services authority will be appointed as acting nearest relative. An application may be made on any of the following grounds in s 29(3):

(a)   that the patient has no nearest relative within the meaning of the Act, or that it is not reasonably practicable to ascertain whether he or she has such a relative, or who that relative is;

(b)   that the nearest relative is incapable of acting as such by reason of mental disorder or other illness;

[7]   (2000) 30 EHRR CD 77.
[8]   [2003] EWHC 1094 (Admin).

(c)   that the nearest relative of the patient unreasonably objects to the making of an application for admission for treatment or guardianship;

(d)   that the nearest relative has exercised, without due regard to the welfare of the patient or the interests of the public, his or her power to discharge the patient from hospital or guardianship, or is likely to do so.

5.14   The MHA 2007 introduces an additional ground in new s 29(3)(e) 'that the nearest relative is otherwise unsuitable to act'. The patient may apply for displacement on any of the above grounds. Section 23 also amends s 29 of the MHA 1983 to provide that where the person nominated by the applicant is, in the court's opinion, not 'suitable' or there is no nomination, the court can appoint any other person it thinks is 'suitable'.

5.15   Section 24 of the MHA 2007 introduces a new right for the patient or (with prior leave of the court) the displaced NR to apply to discharge or vary an order appointing an acting NR. Currently, court appointments of acting NRs are only for a limited period. In future, the court may make an appointment for an indefinite period.

5.16   Section 25 of the MHA 2007 amends s 66 of the MHA 1983 and limits applications to the MHRT from displaced NRs. Such an application may be made only by a NR displaced on grounds of unreasonable objection to admission or exercising the power of discharge without due regard to the welfare of the patient or the protection of the public. A person displaced as the NR because he or she is too ill to act, or unsuitable to act, will not have the right to apply to the MHRT.

THE INDEPENDENT MENTAL HEALTH ADVOCATE

5.17   Section 30 introduces new ss 130A–130D into the MHA 1983. Section 130A(1) places a duty on the Secretary of State and the Welsh Ministers to make such arrangements as they consider reasonable to enable independent mental health advocates ('IMHAs') to be available to help 'qualifying patients'. Section 130A(4) requires that:

'the appropriate national authority shall have regard to the principle that any help available to a patient should, so far as practicable, be provided by a person who is independent of any person who is professionally concerned with the patient's medical treatment.'

The detail of qualifications to be an IMHA and the conditions of approval will be provided in regulations made under s 130A(2).

The Draft Mental Health 1983 (Independent Mental Health Advocacy) Regulations provide that no-one may be appointed to act as an IMHA unless they are of integrity and good character, have appropriate experience or training or an appropriate combination of experience and training, and are able to act independently of both professionals and any person who has requested them to visit and interview the patient. The person must undergo a criminal record check under the Police Act 1997. Regard must be had to whether the person has an appropriate advocacy qualification although the absence of such a qualification does not preclude appointment.

Duties

5.18 The help to be provided by IMHAs is listed in s 130B(1) and (2). It is to include help in obtaining information about and understanding:

(a) the provisions of the Act under which he is subject to compulsion;

(b) any conditions or restrictions to which he is subject by virtue of this Act;

(c) what (if any) medical treatment is given to him or is proposed or discussed in his case;

(d) why it is given, proposed or discussed;

(e) the authority under which it is, or would be, given;

(f) the requirements of this Act which apply, or would apply, in connection with the giving of the treatment to him;

(g) help in obtaining information about and understanding any rights which may be exercised under this Act by or in relation to him.

Finally, help is to be made available (by way of representation or otherwise) in exercising those rights.

5.19 For the purpose of providing help to a patient in accordance with the arrangements, an IMHA is under a duty to comply with any reasonable request from the person appearing to be the NR, the RC, or an AMHP. The patient remains entitled decline help under the arrangements.[9]

Powers

5.20 The powers of IMHAS are listed in s 130B(3). For the purposes of providing help, an IMHA may:

'(a) visit and interview the patient in private;
(b) visit and interview any person who is professionally concerned with his medical treatment;

---

[9] MHA 1983, s 130B(5) and (6).

(c)   require the production of and inspect any records relating to his detention or treatment in any hospital or registered establishment or to any after-care services provided for him under section 117 above;

(d)   require the production of and inspect any records of, or held by, a local social services authority which relate to the patient.'

5.21   The IMCA is not entitled to require production of records unless either:[10]

'(a)   in a case where the patient has capacity or is competent to consent, he does consent; or

(b)   in any other case, the production or inspection would not conflict with a decision made by a donee or deputy or the Court of Protection, and the person holding the records, having regard to such matters as may be prescribed in regulations under section 130A above, considers that—

(i)   the records may be relevant to the help to be provided by the advocate; and

(ii)   the production or inspection is appropriate.'

Qualifying patients

5.22   Qualifying patients are defined in s 130C(2) and (3): They include patients who are:

(a)   liable to be detained under the MHA 1983 (otherwise than under ss 4, 5(2), (5)(4), 135 or 136);

(b)   subject to guardianship under this Act; or

(c)   community patients.

A patient is also a qualifying patient according to s 130C(3) if:

'(a)   not being a qualifying patient falling within subsection (2) above, he discusses with a registered medical practitioner or approved clinician the possibility of being given a form of treatment to which section 57 above applies; or

(b)   not having attained the age of 18 years and not being a qualifying patient falling within subsection (2) above, he discusses with a registered medical practitioner or approved clinician the possibility of being given a form of treatment to which section 58A above applies.'

Section 130C(4) provides that where such a patient is informed that the treatment concerned is proposed in his case, he remains a qualifying patient falling within that subsection until either:

(a)   the proposal is withdrawn; or

---

[10]   MHA 1983, s 130B(4).

(b)   the treatment is completed or discontinued.

Duty to provide information about IMHAs

5.23   A 'responsible person', defined in s 130D(2), has a duty under s 130D(1) to take such steps as are practicable to ensure that:

(a)   the patient understands that help is available to him from an IMHA; and

(b)   how he can obtain that help.

5.24   Where the patient is detained the 'responsible person' means the hospital managers, and the information is to be given as soon as practicable after the patient becomes liable to be detained. If the patient is a community patient the managers of the responsible hospital are the responsible person, and the information is to be given as soon as practicable after the patient becomes a community patient. Where the patient is a conditionally discharged restricted patient, the responsible person is the RC and the information is to be given as soon as practicable after the conditional discharge. If the patient is subject to guardianship, the responsible person is the LSSA and the information is to be given as soon as practicable after the patient becomes subject to guardianship. In any case, where the patient is a qualifying patient because of treatment proposed to be given, the responsible person is the registered medical practitioner or approved clinician with whom the patient first discusses the possibility of being given the treatment concerned.

5.25   Section 134 of the Act is amended by s 30(3) of the MHA 2007 to ensure that hospital managers cannot withhold correspondence between patients and their IMHAs.

HOSPITAL MANAGERS

5.26   The hospital managers are the detaining authority in law.[11] The Draft Revised Code describes their general role as follows:[12]

> 'They have the key responsibility for seeing that the requirements of the Act are followed. In particular they must ensure that patients are detained only as the Act allows, that their treatment and care accord fully with its provisions, and that they are fully informed of, and are supported in exercising, their statutory rights.'

Section 145 defines the hospital managers. As the Draft Code explains:[13]

---

[11]   MHA 1983, ss 6(2) and 40(1).
[12]   Department of Health *Mental Health Act 1983 Draft Revised Code of Practice* (2007), para 33.4. See http://www.dh.gov.uk/en/Consultations.
[13]   Ibid, para 33.3.

'In England and Wales, in general, NHS Hospitals are owned by NHS trusts, NHS foundation trusts and PCTs. For these hospitals the Trusts themselves are defined as the 'managers' for the purposes of the Act.'

If a hospital in Wales is vested in a Local Health Board, the managers are the members of that Board. The three high security special hospitals are owned by the Secretary of State and managers' functions are exercised on behalf of the Secretary of State by the Special Health Authorities set up to manage those hospitals.

5.27 If an establishment is registered under Part 2 of the Care Standards Act 2000 as an independent hospital in which treatment or nursing (or both) are provided for persons liable to be detained under the MHA 1983, the managers are the person or persons registered in respect of the establishment.[14]

5.28 For community patients the managers are those of the responsible hospital where the patient was detained immediately before becoming subject to the CTO, or to which responsibility for the patient has subsequently been assigned.

5.29 Most of the hospital managers' responsibilities may be delegated to officers of the body Trust or Hospital Authority but the power to discharge patients may only be delegated in accordance with s 23.

5.30 The Draft Illustrative Code suggests that 'NHS bodies may find it useful to appoint a committee or subcommittee to undertake the Hospital Managers' functions'.[15] The Trust or Hospital Authority retains the ultimate responsibility for the performance of the managers' duties, and in view of this the committee should, where possible, include members of the Trust or Hospital Authority Board. The committee should report formally to the Board with an account of its activities not less than once a year. For the most part, the managers' responsibilities may be delegated to officers of the body Trust or Hospital Authority but the power to discharge patients may only be delegated in accordance with s 23. Section 23 of the Act gives managers the power to discharge patients from detention. This power can be delegated by NHS Trusts to three or more people who are either non-executive directors of the trust or members of a committee or subcommittee of the trust. The subcommittee may include outside people, but may not include employees of the trust. The Draft Code emphasises that:[16]

'Hospital Managers retain responsibility for the performance of all delegated duties and must ensure that those acting on their behalf are competent to undertake them.'

---

[14] MHA 1983, ss 34 and 145.
[15] Draft Illustrative Code of Practice, para 22.4.
[16] Department of Health *Mental Health Act 1983 Draft Revised Code of Practice* (2007), para 33.9. See http://www.dh.gov.uk/en/Consultations.

5.31 The Draft Revised Code recommends the following approach to powers of discharge of patients in independent hospitals under a contract with an NHS body:[17]

> 'The managers of NHS bodies who have contracted with independent hospitals to treat NHS patients, or to act as their responsible hospital, discharge such patients from detention in those hospitals or from SCT (as the case may be), in the same way as they could discharge patients in their own hospitals. Because of this, the NHS bodies (or the people exercising the functions of hospital managers on their behalf) should take steps to satisfy themselves that the discharge functions are performed by the managers of the relevant independent hospitals appropriately protects the rights of the NHS patients for whom they are responsible.'

The managers of independent hospitals and NHS bodies are advised, where possible, to co-operate over exercising their respective functions in relation to the discharge of NHS patients detained in independent hospitals, but are reminded that they must all take their own decisions, not defer to those of another body.

Duties in relation to the receipt of admission documents

5.32 Applications for compulsory admission are addressed to the managers of the receiving hospital. As the detaining authority it is the Hospital Managers' duty to ensure that the grounds for admitting the patient are valid and that all relevant admission documents are in order.[18] Chapter 12 of the Draft Revised Code of Practice deals with the receipt and scrutiny of documents authorising detention, guardianship or Supervised Community Treatment ('SCT'). The Hospital Managers are responsible for detained patients and patients on SCT. Social Services Authorities are responsible for patients under guardianship. Each should monitor the receipt and scrutiny of documents on a regular basis. The managers must therefore delegate the authority to receive the statutory documents to named officers or to a class of officers. Such a delegation should be formally minuted, and should ensure that there is 24-hour cover from officers with good knowledge of the Mental Health Act. A manager of appropriate seniority should take overall responsibility for reception and scrutiny, and those responsible for scrutinising documents should be clear about what kind of errors on applications and medical recommendations can and cannot be corrected.[19]

---

[17] Department of Health *Mental Health Act 1983 Draft Revised Code of Practice* (2007), para 34.6. See http://www.dh.gov.uk/en/Consultations.

[18] Department of Health *Mental Health Act 1983 Draft Revised Code of Practice* (2007), para 33.13. See http://www.dh.gov.uk/en/Consultations.

[19] Ibid, para 12.10.

Duties to give patients information concerning their rights under the Act and to help from advocates (ss 132, 132A and 130D)

5.33 Section 130D places a duty on the hospital managers to inform patients of their right to advocacy help from IMHAs (see para **5.23** above). Under s 132 the managers have a duty to take such steps as are practicable to ensure that the patient understands under which provision of the MHA 1983 he is detained and the effects of that provision, as well as any rights to apply to a Mental Health Review Tribunal ('MHRT'). These steps must be taken as soon as practicable after the commencement of detention. The managers must also take such steps as are practicable to ensure that the patient understands who has the power of discharge under s 23, the restrictions on the nearest relative's power of discharge under s 25, the nearest relative's right to apply to the MHRT if the RMO bars discharge, the effect of Part 4 of the Act relating to medical treatment, the existence of the Code of Practice, his right to complain to the Mental Health Act Commission under s 120, and, if applicable, his rights in relation to postal packets under s 134. The duty is to give the requisite information both orally and in writing, and the DoH and Welsh Office have produced 'rights leaflets'.

5.34 Section 132A requires the managers of the responsible hospital to take such steps as are practicable to ensure that a community patient understands the effect of the CTO and their right to make an application to a MHRT.[20]

5.35 Sections 130D(5), 132(4) and 132A(3) all provide that, unless the patient otherwise requests, the managers must take such steps as are practicable to a give a copy of any written information to the person appearing to them to be the nearest relative. This must be done when the information is given to the patient or within a reasonable time thereafter, unless the patient objects.

5.36 The duties under ss 130, 132 and 132A are all delegable to hospital staff, but managers should ensure that the staff who carry out the explanation are adequately trained in the Act.

Duty to notify social services when patient admitted on nearest relative application

5.37 Where a patient is detained under ss 2 or 3 on the application of the nearest relative, the managers are under a duty to give notice of that fact to the social services department for the area in which the patient resided immediately prior to admission. This must be done as soon as practicable after admission. The LSSA then has a duty to direct an AMHP to visit and prepare a social circumstances report which is to be forwarded to the managers.[21]

---

[20] As inserted by MHA 2007, Sch 3, para 30.
[21] MHA 1983, s 14.

Responsibilities in relation to Supervised Community Treatment

5.38 Paragraphs 22.9(c) and (d) of the Draft Illustrative Code states that where a RC is contemplating a CTO for a patient:

> 'it is the responsibility of the managers to liaise with the relevant authorities, usually the PCT and the Local Authority, to ensure arrangements are put in place for suitable aftercare services in line with the specifications draw up by the multidisciplinary team.'

5.39 The Draft Code also places responsibility on the managers to ensure that no community patient is detained on recall for longer than 72 hours without having their community treatment order revoked. 'Arrangements should be put in place to ensure that the time of recall is recorded and the length of stay monitored.' The managers also have a duty to ensure a patient is referred to the MHRT as soon as is practicable if their community treatment order is revoked.

Complaints

5.40 All detained patients have the right to complain to the Mental Health Act Commission ('MHAC') provided that they have already complained to the hospital managers, and the managers have been given the opportunity of dealing with the matter using the relevant NHS complaints procedure.[22] Guidance on the arrangements for dealing with complaints about NHS treatment and services is contained in *Supporting Staff, Improving Services – Guidance to support implementation of the National Health Service (Complaints) (Amendment) Regulations 2006 (SI 2006/2084)* for England; and the document *Complaints in the NHS: A Guide to handling complaints in Wales (2004)* for Wales. However, if the complaint relates specifically to the exercise of powers or discharge of duties under the Act, a complaint may be made direct to the MHAC. There is no need for the complaint to have been referred to the managers first.

5.41 Staff have the responsibly of bringing the complaints procedures to the attention of all patients, both orally and in writing, and in the case of detained patients must give equivalent information about the right to complain to the MHAC. If a patient is unable to formulate a complaint, he or she should be given reasonable assistance to do so by staff, including assistance in accessing advocacy. Complaint records should be kept separate from medical records.

Patients' correspondence

5.42 Section 134 of the MHA 1983 allows the Hospital Managers to withhold outgoing mail from detained patients provided the addressee has made a written request to the managers, the patient's RC or the Secretary of State. The fact that mail has been withheld must be recorded in writing and the patient

---

[22] MHA 1983, s 120(1)(b)(i).

must be informed. In the special hospitals managers have wider powers under s 134 to withhold an outgoing postal packet if it is likely:

(i)   to cause distress to the person to whom it is addressed or to any other person (not being a person on the staff of the hospital); or

(ii)   to cause danger to any person.

The managers of a special hospital may also withhold incoming mail if, in their opinion, it is necessary to do so in the interests of the safety of the patient or for the protection of other persons. Managers of special hospitals should have a written policy on the use of this power. Decisions are subject to review by the MHAC.

Transfers of detained and community patients

5.43   Section 19 of the MHA 1983, and the regulations made under it allow the Hospital Managers to transfer a detained patient from one hospital to another.[23] Section 19A provides for responsibility for patients on SCT to be assigned to another hospital, in circumstances to be specified in regulations. Section 17F of the Act and the regulations made under it allow the hospital managers to transfer a patient on SCT who has been recalled to hospital from one hospital to another.

5.44   Transfers are a potential interference with a patient's right of respect for family life under Art 8 of the European Convention. For that reason the Draft Revised Code emphasises that they should be for valid reasons:[24]

> 'Valid reasons for transfer might be clinical – for example, the need for the patient to be in a more suitable environment or in a specialist facility. It could also be to move the patient closer to home to return "out of area" patients to their home areas. It is important to explain the reasons to the patient and where appropriate, family or friends, and to record them.'

The Code underlines that it is important to explain the reasons to the patient and where appropriate, family or friends, and to record the reasons. There might be clinical reasons for transfer such as the need to be in more specialist facility or a more suitable environment, or it might be at the patient's request or to move the patient nearer their home area. For restricted patients, the Hospital Managers' power is subject to the prior agreement of the Home Secretary.

---

[23]   Mental Health (Hospital, Guardianship and Consent to Treatment) Regulations 1983 (SI 1983/893), as amended by Mental Health (Hospital, Guardianship and Consent to Treatment) (Amendment) Regulations 1996 (SI 1996/540), regs 7 and 9.

[24]   Department of Health *Mental Health Act 1983 Draft Revised Code of Practice* (2007), para 33.16. See http://www.dh.gov.uk/en/Consultations.

Duties regarding renewal of detention

5.45 Section 20 of the MHA 1983 provides that the authority to detain a patient under ss 3 or 37 lasts for six months beginning on the day of admission. Within the last two months of the current period of detention, the RC has the power to renew detention. This is done by furnishing a report in the prescribed form to the managers, stating that:

(1) the patient continues to suffer from mental disorder of a nature or degree which makes it appropriate for him to receive medical treatment in a hospital; *and*

(2) it is necessary for the health or safety of the patient or for the protection of other persons that he should receive such treatment which cannot be provided unless he continues to be detained; *and*

(3) appropriate medical treatment is available for him.

5.46 New s 20(5A) requires that before furnishing that report the RC must secure written agreement that the renewal conditions are satisfied from a person who has been professionally concerned with the patient's medical treatment; but who belongs to a profession other than that to which the responsible clinician belongs.[25] The act of furnishing the report has the effect of renewing the detention.[26] When they are duly furnished with the RC's report, the managers must then consider whether to exercise their power of discharge under s 23(2).

The Managers' power of discharge and Managers' Hearings (s 23)

5.47 Section 23 of the MHA 1983 gives Hospital Managers the power to discharge unrestricted patients from detention or from Supervised Community Treatment ('SCT').

Managers' Panels

5.48 Section 23(6) enables the board of any NHS Trust to authorise three or more people to exercise this power, provided they are neither an executive director of the board nor an employee or officer of the trust. The committee may be made up of non-executive directors of the trust and people appointed from outside the trust. Section 45 amends s 23 to allow Foundation Trusts similar powers to those enjoyed by NHS trusts, to delegate the discharge power to any three or more people 'appointed' by the trust board, provided that those persons are neither executive directors nor employees of the trust. Section 45 also introduces a new s 142B the effect of which is that:[27]

---

[25] Inserted by the MHA 2007, s 9(4)(b).

[26] *R v Managers of Warlingham Park Hospital, ex parte B* (1994) 22 BMLR 1, CA.

[27] *Explanatory Notes*, para 181.

'A NHS foundation trust's constitution may not permit its functions under the 1983 Act to be delegated to executive directors or committees of directors unless that is permitted by or under the 1983 Act itself. But the Constitution may permit delegation to other people where that is allowed by or under the 1983 Act.'

The persons registered in respect of an independent hospital retain final responsibility in relation to the managers' power of discharge. They too may delegate their discharge function to a committee or subcommittee. The Draft Code says it is 'desirable that detention is reviewed by people who are neither on the staff of the home nor have a financial interest'.[28]

5.49   Where a patient is liable to be detained for assessment or for treatment in an independent hospital, or is a community patient whose responsible hospital is an independent one, the Secretary of State has a power of discharge. If the patient is being cared for pursuant to a contract with a NHS body, the managers of that body have the power of discharge.[29] The Draft Illustrative Code suggests that where detained patients placed in an independent hospital under a contract with a Trust, the Trust committee which is appointed to undertake Hospital Managers' functions should also monitor the way those functions are performed by the managers of the independent hospital, and both sets of managers should cooperate in exercising their respective discharge functions.[30]

5.50   Chapter 23 of the Draft Illustrative Code of Practice provides detailed guidance on the managers' power of discharge and the managers' duty to ensure that all patients are aware that they may seek discharge by this route, and of the distinction between this and their right to a Mental Health Review Tribunal ('MHRT') hearing.

5.51   Managers may undertake a review at any time at their discretion. The managers must consider holding a review when they receive a request from a patient or when the RC issues a barring certificate opposing a nearest relative's application for the patient's discharge. They might decide that it is inappropriate to hold a review where one has been held recently and there is no evidence that the patient's condition has changed or where a MHRT hearing is either due soon or has been held recently. Managers have a statutory duty to decide whether to exercise their discretion to discharge from detention or a CTO when the RC submits a report renewing detention or SCT. Therefore, a review must be held on renewal, whether or not the patient objects.

5.52   The Draft Code distinguishes between contested where the patient or NR are disputing the need for detention or SCT and uncontested renewal cases where they are not. With uncontested renewals the Code advises the review

---

[28]   Department of Health *Mental Health Act 1983 Draft Revised Code of Practice* (2007), para 34.4. See http://www.dh.gov.uk/en/Consultations.

[29]   MHA 1983, s 23(3) and (3A), as inserted by MHA 2007, Sch 3, paras 10(5) and 10(6).

[30]   Department of Health *Mental Health Act 1983 Draft Revised Code of Practice* (2007), para 34.7. See http://www.dh.gov.uk/en/Consultations.

panel to meet to consider the papers interview the patient and his or her key worker. If the panel agree that the patient should not be discharged the review can be concluded and the outcome recorded in the patient's records.

5.53 With contested cases the recommended procedure very much mirrors that of the MHRT, with the crucial difference that the managers do not have the benefit of a medical member of the decision-making panel. For this reason managers are advised that members will not, as a rule, be qualified to form clinical assessments of their own, and where there is any divergence of view between the managers and the RC about whether the patient reaches the clinical grounds for continued detention especially in relation to risk assessment, the panel should consider an adjournment for further professional advice.[31] This is intended to dissuade the managers from discharging against medical advice.

5.54 Written reports are to be obtained from the RC, in which an essential element will be full information about any history of violence or self-harm, a full risk assessment, the history of the patient's care and treatment, and details of the care plan. The Code recommends that the patient should receive copies of the reports unless the managers consider the information disclosed would be likely to cause serious harm to the physical or mental health of the patient or any other individual. Relatives and carers should be informed of the review and should be invited to attend and put their views to the panel in person. If the patient objects to this a suitable member of the professional care team should be asked to include the relative's or carer's views in a report to the panel. The panel should have before them a copy of the RC's renewal report supplemented by a record of the consultation undertaken by the RC under s 20(5) and the written agreement of that other professional under s 20(5A) that the renewal criteria are met.

Principles

5.55 The Act does not define the criteria or the procedure for reviewing detention. Noting this, the Code sets three principles of fairness, reasonableness and lawfulness which must be satisfied in the conduct of managers' reviews.[32] They must adopt and apply a fair and reasonable procedure appropriate to the important issue of deprivation of liberty. They must not behave in a way which is irrational or *Wednesbury* unreasonable, meaning that they must avoid decisions which no body of Hospital Managers, properly directing themselves as to the law and on the available information, could have made.[33] Finally, they must not act unlawfully. They must interpret and apply the Mental Health Act and any other applicable legislation correctly. They must neither fail to take into account relevant evidence nor take into

[31] Department of Health *Mental Health Act 1983 Draft Revised Code of Practice* (2007), para 34.29. See http://www.dh.gov.uk/en/Consultations.

[32] Ibid, para 34.20.

[33] *Associated Provincial Picture Houses Ltd v Wednesbury Corpn* [1948] 1 KB 223, CA.

account material which is irrelevant. As public authorities exercising functions of a public nature, they must act compatibly with Convention rights under the Human Rights Act 1998.

5.56 In relation to continuation of detention it is important to recognise that mental health detention will be unlawful under Art 5 of the European Convention on Human Rights and the HRA 1998 without objective evidence of a true mental disorder which is of a kind or degree warranting confinement. There must also be regular review to ensure that the conditions justifying detention continue to be met.

5.57 Where a patient is subject to a CTO, Art 8 is likely to be engaged which means that interferences with the right must be in accordance with the law and necessary for one of the goals in Art 8(2), such as the patient's health, for the prevention of crime or to protect the rights and freedoms of others.

5.58 The key issue with detention or SCT is whether the statutory grounds justifying compulsion continue to be met. This entails considering, in this order, the following questions:

- is the patient still suffering from mental disorder?

- if so, is the disorder of a nature or degree which makes treatment in a hospital appropriate, or in the case of a patient on SCT, which makes treatment while liable to recall appropriate?

- is detention in hospital still necessary in the interests of the patient's health or safety, or for the protection of other people, or in the case of a patient on SCT, is liability to recall still necessary in the interest of the patient's health and safety or for the protection of other people?

- in the case of a patient detained under s 3 (or its equivalent) or subject to SCT, is appropriate medical treatment available for the patient?[34]

If, on the evidence, the panel is satisfied that the answer to any of these questions is 'no', the patient should be discharged.

5.59 Where the nearest relative ('NR') has sought to discharge the patient and the RC has issued a barring certificate on grounds that the patient if discharged would be likely to act in a manner dangerous to self or to others, the NR may apply to the Mental Health Review Tribunal. If the patient does not apply to the MHRT but there is a managers' review instead, the managers have to consider whether there is a risk that the patient would act dangerously to self or others. As the Draft Code says, this is a 'more stringent test for continuing detention' since the focus of this question should be 'on the probability of

---

[34] Department of Health *Mental Health Act 1983 Draft Revised Code of Practice* (2007), paras 34.14–34.16. See http://www.dh.gov.uk/en/Consultations.

dangerous acts, such as causing serious physical injury rather than on the patient's general need for safety and others' general need for protection.' The Code then suggests that if the managers disagree with the RC and decide the answer to this question is 'no', 'they should *usually* discharge the patient, and in all cases should ensure that a full risk assessment is carried out when considering discharge'.[35]

Hearing procedures

5.60   Four key points for the hearing procedure are covered in paras 34.26 and 34.28 of the Draft Revised Code. They are:

- the patient should be given a full opportunity, and any necessary help, to explain why he or she wishes to be discharged;

- the patient should be allowed to be accompanied by a friend or representative of his or her own choosing to help in putting his or her point of view to the panel;

- the RC and other professionals should be asked to give their views on: whether the patient's continued detention or continued SCT order is justified; and the factors on which those views are based;

- the patient and the other parties to the review should, if the patient wishes it, be able to hear each other's statements to the panel and to put questions to each other. However, the patient should always be offered the opportunity of speaking to the panel alone.

If the panel conclude that the patient ought to be discharged but arrangements for after-care need to be made, they may adjourn the panel, for a brief period, to enable a full CPA/care planning meeting to take place.

The decision

5.61   The decision and the reasons for it should be recorded, and communicated immediately, both orally and in writing, to the patient, to the nearest relative with the patient's consent, and to the professionals concerned. At least one of the members of the panel should offer to see the patient to explain in person the reasons for the decision. Copies of the papers relating to the review, and the formal record of the decision, should be placed in the patient's records.

---

[35]   Department of Health *Mental Health Act 1983 Draft Revised Code of Practice* (2007), paras 34.19 (emphasis added). See http://www.dh.gov.uk/en/Consultations.

Duties to refer cases to MHRTs

5.62   Duties of managers to refer cases to MHRTs arise under s 68. Under the MHA 1983 if a patient had not applied to a MHRT within the six-month period immediately following admission under s 3, the managers had a duty to refer the case to a MHRT. The aim was to ensure that detained patients who lack capacity should not fall below the radar of the system of review. Currently, a period of detention under s 2 does not count when calculating the six-month period. Section 37 of the MHA 2007 amends s 68, introduces a new requirement to refer six months from 'the applicable day', which is the day on which the patient was first detained, whether that was under s 2 for assessment, s 3 for treatment, or following a transfer from guardianship.[36] The six-month period can be reduced by order made under s 68A by the Secretary of State, in relation to hospitals in England, or the Welsh Ministers, in relation to hospitals in Wales.

5.63   The duty also arose under the MHA 1983 where the authority to detain was renewed and three years (or one year in the case of a child under 16) had elapsed since the patient's case was last considered by a MHRT. The amended s 68 breaks the link between renewal and referral. Now there is a duty to refer if a MHRT has not considered the patient's case in three years (or one year if the patient is under 18). The order making power under new s 68A can be used to reduce the three year and one year periods.

5.64   Patients who are absent without leave at the point at which they should be referred to the MHRT must be referred on their return to hospital.[37] Section 68(7) requires the managers to refer the case of a community patient to the MHRT as soon as possible after the community treatment order is revoked.

5.65   A managers' referral to the MHRT should include a statement containing the information about the patient specified in Sch 1 to the MHRT Rules, which in the case of a restricted patient must also be sent to the Ministry of Justice.

5.66   Section 68(8), which entitles a patient to commission an independent report from a doctor in preparation for a MHRT hearing, is extended to entitle an AC or a doctor to prepare such a report and for that purpose to visit and examine a detained or a community patient and to inspect records.

5.67   The hospital managers are only under a duty to refer to the MHRT in specified circumstances. The Secretary of State for Health has the power under s 67 to refer the case of a Part 2 patient or an unrestricted Part 3 patient at any time. The Draft Code states that: 'Anyone may request such a referral and the Secretary of State will consider each such request on its merits'.[38] The

---

[36]   MHA 1983, s 68(5), as inserted by MHA 2007, s 37(3).

[37]   MHA 1983, s 21(3), as inserted by MHA 2007, s 37(2).

[38]   Department of Health *Mental Health Act 1983 Draft Revised Code of Practice* (2007), para 33.37. See http://www.dh.gov.uk/en/Consultations.

importance of this power is underlined in *R (on the application of H) v Secretary of State for Health.*[39] MH was severely mentally disabled by Down's Syndrome. She lacked mental capacity to consent to admission. She was admitted under s 2 for assessment when her mother became ill and she became increasingly disturbed. The plan was to assess MH's needs in hospital and then find a suitable residential placement where she could be received into guardianship under s 7 of the MHA 1983. MH's mother was her nearest relative. She objected to guardianship. Objection by a nearest relative cannot block detention under s 2, but it can veto detention under s 3 or guardianship. Steps were taken to displace MH's mother as nearest relative by application to the county court on the grounds of unreasonable objection.

5.68   By virtue of s 29(4), if such an application is made during the currency of detention under s 2, the 28-day period authorised by that section is extended until the county court deals with the case. In MH's case the effect of this was to extend her detention under s 2 from 28 days to over two years, and since she had not applied for a MHRT within the first 14 days of her s 2, MH had no right, herself or through a proxy, to seek review of the lawfulness of her detention as required by Art 5(4). Baroness Hale delivered the only speech for a unanimous House of Lords, holding that there was no necessary incompatibility between ss 2 and 29(4) of the MHA 1983 and Art 5(4) as long as either the county court proceedings were determined swiftly or the Secretary of State referred the case to the MHRT under s 67.

5.69   The Draft Illustrative Code of Practice takes the consequences of the House of Lords decision in MH and advises the hospital managers 'always' to consider requesting referral by the Secretary of State where detention is extended pending a displacement decision and the patient is unable for any reason to make a request. The Code advises that:[40]

> 'Hospital managers should consider asking the Secretary of State to make a reference in respect of any patients whose rights under Article 5 of the European Convention on Human Rights might otherwise be at risk of being violated because they are unable (for whatever reason) to have their cases considered by the MHRT.'

In particular they should normally seek a reference where the patient has never had a MHRT hearing or, if there was one, it was a long time ago.

5.70   The Draft Code recognises that the availability of community care facilities and a care plan will often be crucial in determining eligibility for discharge and advises that where a Tribunal hearing has been arranged:[41]

---

[39]   [2005] UKHL 60.

[40]   Department of Health *Mental Health Act 1983 Draft Revised Code of Practice* (2007), para 33.38. See http://www.dh.gov.uk/en/Consultations.

[41]   Ibid, para 30.7.

'Primary care trusts and LSSAs should take reasonable steps to identify appropriate after-care services for patients before their actual discharge from hospital if there is a reasonable prospect of the patient being discharged by hospital managers or the MHRT. Where a tribunal hearing has been arranged for a patient who might be entitled to after-care under section 117 of the Act, the hospital managers should inform the relevant PCT and LSSA.'

Managers' duties in relation to children

5.71 Section 31 adds new s 131A to the MHA 1983. This places hospital managers under a duty to ensure that patients aged under 18 admitted to hospital for mental disorder are accommodated in an environment that is suitable for their age (subject to their needs). This provision comes into force in April 2010. In determining whether the environment is suitable, the managers must consult a person whom they consider to be suitable because of their experience in child and adolescent mental health services cases.

CONCLUSION

5.72 The Nearest Relative and the Hospital Managers will continue to occupy a significant role under the MHA 1983 (as amended), and the new role of IMHAs is to be welcomed. The IMHA will not be a public authority for the purposes of the Human Rights Act 1998. The hospital managers will clearly be a 'public authority' exercising public functions when making decisions about detention or community treatment. More difficult is the situation of the Nearest Relative when making an application for detention. Would the NR be exercising functions of a public nature, sufficient to make them a public body and therefore bound to act in a manner consistent with convention rights. Although a NR might be held to be a public authority, the practical significance of this issue is less marked in relation to the NR than in relation to the AMHP, who has procedural obligations such as interviewing the patient in a suitable manner.

Chapter 6

POWERS OF DETENTION UNDER THE MENTAL HEALTH ACT 1983 AND THE MENTAL CAPACITY ACT 2005

OVERVIEW

6.1   Under the MHA 1983 there were two routes whereby an adult needing in-patient treatment of mental disorder could be admitted: informally under s 131; or under the powers of compulsory admission in ss 2, 3, and 4. In future there will be three:

(1)   informal admission;

(2)   detention under ss 2, 3 or 4; or

(3)   detention under the '*Bournewood*' Deprivation of Liberty procedures in the Mental Capacity Act 2005, Schs 1A and A1.

This chapter outlines what is meant by informal status, and then examines each of these procedures for depriving people of their liberty, explaining the circumstances in which each is appropriate. The chapter also explains the approved clinician's, doctor's, and nurse's holding powers under s 5 to prevent informal patients from leaving hospital.

INFORMAL ADMISSION

6.2   The MHA 1983 is based on the principle that, wherever possible, patients should be admitted to hospital on an informal basis and powers of compulsion should be used as a last resort. Approximately 250,000 admissions to psychiatric hospitals take place every year. Over ninety per cent of all admissions to mental illness and learning disability hospitals and units are informal.[1] Informal admission is provided for in s 131 of the MHA 1983 which states that nothing in the Act:

> 'shall be construed as preventing a patient who requires treatment for mental disorder from being admitted to any hospital or registered establishment in

---

[1]   P Bartlett and R Sandland *Mental Health Law Policy and Practice* (Oxford, 3rd edn, 2007), p 111.

pursuance of arrangements made in that behalf and without any application, order or direction rendering him liable to be detained under this Act.'

Informal patients are free to leave hospital at any time (they need not seek permission from their doctor, approved clinician, or anyone else, although it is desirable to inform the hospital staff), unless a holding power under s 5 is invoked. If staff decide that the s 5 holding power should be invoked, they should explain to the patient in 'neutral terms' the effect of being detained and the safeguards attached to detained patient status. If the patient decides not to remain voluntarily following such an explanation, the choice is between discharge or the holding power. In such a case the Revised Draft Code states that:[2]

> 'It should be made clear to a patient who consents to remain voluntarily in such circumstances that they may withdraw their consent at any time in order to require a decision to be made about discharge or detention.'

If an informal patient who had consented to admission seems to have lost capacity to decide whether to remain in hospital, the Draft Revised Code says that:[3]

> 'it may be necessary to seek an authorisation under the Mental Capacity Act 2005 deprivation of liberty safeguards even if the patient appears happy to remain in hospital.'

The least restrictive alternative

6.3   It is a condition of detention for treatment under s 3(2)(c) that the necessary treatment cannot be provided unless the patient is detained under that section. Hence an application cannot proceed if there are safe and effective ways, other than detention under s 3, in which the necessary treatment may be provided. Those other ways might be informal admission or, after March 2009, admission under the Deprivation of Liberty safeguards in the MCA 2005.

Patients who lack capacity to consent to admission

6.4   Informal admission has traditionally been seen as being not only for patients who were capable of consenting and agreeing to admission, but also for patients who lacked capacity to consent to admission, as long as they were not resisting or protesting. Compliant incapable patients were admitted informally. Detention was reserved for cases where hospitalisation is necessary to prevent risk to self or others, and the patient, whether capable or incapable of consenting, is refusing admission, or is persistently or purposefully seeking to leave hospital.

---

[2]   Department of Health *Mental Health Act 1983 Draft Revised Code of Practice* (2007), para 4.18. See http://www.dh.gov.uk/en/Consultations.

[3]   Ibid.

6.5 This changed with *HL v United Kingdom*[4] (for full discussion of the case see paras **1.32–1.36** above), where the European Court of Human rights held that a procedure prescribed by law must be followed where a mentally disordered person is subject to a degree of control over their residence, treatment, and movement which reaches a degree and intensity sufficient to amount to a deprivation of liberty. Section 131 does not provide a procedure prescribed by law.

Informal admission post-*HL v United Kingdom*

6.6 Informal admission of adult patients will in future apply to two groups: first to those who are capable and consenting to admission; and second, to those who

(a) lack capacity to consent to admission or treatment; and

(b) are not resistant to hospitalisation, and

(c) where the level of control to be exercised over residence, movement, and treatment is insufficient in degree and intensity to amount to a deprivation of liberty.

Patients with capacity who consent

6.7 The Draft Revised Code says that:[5]

'Informal admission to hospital is usually appropriate when a patient who has the capacity to do so consents to admission. But this is not a hard and fast rule.'

The Code goes on to recommend that where a patient presents a 'clear danger to self or others', compulsory admission should be considered even though the patient has expressed willingness to be admitted voluntarily:[6]

'If this is the case, compulsory admission should be considered if the 'patient's current medical state, together with reliable evidence of past experience, indicates a strong likelihood that he or she will have a change of mind about informal admission either prior to or after admission, with a resulting risk to their health or safety or to the safety of other people.'

Hence, detention may be justified, even when the patient has capacity and is consenting, if:

(a) without detention there would be danger to self or others; and

---

[4] (2004) 40 EHRR 761, ECtHR.
[5] Department of Health *Mental Health Act 1983 Draft Revised Code of Practice* (2007), para 4.14. See http://www.dh.gov.uk/en/Consultations.
[6] Ibid, paras 4.14–4.15.

(b)   the patient's history or current behaviour suggests that consent will be withdrawn.

Paragraph 4.16 of the Draft Code emphasises that:

> 'the threat of compulsion should not be used to induce a patient to consent to admission to hospital or to treatment (and might invalidate any apparent consent). In order to do so it would have to amount to duress or undue influence. An explanation of the possibility and consequences of detention and the safeguards attaching to it, which is couched in neutral language, is unlikely to invalidate consent.'

Patients who lack capacity to consent to treatment or admission

6.8   Where a patient aged 16 or over lacks mental capacity to consent to admission or treatment, AMHPs and doctors will need to consider whether the patient could instead safely and effectively be treated informally under the MCA 2005. Note that the deprivation of liberty safeguards under the MCA 2005 do not apply to people under 18. Provided admission to hospital does not involve deprivation of liberty the person may be admitted informally under s 131, if the conditions in s 5 of the Mental Capacity Act 2005 are met. These provide a defence in respect of any act done in connection with care or treatment, provided the person doing the act

(a)   has taken reasonable steps to assess the person's capacity;

(b)   reasonably believes that the person lacks capacity; and

(c)   reasonably believes that the action is in the person's best interests.

Anyone who is to be deprived of his liberty must be subject to a procedure prescribed by law. This will either be by detention under the Mental Health Act 1983, or by *Bournewood* authorisation under the Mental Capacity Act 2005. The answer to the question whether the patient is subject to a deprivation of liberty is the key to deciding whether a person who lacks capacity may be admitted to hospital informally or whether the *Bournewood* safeguards should be used.

Deprivation of liberty

6.9   In *HL v United Kingdom* the court held that the distinction between a deprivation of liberty, which requires authorisation by a procedure prescribed by law, and a restriction of liberty, which does not, was a matter of degree and intensity. The starting point must be the 'concrete situation of the individual' and a whole range of criteria must be taken into account such as the type, duration, effects and manner of implementation of the measure in question.

6.10   In *HL v United Kingdom* the Court found that those having care of HL exercised complete and effective control over his assessment, care, treatment, contacts, movement and residence. He was under constant supervision and control, and was not free to leave the hospital. This amounted to a deprivation of liberty. Since the deprivation of liberty had not been carried out in accordance with a procedure prescribed by law, and HL had not been able to seek speedy review of the lawfulness of his detention, there were breaches of his Convention rights under Art 5(1)(e) and (4).

6.11 In December 2006 the Government issued *Draft Illustrative Guidance on the Bournewood Safeguards*, which will be included, when finalised, in the Mental Capacity Act 2005 Code of Practice. The Draft Guidance states that 'a deprivation of liberty in Article 5 ECHR terms should be avoided if at all possible' and residential care homes and hospitals should:[7]

> 'to the greatest possible extent that safety considerations will allow, seek to operate care regimes that promote a person's control over their daily living and maximise their autonomy. This will both reduce the likelihood of deprivation of liberty arising, and enhance their quality of life.'

The Draft Guidance goes on to advise (at para 11) on steps which will reduce the risk of deprivation of liberty and therefore legal challenge by minimising restrictions within institutions. Decisions should be taken in a structured way, involving the person themselves and their carers, should follow (as appropriate) the Care Programme Approach, Person Centred Planning, Unified Assessment or Single Assessment Process, and should be fully documented. Following the fifth principle in s 1 of the MCA 2005 (see paras **2.40** and **2.41** above), before an authorisation is sought for deprivation of liberty, attempts must always be made to identify ways to meet the person's needs in a less restrictive way.

6.12 However, minimising restrictions on freedom within institutions may not be enough to avoid reaching the level of control needed to deprive someone of their liberty, as is indicated by the decision in *JE v DE (by his litigation friend the Official Solicitor), Surrey County Council and EW*.[8] DE lacked mental capacity to decide where he should live, but had made it abundantly clear that he wished to leave the residential care home where he had been placed by the local authority. Munby J accepted that a deprivation of liberty consisted of both an *objective* element – a person's confinement in a particular restricted space for a not negligible length of time – and a *subjective* element – that the person has not validly consented to the confinement in question.[9] The judge held that the crucial question was not so much whether (and, if so, to what extent) DE's freedom or liberty was or is curtailed *within* the institutional setting. The fundamental issue was:[10]

> 'whether DE was deprived of his liberty to leave the homes where he was placed not in the sense of leaving for the purpose of some trip or outing approved by

7 Department of Health *Draft Illustrative Guidance on the Bournewood Safeguards*, paras 7–8.
8 [2006] EWHC 3459 (Fam).
9 [2006] EWHC 3459 (Fam) at [77], following *Storck v Germany* (2005) 43 EHRR 96, at para 74.
10 [2006] EWHC 3459 (Fam) at [115].

those managing the institution, but rather leaving in the sense of removing himself permanently in order to live where and with whom he chooses.'

Because he was not free to leave he had been deprived of his liberty.

6.13 The Draft Guidance lists the following factors drawn from the Strasbourg case law as 'potentially indicating that a deprivation of liberty is taking place':

(1)   restraint is used, including sedation, to admit a person who is resisting;

(2)   professionals exercise complete and effective control over care and movement for a significant period;

(3)   professionals exercise complete control over assessments, treatment, contacts and residence;

(4)   the person would be prevented from leaving if they made a meaningful attempt to do so;

(5)   a request by carers for the person to be discharged to their care would be refused;

(6)   the person is unable to maintain social contacts because of restrictions placed on access to other people;

(7)   the person loses autonomy because they are under continuous supervision and control.[11]

6.14   The Draft Code of Practice then lists further 'factors which are likely to be taken into account by the courts in deciding whether there is a deprivation of liberty'. These are:

(1)   the person is not allowed to leave the facility – especially where family or friends are prevented from moving them to another care setting;

(2)   the person has no or very limited choice about their life within the care home or hospital;

(3)   the person is unable to maintain contact with the world outside the care home or hospital;

(4)   restraint is used on admission and the person is not realistically subsequently able to leave.[12]

---

[11]   Department of Health *Draft Illustrative Guidance on the Bournewood Safeguards*, para 25.
[12]   Ibid, para 28.

The Joint Committee on Human Rights considered that deprivation of liberty is 'a less flexible and elusive concept than might be thought from the draft illustrative guidance' and:[13]

> 'It is not necessary for all the elements identified in the list of factors contributing to a deprivation of liberty to be present.'

The starting point should therefore be that it is likely there will be a deprivation of liberty if it is known that a person is to be prevented from leaving the place where they are being taken to reside. In England and Wales deprivations of liberty may be authorised by detention under the Mental Health Act or by authorisation under the Mental Capacity Act. For the purposes of the Convention, a deprivation of liberty must be carried out 'in accordance with a procedure prescribed by law'.

'In Accordance with a Procedure Prescribed by Law'

6.15   In *Winterwerp v Netherlands* the European Court of Human Rights held that the notion underlying the phrase 'in accordance with a procedure prescribed by law' in Art 5 ECHR is:[14]

> 'one of fair and proper procedure, namely that any measure depriving a person of his liberty should issue from and be executed by an appropriate authority and should not be arbitrary.'

In *HL v United Kingdom* the Court made important statements about what is required by a procedure prescribed by law. A number of key ingredients of a procedure prescribed by law had been missing in HL's case in the court's opinion. These were:[15]

'(a)   The lack of any formalised admission procedures which indicate who can propose admission, for what reasons and on the basis of what kind of medical and other assessments and conclusions.

(b)   There was no requirement to fix the exact purpose of admission (for example, for assessment or for treatment) and, consistently, no limits in terms of time, treatment or care attach to that admission.

(c)   There was no specific provision requiring a continuing clinical assessment of the persistence of a disorder warranting detention.

(d)   There was no provision for the appointment of a representative of a patient who could make certain objections and applications on his or her behalf, a procedural protection accorded to those committed involuntarily under the 1983 Act and which would be of equal importance for patients who are legally incapacitated and have extremely limited communication abilities.'

---

[13]   House of Lords, House of Commons Joint Committee on Human Rights *Legislative Scrutiny: Mental Health Bill Fourth Report of Session 2006–2007* (HL Paper 40, HC Paper 288), para 86.

[14]   (1979) 2 EHRR 387, at para 45.

[15]   (2004) 40 EHRR 761, at para 120.

The Court found striking 'the lack of any fixed procedural rules by which the admission and detention of compliant incapacitated persons is conducted'. The Deprivation of Liberty authorisations in the MCA 2005 are designed to remedy the failure to provide a procedure prescribed by law.

6.16 The issue of what is required by a procedure prescribed by law was addressed in *Re PS (incapacitated or vulnerable adult)* where Munby J said that where a court was authorising deprivation of liberty, the following minimum requirements must be satisfied in order to comply with Art 5:[16]

'(1) The detention must be authorised by the court on application made by the local authority and *before* the detention commences.
(2) Subject to the exigencies of urgency or emergency the evidence must establish unsoundness of mind of a kind or degree warranting compulsory confinement. In other words, there must be evidence establishing at least a prima facie case that the individual lacks capacity and that confinement of the nature proposed is appropriate.
(3) Any order authorising detention must contain provision for an adequate review at reasonable intervals, in particular with a view to ascertaining whether there still persists unsoundness of mind of a kind or degree warranting compulsory confinement.'

The requirement of authorisation before the detention commences is covered in the MHA 1983 under s 6(1) which provides that a duly completed application under Part 2 with medical recommendations is sufficient authority for the AMHP to authorise the patient to be taken and conveyed to hospital (see para **4.32** above). The MHA 2007 contains a provision introducing a power to take and convey a person to their place of residence under guardianship.[17] No such power is expressly provided in relation to the MCA authorisation procedure.

6.17 It may be that the Government considers it can rely instead on the defence in respect of acts done in connection with care and treatment, involving proportionate restraint in ss 5 and 6 of the Mental Capacity Act 2005. However, it is doubtful whether a retrospective defence can amount to a procedure prescribed by law. In *Storck v Germany* the European Court of Human Rights held that states have an obligation to take positive steps to secure the right to liberty under Art 5 and the right to physical and moral integrity under Art 8. This obligation placed them under a duty to exercise supervision and control over private psychiatric institutions. The court noted that in the sphere of interferences with a person's physical integrity, German law provided for strong penal sanctions and for liability in tort, but went on to say that:[18]

---

[16] [2007] EWHC 623 (Fam) at [23].
[17] MHA 1983, s 18(7), as inserted by MHA 2007, Sch 3, para 3(5).
[18] *Storck v Germany (App no 61603/00)* (2005) 43 EHRR 96, at para 150.

'Just as in cases of deprivation of liberty, the Court finds that such retrospective measures alone are not sufficient to provide appropriate protection of the physical integrity of individuals in such a vulnerable position as the applicant.'

Which procedure to use? The interface between the Mental Health Act 1983 and the Mental Capacity Act 2005

6.18 If deprivation of liberty is necessary this will have to be under either the Mental Health Act or the Mental Capacity Act. Which one to use is a matter of professional judgment, and the interface is not always clear cut. Detention under the Mental Health Act will be appropriate if the person needs deprivation of liberty in order to provide some aspect of their treatment for mental disorder and either:

(a)   they are ineligible for *Bournewood* safeguards; or

(b)   their care cannot be safely and effectively provided using those safeguards.

If AMHPs and doctors are satisfied that a patient can safely and effectively be assessed or treated by relying on the MCA, it is likely to be difficult to demonstrate that the criteria for detaining them under s 3(2)(c) are met. The decision which framework to use is a judgment for the professionals concerned. A person may not be subject to a MCA authorisation unless they are 'eligible', and the 'no refusals' condition is satisfied.

Eligibility for the *Bournewood* safeguards

6.19 The purpose of the eligibility requirement for the MCA Deprivation of Liberty Safeguards under Sch 1A to the MCA 2005 is to mark the interface between cases which can be dealt with under the *Bournewood* authorisations and 'cases where a person is, or might be made, subject to the 1983 Act'.[19]

Patients already subject to the Mental Health Act 1983

6.20 The cases where a person is already subject to the MHA 1983 are relatively straightforward. A person is ineligible for *Bournewood* detention if he is already subject to a hospital treatment obligation[20] under the MHA 1983 and will continue to be detained in hospital under that regime. In such a case there is authority to detain already, so a further application for detention under either legislation is unnecessary.

6.21 A person on leave of absence from detention, subject to guardianship, supervised community treatment or conditional discharge will also be ineligible

---

[19]   *Explanatory Notes*, paras 201–220.
[20]   That is, detained under ss 2, 3, 4, 35, 36, 37, 38, 44, 45A, 47, 48 or 51.

if the authorisation would be inconsistent with an obligation placed on them under the MHA 1983 to reside somewhere else. The Explanatory Notes state that:[21]

> 'a person who is subject to the 1983 Act but who is not in hospital could be subject to an authorisation under these new provisions. This might be necessary for example if a person subject to guardianship who normally lived at home needed respite care in a care home.'

However, *Bournewood* authorisation would not be available if the person is on leave of absence from detention, or subject to SCT or conditional discharge and the authorisation, if given, would be for deprivation of liberty in a hospital for treatment for mental disorder. This means that an authorisation cannot be used as an alternative to the procedures for recall in the MHA 1983.[22]

Patients not already subject to the Mental Health Act 1983 or the Mental Capacity Act 2005

6.22   More difficult is the situation where a person is already subject to neither regime. Schedule 1A states that the person will be ineligible for deprivation of liberty in a hospital, either by order of the Court of Protection or by a *Bournewood* authorisation, if three conditions are met:

(1)   the proposed order of the Court of Protection or *Bournewood* authorisation will authorise the person to be a mental health patient, meaning 'a person accommodated in a hospital for the purpose of being given medical treatment for mental disorder'; or

(2)   the patient objects—
       (a)   to being a mental health patient, or
       (b)   to being given some or all of the mental health treatment; and

(3)   an attorney or deputy has not made a valid decision to consent to each matter to which P objects.[23]

In deciding whether the person objects, regard is to be had to all the circumstances (insofar as they are reasonably ascertainable, including the person's behaviour, their wishes and feelings, and their views beliefs and values. Regard is to be had to circumstances from the past only insofar as it is reasonable to have regard to them. These provisions treat incapable people as if they had capacity to consent but are refusing.

6.23   However, the patient's objection may be overridden, and they still may be subject to the *Bournewood* procedure if their attorney or deputy validly consents to the placement and treatment. The 'no refusals' requirement means

---

[21]   *Explanatory Notes*, para 201.
[22]   Ibid.
[23]   MCA 2005, Sch A1, para 5.

that the attorney or deputy, acting within the scope of their authority, also has the right to block a *Bournewood* authorisation. The only way in which a patient may block a *Bournewood* authorisation is by a valid and applicable advance decision refusing in sufficiently precise terms admission to hospital in circumstances amounting to a deprivation of liberty, or refusing some or all of the treatment proposed to be given. Such an advance directive could only be overridden by detention under the Mental Health Act.

6.24 If deprivation of liberty in hospital is needed to provide the care a patient who lacks capacity needs, considerations should be given first to whether this may be achieved by a *Bournewood* authorisation under the Mental Capacity Act 2005. In order to be eligible, the patient must lack capacity within the meaning of ss 2 and 3 of the MCA 2005, and deprivation of liberty must be necessary in the patient's best interests.

THE MENTAL CAPACITY ACT 2005

6.25 In order to understand the *Bournewood* safeguards and the interface between the MCA and the MHA it is important to understand the basic concepts and instruments of the Mental Capacity Act 2005. Five principles apply to decision-making under the MCA 2005 (see further para **2.39** above). They are:

(1)   a person must be assumed to have capacity unless it is established that they lack capacity;

(2)   a person is not to be treated as unable to make a decision unless all practicable steps to help him to do so have been taken without success;

(3)   a person is not to be treated as unable to make a decision merely because he makes an unwise decision;

(4)   an act done, or decision made, under this Act for or on behalf of a person who lacks capacity must be done, or made, in his best interests;

(5)   before the act is done, or the decision is made, regard must be had to whether the purpose for which it is needed can be as effectively achieved in a way that is less restrictive of the person's rights and freedom of action.[24]

Incapacity

6.26   A patient lacks capacity in relation to a matter if, at the material time he or she is unable to make a decision for him or herself in relation to the matter because of a temporary or permanent impairment of, or disturbance in the

---

[24]   MCA 2005, s 1.

functioning of, the mind or brain.[25] Note that a person lacks capacity 'in relation to a matter', making capacity task specific. A person may be able to make some decisions but not others. Section 2(3) states that lack of capacity cannot be established merely by reference to a person's age or appearance, or 'a condition of his, or an aspect of his behaviour, which might lead others to make unjustified assumptions about his capacity'. These provisions reinforce the presumption of capacity and emphasise that people are not to be treated as incapable because they have a particular diagnosis. Incapacity is to be established on the balance of probabilities, the standard of proof in civil proceedings.

6.27 Section 2 states that a person lacks capacity if they are unable to make a decision, and s 3(1) sets out the test to be met if a person is to be found unable to make the relevant decision. The person must be unable because of a temporary or permanent impairment or disturbance in the functioning of mind or brain:

(1) to understand the information relevant to the decision;

(2) to retain that information;

(3) to use or weigh that information as part of the process of making the decision; or

(4) to communicate his decision (whether by talking, using sign language or any other means).

Relevant treatment information includes information about the reasonably foreseeable consequences of deciding one way or another, or failing to make the decision. A person is not to be regarded as unable to understand the information relevant to a decision if he is able to understand an explanation of it given to him in a way that is appropriate to his circumstances (using simple language, visual aids or any other means). The requirement to be able to retain information is only to retain it long enough to make the relevant decision and the fact that a person is able to retain the information relevant to a decision for a short period only does not prevent him from being regarded as able to make the decision.

Best interests

6.28 It is a principle of the MCA 2005 that any act or decision, for or on behalf of a person who lacks capacity, must be done, or made, in his best interests. Best interests was initially to be determined according to the *Bolam* formula.[26] Treatment was in the best interests of a patient if a responsible body of medical opinion (not necessarily the majority) would consider it to be in the

---

[25] MCA 2005, s 2(1).
[26] *Bolam v Friern Hospital Management Committee* [1957] 2 All ER 118, QBD.

patient's best interests.[27] However, the MCA 2005 and subsequent case-law have modified substantially the approach to determining best interests.

A new approach to best interests

6.29 Since *Re A (Male Sterilisation)*[28] a two-stage 'balance sheet' approach has been employed. The first question is whether the treatment is within 'the *Bolam* range? The second is which treatment provides the most 'significant credit' in the balance sheet of probable advantages over disadvantages. In *JS v an NHS Trust* the Court insisted on a broader concept of best interests, recognising interconnectedness of incapacitated people and their carers and families. The duty of the assessor is to consider and assess the best interests of the patients in the widest possible way to include the medical and non-medical benefits and disadvantages, the broader welfare interests of the patient, their abilities, their future with or without treatment, the impact on their families, and the impact of denial of the treatment.[29] These remain the matters which are to be considered. Section 4 of the MCA 2005 does not redefine best interests. Instead it sets out how they are to be determined.

Section 4 of the Mental Capacity Act 2005

6.30 Section 4 of the MCA 2005 sets out the approach to be adopted in assessing best interests. The person making the determination must not make it merely on the basis of the person's age or appearance, or a condition of his, or an aspect of his behaviour, which might lead others to make unjustified assumptions about what might be in his best interests. The assessor must take into account all the circumstances of which he or she is aware and which might reasonably be regarded as relevant. He or she must consider whether it is likely that the person will at some time have capacity in relation to the matter in question, and, if it appears likely that he will, when that is likely to be.

6.31 The person making the best interests determination must, so far as reasonably practicable, permit and encourage the person to participate, or to improve his ability to participate, as fully as possible in any act done for him and any decision affecting him. The decision-maker must take into account the person's past and present wishes and feelings, his beliefs and values which might be likely to influence his decision, and any other factors which he would be likely to consider if able to do so. If practicable and appropriate the decision maker must consider the views of anyone named by the person to be consulted, any carer or person interested in his welfare, any donee of a lasting power of attorney granted by the person, and any deputy appointed by the Court of Protection.

---

[27] *Re F (Sterilisation: Mental Patient)* [1990] 2 AC 1.
[28] [2000] 1 FLR 549, per Thorpe LJ at 560.
[29] [2002] EWHC 2734 (Fam).

6.32 Where the determination of best interests relates to treatment which those providing health care consider to be necessary to sustain life, the decision-maker must not, in considering whether the treatment is in the best interests of the person concerned, be motivated by a desire to bring about his death. As long as the processes and requirements of s 4 have been fulfilled, and the balance sheet test applied, there is sufficient compliance with the best interests requirement if the decision-maker reasonably believes that what he does or decides is in the best interests of the person concerned.

The defence in relation to acts of care, treatment and restraint done in the best interests of people who lack mental capacity

6.33 Sections 5 and 6 of the Mental Capacity Act 2005 provide a legal defence for anyone who does any act relating to the care or treatment of a person who lacks capacity, provided the act is done in what are reasonably believed to be the patient's best interests. In order for the action to be lawful the person taking it must have taken reasonable steps to determine whether the person has capacity in relation to the relevant decision, must reasonably believe that the person indeed lacks capacity, and must reasonably believe that what they are doing is in the person's best interests. Section 5 acts may include restraint as long as the conditions in s 6 are met. Restraint may be imposed to prevent harm to the patient as long as it is a proportionate response both to the likelihood of harm *to the patient* and the severity of the harm. The defence is not available if the proposed care or treatment intervention is one which has been refused by a valid and applicable advance decision made by the patient while he or she still retained capacity. Restraint cannot be authorised in the interests of protecting others from harm, although there may be occasions when there is overlap, such as where the person is restrained from rushing into a busy road, potentially harming themselves or other road users. Certain, more serious, treatment decisions require the approval of the Court of Protection unless the person has previously made a Lasting Power of Attorney appointing an attorney to make the decision for them, or they have made a valid advance decision refusing the proposed treatment. The Court of Protection must be asked to make decisions relating to withholding or withdrawal of artificial nutrition and hydration ('ANH') from a patient in a permanent vegetative state ('PVS'), organ or bone marrow donation by a donor who lacks mental capacity, non-therapeutic sterilisation (eg for contraceptive purposes) and cases where there is dispute about whether a treatment will be in a person's best interests.[30] Section 37 of the MCA 2005 applies to decisions about providing, stopping or withholding serious medical treatment where there is no-one other than paid carer to consult, the responsible body must appoint an Independent Mental Capacity Advocate ('IMCA') whose submissions must be taken into account in deciding whether to provide the treatment. The IMCA may consider seeking a second opinion. The requirement to consult an IMCA does not apply to treatment which is urgently needed to save a person's life or prevent a serious deterioration in condition. The IMCA requirement applies if any patient is to

---

[30] Ministry of Justice *Mental Capacity Act Code of Practice* (2007), paras 6.18 and 8.18–8.24.

be subject to the *Bournewood* deprivation of liberty safeguards, and also to any patient lacking capacity with no-one other than a paid carer to consult is to be placed in hospital for a period likely to exceed 28 days or in a care home for more than eight weeks. The *Bournewood* deprivation of liberty safeguards will be appropriate only when detention is in the patient's own best interests, and necessary detention for the protection of others should take place under the MHA 1983.

Advance decisions

6.34 Sections 24–26 of the MCA 2005 apply to the making of advance decisions refusing treatment. An advance decision is made by an adult to refuse certain defined treatments, to take effect at some time in the future if and when the person loses capacity to make the decision. In order to be valid the decision has to be made while the person still has capacity to make the treatment decision, it must specify clearly the treatment being refused, and must be clear about the circumstances in which it is to apply. For example, if the refusal applies to blood transfusions, is it to apply even if the treatment is necessary to keep the person alive. If so the decision must be in writing. In order to be applicable an advance decision must apply to the circumstances which have currently arisen. A valid and applicable advance decision is binding on the doctors.

6.35 This means that a patient can refuse specified treatment for mental disorder, or to be admitted to hospital for treatment of mental disorder, and if the decision is valid and applicable it will prevent the person being admitted or given the relevant treatment under the Mental Capacity Act. The *Bournewood* deprivation of liberty procedures cannot be applied unless a 'no refusals' requirement is met. If there is a valid advance directive refusing an aspect of the treatment proposed for a patient who is deprived of his liberty, the no-refusals requirement for the *Bournewood* procedures is not met, because there is a valid refusal. A person may not be restrained and given treatment for mental disorder under ss 5 and 6 of the Mental Capacity Act 2005, if he or she lacks capacity to consent and has, when capable, made a valid advance decision refusing drug treatment for mental disorder. However, an advance decision refusing admission and medication for mental disorder may be overridden by detention and treatment under the Mental Health Act. Unless it is immediately necessary to save the patient's life or to prevent serious deterioration in her or his condition, ECT may not be given to a patient who has made a valid and applicable advance decision refusing the treatment, even if the patient is detained under the MHA 1983.[31]

Lasting powers of attorney

6.36 Section 9 of the MCA 2005 entitles a person (P), while they still have capacity to grant a lasting power of attorney (LPA), conferring on the attorney

---

[31] MHA 1983, ss 58A and 621A.

authority to make decisions about the P's personal welfare and/or their property and affairs. A lasting power of attorney gives the attorney authority to make decisions in circumstances where P no longer has capacity.[32] The powers of an attorney are subject to the principles in s 1 and the provisions on best interests in s 4. An attorney may act to restrain P if the conditions in s 11(2)–(4) are met. These are that:

- P lacks, or the attorney reasonably believes that P lacks, capacity in relation to the matter in question.

- the attorney reasonably believes that it is necessary to do the act in order to prevent harm to P.

- the act is a proportionate response to—
  - the likelihood of P's suffering harm, and
  - the seriousness of that harm.

The attorney restrains P if he:

'(a)   uses, or threatens to use, force to secure the doing of an act which P resists; or
(b)   restricts P's liberty of movement, whether or not P resists; or

if he authorises another person to do any of those things.'

6.37   The fact that a person is subject to the MHA does not prevent someone from granting a LPA as long as he or she retains capacity to do so, nor does it affect the validity of any existing LPA or the authority of an attorney to make decisions. An attorney acting under a LPA is therefore able to take any decisions in relation to the welfare, property or affairs of a person subject to the MHA that they would otherwise be authorised to take, with two exceptions. The attorney will not be able:

(1)   to consent on the patient's behalf to treatment which is regulated by Part 4 of the MHA (including neurosurgery for mental disorder and other treatments under s 57); or

(2)   to take decisions about where a person subject to guardianship is to reside, nor take other decisions which conflict with those of a guardian.[33]

An attorney's authority to make decisions about P's personal welfare extends to 'giving or refusing consent to the carrying out or continuation of a treatment by a person providing health care for P'. The authority does not come into effect unless the attorney reasonably believes that P lacks capacity to make the decision. The authority is also subject to any valid and applicable advance decision to refuse treatment. The decision to give or refuse consent to treatment

[32]   The formalities are specified in s 10 and Sch 1 to the MCA 2005.
[33]   MCA 2005, s 28.

is subject to two further limitations. It does not authorise the giving or refusing of consent to the carrying out or continuation of life-sustaining treatment, unless the instrument contains express provision to that effect, and it is subject to any conditions or restrictions in the instrument conferring the LPA.[34] If there is an attorney, the attorney may consent to deprivation of liberty under the MCA even if the patient objects, but no deprivation of liberty may take place if the attorney objects.

The Court of Protection and court appointed deputies

6.38   Where a person (P) is found to lack capacity in relation to decisions about personal welfare or property and affairs, the Court of Protection may itself make an order taking the decision on P's behalf (s 16(2)(a)), or it may appoint a person (a 'deputy') to make decisions on P's behalf (s 16(2)(b)). The powers of the court under this section are subject to ss 1 (the principles) and 4 (best interests). The court may not make a welfare order under s 16(2)(a) authorising deprivation of liberty if the person is ineligible under Sch 1A to the MCA 2005.[35]

6.39   When deciding whether it is in P's best interests to appoint a deputy, the court must have regard to P's best interests and to the principles that:

(a)   a decision by the court is to be preferred to the appointment of a deputy to make a decision; and

(b)   the powers conferred on a deputy should be as limited in scope and duration as is reasonably practicable in the circumstances.

The court may confer powers or impose duties on a deputy as it thinks necessary or expedient in connection with the appointment. Section 17 provides that the Court's powers in relation to P's personal welfare extend in particular to:

(a)   deciding where P is to live;

(b)   deciding what contact, if any, P is to have with any specified persons;

(c)   making an order prohibiting a named person from having contact with P;

(d)   giving or refusing consent to the carrying out or continuation of a treatment by a person providing health care for P;

(e)   giving a direction that a person responsible for P's health care allow a different person to take over that responsibility.

---

[34]   MCA, s 11(7)–(8).
[35]   MCA 2005, s 16A, as inserted by MHA 2007, s 50.

Deputies may be given all of these powers with the exception of (c) and (e).[36]

6.40 A deputy may not refuse life sustaining treatment on P's behalf. Nor may a deputy make a decision which is inconsistent with a decision made by the attorney or the attorneys of a lasting power of attorney conferred by P, acting within the scope of their authority.[37] Deputies exercise their powers subject to s 1 (principles) and s 4 (best interests), and are not authorised to restrain P unless four conditions are met:

(1) in doing the act, the deputy must be acting within the scope of an authority expressly conferred on him by the court;

(2) the deputy must reasonably believe that P lacks, capacity in relation to the matter in question;

(3) the deputy must reasonably believe that it is necessary to do the act in order to prevent harm to P;

(4) the act must be a proportionate response to—
    (a) the likelihood of P's suffering harm; and
    (b) the seriousness of that harm.[38]

A deputy restrains P if he:

(1) uses, or threatens to use, force to secure the doing of an act which P resists; or

(2) restricts P's liberty of movement, whether or not P resists, or if he authorises another person to do any of those things.

Attorneys and deputies have significant powers to consent to or to refuse deprivation of liberty under the *Bournewood* Deprivation of Liberty safeguards in the Mental Capacity Act 2005. They may override the refusal of a patient who lacks capacity to agree to admission to a hospital or care home. They may also exercise a significant role in relation to patients' rights under the Mental Health Act 1983 (see para **6.77** below).

THE *BOURNEWOOD* DEPRIVATION OF LIBERTY SAFEGUARDS

6.41 Section 50 of the MHA 2007 amends the MCA 2005 to add provisions for the lawful deprivation of liberty of a person with a mental disorder, who lacks capacity to consent, if it is in that person's best interests. Section 50(2)

---

[36] MCA 2005, s 20(2).
[37] MCA 2005, s 20(4)–(5).
[38] MCA 2005, s 20(8)–(11).

inserts two new sections – 4A and 4B – into the MCA 2005. The effect of these will be that deprivation of liberty may only take place under the MCA in one of three situations. These are where:

(1) the deprivation is authorised by a personal welfare decision of the Court of Protection under s 16(2)(a) of the MCA 2005; or

(2) the deprivation is authorised in accordance with the deprivation of liberty procedures set out in Sch A1; or

(3) the deprivation is carried out because it is necessary in order to give life sustaining treatment or to carry out a vital act to prevent serious deterioration in the person's condition 'while a decision as respects any relevant issue is sought from the court'.[39]

6.42 The *Bournewood* provisions for authorisation of deprivation of liberty apply to people who are over 18 (Children are dealt with under the MHA 1983 or under s 25 of the Children Act 1989). The person must lack capacity to consent to the arrangements for their care. Receiving care or treatment in circumstances that amount to a deprivation of liberty must be necessary to protect the person from harm and must be in their best interests.

Procedures for authorising deprivation of liberty in Sch A1

6.43 Schedule A1 (inserted by Sch 7 to the MHA 2007) sets out procedures whereby the managing authority of a hospital or care home may obtain authorisation to deprive someone of their liberty for the purpose of giving them care or treatment. Schedule A1 comes into force in March 2009. The 'managing authority' of the hospital or care home where the mentally incapacitated person is or is about to be deprived of their liberty will be responsible for requesting authorisation for deprivation of liberty from 'the supervisory body'. If an authorisation is obtained those who carry out the detention are protected against liability in battery or for wrongful imprisonment but not against liability in negligence, or for acting beyond the scope of the authorisation.[40]

The managing authority

6.44 The managing authority is responsible for applying for authorisations. In the case of an NHS hospital, the managing authority will be the NHS body responsible for the running of the hospital in which a person is, or is to be, a resident. In the case of a private hospital or care home, the managing authority will be the person registered, or required to be registered, under Part 2 of the Care Standards Act 2000 in respect of the hospital or care home.[41] Managing

---

[39] MCA 2005, s 4B.
[40] MCA 2005, Sch A1, paras 3 and 4.
[41] MCA 2005, Sch A1, paras 167–170.

authorities will require systems to identify when a deprivation of liberty of a mentally incapacitated person may be taking place.

The supervisory body: hospitals

6.45 The supervisory body is responsible for authorising deprivation of liberty. Where the *Bournewood* provisions are applied to a person in a hospital situated in England, the supervisory body will be:

(1) if a PCT commissions the relevant care or treatment, that PCT;

(2) if the National Assembly for Wales or a Local Health Board in Wales commission the relevant care and treatment in England, the National Assembly for Wales;

(3) in any other case, the PCT for the area in which the hospital is situated.[42]

The supervisory body in a case where the *Bournewood* provisions are applied to a person in a hospital situated in Wales will be the National Assembly for Wales unless an English PCT commissions the relevant care and treatment in Wales, in which case the PCT will be the supervisory body.[43]

The supervisory body: care homes

6.46 Whether the care home is situated in England or Wales, the supervisory body will be the local authority for the area in which the person is ordinarily resident. However, if the person is not ordinarily resident in the area of a local authority, the supervisory body is the local authority for the area in which the care home is situated.

Standard authorisations

6.47 A managing authority must request a standard authorisation when it appears to them to be likely that, either currently or at some time during the next 28 days, a present or future resident will be accommodated in their hospital or care home in circumstances that amount to a deprivation of liberty.[44] If a person who is subject to a standard authorisation moves to a different hospital or care home, the managing authority of the new hospital or care home must request a standard authorisation.[45] If a personal welfare order granted by the Court of Protection authorising deprivation of liberty is about to expire and the person will continue to be deprived of their liberty, the managing authority should apply in good time before the expiry of the Court

[42] MCA 2005, Sch A1, para 171.
[43] MCA 2005, Sch A1, para 172.
[44] MCA 2005, Sch A1, para 24.
[45] MCA 2005, Sch A1, para 25–26.

of Protection order for a standard authorisation.[46] Standard authorisations are for a maximum period of 12 months and may be renewed.

Independent persons

6.48 When a person is identified as potentially coming within the scope of the *Bournewood* provisions, the hospital or care home must establish whether there is a suitable independent person to look after their interests. The managing authority must notify the supervisory body if the managing authority concludes that there is nobody, other than a person engaged in providing care and treatment for the relevant person in a professional capacity or for remuneration, whom it would be appropriate to consult in determining the person's best interests. In such a case, the supervisory body must instruct an IMCA to represent the relevant person.[47]

Applications

6.49 The Government has issued a statement of intent regarding regulations which will specify the information to be included in an application for a standard authorisation. The regulations for England will specify that information must be provided as requested on the standard form. It is intended that this should cover information about:

(1) the person, their age, their mental disorder and other relevant health information, ethnicity and issues relevant to carrying out the assessments (an example would be if the person was deaf);

(2) purpose and nature of the proposed deprivation of liberty including relevant care plans and needs assessment;

(3) contact details for the care home or hospital and lead professionals involved and for the person if they currently reside somewhere else;

(4) contact details for family friends and carers to contact for the best interests assessment (to the extent that this information is available);

(5) whether an urgent authorisation has been issued.

Regulations for Wales will be a matter for the National Assembly for Wales which will give careful consideration to cross-border issues.

Qualifying requirements

6.50 Six qualifying requirements must be met for a standard authorisation to be granted. The supervisory body must carry out assessments of whether each

---

[46] MCA 2005, Sch A1, para 27.
[47] MCA 2005, s 39A.

of these requirements is met within 21 days of the request by the managing authority.[48] The qualifying requirements are set out below.

The age requirement

6.51   The person must be 18 or over. Anyone who appears to the supervisory body to be suitable may carry out an age assessment.

The mental health requirement

6.52   The person must be suffering from mental disorder within the meaning of the MHA 1983, which will be any disorder or disability of mind. This is subject to the exception that a person with a learning disability can receive *Bournewood* safeguards whether or not the disability is associated with abnormally aggressive or seriously irresponsible conduct.[49] This assessment has to be carried out by a s 12 doctor or a registered medical practitioner who the supervisory body is satisfied has special experience in the diagnosis and treatment of mental disorder.[50] The Draft Guidance states that where the assessor is s 12 approved, they must also have undertaken basic *Bournewood* / MCA 2005 training. Where the doctor is not s 12 approved, they should have completed MCA 2005 mental health assessor training. Assessing doctors should also possess the published competences for the mental health assessment.[51] When carrying our a mental health assessment the assessor must consider how (if at all) the person's mental health is likely to be affected by his being a detained resident, and notify the best interests assessor of his conclusions.[52]

The mental capacity requirement

6.53   A person meets the mental capacity requirement if he lacks capacity in relation to the question whether or not he should be accommodated in the relevant hospital or care home for the purpose of being given the relevant care or treatment.[53] This should be done in accordance with ss 1–3 of the MCA 2005. The Draft Guidance states that in practice this assessment is likely to be usually undertaken by a doctor,[54] but the draft regulations provide that such assessments may be done by an AMHP, a social worker, a first level nurse in mental health or learning disabilities nursing, an occupational therapist or a chartered psychologist.[55]

---

[48]   Draft Mental Capacity (Deprivation of Liberty: Appointment of Relevant Person's Representative and Assessment) Regulations 2007, reg 19.
[49]   MCA 2005, Sch A1, para 14.
[50]   Draft Mental Capacity (Deprivation of Liberty: Eligibility and Selection of Assessors) Regulations 2007, reg 4.
[51]   Department of Health *Draft Illustrative Guidance on the Bournewood Safeguards*, para 62.
[52]   MCA 2005, Sch A1, para 33.
[53]   MCA 2005, Sch A1, para 15.
[54]   Department of Health *Draft Illustrative Guidance on the Bournewood Safeguards*, para 67.
[55]   Draft Mental Capacity (Deprivation of Liberty: Eligibility and Selection of Assessors) Regulations 2007, reg 5.

The best interests requirement

6.54   Four conditions must be met before the person meets the best interests requirement. The first is that the person is, or is to be, a detained resident. The second is that it is in that person's best interests to be a detained resident. The third condition is that it is necessary for him to be a detained resident in order to prevent harm to himself. Finally, deprivation of liberty must be a proportionate response to:

(a)   the likelihood of the person suffering harm; and

(b)   the seriousness of that harm, for him to be a detained resident.[56]

The Draft Code states that best interests assessments may be carried out by people who are not AMHPs as long as they possess the relevant skills and experience that would enable them to apply for AMHP status if they so wished. A *Bournewood* best interests assessor should also have completed basic *Bournewood* / MCA 2005 training, possess the published competences for *Bournewood* best interests assessors, and have completed specific *Bournewood* best interests assessor training. The draft regulations provide that best interests assessments may be done by an AMHP, a social worker, a first level nurse in mental health or learning disabilities nursing, an occupational therapist or a chartered psychologist.[57]

6.55   The best interests assessor must consult with the managing authority of the hospital or care home and must have regard to any relevant needs assessments and care plans prepared in connection with the relevant person being accommodated in the hospital or care home. The managing authority and supervisory body must provide the best interests assessor with any such needs assessment or care plan that has been undertaken by them, or on their behalf.[58] The best interests assessor must record in writing the name and address of every interested person consulted by him in determining the patient's best interests.[59] The best interests assessor must state the maximum recommended authorisation period, which may not exceed one year. The supervising body may not grant an authorisation for longer than the period recommended in the best interests assessment.[60] The best interests assessor may make recommendations about conditions to be attached to the authorisation, and if the supervisory body accepts such conditions the managing authority must ensure that they are complied with.[61]

---

[56]   MCA 2005, Sch A1, para 16.
[57]   Draft Mental Capacity (Deprivation of Liberty: Eligibility and Selection of Assessors) Regulations 2007, reg 6.
[58]   MCA 2005, Sch A1, para 39.
[59]   MCA 2005, Sch A1, para 40.
[60]   MCA 2005, Sch A1, paras 42 and 51.
[61]   MCA 2005, Sch A1, paras 43 and 53.

Patient Representatives

6.56 Paragraph 131 of Sch A1 requires that the supervisory body must appoint a representative for a person in respect of whom a standard authorisation has been issued. Supervisory bodies are only able to appoint representatives who have been selected for that purpose. The role of the representative is to maintain contact with the person and to support and represent them in matters relating to their deprivation of liberty. The best interests assessor is also responsible for making recommendations about who should be appointed as the person's representative, and this process should begin as soon as the best interests assessor is appointed.[62] The procedure is set out in the Draft Mental Capacity (Deprivation of Liberty: Appointment of Relevant Person's Representative and Assessment) Regulations 2007.

The eligibility requirement

6.57 Whether a person is eligible for deprivation of liberty is to be determined in accordance with the new Sch 1A to the MCA 2005. If the eligibility assessor and the best interests assessor are not the same person, the eligibility assessor must request that the best interests assessor provide him with any relevant eligibility information that the best interests assessor may have.[63]

6.58 A person is ineligible for *Bournewood* detention if s/he is subject to a hospital treatment obligation[64] under the MHA 1983 and will continue to be detained in hospital under that regime. A person will also be ineligible if the authorisation would be inconsistent with an obligation under the MHA 1983 to reside somewhere else. This will affect people who are on leave of absence from detention under the Mental Health Act 1983 or who are subject to guardianship, supervised community treatment or conditional discharge.

6.59 Refusal by the person her or himself will not render that person ineligible to be detained in a residential care home under the *Bournewood* arrangements. This raises an important issue, since the Government intends that people detained in residential care homes will be subject to the charging regime, whereas those detained in hospital will not.

The no refusals requirement

6.60 The 'no refusals' requirement will be met unless one of two situations appertains. The first is that the person has, when capable, made a valid advance decision refusing some or all of the treatment which would be provided if the authorisation were to be granted. The second is where the proposal to place the person in a hospital or care home in circumstances that amount to deprivation of the person's liberty, or to place them in the hospital or care home at all,

---

[62] Draft Mental Capacity (Deprivation of Liberty: Appointment of Relevant Person's Representative and Assessment) Regulations 2007, reg 4.
[63] Ibid, reg 20.
[64] That is detained under ss 2, 3, 4, 35, 36, 37, 38, 44, 45A, 47, 48 or 51.

would be in conflict with a valid decision of an attorney or a deputy appointed by the court. Anybody that the supervisory body considers to be appropriate, by virtue of possessing the skills and experience to perform the role, may undertake the 'no refusals' assessment, including a person conducting one or more of the other assessments.

Issuing the standard authorisation

6.61 The supervisory body must give a standard authorisation if all assessments are positive, and they have written copies of all those assessments. If all the assessments are not positive, the supervisory body must not give a standard authorisation.[65] The Draft Guidance states that:[66]

> 'If, in the light of the assessments, the supervisory body does not give a standard authorisation, it must, as soon as practicable after it becomes apparent to it that it is prohibited from giving the authorisation, notify the managing authority, the relevant person, any IMCA involved and every interested person consulted by the best interests assessor accordingly. It must provide the managing authority, the relevant person and any IMCA involved with copies of those assessments that have been carried out.'

6.62 A standard authorisation must be in writing and must state the following:

(a) the name of the relevant person;

(b) the name of the relevant hospital or care home;

(c) the period during which the authorisation is to be in force;

(d) the purpose for which the authorisation is given;

(e) any conditions subject to which the authorisation is given;

(f) the reason why each qualifying requirement is met.[67]

Urgent authorisations

6.63 Paragraphs 67–83 of Sch A1 provide a procedure for a managing authority to issue an urgent authorisation authorising deprivation of liberty for up to seven days. A managing authority must give an urgent authorisation where it:

---

[65] MCA 2005, Sch A1, para 50
[66] Department of Health *Draft Illustrative Guidance on the Bournewood Safeguards*, para 103.
[67] MCA 2005, Sch A1, paras 54 and 55.

(1)   is required to make a request to the supervisory body for a standard
       authorisation but believes that the need for a person to be deprived of
       liberty is so urgent that it is appropriate to begin the deprivation before
       the request is made; or

(2)   has made a request for a standard authorisation but believes that the need
       for a person to be deprived of liberty has now become so urgent that it is
       appropriate to begin the deprivation before the request is dealt with by the
       supervisory body.[68]

The urgent authorisation must state the name of the person, the name of the
hospital or care home, the period during which the authorisation is to be in
force and the purpose for which the authorisation has been given.[69]

Extensions

6.64   An urgent authorisation may be extended once where an application has
been made for a standard authorisation and there are exceptional reasons why
it has not been possible for the standard authorisation request to be disposed
of, and it is essential for the existing detention to continue until the request is
disposed of.[70] The Draft Guidance says this about extensions:[71]

> 'It is intended that extension should only occur rarely in exceptional
> circumstances. An example of when an extension would be justified might be
> where the supervisory body was satisfied that a person who needed to be contacted
> by the best interests assessor had been uncontactable, that the assessment could
> not be relied upon without their input and that extension for the specified period
> would enable them to be contacted.'

6.65   In this context it is worth mentioning the recent decision of Munby J in
Re PS (incapacitated or vulnerable adult)[72] where he said that where a court
was authorising deprivation of liberty, the following minimum requirements
must be satisfied in order to comply with Art 5:

'(1)   The detention must be authorised by the court on application made by the
        local authority and *before* the detention commences.
(2)   Subject to the exigencies of urgency or emergency the evidence must
        establish unsoundness of mind of a kind or degree warranting compulsory
        confinement. In other words, there must be evidence establishing at least a
        prima facie case that the individual lacks capacity and that confinement of
        the nature proposed is appropriate.

---

[68]   MCA 2005, Sch A1, para 69.
[69]   MCA 2005, Sch A1, para 73.
[70]   MCA 2005, Sch A1, para 77.
[71]   Department of Health *Draft Illustrative Guidance on the Bournewood Safeguards*, para 118.
[72]   [2007] EWHC 623 (Fam) at [23].

(3)   Any order authorising detention must contain provision for an adequate review at reasonable intervals, in particular with a view to ascertaining whether there still persists unsoundness of mind of a kind or degree warranting compulsory confinement.'

Section 4 of the the MHA 1983 allows emergency admission, but requires that an application supported by one medical recommendation be completed prior to admission. This provides authority for the patient to be taken and conveyed to the relevant hospital. There is no procedure here for such emergency applications and there is no provision to take and convey someone to a hospital or care home where they urgently need *Bournewood* detention.

Review by the supervisory body

6.66 Part 8 of Sch A1 (paras 94–118) deal with reviews of standard authorisations. The managing authority is required to monitor each persons case and to request a review if one of the qualifying requirements appears to be reviewable. The person detained may request a review, as may their representative or the managing authority.[73] If such a request is made the supervisory body must carry out a review. They have a discretion themselves to carry out a review at any other time.

6.67 A qualifying requirement may be reviewable on one of three grounds:

(1)   the relevant person does not meet all the qualifying requirements;

(2)   the reason why the relevant person meets a qualifying requirement is not the reason stated in the authorisation;

(3)   there has been a change in the relevant person's case and, because of the change, it would be appropriate to vary the conditions to which the authorisation is subject.

If none of the qualifying requirements appears to the supervisory body to be reviewable, then it need take no further action. The supervisory body must, however, carry out a separate review assessment of any requirement that appears to be reviewable.[74]

Review by the Court of Protection

6.68 Article 5(4) of the European Convention on Human Rights requires that anybody deprived of his liberty must be able to obtain speedy access to a court for to review the lawfulness of their detention and order discharge if detention is not lawful. Paragraph 2 of Sch 8 to the Mental Health Bill inserts a new s 21A into the MCA 2005, giving the Court of Protection jurisdiction for this purpose.

---

[73]   MCA 2005, Sch A1, para 95.
[74]   MCA 2005, Sch A1, paras 103–104.

6.69 Where a standard authorisation has been given the Court of Protection may determine any question relating to:

(a) whether the person meets any of the qualifying requirements;

(b) the period for which the standard authorisation is to be in force;

(c) the purpose for which it has been given; or

(d) the conditions subject to which it has been given.

The court may make an order varying or terminating the authorisation or ordering the supervisory body to vary or terminate it.[75]

6.70 Where an urgent authorisation has been given the court may determine any question relating to:

(a) whether the urgent authorisation should have been given;

(b) the period during which the urgent authorisation is to be in force; or

(c) the purpose for which the urgent authorisation is given.

The court may make an order varying or terminating the urgent authorisation, or directing the managing authority of the relevant hospital or care home to vary or terminate the urgent authorisation.[76]

6.71 When making orders under s 21A, the court may make an order about a person's liability for any act done in connection with the standard or urgent authorisation before its variation or termination, and this includes an order excluding a person from liability.[77]

Monitoring

6.72 Paragraph 153 of Sch A1 confers a regulation making power which will enable a monitoring function for the *Bournewood* safeguards to be established and for a monitoring body or bodies to be designated as having the responsibility for discharging that function. The Government's intention is to formally confer the monitoring function on the three existing Inspectorates (Healthcare Commission, Commission for Social Care Inspection, Mental Health Act Commission) pending the establishment of the new merged regulator, at which point the function would transfer to the merged body. The expectation is that the existing inspectorates will work in a co-ordinated manner to avoid duplication of activity.

---

[75] MCA 2005, s 21A(2)–(3).
[76] MCA 2005, s 21A(4)–(5).
[77] MCA 2005, s 21A(6)–(7).

6.73 The Government intends that the designated monitoring body or bodies for care homes and hospitals in England will be able to:

(1) monitor and report on the operation of the *Bournewood* safeguards;

(2) visit hospitals and care homes;

(3) visit and interview people in hospitals and care homes;

(4) require the production of, and inspect records.

Paragraph 155 of Sch A1 confers a further regulation making power on the monitoring body or bodies to require supervisory bodies and managing authorities of hospitals or care homes to disclose information to the monitoring body or bodies (including data on ethnicity).

6.74 The Government has said that:

> 'the focus of the monitoring will be on the protocols and procedures in place for complying with duties placed on hospitals, care homes, primary care trusts and local authorities and the effect of these protocols and procedures on individual cases. The monitoring function will not negate the role of the Court of Protection.'

The monitoring process will address:

(1) whether the provisions have been applied correctly and in line with guidance in the Code of Practice in cases where authorisation has been requested;

(2) whether guidance in the Code of Practice on identifying those at risk of deprivation of liberty, and on avoiding deprivation of liberty, is being complied with;

(3) whether conditions attached to authorisation and requirements to request review if circumstances change are complied with;

(4) whether appropriate steps are being taken in cases where authorisation has been refused.

Monitoring will not cover:

(1) treatment and care other than as it relates to the deprivation of liberty;

(2) revisiting individual assessments.

The monitoring will not constitute an alternative review or appeal process.

6.75 If neither informal admission nor *Bournewood* authorisation is appropriate to authorise in-patient care without consent, consideration should be given to detention under the powers of compulsory admission in ss 2–4 of the MHA 1983. The Code of Practice on the MCA 2005 suggests that professionals 'may need to think about using the MHA to detain and treat somebody who lacks capacity to consent to treatment (rather than use the MCA)', if:

(1)   it is not possible to give the person the care or treatment they need without doing something that might deprive them of their liberty;

(2)   the person needs treatment that cannot be given under the MCA 2005 (for example, because the person has made a valid and applicable advance decision to refuse an essential part of treatment);

(3)   the person may need to be restrained in a way that is not allowed under the MCA 2005;

(4)   it is not possible to assess or treat the person safely or effectively without treatment being compulsory (perhaps because the person is expected to regain capacity to consent, but might then refuse to give consent);

(5)   the person lacks capacity to decide on some elements of the treatment but has capacity to refuse a vital part of it – and they have done so;

(6)   there is some other reason why the person might not get treatment, and they or somebody else might suffer harm as a result.[78]

The MCA Code stresses that before making an application under the MHA, decision-makers should consider whether they could achieve their aims safely and effectively by using the MCA instead. Compulsory treatment under the MHA is not an option if the patient's mental disorder does not justify detention in hospital, or the patient needs treatment only for a physical illness or disability. The order of preference is informal admission, followed by deprivation of liberty under the MCA, with detention under the MHA the last resort, if the powers available under the MCA are insufficient to manage the risk to the patient or others.

The role of attorneys and deputies in relation to patients subject to the Mental Health Act 1983

6.76 Not only may deputies and attorneys consent to or refuse a *Bournewood* authorisation; they also have a potentially significant role under the MHA 1983. It is good practice for clinicians and others acting under the MHA to try and find out if the patient has an attorney or a deputy. An attorney or a

---

[78]   Department of Constitutional Affairs *Code of Practice on the Mental Capacity Act 2005*, pp 225–226.

deputy may make decisions on behalf of a patient who is subject to detention under the MHA 1983 and may, if they have authority under the LPA or court appointment and the patient lacks capacity to do so, exercise the patient's various rights to apply to a MHRT for discharge. A decision of an attorney or a deputy that results in the patient being in breach of conditions attached to guardianship, a CTO, or conditional discharge may result in the patient being recalled to hospital. As the Draft Code of Practice notes:

'Attorneys and deputies may not exercise the rights of nearest relatives, unless they are themselves the nearest relative (because the rights belong to the nearest relative, not the patient).'

There may be disagreement between the two, for example about whether the attorney should apply to the MHRT or the NR should seek to discharge the patient, but ultimately 'they have different roles, and each must act as they think best'.[79]

POWERS OF COMPULSORY ADMISSION UNDER PART 2

Overview

6.77 There are three powers under Part 2 which enable a person to be admitted compulsorily from the community, s 2 for assessment for up to 28 days, s 4 emergency admission for assessment for up to 72 hours, and s 3 for treatment for up to six months renewable. In the year 2005–2006, of the total of 27,353 patients admitted under Part 2 from the community, 1,208 (5%) were detained under s 4, as against 15,265 (55%) admitted under s 2, and 9,147 (33%) under s 3.[80]

6.78 In addition to people admitted from the community, over the year 6,287 people who were already psychiatric in-patients were admitted under s 2. Of these, 3,425 went direct from informal in-patient status in NHS hospitals and 45 in private hospitals. A further 2,723 informal NHS patients and 104 private patients were held under s 5 of the Act and subsequently admitted for assessment. This makes a total of 21,552 uses of s 2 over the year 2005–2006.[81]

6.79 Whilst under one third of admissions under s 2 take place in hospital, almost half of admissions under s 3 take place in hospital; 9,147 admissions

---

[79] Department of Health *Mental Health Act 1983 Draft Revised Code of Practice* (2007), paras 8.22–8.23. See http://www.dh.gov.uk/en/Consultations.

[80] National Statistics Information Centre NSIC *In-patients formally detained in hospitals under the Mental Health Act 1983 and other legislation, NHS Trusts, Care Trusts, Primary Care Trusts and Independent Hospitals, England: 1995–1996 to 2005–2006* (2007), Table 1. See http://www.ic.nhs.uk/statistics-and-data-collections/health-and-lifestyles/mental-health/in-patients-formally-detained-in-hospitals-under-the-mental-health-act-1983-and-other-legislation-nhs-trusts-care-trusts-primary-care-trusts-and-independent-hospitals;-2005-06).

[81] Ibid, Tables 1 and 4.

from the community as against 8,654 of people who were in-patients when the application was made. Of these, 5,467 were informal in-patients in NHS hospitals and 87 in private hospitals. A further 3,034 NHS and 66 private hospital informal patients were made subject to s 5 holding powers (see paras **6.94–6.103** below) and then detained under s 3. This makes a grand total of 17,791 s 3 detentions.[82]

Admission for assessment

6.80   Section 2 of the Act provides for compulsory admission for assessment for up to 28 days, which is non-renewable. If further detention is necessary, it must take place under s 3 or under the MCA 2005. An application may be made by an AMHP or the patient's nearest relative, supported by two medical recommendations, one of which must come from a doctor approved under s 12 of the MHA 1983 as having expertise in the diagnosis or treatment of mental disorder. The patient must be suffering from mental disorder of a nature or degree which warrants his detention in hospital for assessment or for assessment followed by medical treatment for at least a limited period. In contrast to the position under s 3 admissions, a person with a learning disability who does not exhibit without abnormally aggressive or seriously irresponsible conduct may be detained under s 2 for up to 28 days. This possibility will remain following the entry into force of s 2(2) of the MHA 2007.

6.81   It must also be certified that the patient ought to be detained in the interests of his health *or* safety *or* for the protection of other persons. Where the patient meets the 'mental disorder of a nature or degree' criterion, detention may be implemented if necessary in the interests of the patient's own health (including mental health) and it is not necessary to wait until he or she is overtly dangerous to self or others. It is a common misconception that patients need to present some threat to their own safety or that of others before compulsory admission is possible. The MHA 1983 allows detention on 'strong paternalist' grounds, in the sense that a person may be detained in the interests of their own health.

6.82   The nearest relative (NR) of the patient may not block detention under s 2. If it is proposed to detain the patient under s 3 and the NR objects unreasonably, detention under s 2 is extended until the county court displacement proceedings are terminated. A patient detained under s 2 has the right to apply to the MHRT for discharge once within the first 14 days following admission (see Chapter 9).[83] Treatment for mental disorder of patients detained under s 2 is regulated by Part 4 of the MHA 1983, and treatment for physical disorder by the MCA 2005 (see Chapter 10).

---

[82]   See fn 80, Table 4.
[83]   MHA 1983, s 66(1)(a), (2)(a).

Emergency admission for assessment

6.83   Section 4 of the MHA 1983 provides a power, to be used only in cases of urgent necessity, to admit compulsorily a patient for assessment for up to 72 hours. An application may be made either by an AMHP or the nearest relative and, although it requires only one medical recommendation, the application must state that it is of urgent necessity that the patient be admitted and detained for assessment, and that compliance with the full s 2 procedure would involve undesirable delay. The doctor giving the recommendation need not be s 12 approved. The form on which the medical recommendation is furnished requires information to be given which clarifies the nature of the emergency. It requires the doctor to estimate the delay which would be involved if the full requirements of s 2 were to be complied with, and to state that, in his or her opinion, such delay might result in harm to the patient, those caring for the patient or to other persons.

6.84   Although when it was introduced in 1959 this power was expected to be used only in exceptional circumstances, the equivalent procedure it was used much more frequently than envisaged, and at one time was the most frequently used power of compulsory admission. To ensure that the procedure is only used in genuine emergencies, new time limits were introduced. The applicant must have seen the patient within the previous 24 hours, and the patient must be admitted to hospital within 24 hours beginning with the time when the application was made or the time when he or she was medically examined, whichever is the earlier.[84] The authority to detain lasts for 72 hours from the time of the admission, unless the second medical recommendation required by s 2 is furnished to the managers within that period. The effect of such a conversion is that the 28 day authority to detain is deemed to have begun to run from the time of admission under s 4. Where s 4 is used, the patient is deprived of a fundamental safeguard at the time of initial detention in the form of an expert medical opinion from a doctor experienced in the diagnosis and treatment of mental disorder. Patients detained under s 4 do not have the right to apply to the MHRT, nor do they become subject to the Consent to Treatment provisions in Part 4[85] unless they become liable to be detained under s 2 by the furnishing of the second medical recommendation.

Admission for treatment

6.85   Section 3 of the MHA 1983 provides for compulsory admission for treatment for up to six months renewable under s 20 for a further six months and thereafter for periods of 12 months at a time. The renewal procedure is explained at paras **4.78–4.80** below. An application may be currently made by either the nearest relative or an AMHP and must be supported by medical recommendations given by two medical practitioners one of which must come from a s 12 approved doctor.

---

[84]   MHA 1983, ss 4(5) and 6(1)(b).
[85]   The s 57 second opinion requirement still applies.

6.86   The criteria which must be met are:

(a)   the patient must be suffering from mental disorder of a nature or degree which makes it appropriate for the patient to receive medical treatment in a hospital; and

(b)   it must be necessary in the interests of his health or safety or for the protection of other persons that he should receive such treatment and that it must be the case that the treatment cannot be provided unless he is detained under this section; and

(c)   treatment must be available for the patient which is 'appropriate in his case, taking into account the nature and degree of the mental disorder and all other circumstances of his case'.[86]

The MHA 2007 dispenses with the subcategories of mental disorder for the purposes of s 3 and replaces them with the definition 'any disorder or disability of mind' which will apply to all uses of compulsory powers under the Act (see Chapter 3).

Nature or degree

6.87   In *R v Mental Health Review Tribunal for the South Thames Region, ex parte Smith*[87] Popplewell J held that:

> 'the word nature refers to the particular mental disorder from which the patient suffers, its chronicity, its prognosis, and the patient's previous response to ... treatment. The word degree refers to the current manifestation of the patient's disorder.'

In *Smirek v Williams* Hale LJ said that:[88]

> '[W]here there is a chronic condition, where there is evidence that the patient will deteriorate if medicine is not taken, I find it impossible to accept that it is not a mental illness of a nature or degree which makes it appropriate for the patient to be liable to be detained in hospital for medical treatment if the evidence is that, without being detained in hospital, the patient will not take the treatment.'

The test may therefore be satisfied if there is a patient with an illness of a serious nature, where the patient is not showing any severe symptoms, but where the patient has ceased taking medication and there is a history of serious relapse when medication is stopped. The illness, although not currently of a degree making detention appropriate, may nevertheless be of a sufficiently serious nature to satisfy the test.

---

[86]   MHA 1983, s 3(2)(d), as inserted by MHA 2007, s 4.
[87]   [1999] COD 148.
[88]   [2002] MHLR 38 at para 19.

6.88   The mental disorder must be of a nature or degree making it appropriate for the patient to receive treatment *in a hospital*. This means that the intention must be for the patient to receive treatment as an in-patient. In *R v Hallstrom, ex parte W (No 2)*[89] McCullough J said that:

> 'Admission for treatment under s 3 is intended for those whose condition is believed to require treatment as an in-patient.'

Section 3 cannot therefore be used when the intention is that the patient will be detained for a purely nominal period before being sent home on leave under s 17, and where the true purpose of the admission is to provide authority to impose treatment in the community.

Necessary in the interests of the patient's health or safety or for the protection of others and the treatment cannot be provided unless he is detained under this section

6.89   A patient need not be dangerous to him or herself or others in order to be detained. If detention in hospital is necessary in the interests of only one of the goals listed: health (including mental health) *or* safety, *or* the protection of others, this criterion will be met. The requirement to certify that the treatment cannot be provided without detention reflects the European Convention principle of proportionality or the US principle of the least restrictive alternative, namely that treatment should be provided if possible in the setting which imposes the least restrictions on the patient's freedom.

Availability of appropriate treatment

6.90   The so-called 'treatability test' has been abolished to be replaced under the MHA 2007 by the test of availability of appropriate treatment (see Chapter 3). Section 7 of the MHA 2007 changes the definition of medical treatment to state that it includes 'psychological intervention and specialist mental health habilitation, rehabilitation and care'. The addition of psychological interventions makes clear that treatments for personality disorder such as cognitive behaviour therapy are included within medical treatment. Medical treatment for mental disorder must have the purpose of alleviating, or preventing a worsening of, the disorder or one or more of its symptoms or manifestations. As the definition is inclusive, this is not an exhaustive list, and treatment also clearly includes treatments expressly mentioned in Part 4 of the MHA 1983 such as medicines and Electro Convulsive Therapy.

6.91   A patient who is detained under s 3 has the right to apply to the MHRT for discharge once within the first six months following admission, and once in each period for which the detention is renewed (see Chapter 9).[90] Treatment for

---

[89]   [1986] 2 All ER 306, QBD.
[90]   MHA 1983, s 66(1)(b), (f), (2)(b), (f).

mental disorder of patients detained under s 2 is regulated by Part 4 of the MHA 1983, and treatment for physical disorder by the Mental Capacity Act 2005 (see Chapter 10).

When should s 2 be used and when s 3?

6.92 The question of which admission section should be used is a matter for professional judgment guided by the statutory criteria. The only difference in scope of the respective powers relates to learning disability where abnormally aggressive or seriously irresponsible conduct is needed for detention under s 3 but not s 2. The Draft Revised Code of Practice suggests that pointers to s 2 include the following:

(a) the diagnosis and prognosis of a patient's condition is unclear;

(b) a need to carry out an in-patient assessment in order to formulate a treatment plan;

(c) a judgment is needed as to whether the patient will accept treatment on a voluntary basis following admission;

(d) a judgment has to be made as to whether a particular treatment proposal, which can only be administered to the patient under Part 4 of the Act, is likely to be effective;

(e) the condition of a patient who has already been assessed, and who has been previously admitted compulsorily under the Act, is judged to have changed since the previous admission and further assessment is needed;

(f) the patient has not previously been admitted to hospital either compulsorily or informally and has not been in regular contact with the specialist psychiatric mental health services.

As for s 3, this should be used when the patient is considered to need compulsory admission for the treatment of a mental disorder which is already known to his clinical team, and has been assessed in the recent past by that team. In these circumstances it may be right to use s 3 even where the patient has not previously been admitted as an in-patient.[91]

---

[91] Department of Health *Mental Health Act 1983 Draft Revised Code of Practice* (2007), paras 4.32 and 4.33. See http://www.dh.gov.uk/en/Consultations.

APPLICATION FOR DETENTION OF SOMEONE WHO IS ALREADY AN IN-PATIENT

6.93 A patient who initially consents to admission but later seeks to leave hospital may be restrained from doing so using the doctor's, approved clinician's, or nurse's holding power under s 5 of the MHA 1983.

The doctor's (and AC's) holding power

6.94 Section 5(2) confers a holding power on the registered medical practitioner or Approved Clinician ('AC') in charge of the treatment of an in-patient in any hospital, not necessarily a psychiatric one. Section 9 of the MHA 2007 extends the power to ACs (see Chapter 4). If the doctor or AC considers that an application for compulsory admission needs to be made, s/he should furnish a report to the hospital managers to that effect. Where this happens, the patient may be detained in hospital for a period of 72 hours from the time when the report was furnished.

6.95 In-patient for the purposes of this section does not include anyone who is already liable to be detained or who is a community patient under the MHA 1983. It refers to anyone receiving in-patient care or treatment without being subject to the use of compulsory powers under the MHA 1983 and includes patients who are in hospital by virtue of a *Bournewood* authorisation under the MCA 2005. Section 5 cannot be used for an out-patient attending a hospital's accident and emergency department, and in such cases admission procedures should not be implemented with the sole intention of then using the power in s 5(2).[92] Nor can s 5(2) be used to extend the 72 hours detention of a patient brought to a hospital as a place of safety under ss 135 or 136. The power may be used in the case of a person receiving treatment for a physical condition in a general hospital, provided he or she is an in-patient.

6.96 Section 5(3) permits the doctor or AC in charge of the patient's treatment to nominate 'one (but not more than one) other registered medical practitioner or AC on the staff of the hospital to act for him ... in his absence'. Only one deputy may be nominated at a time, and it is unlawful for the nominated deputy to delegate the power to someone else.[93]

6.97 The purpose of detention is to enable the assessment necessary for admission under either s 2 or s 3 to take place. Section 5(2) should not therefore be seen as an independent power of short term detention but as a *holding power* to enable a full assessment to be made. This being so, arrangements for such an assessment should be set in train immediately the holding power is implemented. The Draft Revised Code states that:[94]

---

[92]   Department of Health *Mental Health Act 1983 Draft Revised Code of Practice* (2007), para 11.9. See http://www.dh.gov.uk/en/Consultations.

[93]   Ibid, paras 11.15 and 11.16.

[94]   Ibid, para 11.23.

'Patients should be released from detention under s 5(2) as soon as—

- a decision is taken not to make an application for admission; or
- the doctor or approved clinician decides that, in fact, no assessment for a possible application needs to be carried out.'

In such a case the Code advises that the patient should be informed that he or she is no longer detained under the holding power, and the decision, the reasons for it, and its time should be recorded. 'The power cannot be renewed, but circumstances may arise where, subsequent to its use and the patient's reversion to informal status, its use can be considered again.'[95] Patients detained under s 5(2) may not be transferred to another hospital under s 19 (because they are not detained by virtue of an application made under Part 2 of the Act).[96]

The nurse's holding power

6.98   The second power is the nurse's holding power under s 5(4). This enables a nurse 'of the prescribed class' to hold an in-patient in a psychiatric ward or hospital for not more than six hours. During that time the doctor or AC in charge of the patient's treatment or his or her deputy should attend to determine whether the managers should be furnished with a report under s 5(2). A nurse of the prescribed class is currently defined as 'a nurse registered in Part 3 (first level nurses trained in the nursing of persons suffering from mental illness) or Part 5 (first level nurses trained in the nursing of persons suffering from mental handicap) or Part 14 (nurses qualified following a course of preparation in learning disabled nursing)' of the professional register established under s 10 of the Nurses, Midwives and Health Visitors Act 1997.

6.99   The Draft Revised Code emphasises that:

'The decision to invoke the power is the personal decision of the nurse who cannot be instructed to exercise this power by anyone else.'[97]

The nurses' holding power can only be used *where the patient is receiving treatment for mental disorder as an in-patient*. The grounds for its use are:

(a)   that the patient is suffering from mental disorder to such a degree that it is necessary for his or her health or safety or for the protection of others that he or she be immediately restrained from leaving hospital; and

(b)   that it is not practicable to secure the immediate attendance of a practitioner (or clinician) for the purpose of furnishing a report under s 5(2).

---

[95]   Department of Health *Mental Health Act 1983 Draft Revised Code of Practice* (2007), para 11.24. See http://www.dh.gov.uk/en/Consultations.
[96]   Ibid, para 11.42.
[97]   Ibid, para 11.29.

6.100 The nurse must record in writing on a statutory form the fact that the above criteria are satisfied, and must deliver the completed form to the managers or their appointed officer as soon as possible after completion but the six hours detention starts to run from the time when the nurse signed the form.[98] The reasons for invoking the power must be entered in the patient's nursing and medical notes and that a local incident report form should be sent to the managers. If, following the exercise of the nurse's holding power, the doctor exercises his holding power under s 5(2) and (5) provided that the 72-hour period runs from the time the nurse furnishes the s 5(4) report to the managers. It is worth noting that this power can be used only where an informal patient is receiving treatment as an in-patient for mental disorder; it cannot, for example, be used on a general hospital ward where the patient is receiving treatment for a physical disorder. A nurse invoking s 5(4) is entitled to use the minimum force necessary to prevent the patient from leaving hospital.[99]

6.101 The nurse's holding power may only be used to restrain the patient from leaving hospital. Where a patient requires restraint or seclusion but is not showing any inclination to leave the hospital, staff may act in reliance on other statutory and common law powers. Section 3(1) of the Criminal Law Act 1967 allows a person to use 'such force as is reasonably in the circumstances in the prevention of crime'. The common law allows for reasonable force to be used in self-defence, for the defence of others, or to prevent a breach of the peace. Reasonable steps to prevent the breach of the peace can include detaining the person against his will.[100] A breach of the peace can take place in either a public or a private place where a person is in fear of being harmed through an assault, an affray, an unlawful assembly or other disturbance.[101] These powers apply regardless of whether the person has capacity. They can only be used to justify detention or restraint within the hospital insofar as it is reasonably necessary, and only for so long as the risk of breach of the peace or crime subsists. Hence, they would not authorise any restraint or seclusion to continue after the risk had passed.

6.102 Sections 5 and 6 of the MCA 2005 provide a legal defence for anyone who takes action that is in the best interests of a person who lacks capacity in relation to the decision to remain in hospital. This includes reasonable restraint where the restraint is imposed to prevent harm to the patient and is a proportionate response both to the likelihood of harm and the severity of the harm. In order for the action to be lawful the person taking it must have taken reasonable steps to determine whether the person has capacity in relation to the relevant decision, must reasonably believe that the person indeed lacks capacity, and must reasonably believe that what they are doing is in the person's best interests.

---

[98] Department of Health *Mental Health Act 1983 Draft Revised Code of Practice* (2007), para 11.27. See http://www.dh.gov.uk/en/Consultations.

[99] Draft Illustrative Code of Practice, para 9.6.

[100] *Albert v Lavin* [1982] AC 546, HL.

[101] *R v Howell* [1982] QB 416, CA.

CONCLUSION

6.103 The MHA 1983 and the MCA 2005 provide ample powers to deprive mentally disordered people of their liberty. As we have seen, a key issue is the interface between the two Acts and the decision when to use which regime. The *Bournewood* Deprivation of Liberty safeguards are complex and voluminous. Schedules A1 and 1A have 205 paras and occupy 53 of the MHA 2007's 168 pages, all for one procedure. The Joint Committee on Human Rights was critical of this complexity:

> 'In *HL v United Kingdom* the Court held (at para 114) that "an important ingredient of lawfulness is that all law must be sufficiently precise to allow the citizen – if need be with appropriate advice – to foresee, to a degree that is reasonable in the circumstances, the consequences which a given action might entail". The proposals to amend the Mental Capacity Act are detailed and complex, and we question whether they will be readily understood.'

This prompts the question whether, and in what circumstances, the simpler and more familiar procedure of guardianship can be used as an alternative to the *Bournewood* authorisation. The MHA 2007 introduces a power to take and convey a person to their place of residence under guardianship.[102] Where the Act gives a power to return a person to a place of required residence, a new s 18(7) complements that with a power to take the person there initially – if they have 'yet to comply with a requirement imposed by virtue of this Act to be in a hospital or place'. Guardianship therefore carries the power to require residence at a specified place, to take and convey the person to that place and to bring them back if they abscond. The guardian can also require the person to attend for treatment, work, training or education at specific times and places, and they can demand that a doctor, approved social worker or another relevant person have access to the person wherever they live. It does not, however, give anyone the right to treat the person without their permission or to consent to treatment on their behalf, although the MCA 2005 would apply if the person lacks capacity.

6.104 The powers of the guardian are discussed in full in Chapter 8. It is clear that they are capable of authorising a degree of control over residence, movement and treatment which could amount to deprivation of liberty. There is nothing in the MHA 1983 to say that guardianship cannot authorise deprivation of liberty, but the MCA Code is emphatic that whilst guardianship confers 'the exclusive right to decide where a person should live ... in doing this they cannot deprive the person of their liberty'. The Code goes on to say that: 'Decision-makers must never consider guardianship as a way to avoid applying the MCA.'[103]

---

[102]   MHA 1983, as amended by the MHA 2007, Sch 3, para 3(5).
[103]   Department of Constitutional Affairs *Mental Capacity Act 2005 Code of Practice* (2007), paras 13.16–13.20.

6.105 The MCA Code goes on to outline the following possible situations in which guardianship might be considered in relation to a mentally disordered person who lacks capacity to make important decisions about their own welfare:

(1)   where it is thought to be important that decisions about where the person is to live are placed in the hands of a single person or authority over a continuing period – for example where there have been long-running or particularly difficult disputes about where the person should live;

(2)   where the person is thought likely to respond well to the authority and attention of a guardian, and so be more willing to comply with necessary treatment and care for their mental disorder (whether they are able to consent to it, or it is being provided for them under the MCA 2005);

(3)   where there is a particular need to have explicit authority for the person to be returned to the place the person is to live (eg a care home).[104]

6.106 By contrast to the *Bournewood* procedures, guardianship has the advantage of clear Convention compliance. If the procedure must be initiated before the patient is removed to hospital or care home, guardianship must be implemented prior to the detention taking place, the *Bournewood* procedures need not. Guardianship is familiar to mental health professionals, and is more accessible to patients, carers, and their advisers. It occupies only a few pages of statute and Code of Practice. It could be used to authorise control of a degree and intensity to amount to a deprivation of liberty. The patient or nearest relative may apply for discharge to the managers or to the MHRT, which is more likely than the Court of Protection to be in a position to meet the requirements of Art 5(4) that access to such review is speedy, and that legal representation is available.[105] The main limitations on using guardianship as an alternative to the *Bournewood* procedures are the exclusion in relation to learning disability without abnormally aggressive or seriously irresponsible conduct, and the right of the nearest relative to block a guardianship application.

6.107 The introduction in March 2009 of a power to initiate a deprivation of liberty under the MCA 2005 will add complication to the interface with the MHA 1983, mostly for the purpose of ensuring that some groups have their liberty removed under the more benign MCA without the stigma of a MHA section. Guardianship may provide an alternative in some cases.

---

[104]   Department of Constitutional Affairs *Mental Capacity Act 2005 Code of Practice* (2007), para 13.20.
[105]   *Megyeri v Germany* (1992) 15 EHRR 584, ECtHR.

Chapter 7

DETENTION OF MENTALLY DISORDERED OFFENDERS

OUTLINE

7.1   This chapter considers police powers relating to mentally disordered people under ss 135 and 136 of the MHA 1983, the factors determining whether a mentally disordered offender will be prosecuted, the special procedures and defences which apply to mentally disordered and mentally vulnerable suspects and defendants, the sentencing and other disposals available in such cases. This chapter considers the powers of the criminal courts to remand mentally disordered defendants to hospital for treatment and for reports, as well as their power to impose hospital orders under s 37 or hospital directions under s 45A of the MHA 1983. The Secretary of State for Justice has assumed the roles formerly occupied by the Home Secretary in relation to the power to transfer mentally disordered prisoners to psychiatric hospital, and the Home Office Mental Health Unit has been transferred to the Ministry of Justice. Where a crown court makes a hospital order under MHA 1983, s 37 in respect of a mentally disordered offender it may attach a restriction order under s 41 where it is necessary for the protection of the public from serious harm to impose restrictions on discharge. Where a crown court makes a hospital direction it attaches a restriction direction. Where a prisoner is transferred to hospital, the Minister of Justice may impose a restriction direction. The Ministry of Justice Mental Health Unit supervises the care of offenders who are subject to restriction orders and restriction directions. The MHA 2007 applies the new broad definition of mental disorder to all these powers including the hospital direction which has hitherto only been available for patients with psychopathic disorder. The 2007 Act also removes the possibility for a restriction order to be time limited and provides that all restriction orders shall in future be without limit of time. This provision is already in force. Finally, this chapter considers the MHA 2007 amendments to the rights of victims of crimes committed by mentally disordered offenders under the Domestic Violence, Crime and Victims Act 2004.

BACKGROUND

7.2   Criminal justice policy towards mentally disordered people rests on three basic principles. The first, exemplified in the Police and Criminal Evidence Act 1984, is that mentally disordered suspects should be subject to special safeguards surrounding their treatment in custody, since they may be particularly prone to make false confessions; the second, elaborated in *Home Office Circular 66/90* is that mentally disordered suspects and offenders should be diverted away from the penal system and into the health and social care system. Two ideas underpin the second principle: the first that mental disorder may reduce the person's culpability for their criminal acts; the second that they will be vulnerable to suicide and self harm. The third principle, which has come to dominate the discourse of mental health law reform since the early 1990s, is that the public require protection against the risk posed by mentally disordered people.

7.3   It is estimated that a significant proportion of the prison population suffer from mental health problems, with over half of female and three quarters of male prisoners suffering from personality disorders, neurotic disorders being found in 40% of male prisoners and 76% in females. Six per cent of male sentenced prisoners and 13% of all female prisoners were estimated to have a schizophrenic illness, and between 1 and 2% of prisoners have affective psychosis.[1] Given these high levels of psychiatric morbidity in the prison population, and the high risk of suicide and self-harm, it is important to recognise the limits of any policy of diversion of mentally disordered offenders from prison to hospital.

7.4   The prison population in England and Wales is over 80,000, and the total number of in-patient beds in psychiatric hospitals is around 30,000. On 31 March 2006 there were 14,600 patients detained in hospital, of whom 12,100 were in NHS hospitals (including the three high security special hospitals Ashworth, Broadmoor and Rampton), and 2,500 in private hospitals. In 2005–2006 there were 27,353 admissions under powers of detention in the Mental Health Act 1983, 1,664 of which occurred under the offender provisions of the Act. Both the prison system and the psychiatric hospital system are running at full stretch, and the capacity of the psychiatric system to cope with treating greater numbers of mentally disordered offenders is strictly limited. Those who are transferred from prison to hospital tend to be people who are exhibiting acute symptoms of mental illness of a psychotic nature, or people with personality disorders who are perceived to pose a risk to the public requiring continued detention, are nearing the end of determinate sentence, and whose detention can only be continued if transferred to hospital under the MHA 1983.

---

[1]   C Brooker, J Repper, C Beverley, M Ferriter and N Brewer *Mental Health Services and Prisoners: A Review* (2002), p 8. See http://www.dh.gov.uk/en/Publicationsandstatistics/ Publications/PublicationsPolicyAndGuidance/DH_4084149.

POLICE POWERS TO REMOVE A MENTALLY DISORDERED PERSON TO A PLACE OF SAFETY: MENTAL HEALTH ACT 1983, SS 135–136

7.5   This section considers powers to remove to a 'place of safety' a person who is reasonably believed to be suffering from mental disorder, either with a warrant, from private premises (s 135) or by a police office either from a public place (s 136). The purpose of removal to a place of safety is to enable the person to be assessed by an AMHP and a doctor.

Power to obtain a warrant to enter premises

7.6   Section 135(1) of the MHA 1983 confers a power on a magistrate to issue a warrant authorising a police office to enter private premises, using force if necessary, and, 'if thought fit', to remove a person to a place of safety with a view to the making of an application under Part 2, or of other arrangements for his treatment or care. A warrant may only be granted where an information has been laid on oath by an AMHP stating reasonable cause to suspect that a person believed to be suffering from mental disorder has been or is being ill-treated, neglected or kept otherwise than under proper control, or is living alone and unable to care for himself. The Draft Revised Code suggests that local authorities should issue guidance to AMHPs on how and when to use the power to apply for a warrant.[2]

7.7   Section 135(2) confers a similar power on magistrates, to grant a warrant authorising entry by any constable, if need be by force, onto premises to remove a patient who is 'liable to be taken or retaken' under English or Scottish mental health legislation. An information must have been laid by a constable, AMHP or other person authorised to take or retake the patient, to the effect that:

(a)   there is reasonable cause to believe that the patient is to be found on premises within the jurisdiction of the justice; and

(b)   that admission to the premises has been refused or that a refusal of such admission is apprehended.

The Draft Revised Code suggests that when a warrant under s 135(2) is used to gain access it is good practice for the police officer to be accompanied by a person authorised by the hospital, and for patients on SCT, if practicable, this should be a member of the multi-disciplinary team. Good planning should mean that it is 'almost never' necessary to use a police station as a place of safety under s 135.[3] During 2005–2006 there were 382 admissions to hospitals under s 135, 224 men and 158 women.

---

[2]   Department of Health *Mental Health Act 1983 Draft Revised Code of Practice* (2007), para 9.2. See http://www.dh.gov.uk/en/Consultations.

[3]   Ibid, paras 9.7 and 9.9.

Police power to remove from a public place to a place of safety

7.8　Section 136 of the MHA 1983 empowers a constable who finds a person in 'a place to which the public have access' who appears to be mentally disordered and to require immediate care and control, may, if he thinks it is necessary in that person's interests or for the protection of others, take that person to a place of safety. The person need not be diagnosed by a doctor as mentally disordered; the constable need only have a reasonable belief that the patient suffers from 'any disorder or disability of mind'. The purpose of removal is to enable the person to be examined by a doctor and interviewed by an AMHP and for any necessary arrangements for his treatment or care to be made. The authority for detention under s 136 and s 135 expires when these arrangements have been made or after 72 hours, whichever is the earlier.

7.9　The s 136 power may be exercised in a public place. In *Carter v Metropolitan Police Comr*[4] the Court of Appeal held that the communal balcony of a block of flats was a place to which the public have access. Police powers to enter private premises to prevent a breach of the peace are preserved by s 17(6) of the Police and Criminal Evidence Act 1984, provided any police action is a proportionate response in all the circumstances.[5]

Place of safety

7.10　A place of safety is defined in s 135(6) as residential accommodation provided by a local social services authority, a hospital, a police station, independent hospital or care home for mentally disordered persons, or any other suitable place the occupier of which is willing temporarily to receive the patient. As a general rule the Code expresses a preference for detention of a person thought to be suffering from mental disorder in a hospital rather than a police station, stating that:[6]

> 'Every effort should be made to ensure that a police station is used only on an exceptional basis in cases, for example, where the person's behaviour would pose an unmanageably high risk to other patients, staff or users of a health care setting. Subject to any physical health care needs, it is preferable for a person thought to be suffering from mental disorder to be detained in a hospital, or other health care setting, where mental health services are provided.'

In formulating local policy, regard is to be had to the impact different types of place of safety may have on the person and on the outcome of the assessment.

---

[4]　[1975] 1 WLR 507, CA.
[5]　*McLeod v United Kingdom* (1998) 27 EHRR 493, ECtHR.
[6]　Department of Health *Mental Health Act 1983 Draft Revised Code of Practice* (2007), para 9.19. See http://www.dh.gov.uk/en/Consultations.

7.11 The LSSA, hospitals and the Chief Constable should establish a clear policy for using the power and identifying appropriate facilities for the safe containment and rapid assessment of the person removed. The policy should define responsibilities for:[7]

> '• commissioning and providing facilities in health care settings for the safe accommodation of people requiring assessment and the levels of security which such facilities should be capable of providing through physical design and staffing;
>
> • providing prompt assessment and, where appropriate, admission to hospital for treatment;
>
> • securing the attendance of police officers where appropriate for the patient's health or safety or the protection of others;
>
> • the safe, timely and appropriate conveyance of the person to and between places of safety;
>
> • deciding whether it is appropriate to transfer the person from the place of safety to which they have been taken to another place of safety;
>
> • the release, transport and follow-up of people assessed under ss 135 or 136 who are not then admitted to hospital or immediately accommodated elsewhere.'

The policy should include provisions for the use of s 136 to be monitored so that a check can be made of how and in what circumstances it is being used, including its use in relation to black and minority ethic communities and children.[8] If the person removed to a place of safety is already subject to supervised community treatment ('SCT'), conditional discharge or, on leave of absence and recall to hospital may need to be considered. The patient's clinical supervisor should be contacted as soon as possible.[9]

7.12 Section 44 of the MHA 2007 amends ss 135 and 136 to provide that a person who has been removed to one place of safety may be transferred to another one within the 72-hour time limit. This provision will come into force in April 2008. This will mean that a person could initially be detained in a police cell but be removed to a hospital for further assessment, still within the authority of s 136, without need for fresh authority to detain from some other provision of the Act. The 72-hour period runs from arrival at the first place of safety. There were attempts in the House of Lords to reduce the maximum period to 24 hours, but the Minister of State rejected these on the basis of 'emerging evidence' collected by the independent Police Complaints Commission suggesting that whilst the average period spent in police custody under s 136 was 10 hours, and most people were released after 18 hours, 'some people need to be detained for longer than 24 hours'.[10]

---

[7]   Ibid, para 9.15.
[8]   Ibid, para 9.38.
[9]   Ibid, para 9.51.
[10] *Hansard,* HL Deb, vol 689, cols 1468–1469.

7.13 In *R (on the application of Anderson) v Inner North Greater London Coroner*, Collins J held that:[11]

> 'The powers contained in s 136 of the 1983 Act to remove to a place of safety inevitably require that the person concerned can be kept safe in the sense that harm to himself or others is prevented until he can be seen by a doctor and, if necessary, given some form of sedation ... A police officer in exercising his powers under s 136 is entitled to use reasonable force. If someone is violent, he can be restrained.'

Part 4 of the Act does not apply to persons detained under ss 135 or 136. In *R (on the application of Munjaz) v Mersey Care NHS Trust* Hale LJ said this:[12]

> 'There is a general power to take such steps as are reasonably necessary and proportionate to protect others from the immediate risk of significant harm. This applies whether or not the patient lacks the capacity to make decisions for himself. But where the patient does lack capacity, there is also the power to provide him with whatever treatment or care is necessary in his own best interests.'

A person aged 16 or over can be given necessary treatment using proportionate restraint if they lack capacity to consent and the treatment is administered in accordance with ss 5 and 6 of the MCA 2005.

7.14 During 2005–2006 there were 5,495 admissions under s 136 where the place of safety was a hospital, 3,092 men and 2,403 women. 72 per cent of the 5,385 patients taken to hospital under s 136 for whom outcome figures were available became informal patients after assessment, and the remaining 28 per cent were detained under Part 2.[13] There are no figures relating to the use of police stations as places of safety. Where an individual has been arrested by the police under s 136 he is entitled to have another person informed of his arrest and whereabouts, and where he is detained in a police station as the place of safety he has a right of access to legal advice.[14] Code of Practice C issued under the Police and Criminal Evidence Act 1984 ('PACE Code C') governs the detention, treatment and questioning of persons by police officers, and applies to people removed to a police station under s 136.

7.15 PACE Code C emphasises the 'imperative' requirement that a mentally disordered or otherwise mentally vulnerable person detained under s 136 be assessed as soon as possible. If that assessment is to take place at the police station, an AMHP and a doctor must be called to the station as soon as possible in order to interview and examine the detainee. Once the detainee has

---

[11]   [2004] EWHC 2729 (Admin).

[12]   [2003] EWCA Civ 1036 at [46].

[13]   National Statistics Information Centre NSIC *In-patients formally detained in hospitals under the Mental Health Act 1983 and other legislation, NHS Trusts, Care Trusts, Primary Care Trusts and Independent Hospitals, England; 1995–1996 to 2005–2006* (2007), Tables 1 and 5. See http://www.ic.nhs.uk/statistics-and-data-collections/health-and-lifestyles/mental-health/in-patients-formally-detained-in-hospitals-under-the-mental-health-act-1983-and-other-legislation-nhs-trusts-care-trusts-primary-care-trusts-and-independent-hospitals;-2005-06.

[14]   Police and Criminal Evidence Act 1984, ss 56, 58; Mental Health Act Code, para 10.9.

been interviewed, examined and suitable arrangements made for their treatment or care, they can no longer be detained under s 136. The Code also states that a detainee must be immediately discharged from detention under s 136 if the examining doctor concludes they are not mentally disordered within the meaning of the Act.[15]

7.16 Whether or not the person has been detained under s 136, if he or she appears to be suffering from a mental disorder the custody officer must make sure the person receives appropriate clinical attention as soon as reasonably practicable. Where an assessment under s 136 is taking place at a police station the custody officer must consider whether an appropriate health care professional should be called to conduct an initial clinical check on the detainee. This applies particularly when there is likely to be any significant delay in the arrival of a suitably qualified medical practitioner. If a detainee requests a clinical examination, an appropriate health care professional must be called as soon as practicable to assess the detainee's clinical needs.[16]

THE DECISION TO PROSECUTE

7.17 The decision to proceed with a criminal investigation in respect of a mentally disordered suspect will be taken by the police in the first instance in the light of the public interest as defined in the *Code for Crown Prosecutors*.[17] The decision to prosecute a mentally disordered suspect triggers the use of special interview procedures, may lead to the use of special procedures at trial, may involve decisions about criminal responsibility, and may culminate in the use of a hospital rather than a penal disposal. In most cases, the Crown Prosecution Service ('CPS') are responsible for deciding whether a person should be charged with a criminal offence, and if so, what that offence should be, and the decision is made in accordance with the *Code for Crown Prosecutors* and the Director of Public Prosecutions *Guidance on Charging*. The CPS applies a two-stage test. The first question is evidentiary and asks whether there is a 'realistic prospect of conviction' or in other words whether a jury or bench of magistrates or judge hearing a case alone, properly directed in accordance with the law, is more likely than not to convict the defendant of the charge alleged. The second question is whether a prosecution is needed in the public interest. The general principle here is that:[18]

> 'A prosecution will usually take place unless there are public interest factors tending against prosecution which clearly outweigh those tending in favour, or it appears more appropriate in all the circumstances of the case to divert the person from prosecution.'

---

[15] Police and Criminal Evidence Act Code of Practice C, para 3.16.
[16] Ibid, paras 9.3–9.8.
[17] Crown Prosecution Service (2004).
[18] Crown Prosecution Service *Code for Crown Prosecutors* (2004), para 5.1 (available at http://www.cps.gov.uk/publications/prosecution/index.html).

7.18   The *Code for Crown Prosecutors* states that factors weighing against proceeding to trial could include where:[19]

'(1)   prosecution is likely to have a bad effect on the victim's physical or mental health, always bearing in mind the seriousness of the offence; or

(2)   the defendant is elderly or is, or was at the time of the offence, suffering from significant mental or physical ill health, unless the offence is serious or there is real possibility that it may be repeated ... Crown Prosecutors must balance the desirability of diverting a defendant who is suffering from significant mental or physical ill health with the need to safeguard the general public.'

So if the offence is not serious and is unlikely to be repeated the public could be adequately safeguarded by a decision to admit as a voluntary patient or under civil powers rather than proceed to prosecution. The decision to investigate a criminal offence will be made by the police in the light of this guidance. The weightiest factor in the decision to prosecute a mentally disordered suspect rather than divert them from the criminal justice system will be the seriousness of the alleged offence. If the police decide to proceed to interview a mentally disordered or mentally vulnerable suspect in relation to a criminal offence, an 'appropriate adult' must be present.

THE APPROPRIATE ADULT

7.19   If a detainee in a police station is mentally disordered or otherwise mentally vulnerable, the custody officer must, as soon as practicable, inform an 'appropriate adult' of the grounds for their detention and their whereabouts, and ask the adult to come to the police station to see the detainee.[20] PACE Code C recognises the vulnerability of mentally disordered suspects, observing that whilst they:[21]

'are often capable of providing reliable evidence, they may, without knowing or wishing to do so, be particularly prone to provide information which is unreliable, misleading or self-incriminating. Special care should therefore be exercised in questioning such a person and the appropriate adult should always be involved if there is any doubt about a person's mental state or capacity.'

PACE Code C refers to appropriate adults being necessary for mentally vulnerable detainees who, because of mental state or capacity, may not understand the significance of what is said, of questions and their replies, as well as for those suffering from mental disorder meaning 'mental illness, arrested or incomplete development of mind, psychopathic disorder and any other disorder or disability of mind'. The Code states that when the custody

---

[19]   Police and Criminal Evidence Act Code of Practice C, para 5.10f–g.
[20]   Ibid, para 3.15.
[21]   Ibid, *Notes for Guidance*, para 11C.

officer has any doubt about the mental state or capacity of a detainee, that detainee should be treated as mentally vulnerable and an appropriate adult called.

7.20 The primary role of the appropriate adult is to ensure that no undue pressure is put on the suspect. The appropriate adult is not to act simply as an observer and this is to be explained to him or her. The Code states that the role has three aspects:

(1) to advise the person being questioned;

(2) to observe whether or not the interview is being conducted properly and fairly; and

(3) to facilitate communication with the person being interviewed.[22]

7.21 An appropriate adult in the case of someone who is mentally disordered or mentally vulnerable can be:

(i) a relative, guardian or other person responsible for their care or custody;

(ii) someone experienced in dealing with mentally disordered or mentally vulnerable people but who is not a police officer or employed by the police; or

(iii) failing these, some other responsible adult aged 18 or over who is not a police officer or employed by the police.[23]

Explanatory Note 1D of PACE Code C states that it may be appropriate if the appropriate adult is someone with qualifications in looking after mentally disordered people, but that if the suspect prefers a relative to a better qualified stranger, that wish should 'if practicable' be respected. A person should not be the appropriate adult if they are suspected of involvement in the offence, a victim, a witness or otherwise involved in the investigation. Nor should someone be an appropriate adult if they have received admissions in relation to the offence from the suspect, as appropriate adults are not covered by legal professional privilege. A solicitor or independent custody visitor may not be an appropriate adult if they are present in the police station in either of those capacities.[24]

7.22 Unless an urgent interview can be authorised by a superintendent or higher rank, a mentally disordered person must not be interviewed or asked to sign a statement without an appropriate adult attending.[25] The only exception is where an officer of at least the rank of superintendent certifies that delay will

---

[22] Ibid, para 11.17.
[23] Ibid, para 1.7(b).
[24] *Police and Criminal Evidence Act Code of Practice C, Explanatory Notes 1B–1E.*
[25] *Police and Criminal Evidence Act Code of Practice C, para 11.15.*

involve a serious risk of interference with evidence, harm to persons or serious loss or serious damage to property. Even then questioning may not continue in the absence of the appropriate adult once sufficient information to avert the risk has been received. A record must be made of the grounds for any decision to begin an interview in such circumstances.[26]

CONSEQUENCES OF FAILURE TO HAVE AN APPROPRIATE ADULT PRESENT AT INTERVIEW

7.23   Three sections of the Police and Criminal Evidence Act 1984 relate to the admissibility of confession evidence. Only s 77 refers directly to any form of mental disorder. Although the PACE Code refers to mental vulnerability and mental disorder in general, s 77 of the Police and Criminal Evidence Act 1984 refers to the narrower concept of mental handicap ('arrested or incomplete development of mind which includes significant impairment of intelligence and social functioning'), stating that where the case against a defendant depends wholly or substantially on a confession by him and the judge is satisfied (a) that he is mentally handicapped; and (b) that the confession was not made in the presence of an independent person the judge must warn the jury that there is a special need for caution before convicting the accused in reliance on the confession. The decision as to whether a suspect is mentally handicapped is to be based on medical evidence.[27] Although a solicitor cannot be an appropriate adult, a solicitor was held to be an independent person for the purposes of this section in *R v Lewis*.[28] Section 77 of the Police and Criminal Evidence Act 1984 merely requires the judge to warn the jury of the need for caution before relying on a confession, and the warning is only required where the suspect was mentally handicapped and an appropriate adult was not present.

7.24   Sections 76 and 78 allow for confessions to be excluded entirely, and one of the grounds on which they may be excluded is failure to provide an appropriate adult. Section 76(2) provides that where it is represented to the court that a confession may have been (a) obtained by oppression of the person who made it; or (b) in consequence of anything said or done which was likely, in the circumstances existing at the time, to render the confession unreliable, the burden is on the prosecution to show beyond reasonable doubt that the confession was not improperly obtained (notwithstanding that it may be true). Failure to secure the presence of an appropriate adult is unlikely to amount to oppression, unless there is a strong degree of hectoring of a mentally vulnerable suspect. However, it may amount to something said or done which was likely to render the confession unreliable under s 76(2)(b).[29]

---

26   Police and Criminal Evidence Act Code of Practice C, paras 11.1(a), 11.18–11.20.
27   *R v Ham* (1995) 36 BMLR 169, CA.
28   [1996] Crim LR 260, CA.
29   See *R v Everett* [1988] Crim LR 826, CA; and *R v Moss* (1990) 91 Cr App R 371, CA.

7.25 Under s 78(1) the court may refuse to allow evidence on which the prosecution proposes to rely to be given if it appears to the court that, having regard to all the circumstances, including the circumstances in which the evidence was obtained, the admission of the evidence would have such an adverse effect on the fairness of the proceedings that the court ought not to admit it. The attitude of the courts to the effect of failure to provide an appropriate adult on fairness has varied. In some cases it has led to exclusion,[30] in others not.[31]

ASSESSMENT OF MENTALLY DISORDERED OFFENDERS

7.26 The Mental Health Act Code of Practice asserts that:[32]

> 'People subject to criminal proceedings have the same right to psychiatric assessment and treatment as other citizens. Any person who is in police or prison custody, or who is before the courts charged with a criminal offence, and who is in need of medical treatment for mental disorder should be considered for admission to hospital. Such people may be at greatest risk of self-harm while in custody.'

Moreover, the Code makes it clear that a prison health care centre is not a hospital within the meaning of the MHA 1983. As it is not a hospital and as prisoners are not detained under the MHA 1983 they may not be given treatment for mental disorder without consent using the powers and second opinion safeguards in Part 4 of the 1983 Act.[33]

7.27 But there is convergence in the regimes in terms of legal powers to treat without consent. Treatment for mental disorder may be given to prisoners using restraint and force under ss 5 and 6 of the Mental Capacity Act 2005 if the person lacks capacity and restraint and treatment are necessary and proportionate responses to prevent harm to the patient. Although ss 5 and 6 are said to codify the common law doctrine of necessity, the statute and supporting Code of Practice show clearly that treatment necessary to prevent harm to the patient may be given without consent outside hospital settings, using force or the threat of force if necessary, where the patient lacks capacity. Under common law, treatment which is immediately necessary and a proportionate response to prevent the patient from harming others may be given using restraint, whether or not the person retains capacity.[34]

---

[30]   See *R v Aspinall* (1999) 2 Cr App R 115, CA.
[31]   See *R v Law-Thompson* [1997] Crim LR 674, CA.
[32]   Department of Health *Mental Health Act 1983 Draft Revised Code of Practice* (2007), para 36.2. See http://www.dh.gov.uk/en/Consultations.
[33]   Ibid, para 36.2.
[34]   *R (on the application of Munjaz) v Mersey Care NHS Trust; R (on the application of S) v Airedale NHS Trust* [2003] EWCA Civ 1036, CA.

7.28   Even after a decision has been made to proceed to trial for a criminal offence there are still ample opportunities for mentally disordered offenders to be diverted away from the prison system to psychiatric hospital (be that high, medium, or low security) or to psychiatric supervision in the community. The MHA 1983 also provides remand powers to enable psychiatric assessment to take place in hospital rather than prison.

REMAND TO HOSPITAL

7.29   The MHA 1983 introduced three remand powers for mentally disordered offenders: the power to remand an accused person for reports on his mental condition under s 35, which was used 135 times in 2005–2006; the power to remand for psychiatric treatment under s 36, used 17 times in 2005–2006; and the power to impose an interim hospital order under s 38, used an unknown number of times in 2005–2006. As Bartlett and Sandland note:[35]

> 'When the numbers remanded under both sections [35 and 36] are compared to the thousands of mentally disordered people remanded to prison for medical assessments, the underuse of the power to remand to hospital is truly shocking.'

7.30   There are certain common features to the remand powers. No court can make a remand order unless it is satisfied, on the evidence of the doctor or approved clinician ('AC') who would be responsible for making the report[36] (or who would be in charge of his case,[37] or some other person representing the hospital managers, that arrangements have been made for the patient's admission to hospital within a period of seven days after the remand order has been made. Remand is for 28 days in the first instance, but the accused may be further remanded for two further 28-day periods up to a maximum of twelve weeks in all. The court can extend the remand of someone remanded under s 35 in his absence (as long as he is represented in court) if it is satisfied on the evidence of the doctor or the 'approved clinician' ('AC') preparing the report, that a further remand is necessary in order to complete the psychiatric assessment.[38]

7.31   In the case of someone remanded for treatment under s 36, remand may be extended if the court is satisfied on the report of the AC who would be in charge of treatment that further remand is warranted. A person remanded for reports is entitled to commission at his own expense an independent report from a doctor or any other AC, and to apply to the court for his remand to be terminated. However, remand patients have no right to apply for discharge to a Mental Health Review Tribunal ('MHRT').

---

[35]   P Bartlett and R Sandland *Mental Health Law Policy and Practice* (OUP, 3rd edn, 2007), p 220.

[36]   MHA 1983, s 35(4).

[37]   MHA 1983, s 36(7).

[38]   MHA 1983, s 35(5), (6).

REMAND FOR A PSYCHIATRIC REPORT UNDER S 35

7.32 In recognition of the fact that remand to prison may lead to a high risk of suicide in mentally vulnerable people, s 35 of the Act provides for remand to hospital for reports where the court is satisfied that:

(a) there is reason to suspect that the accused is suffering from mental disorder; and

(b) it would be impracticable for a report to be made on his mental condition if he were remanded on bail.

A Crown Court may remand an accused person awaiting trial or who has been arraigned for an offence punishable by imprisonment and has not yet been sentenced. In relation to the magistrates, 'accused person' has two meanings. First, it includes anyone who has been convicted by the court of an offence punishable with imprisonment. Second, it includes any person charged with such an offence if the court is satisfied that either:

(a) he did the act or made the omission charged; or

(b) he has consented to the making of the remand.

Evidence is required from one doctor, who must be approved by the Secretary of State as having special experience in the diagnosis or treatment of mental disorder.[39] The diagnostic threshold for remand is not high. There need only be reason to suspect that the accused is suffering from mental disorder, meaning 'any disorder or disability of mind'.

7.33 A report prepared under s 35 should contain a statement of whether a patient is suffering from mental disorder identifying its relevance to the alleged offence. The report should not comment on guilt or innocence, but should include relevant social factors and any recommendations on care and treatment including where and when it should take place and who should be responsible. Section 10(2) of the MHA 2007 allows reports to be prepared not just by doctors but also by approved clinicians who might be nurses, psychologists, social workers or occupational therapists.

7.34 A person remanded under s 35 is not subject to the consent to treatment provisions in Part 4 of the Act and therefore retains the common law right to refuse treatment.[40] The Code of Practice advises that where a patient remanded under s 35 is thought to be in need of medical treatment for mental disorder under Part 4 of the Act, consideration ought to be given to referring the patient back to court with an appropriate recommendation, and with an assessment of whether the patient is in a fit state to attend court. It goes on to suggest that if

---

[39]   MHA 1983, s 54(1).
[40]   MHA 1983, s 56(1)(b).

there is delay in securing a court date, and depending on the patient's mental condition, consideration should be given to whether the patient meets the criteria of s 3. There are various legal issues in relation to detaining a remanded person under civil powers in order to acquire a right to treat compulsorily, most notably that Parliament clearly provided a separate power to remand for treatment which is subject to stricter criteria, and a patient could appeal successfully against detention under the civil powers, but still remain detained under the remand power.[41]

7.35 The MCA 2005 introduces the possibility that a person remanded for reports could be given treatment without consent for mental disorder. Under s 5 a defence is available, in relation to any action based on treatment without consent, to anyone who has taken reasonable steps to carry out an assessment of a patient's capacity, reasonably believes that the person lacks capacity, and reasonably believes that the treatment is in the person's best interests. Restraint (use or threat of force) can also be justified if necessary and proportionate to prevent harm to the incapacitated person under s 6 of the MCA 2005. Under s 3 of the MCA 2005 a person's capacity is to be assessed by asking whether there is any mental disability (disturbance or disability of mind or brain) which renders him unable to communicate a decision, unable to understand and retain relevant treatment information, or unable to use and weigh that information in the balance as part of the process of arriving at a decision. This definition may mean that a person who retains cognitive function and can communicate and understand and retain treatment information long enough to make a decision may still lack capacity if some emotional disturbance of mental functioning, such as depression, renders them unable to weigh the information in the balance to make a decision. Intervention under the MCA may only be carried out where in the patient's best interests, although the definition of best interests, which includes social and psychological interests is capable of being interpreted so as to protect others. It can be argued that it is in X's interest that X be prevented from assaulting others or provoking them to assault him.

REMAND FOR TREATMENT UNDER S 36

7.36 Remand for treatment may be used to provide treatment before trial and hence potentially avoid an accused person being found unfit to plead. The definition of accused person for this power is any person who is in custody awaiting trial for an offence punishable with imprisonment (other than murder), or who at any time before sentence is in custody in the course of a Crown Court trial. A remand order for treatment may only be made by the Crown Court on the evidence of two doctors, one of whom must be approved by the Secretary of State as having special experience in the diagnosis or

---

[41] Department of Health *Mental Health Act 1983 Draft Revised Code of Practice* (2007), para 9.2. See http://www.dh.gov.uk/en/Consultations. For a critical view see P Fennell 'Double detention under the Mental Health Act 1983: a case of extra Parliamentary legislation' (1991) *Journal of Social Welfare and Family Law* 194.

treatment of mental disorder. The court must be satisfied that the accused is suffering from mental disorder ('any disorder or disability of mind') of a nature or degree which makes it appropriate for him to be detained in hospital for medical treatment. The MHA 2007 broadens the definition of mental disorder which applies to remands for treatment, which used to be available only for mental illness or severe mental impairment. The test now is that:

(a) the patient is suffering from mental disorder of a nature or degree which makes it appropriate for him to be detained in a hospital for medical treatment; and

(b) appropriate medical treatment is available to him.

Section 36 was only used seventeen times in 2005–2006. It remains to be seen whether the broader definition of mental disorder will lead to an increase in its use.

7.37 Because the sentence is fixed by law, a person accused of murder cannot be remanded for treatment under s 36 (see s 36(2)). However, s 3(6A) of the Bail Act 1976 allows the court to impose the following conditions of bail:

(a) that the accused must undergo examination by two doctors for psychiatric reports to be prepared; and

(b) that he must attend an institution or place as the court directs for that purpose and comply with any other directions from the doctors.

A person remanded for treatment is subject to Part 4 of the MHA 1983 and so may be given medicine for mental disorder or Electro Convulsive Therapy ('ECT'), subject to the statutory second opinion procedure in ss 58 and 58A (see paras **10.30**–**10.38** below). An accused person remanded for treatment has no right to apply for discharge to a Mental Health Review Tribunal ('MHRT').

INTERIM HOSPITAL ORDER UNDER S 38

7.38 Either the Crown Court or a magistrate's court may make an interim hospital order on the evidence of two doctors (one of whom must be approved under s 12) that the relevant criteria are met. Currently the court must be satisfied that the diagnostic criterion is met, that the offender is suffering from mental illness, psychopathic disorder, severe mental impairment or mental impairment. The court must also be satisfied that there is reason to suppose that the mental disorder is such that it may be appropriate for a hospital order to be made. The MHA 2007 will open the possibility for patients suffering from any disorder or disability of mind to be subject to interim orders.

7.39 The court must be satisfied on the evidence of the 'responsible clinician' ('RC') who would have overall responsibility for his case' or the hospital managers that arrangements have been made for the patient's admission to hospital within 28 days.[42] An interim hospital order is for an initial period of twelve weeks which may be renewed at 28 day intervals thereafter up to a maximum of twelve months on the written or oral evidence of the 'responsible clinician'. The court may terminate the order if, having considered the evidence of the responsible clinician, it decides to deal with the offender in some other way. The court can renew the interim order or make a full hospital order in the absence of the patient, provided he is represented in court.[43]

7.40 A patient on an interim hospital order is subject to the consent to treatment provisions in Part 4 of the Act, and so may be given medicine for mental disorder or Electro Convulsive Therapy, subject to the statutory second opinion procedure in ss 58 and 58A. Patients on interim hospital orders are not entitled to apply to a MHRT for discharge.

MENTAL CONDITION AT THE TIME OF THE OFFENCE

7.41 The offender's mental condition at the time of the offence can have a bearing on disposal of a mentally disordered offender. Mentally disordered offenders have traditionally been exempt from ordinary penal measures on the grounds that they are not criminally responsible for their behaviour (not guilty by reason of insanity), that their responsibility for doing or being a party to a homicide is diminished by abnormality of mind (diminished responsibility), or that they are unable to understand the course of the proceedings at their trial and contribute to their defence (unfit to plead). Each of these may lead to a psychiatric rather than a penal disposal.

THE INSANITY DEFENCE

7.42 Section 2 of the Trial of Lunatics Act 1883 provides for a special verdict of not guilty by reason of insanity to be returned where a person who was insane at the time the offence was committed. The definition of insanity remains the *McNaghten* rules laid down by Tindal CJ in the decision of the House of Lords in *McNaghten's Case*. For the defence to be made out:[44]

> 'It must be clearly proved that, at the time of committing the act, the accused was labouring under such a defect of reason from disease of the mind that he did not know the nature and quality of the act, or so as not to know that what he was doing was wrong.'

A person must be labouring under a very severe defect of reason to be entitled to the defence not to know the nature and quality of their act (the example

---

[42] MHA 1983, s 38(4).
[43] MHA 1983, s 38(2), (6).
[44] *McNaghten's Case* [1843–60] All ER Rep 229, HL.

often given is chopping someone with an axe believing them to be a block of wood). Similarly, there must be a severe defect of reason if someone knows the nature and quality of their act (for example, killing someone), but does not know that it is wrong. Professor Mackay succeeded in persuading the Royal Court of Jersey in *Attorney-General v Prior*[45] to adopt a definition of insanity more in keeping with modern medical thinking. A person would be entitled to the insanity defence if:

> 'at the time of the offence, his unsoundness of mind affected his criminal responsibility to such a degree that jury consider that he ought not to be found criminally responsible.'

The insanity defence is used between 10 and 15 times per year, and is most often used with serious offences against the person. If the offence is homicide, the defence is more likely to plead guilty to manslaughter on grounds of diminished responsibility rather than rely on the insanity defence.

7.43 Concerns were raised by cases where the insanity defence was imposed when the defendant suffered from epilepsy[46] or hypoglycaemia[47] rather than what psychiatrists would accept as a true mental disorder in accordance with modern principles of medicine. Section 1 of the Criminal Procedure (Insanity and Unfitness to Plead) Act 1991 provides that that a jury shall not return a special verdict except on the written or oral evidence of two medical practitioners, one of whom must be approved under s 12. This effectively means that unless a psychiatrist certifies that the person is suffering from a true mental disorder there will not be a special verdict.

7.44 Since the Criminal Procedure (Insanity and Unfitness to Plead) Act 1991 a Crown Court which finds a defendant not guilty by reason of insanity is no longer bound to impose a restriction order without limit of time. The Domestic Violence, Crime and Victims Act 2004 inserts a new s 5 into the Criminal Procedure (Insanity) Act 1964 setting out the three disposal options available to the court:

(1) a hospital order under s 37 of the MHA 1983, which can be accompanied by a restriction order under s 41;

(2) a supervision order; or

(3) absolute discharge of the accused.[48]

Where the sentence for the offence is fixed by law the 1991 Act provides that there must be a restriction order without limit of time if the Mental Health Act

---

[45]   *A-G v Prior* 2001 JLR 146, Jersey RC.
[46]   See *R v Sullivan* [1983] 2 All ER 673, HL.
[47]   As in *R v Hennessy* [1989] 2 All ER 9, CA.
[48]   Domestic Violence, Crime and Victims Act 2004, s 24.

criteria for making a restriction order are met.[49] If those criteria are not met, the court may only make a supervision order or discharge the defendant absolutely. Absolute discharge is most likely to apply in a case where the defendant is found unfit to plead because of a physical disorder rather than a case where the defendant is found on psychiatric evidence to be not guilty by reason of insanity.

Supervision order

7.45 A supervision order requires the supervised person to be under the supervision of a supervising officer (social worker or probation officer) for a specified period of not more than two years. A supervision order may require the supervised person to submit to treatment by or under the direction of a registered medical practitioner. The court may only make a supervision order if satisfied that, having regard to all the circumstances of the case, the making of such an order is the most suitable means of dealing with the accused, that the supervising officer is willing to supervise, and that arrangements have been made for the treatment which will be specified in the order.

7.46 The court must be satisfied on the evidence of two doctors, one of them s 12 approved, that the mental condition of the supervised person requires and may be susceptible to treatment; but is not such as to warrant the making of a hospital order under s 37 of the MHA 1983. A supervision order may include a condition that the supervised person shall submit to medical treatment aimed at improving his mental condition. This may be either treatment as a non-resident patient at a specified institution or treatment under the direction of a specified doctor.

7.47 A supervision order may also include a condition that the supervised person submit to medical treatment designed to improve his medical condition other than his mental condition. This may be either treatment as a non-resident patient at a specified institution or treatment under the direction of a specified doctor. This option is only available where the court is satisfied on the written or oral evidence of two or more doctors that because of his medical condition, other than his mental condition, the supervised person is likely to pose a risk to himself or others; and the condition may be susceptible to treatment.

7.48 If the doctor in charge of mental or other medical treatment considers that the treatment may be more conveniently given in or at an institution or place which is not specified in the original order where the person will receive treatment under the direction of a doctor, he may, with the consent of the supervised person, make arrangements for that treatment to take place. This may include treatment as a resident patient. Notice must be given to the supervising officer. The supervised person's consent is required for the change of arrangement, but once the change is made, the treatment provided for by the arrangements shall be deemed to be treatment to which he is required to submit

---

[49] Criminal Procedure (Insanity and Unfitness to Plead) Act 1991, Sch 1, para 2(2).

in pursuance of the supervision order. A supervision order may also include requirements as to residence but before imposing a residence requirement, the court must consider the home surroundings of the supervised person.

7.49 The insanity defence is available in respect of any offence. The legislation on the special verdict applies to Crown Court trials. White (1991) has argued that the insanity defence is also available in the Magistrates' Court and that a defendant who establishes it there is entitled to an acquittal. The argument has been accepted by some magistrates.

THE PLEA OF DIMINISHED RESPONSIBILITY

7.50 Section 2 of the Homicide Act 1957 provides for the plea of diminished responsibility to a charge of murder. The effect of a successful plea is that a homicide conviction is reduced from murder with a mandatory life sentence, to manslaughter where the sentence is within the judge's discretion. However, this does not necessarily mean that a hospital order will be imposed. The jury must be satisfied on the balance of probabilities that the accused is suffering from such abnormality of mind (whether arising from a condition of arrested or retarded development of mind or any inherent cause or induced by disease or injury) as substantially impaired his mental responsibility for his acts or omissions in doing or being a party to the killing. The court will accept pleas of guilty to manslaughter except in cases where medical opinion is divided or is open to challenge.[50]

7.51 The first question is whether there is an abnormality of mind. This is a question for the jury to decide on the balance of probabilities, based on medical evidence.[51] In *R v Byrne* where Lord Parker CJ contrasted 'abnormality of mind' with 'defect of reason' in the *McNaghten* rules stating that abnormality of mind means:[52]

> '[A] state of mind so different from that of ordinary human beings that the reasonable man would term it abnormal. It appears to us to be wide enough to cover the mind's activities in all its aspects, not only the perception of physical acts and matters and the ability to form a rational judgment whether an act is right or wrong, but also the ability to exercise will-power to control physical acts in accordance with that rational judgment.'

The Court in *Byrne* held that a man with a personality disorder could be suffering from an abnormality of mind.

7.52 The second question is whether the abnormality of mind arises from a condition of arrested or retarded development of mind or any inherent cause or induced by disease or injury. Arrested or retarded development of mind

---

[50] *R v Cox* (1968) 52 Cr App R 130, CA; *R v Vinagre* (1979) 69 Cr App R 104, CA.
[51] (1979) 69 Cr App R 104, CA.
[52] *R v Byrne* [1960] 3 All ER 1 at 5, CA.

includes learning disability. Any inherent cause could include personality disorders. Induced by disease could psychotic illnesses with strong delusions and hallucinations, depressive illness, and severe reactive depression. Induced by injury would include mental disorder brought on by head injury.

7.53 In *R v Dietschmann*[53] the House of Lords held that a defendant who had an abnormality of mind and was under the influence of drink or drugs did not have to establish that even if he had not had any drink or drugs he would still have killed as he did. Section 2(1) refers to substantial impairment which does not require the abnormality of mind to be the sole cause of the defendant's acts in doing the killing. The abnormality of mind does not have to be the sole cause of the impaired responsibility.

7.54 The third issue is whether the defendant's 'responsibility' was 'substantially impaired'. The first question here is what is meant by 'responsibility' in *R v Byrne* Lord Parker CJ offered this definition:[54]

> '[T]he expression 'mental responsibility for his acts' points to a consideration of the extent to which the accused's mind is answerable for his physical acts which must include a consideration of the extent of his ability to exercise will-power to control his physical acts.'

This meant that the defence was available to someone with a personality disorder.

7.55 On the question of 'substantially', in *R v Lloyd*, Edmund Davies J said this:[55]

> 'Substantial does not mean total, that is to say, the mental responsibility need not be totally impaired, so to speak, destroyed altogether. At the other end of the scale substantial does not mean trivial or minimal. It is something in between and Parliament has left it to you and other juries to say on the evidence was the mental responsibility impaired, and, if so, was it substantially impaired?'

The Mental Health Act Commission ('MHAC') report that 'the number of diminished responsibility verdicts peaked about 25 years ago and has been tailing away ever since'. The MHAC also report that of the 515 diminished responsibility verdicts between 1992 and 2002–2003 182 (35 per cent) resulted in prison sentences rather than hospital. After 1999–2000 'other' manslaughter verdicts (most likely provocation) account for over 80 per cent of hospital orders.[56]

---

53   *R v Dietschmann* [2003] UKHL 10, [2003] 1 All ER 897, HL.
54   [1960] 3 All ER 1 at 5.
55   *R v Lloyd* [1967] 1 QB 175 at 178.
56   Mental Health Act Commission *In Place of Fear* (Eleventh Biennial Report 2003–2005, TSO, 2005), p 369; Mental Health Act Commission *Placed Among Strangers* (Thirteenth Biennial Report 2005–2007, TSO, 2007), pp 375–376.

THE PLEA OF INFANTICIDE

7.56   Infanticide is defined in s 1(1) of the Infanticide Act 1938 as:

'Where a woman by any wilful act or omission causes the death of her child being a child under the age of twelve months, but at the time of the act or omission the balance of her mind was disturbed by her not having fully recovered from the effect of giving birth to the child or by reason of the effect of lactation consequent upon the birth of the child, then ... she shall be guilty ... of infanticide, and may for such offence be dealt with and punished as if she had been guilty of the offence of manslaughter of the child.'

This replaced the definition in the Infanticide Act 1922 which only applied to a 'newly born' child. It enables women charged with child killing when in the throes of post-natal depression or any other severe mental illness to escape conviction for murder.

UNFITNESS TO PLEAD

7.57   A defendant in a Crown Court will be under disability in relation to his or her trial ('unfit to plead') if unable to plead to the indictment, to understand the proceedings so as to be able to challenge jurors, to understand and give evidence, and to make a proper defence.[57] If the defendant raises the issue, the burden is on him or her to satisfy the judge on the balance of probabilities. If the issue is raised by the prosecution, the prosecution must satisfy the judge beyond reasonable doubt that the defendant is under disability.[58]

7.58   Section 4A(2)(b) of the Criminal Procedure (Insanity and Unfitness to Plead) Act 1991 provides for 'a trial of the facts' to take place where a defendant is found to be unfit to plead. A full trial will not take place, but a jury will be required to determine whether they are satisfied beyond reasonable doubt that the defendant did the act or made the omission charged against him as an offence regardless of the existence of any necessary mens rea. If they are satisfied that the defendant did the act or made the omission charged, they must make a finding to that effect; if they are not so satisfied, they are obliged to return a verdict of acquittal. Where the defendant is found guilty 'on the facts', the powers of sentence are the same as for a special verdict of not guilty by reason of insanity.

7.59   Paragraph 13 of *Home Office Circular 93/91* states:

---

[57]   *R v Pritchard* (1836) 7 C & P 303.
[58]   Criminal Procedure (Insanity) Act 1964, s 4, as amended by Domestic Violence, Crime and Victims Act 2004, s 22.

'Where an accused person is found unfit to be tried he should always be legally represented during the trial of the facts. There may be cases where the accused, because of his mental disorder, repudiates his legal representative prior to, or during the trial of the facts.'

The court should appoint a lawyer to put the case for the accused who may properly be entrusted to pursue his or her interests. This could include someone who has previously represented the accused or any other person whom the court considers appropriate, for example a solicitor known to the court to have experience in such matters. The Official Solicitor has let it be known that he is prepared to act as the legal representative of an accused person during a trial of the facts.

7.60 The Domestic Violence, Crime and Victims Act 2004 has made a number of changes. First, as we have seen it reduces to three the disposal options available to the court:

(1) hospital order under s 37 with or without restrictions;

(2) a supervision order; or

(3) an absolute discharge.

Second, it clarifies that for a hospital order to be made the criteria in s 37 need to be satisfied. If a restriction order is to be imposed it must be necessary for the protection of the public from serious harm. Third, the court can direct admission, and does not have to rely on the Secretary of State to do so. Fourth, in appropriate cases remand powers under ss 35, 36 and interim orders under s 38 are available to the court. Finally, the Home Secretary is empowered to remit for trial a patient detained under ss 37 or 41 following a finding of unfitness to plead, if satisfied that they can now properly be tried.

MENTAL CONDITION AT TIME OF SENTENCING

7.61 The effect of mental disorder on criminal responsibility or fitness for trial is confined to small numbers of cases. Its effect on sentencing disposal is manifest in many thousands of cases. In some of these the result will be that an offender is not imprisoned but is instead admitted to hospital under Part 3 of the MHA 1983. In others, especially where there is a personality disorder, the result may be an enhanced prison sentence under the Criminal Justice Act 2003. Once a defendant is convicted or has been found to have committed the act constituting the offence, they may be given a community disposal, a prison sentence or a hospital order. A patient may be diverted to the psychiatric system at the sentencing stage. This may be done under the MHA 1983 by a hospital or a guardianship order or by using a community order under the Criminal Justice Act 2003.

7.62 Since the MHA 1959, hospital orders have been a key method of disposal of mentally disordered offenders. Department of Health figures show a long-term decline in unrestricted hospital orders over the lifetime of the MHA 1983. In 1995–1996, 536 such orders were made, since then the annual figure has been between 300 and 350, the number for 2005–2006 being 322, with a further 322 hospital order with restrictions on discharge being imposed.[59]

7.63 The key question in the decision to impose a hospital order is whether the offender is suffering from mental disorder *at the time of sentencing*, not whether his mental disorder had any bearing on the offending behaviour. In making a hospital order the court is not concerned with criminal responsibility or the defendant's fitness to participate in the trial; the person has usually already been tried and convicted. The only relevant considerations are his mental condition and the need for psychiatric treatment in hospital at the time of sentencing. The MHA 1983 also provides for the transfer of mentally disordered prisoners (whether on remand or serving a sentence) from prison to hospital on the authority of a Home Secretary's warrant. In 2005–2006 704 prisoners were transferred from prison to hospital.

7.64 The Criminal Justice Act 2003 now provides a general framework for sentencing offenders, with disposals ranging from community sentences to provisions for sentencing dangerous offenders. Hospital orders and transfers to psychiatric hospital from prison continue to be governed by the MHA 1983. Section 142(1) of the Criminal Justice Act 2003 requires any court dealing with an offender to have regard to five purposes of sentencing. These are:

(1)   the punishment of offenders;

(2)   the reduction of crime (including its reduction by deterrence);

(3)   the reform and rehabilitation of offenders;

(4)   the protection of the public; and

(5)   the making of reparation by offenders to persons affected by their offences.

This section does not apply to offenders under 18, to offenders convicted of murder, of certain firearms offences or offences requiring a custodial sentence, who are subject to the dangerous offender provisions in ss 225–228 of the Act,

---

[59]   National Statistics Information Centre (NSIC) *In-patients formally detained in hospitals under the Mental Health Act 1983 and other legislation, NHS Trusts, Care Trusts, Primary Care Trusts and Independent Hospitals, England; 1995–1996 to 2005–2006* (2007). See http://www.ic.nhs.uk/statistics-and-data-collections/health-and-lifestyles/mental-health/in-patients-formally-detained-in-hospitals-under-the-mental-health-act-1983-and-other-legislation-nhs-trusts-care-trusts-primary-care-trusts-and-independent-hospitals;-2005-06.

or where the court makes a hospital order, an interim hospital order or a hospital direction under Part 3 of the MHA 1983.

The hierarchy of sentencing severity

7.65　The least serious offences should be dealt with by a fine or a discharge. Those where the purposes of sentencing would not be met by such leniency, are to be dealt with by a community sentence. A community sentence may only be imposed if the court considers that the offence, or the combination of the offence and one or more offences associated with it, is serious enough to warrant such a sentence.[60] A further threshold is s 151, which requires that a community order must be in the interests of justice and the offender must, since the age of 16, have been fined on three or more occasions, even though their offence may not be serious enough to justify a community sentence and their previous convictions would not justify such a sentence. The Sentencing Guidelines Council advises 'great care ... in assessing whether a community sentence is appropriate, since failure to comply with conditions could result in a custodial sentence'.[61] A court may only impose a prison sentence if it considers a community sentence would be insufficient, and the offence is so serious that neither a fine alone nor a community sentence can be justified for the offence or the offences associated with it.

The community order

7.66　Section 177 sets out 12 forms of community order which a court may attach to a community sentence for an offender over the age of 18. These include:

(i)　an unpaid work requirement (s 199);

(ii)　an activity requirement (s 201);

(iii)　a programme requirement (s 202);

(iv)　a prohibited activity requirement (s 203);

(v)　a curfew requirement (s 204);

(vi)　an exclusion requirement (s 205);

(vii)　a residence requirement (s 206);

(viii) a mental health treatment requirement (s 207);

---

[60]　CJA 2003, s 148(1).
[61]　Sentencing Guidelines Council *New Sentences: Criminal Justice Act 2003 Guideline*. See http://www.sentencing-guidelines.gov.uk/docs/New_sentences_guideline1.pdf.

(ix) a drug rehabilitation requirement (s 209);

(x)   an alcohol treatment requirement (s 212);

(xi) a supervision requirement (s 213); and

(xii) in a case where the offender is aged under 25, an attendance centre requirement (s 214).

Of greatest interest here is the 'mental health treatment requirement'.[62] A court may not impose a mental health treatment requirement unless satisfied on the evidence of a s 12 doctor that the offender's mental condition requires and may be susceptible to medical treatment but not so as to warrant a hospital or guardianship order. The court must be satisfied that arrangements have or can be made for the treatment intended to be specified in the order, and the offender must have expressed willingness to comply with the requirement.

Powers under a mental health treatment requirement

7.67 A mental health treatment requirement requires the offender to submit, during a period specified in the order, to treatment by or under the supervision of a doctor or a chartered psychologist (or both) 'with a view to the improvement of the offender's mental condition'. A community order can require treatment as an out-patient where the offender must accept treatment as a non-resident patient at any institution specified in the order, or treatment by or under the direction of such registered medical practitioner or chartered psychologist as may be specified. Treatment may be required as a resident patient in an independent nursing home or care home within the meaning of the Care Standards Act 2000 or a hospital, but not in a high security hospital. Beyond the above listed specifications, the court may not specify in the order the nature of the treatment to be given.

7.68 Section 208 empowers the doctor or psychologist in charge of treating an offender's mental condition under a mental health treatment requirement to arrange transfer where the offender consents and where the clinician is of the opinion that part of the treatment given by or under the direction of a doctor or a psychologist can be better or more conveniently given in or at an institution or place which is not specified in the relevant order. The requirement to accept treatment at the new location applies as if it had been part of the original order. Interestingly, the arrangements to transfer may provide for the offender to receive part of his treatment as a resident patient in an institution or place 'notwithstanding that the institution or place is not one which could have been specified for that purpose in the relevant order'. It is not clear whether this is intended to authorise admission to a high security hospital, which is not a power available to the court on making the initial order.

---

[62] CJA 2003, s 207.

Breach

7.69 Section 179 and Sch 8 deal with breach. Schedule 8 provides that where the responsible officer considers that an offender has failed to comply with a community order without reasonable excuse, he must issue a warning specifying the breach, stating that it is unacceptable, and that if there is a further breach within 12 months the offender will be liable to be brought before a court. If, within that period, the responsible officer considers there has been a further breach without reasonable excuse, he must lay an information before the magistrates or bring the matter before a Crown Court. The court may then deal with the offender as if for the original offence by attaching more onerous requirements to the community sentence, or by imprisoning the offender if the original offence was punishable by imprisonment. If an offender over 18 has willfully and persistently failed to comply with the requirements of the order, the magistrates or the Crown Court may impose a sentence for the original offence of up to 51 weeks even though that offence was not punishable by imprisonment. In deciding what to do in the event of persistent and willful non-compliance, the court must take into account the extent to which the offender has complied with the requirements of the community order.

The requirement of a medical report prior to imprisonment

7.70 Section 157 requires any court to obtain and consider a medical report before passing a custodial sentence on an offender who is or who appears to be mentally disordered within the meaning of the MHA 1983. The medical report may be made orally or in writing by a doctor approved under s 12 of the MHA 1983 by the Secretary of State as having special experience in the diagnosis or treatment of mental disorder. However, the obligation is not absolute and does not apply if, in the circumstances of the case, the court is of the opinion that it is unnecessary to obtain a medical report, or in any case where the sentence is fixed by law.

7.71 Where the offender appears to be mentally disordered, unless the sentence is fixed by law, the court must consider any information (whether or not it is in a report) relating to the offender's mental condition and the likely effect of a custodial sentence on the person's mental condition and on any treatment which may be available for it. Failure to obtain and consider a report does not invalidate any custodial sentence, but any court considering an appeal against sentence must obtain a medical report if none was obtained by the court below, and must consider any report obtained by it or by the court below.

7.72 Sections 224–236 of the Criminal Justice Act 2003 contain provisions relating to allowing dangerous offenders guilty of specified serious offences to be sentenced to life imprisonment, imprisonment for public protection or an extended sentence. Schedule 15 specifies the sexual and violent offences which render an offender eligible for dangerous offender sentencing. Section 37(1A) of the Mental Health Act 1983 provides that nothing in ss 225–228 of the Criminal Justice Act 2003 shall prevent a court from making a hospital order under s 37(1) of the MHA 1983. So if the court is satisfied that the criteria for making a hospital order are met, an offender need not be dealt with under the dangerousness sentencing provisions of the 2003 Act.

7.73 If an offender has committed a specified offence and meets the criterion of dangerousness, the court must impose a life sentence, imprisonment for public protection or an extended sentence. An offender is dangerous where the court is 'of the opinion that there is a significant risk to the public of serious harm occasioned by the commission by him of serious offences'. 'Serious harm' means death or serious personal injury, whether physical or psychological. Section 229 governs the way in which the courts are to assess dangerousness. In all cases the court must take into account any available information before it about the offences, about any pattern of behaviour of which it may form part, and about the offender. Section 229(3) creates a presumption of dangerousness where an offender over 18 has previously been convicted of a relevant offence. The court must assume risk of serious harm to the public unless the court considers, after considering the information outlined above that it would be unreasonable to conclude that there is such a risk. The dangerous offender provisions are beyond the scope of this book. Suffice to say that offenders with personality disorders are more likely than their mentally ill counterparts to receive a dangerous offender sentence.

7.74 As noted above, nothing in ss 225–228 of the Criminal Justice Act 2003 prevents a court from making a hospital order under s 37(1) of the MHA 1983. So if the court is satisfied that the criteria for making a hospital order are met, an offender need not be dealt with under the dangerousness sentencing provisions of the 2003 Act and may be given a hospital order instead.

THE HOSPITAL ORDER (MHA 1983, S 37)

7.75 A hospital order sentences a mentally disordered person to detention in hospital for treatment rather than in gaol. A hospital order may be imposed without restrictions in which case the patient's responsible clinician ('RC') may discharge the patient without recourse to higher authority, and the detention is renewed in the same way as detention under s 3. If a restriction order is imposed by a Crown Court (see paras **7.82–7.89** below) this will be without limit of time, and there is no need for the RC to renew detention. The patient may not be discharged by the RC. Only the Home Secretary or the MHRT may direct discharge. In 1995–1996, 536 hospital orders without restrictions on discharge were made. This figure has declined to 322 in 2005–2006. At the same time the number of restriction orders was 321 in 1995–1996, declined to 235 in 2003–2004 and has since risen to 322 in 2005–2006. This is the first time that there have been equal numbers of non-restricted and restricted hospital orders made during the year.

7.76 If sent to prison a mentally disordered person can only be treated under the terms of ss 5 and 6 of the Mental Capacity Act 2005 which authorise treatment without consent of a person who lacks capacity and who needs treatment in his own best interests, and authorise restraint of a mentally incapacitated person where necessary and a proportionate response to prevent harm to the person. A person, whether or not they lack capacity, may also be treated without consent under common law, where restraint and treatment may be authorised where they represent the minimum force necessary to prevent that person from harming others. People who are detained under the MHA 1983 may be given treatment without consent subject to the second opinion safeguards in Part 4.

7.77 A hospital order may be made by magistrates or by the Crown Court. The Crown Court can make an order if the person is convicted of an offence punishable with imprisonment, except in the case of murder (for which the sentence is fixed by law). A magistrates' court can make a hospital order without recording a conviction if the person is suffering from mental illness or severe mental impairment, and the court is satisfied that he committed the act with which he is charged.[63] One of the two doctors giving evidence must be approved under s 12 of the MHA 1983. An order authorises detention for up to six months in the first instance, renewable for a further six months, and then for periods of one year at a time. Under the MHA 2007 the old categories of mental disorder will cease to be relevant and the court will be required to be satisfied that:

(a)   the offender is suffering from mental disorder ('any disorder or disability of mind') of a nature or degree making it appropriate for him to be detained in hospital for medical treatment; and

(b)   that appropriate treatment is available for him.

The court must also be of the opinion, having regard to all the circumstances, including the nature of the offence and the character and antecedents of the offender, and to other methods of dealing with him, that the most suitable method of disposing of the case is by means of a hospital order.

7.78 Even if the criteria for making a hospital order are met, the court still has considerable discretion to consider other alternatives such as a dangerous offender sentence. Guidance was given by the Court of Appeal in *R v Birch* on the circumstances where prison might be chosen as an alternative for a patient found to be suffering from mental disorder.[64] The first is where the offender is dangerous and there is no suitable secure hospital bed. The second is where there was an element of culpability for the offence which merited punishment. This might happen where there is no connection between the mental disorder and the offence, or where the offender's responsibility for the offence 'is diminished but not extinguished'. In *R v Drew*[65] the House of Lords held that under both national law and the European Convention case-law a sentence of

---

[63]   MHA 1983, s 37(3).
[64]   (1989) 11 Cr App R (S) 202 at 215, CA.
[65]   [2003] UKHL 25.

imprisonment could be imposed on a mentally disordered defendant who was criminally responsible and fit to be tried.

7.79 Appropriate treatment can include psychological treatment, care, habilitation and rehabilitation and is defined as treatment which is intended to alleviate or prevent deterioration in the patient's condition. The new definition of mental disorder means that people with learning disability, people with mental illness and people with personality disorders (who are thought to benefit most from psychological interventions such as cognitive behaviour therapy) may be detained if their disorder is of a nature or degree making it appropriate for them to be detained for treatment.

7.80 A hospital order cannot be made unless the court is satisfied, on the evidence of the approved clinician who would have overall responsibility for his case or the hospital managers, that arrangements have been made for the patient's admission to hospital within 28 days. Thus the hospital has the discretion to decide whether to admit an offender; in some cases under the MHA 1959, mentally disordered people were sentenced to imprisonment because hospitals refused to accept them. Section 39 of the MHA 1983 therefore, empowers a court considering making a hospital order, an interim hospital order, or a hospital direction with a restriction direction to request the Primary Care Trust or Health Authority where the person resides or last resided or any other Health Authority or PCT which appears to be appropriate to furnish the court with such information as they can reasonably obtain with respect to the hospital or hospitals in their area or elsewhere where arrangements could be made for the admission of the offender. The Trust or Authority approached by the Court must comply with any such request.

7.81 The effect of a hospital order is similar to that of an admission for treatment as a non-offender under s 3. Detention is renewed under s 20, the patient has the right to apply for discharge to the MHRT on the same basis as a patient detained under s 3, and treatment for mental disorder is subject to Part 4 of the MHA 1983. The most important difference is that a hospital order patient cannot be discharged by his nearest relative. A hospital order can be made with or without a s 41 'restriction order' imposing restrictions on discharge.

RESTRICTION ORDER (MHA 1983, S 41)

7.82 Where a hospital order has been made, a Crown Court may make a restriction order. A magistrates' court has no power to make a restriction order, but if the criteria are met, it may commit an offender over fourteen years of age to the Crown Court where a restriction order can be made. The evidence of one of the two doctors supporting the hospital order must have been given orally. In 2005–2006 Department of Health figures indicate that 322 hospital orders with restriction orders were made by courts. Home Office data show that in

1995, 1,548 patients subject to restriction orders were resident in hospitals under detention, including 264 women. By 2005 that figure had risen to 2,344, 411 of whom were women.[66]

7.83   The grounds for making a restriction order are that it appears to the court, having regard to the nature of the offence, the antecedents of the offender, and the risk of his committing further offences if set at large, that a restriction order is necessary for the protection of the public from serious harm. The Court of Appeal in *R v Birch*[67] held that the sentencing court is required to assess the seriousness of the risk not that he will re-offend, but the risk that if he does, the public will suffer serious harm. The harm in question need not be limited to personal injury, nor need it relate to the public in general, but the potential harm must be serious, and a high possibility of the recurrence of minor offences will not be sufficient.

7.84   Where the medical opinion is unanimous that a restriction order should be imposed and there is a secure bed, a decision not to impose a hospital order should not be made because of concerns about risk to the public should the offender be released.[68] However, if the doctors giving medical evidence are not unanimous about a hospital disposal, the sentencing decision is for the judge to resolve in the light of all the evidence and the circumstances of the case.[69]

7.85   The MHA 1983 provided for restriction order to be made for either a specified period or without limit of time. The possibility of a time limited restriction order has been removed by s 40(1) of the Mental Health Act 2007.

7.86   The effect of a restriction order is that a patient does not have to have his or her detention renewed by the hospital managers. Detention carries on, subject to a requirement on the responsible clinician to submit a report at least once a year 'on that person'. The patient cannot be granted leave of absence, transferred or discharged by the responsible clinician or hospital managers without the consent of the Secretary of State for Justice. This is dealt with by the Mental Health Unit in the Ministry of Justice. If the patient is discharged with Home Office permission this may be absolutely or subject to conditions. Except in rare cases (such as extreme age) where the offender is assessed as posing no risk, conditional discharge will be the route chosen.

7.87   Restriction order patients used to have only limited rights to challenge detention. A patient detained for treatment under the civil power (s 3) or by a criminal court under a hospital order (s 37), has the right to apply to a Mental Health Review Tribunal ('MHRT') to seek discharge. The MHRT must order discharge if not satisfied that the patient is suffering from mental disorder of a nature or degree warranting detention. Under the MHA 1959 restriction order patients did not have this right. They could only ask the Home Secretary to

---

[66]   Home Office *Statistics of Mentally Disordered Offenders 2005* (Statistical Bulletin 05/07), p 4.
[67]   (1989) 11 Cr App R (S) 202.
[68]   *R v Howell* (1985) 7 Cr App R (S) 360, CA.
[69]   *R v Reid* [2005] EWCA Crim 392, CA.

refer their case to a MHRT, and the tribunal did not have the power to order release, only to advise the Home Secretary to exercise his power of discharge.

7.88 The MHRT's lack of power to order discharge was held in *X v United Kingdom*[70] to breach the requirement in Art 5(4) that a person detained because of unsoundness of mind must be able, at intervals, to seek review of the lawfulness of their detention before a court or tribunal *with the power to order release*. The MHA 1983 now authorises a MHRT to order the absolute or conditional discharge of a restriction order patient if not satisfied that the conditions of detention are met (mental disorder of a nature or degree warranting confinement). This introduced the possibility that an offender patient might persuade a tribunal to discharge him when the Home Office (now the Ministry of Justice) Mental Health Unit still considered discharge to pose too great a risk, hence removing the absolute control exercised by the Ministry of Justice over the duration of detention of offenders sentenced to restriction orders without limit of time.

7.89 In *R v A*[71] the Court of Appeal held that the risk that an offender might be released prematurely by a MHRT is not a ground for a court to pass a life sentence rather than making a restriction order, since the composition and powers of the MHRT and the Parole Board panels are 'closely analogous'. Each consists of a legally qualified president who has experience in the criminal courts, a psychiatrist and a lay member. The figures show that since 1990 the MHRT gives many more conditional discharges than the Home secretary. In 2002, of the 357 conditional discharges of restricted patients 280 were by the MHRT and 77 were by the Home Office Mental Health Unit. This has been the pattern for the past decade.

Conditional discharge

7.90 The restriction order with its conditional discharge option is seen as an effective means of risk management. Re-offending rates in terms of serious sexual offences or violent offences of the 717 patients conditionally discharged between 1999 and 2003 are assessed by the Home Office as averaging 2 per cent.[72]

7.91 A restriction order patient can be discharged by the Secretary of State for Justice or a MHRT either absolutely or subject to conditions. If the patient is given an absolute discharge, both the hospital and restriction orders cease to have effect, and he cannot be recalled to hospital. A conditionally discharged restricted patient may, for example, be directed to live in a specified place, to attend for treatment, and to accept treatment by or under the direction of the responsible clinician. Because it may be a condition of discharge that the patient must accept treatment for mental disorder, a conditionally discharged

---

[70] (1981) 4 EHRR 188, ECtHR.
[71] [2005] EWCA Crim 2077, CA.
[72] Home Office *Statistics of Mentally Disordered Offenders 2005* (Statistical Bulletin 05/07), p 14.

restricted patient is not eligible to seek review of treatment by a second opinion doctor under Part 4 of the MHA 1983.

GUARDIANSHIP ORDER (MHA 1983, S 37)

7.92 As Jones points out, 'Little use has been made of guardianship orders by the courts', with figures running at under 30 cases per year.[73] The diagnostic criteria for making an order are that the offender must be sixteen or over, and suffering from any disorder or disability of mind warranting reception into guardianship. The court has wide discretion to decide whether guardianship is 'suitable', since it must be of the opinion, having regard to all the circumstances, including the nature of the offence and the character and antecedents of the offender and to other methods of dealing with him, that the most suitable method of disposing of the case is by means of a guardianship order.

7.93 The medical evidentiary requirements for making a guardianship order are virtually the same as for making a hospital order. The court enjoys similar powers to request information to those available for hospital order cases request. Under s 39A, a court considering making a guardianship order will be empowered to request the local social services authority (or any other social services authority considered by the court to be appropriate):

(a) to inform the court whether it or any person authorised by it is prepared to receive the patient into guardianship; and

(b) if so, to give such information as it reasonably can about how it or the other person could be expected to exercise guardianship powers.

TRANSFER TO HOSPITAL OF SENTENCED PRISONERS (SS 47 AND 49)

7.94 Section 47 allows for the transfer of a sentenced prisoner to hospital by Home Secretary's direction. Section 49 empowers the Home Secretary to attach a restriction direction, imposing restrictions on discharge. By far the majority of transfers are subject to restrictions. In 1995–1996, 222 patients were transferred under ss 47 and 49. In 2005–2006 the figure was 273. The equivalent figures for s 47 transfers without restrictions were 31 for 1995–1996 and 56 for 2005–2006.[74] In 1995, 402 prisoners were resident in hospital having been

---

[73] Ibid, p 230.

[74] National Statistics Information Centre (NSIC) *In-patients formally detained in hospitals under the Mental Health Act 1983 and other legislation, NHS Trusts, Care Trusts, Primary Care Trusts and Independent Hospitals, England; 1995–1996 to 2005–2006* (2007). See

transferred under ss 47 and 49 restrictions. Since 2003 the numbers of in-patients have begun to rise significantly, the total for 2005 being 561.[75]

7.95 If no restriction direction is made, detention lasts for up to six months, renewable for six months and then for periods of one year at a time. If a restriction direction is made, the restrictions expire on the earliest date on which the offender would have been released from prison (the earliest release date); thereafter, the patient is detained as if he were a patient under a s 37 hospital order without restrictions, and may be discharged by the clinical supervisor or the Mental Health Review Tribunal without recourse to the Ministry of Justice.

7.96 Before issuing a direction the Secretary of State for Justice must be satisfied that the prisoner is:

(a)   suffering from mental disorder (any disorder or disability of mind); and

(b)   the mental disorder is of a nature or degree which makes it appropriate for him to be detained in hospital for medical treatment; and

(c)   that appropriate medical treatment is available for him; and

(d)   having regard to the public interest and to all the other circumstances, a transfer is expedient.

The direction must be based on two medical reports, one from a doctor approved under s 12.

7.97 The initial version of the Mental Health Act Code of Practice (1993) stated that the need for in-patient treatment of a prisoner must be identified and acted on swiftly, and contact made urgently between the prison doctor and the hospital doctor. It also emphasises that the transfer of a prisoner to hospital should not be delayed until close to his release date, since a transfer in such circumstances may well be seen by the prisoner as being primarily intended to extend his detention.[76] These paragraphs no longer appear in the Code, but have been replaced by a short statement that:[77]

> 'The need for in-patient treatment for a prisoner should be identified and acted upon quickly and contact made immediately with the responsible PCT by Prison Health Care staff.'

http://www.ic.nhs.uk/statistics-and-data-collections/health-and-lifestyles/mental-health/in-patients-formally-detained-in-hospitals-under-the-mental-health-act-1983-and-other-legislation-nhs-trusts-care-trusts-primary-care-trusts-and-independent-hospitals;-2005-06.

[75]   Home Office *Statistics of Mentally Disordered Offenders 2005* (Statistical Bulletin 05/07), p 4.

[76]   Department of Health and Welsh Office *Mental Health Act 1983 Code of Practice*, paras 3.12–3.13.

[77]   Department of Health *Mental Health Act 1983 Draft Revised Code of Practice* (2007), para 36.25. See http://www.dh.gov.uk/en/Consultations.

The Mental Health Act Commission have expressed their continuing concern that transfers late in the sentence are distorting mental health law by using it for primarily public protection purposes, and that transfer should take place as soon as is therapeutically indicated rather than being delayed until risk is the primary factor.[78]

Restriction direction

7.98 Where the Secretary of State for Justice thinks fit, he may attach to a transfer direction a restriction direction. If a restriction direction is not given, or once it expires because the prisoner's earliest release date has passed, the offender is detained 'as if' under a hospital order without restrictions, sometimes known as 'a notional s 37'. Patients transferred from prison to hospital are entitled to make applications to have their cases referred to MHRTs. If the Secretary of State for Justice is notified by the clinical supervisor, another clinician or the MHRT that the offender no longer requires treatment in hospital, he has two options: he can either discharge an offender who would have been eligible for release on parole had he remained in prison, or he can direct that he be returned to prison to serve the remainder of his sentence. This means that the Secretary of State for Justice retains greater control over the duration of detention of a transferred prisoner with a restriction direction than he does over a restriction order patient. To comply with Art 5 of the European Convention a tribunal must have the power to discharge a restriction order patient, but because a transferred person is a prisoner, the Secretary of State for Justice may remit them to prison to serve out their term. This fact was undoubtedly one of the inspirations behind the introduction of the hybrid order under s 45A (discussed below).

TRANSFER OF UN-SENTENCED PRISONERS TO HOSPITAL (S 48)

7.99 Section 48 provides the same power of transfer from prison to psychiatric hospital of civil prisoners, remand prisoners and prisoners detained under Immigration legislation. Under the MHA 2007 the Secretary of State for Justice will have to be satisfied:

(a) that the person is suffering from mental disorder (again the new braod definition of any disorder or disability of mind) of a nature or degree which makes it appropriate for him to be detained in hospital for medical treatment; and

(b) he is in urgent need of such treatment; and

(c) appropriate medical treatment is available for him.

---

[78] Mental Health Act Commission *Placed Among Strangers* (Thirteenth Biennial Report 2005–2007, TSO, 2007), pp 382–383.

The same requirements for medical reports apply to s 48 as apply to a transfer direction under s 47. The main difference between ss 47 and 48 is that for the latter the need for treatment must be urgent.

7.100 In 1995–1996 there were 359 transfers of un-sentenced prisoners with restriction directions, and 51 without. In 2005–2006 there were 361 with restrictions and 14 without.[79] In 1995, 183 prisoners were resident in hospital having been transferred under s 48 with s 49 restrictions. The figures since have been between 140 and 190 per year. The total population for 2005 was slightly up at 218.[80] Under the MHA 1983 the power was confined to people with mental illness or severe mental impairment. The MHA 2007 extends it to patients with any form of disorder or disability of mind. This may prove important and may lead to increased use, since transfer of remand prisoners is an important power to rescue people who may be at risk of suicide or self harm due to mental illness such as depression but who equally might need urgent treatment to prevent risk to self or others brought on by personality problems. Patients transferred under s 48 may be given treatment under the regime of powers and second opinions in Part 4 of the MHA 1983.

HOSPITAL DIRECTIONS AND RESTRICTION DIRECTIONS (S 45A)

7.101 Section 45A, introduced into the MHA 1983 by the Crime (Sentences) Act 1997 provides for a 'hybrid order' whereby a mentally disordered offender may be given a sentence of imprisonment coupled with an immediate direction to hospital. Initially confined to people with a personality disorder diagnosis, the MHA 2007 extends this to people with any disorder or disability of mind. The conditions which must be met before a court may impose a hospital and restriction direction are that there must be written or oral evidence from two doctors:

(a)   that the offender is suffering from mental disorder;

(b)   that the mental disorder from which the offender is suffering is of a nature or degree which makes it appropriate for him to be detained in a hospital for medical treatment; and

(c)   that appropriate medical treatment is available for him.

---

[79]   National Statistics Information Centre (NSIC) *In-patients formally detained in hospitals under the Mental Health Act 1983 and other legislation, NHS Trusts, Care Trusts, Primary Care Trusts and Independent Hospitals, England; 1995–1996 to 2005–2006* (2007). See http://www.ic.nhs.uk/statistics-and-data-collections/health-and-lifestyles/mental-health/in-patients-formally-detained-in-hospitals-under-the-mental-health-act-1983-and-other-legislation-nhs-trusts-care-trusts-primary-care-trusts-and-independent-hospitals;-2005-06.

[80]   Home Office *Statistics of Mentally Disordered Offenders 2005* (Statistical Bulletin 05/07), p 4.

The result of this is that, although directed initially to hospital, the offender has the legal status of prisoner rather than patient. This means that in the event of the mental disorder being successfully treated before the expiry of the prison sentence the offender can be returned to prison to serve the remainder of the tariff sentence. The offender is given a prison sentence which is calculated in accordance with normal sentencing principles, but is directed to hospital in the first instance. If he recovers prior to the expiry of the sentence, he will be remitted to prison to serve the remaining sentence. This avoids the problem of the MHRTs discharging patients 'early', because if the offender is no longer mentally disordered, the Home Secretary has the ultimate say in whether he returns to prison. The hybrid order was initially confined to patients with psychopathic disorder, but the MHA 2007 extends it to anyone suffering from mental disorder in the broad sense of 'any disorder or disability of mind'.

7.102 The MHAC have criticised of the Home Office for its suggestion that hybrid orders 'could provide a punitive element in the disposal … to reflect the offenders whole or partial responsibility'.[81] They adopt Bartlett and Sandland's argument that it is purportedly the aim of mental health disposals to divert the mentally disordered from punitive sanctions and the hybrid orders require clinicians to become involved in determining levels of criminal responsibility and to engage in the process of deciding what is a suitable punishment.[82]

7.103 Home Office Guidance has dropped reference to criminal responsibility, preferring instead to stress that the power should be used in two situations. First is where the alternative would be a mandatory life sentence under the 'two strikes and you're out' provision in s 109 of the Powers of Criminal Courts (Sentencing) Act 2000 which provides, absent exceptional circumstances, for a mandatory life sentence on conviction of a second serious offence. Mental disorder is not an exceptional circumstance. The second situation is where it would be the most effective way to protect the public from further harm.[83] If the Home Office entertained hopes that this provision would be widely used, they have been disappointed. The courts have not used the power extensively. Since 2000, the total number of patients in hospital in any year under a hospital direction and restriction direction has never risen above 11.

7.104 The MHAC remain concerned that hybrid orders if they are to be used at all should not become the normal disposal for any mentally disordered offender whom the court views as criminally responsible to some degree. They are also worried about imposition of punishment alongside medical treatment may undermine treatment compliance and foster a sense of 'doing time'.

---

[81]　Mental Health Act Commission *In Place of Fear* (Eleventh Biennial Report 2003–2005, TSO, 2006), pp 389–394.

[82]　P Bartlett and R Sandland *Mental Health Law Policy and Practice* (OUP, 3rd edn, 2007).

[83]　Home Office *Guidance on the Crime Sentences Act 1997*, para 3.

Moreover, since mental illness may be relapsing and episodic a return to prison might trigger relapse and result in a form of ping pong between prison and hospital throughout the tariff period.[84]

VICTIMS

7.105 In keeping with the general move to increase the legal rights of victims of crime to make representations in relation to disposal and release, ss 36–38 of the Domestic Violence, (Crime and Victims) Act 2004 provide that where a person convicted of a violent or sexual offence defined in s 45 of the 2004 Act is given a hospital order with restrictions or a hospital and limitation direction the local probation board must take all reasonable steps to ascertain whether the person who appears to be the victim of the offence or who appears to act for the victim wishes to make representations about whether the offender should be subject to any conditions if discharged or wishes to receive information about any conditions which may be imposed. If the person makes representations, the local probation board must forward them to the body making the decision on discharge.

7.106 Section 48 of, and Sch 6 to, the Mental Health Act 2007 significantly amend Chapter 2 of Part 3 of the Domestic Violence, Crime and Victims Act 2004. These provisions entitle a victim or any person acting for a victim of a sexual or violent offence where the offender is subject to a restriction order or and restriction direction, to be notified of their right to make representations to the local probation board about whether the patient should be subject to any conditions in the event of his conditional discharge from hospital and if so what those conditions should be. Schedule 6 to the MHA 2007 extends this right to victims of sexual or violent offences where the offender is sentenced to a hospital order without restrictions, or is given a transfer direction without restrictions.

7.107 In such cases the victim or representative is entitled to make representations as to what conditions the patient should be subject to in the event of his discharge from hospital under a community treatment order.[85] The victim or representative is entitled to receive information about any conditions that are imposed on discharge.[86] Furthermore, where the offender is subject to a hospital order without restrictions, the victim may ask to make representations or to receive information, and if they do so the probation board must notify the victim of the hospital's name and address and the hospital must be notified of the victim's address.[87] The probation board is required to forward any representations made to the person or body

---

[84] Mental Health Act Commission *In Place of Fear* (Eleventh Biennial Report 2003–2005, TSO, 2006), pp 392–393.

[85] Domestic Violence, Crime and Victims Act 2004, s 36(5).

[86] Domestic Violence, Crime and Victims Act 2004, s 36(6).

[87] Domestic Violence, Crime and Victims Act 2004, s 36A.

responsible for determining matters to do with discharge, ending of restrictions, conditional discharge or discharge subject to a community treatment order.

7.108 The changes to the Domestic Violence, Crime and Victims Act 2004 require responsible clinicians, Mental Health Review Tribunals, and the Secretary of State (in the case of a restricted patient) when considering whether to discharge to notify the hospital managers who must notify the local probation board, and give victims the chance to make representations and information about discharge and conditions. Since the 2004 Act came into force MHRTs have been granting rights to victims to make representations in relation to discharge and conditions of discharge. The changes to the Domestic Violence, Crime and Victims Act 2004 are significant in that they require responsible clinicians of all offender patients who have committed sexual or violent offences to consider the victim's representations before discharging either conditionally or under a community treatment order. Tribunals too must consider the victim's representations.

CONCLUSION

7.109 The Department of Health's *Offender Mental Health Care Pathway (2005)* provides a best practice template and aims to meet two targets: first, no one with acute severe mental illness should be in prison; and, second, prisons should be safe places for other people with mental health problems, with a particular focus on the creation of in reach services and suicide prevention. With a prison population now over 80,000, limited capacity in the psychiatric services, and overcrowding rife in British jails, these goals are far from realisation. The small numbers transferred from prison of around 800 per year represents less than one per cent of the prison population. The 3,500 restricted patients equal just over four per cent of the prison population. It cannot seriously be doubted that there are many people in the prison system who are in need of hospital treatment for mental disorder.

7.110 This chapter has examined the mechanisms for diverting mentally disordered offenders from the penal system to the mental health system, and has revealed a certain convergence between the powers of detention under the respective regimes. Mental health law and penal law each provide a range of options for indeterminate detention with closely supervised discharge either via MHA restriction orders or CTOs, or CJA dangerousness sentences followed by release on licence subject to close supervision. The advantage of indeterminate detention has been transplanted from the psychiatric system to the penal system. Before a prisoner assessed as high risk for causing serious harm emerges from prison following a determinate sentence, he may be transferred to hospital under s 47. If he falls through the net and is released, he or she will be subject to the Multi-Agency Public Protection Panel system established by the Criminal Justice and Court Services Act 2000. These are joint committees including police, probation, health, social services and housing to assess and manage risks posed by violent or sexual offenders. These are intended to identify people who may require admission to hospital under civil powers on grounds of risk before they commit an offence.

7.111 Mental health and penal law each have a network of community powers with the capacity to impose significant limits on freedom of movement, to choose residence, and to refuse treatment for mental disorder alcoholism or drug addiction. In addition any condition may be attached to a patient's community treatment order which is either necessary or appropriate to secure that the patient receives medical treatment or to prevent risk to self or others. This could include the power to impose a curfew or restrictions of movement on an individual. Here we see strong cross-fertilisation between conditional discharged restricted patient status, anti social behaviour orders ('ASBOs') under the Crime and Disorder Act 1998, community orders under the Criminal Justice Act 2003, and community treatment orders under the Mental Health Act. Obligations under a community treatment order may only include such limits on behaviour as are necessary to manage risk, not exactly an onerous restriction of the range of conditions which may be applied. The range of controls available under all of these measures has effectively meant that anyone subject to them is broadly in a similar position to a conditionally discharged restricted patient. Compulsory Community powers are considered in Chapter 8.

Chapter 8

COMPULSORY POWERS IN THE COMMUNITY

OVERVIEW

8.1   Under the Mental Health Act 1983 there were three compulsory powers over patients in the community:

(1)   guardianship under ss 7 or 37;

(2)   extended leave under s 17;

(3)   after-care under supervision under ss 25A–25J, repealed and replaced by ss 17A–17G which introduce the new 'community treatment orders' ('CTOs') also referred to in the MHA 2007 as supervised community treatment ('SCT').

Neither guardianship nor after-care under supervision is much used (see note to para **2.24** above). Section 17 leave is the most frequently used vehicle for imposing control over patients in the community. The main reason for its attractiveness is its simplicity. It is granted and may be revoked on the authority of a single clinician. The ultimate sanction for non-compliance is detention, if the clinician considers continued non-compliance will make it necessary to recall the patient for the patient's health or safety or for the protection of others. The difficulty is that, in order for recall to be an effective sanction, there must be a bed available for the patient to be recalled to.

8.2   The most relevant Convention case law on compulsion in the community is the 1988 Commission decision in *L v Sweden,* where a decision provisionally to release someone who had been detained in a psychiatric hospital was held to constitute a potential interference with his right to respect for private life. However, the Commission declared the application manifestly ill-founded, that the measure was justified in the interests of the person's health under Art 8(2) and that the applicant could not be said to have an 'arguable claim' of a violation of Art 8.[1] If compulsory powers are necessary on grounds of health,

---

[1]   *(Application 10801/84)* Decisions and Reports of the European Commission of Human Rights, vol 45, pp 181–189 (Decision of 20 January 1986 on admissibility). Report of the Commission (adopted on 3 October 1988), para 93.

to prevent crime, or to protect the rights and freedoms of others, the interference can be justified provided it is necessary in a democratic society and is done in accordance with law.

8.3   This Chapter considers guardianship and guardianship orders under ss 7 and 37, extended leave under s 17, Supervised Community Treatment ('SCT') under ss 17A–17G, and conditional discharge of restricted patients under Part 3 of the MHA 1983. Before discussing these powers it is important to understand the policy and legal framework of community care services for mentally disordered people and their carers.

THE LEGAL AND POLICY FRAMEWORK OF COMMUNITY CARE

8.4   Before the decision is taken to discharge or grant leave to a patient, or place a patient under SCT, the RC is responsible for ensuring, in consultation with the other professionals concerned, that the patient's needs for health and social care are fully assessed and the care plan addresses them. The RC is also responsible for ensuring that:

(1)   a proper assessment is made of risks to the patient or other people and that plans, services and support are available to manage any risks;

(2)   in the case of offender patients, the circumstances of any victim and their families are taken into account; and

(3)   consideration is given to whether the patient meets the criteria for guardianship or Supervised Community Treatment.[2]

The administrative framework within which care is to be provided is the Care Programme Approach ('CPA'), based on United States models of care management.

Care programme approach

8.5   All service users, whether or not they have been detained, who have been in contact with the specialist psychiatric service are entitled to be dealt with under the CPA. The CPA requires a risk assessment, a needs assessment, a written care plan which will be regularly reviewed and a key worker (now known as a care co-ordinator). In 1996 the CPA was extended to all patients receiving care from the specialist psychiatric services.[3] The current guidance on

---

2   Draft Illustrative Code, paras 27.5–27.6.
3   NHS Executive *Audit Pack for Monitoring the Care Programme Approach: Background and Explanatory Notes* (NHS Executive, 1996, HSG 96(6)).

the CPA is *Modernising the Care Programme Approach*.[4] This provides that there are two levels of CPA, standard and enhanced. Standard CPA is for people whose mental illness is less severe or who have low risk factors or have an active informal support network. But a major reason why a patient with a severe mental illness will be found to have low risk factors is if they are receiving intensive support from their informal support network. Their needs may be great but they will be assigned to standard CPA and this will be significant because CPA is used as a rationing tool, and some social services authorities have tried to limit services to both patients and carers to those who are on enhanced CPA. People are on enhanced CPA if their mental disorder is assessed as posing a potential risk to their own safety or to that of other people. Resources follow risk. The Government is currently discussing proposals to dispense with standard CPA and introduce a new system whereby eligibility would be restricted to those currently on enhanced CPA. In *R (on the application of HP) v London Borough of Islington* it was held to be unlawful to rule out providing services under s 47 of the National Health Service and Community Care Act 1990 because someone was not eligible for CPA.[5]

Section 117 of the Mental Health Act 1983

8.6   Section 117 of the MHA 1983 places a duty jointly on Primary Care Trusts and social services authorities, in co-operation with relevant voluntary agencies, to provide after-care services for patients who have been detained in hospital for treatment under s 3, under a s 37 hospital order with or without restrictions, under a s 45A hospital direction, or following transfer from prison under ss 47 or 48 with or without restrictions. The duty applies when the patient ceases to be detained and leaves hospital, whether or not immediately after so ceasing. The duty continues until the health and local social services authorities are satisfied that the person concerned is no longer in need of such services, 'but they shall not be so satisfied in the case of a community patient while he remains such a patient'.[6] Patients on SCT remain entitled to s 117 after-care services throughout the duration of their Community Treatment Order ('CTO').

8.7   Section 117 services are community care services under s 46 of the National Health Service and Community Care Act 1990. Section 47 provides that where it appears to a local authority that any person for whom they may provide or arrange to provide community care services may be in need of any such services, the authority:

(a)   shall carry out an assessment of his needs for those services; and

---

4   Care Programme Approach Association *The Care Programme Approach Handbook* (Chesterfield, 2003).
5   *R (on the application of HP) v London Borough of Islington* [2004] EWHC 7 (Admin).
6   MHA 1983, s 117(2).

(b) having regard to the results of that assessment, shall then decide whether his needs call for the provision by them of any such services.[7]

There is a two stage process of needs assessment followed by a care provision decision. A person for whom the LSSA is responsible, who is being considered for discharge, extended leave or a CTO will be someone who appears to the local authority to be in potential need of community care services. Local authorities may lawfully employ eligibility criteria.[8] Unlike other community care services, for which the service user may be charged, it is unlawful to charge for s 117 after-care.[9]

8.8   In *R (on the application of H) v Secretary of State for the Home Department*[10] the House of Lords ruled on the nature of the health authority's duty when a MHRT defers a patient's conditional discharge, pending the provision of community care services, which in this case included supervision by a psychiatrist. The House of Lords held that:

> 'The duty of the health authority, was not absolute, whether it arose under s 117 of the 1983 Act or in response to the tribunal's order. The authorities had to use their best endeavours to procure compliance with the conditions laid down by the tribunal. This they had done.'

The authorities were not under an absolute duty to secure compliance with a MHRT's order for deferred discharge. They had not been able to find a psychiatrist who considered that IH could be safely supervised in the community. The House left open the question whether a clinician who declines to supervise a community patient could be a hybrid public authority for the purposes of the Human Rights Act 1998.

Relevant authorities

8.9   In *R v Mental Health Review Tribunal, ex parte Hall* Scott Baker LJ held that:[11]

> 'For the purposes of s 117 of the 1983 Act, the relevant health and social services authorities were those for the area where the patient was ordinarily resident at the time of his detention, unless he had no place of residence. In the latter case, the relevant authorities would be those of the area where the patient was sent on discharge, but the placing authority where the patient resided did not cease to be the appropriate local social services authority by virtue of the fact that he was sent to a different authority on discharge.'

---

[7]   National Health Service and Community Care Act 1990, s 47.
[8]   *R v Gloucestershire County Council, ex parte Barry* [1997] 2 All ER 1, HL.
[9]   *R v Manchester City Council, ex parte Stennett* [2002] UKHL 34, [2002] 4 All ER 124, HL.
[10] [2003] UKHL 59.
[11] [1999] 3 All ER 132, QBD.

Carers' rights

8.10 Many mentally disordered service users depend on the support of carers to enable them to survive in the community without need for frequent admission to hospital. The National Service Frameworks for Mental Health for England and Wales emphasise service user and carer involvement in the planning and delivery of services and ideals of equity and empowerment.[12]

8.11 A carer is someone who provides or intends to provide a substantial amount of care to a disabled person (including someone disabled by mental disorder) on a regular (not necessarily frequent) basis. Caring for someone with a mental illness may not involve hands-on physical or practical care on a regular basis, but it does require constant vigilance, and if relapse seems imminent or actually occurs, intense support of an emotional and a practical nature. The physical and psychological impact on carers can be significant. The final requirement to be a carer is that the person must not be a paid professional carer, and must indicate the wish to be a carer of the patient. The Practice Guidance states that 'willingness'[13] to care 'should not be assumed', and that carers should have the 'freedom to choose the nature of the tasks they will perform and how much time they will give to their caring role'.

8.12 The Carers (Recognition and Services) Act 1995 provides that during a community care needs assessment local authorities must consider whether there are any carers, and, where they think it appropriate, must consult those carers. Section 1(2) of the 1995 Act provides that the carer may request the local authority, before they make a service provision decision, to carry out an assessment of the carer's ability to provide and continue to provide care.

8.13 The Carers and Disabled Children Act 2000 entitles the carer to an assessment of their own need for support services to enable them to carry on caring for the person, a move towards recognising the carer as a separate entity from the cared for person. A carer's assessment may be requested even if the disabled person refuses a community care assessment for themselves. Where a carer asks for an assessment, the local authority must carry one out, deciding first whether the carer has needs in relation to the care being provided, secondly whether those needs could be wholly or partly satisfied by local authority services, and thirdly whether to provide services to the carer. The right to a

---

[12] Department of Health *National Service Framework for Mental Health England* (1999) at http://www.dh.gov.uk/PolicyAndGuidance/HealthAndSocialCareTopics/ HealthAndSocialCareArticle/fs/en?CONTENT_ID=4070951&chk=W3ar/W; Welsh Assembly Government *National Framework for Adult Mental Health Services in Wales* (2001) at http://www.wales.nhs.uk/sites3/docmetadata.cfm?orgid=438&id=48286&pid=11071; Welsh Assembly Government *Mental Health Policy Guidance: The Care Programme Approach for Mental Health Service Users* (2003) at http://www.wales.nhs.uk/sites3/Documents/438/ mental%2Dhealth%2Dpolicy%2Dimple%2Dguide%2De%2Epdf; Welsh Assembly Government *Revised National Service Framework for Adult Mental Health Services Wales* (2005) at http://www.wales.nhs.uk/sites3/page.cfm?orgid=438&pid=11071.

[13] Department of Health *Practice Guidance under the Carers and Disabled Children Act 2000* (2000), para 68. See www.carers.gov.uk/pdfs/practiceguidecarersparents.pdf.

separate assessment can be particularly important where the care recipient has mental disorder and may refuse a community care assessment. The Act recognises that often the best way of supporting the carer is to provide breaks from the caring role, through 'respite care', which may involve providing services to the cared for person. Section 2(3) provides that although a service is provided to the carer, it may take the form of a service delivered to the person cared for, as long as it does not include anything 'of an intimate nature'.

8.14 The Carers (Equal Opportunities) Act 2004 introduced an obligation on social services to inform carers of their right to an assessment, thereby obliging authorities to be proactive in their work practices. The Act also seeks to combat social exclusion by requiring carers' assessments to consider whether the carer works or wishes to work and is undertaking, or wishes to undertake, education, training or any leisure activity. The 2004 Act is designed to provide state support to enable the carer to work.

COMPULSORY POWERS IN THE COMMUNITY

Guardianship

8.15 Guardianship applications in respect of non-offender patients are made under s 7. Either the nearest relative or an AMHP may apply. Two medical recommendations are necessary. The nearest relative may block a guardianship application but unreasonable objection will be grounds for displacement by the county court under s 29. The patient must be suffering from mental disorder of a nature or degree warranting reception into guardianship. In addition, guardianship must be necessary in the interests of the patient's welfare or for the protection of others. Section 8 of the Act sets out the three powers conferred on the guardian:

(1) to require the patient to live at a place specified by the guardian. The person may be taken and conveyed to the place of residence and may be returned there if she or he absconds;

(2) to require the patient to attend at specified places for medical treatment, occupation, education or training. If the patient refuses to attend, the guardian is not authorised to use force to secure attendance, nor does the Act enable medical treatment to be administered in the absence of the patient's consent (although it may be under ss 5 and 6 of the Mental Capacity Act 2005 if the patient lacks capacity to consent); or

(3) to require access to the patient to be given at the place where he or she is living to persons detailed in the Act. A refusal without reasonable cause to permit an authorised person to have access to the patient is an offence under s 129 but no force may be used to secure entry.

Although guardianship was the flagship community power of both the MHA 1959 and the MHA 1983 in terms of providing the underpinning of compulsion necessary to enforce community care, it has never been much used.

8.16 In England about 900 patients are subject to guardianship at any time, and around 450 new cases are initiated each year (National Statistics Information Centre 2006: Tables 1–2).[14] In 2006 in England there were 934 people under s 7 guardianship, and 45 under guardianship orders made by a criminal court under s 37. For Wales the equivalent figures for 2005 were 85 people under s 7 guardianship, and 21 under guardianship orders made by a criminal court under s 37.[15]

Guardianship orders

8.17 As Jones points out, 'Little use has been made of guardianship orders by the courts', with figures running at under 30 cases per year.[16] The diagnostic criteria for making an order are that the offender must be sixteen or over, and suffering from any disorder or disability of mind warranting reception into guardianship. The court has wide discretion to decide whether guardianship is 'suitable', since it must be of the opinion, having regard to all the circumstances, including the nature of the offence and the character and antecedents of the offender and to other methods of dealing with him, that the most suitable method of disposing of the case is by means of a guardianship order.

8.18 The guardian under a guardianship order has the same powers as a guardian under Part 2.[17] The medical evidence required for a guardianship order is the same as for making a hospital order. The court enjoys similar powers to request information to those available for hospital order cases. Under s 39A, a court considering making a guardianship order will be empowered to request the local social services authority (or any other social services authority considered by the court to be appropriate):

(a) to inform the court whether it or any person authorised by it is prepared to receive the patient into guardianship; and

(b) if so, to give such information as it reasonably can about how it or the other person could be expected to exercise the powers of guardian in relation to the offender.

---

[14] National Statistics Information Centre *Guardianship under the Mental Health Act 1983* (2006) at http://www.ic.nhs.uk/statistics-and-data-collections/health-and-lifestyles/mental-health/guardianship-under-the-mental-health-act-1983-england-2006.

[15] Local Government Data Unit Wales (2005) and Personal Social Services Statistics Wales (2005) *People who are subject to guardianship under Section 7 or Section 37 of the Mental Health Act 1983.* See www.uneddatacymru.gov.uk/Documents/.

[16] Ibid, p 230.

[17] MHA 1983, s 40(2).

8.19   The small numbers under guardianship may change now that the MHA 2007 extends guardianship to anyone who suffers from 'any disorder or disability of mind', although the exclusion in relation to learning disability without abnormally aggressive or seriously irresponsible conduct remains. Moreover, Sch 3, para 3(5) broadens the powers of the guardian by introducing a new power to take and convey a person to their required place of residence under guardianship alongside the power which already exists to return a guardianship patient who has absconded to their place of residence.

Section 17 leave

8.20   Under s 17 the RC may grant either indefinite leave or leave for a specified period, subject to such conditions as he or she considers necessary in the interests of the patient or for the protection of others. Where it appears to the RC to be necessary in the interests of the patient's health *or* safety *or* for the protection of others, the patient may be recalled from leave by the RC giving notice in writing to the patient or person in charge of him or her. The MHA 2007 preserves the RC's power to send on leave under s 17, but it is intended that its role will be reduced and supplanted by the CTO under s 17A. To reinforce this policy, a RC considering granting leave for more than seven days must first consider whether the patient should be 'dealt with' under s 17A by a community treatment order ('CTO') instead.[18]

8.21   The 1990s saw increasing legal recognition of the problem of the 'revolving door' patient, who gets well on medication but, once discharged, ceases to take it and relapses. Instead of using mental health guardianship to provide a framework for compulsion in the community, the psychiatric profession's preferred solution is s 17 leave. A patient can be required to accept medication as a condition of leave and recalled to hospital in the event of non-compliance. Detention must be renewed at intervals, and a problem came if the patient was in the community when the time came to renew detention. To overcome this, patients would be recalled from the community to hospital for one night to have their detention renewed, and would then be sent on leave for a further six or twelve months until the detention next required renewal. By this ingenious device, a long-term community treatment order was fashioned out of the power to grant leave from detention. However, the obligation to accept treatment whilst resident in the community could only be imposed on someone who has already been detained, since only a detained patient can be granted leave.

8.22   In *R v Hallstrom, ex parte W (No 2)*[19] McCullough J declared unlawful two widely used practices in psychiatry. The first was that of compulsorily admitting patients for treatment under s 3 of the Mental Health Act 1983 when there was no intention that they should receive in-patient treatment for mental disorder. Such patients would be sent on leave under s 17 of the Act shortly

---

[18]   MHA 1983, s 17(2A) and (2B), inserted by MHA 2007, s 33(2).
[19]   [1986] 2 All ER 306.

after admission, subject to the condition that they took their medication. This was declared unlawful on the grounds that one of the conditions of admission is that the patient must need treatment in hospital for their mental disorder and that the treatment cannot be provided unless they are detained. It remains unlawful to detain a patient in the first place when there is no intention to provide any in-patient treatment.

8.23   The second practice at issue in *Hallstrom* was that of returning patients on leave under s 17 to hospital for one night, renewing their detention and discharging them the next day subject to the condition that they continued to take their medication. The judge held that a patient's detention could not be renewed unless it was intended that they should receive treatment in hospital as an in-patient. The implication of this was a limit on the duration of a patient's subjection to compulsory powers in the community. Legislation providing for supervised discharge, introduced to overcome the effect of *Hallstrom*, has been little used.

8.24   Subsequent case-law has almost completely reversed the effect of *Hallstrom*. It provides that a patient's detention can be renewed as long as a patient needs some treatment at a hospital, not necessarily as an in-patient. In *B v Barking Havering and Brentwood Community Healthcare NHS Trust*[20] the Court of Appeal held that it was lawful to renew detention of a patient even though she spent only two nights a week in hospital, Lord Woolf holding that (at para 113):

> 'As long as treatment viewed as a whole involves treatment as an in-patient the requirements of the section can be met.'

Then in *R (on the application of DR) v Mersey Care NHS Trust*[21] the patient was receiving no in-patient treatment whilst on leave, but was receiving treatment in hospital as an out-patient. Justice Wilson held that the only relevant question to renewal was whether a significant component of the treatment of the plan for the claimant was for treatment in hospital. That treatment did not have to be as an in-patient.

8.25   In *R (on the application of S) v Mental Health Review Tribunal*[22] the patient was residing at her home on s 17 leave on condition that she attend weekly sessions with her psychologist and attended ward rounds once per month. The purpose of the ward round requirement was to give the patient the necessary motivation and encouragement to progress in the community. Pitchford J held that the MHRT had acted lawfully in declining to discharge on the grounds that some treatment in hospital was still required.

8.26   By the time these later cases were decided, supervised discharge had already been introduced by the Mental Health (Patients in the Community)

---

[20]   [1999] 1 FLR 106, CA.
[21]   *R (on the application of DR) v Mersey Care NHS Trust* [2002] EWHC 1810 (Admin).
[22]   [2004] EWHC 2958 (Admin), [2004] MHLR 355.

Act 1995 inserting into the MHA 1983 new ss 25A–25H, following the exposure of failures of community care in cases such as that of Christopher Clunis. Supervised discharge has been little used. In *R (on the application of DR) v Mersey Care NHS Trust*, which so markedly increased the scope of extended leave, the argument was put that supervised discharge should have been at least considered, if not used in preference to extended leave. The judge rejected this argument, stating that it was a:[23]

> '[C]entral feature, regarded by many as a central deficiency, of the provisions for after-care under supervision that, although under section 25D (3)(b) and (4) a patient can be required to attend the place where he is due to receive the treatment and to allow himself to be conveyed there, he cannot be required to actually take the medication. If he refuses to take it, the power to administer it compulsorily arises only when he has again been made liable to be detained by the properly cumbersome procedures set by s 3 of the Act.'

The Mental Health Act 2007 repeals ss 25A–25J of the MHA 1983 and replaces them with a new regime of powers (ss 17A–17G) to impose supervised community treatment ('SCT').

SUPERVISED COMMUNITY TREATMENT ('SCT')

8.27   The new provisions on SCT will come fully into force in October 2008. To be eligible for SCT the patient must be liable to be detained in hospital under s 3 or, if a Part 3 patient, be subject to a hospital order, a hospital direction, or a transfer direction without restrictions. SCT is also available for patients treated as being subject to s 3 or subject to an unrestricted hospital order or transfer direction, following transfer from Northern Ireland, Scotland, the Isle of Man or the Channel Islands.[24] A patient who is subject to SCT is known as a 'community patient'.

8.28   Section 17A(1) gives the RC the power, 'by order in writing' to 'discharge a detained patient from hospital subject to his being liable to recall in accordance with section 17E'. This is called a 'community treatment order' ('CTO').[25] The RC must be of the opinion that:

(a)   the patient is suffering from mental disorder (any disorder or disability of mind) of a nature or degree which makes it appropriate for him to receive medical treatment;

(b)   it is necessary for his health or safety or for the protection of other persons that he should receive such treatment;

---

[23]   [2002] EWHC 1810 (Admin) at [33].

[24]   Department of Health *Mental Health Act 1983 Draft Revised Code of Practice* (2007), para 28.4. See http://www.dh.gov.uk/en/Consultations.

[25]   MHA 1983, s 17A(3).

(c)   subject to his being liable to be recalled, such treatment can be provided without his continuing to be detained in a hospital;

(d)   it is necessary that the responsible clinician should be able to exercise the power to recall the patient to hospital (the Bill said necessary for the patient's health or safety or for the protection of others – the Act simply says necessary); and

(e)   appropriate medical treatment is available for him.

All of the above criteria must be satisfied for a patient to be eligible for SCT.

8.29   The order will be made by the patient's Responsible Clinician ('RC'). The RC may not make a CTO without a written statement from an AMHP agreeing with the RC's opinion and that it is appropriate to make the order. When considering an order the RC must give priority to the risk of deterioration, and the risk of non-compliance with medication if the patient were not to remain in detention. When considering whether a person should be liable to recall under s 17E, the RC must:[26]

> '*in particular*, consider, having regard to the patient's history of mental disorder and any other relevant factors, what risk there would be of a deterioration of the patient's condition if he were not detained in a hospital (as a result, for example, of his refusing or neglecting to receive the medical treatment he requires for his mental disorder).'

Conditions

8.30   The Mental Health Bill 2006 listed specific types of condition which might be imposed in a CTO, as follows:

(a)   that the patient reside at a particular place;

(b)   that the patient make himself available at particular times and places for the purposes of medical treatment;

(c)   that the patient receive medical treatment in accordance with the responsible clinician's directions;

(d)   that the patient makes himself available for examination;

(e)   that the patient abstain from particular conduct.

Most noteworthy on the list of conditions was the obligation to receive medical treatment, rather than as before to attend a specified place for the purpose of medical treatment, and the obligation to desist from specified conduct, a condition which led to the contention that this amounts to the psychiatric

---

[26]   MHA 1983, s 17A(6). [Emphasis added].

equivalent of the anti-social behaviour orders ('ASBOs') introduced by s 1 of the Crime and Disorder Act 1998. Section 32 of the Mental Health Act 2007 does not list the types of condition which may be applied.

8.31 Without listing the types of condition, the MHA 2007 requires that a community treatment order must 'specify conditions to which the patient is to be subject'. Any conditions must be agreed between the RC and the AMHP. The only limitation on the scope of the conditions is that the RC and AMHP must agree that they are 'necessary or appropriate' for:

(a) ensuring that the patient receives medical treatment;

(b) preventing risk of harm to the patient's health or safety;

(c) protecting other persons.[27]

Although the abandonment of the list approach to powers was heralded as a major concession by the Government, the new provisions confer wide discretionary power. The Draft Revised Code of Practice refers to the requirement that the patient abstain from specified conduct and says that it might be appropriate:[28]

> 'If necessary for one or more of the purposes above, conditions might cover the arrangements for treatment in the community, and where the patient is to live. For some patients, they might cover matters such as the avoidance of illegal drugs, if that is a known risk factor. It might be appropriate to require a patient to try to avoid certain high risk situations known to place them at high risk of harm. The reasons for any condition should of course be explained to the patient and others, as appropriate, and recorded in the patient's notes.'

The position is no different under the 2007 Act where any similar condition could easily be justified.

8.32 There are several disturbing factors of this power from a human rights point of view. First, the scope of the conditions and limitations on personal freedom is left to the discretion of health care professionals, subject only to loose requirements as to purpose which would allow conditions that the patient desist from specified conduct. This was supposedly one of the Government's concessions during the debates on the 2006 Bill. The MHA 2007, if anything, allows more scope for expansion of the powers, as long as they can be necessary or appropriate for treatment or to prevent risk to self or others. The 'necessary or appropriate' test is lax indeed. 'Necessary and appropriate' would have required the professionals to address their minds to whether the

---

[27] MHA 2007, s 32.
[28] Department of Health *Mental Health Act 1983 Draft Revised Code of Practice* (2007), para 28.19. See http://www.dh.gov.uk/en/Consultations.

conditions were necessary and whether they are appropriate. As it is one may question what sort of condition might not be necessary but would be appropriate and vice versa.

8.33 There is no power to seek review before the MHRT of the need for specified conditions, although the patient may apply to the MHRT on the grounds that one or more of the conditions for making an order are not met. The MHRT must direct discharge if it is not satisfied that:

(1) the patient is then suffering from mental disorder or mental disorder of a nature or degree which makes it appropriate for him to receive medical treatment; or

(2) that it is necessary for his health or safety or for the protection of other persons that he should receive such treatment; or

(3) that it is necessary that the responsible clinician should be able to exercise the power to recall the patient to hospital; or

(4) that appropriate medical treatment is available for him.[29]

In deciding whether it is satisfied that the power of recall is necessary the MHRT must *in particular* consider having regard to the patient's history of mental disorder and any other relevant factors, what risk there would be of a deterioration of the patient's condition if he were to continue not to be detained in a hospital (as a result, for example, of his refusing or neglecting to receive the medical treatment he requires for his mental disorder).

8.34 The tribunal is also under a duty to discharge on an application by the nearest relative if not satisfied that the patient if discharged would be likely to act in a manner dangerous to self or to others. The RC and AMHP must consider the restrictions 'necessary *or* appropriate' not 'necessary *and* appropriate'. It is not hard to envisage circumstances where a condition that the patient desist from a specified conduct could be deemed necessary or appropriate to protect others. It is quite possible that the list will re-emerge in the Code of Practice.

8.35 Failure to comply with conditions will not lead to automatic recall, but a patient who fails to comply with any of the conditions may be recalled to hospital and held there for up to 72 hours. If they do not agree to comply within that period, the community treatment order will be revoked and they will resume status as a detained patient.

8.36 CTOs potentially engage the right of respect for privacy under Art 8. Interferences with Art 8 rights may be justified if carried out in the interests of the patient's health or to protect the rights and freedoms of others. There will

---

[29] MHA 2007, Sch 3, para 21.

be no breach of Art 8 if the CTO is made in accordance with the law and is necessary in a democratic society for one of the purposes listed in Art 8(2).[30] A patient subject to SCT is known as a 'community patient'.[31]

Power to recall to hospital from s 17 leave or from a CTO (ss 17 and 17E)

8.37 A patient who is on s 17 leave from a hospital may have their leave revoked and be recalled to the hospital where they were detained if the RC considers it necessary in the interests of the patient's health or safety or for the protection of other persons. Revocation and recall are by the RC giving notice in writing 'to the patient or to the person for the time being in charge of the patient'.[32]

8.38 A community patient may be recalled to any hospital[33] if in the RC's opinion:

(a)   the patient requires medical treatment in hospital for his mental disorder; and

(b)   there would be a risk of harm to the health or safety of the patient or to other persons if the patient were not recalled to hospital for that purpose.

A patient may also be recalled for breach of a condition of a CTO, although this is not a necessary condition of recall.

8.39 The RC may also recall a community patient to hospital if the patient fails to comply with a condition of the CTO. Section 17B requires that CTOs specify conditions to which a community patient will be subject. A CTO must contain conditions that the patient must make himself available for medical examination to determine whether the CTO should be extended, and secondly to allow a Second Opinion Approved Doctor ('SOAD') to issue a certificate authorising treatment under Part 4A. Apart from these mandatory conditions any other conditions may be imposed, provided an AMHP agrees they are necessary or appropriate to ensure that the patient receives medical treatment, to prevent harm to the patient's health or safety, or to protect others.

8.40 The Explanatory Notes on the MHA 2007 state that:[34]

---

[30]   *(Application 10801/84)*, Decisions and Reports of the European Commission of Human Rights, vol 45, pp 181–189 (Decision of 20 January 1986 on admissibility). Report of the Commission (adopted on 3 October 1988).

[31]   MHA 2007, s 17A(3).

[32]   MHA 1983, s 17(4).

[33]   MHA 1983, s 17E(3) provides that: 'The hospital to which a patient is recalled need not be the responsible hospital.'

[34]   MHA 1983, s 17B(6) and *Explanatory Notes*, para 113.

'Other than the conditions about availability for examination, the conditions specified under section 17B are not in themselves enforceable but, if a patient fails to comply with any condition, the RC may take that into account when considering if it is necessary to use the recall power.'

However, provided the recall criteria are met, the patient may still be recalled even if he or she is complying with the conditions.[35] A community patient can be recalled to a hospital even though he is already in the hospital at the time when the power of recall is exercised.[36]

8.41   The power of recall is exercisable by notice in writing to the patient, which is sufficient authority for the managers of that hospital to detain the patient. A patient who has been recalled under ss 17(4) or 17E can be taken and conveyed to hospital by any AMHP, officer on the staff of the hospital, any constable or by any person authorised in writing by the responsible clinician or the hospital managers. The RC is responsible for co-ordinating the recall, which is designed to provide a means to respond to evidence of relapse or high risk behaviour before it becomes critical and leads to the patient or other people being put at risk. The Draft Revised Code states that:[37]

'Particular attention should be paid to carers and relatives when they raise a concern that the patient is not complying with the conditions or their mental health appears to be deteriorating. The community team needs to give due weight to those concerns and any requests made by the carers or relatives in deciding what action to take. Carers and relatives are typically in much more constant contact with the patient than professionals, even under well-run care plans.'

Power to revoke a community treatment order (s 17F)

8.42   Recalling a patient from leave under s 17(4) automatically revokes the leave and the patient resumes detained patient status in the hospital from which they were granted leave. By contrast, recalling a community patient means that the patient may be detained in a hospital for up to 72 hours immediately following return to hospital. A separate decision under s 17F is necessary to revoke a CTO. The RC may revoke a CTO by order in writing if of the opinion that the conditions for detention under s 3(2) are satisfied in respect of the patient. An AMHP must agree with that opinion and that it is appropriate to revoke the order. If a CTO is revoked, the patient reverts to detained patient status and is treated for the purposes of renewal of detention as if they had been admitted for treatment on the date of the order being revoked.[38]

8.43   The RC may 'release' the patient at any time during the 72 hours in which case the patient remains subject to the CTO.[39] If the CTO has not been

---

[35]   MHA 1983, s 17B(7).

[36]   MHA 1983, s 17E(4).

[37]   Department of Health *Mental Health Act 1983 Draft Revised Code of Practice* (2007), para 28.32. See http://www.dh.gov.uk/en/Consultations.

[38]   MHA 1983, s 17G.

[39]   MHA 1983, s 17F(5) and (7).

revoked by the end of the 72-hour period and the patient is still in hospital, he must be released. Again, the patient remains subject to the CTO.[40] 'Released' means 'released from that detention (and accordingly from being recalled to hospital)',[41] it does not mean that the patient is discharged from the CTO. The patient remains liable to s 17E recall.

Power to renew a community treatment order (s 20A)

8.44 Within the last two months of a community treatment order the RC must:

(1) examine the patient; and

(2) consult 'one or more other persons who have been professionally concerned with the patient's medical treatment';

(3) if there is a written statement from an AMHP agreeing that the renewal conditions are met and it is appropriate to do so submit to the hospital managers a report renewing the CTO.

The renewal conditions are:

(1) the patient is suffering from mental disorder of a nature or degree which makes it appropriate for him to receive medical treatment;

(2) it is necessary for his health or safety or for the protection of other persons that he should receive such treatment;

(3) subject to his continuing to be liable to be recalled, such treatment can be provided without his being detained in a hospital;

(4) it is necessary that the responsible clinician should continue to be able to exercise the power of recall; and

(5) appropriate medical treatment is available for him.

Furnishing the report has the effect of renewing the CTO for six months if it is the first renewal, and for 12 months in the case of the second or subsequent renewals.[42]

Authority to treat community patients

8.45 Section 35 of the MHA 2007 introduces a new Part 4A into the Mental Health Act 1983 providing authority to treat community patients without their

---

[40] MHA 1983, s 17F(6) and (7).
[41] MHA 1983, s 17F(8)(b).
[42] MHA 1983, s 20A, as inserted by MHA 2007, s 34(3).

consent. New ss 64A–64K authorise 'relevant treatment' (medicines for mental disorder or Electro Convulsive Therapy ('ECT')) to be given to a community patient who has not been recalled to hospital. Medicine may be given in the community, not necessarily in a hospital or clinic. ECT can only safely be given in hospital. Part 4A applies aspects of the decision-making framework of the Mental Capacity Act 2005 to treatment under the Mental Health Act and permits treatment in the community of a community patient if:

(a) if the treatment is immediately necessary and the patient is capable and consents to the treatment;

(b) if the treatment is immediately necessary and there is consent from someone authorised under the Mental Capacity Act to make decisions on the patient's behalf;

(c) if the patient lacks capacity and force is not necessary to secure compliance; or

(d) if emergency treatment needs to be given, using force if necessary, to a patient who lacks capacity.

8.46 The effect of these changes is explained in Chapter 10. Safeguards are provided in the shape of a 'certificate requirement' from a second opinion doctor appointed for the purposes of Part 4A. If the treatment is medicines for mental disorder, a certificate is not required until the expiry of one month from the date the community treatment order was made.[43] A certificate is not required where the treatment is 'immediately necessary' and the patient has capacity and consents. Nor is one required if the treatment is 'immediately necessary' and there is consent from a person exercising a lasting power of attorney or from a Deputy appointed by the Court of Protection. Finally, no certificate is required where emergency treatment is given under s 64G.[44] The test of 'immediate necessity' depends on the treatment. The certificate requirement is met where a Second Opinion Appointed Doctor ('SOAD') appointed to act under Parts 4 and 4A has certified that it is appropriate for the medicines to be given subject to conditions specified in the certificate.

CONDITIONALLY DISCHARGED RESTRICTED PATIENTS

8.47 The restriction order and restriction direction with their conditional discharge option are seen as effective means of risk management. Re-offending

---

[43] MHA 1983, s 64B(4).
[44] MHA 1983, s 64B(3).

rates in terms of serious sexual offences or violent offences of the 717 patients conditionally discharged between 1999 and 2003 are assessed by the Home Office as averaging 2 per cent.[45]

8.48   A patient subject to Ministry of Justice restrictions on discharge can be discharged by the Minister of Justice or a MHRT either absolutely or subject to conditions. If the patient is given an absolute discharge, both the hospital and restriction orders cease to have effect, and he cannot be recalled to hospital. If a patient's discharge is conditional, he may, for example, be directed to live in a specified place, to attend for treatment, and to accept treatment by or under the direction of the responsible clinician. Because it may be a condition of discharge that the patient must accept treatment for mental disorder, a conditionally discharged restricted patient is not eligible to seek review of treatment by a second opinion doctor under Part 4 of the MHA 1983. The patient may apply to the MHRT for absolute discharge.

8.49   The Ministry of Justice say they should be notified by the responsible clinician in the case of a conditionally discharged patient where:

(1)   there appears to be a risk to the public;

(2)   contact with the patient is lost;

(3)   the patient is unwilling to co-operate with supervision;

(4)   the patient needs further in-patient treatment; or

(5)   the patient is charged with an offence.

A conditionally discharged restricted patient may be recalled to hospital by the Minister of Justice or by the RC at any time whilst the restriction order is in force but, unless it is an emergency recall, there must be medical evidence of mental disorder warranting confinement *Kay v United Kingdom*.[46] The patient must be informed that he or she is being recalled to hospital at the time, and a further explanation of reasons for recall must be given as soon as is reasonably practicable.[47] The case of a conditionally discharged restricted patient who is recalled to hospital must be referred by the Minister of Justice to a MHRT within a month of his return to hospital.

CONCLUSION

8.50   The Government's intention is clearly that the new CTO power introduced by the MHA 2007 will replace s 17 leave for any compulsion in the

---

[45]   Home Office *Statistics of Mentally Disordered Offenders 2005* (Statistical Bulletin 05/07), p 14.
[46]   (1994) 40 BMLR 20, EComHR.
[47]   RM Jones *Mental Health Act Manual* (Sweet and Maxwell, 10th edn, 2006), p 266.

community lasting longer than seven days. Patients subject to each of these powers are entitled to apply for discharge to the MHRT (see Chapter 9). Their treatment without consent is regulated by Part 4 in the case of s 17 patients and Part 4A in the case of CTO patients (see Chapter 10).

8.51 Detention as an in-patient is governed by Art 5. Compulsory community treatment falls under Art 8. Article 8 contains no explicit procedural requirement, but the decision-making process leading to interference must be fair and such as to afford due respect to the interests safeguarded by Art 8. Where guardianship or other community compulsion includes a duty to reside at a specified place enforceable by a power to take and convey, a requirement to grant access to professionals, and any requirement connected with medical treatment or the management of risk, there is a question whether civil rights and obligations are engaged.[48]

8.52 The Joint Committee on Human Rights noted that there is no procedure on the face of the statute requiring objective medical evidence to be presented to a competent authority. The CTO should be signed by the responsible clinician and the AMHP and sent to the Hospital Managers. Regulation 6 of the Draft Mental Health (Hospital, Guardianship and Treatment) Regulations 2008 provide that a CTO must be on prescribed documentation and that the RC must, as soon as reasonably practicable, furnish the managers of the responsible hospital with a copy of the order. The CTO will be effective from the date on which the patient is discharged from detention. The Draft Revised Code of Practice states that:[49]

> 'There are no provisions in the Act for community treatment orders and related documents to be rectified once made. Hospital managers should nonetheless ensure that arrangements are in place to check that they have been properly completed, as errors in them may invalidate managers' authority to detain a patient recalled to hospital.'

The Joint Committee considered that a procedure should be on the face of the statute. Furthermore, the potential breadth of conditions may well mean that a civil right could be infringed engaging the protection under Art 6 of speedy access to an independent court in determination of civil rights and obligations, or at the very least that the procedural obligation under Art 8 might be engaged.[50]

---

[48] As has been held in relation to public law issues in family law such as placement of children in care or placing them for adoption or fostering: *Olsson v Sweden* (1988) 11 EHRR 259; *Keegan v Ireland* (1994) 18 EHRR 342; and *Eriksson v Sweden* (1989) 12 EHRR 183. See N Mole *Council of Europe Guide to Article 6*. See http://hrls.echr.coe.int/uhtbin/cgisirsi.exe/x/0/0/5?searchdata1=human+rights+handbooks%7b440%7d.

[49] Department of Health *Mental Health Act 1983 Draft Revised Code of Practice* (2007), para 12.14. See http://www.dh.gov.uk/en/Consultations.

[50] House of Lords, House of Commons, Joint Committee on Human Rights *Legislative Scrutiny: Mental Health Bill: Fourth Report of Session 2006–2007* (HL Paper 40, HC Paper 288, 4 February 2007), paras 48–51.

Chapter 9

DISCHARGE AND REVIEW OF THE LAWFULNESS OF DETENTION BY MENTAL HEALTH REVIEW TRIBUNALS AND THE COURTS

OVERVIEW

9.1 An unrestricted patient detained under the MHA 1983 may be discharged by the Responsible Clinician ('RC') (see paras **4.66–4.67** above), by the nearest relative (NR) (see para **5.6** above), by the Hospital Managers (see paras **5.51–5.55** above), or by the MHRT. Only the Minister of Justice or a Mental Health Review Tribunal ('MHRT') may discharge a restriction order patient. The Minister of Justice has the final say on discharge of restriction direction, or hospital direction patients. Patients detained for longer than 72 hours under the 1983 Act have the right to apply to a MHRT to seek review of the lawfulness of detention. If the patient does not apply within specified periods the case must be automatically referred to the MHRT. Article 5(4) of the European Convention on Human Rights states that everyone deprived of liberty:

> 'by arrest or detention shall be entitled to take proceedings by which the lawfulness of his detention shall be decided speedily by a court and his release ordered if the detention is not lawful.'

The Strasbourg Court has recognised in light of 'the gravity of detention in a psychiatric hospital'[1] that Art 5(4) also requires that the patient have an effective remedy, and it must be possible to maintain a challenge to the lawfulness of detention even if it has already terminated. This Chapter considers the power of discharge, and the respective roles of MHRTs and the courts in reviewing the lawfulness of psychiatric detention.

Mental Health Review Tribunals ('MHRTs')

9.2 MHRTs were established under the Mental Health Act 1959 with the task of reviewing the continued need for the detention of the patient, and were empowered to direct discharge. The legal member chairs the hearing, is responsible for ensuring that the proceedings are conducted fairly in accordance with the MHA 1983 and the MHRT Rules, and advises on any

---

[1]   *Herz v Germany (Application 44672/98)* Judgment of 12 June 2003, ECtHR.

points of law. The legal member also takes responsibility for drafting the reasons for the decision, following discussion with the other members. The medical member performs two roles. Prior to the hearing he or she must 'examine the patient and take such other steps as he or she considers necessary to form an opinion of the patient's mental condition'. At the hearing the medical member shares judicial responsibility with the other members and must decide whether or not the patient should remain in detention. The medical member advises the tribunal on medical matters. The third category of member is 'lay members', although this term does not appear in the 1983 Act which refers to 'members who are neither legal nor medical members'. These are persons 'having such experience in administration, such knowledge of social services or such other qualifications or experience as the Lord Chancellor considers suitable'. The lay member is there to provide balance by representing the social view rather than bringing to bear legal or medical professional expertise.

9.3   Chapter 5 of the MHA 2007 amends the provisions of the MHA 1983 on MHRTs, introducing new provisions for automatic referrals (see paras **5.72–5.80** above), and abolishing the regional structure for England to create a single MHRT for England and a single one for Wales, each with a President appointed from among the legal members. New provisions are introduced for MHRT review of CTOs, and to remove the soon to be redundant jurisdiction of the MHRT in relation to patients reclassified from one form of disorder to another.

The role of the MHRT

9.4   In *R v Canons Park Mental Health Review Tribunal, ex parte A*, Sedley J said that the MHRT is:[2]

> 'a body charged with reviewing the operative decisions of the responsible authorities to detain the patient, and its functions are to reappraise the patient's condition at the time of the hearing and in the light of its findings do one of three things – to direct discharge as of right, to direct discharge in the exercise of its discretion, or to do neither.'

In essence the MHRT's task is to determine whether at the time of the hearing, the criteria justifying detention continue to be met. It was envisaged that the lawfulness of initial admission and renewal of detention would continue to be a matter to be dealt with in the High Court by way of judicial review or habeas corpus.[3]

---

[2]   [1994] 1 All ER 481 at 490.

[3]   *R v Hallstrom and another, ex parte W* (1985) 2 BMLR 54, [1985] 3 All ER 775; and *R v North West Thames Mental Health Review Tribunal, ex p Cooper* (1990) 5 BMLR 7, QBD.

Article 5(1) and discharge powers

9.5   In *Winterwerp v Netherlands* the Strasbourg Court held that the lawfulness of continued psychiatric detention under Art 5(1)(e) depends on the persistence of unsoundness of mind of a nature or degree warranting confinement. This means that all those with a power of discharge, particularly the RC, must keep under review the continued need for detention, and if the criteria for detention are not met, must discharge the patient. However, before doing so the RC must carry out a full risk assessment, must formulate a care plan (see paras **4.82–4.83** above), and must give victims of certain offender patients the right to make representations (see paras **7.105–7.108** above).

Article 5(4) and review of the lawfulness of detention

9.6   Whilst *Winterwerp* is the classic case on Art 5(1)(e), *X v United Kingdom*[4] has equivalent status in relation to the right to take proceedings to challenge the lawfulness of detention under Art 5(4). If the detention was ordered by a court, the requirement of speedy review does not apply during the initial stages of detention, but there must be periodic opportunities for the detained person to assert, before a court with the power of discharge, that the conditions of detention no longer apply. In *X v United Kingdom* this was held to mean that:[5]

> 'A person of unsound mind compulsorily confined in a psychiatric institution for an indefinite or lengthy period is in principle entitled, at any rate where there is no automatic review of a judicial character, to take proceedings before a court at reasonable intervals to put in issue the lawfulness ... of his detention, whether that detention was ordered by a civil or criminal court, or by some other authority.'

The expectation here is that the norm will be automatic review of a judicial character, but that where that is not present the patient must have the right to take proceedings at reasonable intervals. Under the MHA 1959 there was no automatic review of a judicial character. Referrals were introduced by the MHA 1983, in recognition that some patients might lack the necessary capacity or motivation to apply themselves due to their disorder.

Scope of the review

9.7   The review must be able to consider whether, on the facts, the *Winterwerp* criteria for lawful detention are still met. In *X v United Kingdom*, the Court held that:[6]

> 'The right guaranteed by Article 5(4) to test the lawfulness of detention does not incorporate a right for the court to substitute its discretion for that of the decision-making authority; but the scope of the judicial review must be sufficient to enable enquiry to be made whether, in the case of detention of a mental patient, the reasons which initially justified the detention continue thereafter to subsist.'

---

[4]   (1981) 4 EHRR 188.
[5]   (1981) 4 EHRR 188, at para 52.
[6]   (1981) 4 EHRR 188, at para 53.

This means that the court must be able to rule on the applicability of the *Winterwerp* criteria in the patient's case. Is there, at the time of the hearing, a true mental disorder which is of a kind or degree warranting detention?

9.8 The applicant in *X v United Kingdom* was a restricted patient. Under the MHA 1959, the only judicial body which could look at the substantive justification for detention was the MHRT, but the MHRT had no power to direct discharge if the criteria were found not to be met. They could only give advice to the Home Secretary. This was held to be a breach of Art 5(4). Although the High Court could have discharged the patient by way of habeas corpus or judicial review, these avenues considered the formal legality rather than the substantive factual and diagnostic justification for detention. In its implementation of the ruling in *X v United Kingdom*, the MHA 1983 extended the right to apply to the MHRT for discharge to restricted patients, and also to non-offender patients detained for up to 28 days under s 2.

9.9 In order to be a competent court for the purposes of reviewing the lawfulness of detention, the review must be sufficient in scope to address the *Winterwerp* criteria and the court or tribunal must have the power to direct discharge. *X v United Kingdom* meant that the Home Office lost the final word in the discharge of restriction order patients. The decision as to discharge was now for the judicial body, the MHRT, and was no longer an administrative decision within the sole province of the minister (then the Home Secretary, now the Minister of Justice). Instead of having the final word, the Minister of Justice, through the Mental Health Unit is now a party to MHRT proceedings relating to restricted patients, and their rights as party have been asserted by the Home Office with vigour before Tribunals and in judicial review. With restriction direction patients transferred from prison or on a hospital direction, the Minister of Justice retains the final say on discharge. As a safeguard for the public interest, tribunals in restricted cases are chaired by a judge rather than a solicitor or barrister. These developments have inevitably made the proceedings more formal, and potentially more adversarial.

9.10 In *Reid v United Kingdom*[7] the ECHR elaborated further on the features of a competent court. For the purposes of Art 5(4), the body does not necessarily have to be a court of law of the classic kind integrated within the standard judicial machinery of the country. MHRTS are courts for the purposes of this provision. The most important feature is independence from the executive and the parties to the case. Secondly, the safeguards must be 'appropriate to the kind of deprivation of liberty in question.' This means there must be a 'judicial procedure', the forms of which may vary but which must include the competence to 'decide' the lawfulness of the detention and to order release if the detention is not lawful.[8] Finally, review of the 'lawfulness' of detention must be carried out in light not only of domestic law requirements but also of the text of the Convention, the general principles embodied therein

---

[7] (2003) 37 EHRR 9, ECtHR.

[8] *Weeks v United Kingdom (Application 9787/82)* (1987) 10 EHRR 293, at para 61.

(including proportionality) and the aim of the restrictions permitted by para (1)(e).[9] This task is shared by the MHRT which reviews the current need for continued detention, and the courts which have jurisdiction to review the lawfulness of the initial decision to detain, by habeas corpus, judicial review or civil action for the tort of false imprisonment. Damages may be obtained if a person is imprisoned (the Convention equivalent is deprived of liberty) and there is no lawful authority to justify it.[10]

Habeas corpus

9.11   The writ of habeas corpus requires the detaining body to show lawful justification for a detention, and the detainee is entitled to release if such justification is lacking. The scope of the court's inquiry in habeas corpus applications is to review the facial validity of the application and medical recommendations, and to consider any irregularities which go to the jurisdiction of the detaining body. Reviewing whether the documents show sufficient authority is carried out in the context that if any of the statutory documents is incorrect or defective it may be amended within the first 14 days following admission.[11] Examples of irregularities going to jurisdiction are where a key jurisdictional fact is missing as, for example, if a magistrates' court made a hospital order in a case of an offender convicted of a non-imprisonable offence. In *R v Board of Control, ex parte Rutty*[12] habeas corpus was granted because the power to detain could only be used on someone who was 'found neglected' and Kathleen Rutty had been living at all times in institutional care. A key jurisdictional fact was missing. In *Re S-C (mental patient: habeas corpus)*,[13] the ASW, knowing that the father, who was the nearest relative, objected to s 3 admission, had consulted the mother, who did not. Since an objection by the NR deprives the managers of jurisdiction to detain, habeas corpus was granted on the basis of want of jurisdictional fact. Sir Thomas Bingham held that habeas corpus was appropriate since:

> 'There was no attempt being made to overturn an administrative decision. The object is simply to show that there was never jurisdiction to detain the appellant in the first place.'

On the evidence this was plainly made out.

9.12   Although an application for habeas corpus takes priority over any other High Court business, the scope of the review which it allows means that it cannot examine whether the person is still suffering from a true mental disorder of a kind or degree warranting detention for the purposes of Art 5(4). In *X v United Kingdom* a duly completed recall warrant was held sufficient to defeat a habeas corpus application. The Strasbourg Court held that although habeas

---

9   *Brogan v United Kingdom* (1988) 11 EHRR 117, ECtHR.
10   *R v Deputy Governor of Parkhurst Prison, ex parte Hague* [1991] 3 WLR 340.
11   MHA 1983, s 15.
12   [1956] 2 QB 109.
13   [1996] 1 All ER 532, CA.

carried a power of discharge as required by Art 5(4), the scope of review which
it permitted was insufficient for the purposes of that Article.

Judicial review

9.13   The purpose and limits of judicial review were described as follows by
Lord Hailsham in *Chief Constable of North Wales Police v Evans*:[14]

> '[T]o ensure that the individual is given fair treatment by the authority to which he
> has been subjected ... it is no part of that purpose to substitute the opinion of the
> judiciary or individual judges for that of the authority constituted by law to decide
> the matter in question.'

Judicial review does *not* challenge the merits of the decision, since the doctrine
of the separation of powers requires them to avoid usurping functions given to
the decision-maker by statute. The process is governed by s 31 of the Supreme
Court Act 1981 and Parts 8 and 54 of the Civil Procedure Rules which govern
the way that courts exercise supervisory jurisdiction over the proceedings and
decisions of bodies performing public law duties or functions.

9.14   There are six basic grounds for judicial review:

(1)   **Illegality / Error of Law**
      The decision maker must understand correctly the law that regulates his
      decision-making power and must give effect to it.

(2)   **Procedural Impropriety**
      This means more than failure to observe basic rules of natural justice
      (audi alteram partem, nemo judex in causa sua) or failure to act with
      procedural fairness towards the person affected. It also includes failure by
      an administrative tribunal to observe procedural rules.

(3)   **Irrationality / *Wednesbury* unreasonableness**[15]
      Where the decision is so outrageous in its defiance of logic or accepted
      moral standards that no sensible person who had applied his mind to the
      question to be decided could have arrived at it.

(4)   **Abuse of Power**
      This includes failing to have regard to relevant considerations, taking
      account of irrelevant considerations, acting for an improper purpose, or
      following a policy unduly rigidly without allowing for exceptional
      circumstances.

(5)   **Human Rights Act 1998**
      Challenges may be brought by way of judicial review alleging that actions
      of public bodies have violated a person's Convention rights.

----

[14]   [1982] 1 WLR 1155 at 1160, HL.

[15]   *Associated Provincial Picture Houses Ltd v Wednesbury Corpn* [1948] 1 KB 223, CA.

(6) **EC Law**
EC Law challenges based on the infringement of enforceable Community rights under the European Communities Act 1972.

The MHRT's jurisdiction is confined to reviewing the patient's condition at the time of the hearing and determining whether detention is still necessary. If a person wishes to challenge the validity of the decision to detain in the first place or the renewal of detention the correct avenue will be judicial review. Although there is a procedure for appeal by cased stated from the MHRT it has been much more common for parties aggrieved by a MHRT decision to seek judicial review.

Speedy review of the lawfulness of detention

9.15 Article 5(4) entitles anyone detained on grounds of unsoundness of mind to take proceedings by which the lawfulness of their detention shall be decided speedily by a court and their release ordered if their detention is not lawful. If the initial decision was ordered by administrative procedure, the review must be available 'speedily' following the detention.

9.16 In *Reid v the United Kingdom*[16] the Court found a breach of the speediness requirement in Art 5(4). Reid applied for release in April 1994, and the House of Lords finally determined his appeal almost four years later. The speediness requirement in Art 5(4) applies to appellate instances as well as the initial review, so time continues to run until all appeals or judicial review proceedings are determined. The Strasbourg Court does not rule on speediness by stating that a particular time delay (three months for example) is or is not compatible with Art 5(4). Instead it asks whether, on the facts of the individual case, there was a failure to proceed with reasonable despatch having regard to all the material circumstances.

9.17 In *R (on the application of C) v Mental Health Review Tribunal*[17] C's case was listed for a date precisely eight weeks after his application. The MHRT Chairs had adopted a policy of seeking to bring all cases on within eight weeks. The MHRT administration had translated this into a practice of giving all applicants a hearing date precisely eight weeks from the date of the application. The Court of Appeal held this was incompatible with Art 5(4), unless this was the only practicable way of ensuring that individual cases are determined as speedily as their individual circumstances reasonably permit. In *R (on the application of K) v Mental Health Review Tribunal*[18] Stanley Burnton J held that the right of seven applicants to a speedy hearing under Art 5(4) had been breached and that the evidence before him indicated the basic responsibility for the delays experienced by patients was that of central government rather than the tribunal chairmen or their staff.

---

[16] (2003) 37 EHRR 9, ECtHR.
[17] [2002] 1 WLR 176, CA.
[18] [2002] EWHC 639 (Admin).

9.18   Following the friendly settlement in *Roux v United Kingdom*[19] the UK Government agreed that a new r 29(cc) should be introduced for cases of recall of conditionally discharged restricted patients, whereby the tribunal would be required to fix a date between five and eight weeks from the date of reference. *R (on the application of B) v Mental Health Review Tribunal*[20] concerned delay of eight months in the hearing of a recalled restricted patient. Scott Baker J held that there had been a breach of Art 5(4), and that the underlying problem was a lack of case management on the tribunal's part. At each stage the tribunal ought to have had in mind the delay which had accrued and given directions against that background. The longer the delay, the more aggressive the directions would have to be in order to ensure an early disposal of the case. There would come a time where the convenience of expert witnesses had to cede to the need for the tribunal to conclude a substantive hearing. No adequate explanation had been given for the delays.

BURDEN OF PROOF

9.19   For the first 40 years of its existence the MHRT operated under a reverse of the normal common law presumption that it is for those carrying out the detention to justify it, rather than for the detainee to justify his or her freedom. A patient would only be entitled to discharge if he or she could satisfy the MHRT that he or she was no longer suffering from mental disorder of a nature or degree warranting confinement. This faced patients with the considerable burden of establishing a negative, the absence of mental disorder of a nature or degree making detention for medical treatment appropriate. In a series of cases decided prior to the coming into force of the Human Rights Act 1998 the courts emphasised the importance of this reverse burden of proof. In *R v Canons Park Mental Health Review Tribunal, ex parte A* the majority in the Court of Appeal held that a tribunal was only required to direct discharge:[21]

> 'if it is satisfied of a negative, because the tribunal is not intended to duplicate the role of the medical officer, whose diagnosis stands until the tribunal is satisfied that it is wrong.'

9.20   There were signs from the Strasbourg institutions that the burden of proof might be incompatible with Convention rights. The stipulation in *X v United Kingdom* that an Art 5 court must conduct an inquiry whether the reasons which initially justify detention continue to subsist implies that the court ought to be satisfied they are met. In *James Kay v United Kingdom*, the European Commission on Human Rights declared admissible a complaint where one of the applicant's contentions was that the tribunal could not

---

[19]   *(Application 25601/94)* Decision of 4 September 1996, ECtHR.
[20]   [2002] EWHC 1553 (Admin).
[21]   [1994] 2 All ER 659, CA. The reverse burden was also emphasised in *Perkins v Bath District Health Authority; R v Wessex Mental Health Review Tribunal, ex parte Wiltshire County Council* (1989) 4 BMLR 145, CA; and *R v Merseyside Mental Health Review Tribunal, ex parte K* [1990] 1 All ER 694, (1989) 4 BMLR 60, CA.

provide an effective remedy 'because it does not have to find positive evidence that the patient is suffering from mental disorder'.[22] One of the first declarations of incompatibility granted under the Human Rights Act 1998 was *R (on the application of H) v London North and East Region Mental Health Review Tribunal (Secretary of State for Health intervening)*[23] where the Court of Appeal held that the positioning of the burden of proof under ss 72 and 73 on the applicant to satisfy the tribunal of the absence of detainable mental disorder was incompatible with Art 5 of the ECHR.

9.21 The Government introduced a remedial order to rectify the incompatibility. Under the amended s 72(1)(b) a patient is entitled to discharge if the MHRT is not satisfied:[24]

'(i)   that the patient is then suffering from mental disorder of a *nature or degree* which makes it appropriate for him to be *liable to be detained* in hospital for medical treatment; or

(ii)   that it is necessary for the health or safety of the patient or for the protection of other persons that he should receive such treatment; or

(iia) that appropriate medical treatment is available for him; or

(iii) in the case of an application by the nearest relative following the barring of a discharge order, that the patient if released would be likely to act in a manner dangerous to himself or to other persons.'

The MHRT must discharge if not satisfied that any one of conditions (i)–(ii) or (iia) is met, or in the case of a nearest relative application if not satisfied that condition (iii) is met.

Standard of proof

9.22 In *R (on the application of N) v Mental Health Review Tribunal (Northern Region)*[25] the Court of Appeal affirmed that the standard of proof was the balance of probabilities and considered this to be 'compliant with the ECHR case-law requiring it to be "reliably shown" that detention was justified.' The court recognised that standard of proof had a potential part to play in the decision-making process, 'even in relation to issues that were the subject of judgment and evaluation.' 'Standard of proof' and 'balance of probabilities' are words which go naturally with the concept of evidence relating to fact, but in the Court's view were less than perfect with evaluative assessments where it was best to speak of the 'burden of persuasion'. MHRTs should approach the entire range of issues by reference to the standard of proof on the balance of probabilities, whilst recognising that in practice the standard of proof will have

---

22   *(Application 17821/91)* Decision of 7 July 1993, ECtHR.

23   [2001] 3 WLR 512, CA. See also *Lyons v The Scottish Ministers* (unreported) 17 January 2002, First Division of Scottish Court of Session.

24   MHA 1983, ss 72 and 73, as amended by Mental Health Act 1983 (Remedial) Order 2001 (SI 2001/3712), and MHA 2007, Sch 1, para 14 and s 4(8)(a).

25   [2005] EWCA Civ 1605, 88 BMLR 59, CA.

a much more important part to play in the determination of disputed issues of fact than it will generally have in matters of judgment as to appropriateness and necessity.

Congruence between admission and discharge criteria

9.23   The Court of Appeal decision in *R (on the application of H) v London North and East Region Mental Health Review Tribunal (Secretary of State for Health intervening)* is not only important because the burden of proof was held to be incompatible with Art 5(4), but also because the Court held that Art 5(4) required congruence between the criteria for admission and discharge (per Lord Phillips MR):[26]

> 'So far as Article 5(4) is concerned, it seems to us axiomatic that if the function of the tribunal is to consider whether the detention of the patient is lawful, it must apply the same test that the law required to be applied as a precondition to admission unless it be the case that the patient can lawfully be detained provided some other test is satisfied.'

There is one area of incongruence between the admission and discharge criteria for s 3, where patients may only be detained if:

(1)   they are suffering from mental disorder of a nature or degree which makes it appropriate for them to receive medical treatment in a hospital treatment; and

(2)   treatment is necessary for their own health or safety or for the protection of other persons and it cannot be provided unless they are detained.

The MHRT only comes under a duty to discharge if not satisfied that the patient is then suffering from mental disorder of a nature or degree which makes it appropriate for him to be *liable to be detained* in hospital for medical treatment. This means that the MHRT does not come under a duty to discharge where it is not satisfied that detention is still necessary. That duty only applies where it is not satisfied that it is necessary for the patient to be liable to be detained. Hence, the MHRT is not under a duty to discharge a patient who is on extended leave in the community if it is satisfied that the patient still needs the discipline of liability to recall under s 17. The Mental Health (Amendment) Bill 1981 would have entitled a patient to discharge if their mental disorder was not of a nature or degree requiring *detention*. The phrase 'liable to be detained' was retained from the MHA 1959 and introduced in the MHA 1983 as a result of the intervention before the Special Standing Committee of the late James Cooke, then Chairman of the South East Thames MHRT, who argued that the MHRT should not be obliged to discharge someone who was on s 17 leave.

---

[26]   [2001] 3 WLR 512 at [31].

9.24 Despite the incongruence between admission and discharge criteria the criteria for renewal of detention by the RC are congruent with the criteria for admission. For renewal it must be necessary for the health or safety of the patient or for the protection of others that he receives treatment and it must be the case that it cannot be provided unless he is detained.[27] However, in *B v Barking Havering and Brentwood Community Healthcare NHS Trust*[28] the Court of Appeal held that the words 'unless he continues to be detained' mean 'unless he continues to be liable to be detained' rather than 'unless he continues to be actually detained.' Accordingly, the conditions of renewal can be satisfied even in relation to a patient who is no longer actually detained but has been granted leave of absence under s 17.

Organisation of the MHRT

9.25 Section 38(2) of the MHA 2007 introduces a new s 65(1) into the MHA 1983 providing that there shall in future be a MHRT for England and a separate MHRT for Wales, each headed up by a President.[29] The panel for each hearing will be presided over by a legal chairman. This reverses the 1983 Act terminology where there were Regional Chairmen and the panel for each MHRT hearing was presided over by a president.

9.26 The purpose of the MHRTs is set out in s 65(1A) 'to deal with applications and references by and in respect of patients under ... this Act'. The tribunal's duties may be performed by three or more of its members. At least one must be a 'legal member', one a 'medical member' and one a member who is neither a legal nor a medical member.[30] The legal members are appointed by the Minister of Justice and are persons whom the Minister considers to have suitable legal experience. The Minister must appoint one legal member to be the President in each of England and Wales. The President is responsible for appointing the tribunal members who are to hear a particular case.[31] He or she is empowered to deal with matters which are preliminary or incidental to the hearing, and may take steps to ensure that each case is given prompt consideration.[32]

The panel for a hearing

9.27 Where a tribunal is appointed to hear a particular case, the legal member is the chairman of that tribunal and has wide discretion in the conduct of the proceedings. In the case of a restricted patient, the legal member must be chosen from a panel of legal members who have been approved by the Lord Chancellor to hear such cases.[33] The intention of this provision is to

---

27   MHA 1983, s 20(4)(c).
28   [1999] 1 FLR 106, CA.
29   MHA 1983, Sch 2, para 3, as inserted by MHA 2007, s 38(6).
30   MHA 1983, s 65(3) and Sch 2, para 4.
31   MHA 1983, Sch 2, paras 3 and 4.
32   Mental Health Review Tribunal Rules 1983, SI 1983/942, rr 5, 13.
33   Mental Health Review Tribunal Rules 1983, SI 1983/942, r 8(3).

ensure that persons presiding over tribunals in cases of patients who have been convicted of serious offences have 'substantial judicial experience in the criminal courts'. The medical members are psychiatrists who are nominated by the Secretary of State for Health on recommendation by the health authorities. The medical member has a duty to examine the patient prior to the proceedings and to form an opinion about the patient's mental condition (r 11). The other tribunal members are neither legal members nor medical members. They are appointed by the Minister of Justice after consultation with the Secretary of State for Health and are persons having experience in administration or social services, or who are persons with other experience or qualifications which are considered suitable.

Disqualifications

9.28   Rule 8(2) of the MHRT rules precludes a tribunal member from serving on a particular case if he or she is a member or an officer of the responsible authority or if he or she has recently treated the patient or has some other close acquaintance or connection with him.[34] A member is not disqualified by virtue of having heard a previous tribunal application by the same patient.[35] In *R (on the application of M) v Mental Health Review Tribunal* the court held that In the circumstances, a fair-minded and informed observer, having taken account of all the facts of the case, would not have said that there was a real possibility of bias on the part of the judge President of the MHRT, who had just over a year previously sentenced the patient to a hospital order with restrictions under the MHA 1983.[36] In *R (on the application of D) v West Midlands and North West Mental Health Review Tribunal*[37] the issue was whether the medical member of the Tribunal was sufficiently independent as he was employed as a Consultant Psychiatrist by Mersey Care NHS Trust ('Mersey Care'), which was the 'mega' Trust that was responsible for detaining the claimant. The doctor had never worked in the hospital in which the claimant was detained and he did not know the claimant or any of the medically qualified or other witnesses at the hearing. It was not suggested that there was any actual bias on the part of the medical member. The Court of Appeal held that the wording of r 8 did not lead to the conclusion that the doctor was disqualified from sitting on the tribunal. He was not a member of the trust, and the meaning of the word 'officer' would depend on the context. In the present context it was natural to exclude those who managed the affairs of the authority in question. Moreover, no appearance of bias arose simply from the fact that the doctor was employed by the trust. Indeed, Lord Phillips MR, delivering the judgment of the court, described the contention that the doctor might have been biased as absurd, and

---

[34]   Mental Health Review Tribunal Rules 1983, SI 1983/942, r 8(2).
[35]   *R v Oxford Regional Mental Health Review, ex parte Mackman* (1986) *The Times*, 2 June.
[36]   [2005] EWHC 2791 (Admin).
[37]   *R (on the application of D) v West Midlands and North West Mental Health Review Tribunal* [2004] EWCA Civ 311, CA.

expressed the court's wonderment that the proceedings had ever been brought.[38] Appended to the Court of Appeal's decision is the Guidance issued by the MHRT on conflict of interest.

Tribunal clerks and tribunal assistants

9.29 Tribunal clerks are responsible for the administration of the tribunals, and advise on matters such as the appointment of tribunal members and administrative issues. The clerk exercises some administrative powers on behalf of the tribunal: he or she receives the application from the patient; sends out the necessary notices; obtains the responsible authority's statement and sends copies to the applicant, the applicant's representative and any other person who is entitled to receive it; arranges the time and place of the hearing; pays expenses and informs the applicant and other interested persons of the tribunal's decision. Tribunal assistants perform the role of usher and note-taker.

Entitlement to apply for a MHRT hearing

9.30 Under the MHA 1959, only patients detained following admission for treatment (now s 3) or under a hospital order (now s 37) were eligible to apply for discharge to a tribunal. Restricted patients could ask the Secretary of State for their case to be referred to the tribunal, but the jurisdiction of the tribunal in these cases was purely advisory. In *X v the United Kingdom*,[39] the European Court held that this advisory role breached Art 5(4) of the Convention. Following that ruling the UK Government empowered tribunals to direct the discharge of restriction order patients.[40] The MHA 1983 also introduced new rights for patients detained for up to 28 days' assessment, and for restricted patients to apply to a MHRT, as well as automatic referrals where patients had not applied.[41]

Part 2 patients

9.31 A patient admitted for assessment under s 2 may apply once within the first 14 days of detention.[42] In *R v South Thames Mental Health Review Tribunal, ex parte M*[43] Collins J explained a patient's tribunal entitlement where he or she is initially detained under s 2, but then detained under s 3 before the MHRT has heard the application for discharge from s 2. The MHRT hears the appeal as if it were an appeal against detention under s 3, and the patient's right to apply for a Tribunal under s 66(1)(b) in the first period of detention after his change of status is unaffected. A patient admitted for treatment under s 3 may apply once in the first six months, and thereafter once in every period for which

---

38   [2004] EWCA Civ 311 at [46].
39   (1981) 4 EHRR 178, 1 BMLR 98, ECtHR.
40   MHA 1983, s 73.
41   MHA 1983, s 66(1)(a), (2)(a), 68 and 70.
42   MHA 1983, s 66(1)(a) and (2)(a).
43   (unreported) 3 September 1997 (CO/2700/97), QBD.

the detention is renewed.[44] Patients subject to guardianship may apply once in the first six months, and thereafter once in every period for which the guardianship is renewed.[45] Patients who are transferred from guardianship to hospital may apply within six months of the transfer, and once during each period where detention is renewed. In such cases the renewal date is six months from the date of acceptance or the original guardianship application.[46] Patients who are subject to SCT may apply once within six months of the making or revocation of a CTO and once within every period for which the CTO is renewed.[47] Where a detained patient absents her or himself without leave, and a report under s 21B is furnished by the RC to the managers extending or renewing detention or a CTO, the patient may apply once within the period for which the detention or CTO is extended or renewed.[48]

Rights of Nearest Relatives ('NRs') or patients detained under Part 2

9.32   Where the NR has sought to discharge the patient and the RC has issued a barring certificate, the NR may apply for a tribunal hearing within 28 days.[49] Where the NR has been displaced by order of the county court on grounds of unreasonable objection to admission for treatment or guardianship or exercising the power of discharge without regard to the welfare of the patient or the public interest, he or she may apply to the tribunal once within every 12-month period during which the order remains in force.[50] A NR displaced on grounds of unsuitability or being too ill to act as NR will not have the right to apply to the MHRT.

Automatic references

9.33   Section 37 of the MHA 2007 amends s 68 to introduce a requirement to refer to the MHRT the case of any patient who has not applied for a hearing within six months from 'the applicable day', which is the day on which the patient was first detained, whether that was under s 2 for assessment, s 3 for treatment, or following a transfer from guardianship.[51] The duty to refer also arose under the MHA 1983 where the authority to detain was renewed and three years (or one year in the case of a child under 16) had elapsed since the patient's case was last considered by a MHRT. The amended s 68 breaks the link between renewal and referral. Now there is a duty to refer if a MHRT has not considered the patient's case in three years (or one year if the patient is under 18). The six-month, three-year and one-year periods can be reduced by

44   MHA 1983, ss 66(1)(b), (2)(b), (1)(f), (2)(f) and 20(2).
45   MHA 1983, ss 66(1)(c), (2)(c), (1)(f), (2)(f), and 20(2).
46   MHA 1983, ss 66(1)(e), (2)(e) and 19(2)(d).
47   MHA 1983, s 66(1)(ca), (1)(cb), (1)(fza), (2)(ca), (2)(cb), and (2)(fza).
48   MHA 1983, s 66(1)(fa), (1)(faa), (2)(f) and (fza).
49   MHA 1983, s 66(1)(g) and (2)(d).
50   MHA 1983, s 66(1)(h) and (2)(g).
51   MHA 1983, s 68(5), as inserted by MHA 2007, s 37(3).

order made under s 68A by the Secretary of State, in relation to hospitals in England, or the Welsh Ministers, in relation to hospitals in Wales.

Reference by the Secretary of State for Health

9.34   The case of a Part 2 or a non-restricted patient may be referred by the Secretary of State for Health under s 67. The Secretary of State for Health has the power under s 67 to refer the case of a Part 2 patient or an unrestricted Part 3 patient at any time. The Draft Code states that: 'Anyone may request such a referral and the Secretary of State will consider each such request on its merits.'[52]

Part 3 patients

9.35   Hospital order patients and their NRs may apply to the tribunal within the second six-month period, and thereafter once in every 12-month period.[53] Guardianship order patients and their NRs may apply once within the first six months of the guardianship order, and once in every period for which it is renewed.[54] Restriction order, restriction direction and hospital direction patients may apply once within the second six-month period following the restriction order, and thereafter once in every 12-month period.[55] Transfer direction patients detained under ss 47, 48 or 47 and 49, may apply to the tribunal within six months of the making of the direction, and thereafter at the same intervals as restriction order patients.[56] Their nearest relative may only apply if they are subject to a transfer direction without restrictions. Patients who have been conditionally discharged are entitled to apply for absolute discharge once in every two-year period. The date on which a patient is considered conditionally discharged is the date of actual release from detention in hospital.[57]

References by the Minister of Justice

9.36   The Minister of Justice may at any time refer the case of a restricted patient to a MHRT and has a duty to do so if the patient's case has not been considered by a MHRT, whether on his own application or otherwise, within the last three years. The minister must refer the case of a recalled conditionally discharged patient to a tribunal within one month of recall. Following the friendly settlement in *Roux v United Kingdom*[58] the UK Government agreed that a new r 29(cc) should be introduced to the MHRT Rules for cases of recall

---

[52]   Department of Health *Mental Health Act 1983 Draft Revised Code of Practice* (2007), para 33.37. See http://www.dh.gov.uk/en/Consultations.

[53]   MHA 1983, ss 66(1)(f), (2)(f), 40(4), Sch 1, Pt 1, paras 2, 6 and 9.

[54]   MHA 1983, s 69(1)(b) and 66(1)(f), (2)(f), 40(4), Sch 1, Pt 1, paras 2, 6 and 9.

[55]   MHA 1983, s 70.

[56]   MHA 1983, s 69(2)(b).

[57]   *R v Cannons Park Mental Health Review Tribunal, ex parte Martins* (1995) 26 BMLR 134, QBD.

[58]   *(Application 25601/94)* Decision of 4 September 1996, ECtHR.

of conditionally discharged restricted patients, whereby the tribunal would be required to fix a date between five and eight weeks from the date of reference. *R (on the application of B) v Mental Health Review Tribunal*[59] concerned delay of eight months in the hearing of a recalled restricted patient. Scott Baker J held that there had been a breach of Art 5(4), and that the underlying problem was a lack of case management on the tribunal's part. At each stage the tribunal ought to have had in mind the delay which had accrued and given directions against that background. The longer the delay, the more aggressive the directions would have to be in order to ensure an early disposal of the case. There would come a time where the convenience of expert witnesses had to cede to the need for the tribunal to conclude a substantive hearing. No adequate explanation had been given for the delays.

9.37   It should be noted that the practice which has been widely employed of bringing restricted patients back to hospital under ss 2 or 3 of the Act has been accepted as an appropriate alternative to recall in certain circumstances. In *R v North West London Mental Health NHS Trust, ex p S*,[60] the Court of Appeal held that the power to admit under s 3 was not excluded by the provisions of Part 3, and the rights of a patient detained under that power exist, including those of access to the tribunal under s 66, whether or not he happened also to be a conditionally discharged restricted patient. If he were discharged by the tribunal, it would be a discharge in relation to his liability to detention under s 3 which would in no way affect the Minister of Justice's power to recall him as a restricted patient. The independent operability of Parts 2 and 3 has important consequences for patients remanded by a criminal court for reports under s 35 of the MHA 1983. Section 56 of the Act provides that people remanded under s 35 are not subject to the provisions of Part 4 which authorise treatment without consent. In order to circumvent this, some psychiatrists have arranged for the admission of the patient under s 3 of the Act which does authorise treatment without consent under Part 4.[61] In *Dlodlo v Mental Health Review Tribunal for South Thames Region*[62] the patient had been conditionally discharged and re-admitted to hospital under s 3 of the MHA 1983. The Home Secretary recalled him to the hospital where he was already detained under s 3. The Court of Appeal held that the wider power of the Secretary of State may be exercised even if the person is already present and under detention at the hospital to which he is being recalled.

Legal aid

9.38   The rights of patients to put forward their cases for discharge in MHRT proceedings were enhanced by the introduction in 1983 of new tribunal rules, and by the extension of legal aid in the form of assistance by way of controlled

---

[59]   [2002] EWHC 1553 (Admin).
[60]   [1997] 4 All ER 871, (1997) 39 BMLR 105, CA.
[61]   See also *R (on the application of Wirral Health Authority) v Finnegan* [2001] All ER (D) 52 (Mar); confirmed by the Court of Appeal at [2001] EWCA Civ 1901.
[62]   (1996) 36 BMLR 145, CA.

representation (formerly called ABWOR) to MHRT proceedings. The means test in respect of controlled legal representation for MHRTs has been abolished.[63]

POWERS AND DUTIES IN RELATION TO DISCHARGE OF UNRESTRICTED PATIENTS

9.39   In respect of non-restricted patients, the tribunal has a general discretion to discharge a patient from liability to detention or guardianship in any case.[64] Section 72(2) which specified factors which must be considered by the MHRT in exercising the discretion, including the likelihood of medical treatment alleviating or preventing deterioration of the patient's condition, is repealed by s 4(8) of the MHA 2007. Nevertheless the discretion remains, and the MHRT must give reasons for exercising it. Where there has been risk to self or to others, the MHRT will still have to consider and spell out what treatment is considered necessary and satisfy itself that this would be available without the need for the patient to remain liable to be detained.[65] The circumstances in which a MHRT comes under a duty to discharge an unrestricted patient are set out in s 72(1). Paragraph 23(4) of Sch 3 to the MHA 2007 introduces a new subs (3A) which provides that nothing in s 72(1) requires a tribunal to direct the discharge of a patient just because they think it might be appropriate for the patient to be discharged (subject to the possibility of recall) under a CTO. If they think that, the tribunal may recommend that the RC consider a CTO, and may (but need not) further consider the patient's case if the responsible clinician does not make an order.

Duty to discharge s 2 patients

9.40   The tribunal must discharge a patient admitted under s 2 if they are not satisfied *either*:

(1)   that he is then suffering from mental disorder or from mental disorder of a nature or degree which warrants detention in hospital for assessment; or

(2)   that his detention is justified in the interests of his health or safety or the protection of others.[66]

The criteria for discharge correspond with the criteria for admission. The tribunal *must* discharge a patient if they are not satisfied that he is then suffering from mental disorder of a nature or degree warranting detention for assessment. In criterion (2), 'interests of his own health or safety' is an

---

[63]   Legal Advice and Assistance (Amendment) Regulations 1994, SI 1994/805.

[64]   MHA 1983, s 72(1).

[65]   *R (on the application of East London and the City Mental Health NHS Trust) v Mental Health Review Tribunal* [2005] EWHC 2329 (Admin), per Collins J at [19]–[20].

[66]   MHA 1983, s 72(1)(a).

alternative to 'the protection of other persons'. The tribunal may continue to detain the patient if only one of the grounds – health *or* safety *or* the protection of others – is fulfilled.

Patients detained under ss 3 or 37

9.41   The tribunal has a duty to discharge a patient detained under ss 3 or 37 if it is *not* satisfied:

(i)   that he is then suffering from mental disorder or from mental disorder of a nature or degree which makes it appropriate for him to be liable to be detained in a hospital for medical treatment; or

(ii)   that it is necessary for the health of safety of the patient or for the protection of other persons that he should receive such treatment; or

(iia)   that appropriate medical treatment is available for him; or

(iii)   in the case of an application by the nearest relative following the barring of a discharge order, that the patient, if released, would be likely to act in a manner dangerous to other persons or to himself.[67]

If the MHRT is not satisfied that any one of these grounds applies, they are under a duty to discharge. The terms 'nature or degree' in relation to mental disorder are disjunctive. In other words a person can have a detainable mental disorder which although not currently exhibiting symptoms of a degree justifying detention, nevertheless is of such a serious nature that detention is warranted.[68] The tribunal must discharge if it is not satisfied that the treatment is necessary for the health *or* safety of the patient *or* for the protection of other persons. If it is necessary for one of these reasons, that will be enough to justify continued detention, provided the availability of appropriate treatment test has been met. Cases like *R v Canons Park Mental Health Review Tribunal, ex parte A*,[69] *Reid v Secretary of State for Scotland*,[70] and *Reid v United Kingdom*[71] show a trend towards requiring tribunals to apply discharge criteria which mirror the admission criteria. Note here that the mental disorder must be of a nature or degree which makes it appropriate for the patient to be *liable to be detained* in hospital, not of a nature or degree making detention appropriate. The discharge criteria do not mirror the admission criteria in this respect.

---

[67]   MHA 1983, s 72(1)(b).

[68]   *R v Mental Health Review Tribunal for the South Thames Region, ex parte Smith* (1998) 47 BMLR 104.

[69]   [1995] QB 60, CA.

[70]   [1999] 2 WLR 28, HL.

[71]   (2003) 37 EHRR 9, ECtHR.

Patients subject to community treatment orders

9.42   The MHRT must direct the discharge of a community patient if they are not satisfied:

(i)   that he is then suffering from a mental disorder or mental disorder of a nature or degree which makes it appropriate for him to receive medical treatment; or

(ii)   that it is necessary for his health or safety or for the protection of other persons that he should receive such treatment; or

(iii)   that it is necessary that the responsible clinician should be able to exercise the power under s 17E(1) to recall the patient to hospital; or

(iv)   that appropriate medical treatment is available for him; or

(v)   in the case of an application by the nearest relative following barring of a discharge order, that the patient, if discharged, would be likely to act in a manner dangerous to other persons or to himself.

When determining whether it is necessary that the RC should have the power of recall, the MHRT must:[72]

> 'in particular, consider, having regard to the patient's history of mental disorder and any other relevant factors, what risk there would be of a deterioration of the patient's condition if he were to continue not to be detained in a hospital (as a result, for example, of his refusing or neglecting to receive the medical treatment he requires for his mental disorder).'

The MHA 2007 does not empower the patient to seek review of specific conditions before the MHRT. That will only be possible by judicial review.

Guardianship patients

9.43   MHRTs have a general discretion to discharge a guardianship patient in any case, and must so direct if satisfied:

(a)   that the patient is not then suffering from mental disorder; or

(b)   that it is not necessary in the interests of the welfare of the patient, or for the protection of other persons, that the patient should remain under such guardianship.

Unlike patients detained in hospital there is no specification as to the nature or degree of the disorder. In criterion (b), 'the interests of the welfare of the patient' is wider than the corresponding term 'for the health or safety of the

---

[72]   MHA 1983, s 72(1A), as inserted by MHA 2007, Sch 3, para 21(3).

patient' which is applicable to detained patients. It should be noted that the burden of proof in relation to guardianship remains as before on the patient. There will be an issue of compatibility with Art 5(4) if the new possibilities to take and convey a person to a place of required residence and to return them there are used to amount in effect to a deprivation of liberty. In relation to people under guardianship who are not subject to sufficient control to be deprived of their liberty, there are equally compelling arguments for removing the reverse burden of proof. In *R (on the application of SC) v Mental Health Review Tribunal* Munby J said that when concerned with the exercise by State authorities of compulsory powers in relation to persons suffering from mental disorder, increased vigilance is called for in reviewing whether the Convention has been complied with.[73] The judge accepted that MHRT decisions in relation to conditionally discharged restricted patient could engage Art 8 and Art 6 as the patient could be required to reside at a specified place, was required to comply with the directions of the RMO and could be recalled to hospital. If civil rights and obligations under Art 8 are engaged, any interference with private life authorised by the MHRT must be in accordance with law, which must be foreseeable in its effects, and the MHRT is acting as an independent and impartial tribunal for the purposes of Art 6. In such a situation where the State is interfering with private life, it should be for the State to bear the burden of justifying the interference.

Nearest Relative applications

9.44 Where the nearest relative of a patient applies for discharge, the tribunal must discharge if it is satisfied that the patient would not, if discharged, be likely to act in a manner dangerous to self or to others. This is based on the principle that the family is permitted to take responsibility for the health needs of their loved one, but they are not entitled to take over the role of protecting society and the patient from dangerous conduct: this is the function of the State.[74]

Discharge on a future date

9.45 Section 72(3) empowers the tribunal to direct the discharge of a patient on a future date specified in the direction. The power is not available for restricted patients.[75] In *R v Mental Health Review Tribunal for North Thames Region, ex parte Pierce* Harrison J held that that s 72 operates in the following way:[76]

> 'The tribunal deals first with the principle whether or not to direct discharge. If (i), the patient is not suffering from mental disorder of a nature or degree making treatment in hospital appropriate, or (ii), detention is not necessary in the interests

---

[73] [2005] EWHC 17 (Admin) at [54].
[74] *R v Mental Health Review Tribunal for North Thames Region, ex parte Pierce* (1996) 36 BMLR 137.
[75] *Grant v Mental Health Review Tribunal* (1986) *The Times*, 28 April, QBD.
[76] (1996) 36 BMLR 137.

of his health or safety or for the protection of others, applies, they are obliged to direct discharge. If not, they have to decide whether to direct discharge in the exercise of their discretion. Having decided whether or not to direct discharge, the tribunal has to decide whether that discharge should be immediate or should be delayed under s 72(3).'

Reasons for directing discharge on a future date would include setting up community support. Discharge on a future date means that the discharge takes place on that date, whether or not the services are in place. The Court of Appeal has held that the MHRT must therefore give careful consideration to the likelihood that the services will be available within that time:[77]

'If the tribunal is in doubt as to whether suitable after-care arrangements will be made available, it is difficult to see how they can specify a specific date on which to discharge. In cases of doubt, the safer course is to adjourn. On the facts of the case, the tribunal could not reasonably have assumed that the services would be provided as soon as H was discharged into the community.'

For that reason alone the Court of Appeal held the tribunal's decision to be *Wednesbury* unreasonable.

Recommendations with the power to reconvene

9.46 The MHRT has power to recommend leave of absence, transfer to another hospital or into guardianship and to reconsider the case in the event of the recommendation not being complied with.[78] Where a decision with recommendations is made, the tribunal must specify the period at the end of which it will consider the case further if the recommendations are not complied with. If it appears to the tribunal that they have not been complied with, the tribunal may reconvene the proceedings after giving 14 days' notice.[79] In *Mental Health Review Tribunal v Hempstock* Kay J held that MHRTs have all the powers at the time of further consideration that they had originally. They can order immediate discharge, or future discharge. Although the circumstances in which they might exercise the power might be rare, the powers were available for consideration.[80] The MHRT may also recommend that the RC consider a CTO may (but need not) further consider the patient's case if the RC does not make an order.[81] It should be noted that these are the only express powers to make recommendations which the tribunal has been granted under the Act. There is no power to make other recommendations, such as changes of medication, and these can be confusing and dangerous for those who have to implement tribunals' findings. Tribunals should therefore exercise extreme caution, and a self-denying ordinance may be the preferred course.[82]

---

[77] [2002] EWCA Civ 923.

[78] MHA 1983, s 72(3)(a) and (b).

[79] Mental Health Review Tribunal Rules 1983, SI 1983/942, rr 24(4), 25(2).

[80] (1997) 39 BMLR 123.

[81] MHA 1983, s 78(3A), as inserted by MHA 2007, Sch 3, para 21(4).

[82] Blom-Cooper, Grounds et al *The Case of Jason Mitchell: Report of the Independent Inquiry* (Duckworth, 1996), chap 9.

POWERS WITH REGARD TO RESTRICTION ORDER PATIENTS

General

9.47 In cases involving restricted patients, MHRTs have no overriding discretion to discharge. They may only do so when they are satisfied that the relevant statutory criteria are met. One of the circumstances where a restricted patient's case must be referred to a MHRT is following recall to hospital by the Home Secretary. Here the MHRT's function is to consider the justification for detention at the time of the hearing, not whether the recall was justified. But events prior to recall might be relevant to the decision as to whether the patient currently meets the criteria for continued detention. In *R v Merseyside Mental Health Review Tribunal, ex parte Kelly*, the patient had been recalled after a number of criminal allegations were made against him. Proceedings were not taken in relation to these allegations and he denied them. The medical evidence of his RMO assumed that he was guilty and concluded that it was difficult to assess the risk presented by the patient, given his denials. Keene J concluded that it was:[83]

> 'unfair procedurally for the tribunal to prevent cross-examination of the RMO about the factual basis for his conclusions and to prevent evidence being led by the applicant on the same topic. If that factual basis could not be tested in that way, one can only wonder how it was that the applicant would be able to conduct his case in a proper manner with any prospect at all of success.'

Absolute discharge

9.48 Section 73(1) requires the MHRT to direct the absolute discharge of the patient if they are not satisfied:

(a)   –

    (i)   that he is then suffering from mental disorder or from mental disorder of a nature or degree which makes it appropriate for him to be liable to be detained in a hospital for medical treatment; *or*

    (ii) that it is necessary for the health of safety of the patient or for the protection of other persons that he should receive such treatment; *or*

    (iia) that appropriate medical treatment is available for him; *and*

(b)   that it is appropriate for the patient to remain liable to be recalled to hospital for further treatment.

Even if a tribunal is not satisfied that a patient is mentally disordered at the time of the hearing, it must direct conditional discharge unless satisfied that it

---

[83]   (1997) 39 BMLR 114.

is not appropriate for the patient to remain liable to recall.[84] In *R (on the application for the Secretary of State for the Home Department) v Mental Health Tribunal* Moses J said that:

> 'It might very well be in such a case that, whilst a Tribunal would not be satisfied at one particular moment that someone was suffering from a psychopathic disorder, later on symptoms might emerge which would make it highly appropriate and indeed necessary for such a patient to be recalled to hospital'.

There must be an express finding that it is not appropriate for the patient to remain subject to recall for further treatment. In *R (on the application for the Secretary of State for the Home Department) v Mental Health Tribunal* Pill LJ said:[85]

> 'The possible consequences for the safety of members of the public and the patient, when an order for absolute discharge is made are such that the question of liability to be recalled must be dealt with expressly. A failure to deal with the requirement of s 73(1)(b) is a fatal flaw to the tribunal's decision.'

Reasons for preferring absolute discharge to conditional discharge should be given, and such decisions are open to challenge by the Secretary of State by way of judicial review.[86] The effect of an absolute discharge is that both the hospital order and the restriction order are discharged.[87]

Conditional discharge

9.49   Section 72(2) requires the MHRT to direct conditional discharge where it is satisfied that the patient needs to be subject to recall but is not satisfied that the patient has mental disorder of the requisite nature or degree, that detention is necessary for health safety or the protection of others, or that appropriate treatment is available. In *Secretary of State for the Home Department v Mental Health Review Tribunal for Wales*,[88] it was held that a tribunal must be satisfied that the patient should be released from hospital before directing conditional discharge. In *R (on the application of Secretary of State for the Home Department) v Mental Health Review Tribunal*[89] Collins J upheld a challenge by the Home Office to a decision to discharge a patient to a 24-hour staffed hostel which he would only be able to leave under escort. This would amount to a deprivation of liberty rather than a discharge, and therefore the MHRT had no jurisdiction to make such an order. See also *R (on the application of G) v Mental Health Review Tribunal* where it was held that a condition of residence in a rehabilitation flat within the hospital grounds could be a deprivation of

---

[84]   *R v Merseyside Mental Health Review Tribunal, ex parte K* [1990] 1 All ER 694, (1989) 4 BMLR 60, CA.

[85]   [2001] EWHC Admin 849.

[86]   *R (on the application of the Secretary of State for the Home Department) v Mental Health Review Tribunal* [2005] EWCA Civ 1616.

[87]   MHA 1983, s 73(3).

[88]   [1986] 1 WLR 1170, [1986] 3 All ER 233.

[89]   [2004] EWHC 2194 (Admin).

liberty. Collins J held that the lack of any changes in regime or accommodation led inexorably to the conclusion that there was a deprivation of liberty.[90]

Conditions

9.50   The patient must abide by any conditions laid down by the tribunal or subsequently imposed by the Minister of Justice. A patient who is conditionally discharged may be recalled to hospital by the Minister. The Minister may also vary any condition which has been imposed either by the MHRT or by himself.[91] It should be noted that the MHRT is not obliged to lay down specific conditions when it makes its order for conditional discharge. However, in practice it is unlikely that a patient will be conditionally discharged without conditions being imposed either by the MHRT or by the Home Secretary. The rationale of the power of recall rests on the opportunity to detect any deterioration in the patient's condition and to intervene before any further offence is committed.

Power to defer conditional discharge

9.51   The power to defer a conditional discharge differs significantly from the power to delay a discharge in the case of a non-restricted patient (see para **9.45** above). Where a tribunal delays the discharge of an unrestricted patient, it makes an order for discharge which is to take effect at a specified date in the future; discharge must be effected on or before that date, irrespective of whether arrangements for the patient's care have been completed. On the other hand, where a tribunal considering the case of a patient subject to a restriction order defers a direction for his conditional discharge, it postpones the coming into effect of the discharge direction until arrangements are made to its satisfaction. In *Secretary of State for the Home Department v Mental Health Review Tribunal for the Mersey Regional Health Authority* it was held that the tribunal cannot defer a conditional discharge until arrangements are made for admission to another hospital.[92]

9.52   The difficulty with the power of deferred conditional discharge is that it can result in an impasse where the MHRT suggests conditions which for one reason or another are not met by the relevant authorities. The classic Convention case on this is *Johnson v United Kingdom*.[93] Johnson was found by three tribunals (1989, 1990 and 1991) not to be suffering from mental disorder, but his conditional discharge was deferred until a suitable hostel could be found. However, no hostel was found, and he was finally released following a tribunal hearing in 1993. The European Court held that there had been a breach of Art 5(1). The court rejected the argument that a finding by an expert authority that a person is no longer suffering from the form of mental illness which led to his confinement must inevitably lead to his immediate and

---

[90]   [2004] EWHC 2193 (Admin).
[91]   MHA 1983, s 73(4), (5).
[92]   [1986] 1 WLR 1170, [1986] 3 All ER 233.
[93]   (1997) 27 EHRR 296.

unconditional release into the community. This would be an unfortunate curtailment of the expert authority's discretion to assess, part of the 'margin of appreciation' left to the national authorities. Nevertheless, discharge must not be unreasonably delayed, and there must be safeguards, including remedies of a judicial nature to ensure that discharge is not unduly delayed.

9.53 The classic British case on this issue is now the decision of the House of Lords in *R (on the application of H) v Secretary of State for the Home Department*[94] which concerned a patient with a diagnosis of paranoid psychosis. He had a MHRT hearing in June which was adjourned until Dec 1999 at the latest for a full care plan to be drawn up for the patient's conditional discharge. The consultant forensic psychiatrist of the North London Forensic Service, which provided psychiatric services on behalf of the authority, took the view, shared by all his colleagues, that 'a proposed conditional discharge ... direct into the community was clinically inappropriate, and unsafe'. He was willing to admit the appellant to his medium secure unit, but he and his colleagues declined to supervise the appellant as named forensic psychiatrist on conditional discharge. Transfer to the regional secure unit in question was precluded by the Home Secretary withholding consent. The tribunal reconvened on 3 February 2000, and directed the applicant's deferred conditional discharge. The tribunal expressed itself satisfied that the patient was not then suffering from mental disorder of a nature or degree which made it appropriate for the patient to be liable to be detained in a hospital for medical treatment. The tribunal was also satisfied that, if suitable after-care arrangements could be put in place, it would not be necessary in the interests of the patient's health or safety or for the protection of others that he should receive such treatment. They considered that the patient should remain liable to recall. However, because of the risk factors involved, the tribunal deferred the discharge until suitable arrangements could be made for after-care supervision in the community.

9.54 Further unsuccessful attempts were made by the health authority to find a psychiatrist willing to supervise the appellant but without success and his detention continued. The House of Lords held that in order to ensure compatibility with Art 5(4) a decision to defer conditional discharge should be treated as a provisional decision, and the tribunal should monitor progress towards implementing it so as to ensure that the patient is not left 'in limbo for an unreasonable length of time'. The tribunal should meet after an appropriate interval to monitor progress in making these arrangements if they have not been put in place. Once the arrangements have been made, the tribunal can direct a conditional discharge without a further hearing. If problems arise with making arrangements to meet the conditions, the tribunal may:

(1)   defer for a further period;

(2)   amend or vary the proposed conditions;

---

[94]   [2003] UKHL 59.

(3)   order conditional discharge without specific conditions, thereby making patient subject to recall;

(4)   decide that patient remain detained in hospital for treatment.

9.55   The House of Lords went on to hold that the duty of the health authority, whether under s 117 of the MHA 1983 or in response to the tribunal's order of deferred conditional discharge, was to use its best endeavours to procure compliance with the conditions laid down by the tribunal. This it had done. It was not subject to an absolute obligation to procure compliance and was not at fault in failing to do so. It had no power to require any psychiatrist to act in a way which conflicted with the conscientious professional judgment of that psychiatrist. Thus, the appellant could base no claim on the fact that the tribunal's conditions were not met. This conclusion made it unnecessary to address the question on which the House heard argument, but which was not considered below, whether in a context such as this psychiatrists were or could be a hybrid public authority under s 6 of the Human Rights Act 1998. Determination of that question was best left to a case in which it is necessary to the decision. It is suggested that even if a clinician in such a situation is a public authority, a decision not to act as a responsible clinician would not be held to breach Art 5 if it were taken in a genuine and bona fide exercise of clinical judgment.

Recommendations

9.56   Section 72(3), which gives MHRTs power to make recommendations and reconvene if these are not complied with, does not apply to restricted patients.[95] Although the Home Office has indicated that it will be happy to receive recommendations in restriction order cases, the tribunal has no power to reconvene in the event of their not being complied with. Nor may the tribunal adjourn a restricted patient hearing *solely* to gather information relating to making a recommendation, although there is nothing to stop it gathering such information if it adjourns to obtain further information on a matter within its jurisdiction (discharge).[96] Rule 25(2) of the Tribunal Rules has been amended to make it clear that it was not intended for MHRTs to be able to reconvene to consider recommendations.[97] As for the duties of health and social services under s 117, in *R (on the application of W) v Doncaster Metropolitan Borough Council*[98] Stanley Burnton J held that the authority's duty was, before actual discharge, to endeavour to put in place the arrangements required by the tribunal as conditions of a conditional discharge, or which the tribunal required to be satisfied before a deferred discharge took effect, or which the tribunal provisionally decided should be put in place.

---

[95]   *Grant v Mental Health Review Tribunal* (1986) *The Times*, 28 April, QBD.
[96]   *R (on the application of the Secretary of State for the Home Department) v Mental Health Review Tribunal* (unreported) 2000 (CO/1928/2000).
[97]   MHRT (Amendment) Rules 1998, SI 1998/1189, r 2(3).
[98]   [2003] EWHC 192 (Admin).

9.57   In *R (on the application of H) v Mental Health Review Tribunal*[99] Stanley Burnton J held that the power to make recommendations is expressly qualified. There is no power to make recommendations with a view to anything else than facilitating future discharge. Where discharge is not in contemplation, the Convention does not require the MHRT to give reasons for not making recommendations. The applicant was detained under s 3 in an institution remote from his mother's home. The tribunal found that the patient continued to require detention and that this could only be provided in conditions of high security. The applicant argued that the tribunal had breached Art 8 of the Convention because it had failed to make a recommendation in relation to the patient that she live at home, and had failed to give reasons for that failure. Stanley Burnton J held that there was no evidence to justify making a recommendation of transfer. In those circumstances the absence of any reasons was wholly explicable.

9.58   In *R v Secretary of State for the Home Department, ex parte Harry*[100] the MHRT recommended transfer from a special hospital to a regional secure unit. The patient's RMO subsequently made a proposal for the patient to be granted a period of trial leave. The Home Office submitted the proposal to the Advisory Board on Restricted Patients (sometimes known as the Aarvold Board after Sir Carl Aarvold, chair of the committee which recommended its establishment following the *Graham Young* case in the 1970s). After considering a report from a non-medical member of the board that Harry was still as dangerous as ever, the Home Office did not approve the leave. The applicant sought judicial review of the Home Secretary's decisions:

(a)   to refer the proposal to the board; and

(b)   to act on its recommendations.

The court held that the MHA 1983 entrusted the Home Secretary with the task of deciding whether to consent, and he could not deprive himself of further information if he considered it to be required; the only limitation on his freedom to consult and act on the board's recommendation was his obligation to act in a procedurally fair manner. The patient should be furnished with the report, given the gist of its contents, and invited to make representations on it to the Board. He should also have been furnished with the advice note and invited to make representations to the Secretary of Home Secretary.

Status of recommendations

9.59   The fact that a MHRT has made a recommendation with funding implications does not mean that the NHS commissioning bodies are obliged under the Human Rights Act 1998 to fund it. In *R (on the application of F) v*

99   [2002] EWHC 1522 (Admin).
100   [1998] 3 All ER 360, QBD.

Oxfordshire Mental Healthcare NHS Trust[101] the tribunal recommended transfer to a RSU, and recommended that the patient go to a unit in Manchester where her parents lived and where she wanted to go, rather than the Oxford unit with which the Trust contracted for its secure psychiatric provision, and which was in the area of her index offence, described as horrific. The Manchester placement would necessitate a costly extra-contractual referral. The Trust set up a forum to decide on funding declined to fund the Manchester placement. The applicant sought judicial review arguing that her rights to family life under Art 8 were engaged by the denial of an extra-contractual referral, and this meant that the forum had to attach sufficient weight to the opinion of her current RMO who was in favour of Manchester. Sullivan J held that the forum was not obliged, either as a matter of proportionality or rationality, to accept the RMO's view. Fairness required that the claimant should have the opportunity to tell the forum in writing why it was contended that resources should be allocated to her. If Art 8 was engaged a balancing Act had to be carried out under Art 8(2):

'in a world where the funds available for medical treatment are limited and where granting a patient's request will inevitably mean that other patients will be disappointed. They will have to wait longer or be denied pain-killing drugs.'

The judge went on to say that:[102]

'Decisions on funding affect lives, not just liberty. That is a good reason not to judicialise them. They are agonisingly difficult decisions, and they will not be made any easier or better by being encumbered with legalistic procedures.'

The courts have traditionally been unwilling to involve themselves in decisions about the allocation of resources in health care generally. This case applies that principle in the mental health context.

PATIENTS SUBJECT TO A RESTRICTION DIRECTION (INCLUDING HOSPITAL DIRECTIONS WITH LIMITATION DIRECTIONS)

Role of the MHRT

9.60 Patients transferred from prison to hospital, including those transferred under s 48, have the right to apply to the MHRT. Where a patient has been transferred from prison to a hospital under a restriction direction, or is detained under a hospital direction, the tribunal is not empowered to order his discharge. This is because, technically, the patient is still subject to his sentence and thus any decision regarding his discharge must be taken by the Minister of Justice. The legislation gives the final decision to the Minister of Justice as to whether the patient is discharged or remitted to prison. Under the MHA 1983

---

[101] [2001] EWHC Admin 535.
[102] [2001] EWHC Admin 535 at [76]–[80].

the tribunal's role is limited to notifying the Minister of Justice whether the patient would be entitled to be absolutely or conditionally discharged had he been subject to a restriction order. Thus, the tribunal must consider the same statutory criteria that apply to a patient subject to a restriction order.[103]

Notification of entitlement to absolute discharge

9.61   If the Minister of Justice is notified that the patient would be entitled to be absolutely discharged, he may, within 90 days, consent to the discharge and the tribunal must accordingly discharge the patient. If, at the end of the 90-day period, the Minister has not given his consent, the hospital managers must transfer the patient back to prison or to the other institution from where he came; the patient would then serve the remainder of his sentence or be dealt with as if he had not been transferred to hospital. The logic of this provision is that if the person is entitled to an absolute discharge, there is no case for continuing to detain him in a hospital. The issue becomes whether the person is dangerous and requires further detention in prison to complete his sentence or whether he can be released. Section 74 makes this a matter for the Minister.

Notification of entitlement to conditional discharge

9.62   Where the tribunal notifies the Minister of Justice that the patient would be entitled to be conditionally discharged it may add a recommendation that the patient should remain in hospital if his discharge is not approved. As with absolute discharge, if, within 90 days, the Minister gives his consent, the tribunal must conditionally discharge the patient; it may defer the direction for conditional discharge in the same way as for patients subject to a restriction order.[104] Section 74(3) provides that if the Minister does not give his consent and the tribunal has not recommended that the patient should remain in hospital, then the hospital managers must return him to the prison or other institution from which he came. If the tribunal has recommended that the patient should remain in hospital if not discharged, then he cannot be returned to prison. The logic of this is that for the patient who is entitled to conditional discharge but is not so discharged there is a choice to be made: whether he would benefit from further hospital care as opposed to prison confinement. The MHRT assists the Minister in this choice by making appropriate recommendations.

9.63   This means that the patient who is declared suitable for discharge from mental health detention can have that discharge blocked and be returned to prison unless the Minister consents to the implementation of the tribunal's decision of entitlement to discharge. Hence, a patient could be remitted to prison in such a case, and have to seek review of the continued need for their detention via the Parole Board which has the power to release them. If the MHRT has recommended the patient should remain in hospital if not

---

[103]   MHA 1983, s 74(1).
[104]   MHA 1983, s 74(1)(b), (2), (6) and (7).

discharged, they remain in hospital and are still entitled to review by the Parole Board by virtue of s 74(5A), introduced following a declaration of incompatibility in *R (on the application of D) v Secretary of State for the Home Department.*[105] Stanley Burnton J held s 74(3) to be incompatible with Art 5 of the ECHR in relation to discretionary lifers where the tribunal recommended that they remain in hospital if not discharged, on the grounds that it deprived them of their right to Art 5(4) review. Section 74(5A) provides that if the Parole Board make a direction or recommendation by virtue of which the patient would become entitled to be released, any restriction or limitation direction ceases to have effect 'at the time when he would become entitled to be so released'.

CONDITIONALLY DISCHARGED PATIENTS

9.64   Section 75 of the MHA 1983 gives the right to conditionally discharged patients to apply to tribunals; such patients did not have a right to a tribunal hearing under the MHA 1959. The tribunal has the power to change the conditions, or to discharge absolutely. The tribunal may vary any condition by which the patient must abide or impose a new condition.[106] Thus, the tribunal may change a condition in accordance with a change in the patient's circumstances or remove a condition if it is no longer necessary. In *R (on the application of SC) v Mental Health Review Tribunal* Munby J agreed that decisions under s 75 could engage Arts 6 and 8. This means that any interference with private life authorised by the MHRT must be in accordance with law, which must be foreseeable in its effects, and that the MHRT is acting as an independent and impartial tribunal for the purposes of Art 6. Whilst Munby J accepted that Arts 6 and 8 were engaged, he dismissed the application on the grounds that, whilst s 75(3) lays down no criteria for the exercise of the discretion it bestows, it was sufficiently foreseeable in it effects. Munby J said that MHRTs exercising the s 75(3) power:[107]

> '[W]ill need to consider such matters as the nature, gravity and circumstances of the patient's offence, the nature and gravity of his mental disorder, past, present and future, the risk and likelihood of the patient re-offending, the degree of harm to which the public may be exposed if he re-offends, the risk and likelihood of a recurrence or exacerbation of any mental disorder, and the risk and likelihood of his needing to be recalled in the future for further treatment in hospital. The Tribunal will also need to consider the nature of any conditions previously imposed, whether by the Tribunal or by the Secretary of State, the reasons why they were imposed and the extent to which it is desirable to continue, vary or add to them.'

---

[105]   [2002] EWHC 2805 (Admin), [2003] MHLR 193. See also *Benjamin v United Kingdom* (2003) 36 EHRR 1, ECtHR. Section 74(5A) was introduced by the Criminal Justice Act 2003, s 295.
[106]   MHA 1983, s 75(3)(a).
[107]   [2005] EWHC 17 (Admin) at [57].

The tribunal's general statutory role is to review the justification for detaining the patient or for otherwise restricting his liberty. Only in the most exceptional circumstances will the tribunal be likely to conclude that its duty is to impose upon the patient conditions more restrictive than those already imposed by the Minister of Justice or by a previous tribunal. The MHRT may direct that the restriction order, restriction direction, or limitation is lifted. The patient will then cease to be liable to be detained under the hospital order or transfer direction and will not be subject to recall to hospital.[108]

PRE-HEARING PROCEDURES

Application

9.65 An application must be made to the MHRT in writing and signed by the applicant or any person authorised by him to do so on his behalf. Where possible it should contain specified information, including the patient's name and address and the address of the hospital, but if any of this information is not included, it must, so far as is practicable, be provided by the responsible authority or the Home Secretary if requested by the MHRT.[109]

Notice of the application

9.66 Rule 4 requires that notice must be given to the patient (if not the applicant), to the responsible authority, and to the Home Secretary in the case of a restricted patient. Failure to give notice to the Home Secretary in a restricted case invalidates the proceedings. In *R (on the application of the Secretary of State for the Home Department) v Mental Health Review Tribunal* Owen J quashed the decision of a MHRT where the Home Office had not had notice because the effect of failure to notify is to undermine the statutory scheme and remove the essential mechanism for safeguarding the public interest.[110]

The responsible authority's report

9.67 Rule 6 requires that the responsible authority's statement, including biographical information, an up-to-date medical report, and, insofar as is reasonably practicable to provide it, an up-to-date social circumstances report, must be sent within three weeks, or two weeks if the patient is a recalled conditionally discharged patient.[111] If the hearing concerns a s 2 patient, the hearing must be within seven days of receipt of the application and duty of the

---

[108] The power to lift a limitation direction or restriction direction is added to s 75(3) by s 41 of the MHA 2007.

[109] Mental Health Review Tribunal Rules 1983, SI 1983/942, r 3.

[110] [2004] EWHC 650 (Admin), applying the House of Lords ruling in *Secretary of State for the Home Department v Oxford Regional Mental Health Review Tribunal* [1987] 3 All ER 8, HL.

[111] Mental Health Review Tribunal Rules 1983, SI 1983/942, r 6 and Sch, r 29(c), as amended by MHRT (Amendment) Rules 1998, SI 1998/1189.

responsible authority is to provide such of the above information as can reasonably be provided in the time available.[112]

Disclosure of information to the applicant, the patient, the responsible authority and the Secretary of State

9.68 The responsible authority may set aside parts of its statement which it considers should not be disclosed, but the final decision as to whether the patient should see these is for the tribunal. In practice, there is much more disclosure since the MHA 1983. Information can only be withheld if its disclosure would adversely affect the health or welfare of the patient or others, and reasons have to be given by the responsible authority. MHRT must then consider if disclosure would have adverse effect claimed and, if satisfied that it would, must record in writing its decision not to disclose. The patient has the right to submit comments on any documents released to him.[113]

9.69 Rule 12 requires the MHRT to disclose in full every document it receives to the applicant, the patient if he or she is not the applicant, the Secretary of State and the responsible Authority. Each has the right to submit written comments on any document released to them.

9.70 If any document is withheld from the applicant or the patient it must be disclosed to their representative provided the representative is:

(i)   a barrister or solicitor;

(ii)   a doctor; or

(iii)   a person whom the tribunal considers suitable by reason of his experience or professional qualification.

The information must not be disclosed to the applicant or patient without the authority of the MHRT and must not be used otherwise than in connection with the application. In a case involving a restricted patient, the Secretary of State is entitled to all relevant documents received by the tribunal. Breach of this requirement will invalidate the proceedings.[114]

Parties

9.71 The following are parties to the proceedings: the applicant, the patient, the responsible authority, any person who has received notice of the proceedings in accordance with rr 7 or 31(c) and any person who is added as a party by direction of the tribunal.[115]

---

[112]   Ibid, rr 31(a) and 32.
[113]   Ibid, rr 6(4)(5) and 12(1)–(2).
[114]   *Campbell v Secretary of State for the Home Department* [1988] 1 AC 120, HL.
[115]   Mental Health Review Tribunal Rules 1983, SI 1983/942, r 2.

Notice to other persons interested

9.72   Rule 7 requires notice of the proceedings to be given to a list of persons or bodies including the registration authority if the patient is in a private establishment, to the guardian, the nearest relative, any health authority with the power of discharge. Notice will also need to be given to anyone exercising a lasting power of attorney or acting as a deputy in respect of the person. Rule 7(f) requires notice to be given to any person who, in the opinion of the MHRT, should have an opportunity of being heard. In *R (on the application of T) v Mental Health Review Tribunal* Scott Baker J dismissed an application for judicial review of a decision not to make a victim a party by giving her notice of the proceedings under r 7.[116] In the light of the Domestic Violence, Crime and Victims Act 2004 the MHRTs have determined that victims of violent or sexual offences should be notified of the hearing under r 7 as persons who in the opinion of the tribunal 'should have the opportunity of being heard.' The Guidance states that there will be a presumption in favour of the victim having the right to give evidence.[117] Rule 5 empowers the Regional Chairman to exercise the power to give notice at any time up to the hearing. Once notice is given, the victim becomes a party and is entitled to be represented, and may be accompanied by any other person under r 10. The manner of presentation of evidence will be determined by the tribunal or by the regional chairman in advance of the hearing. Issues such as:

- will evidence be heard in the presence of the other parties? *or*

- will there be cross examination?

will be determined pre-hearing.

9.73   The Domestic Violence, Crime and Victims Act 2004 procedures apply to offences after July 2005, but the MHRT has determined that similar rights will also be conferred on victims of offences occurring prior to that date. The Act applies to violent or sexual offences where the offender is subject to:

(a)   a hospital order with or without restrictions following conviction, finding of not guilty by reason of insanity or finding of unfitness to plead;

(b)   a hospital direction with or without a limitation direction; or

(c)   those sentenced to 12 months or more imprisonment for sexual or violent offence and made subject of a transfer direction with or without a restriction direction under ss 47 and 49.

---

[116]   [2001] EWHC Admin 602.
[117]   See http://www.mhrt.org.uk.

Victims are entitled to make representations as to conditions to be attached to conditional discharge or a CTO if the patient is to be discharged into the community. Conditions relevant to victims would include 'no contact' conditions or exclusion zones.

Notice of the hearing

9.74   Under r 20 the tribunal must give at least 14 days' notice of the date, time and place of the hearing to all parties, their representatives and, in the case of a restricted patient, the Home Secretary; the period of notice may only be reduced if all the parties consent.[118] In *Campbell v Secretary of State for the Home Department*, the MHRT proceedings were declared invalid because the Home Secretary had not been informed in advance of the date of the tribunal hearing and had received the independent psychiatric report only on the very day of the hearing. Rule 20 does not apply to references by the Secretary of State under s 75(1) following recall.[119]

Representation

9.75   Where there is representation, it is usually the patient who is legally represented, although in restricted cases the Home Office may engage a lawyer to put its case for continued detention. Rule 10(1) provides that:

> 'any party may be represented by any person whom he has authorised for that purpose not being a person liable to be detained or subject to guardianship or after-care under supervision under the Act or a person receiving treatment for mental disorder at the same hospital or mental nursing home as the patient.'

Rule 10(2) states that:

> 'Any representative authorised in accordance with paragraph (1) shall notify the tribunal of his authorisation and postal address.'

Often the responsible authority's views are represented at the hearing by the RMO, but and although the responsible authority is entitled to put questions to anyone appearing before the tribunal, the RMO is not the responsible authority. However, if the RMO wishes to be able to question and cross-examine witnesses and represent in that sense, then the tribunal must be notified to that effect. In *R (on the application of Mersey Care NHS Trust) v Mental Health Review Tribunal*[120] Sullivan J held that the RMO (now the RC) is entitled to put questions to other witnesses, but only if he or she has notified the tribunal that he or she has been authorised by the responsible authority to represent them.

---

[118]   Mental Health Review Tribunal Rules 1983, SI 1983/942, rr 10(4) and 20.
[119]   Mental Health Review Tribunal Rules 1983, SI 1983/942, r 29(a), as amended by MHRT (Amendment) Rules 1998, SI 1998/1189.
[120]   [2003] EWHC 1182 (Admin).

Medical examination of the patient

9.76 Rule 11 places the medical member of the panel under a duty, prior to the hearing, to examine the patient and take any other steps which he considers necessary to form an opinion of the patient's mental condition; these may include examining the patient's medical records. In practice, the medical member examines the patient before the hearing and presents his opinion to the other two members when they convene. He or she may provide a written report or, more commonly, will discuss her or his opinion with them during their deliberations. Note that, under r 11, the medical member may also make notes from the medical records and copies of them. Where the notes or copies of the records are submitted to the tribunal, the authorised representative is entitled under r 12(3) to receive copies of them. They must also be disclosed to the applicant unless withheld by the tribunal under r 12(2). At the initial meeting with the patient to receive instructions the patient's representative should obtain the written authority of the patient to apply for access to the patient's health records.

9.77 In *R (on the application of S) v Mental Health Review Tribunal*[121] Stanley Burnton J rejected an application for judicial review on grounds of incompatibility of r 11 with Art 5(4) of the Convention. The claimant believed that all psychiatrists viewed him unfavourably. He instructed his solicitors to inform the regional chairman that he objected to being seen before the hearing by the medical member and requested that r 11 not be applied. The chairman replied that r 11 was mandatory. The claimant sought judicial review of the decision, contending that the mandatory requirement in r 11 was incompatible with his rights under Art 5(4) to an independent and impartial judicial determination of the lawfulness of his detention. Stanley Burnton J held that as a matter of domestic law there could be no objection to the expression of a provisional opinion by a medical member of a tribunal to his colleagues, provided that the other members were aware that it was a provisional opinion and treated it as such, and provided they knew that they were free to disagree with it if the evidence and submissions before them led to a different conclusion.

9.78 Moreover, on the proper interpretation of the relevant Strasbourg jurisprudence,[122] r 11 was not inconsistent with Art 5(4). Impartiality in the present context required a member of a tribunal not to have a preconceived concluded opinion on the merits of the claimant's case. A provisional view formed before the commencement of the hearing was not necessarily objectionable, unless an otherwise impartial and independent member of a tribunal has a preconceived opinion or expresses himself in such a way as to give rise to a reasonable apprehension that he had a preconceived concluded opinion.

---

[121] [2002] EWHC 2522 (Admin).
[122] *DN v Switzerland (Application 27154/95)* Decision of 29 March 2001, ECtHR.

9.79   In *R (on the application of RD) v Mental Health Review Tribunal*[123] *t*he medical member examined the patient and, at the outset of the hearing, the President gave an account of the medical member's interview with RD reporting a 'preliminary view' that:[124]

> '[RD] appeared to be ready for transfer to medium security, but because of the length of time at Broadmoor, the lack of testing in the community, and concern about how he would manage in the community, he would appear to need the regime of a secure unit rather than community living.'

The President said that this was 'a very preliminary view, subject to anything we hear today'. RD argued that whilst it was legitimate for the medical member to communicate an opinion about the patient's mental state, it was not legitimate for her to communicate an opinion as to whether he should be discharged. Munby J rejected this argument stating that:[125]

> 'The communication by the medical member of her 'very preliminary' view was manifestly lawful, notwithstanding that it went to the ultimate issue and not merely to the question of RD's mental condition. There is nothing in r 11 to disable the medical member from doing what she (like the other members of the Tribunal) would otherwise plainly be entitled to do, namely to discuss all aspects of the case with the other members of the Tribunal before the hearing and to express to them her preliminary views either on the case as a whole or on any particular aspect of the case, just as there is nothing in rule 11 to disable the medical member (like the other members of the Tribunal) from expressing to the parties at the outset of the hearing her preliminary views either on the case as a whole or on any particular aspect of the case. The contrary, in my judgment, is simply unarguable.'

This means that a 'preliminary view' may be expressed not only on the patient's mental state and also, as long as it is made very clear that it is a preliminary view, on the question of whether the patient should be discharged.

9.80   In a case where a MHRT makes its decision on the basis of some point in the opinion of its own medical member on which evidence has not been put before it, it must make the applicant or his representative aware of the views of the medical member and give the patient the opportunity to address them. If material evidence is contained in the medical member's report which is not apparent in any document made available to the parties, the report or its substance should be disclosed.[126]

---

[123]   [2007] EWHC 781 (Admin).
[124]   [2007] EWHC 781 (Admin) at [13].
[125]   [2007] EWHC 781 (Admin) at [19].
[126]   *R v Mental Health Review Tribunal, ex parte Clatworthy* [1985] 3 All ER 699, QBD. See also *R v Mental Health Review Tribunal (Mersey Region), ex parte Davies* (unreported) 21 April 1986, QBD.

Independent psychiatric report

9.81   The applicant may engage a psychiatrist to provide an independent report on his medical condition. A copy of each independent report should be sent to the MHRT no later than seven days before the hearing, since late submission may lead to the need for an adjournment. A psychiatrist who provides such a report owes a duty of confidence to the patient. However, this confidential duty is subject to the exception described by Sir Stephen Brown P in *W v Egdell*:[127]

> 'A consultant psychiatrist who becomes aware, even in the course of a confidential relationship, of information which leads him, in the exercise of what the court considers a sound professional judgment, to fear that such decisions may be made on the basis of inadequate information and with a real risk of consequent danger to the public, is entitled to take such steps as are reasonable in all the circumstances to communicate the grounds of his concern to the responsible authorities.'

The doctor may disclose the information to the responsible authorities even where the patient has withdrawn his application.

The power to issue directions

9.82   Rule 13 empowers the tribunal to give such directions as it thinks fit to ensure the speedy and just determination of the application, hence providing the MHRT with the ability to comply with the speediness requirement in Art 5(4).

Evidence

9.83   Rule 14(2) empowers the MHRT to receive any document or information in evidence, notwithstanding that it would be inadmissible in a court of law. This has been held to include the power to receive a written statement from victims in cases involving offender patients. Victims may make a statement in writing which can be received under r 14.[128] In *R (on the application of N) v Mental Health Review Tribunal (Northern Region)* Munby J sounded a note of caution in relation to hearsay evidence:[129]

> 'In relation to past incidents which are centrally important to the decision it has to take, the tribunal must bear in mind the need for proof to the civil standard of proof; it must bear in mind the potential difficulties of relying on second or third hand hearsay; and if the incident is really fundamental to its decision it must bear in mind fairness may require the patient to be given the opportunity to cross examine the relevant witness if their evidence is to be relied upon.'

---

[127]   *W v Egdell* [1990] Ch 359, [1989] 1 All ER 1089, ChD; [1990] 1 All ER 835, CA.
[128]   *R (on the application of T) v Mental Health Review Tribunal* [2001] EWHC Admin 602.
[129]   [2005] EWHC 587 (Admin) at [129].

There is a power to subpoena witnesses under r 14(1) and failure to comply with a subpoena will amount to a contempt of court. Subpoenas are rarely used. The general power to issue directions under r 13 is usually sufficient to secure any necessary information or evidence.

HEARING PROCEDURE

9.84 Unless the patient requests otherwise, the tribunal sits in private. It must sit in public if the patient requests it and if it is satisfied that a public hearing would not be contrary to the patient's interests.[130] The tribunal has a general discretion to conduct the proceedings in the manner that it considers suitable, bearing in mind the health and interests of the patient. It is felt that an informal *atmosphere* encourages the parties to discuss the case openly with a minimum of confrontation, but the *procedures* may be informal only to the extent that the following statutory rules permit. The tribunal chairman must explain at the beginning of the hearing the procedure to be followed. At this point, the representative may put to the tribunal any requests regarding the procedure, such as the presence throughout the proceedings of any particular person or the calling of a particular witness.[131]

The interview with the patient

9.85 Although r 22(2) states only that the tribunal must interview the patient if he so requests and without the presence of any other person, again if requested, and while it is theoretically possible for the tribunal to determine the application without interviewing the patient, in practice the tribunal always interviews the patient before reaching a decision irrespective of a specific request, unless the patient positively objects. This last circumstance provides the rule with its *raison d'être*: where a case is referred automatically to the tribunal the patient may refuse to participate in the proceedings; r 22(2) permits the tribunal to reach a decision without interviewing the patient.

Rights of the applicant, the patient, and the responsible authority

9.86 Unless they are excluded from the proceedings, the applicant, the patient (where he is not the applicant) and the responsible authority have the following rights:

(a) to give evidence to the tribunal;

(b) to hear each other's evidence and to put questions to each other;

---

[130] Mental Health Review Tribunal Rules 1983, SI 1983/942, r 21(1); *Pickering v Liverpool Daily Post and Echo Newspapers plc* [1991] 1 All ER 622, (1991) 6 BMLR 108, HL.
[131] Mental Health Review Tribunal Rules 1983, SI 1983/942, r 22.

(c)   to call witnesses and to question any witness or other person appearing before the tribunal.[132]

If the applicant or patient is excluded from the hearing, his authorised representative is entitled to remain throughout the hearing and has the same rights with respect to the hearing as the person s/he represents.[133]

Rights of other parties or persons

9.87   Any other party or, with the tribunal's permission, any other person may appear at the hearing and take such part in the proceedings as the tribunal thinks proper. However, they do not have specific rights with regard to giving and hearing evidence and calling and questioning witnesses as do the applicant, the patient, and the responsible authority.[134]

Right of applicant and patient to address the tribunal

9.88   After all the evidence has been given, the applicant and, where s/he is not the applicant, the patient, have the opportunity to address the tribunal. This allows the applicant, the patient or the representative to sum up the case and to add any final points.[135]

Adjournment

9.89   The tribunal may adjourn a hearing at any time and may do so in order to obtain further information or for such other reason as it thinks appropriate (r 16(1)), and will normally grant a request for adjournment by a representative if there are reasonable grounds for it. Although the second limb of r 16 allows an adjournment for such other purposes as the tribunal may think necessary, the tribunal has no power to adjourn to give the patient's condition an opportunity to improve or to see whether an improvement already made is sustained. The purpose of the power to adjourn is primarily to obtain information about the patient's current condition. Where the tribunal is satisfied that the criteria for discharge are not met at the time of the hearing, it has no power to adjourn to give the patient's condition an opportunity to improve.[136]

9.90   In *R (on the application of B) v Mental Health Review Tribunal*[137] Scott Baker J held that where there is an adjournment the MHRT should fix a time-limit within which the reconvened hearing will take place, with clear direction to ensure that relevant expert evidence is obtained in time. He also

---

[132]   Mental Health Review Tribunal Rules 1983, SI 1983/942, r 22(4).

[133]   Mental Health Review Tribunal Rules 1983, SI 1983/942, rr 21(4) and 10(4).

[134]   Mental Health Review Tribunal Rules 1983, SI 1983/942, r 22(4).

[135]   Mental Health Review Tribunal Rules 1983, SI 1983/942, rr 22(5) and 10(4).

[136]   *R v Nottingham Mental Health Review Tribunal, ex parte Secretary of State for the Home Department* (1988) *The Times*, 12 October, CA.

[137]   [2002] EWHC 1553 (Admin).

held that experts should meet to narrow any differences of opinion and that adjournments should not be granted without giving the patient's representative an opportunity to be heard. An adjournment which is not requested by the patient may interfere with the patient's right to a speedy determination of the case. Brief reasons should also be given for any decision to adjourn.

9.91 In *R (on the application of X) v Mental Health Review Tribunal*[138] Collins J held that whilst the MHRT has the power of its own motion to adjourn to obtain information, it should not do so unless it regards it as necessary to do justice and reach the right result in the case. This required a balance to be struck between the need for any information and any delay which will occur in the determination of the case.

9.92 The MHRT may only adjourn to obtain information for a purpose which is within its jurisdiction. Hence the tribunal may not adjourn a restricted patient hearing *solely* to gather information relating to making a recommendation, although there is nothing to stop it gathering such information if it adjourns to obtain further information on a matter within its jurisdiction (discharge).[139] Rule 25(2) of the MHRT Rules has been amended to make it clear that it was not intended for MHRTs to be able to reconvene to consider recommendations in restricted cases.[140] Compare this with the power to defer conditional discharge under s 73 until such arrangements as appear to be necessary for that purpose have been made to the tribunal's satisfaction.

THE MHRT DECISION

9.93 Rule 23(1) of the MHRT Rules[141] provides that the tribunal's decision is reached by a majority vote, the President having a second or casting vote where there is equality of votes. The decision must be recorded in writing, and must be signed by the president and must give the reasons for the decision. In most cases the decision will be unanimous. Although the President signs the decision, it is the decision of the tribunal, and the reasons are the reasons of the tribunal, so all members, not just the legal chairman should participate in the formulation of the tribunal's reasons. If the MHRT's decision is reviewed it will be the decision of the whole tribunal which will be reviewed, not just that of the legal member, so it is important for the other members to have the ownership of the decision which comes from participating in drawing up the decision and the reasons for it. The above rules apply to provisional decisions, as well as to recommendations and, the case law suggests, to decisions to adjourn or not to adjourn, for which reasons should be given.[142]

---

[138] [2003] All ER (D) 160 (May).
[139] *R (on the application of the Secretary of State for the Home Department) v Mental Health Review Tribunal* (2000) 63 BMLR 181, QBD.
[140] MHRT (Amendment) Rules 1998, SI 1998/1189, r 2(3).
[141] Mental Health Review Tribunal Rules 1983, SI 1983/942.
[142] Mental Health Review Tribunal Rules 1983, SI 1983/942, r 23(3).

9.94 In a decision to discharge the tribunal must give reasons why they are or are not satisfied that the patient is suffering from mental disorder of the relevant nature or degree for detention, guardianship or supervised discharge, or why they are or are not satisfied that detention, guardianship, or supervised discharge is justified. Similarly, they must give reasons in a restriction order case why they are or are not directing absolute or conditional discharge.[143] As Jack Beatson QC summed it up in *R (on the application of Warren) v Mental Health Review Tribunal (London and North East Region)*:[144]

> 'the tribunal's reasons must address the diagnostic question of whether there is mental disorder and the policy question of whether it is safe to discharge.'

9.95 The early case-law on the 1983 Act – *Bone v Mental Health Review Tribunal*,[145] *R v Mental Health Review Tribunal, ex parte Clatworthy*[146] and *R v Mental Health Review Tribunal, ex parte Pickering*[147] – held that reasons must not be mere rehearsals of the statutory criteria, must be adequate and intelligible, and must reasonably be said to deal with the substantial points that have been raised. It has to be possible to read from the reasons the issue to which they are directed. Where there is a conflict of evidence the reasons have to reveal why the tribunal had accepted the evidence of one party and not the other. The overriding question was:

> 'Is the tribunal providing both parties with the materials which will enable them to know that the tribunal has made no error of law in reaching its finding of fact?'

9.96 In *R (on the application of Ashworth Hospital Authority) v Mental Health Review Tribunal for West Midlands and Northwest Region*,[148] the Court of Appeal upheld Stanley Burnton J's decision to quash as *Wednesbury* irrational the tribunal's direction to discharge the patient immediately where the preponderance of the medical evidence was against it, and the tribunal's reasons showed that they had not give adequate attention to the need for and availability of after-care support. The court held that reasons must deal with the entirety of its decision and not merely whether there is mental disorder of the relevant nature or degree and whether it is safe to discharge. Hence reasons would have to be given for not adjourning to see if adequate after-care could be arranged. Dyson LJ held that where the tribunal is required to resolve a difference of opinion between experts as to whether the patient should be discharged it is important that the tribunal should state which, if any of the expert evidence it accepts and which it rejects, giving reasons. The reasons must at least indicate the reasoning process by which they have decided to accept

---

143 Mental Health Review Tribunal Rules 1983, SI 1983/942, r 23(2).

144 *R (on the application of Warren) v Mental Health Review Tribunal (London and North East Region)* [2002] EWHC 811 (Admin).

145 *Bone v Mental Health Review Tribunal* [1985] 3 All ER 330, per Nolan J.

146 *R v Mental Health Review Tribunal, ex parte Clatworthy* [1985] 3 All ER 699 at 703, per Mann J.

147 *R v Mental Health Review Tribunal, ex parte Pickering* [1986] 1 All ER 99 at 104, per Forbes J.

148 *R (on the application of Ashworth Hospital Authority) v Mental Health Review Tribunal for West Midlands and Northwest Region* [2002] EWCA Civ 923.

some and reject other evidence. The reasons given for deciding to accept the evidence of one doctor and reject that of the other experts were 'wholly inadequate'. Moreover, the tribunal was required to give reasons for not adjourning to see whether adequate after-care arrangements could be made, or not making an order for deferred discharge.

9.97   The decision may be, and often is, given immediately after the hearing. In any case, the tribunal's written decision together with the reasons for it must be sent to all the parties within seven days of the hearing.[149] An exception may be made in cases where the tribunal considers that full disclosure would adversely affect the health or welfare of the patient or others. In such cases the tribunal may communicate its decision to the patient in any other appropriate manner. A patient's authorised representative must receive the full recorded reasons for the decision, but the tribunal may require him not to disclose some of those reasons to the patient.

9.98   It is important to remember that the decision and reasons will be studied closely by the parties to the tribunal, the patient and/or the representative, the hospital, and, in the case of a restricted patient, the Home Office. Those dissatisfied with the decision may well be seeking grounds for judicial review. Each member has a vital contribution to make to the formulation of the decision and the reasons. It is essential, therefore, that the decision is taken by the three members of the tribunal either unanimously or, in extremis by a majority, and that each participate and accept responsibility for it. It is also crucial that the process of agreeing its wording is not delegated to or reserved to the legal chairman.

Effects of a MHRT decision

9.99   Although the decision of a tribunal to terminate detention makes further detention under that authority unlawful, it does not necessarily prevent a fresh application being made for detention or guardianship.[150] In *R (on the application of Von Brandenburg (aka Hanley)) v East London and the City Mental Health NHS Trust*[151] the House of Lords rejected the argument that the test for compulsory admission following discharge by a tribunal had to be based on a 'material change of circumstances'. Instead what was necessary was that the social worker had to have information which had not been available to the tribunal. Lord Bingham of Cornhill said that:[152]

'An [AMHP] may not lawfully apply for the admission of a patient whose discharge has been ordered by the decision of a MHRT of which the [AMHP] is aware unless the [AMHP] has formed the reasonable and bona fide opinion that

---

[149]   Mental Health Review Tribunal Rules 1983, SI 1983/942, r 24.
[150]   *Bath and North East Somerset Council v Crowsley* (unreported) 8 December 1999 (CO/3384/99).
[151]   [2003] UKHL 58.
[152]   [2003] UKHL 58 at [10].

he has information not known to the tribunal which puts a significantly different complexion on the case as compared with that which was before the tribunal.'

In such a case the AMHP may properly apply for the admission of a patient, subject of course to obtaining the required medical support, notwithstanding a tribunal decision directing discharge. The position of the patient's nearest relative, in those cases where he or she makes the application with knowledge of the tribunal decision, does not differ in principle from that of the AMHP, although the NR could not in many cases be expected to be familiar with the evidence or appreciate the grounds on which the tribunal had based its decision.

Applying for a stay of a MHRT decision

9.100 Where the hospital authorities consider that a tribunal decision may have been arrived at due to an error of law, the appropriate course will usually be to apply for a stay of the tribunal decision, rather than to encourage re-sectioning. In *R (on the application of Ashworth Hospital Authority) v Mental Health Review Tribunal for West Midlands and Northwest Region* Dyson LJ held that since the tribunal is a court for the purposes of Art 5(4), the fact that the professionals have been advised that there are substantial grounds for saying that the tribunal's decision is arguably unlawful is not a sufficient ground for sanctioning as lawful a decision to resection a patient in the absence of material circumstances of which the tribunal was not aware when it made the decision.[153] An application to the High Court for a stay was the correct course in such a case.

CONCLUSION

9.101 The period since the MHA 1983 has seen a remarkable development of case-law in relation to MHRTs, resulting from judicial review applications not only from patients, but also from hospital authorities, the Home Secretary and victims, all seeking to assert their rights and prerogatives. One result has been that MHRTs may have many parties appearing before them, each offering different perspectives on whether the patient is fit for discharge. The MHRT has been affected by the MHA 2007 in six main ways. First, its organisation has been changed so that England and Wales each have a separate unitary MHRT with its own President. Second, the panel for each hearing is presided over by a chairman, not a President. Third, the discharge criteria are altered by new broad definition of mental disorder and the condition that appropriate treatment must be available. Fourth, the jurisdiction to reclassify as suffering from a different form of disorder is abolished. Fifth, a new jurisdiction over CTO patients is introduced. Sixth, changes to the Domestic Violence, Crime and Victims Act 2004 mean that victims of certain crimes committed by

---

[153]   *R (on the application of Ashworth Hospital Authority) v Mental Health Review Tribunal for West Midlands and Northwest Region* [2002] EWCA Civ 923.

mentally disordered offenders are entitled to make representations to MHRTs and in certain cases to appear before them.

Chapter 10

CONSENT TO TREATMENT FOR MENTAL DISORDER

OVERVIEW

10.1 Part 4 of the MHA 1983 introduced a framework of powers to administer treatment for mental disorder without consent, subject to a system of second opinion safeguards. Those imposing treatment without consent and the Second Opinion Appointed Doctors ('SOADs') who act under Part 4 of the Act are public authorities for the purposes of the Human Rights Act 1998 and must act compatibly with Convention rights. Section 57 specifies the treatments, psychosurgery and surgical hormone implants for the reduction of male sex drive, which cannot be given without both the patient's valid consent and a second opinion that the treatment is appropriate. This procedure must be observed whether or not the patient is detained. Section 58 authorises treatment without consent. Section 58 applies only to patients who are liable to be detained under powers authorising detention for more than 72 hours, and who are not conditionally discharged restricted patients, or remand patients subject to s 35. Section 58 treatments were medicines for mental disorder (specified in s 58(1)(b)) and Electro Convulsive Therapy ('ECT' – added by regulations under s 52(1)(a)). Section 58 treatments require either the patient's consent or a certificate from a second opinion appointed doctor stating that the patient is either (a) incapable of consenting, or (b) capable and refusing, but that the treatment ought to be given. In deciding whether the treatment ought to be given the SOAD under the MHA 1983 had to have regard to the likelihood that it will 'alleviate or prevent deterioration in the patient's condition'. The MHA 2007 replaces this test with the test that 'it is appropriate for the treatment to be given'.[1] Another important change to Part 4 relates to the removal of ECT from s 58 and its subjection to a separate procedure under s 58A. This provides that, except in an emergency threatening life or serious deterioration in the patient's condition, ECT may not be given to a capable patient who is refusing the treatment.

ECT

10.2 During the debates on the 1982 Bill there was some lobbying to make ECT subject to the s 57 procedure, hence requiring consent before it could be given. The Government responded by making ECT subject to s 58 by regulation rather than on the face of the Act thus leaving themselves the option

---

[1]   MHA 1983, ss 57(2)(b), 58(3)(b), 58A(5)(b), as inserted by MHA 2007 s 6(2).

to move it to the s 57 category, without resort to amending legislation, if experience showed the need.[2] Instead of making ECT subject to s 57 where it could only be given with the consent of a capable patient, the MHA 2007 creates a third procedure under s 58A whereby ECT can be given without the patient being capable and consenting, but cannot be given where the patient has capacity and is refusing it. The MHA 2007 removes ECT from s 58 and creates a new second opinion regime under s 58A whereby ECT may not be given to a patient who has capacity and is refusing, although it may, in specified circumstances, be given to a person who lacks capacity. Section 58A applies to patients who are liable to be detained under powers authorising detention for more than 72 hours, and who are not conditionally discharged restricted patients or subject to remand under s 35. Section 58A also applies to informal (non-sectioned) patients who are under 18. The MHA 2007 means that there are three second opinion regimes under Part 4, with the capacity to move specified treatments from one group to another by regulations.

Treatment without a prior second opinion

10.3 Part 4 also provides for emergency treatment without prior second opinion (s 62), and for treatments other than those specified in ss 57 and 58, to be administered without consent if given by or under the direction of the RMO (s 63). These powers pass to the Approved Clinician ('AC') in charge of treatment under the MHA 2007. Section 62(1A) authorises emergency ECT without compliance with s 58A if the treatment is immediately necessary to save the patient's life; or is not irreversible and is immediately necessary to prevent a serious deterioration of his condition.[3]

Part 4A

10.4 Patients who have been on a CTO, but have been recalled to hospital are treated for mental disorder under ss 58 and 58A.[4] The treatment of non-recalled community patients who remain in the community is governed by Part 4A of the MHA 1983 introduced by s 35 of the MHA 2007. Part 4A regulates treatment for mental disorder of mentally capable, mentally incapable and child patients who are subject to CTOs and who have not been recalled to hospital. The basic principle is that a patient with capacity (or competence if a child) may only be given treatment in the form of medicine for mental disorder if they consent and there is a certificate authorising the treatment from a SOAD. If the patient is capable and refusing treatment may only be given without consent by recalling the patient. For the purposes of Part 4 capacity means capacity to understand the nature purpose and likely effects of the treatment. Part 4A employs the concept of capacity in ss 2 and 3 of the MCA 2005, and authorises attorneys or deputies to consent to treatment on a community patient's behalf.

---

[2]   Speech of Kenneth Clarke, *Hansard*, HC Deb, vol 29, ser 6, col 87 (18 October 1982).
[3]   Inserted by MHA 2007, s 28(6).
[4]   MHA 1983, s 56(4), as inserted by MHA 2007, s 34.

The Interface between Parts 4 and 4A and the Mental Capacity Act 2005

10.5 Section 28 of the MCA 2005 states that nothing in the MCA authorises anyone to give a patient medical treatment for mental disorder, or to consent to a patient's being given medical treatment for mental disorder, if, at the time when it is proposed to treat the patient, his treatment is regulated by Part 4 of the Mental Health Act 1983. This means that the power under s 5 of the MCA 2005 to administer treatment in the best interests of an incapacitated patient does not apply in relation to treatment for mental disorder regulated by Part 4. Treatment regulated by Part 4 includes treatments under s 57 requiring the consent of a capable patient and a favourable second opinion. By definition a patient who lacks capacity may not be given these treatments, and no-one other than the patient can consent to them, so only s 57 of the MHA 1983 can apply. Treatment may be given under the second opinion procedures in ss 58 and 58A to detained patients without their consent. The effect of s 28 is that only patients already detained under the MHA 1983 who fall within the scope of s 56 (see para **10.12** below) may not be given treatment for mental disorder under s 5 of the MCA 2005. Nor may an attorney, deputy or the Court of Protection consent to such treatment on their behalf. Treatment for physical disorder is not regulated by Part 4, and so detained patients who lack capacity may be given treatment for physical ailments under the provisions of the MCA 2005 (see para **6.33** above).

10.6 The MHA 2007 amends s 28 of the MCA 2005 to take account of the new provisions on ECT in s 58A, and the new rules on treatment in the community in Part 4A. Section 28(10) of the MHA 2007 inserts a new subs (1A) into s 28 of the MCA 2005. This states that the exclusion of the MCA does not apply in relation to s 58A treatments if the patient comes within s 58A(7). Section 58A(7) provides that:

> 'This section shall not by itself confer sufficient authority [for an informal patient under 18 to be given ECT] if he is not capable of understanding the nature, purpose and likely effects of the treatment (and cannot therefore consent to it).'

The effect of this appears to be that whilst it is necessary to have a SOAD certify that a child patient is capable of consenting to ECT, if the child is informal and lacks capacity, treatment may be given under s 5 of the MCA 2005 (see para **6.33** above).

10.7 Where treatment for mental disorder is given to a community patient under s 64B of Part 4A, new s 28(1B) prohibits treatment from being given under s 5 of the MCA 2005, which does not apply.[5] Section 28 defines where each Act applies in relation to patients who are detained or subject to SCT. It does not give guidance on what to do where a mentally disordered person lacks

---

5   MCA 2005, s 28(1B), as inserted by MHA 2007, s 35(4) and (5).

mental capacity and is not already subject to compulsory powers. Guidance on this issue is found in the Mental Capacity Act Code of Practice.[6]

HUMAN RIGHTS AND TREATMENT WITHOUT CONSENT

10.8   Approved clinicians , other clinicians in charge of treatment, and SOADs providing second opinions for the purposes of Parts 4 and 4A are performing functions of a public nature, and are public authorities for the purposes of the Human Rights Act 1998. They must therefore act compatibly with Convention rights.[7] Treatment without consent potentially engages Arts 3 and 8 of the European Convention on Human Rights. Remedies are available for infringement of these rights under English law. In *R (on the application of Wilkinson) v Responsible Medical Officer Broadmoor Hospital* Hale LJ said that proceedings in respect of forcible treatment of detained patients may brought by way of an ordinary action in tort, an action under s 7(1) of the Human Rights Act 1998, or by judicial review. ACs, whether proposing treatment for the purposes of ss 57, 58 and 58A, or administering treatment under ss 62 or 63, owe a duty of care to patients.[8]

Article 3

10.9   Article 3 provides that:

> 'No-one shall be subjected to torture or to inhuman or degrading treatment or punishment.'

This is an absolute right. In *Herczegfalvy v Austria*, the applicant complained of breaches of Arts 3 and 8, in that he had been tied to a bed, given strong anti-psychotic medication and forcibly fed, all without his consent and contrary to his wishes. The European Court held that the position of inferiority and powerlessness typical of patients confined in psychiatric hospitals called for increased vigilance in reviewing compliance with Convention rights, and that the protection of Art 3 extended to 'therapeutic methods to be used, if necessary by force, to preserve the physical and mental health of patients who are entirely incapable of deciding for themselves'. However, the Court admitted that:[9]

> 'The established principles of medicine are in principle decisive in such cases; as a general rule, a measure which is a therapeutic necessity cannot be regarded as inhuman or degrading. The Court must nevertheless satisfy itself that the medical necessity has been convincingly shown to exist.'

---

[6]   *Mental Capacity Act 2005 Code of Practice*, chap 13.
[7]   *Draft Code of Practice*, para 18.3.
[8]   *R (on the application of Wilkinson) v Responsible Medical Officer Broadmoor Hospital* [2001] EWCA Civ 1545, per Hale LJ at [68].
[9]   (1992) 15 EHRR 437, at para 82.

In *R (on the application of Wilkinson) v Responsible Medical Officer Broadmoor Hospital*, Hale LJ concluded from *Herczegfalvy* that:[10]

> 'forcible measures inflicted upon an incapacitated patient which are *not* a medical necessity may indeed be inhuman or degrading. The same must apply to forcible measures inflicted upon a capacitated patient.'

For treatment to breach Art 3 its effects must reach a minimum level of severity entailing physical injury or recognised psychiatric injury. In *R (on the application of N) v Dr M and others* the Court of Appeal held that the key questions in determining whether treatment is a 'therapeutic necessity' include:

(a) how certain is it that the person suffers from a treatable mental disorder;

(b) how serious the disorder is;

(c) how serious a risk is presented to others;

(d) how likely is it that, if the patient does suffer from such a disorder, the proposed treatment will alleviate the condition;

(e) how much alleviation there is likely to be;

(f) how likely it is that the treatment will have adverse consequences for the patient; and

(g) how severe may they be.[11]

Article 8

10.10 Article 8 protects the right to respect for private life, which includes the right to physical integrity. This right is not absolute and may be interfered with by the state if justified under Art 8(2). In *Storck v Germany* the European Court held that:[12]

> 'even a minor interference with the physical integrity of an individual must be regarded as an interference with the right of respect for private life under Article 8, if it is carried out against the individual's will.'

The Court went on to say that states had an obligation to secure to their citizens the right to physical and moral integrity, and this meant a duty to exercise effective supervision and control over treatment in private psychiatric institutions.[13] This positive duty under Art 8 applies equally to supervision and control over state institutions. Retrospective regulation by tort action or

---

[10] [2001] EWCA Civ 1545 at [79].
[11] *R (on the application of N) v Dr M and others* [2002] EWCA Civ 1789.
[12] (2005) 43 EHRR 96, at para 143.
[13] (2005) 43 EHRR 96, at para 150.

criminal prosecution is not enough.[14] Regulation must be directed at Convention compliance, and the issue of whether any treatment without consent has been given in compliance with Art 8(2).

10.11 Article 8(2) allows public authorities to interfere with the rights guaranteed in Art 8(1) if the interference is in accordance with the law and is necessary in a democratic society in the interests of national security, public safety or the economic well-being of the country, for the prevention of disorder or crime, for the protection of health or morals, or for the protection of the rights and freedoms of others. In *Herczegfalvy* the court applied the same test of therapeutic necessity to Art 8 and again concluded that 'according to the psychiatric principles generally accepted at the time, medical necessity justified the treatment in issue', attaching 'decisive weight to the lack of specific information capable of disproving the Government's opinion that the hospital authorities were entitled to regard the applicant's psychiatric illness as rendering him entirely incapable of taking decisions for himself.'[15] Medical interferences with the right of respect for physical integrity must be in accordance with law and *therapeutically necessary* in a democratic society (ie proportionate) for protection of public safety, prevention of disorder and crime, the protection of health or the rights and freedoms of others. In accordance with law under Art 8(2) is not as stringent as in accordance with a procedure prescribed by law under Art 5(1), but there must be effective supervision and review, and to be in accordance with law any powers should be transparent and predictable in their effects.

PART 4

Application

10.12 Section 34 of the MHA 2007 introduces a new s 56 to the MHA 1983, setting out the categories of patient to whom Part 4 applies. Section 57 applies to all patients, whether detained, deprived of their liberty under the *Bournewood* safeguards, or informal. Sections 58 and 58A apply to patients who are liable to be detained, with the exception of the following patients, listed in s 56:

(a) admitted under s 4 of the Act, where a second medical recommendation has not been issued to convert to a s 2 detention;

(b) liable to be detained under the AC's (s 5(2)) or the nurse's (s 5(4)) holding power;

(c) remanded to hospital for assessment by a criminal court under s 35 of the MHA 1983;

---

[14] (2005) 43 EHRR 96.
[15] *Herczegfalvy v Austria (Application 10533/83)* (1992) 15 EHRR 437, at paras 83, 86.

(d) detained in a place of safety under ss 135 or 136;

(e) detained in a place of safety (ss 37(4) or 45A(4)) pending admission to hospital under a hospital order or a hospital direction; and

(f) conditionally discharged restricted patients for whom acceptance of treatment may be a condition of discharge.[16]

A community patient is not subject to the provisions of Part 4 of the MHA 1983 (except s 57 which applies to any patient) unless recalled to hospital for treatment under s 17E.[17] The s 58A procedure for ECT applies to patients under 18 whether they are detained or informal.[18]

Medical treatment for mental disorder

10.13 Parts 4 and 4A apply to treatment for mental disorder. Treatment without consent for physical disorder is governed by the Mental Capacity Act 2005. Section 145(1) provides an inclusive definition of 'medical treatment for mental disorder' which 'includes nursing, psychological intervention and specialist mental health habilitation, rehabilitation and care.'[19] These interventions are included, but others not listed, such as medicines or ECT, are not excluded. Section 7(3) inserts a new s 145(4) which states that:[20]

'Any reference in this Act to medical treatment, in relation to mental disorder, shall be construed as a reference to medical treatment the purpose of which is to alleviate, or prevent a worsening of, the disorder or one or more of its symptoms or manifestations.'

This provision acknowledges the Court of Appeal decision in *B v Croydon Health Authority*[21] that treatment for mental disorder includes treatment designed to address the symptoms and sequelae as well as the 'core disorder'. Section 145(4) also requires that treatment have the 'purpose', rather than, as before, the likely effect, of alleviating or preventing deterioration in the patient's condition.

10.14 The Explanatory Notes list among practical examples of psychological interventions 'cognitive therapy, behaviour therapy and counselling'. 'Habilitation' and 'rehabilitation' refer to interventions designed to improve or modify patients' physical and mental abilities and social functioning. The distinction between habilitation and rehabilitation depends in practice on the extent of

---

[16] As inserted by MHA 2007, s 34.
[17] MHA 1983 s 56(4), as inserted by MHA 2007, s 34.
[18] MHA 1983 s 56(5), as inserted by MHA 2007, s 34(2).
[19] As amended by MHA 2007, s 7(2).
[20] MHA 1983 s 145(4), as inserted by MHA 2007, s 7(3).
[21] [1995] 1 All ER 683, CA.

patients' existing abilities – 'rehabilitation' is appropriate only where the patients are relearning skills or abilities they have had before.[22]

The concept of authority to treat in Part 4

10.15 The Scheme of Part 4 is as follows. There must be 'authority to treat' a patient. The most obvious 'authority to treat' is the valid consent of an adult or child patient who has capacity (or competence). For treatments subject to s 57, the authority to treat comes from the patient's consent, and the s 57 procedures set the procedural and other conditions required to act on that authority. For informal child patients under 18 who lack capacity to consent to ECT the authority comes from the MCA 2005 if they are between 16 and 18, or from parental or court consent if they are under 16 and lack *Gillick* competence, and the procedures in s 58A set conditions on the exercise of that authority.[23] For detained patients the authority to treat comes from s 63 unless the treatment is covered by the procedures in ss 57, 58 or 58A.

It is appropriate for the treatment to be given

10.16 The new test for deciding under ss 57, 58 and 58A whether treatment may lawfully be given is 'that it is appropriate for the treatment to be given.'[24] The test employed under the MHA 1983 was that 'the treatment ought to be given having regard to the likelihood that it will alleviate or prevent deterioration in the patient's condition.' Section 57 treatments may not be carried out unless the patient consents and a SOAD states that it is appropriate for the treatment to be given. Treatment without consent may not be authorised under ss 58 or 58A unless it is appropriate for the treatment to be given. The policy intention appears to be that there will not be much difference in practice between the two tests in relation to treatment without consent. 'Medical treatment for mental disorder' under the MHA 1983 has been held to include not merely treatment directed at the core disorder, but also treatment of the 'symptoms and sequelae' of the disorder.[25] For the purposes of Part 4 it is appropriate for treatment to be given to a patient 'if the treatment is appropriate in his case, taking into account the nature and degree of the mental disorder from which he is suffering and all other circumstances of his case'.[26] Paragraph 2A4 of the Draft Illustrative Code issued to accompany the Mental Health Bill 2006 emphasised that the intent and purpose of the medical treatment must be:

> 'to alleviate, prevent deterioration in or otherwise manage the disorder itself, its symptoms or manifestations or the behaviours arising from it.'

[22] *MHA 2007 Explanatory Notes*, para 39.
[23] MHA 1983, s 58(7).
[24] MHA 2007, s 12(2).
[25] *B v Croydon Health Authority* [1995] 1 All ER 683, CA.
[26] MHA 1983 s 64(3), as inserted by MHA 2007, s 6(3).

In *R (on the application of PS) v Responsible Medical Officer*[27] Silber J held that Art 3 would only be contravened by the administration of medicine against a patient's will where:

(a) the proposed treatment reached the minimum level of severity for ill-treatment, taking into account all the circumstances, including positive and adverse physical and mental consequences, the nature and context of the treatment, the manner and method if its execution, its duration, and if relevant the age sex and health of the patient; and

(b) medical and therapeutic necessity for the treatment had not been convincingly shown to exist.

In determining whether treatment is appropriate, the AC or SOAD must consider whether it is medically and therapeutically necessary and in the patient's best interests.

Capacity under Part 4

10.17 Capacity is relevant to all the second opinion procedures, but of central importance to ss 57 and 58A. The assessment of a patient's capacity to make a decision about medical treatment is a matter for clinical judgment, guided by current professional practice and subject to legal requirements. It is the personal responsibility of any doctor or other professional proposing to treat a patient to determine whether the patient has capacity to give a valid consent. Any assessment of capacity has to be made in relation to a particular treatment, that capacity in an individual with a mental disorder can be variable over time and should be assessed at the time the treatment is proposed, and all assessments of an individual's capacity should be fully recorded in the patient's medical notes. The explanation of the treatment given by the AC should be appropriate to the level of the patient's assessed ability. Although refusal of ECT by a detained patient with capacity operates as a bar to ECT under s 58A, the same is not true in relation to medicines for mental disorder. With medicines under s 58, a capable patient's refusal is not a bar, but is an important factor to be taken into account in deciding whether the treatment is appropriate, clinically necessary and in the patient's best interests.[28]

10.18 The concept of capacity employed in Part 4 remains as it was under the MHA 1983, 'that the patient is capable of understanding the nature, purpose and likely effects of the treatment'. Under ss 2 and 3 of the MCA 2005 a person lacks capacity if unable to make a decision for her/himself because of an impairment of, or disturbance in the functioning of, the mind or brain. A person is unable to make a decision if he or she is unable:

(a)   to understand the information relevant to the decision;

---

[27]   [2003] EWHC 2335 (Admin). See also Mental Health Act Commission *Guidance for RMOs following the PS Case* (available at www.mhac.org.uk).

[28]   *R (on the application of PS) v Responsible Medical Officer* [2003] EWHC 2335 (Admin).

(b)   to retain the information;

(c)   to weigh the information in the balance as part of the process of arriving at a decision; or

(d)   to communicate the decision either by talking using sign language or any other means.

The Draft Illustrative Code which accompanied the Mental Health Bill said that 'to all intents and purposes the test of capacity to be used under Part 4 is the same as in Part 4A and therefore in the MCA'.[29] As a strict matter of law this was not accurate. Section 64K(2) provides that for the purposes of Part 4A references to a patient who lacks capacity are to a patient who lacks capacity within the meaning of the MCA 2005. Part 4 uses its own definition of capacity, 'capable of understanding the nature, purpose and likely effects of the treatment'. The Draft Revised Code of Practice eschews such specific guidance, stating that whilst:[30]

> 'Previous versions of this Code have contained extensive general guidance on what constitutes consent to treatment and capacity to give such consent. Authoritative guidance on these matters is now more widely elsewhere. And since the issues are generic to medical treatment in general, not just to treatment for mental disorder, the Code no longer attempts to give such guidance.'

The concepts of capacity employed in Parts 4 and 4A are different in wording, and it remains to be seen whether there will be a difference in practice.

10.19 The Code of Practice on the MHA 1983 advised that to be capable for Part 4 purposes an individual must have the ability to:

- understand what medical treatment is and that somebody has said that he needs it and why the treatment is being proposed;

- understand in broad terms[31] the nature of the proposed treatment;

- understand its principal benefits and risks;

- understand what will be the consequences of not receiving the proposed treatment; and

- possess the capacity to make a choice.'[32]

---

[29]   *Draft Code of Practice*, para 18.33.
[30]   Department of Health *Mental Health Act 1983 Draft Revised Code of Practice* (2007), para 25.2. See http://www.dh.gov.uk/en/Consultations.
[31]   *Chatterton v Gerson* [1981] 1 QB 432, (1980) 1 BMLR 80, QBD.
[32]   *Mental Health Act 1983 Code of Practice* (1993), para 15.10.

In *R v Mental Health Commission, ex parte X* Stuart Smith LJ noted (obiter) that 'the words are "capable of understanding", and not "understands". Thus the question is capacity and not actual understanding.'[33]

Despite this literal approach, the advice from the Mental Health Act Commission ('MHAC') to SOADs remains that in assessing validity of consent they should look not just at capacity to understand in the abstract, but at actual understanding of the treatment proposal in question. The MHAC's approach is correct.[34] In *Re R (a minor)* Lord Donaldson said that capacity entails:[35]

> '[N]ot merely an ability to understand the nature of the proposed treatment – in this case compulsory medication – but a full understanding and appreciation both of the treatment in terms of intended and possible side effects and, equally important, the anticipated consequences of failure to treat.'

It is not necessary 'to understand the precise physiological process involved before he can be said to understand the nature and likely effects'.[36] Nevertheless, the Mental Health Act threshold of capacity does not expressly include the issue of weighing the information in the balance as part of the process of making a decision, although there are suggestions that despite the clear difference in wording, the courts will expect similar factors to be considered.

10.20 A convergence between the MHA and MCA concepts of capacity seems likely from the statement of Hale LJ in *R (on the application of Wilkinson) v Responsible Medical Officer Broadmoor Hospital*[37] referring to the common law test of capacity in *Re MB (an adult: medical treatment)* and commenting that: 'It would be equally suitable for assessing capacity for the purpose of section 58(3)(b) of the Mental Health Act 1983.'[38] The test in *Re MB* is:[39]

> 'A person lacks capacity if some impairment or disturbance of mental functioning renders the person unable to make a decision whether to consent to or refuse treatment. The inability to make a decision will occur when:
>
> (a)   the patient is unable to comprehend and retain the information which is material to the decision, especially as to the likely consequences of having or not having the treatment in question;
> (b)   the patient is unable to use the information and weigh it in the balance as part of the process of arriving at a decision ...'

---

33   (1988) 9 BMLR 77 at 85.
34   P Fennell 'Sexual Suppressants and the Mental Health Act 1983' [1988] Crim LR 660.
35   [1991] 4 All ER 177 at 187, CA.
36   Ibid, per Stuart Smith LJ.
37   [2001] EWCA Civ 1545, [2002] 1 WLR 419, CA.
38   [2001] EWCA Civ 1545 at [65]–[66].
39   [1997] 2 FLR 426 at 437. This was closely modeled on the test proposed by the report of the investigation headed by Baroness Hale when she was at the Law Commission: *Mental Incapacity*, Law Com No 231 (TSO, 1995), paras 3.2–3.19.

The *Re MB* test forms the basis of the statutory test in ss 2 and 3 of the MCA 2005. If Baroness Hale's approach is followed, the courts will apply similar criteria to assessing capacity under the MHA, despite the differences in wording. In the same judgment Hale LJ recognised that:[40]

> 'Our threshold of capacity is rightly a low one. It is better to keep it that way and allow some non- consensual treatment of those who have capacity than to set such a high threshold for capacity that many would never qualify.'

It is not clear from the context of this statement whether her Ladyship was referring to the MHA test, the common law test, or both. On the face of it the MHA concept of incapacity presents a lower threshold than the MCA test. The issue is only likely to be of great practical significance in relation to s 58A where ECT may not be given in the face of a refusal by a patient who can understand the nature purpose and likely effects of the treatment, the argument being that the MHA standard of capacity applies to the right to refuse ECT rather than the potentially more exacting MCA test. In relation to adults it is for the AC or a SOAD to certify that the patient is capable and consenting to ECT. For children under 18 only a SOAD can certify capacity and consent.

Refusal of a patient with capacity not a bar to treatment under s 58

10.21 Although refusal of ECT by a capable patient is a bar to treatment under s 58A, under s 58, medication can be given to a refusing patient who is capable of understanding its nature purpose and likely effects, if it is 'appropriate to give it'. The European Committee for the Prevention of Torture and Inhuman or Degrading Treatment ('CPT') exists to police compliance with Art 3 by Council of Europe Member States. They have issued a set of Standards, the CPT standards, which establish the principle that even though a person is detained, they must still be placed in a position to give or withhold consent to treatment:[41]

> 'Patients should as a matter of principle be placed in a position to give their free and informed consent to treatment to treatment. The admission of a person to a psychiatric establishment on a involuntary basis should not be construed as authorising treatment without his consent. It follows that every competent patient, whether voluntary or involuntary, should be given he opportunity to refuse treatment or other medical intervention. Any derogation for this fundamental principle should be based upon law and only relate to clearly defined exceptional circumstances.'

To escape criticism by the CPT a Member State has to ensure that treatment without consent is based on law and only relates to strictly defined exceptional circumstances.

---

[40]   [2001] EWCA Civ 1545 at [80].
[41]   The European Committee for the Prevention of Torture and Inhuman or Degrading Treatment *The CPT Standards* Chap VI, para 41.

10.22 Article 12 of Council of Europe Recommendation (2004)10 concerning the protection of the human rights and dignity of persons with mental disorder (not ratified by the United Kingdom), provides that treatment of a mentally disordered person must be with consent if the patient is capable, and must be authorised by a representative, authority, person or body provided for by law. Treatment in emergencies may be carried out without such authority only when medically necessary to avoid serious harm to the health of the individual concerned, or to protect the safety of others. It was argued in *R (on the application of B) v Dr SS RMO Broadmoor Hospital, and others*[42] that s 58 was incompatible with Arts 3 and 8 in that it authorised treatment without consent of a capable person and did not define without sufficient precision the circumstances in which treatment may be given without consent. The test under s 58 was that the treatment was likely to alleviate or prevent deterioration. The Court of Appeal held that capacity is not the critical factor in determining whether treatment can lawfully be administered without consent under Arts 3 or 8. It was contended for the applicant that instruments such as the CPT Standards and the Council of Europe Recommendation showed a developing international consensus that the threshold criteria for overriding competent refusal should be that the treatment is necessary to protect other persons from serious harm, or where without such treatment, serious harm is likely to result to the patient's health. This argument was rejected by the court, which refused a declaration of incompatibility.

The Approved Clinician ('AC') or other person in charge of treatment

10.23 Under the MHA 1983 the RMO was responsible for deciding whether the patient had capacity to consent to treatment and was consenting to it, and for setting in motion the second opinion process. Section 12 transfers these powers to the AC, or (in the case of s 57 treatments) 'other person', in charge of the treatment in question. Even if treatment may lawfully be given without consent to a detained or SCT patient, consent should always be sought. The Draft Revised Code of Practice states that:[43]

> 'It remains the responsibility of people who actually administer treatment to ensure that they have lawful authority to do so, whether under this Act or otherwise, and to comply with their other professional and ethical obligations.'

The Explanatory Notes to the MHA 2007 Act state that:[44]

> 'In the majority of cases the AC in charge of the treatment will be the patient's RC, but where, for example, the RC is not qualified to make decisions about a particular treatment (e.g. medication if the RC is not a doctor or a nurse

---

[42] [2005] EWHC 1936 (Admin); [2006] EWCA Civ 28.
[43] Department of Health *Mental Health Act 1983 Draft Revised Code of Practice* (2007), para 25.11. See http://www.dh.gov.uk/en/Consultations.
[44] *Explanatory Notes to the MHA 2007*, para 57.

prescriber) then another appropriately qualified professional will be in charge of that treatment, with the RC continuing to retain overall responsibility for the patient's case.'

Where the person in charge of a particular treatment is not the patient's RC, they should ensure that the RC is kept informed about the treatment and that treatment decisions are discussed with the RC.

10.24 The person in charge of a treatment must be an AC where treatment is given:

(a)   under s 58;

(b)   under s 58A to a person other than an under 18-year-old who is an informal patient; or

(c)   to a patient subject to Part 4A who lacks capacity.

The person in charge of treatment may be an appropriately qualified professional who need not be an AC where the treatment is given:

(a)   under s 57;

(b)   under s 58A to an informal patient who is under 18 years old; or

(c)   under Part 4A to a patient with capacity.

To ensure that there is an independent assessment of whether treatment should be given, s 12 also amends Part 4 of the MHA 1983 so that the patient's RC and the person in charge of their treatment are excluded from being the registered medical practitioner to give the second opinion required by ss 57, 58, and 58A (the SOAD).[45] These professionals are also prevented from being one of the persons the SOAD has a statutory duty to consult.[46]

10.25 Where the treatment is medicine under s 58, in addition to certifying that the patient is capable and has consented, the AC must give a brief description of the treatment consented to. The Draft Code of Practice requires the AC to indicate on Form 38 the drugs prescribed by the classes described in the British National Formulary ('BNF'), the method of their administration, and the dose range, indicating the dosages if they are above the BNF limit.[47] The BNF is not the only prescribing guide available to doctors, but it has played an important part in the second opinion process. Not only do ACs describe the drugs consented to in terms of BNF categories, so too do the SOADs when they authorise treatment without consent. The BNF is published jointly by the

---

[45]   MHA 1983, ss 57(2)(a), 58(3)(b) and 58A(5).
[46]   MHA 1983, ss 57(3)(b), 58(4) and 58A(6)(b).
[47]   Department of Health *Mental Health Act 1983 Draft Revised Code of Practice* (2007), para 25.37. See http://www.dh.gov.uk/en/Consultations.

British Medical Association and the Royal Pharmaceutical Society and updated biannually. It describes the effects and side effects of each drug, specifying recommended maximum dosage levels, determined on the advice of medical advisers working mainly from the manufacturer's data sheet, and produced after the available information has been considered by the Committee for the Safety of Medicines in the process of deciding to give the drug a product licence. Some of the less sedative anti-psychotics have no BNF recommended maximum. The BNF is intended for the guidance of doctors, pharmacists and others who have the necessary training to interpret the information it provides. Each category (for example 4.2.1 anti-psychotic drugs, or 4.2.2 depot anti-psychotics) includes a large number of different drugs, so this method of describing treatment consented to confers considerable scope for the RMO to change medication within categories, or to give more than one drug within the same category at the same time. The Royal College of Psychiatrists has issued guidance on high dose anti-psychotics.[48]

10.26 The AC is the gatekeeper of the system, since where a patient agrees to treatment the decision about capacity will determine whether there will be a second opinion, and where the patient disagrees a second opinion will only be needed if the AC decides to persist with the treatment. It scarcely upholds the principle of self-determination if an AC accepts the consent of a patient who does not understand the decision being made, or who has not been given information about the treatment's nature, purpose, and effects. Here the Commissioners who visit and interview detained patients in hospital play a potentially important role. If they come across someone who is described as capable and consenting by the AC in charge of treatment, but who is in their view incapable, they may ask the RMO to refer the case for a second opinion. If a second opinion is required because the patient cannot consent or is refusing, it is the personal responsibility of the AC in charge of treatment to ensure that a second opinion visit is requested. Requests for a second opinion are made to the Mental Health Act Commission ('MHAC') who administer and monitor the system.

SECOND OPINION PROCEDURES

10.27 There are now three categories of second opinion treatment under Part 4:

(1) Section 57 treatments which cannot be given unless a patient certified to be capable has consented and a SOAD has certified that it is appropriate for the treatment to be given;

(2) Section 58A treatments (currently ECT) which may not be given if a capable patient has refused them. ECT, however, may be given subject to a second opinion where the patient lacks capacity, it is appropriate to give

---

[48] See http://www.rcpsych.ac.uk/files/pdfversion/CR138.pdf.

the treatment, and giving it does not conflict with a valid and applicable advance decision refusing it, or a refusal by an attorney or a deputy with power to do so; and

(3) Section 58 treatments where, whether the patient is—
     (a) incapable of consenting; or
     (b) capable and refusing,
     medicines for mental disorder may be given without consent if appropriate.

Section 57

10.28 The 'special treatments', so called because of their potential long-term effects and the ethical issues they raise, require true consent and a second opinion. They are psychosurgery or surgical implants of hormones to reduce male sex drive. The Government's interpretation of how this section works is that the patient's consent provides authority to treat, with s 57 providing additional safeguards (subject to s 62) before the treatment can lawfully be given. The procedure applies to all patients, whatever their legal status. The decision as to the patient's capacity and the existence of valid consent is made by a team of three people, a psychiatrist and two others, appointed by the Mental Health Act Commission ('MHAC'). They must certify that the patient is capable of understanding the nature, purpose and likely effects of the treatment and has consented to it. Even if the patient has given valid consent, the treatment may not proceed unless the medical member of the team certifies that it is appropriate for the treatment to be given.[49] The non-medical members of the appointed panel have no involvement in the second part of the decision. However, before deciding that the treatment is appropriate, the SOAD must consult two other people who have been professionally concerned with the patient's medical treatment, one of whom must be a nurse, and the other neither a nurse nor a doctor. Neither may be the responsible clinician ('RC') or the person in charge of the treatment in question.[50]

Interface with the Mental Capacity Act 2005

10.29 As the Code of Practice on the Mental Capacity Act 2005 emphasises, the combined effect of s 57 of the MHA 1983 and s 28 of the MCA 2005, is:[51]

> 'effectively that a person who lacks capacity to consent to s 57 treatment may not be given it. Healthcare staff cannot use the MCA as an alternative way of giving these kinds of treatment.'

---

[49] MHA 1983, s 57(2)(b). The certificate authorising treatment to proceed is Form 37 of Sch 1 to the Mental Health (Hospital, Guardianship and Consent to Treatment) Regulations 1983, SI 1983/893.
[50] MHA 1983, s 57(3).
[51] *Mental Capacity Act 2005 Code of Practice*, para 13.51.

Section 58

10.30 Section 58 applies to medicines for mental disorder, but the patient only becomes eligible for a second opinion if:[52]

> 'three months or more have elapsed from the first occasion in that period [of detention] when medicine was administered to him by any means for his mental disorder.'

Medication does not necessarily have to be administered continuously throughout the three months. This is the so-called 'stabilising period', a result of lobbying by the Royal College of Psychiatrists, during which medicine may be given at the direction of the AC in charge of treatment without consent or a second opinion. The Secretary of State, Kenneth Clarke, described its rationale in these terms:[53]

> 'The danger against which everyone wished to protect patients was the continuing course of heavy drug therapy, which has to be resorted to and can be beneficial in some cases. There are different views about that sort of treatment and it was felt that some safeguards were required. If we start applying safeguards from the moment any drug treatment is embarked upon there will be difficulties. There will be no time to see whether the treatment is working and the patient may object bitterly, because he does not understand that it will do him good.'

The Draft Code of Practice states the rationale as being to enable the AC in charge of the medication to develop a treatment programme suitable for the patient's needs. The Joint Committee on Human Rights considered that:[54]

> 'Three months is a long time to be in receipt of compulsory psychiatric treatment without the opportunity for review and supervision of the responsible clinician's decision to impose that treatment, and we consider it doubtful whether the Government's obligation under Article 8 to provide effective supervision and review of treatment without consent is discharged by such a long waiting time.'

10.31 Paragraph 25.14 of the Draft Code emphasises that it should not be assumed that a patient subject to the Act lacks capacity to consent to any or all of their treatment. For detained and SCT patients, the patient's consent should be sought for all proposed treatments, even if they may lawfully be given under the Act without consent. It is the personal responsibility of the person in charge of the treatment to ensure that valid consent has been sought. The interview at which such consent was sought should be properly recorded in the patient's notes. This complies with the principle in the CPT standards that even though a person is detained, they must still be placed in a position to give or

---

[52]   MHA 1983, s 58(1)(b).
[53]   Kenneth Clarke, *Hansard*, HC Deb, vol 29, ser 6, col 86 (18 October 1982).
[54]   House of Lords, House of Commons Joint Committee on Human Rights *Legislative Scrutiny: Mental Health: Bill Fourth Report of Session 2006–2007* (HL Paper 40, HC Paper 288, 4 February 2007), para 66.

withhold consent to treatment.[55] So, even though medicines may be given without consent during the first three months, the Draft Code of Practice advises that the AC in charge of medication should ensure that the patient's valid consent is sought before it is administered. Moreover, refusal or withdrawal of consent should be taken into account when deciding whether to proceed with treatment:[56]

> 'The patient's consent or refusal should be recorded in the case notes. If such consent is not forthcoming or is withdrawn during this period, the approved clinician in charge of the medication must consider whether to proceed in the absence of consent, to give alternative treatment or no further treatment.'

Capacity and consent to treatment under s 58 may be certified either by the AC in charge of treatment or a SOAD on Statutory Form 38.[57]

Role of the Second Opinion Appointed Doctor ('SOAD') under s 58

10.32 The position of the MHAC appointed SOAD is different from that of the AC in charge of treatment. The SOAD does not carry out the treatment or order others to carry it out. As Hale LJ put it in *R (on the application of Wilkinson) v Responsible Medical Officer Broadmoor Hospital*:[58]

> 'the SOAD performs a statutory watchdog function on behalf of the public, to protect detained patients who are in an especially vulnerable position. This is a function which must be subject to judicial review.'

The SOAD's role under the s 58 procedure is to safeguard the patient's rights under Arts 3 and 8, to interview the patient and determine whether he or she is capable of giving valid consent. If the patient is refusing treatment or is not capable of giving consent, the SOAD has to determine whether the proposed treatment is appropriate and should be given. The Draft Code of Practice reiterates the principle from *R (on the application of Wilkinson) v Responsible Medical Officer Broadmoor Hospital*[59] that the SOAD acts as an individual and must reach his or her own judgment as to whether the proposed treatment is appropriate in the light of the general consensus about treatment for the condition in question. In reaching this judgment the SOAD should consider not only the therapeutic efficacy of the proposed treatment but also, where a capable patient is withholding consent, the reasons for such withholding, which

---

[55]   The European Committee for the Prevention of Torture and Inhuman or Degrading Treatment *The CPT Standards* Chap VI, para 41.

[56]   Department of Health *Mental Health Act 1983 Draft Revised Code of Practice* (2007), para 25.48. See http://www.dh.gov.uk/en/Consultations.

[57]   Mental Health (Hospital, Guardianship and Consent to Treatment) Regulations 1983, SI 1983/893, reg 16(2)(b) and Sch 1.

[58]   [2001] EWCA Civ 1545, [2002] 1 WLR 419. See also *R v Mental Health Commission, ex parte X* (1988) 9 BMLR 77, QBD.

[59]   [2001] EWCA Civ 1545, [2002] 1 WLR 419.

should be given their due weight.[60] This reflects the ruling in *R (on the application of PS) v Responsible Medical Officer*[61] that refusal on the part of a capable patient was not a bar to treatment under s 58 but was a very important factor to be taken into account, in deciding the questions of medical necessity and best interests, which must be addressed by ACs and SOADs in deciding that treatment is appropriate.

10.33 Before making the decision the SOAD must consult two other people who have been professionally concerned with the patient's medical treatment, one of whom must be a nurse, and the other neither a nurse nor a doctor. Neither may be the RC or a doctor. The Draft Code advises that the SOAD should seek the opinion of about the nature of the patient's disorder and problems, the appropriateness of various forms of treatment including that proposed, and the patient's likely response to different types of treatment. The SOAD should take into account any previous experience of comparable treatment of a similar episode of disorder. The SOAD should give due weight to the opinion, knowledge, experience and skill of those consulted.[62]

Reasons

10.34 In *R (on the application of Wooder) v Feggetter*, the Court of Appeal held that fairness requires the SOAD to give in writing the reasons for his opinion when certifying under s 58 that a detained patient should be given medication against his will, and that these reasons should be disclosed to the patient unless the SOAD or the RMO considers that such disclosure would be likely to cause serious harm to the physical or mental health of the patient or any other person.[63] Brooke LJ said that the law would not require a SOAD to 'dot every "i" and cross every "t" when giving reasons'. It would suffice if clear reasons are given on the substantive points on which the clinical judgment was made that the treatment is appropriate. Judicial review would only be available if a patient could show a real prospect of establishing that a SOAD has not addressed any substantive point which he should have addressed, or that there is some material error underlying the reasons given.[64] The SOAD must therefore give reasons which address the substantive points upon which the SOAD reached the decision, and the MHAC has produced useful guidance for SOADS on the issues to be addressed in a statement of reasons.[65] The reasons must be given as soon as practicable to the RC or the AC in charge of treatment, not direct to the patient, and must state whether the SOAD

---

[60] Department of Health *Mental Health Act 1983 Draft Revised Code of Practice* (2007), para 26.4. See http://www.dh.gov.uk/en/Consultations.

[61] [2003] EWHC 2335 (Admin). See also Mental Health Act Commission *Guidance for RMOs following the PS Case* (available at www.mhac.org.uk).

[62] Department of Health *Mental Health Act 1983 Draft Revised Code of Practice* (2007), para 26.5. See http://www.dh.gov.uk/en/Consultations.

[63] [2002] EWCA Civ 554, per Brooke LJ at [34]. Sedley LJ (at para [49]) considered that the duty to give reasons could equally be founded on Art 8 of the ECHR.

[64] Ibid at [34].

[65] Mental Health Act Commission *Guidance to SOADs following the Wooder Case*, paras 9 and 10 (accessible at www.mhac.org.uk).

considers disclosure of those reasons to the patient would be likely to cause serious harm to the physical or mental health of the patient or any other person. The duty to provide reasons applies equally to treatment without consent under s 58A or under Part 4A.

Interface with the Mental Capacity Act 2005

10.35 If the patient is not capable of consenting but has made a valid and applicable advance refusal of s 58 treatment, this is not binding, but must be taken into account in determining appropriateness and best interests. The same applies to an advance statement requesting an alternative treatment, which should be given 'due weight'.[66] The MCA Code of Practice says that staff should consider whether they could use a different type of treatment which the patient has not refused in advance. If healthcare staff do not follow an advance decision, they should record in the patient's notes why they have chosen not to follow it.[67] Even if a patient is being treated without their consent for mental disorder under Part 4, an advance decision to refuse other forms of treatment may still be valid.

Section 58A

10.36 Section 27 of the MHA 2007 inserts a new s 58A which provides that ECT and any other treatment provided for by regulations made under subs (1)(b), can only be given when the patient either gives consent, or is incapable of giving consent. Section 58A states that, subject to the possibility of emergency treatment under s 62, ECT may not be given unless one of three circumstances applies:

(1)   where the patient is over 18, has consented, and either the AC in charge of treatment or a SOAD certifies that the patient is capable of understanding the nature purpose and likely effects of the treatment;

(2)   where the patient is under 18, has consented, and a SOAD has certified both—

    (a)   that the patient is capable of understanding the nature purpose and likely effects and has consented, and

    (b)   that it is appropriate for the treatment to be given;

(3)   where a SOAD has certified that the patient is not capable of understanding the nature purpose and likely effects of ECT but it is appropriate for the treatment to be given, and giving it would not conflict with a valid and applicable advance decision refusing it or a decision by someone holding a lasting power of attorney, a deputy or the Court of Protection.

---

[66]   Department of Health *Mental Health Act 1983 Draft Revised Code of Practice* (2007), para 26.4. See http://www.dh.gov.uk/en/Consultations.

[67]   Department of Constitutional Affairs *Mental Capacity Act 2005 Code of Practice*, para 13.37.

As with medicines, the AC in charge of treatment certifies that an adult patient is capable and has consented. If the patient is under 18 the certificate of capacity and consent must come from a SOAD, who must go on to certify that it is appropriate for the treatment to be given. When s 58A of the MHA 2007 comes into force ECT will no longer be able to be given without consent to an adult patient with capacity or a competent child patient who is refusing the treatment, unless it is an emergency covered by s 62(1A).

Treatment without consent of patients lacking capacity or competence

10.37 The threshold of capacity assumes great importance under s 58A. If capable a patient is entitled to refuse ECT; if incapable, it can be given subject to a second opinion. If a patient understands in broad terms the nature, purpose and likely effects of ECT and is refusing it, thereby passing the MHA 1983 capacity test, will he or she nevertheless be deemed incapable if he or she is so depressed that he or she wants to die and does not care if ECT is thought necessary to save his or her life? Under the common law test she might be said to be incapable by virtue of a disorder or disability of the mind or brain of using the information to weigh it in the balance to arrive at a decision. If found incapable, the patient could be given ECT subject to a second opinion under s 58A(5). If a patient is incapable of understanding the nature, purpose and likely effects of ECT, and there is no valid and applicable advance decision refusing it, it may nevertheless be authorised by a SOAD if it is appropriate for ECT to be given. Before issuing the certificate the SOAD must consult with two persons who have been professionally concerned with the patient's medical treatment; one must be a nurse and the other shall be neither a nurse nor a doctor nor the patient's RC or the AC in charge of the treatment.[68]

Emergency treatment under s 62

10.38 Section 62 applies to ensure that a patient, including one who is not consenting, can still receive treatment in the urgent circumstances set out in s 62(1)(a) and (b) if there is insufficient time to apply the 58A procedure. As Jones notes, since ss 57, 58 or 58A do not apply to treatments given under s 62, there is no requirement to certify capacity, but that it is good practice to record issues relating to capacity and the patient's attitude to treatment in the clinical notes.[69] Whether or not the patient is capable s 62(2) applies to authorise ECT in an emergency where immediately necessary to save life or prevent serious deterioration in the patient's condition.[70] It is difficult to envisage an emergency where the patient immediately needs ECT for one of these reasons yet retains decision-making capacity.

---

[68]   MHA 1983, s 58A(6).
[69]   RM Jones *Mental Health Act Manual* (Sweet and Maxwell, 10th edn, 2006).
[70]   MHA 1983, s 62(2), as amended by MHA 2007, s 28(6).

Interface with the Mental Capacity Act 2005

10.39 A certificate may not be given if it would conflict with a valid and applicable advance decision made by the patient when capable, a decision by a health care attorney, by a deputy, or by the Court of Protection. Section 58A protects refusal by valid and applicable advance decisions, proxy decision-makers, and the Court of Protection. The Draft Code advises that before issuing a certificate under s 58A that ECT may be given to a patient who is not capable of consenting, the SOAD should make inquiries and confirm so far as is practicable with the patient, staff and other persons known to the patient whether there is a valid and applicable advance decision refusing ECT or whether an attorney or a deputy has been appointed under the MCA 2005, or whether there is a valid order of the Court of Protection that treatment with ECT should not be given to the patient.[71] It is for the SOAD to confirm whether the advance decision is valid and applicable. In order to be valid the patient has to have been capable when it was made. In order to be applicable it has to refuse ECT in the circumstances which have now arisen. If ECT is necessary to sustain life, the advance decision must be in writing, and must clearly specify that it is intended to refuse ECT even if given as a life-sustaining treatment.

10.40 Section 58A(7) states that:

> 'this section shall not by itself confer sufficient authority for a patient who falls within s 56(5) above to be given a form of treatment to which this section applies if he is not capable of understanding the nature, purpose and likely effects of the treatment (and cannot therefore consent to it).'

Section 56(5) extends the protection of s 58A to informal child patients who are neither detained nor subject to a CTO. The intention here is that the authority to treat an informal child patient must come from somewhere other than s 58A itself. This means that where a patient is between 16 and 18 and lacks competence, treatment may be given under ss 5 or 6 of the MCA 2005, or with the consent of someone with parental responsibility or the Court of Protection. The MCA provides the authority to treat a patient between 16 and 18, and ss 58A and 62, which are intended to apply additionally, lay down the procedures and criteria for exercising that authority to treat without consent. Similarly, if a patient is under 16 and being treated with parental consent, the parental consent provides the authority to treat, and ss 58A and 62 apply additional safeguards to the exercise of that authority.

Consent and withdrawal of consent to a plan of treatment

10.41 Section 59 provides that the patient's consent or a second opinion under ss 57, 58 or 58A may authorise a plan of treatment under which one or more of the forms of treatment mentioned in the relevant section may be given.

---

[71] Department of Health *Mental Health Act 1983 Draft Revised Code of Practice* (2007), para 26.6. See http://www.dh.gov.uk/en/Consultations.

Section 60 allows a patient to withdraw consent at any time before the completion of the plan of treatment consented to. If this happens, subject to the emergency provisions of s 62, a second opinion will be required before the treatment can be resumed. Section 29 of the 2007 Act introduces new subss (1A)–(1D) into s 60. Subsections (1A) and (1B) apply where the patient has given consent, but before completion of the treatment ceases to be capable of understanding its nature, purpose and likely effects. Subject to the possibility of emergency treatment under s 62, the patient is treated as having withdrawn consent and the relevant second opinion procedure must be undertaken afresh. Subsections (1C) and 1D) apply where a certificate has been given under ss 58 or 58A that the patient is not capable of understanding the nature, purpose and likely effects of the treatment to which the certificate applies, but before the completion of the treatment, the patient becomes capable. In such a case, again subject to the possibility of emergency treatment under s 62, the certificate ceases to apply to the treatment and the relevant second opinion procedure must be undertaken afresh as if the remainder of the treatment were a separate form of treatment. The Draft Code of Practice states that where the patient withdraws consent a clear explanation should be given and recorded in the patient's records, of the likely consequences of not receiving the treatment; that, for s 58 treatments, a second opinion under Part 4 of the Act may or will be sought in order to authorise treatment in the continuing absence of the patient's consent, and finally of the power of the clinician in charge of the treatment to begin or continue urgent treatment under s 62.[72]

Section 61: reports on condition of patients who have had treatment following a second opinion

10.42 A prime concern behind the enactment of s 61 was to ensure that patients were not subject to heavy drug regimes for prolonged periods. Section 61 requires the AC or other person in charge of the treatment to report to the MHAC on the treatment and condition of anyone given treatment following a second opinion under ss 57, 58 or 58A or, following recall from SCT, under s 62A in accordance with a Part 4A certificate. A report must be given on subsequent occasion when the authority for the patient's detention or SCT is renewed. If the patient is subject to a restriction order, restriction direction or limitation direction and the treatment is within the first six months following the order or direction, a report must be furnished at the end of that six-month period. If the treatment takes place later than six months from the date of the order or direction the report is due the next time the RC submits a twelve-monthly report to the Secretary of State. A report may also be required at any other time if directed by the MHAC.

Section 62: Emergency Treatment

10.43 Section 62 is intended to allow treatment to be given if a second opinion cannot be arranged sufficiently speedily to cope with an emergency, whilst at

---

[72] Ibid, para 25.29.

the same time protecting patients against hazardous or irreversible treatments. The application of s 62 is not limited by any requirement that the patient must lack decision-making capacity. It applies whether or not the patient is capable in the terms of Part 4. It applies to informal patients where ss 57 or 58A is applicable. Treatment which would in normal circumstances require a second opinion may be given in emergencies defined in s 62 without prior compliance with the second opinion procedures. Section 62(1) states that ss 57 and 58 do not apply to any treatment which is:

'(a) immediately necessary to save the patient's life; or
(b) which (not being irreversible) is immediately necessary to prevent a serious deterioration in his condition; or
(c) which (not being irreversible or hazardous) is immediately necessary to alleviate serious suffering by the patient; or
(d) which (not being irreversible or hazardous) is immediately necessary and represents the minimum interference necessary to prevent the patient behaving violently or being a danger to himself or others.'

Section 62(1A) provides that ECT may be given without compliance with s 58A if immediately necessary on grounds (a) or (b) to save life, or, not being irreversible, immediately necessary to prevent serious deterioration in the patient's condition. ECT is not regarded as an irreversible treatment. Section 62 applies whether or not the patient retains capacity. Any treatments made subject to s 58A in the future by regulations under s 58A(1)(b) may be given in an emergency on the full range of grounds specified in (a)–(d) above. Section 62(2) provides that withdrawal of consent by the patient or withdrawal by the MHAC of a certificate authorising treatment does not preclude the continuation of any treatment or of treatment under any plan pending compliance with ss 57, 58 or 58A above if the AC in charge of the treatment considers that the discontinuance of the treatment or of treatment under the plan would cause serious suffering to the patient.

10.44 The Draft Code of Practice stresses that s 62 treatment must be given by or under the direction of the AC or person in charge of the treatment, who must be an AC if the patient is detained. Treatment must be immediately necessary to achieve one of the objects specified in the section. These are strict tests. The Draft Revised Code emphasises that:[73]

'It is not enough that there is an urgent need for treatment, or that the clinicians involved believe it is necessary or beneficial. The practitioner in charge of the treatment, or other appropriately qualified person, is responsible for judging whether treatment would meet one of the relevant tests.'

The MHAC has consistently maintained that where s 62 is invoked, 'a request should simultaneously be made for a second opinion, so that repeated use does not arise,' having noted a case where no fewer than 12 ECT treatments were

---

[73]   Ibid, para 25.75.

given to a patient under s 62.[74] The Draft Code provides that urgent treatment given under s 62 can only continue for as long as it is immediately necessary to achieve the statutory objective, and before deciding to give treatment under s 62 the AC should wherever possible discuss the issue with others involved with the patient's care. A treatment is deemed irreversible if it has unfavourable irreversible physical or psychological consequences, and hazardous if it entails 'significant physical hazard'.[75] The person in charge of the treatment, or other appropriately qualified person, is responsible for judging whether treatment falls into either of these categories, and whether therefore the Act allows it to be given, having regard to generally accepted medical opinion. The Draft Code requires hospital managers to monitor the use of s 62 in their hospital, including requiring completion of a form giving details of the treatment, why it is of urgent necessity to give the treatment, the duration of the treatment and the subheading of s 62 under which treatment was given.[76] The National Institute of Clinical Excellence has now produced a recommended list of medications to achieve 'rapid tranquillisation' which includes Lorazepam, a strong sedative, Haloperidol an old- style antipsychotic, and Olanzapine, a more modern 'a-typical antispychotic' designed to have fewer Parkinsonian side-effects that the old style anti-psychotics.[77]

Section 62A: treatment of CTO Patients on recall or revocation

10.45 Section 62A applies where a community patient is recalled under s 17E, or where the CTO is revoked under s 17F. For the purposes of s 58 the patient is to be treated as if he had remained liable to be detained since the making of the CTO. This means that if there was a certificate covering s 58 treatment before the CTO was made which covers the patient's current treatment, there is no need for a new s 58 certificate on recall. If the period from the time the patient first received medication during that period of detention is less than three months then a new s 58 certificate will not be required until that three-month period has elapsed. On recall to hospital, a patient may be given treatment which would otherwise require a certificate under ss 58 or 58A (medicines or ECT) on the basis of a certificate given by a SOAD under the new Part 4A of the MHA 1983. However, that certificate must specify the treatment as being appropriate to be given on recall, and giving the treatment would not be contrary to any condition in the certificate. If a patient's CTO is revoked, so that the patient is once again detained in hospital for treatment, treatment can be given on the basis of a Part 4A certificate only until a s 58 or s 58A certificate can be arranged. If the Part 4A certificate does not specify any

---

[74] Mental Health Act Commission *First Biennial Report 1983–1985* (HMSO, 1985), p 40; *Second Biennial Report 1985–1987* (HMSO, 1987), p 23.

[75] MHA 1983, s 62(3).

[76] Department of Health *Mental Health Act 1983 Draft Revised Code of Practice* (2007), para 25.79. See http://www.dh.gov.uk/en/Consultations.

[77] National Institute for Clinical Excellence *Violence: The Short Term Management of Disturbed/Violent Behaviour in In-Patient Psychiatric Settings* (Clinical Guideline 25, February 2005), pp 47–59.

such treatment, then ECT or medicines cannot be given on recall unless or until their administration is permitted under Part 4.

10.46 A Part 4A certificate will not provide authority to give s 58A type treatment to a patient who has capacity or competence to consent but who refuses consent when recalled or when the community treatment order is revoked.[78] A s 58 or s 58A certificate is not required in circumstances where discontinuing the treatment or the plan of treatment at that point would cause serious suffering to the patient,[79] or the treatment is immediately necessary under s 62, or, if the treatment is medicine, the patient is still within the period before which a certificate is required, ie either one month has not elapsed from the time when the CTO was made or the three-month period from when medication was first given to the patient during that period of detention has not elapsed.

Section 63: general power to treat detained patients without consent

10.47 An important concern behind Part 4 was to clarify the powers of staff to treat without consent. Section 63 provides that any medical treatment for mental disorder not specifically identified under ss 57, s 58 or s 58A as requiring a second opinion may be given to a detained patient without consent by or under the direction of the AC in charge of treatment. In *R (on the application of B) v Ashworth Hospital Authority* Baroness Hale said that the MHA 1983:[80]

> 'enacted the general power in s 63, defined in s 56 the patients to whom it applied, and provided safeguards for the most controversial treatments specified in or under ss 57 and 58.'

Hence s 63 provides a general power to treat detained patients without consent for mental disorder, s 58 and s 58A provide procedures and safeguards attending the administration of medicines or ECT without consent, and s 62 provides for emergency treatment without a prior second opinion. 'Medical treatment for mental disorder' is defined broadly and extends beyond those treatments which require a second opinion. In Lord Elton's words, spoken in the Lords debate in 1982, s 63 was included 'to put the legal position beyond doubt ... for the sake of the psychiatrists, nurses and other staff who care for these very troubled patients.' When faced with the criticism that this provision might authorise a disturbingly wide range of interventions, Lord Elton emphasised that this provision was not intended to apply to 'borderline' or 'experimental' treatments but:[81]

---

[78] See MHA 1983, s 62A(4) and Department of Health *Explanatory Notes to the MHA 2007*, para 128.

[79] MHA 1983, s 62A(6).

[80] *R (on the application of B) v Ashworth Hospital Authority* [2005] UKHL 20 at [26].

[81] *Hansard*, HL Deb, vol 426, ser 5, cols 1064–1065 and 1071 (1 February 1982).

'things which a person in hospital for treatment ought to undergo for his own good and for the good of the running of the hospital and for the good of other patients ... perfectly routine, sensible treatment.'

10.48 Subsequent case-law has made it clear that force-feeding patients suffering from anorexia nervosa or other eating disorders can be treatment for mental disorder covered by s 63. Anorexia nervosa is viewed as a mental illness, and therefore force feeding could be seen as a treatment of that disorder. In *Re KB (adult) (mental patient: medical treatment)*, Ewbank J said that 'relieving symptoms was just as much part of treatment as relieving the underlying cause'.[82] *B v Croydon Health Authority* differed from *Re KB* in that the patient suffered from a borderline personality disorder rather than anorexia, but the Court of Appeal held that s 63 applied to treatment directed at the symptoms or sequelae of mental disorder just as much as to treatment directed to remedying B's underlying personality disorder which caused her compulsion to harm herself by not eating.[83] The self-harm by starvation was a symptom of the underlying disorder. In *R v Collins and Ashworth Hospital Authority, ex parte Brady*[84] the court held that it would be lawful under s 63 to feed forcibly a patient on hunger strike. The pursuit of the hunger strike was held to be a manifestation of his histrionic personality disorder which led him to embark on dramatic conflicts with authority.

10.49 In *Tameside and Glossop Acute Services Trust v CH*,[85] s 63 was held to authorise use of reasonable force to secure delivery of a baby by Caesarean section as a treatment for mental disorder, where the mother was detained under s 3. The doctors feared placental failure. Administering a Caesarean was held to be a treatment for mental disorder for the following reasons. CH's schizophrenia could only be treated by tranquillisers rather than anti-psychotic drugs, because the latter would cross the placental barrier and might damage the foetus. It was therefore in the interests of her mental health that her pregnancy be brought to a swift conclusion to enable the new drug regime to start. It was also in CH's interests that the baby be born alive, since if it were not she would blame herself and the doctors and this would exacerbate her schizophrenic illness. This case stretched the concept of treatment for mental disorder to the very limit. *St George's Healthcare NHS Trust v S*[86] represented a step back from the *CH* position. Here the Court of Appeal held that a person who is detained under the Act cannot be forced to undergo medical procedures unconnected with her mental condition unless she is deprived of capacity to decide for herself, in which case the treatment could be authorised under

---

[82] *Re KB (adult) (mental patient: medical treatment)* (1994) 19 BMLR 144 at 146.
[83] [1995] 1 All ER 683, CA.
[84] [2000] Lloyd's Rep Med 355.
[85] [1996] 1 FLR 762, FD. See also *Norfolk and Norwich Healthcare (NHS) Trust v W* [1996] 2 FLR 613; and *Rochdale Healthcare (NHS) Trust v C* [1997] 1 FCR 274, where force was authorised at common law to administer a Caesarean. These cases are discussed in E Fegan and P Fennell 'Feminist Perspectives on Mental Health Law' in S Sheldon and M Thomson (eds) *Feminist Perspectives on Health Care Law* (Cavendish, 1998), at pp 87–94.
[86] [1998] 3 All ER 673, CA.

common law now superseded by the MCA 2005. If the treatment is needed to cope with a physical cause or symptom or consequence of the disorder, it can be a treatment for mental disorder.[87]

10.50 Section 63 was not intended to apply to controversial treatments like force-feeding or Caesarean sections, but the Department of Health has resisted extending the second opinion procedures in s 58 by regulation to include force feeding. The Department has been content to leave the position as it is.[88] Forcible feeding is potentially a breach of Arts 3 and 8.[89] The Joint Committee on Human Rights asked the Government whether it considered it necessary to provide more effective supervision and review of decisions to forcibly feed a patient than is currently provided by s 63. The Government response was that:[90]

> 'While s 58 provides an additional safeguard of a SOAD (Second Opinion Approved Doctor) in relation to certain treatments, there is no requirement in the Convention for a second opinion. With respect to the Committee, the key question is whether the provisions of the Act which provide for the forcible feeding of patients without consent, with or without a second opinion, are compatible with the Convention. The Department considers that they are.'

It seems anomalous and arbitrary that similar safeguards are not applicable to forcible feeding by naso-gastric tube given its invasiveness by comparison with other treatments covered by second opinion procedures under Part 4.

Seclusion

10.51 Although there have at various points in recent history been calls to ban seclusion, it has retained its place as an accepted psychiatric practice, to the extent that the present day Code of Practice on the Mental Health Act 1983, whilst not regarding it as 'a treatment technique', describes it as falling within the broad legal definition of 'medical treatment', a position confirmed by the Court of Appeal and the House of Lords in *R (on the application of Munjaz) v Mersey Care NHS Trust* where Lord Bingham said that:[91]

> 'medical treatment is in my opinion an expression wide enough to cover nursing and caring for a patient in seclusion, even though seclusion cannot properly form part of a treatment programme.'

The NICE Guidance on the management of violence in psychiatric settings states that:[92]

---

[87]   DoH and Welsh Office *Code of Practice on the Mental Health Act 1983* (TSO, 1998), para 16.5.
[88]   (1995) 145 NLJ 319–320.
[89]   *Nevmerzhitsky v Ukraine (Application 54825/00)* Judgment of 5 April 2005, ECtHR.
[90]   House of Lords, House of Commons Joint Committee on Human Rights *Legislative Scrutiny: Mental Health Bill Fourth Report of Session 2006–2007* (HL Paper 40, HC Paper 288, 4 February 2007), para 80 and App 3, para 67.
[91]   [2003] EWCA Civ 1036; [2005] UKHL 58 at [20].
[92]   Emphasis added.

'These interventions are *management strategies* and are *not* regarded as *primary treatment techniques*.'

Although legally these are 'treatments for mental disorder', in reality they are legally sanctioned treatments *of mentally disordered people*. The courts have been willing to accept that treatment designed to prevent harm to others can be in the best interests of the patient.

10.52 The Code of Practice on the Mental Health Act 1983 defines seclusion as:

'the supervised confinement of a patient in a room, which may be locked to protect others from significant harm. Its sole aim is to contain severely disturbed behaviour which is likely to cause harm to others.'

The Code further prescribes a number of principles that seclusion should only be used as a last resort and for the shortest period possible, a reflection of principles of both common law (necessity) and of the European Convention case-law (proportionality). The Code states that seclusion should never be used as a punishment or threat, as part of a treatment programme, because of shortage of staff or where there is a risk of suicide or self-harm.[93]

10.53 *R (on the application of Munjaz) v Mersey Care NHS Trust* was a challenge to Ashworth's seclusion policy, which provided for one daily medical review after the third day, in contrast to the Code of Practice recommendation of four-hourly review by a doctor. Furthermore, the Ashworth policy did not meet the requirement of the Code that a patient should have a review after two hours, and that one of the nurses reviewing the seclusion must not have been involved in the original decision to seclude. The 'independent' nurse requirement under the Code applies 'where practicable'. The House of Lords by a majority held that the Code was not mandatory and could be departed from if there was a cogent reason for doing so. Lord Hope considered that Ashworth's status as a high security special hospital justified the departure from the Code:[94]

'If good reasons are required for departing from the system that the Code sets out for the monitoring and review of the use of seclusion, there are ample grounds for thinking that they have been well demonstrated at Ashworth. There is no doubt that the situation there differs from that in the generality of institutions in which mental patients who are severely disturbed may find themselves. As the introduction to Ashworth's Policy states, special considerations need to be applied to the use of seclusion in a high security hospital, bearing in mind that the very reason why patients are there is because they cannot be dealt with by mental health services elsewhere in a way that will protect others from harm. The Code does not address this problem. Nor is it designed to do so.'

---

[93] *Mental Health Act Code of Practice* (1998), para 19.16.
[94] [2005] UKHL 58 at [70].

Lord Bingham in *Munjaz* accepted that improper use of seclusion might breach the right of respect for private life under Art 8, but refused to accept that there would be any breach if it were 'properly used', 'as the only means of protecting others from violence or intimidation and it is used for the shortest time possible':[95]

> 'A detained patient, when in his right mind or during lucid intervals, would not wish to be free to act in such a way and would appreciate that his best interests were served by his being prevented from doing so.'

On the assumption that Art 8 might be engaged, Lord Bingham then considered seclusion could be necessary to meet one of the legitimate grounds for interference in Art 8(2), whether it would be a proportionate response, and whether it would be in accordance with law:[96]

> 'Seclusion under the policy is plainly necessary for the protection of health or morals, or for the protection of the rights and freedoms of others, properly used the seclusion will not be disproportionate because it will match the necessity giving rise to it. The procedure adopted by the Trust does not permit arbitrary or random decision-making. The rules are accessible, foreseeable and predictable. It cannot be said ... that they are not in accordance with or prescribed by law.'

The majority in the House of Lords accepted that Ashworth had considered the issues carefully before adopting its own seclusion policy which was at variance with the Code, that the Code could be departed from if there was a cogent reason to do so, and that Ashworth's policy complied with Arts 3 and 8.[97]

PART 4A: AUTHORITY TO TREAT IN THE COMMUNITY

10.54 Section 35 introduces a new Part 4A (ss 64A–64K) into the MHA 1983 to regulate the giving of 'relevant treatment' (ie treatments not governed by s 57) of community patients whilst they are in the community, in other words 'when they are not recalled to hospital'.[98] Treatment of community patients recalled to hospital is governed by s 62A (see paras **10.45** and **10.46** above). The basic principle is that a patient with capacity (or competence if a child) may only be given treatment in the form of medicine for mental disorder or ECT if they consent and there is a certificate authorising the treatment from a SOAD. If the patient is capable and refusing treatment may only be given without consent by recalling the patient and treating under s 62A. Sections 64A–64K authorise 'relevant treatment' to be given to a community patient who has not been recalled to hospital. Sections 64A–64K set out the circumstances in which

---

[95]   [2005] UKHL 58 at [32].

[96]   [2005] UKHL 58 at [33]–[34].

[97]   In *Ramirez Sanchez v France (App no 59450/00)* Judgment of the European Court of Human Rights of 27 January 2005, the Court held that in certain cases prisoners were entitled to a remedy to enable applicant to contest decision to place in solitary confinement.

[98]   *Explanatory Notes to the MHA 2007*, para 129.

treatment for mental disorder (other than treatments covered by s 57) may be given to an adult or child community patient in the community (not necessarily in a hospital or clinic). They apply parts of the decision-making framework of the MCA 2005 to treatment under the MHA 1983 and authorise treatment in the community without the consent of an incapable patient:

(a)   if there is consent from someone authorised under the MCA 2005 to make decisions on the patient's behalf;

(b)   if the patient lacks capacity and force is not necessary to secure compliance; or

(c)   if emergency treatment needs to be given, using force if necessary, to a patient who lacks capacity.

Relevant treatment

10.55 Relevant treatment for the purposes of Part 4A is any treatment for mental disorder which is not covered by s 57 (ie is not psychosurgery or surgical hormone implants to reduce male sex drive).[99] In practice 'relevant treatment' will probably be most frequently applied to the administration of medicines for mental disorder, although ECT can be a relevant treatment too. Relevant treatment may be given by or under the direction of the responsible clinician to an adult patient (ie one over 16) under s 64B, or to a child under s 64E. There must be authority to give the treatment. In addition, for s 58 or s 58A type treatments, unless one of the exceptions applies, the 'certificate requirement' must be met. Treatment is a s 58 or s 58A type treatment if ss 58 or 58A would have applied to it if the patient had remained liable to be detained instead of being on a CTO.[100]

Authority to treat under Part 4A

10.56 Before treatment may be given under Part 4A there must be 'authority to treat'. There is authority to give treatment to a patient over 16 if:

(a)   the patient has capacity and consents to it being given; or

(b)   a donee of a lasting power of attorney, or a deputy appointed by the Court of Protection, or the Court of Protection itself, consents to it on his behalf; or

(c)   Section 64D (treatment for adult patients lacking capacity) or s 64G (emergency treatment for patients lacking capacity) applies.[101]

---

[99]   MHA 1983, s 64A, introduced by MHA 2007, s 35.
[100]   MHA 1983, s 64C(3).
[101]   MHA 1983, s 64C(2).

For a child under 16 there is authority to treat if:

(a)   the patient is competent and consents to it being given; or

(b)   it is authorised by s 64F (treatment for child patients lacking competence); or

(c)   the treatment is emergency treatment under s 64G.[102]

No one can consent or refuse on the patient's behalf if they are under 16, since they are ineligible to appoint an attorney and there is no jurisdiction to appoint a deputy for them. The test of capacity for both adult and child patients is that set out in ss 2 and 3 of the MCA 2005, not the test used in relation to Part 4 (see paras **10.17–10.20** above). Treatment of child community patients under Part 4A is dealt with in Chapter 11 below at paras **11.51–11.59**.

The certificate requirement

10.57 The certificate requirement must be met if the treatment is medicines for mental disorder or ECT, unless one of the exceptions applies. The certificate requirement is met where a SOAD under Part 4 of the MHA 1983 has certified that it is appropriate for the medicines to be given subject to such conditions as may be specified in the certificate. The conditions in the certificate must be satisfied before the certificate requirement can be met in respect of a treatment.[103] The certificate may relate to a plan of treatment where a patient is to be given one or more treatments covered by s 58. The Explanatory Notes state that:[104]

> 'For medication, a certificate is not required immediately, but must be in place within one month from when a patient leaves hospital under a CTO, or three months from when the medication was first given to the patient (whether that medication was given in the community or in hospital), whichever is later.'

The SOAD must certify in writing that it is appropriate for the treatment to be given. On the certificate the SOAD may specify that certain treatment can be given to the patient only if certain conditions are satisfied. The Explanatory Notes give the example that:[105]

> '[T]he SOAD could specify that a particular antipsychotic and dosage can only be given in the community if the patient retains capacity to consent to it. The SOAD can also specify whether and if so what treatments can be given to the patient on recall to hospital and the circumstances in which the treatment can be given. For example, the SOAD can specify, if appropriate, that an antipsychotic can be given to the patient on recall without the patient's consent.'

---

[102]   MHA 1983, s 64E.
[103]   MHA 1983, s 64C(4).
[104]   *Explanatory Notes to the MHA 2007*, para 133.
[105]   Ibid, para 134.

If the certificate specifies conditions the treatment may only be given in accordance with those conditions.

10.58 The exceptions where the certificate requirement need not be met are as follows:

(1) it need not be met until the expiry of one month from the date the community treatment order was made;[106] or

(2) if the treatment is emergency treatment given under s 64G (see para **10.61** below); or

(3) if treatment is immediately necessary and the patient is capable (or if a child under 16 is 'competent') and consents to it; or

(4) if treatment is immediately necessary and a donee of a lasting power of attorney or a deputy appointed by the Court of Protection has consented to it.[107]

10.59 The full s 62 criteria apply in determining whether s 58 treatment (medicine for mental disorder) is 'immediately necessary':

(a) to save the patient's life; or

(b) to prevent a serious deterioration in the patient's condition and is not irreversible; or

(c) to prevent serious suffering by the patient and is not irreversible or hazardous; or

(d) to prevent the patient from behaving violently or being a danger to himself or others, as long as the treatment is the minimum interference necessary, and is neither irreversible nor hazardous.[108]

Irreversible means having unfavourable irreversible physical or psychological consequences, and hazardous means entailing significant physical hazard.[109] If the treatment is ECT it is 'immediately necessary' if it falls within (a) or (b) above; if it is any s 58A treatment by virtue of regulations under s 58A(1)(b) criteria (a)–(d) apply in determining whether it is immediately necessary.[110]

---

[106] MHA 1983, s 64B(4).
[107] MHA 1983, s 64B(3).
[108] MHA 1983, s 64C(5).
[109] MHA 1983, s 62(3).
[110] MHA 1983, s 64C(6).

Treatment without force of adult patients who lack capacity

10.60 Section 64D authorises the approved clinician in charge of the patient's treatment to give or direct the giving of relevant treatment, subject to the following conditions. First, the AC must follow the steps outlined in s 5(1)(a) and (b)(i) of the MCA 2005, namely:

(a) take reasonable steps to establish whether the patient lacks capacity to consent to the treatment; and

(b) when giving the treatment, must reasonably believe that the patient lacks capacity to consent to it.

Second, giving the treatment must not conflict with a valid and applicable advance decision,[111] or a decision of an attorney or deputy or the Court of Protection. Third, the AC must either have no reason to believe that the patient objects to the treatment being given, or if he does have reason to believe that the patient objects, it must not be necessary to use force in order to give the treatment. Section 64J states that in deciding whether there is reason to believe that a patient objects, the relevant person must consider all the circumstances so far as they are reasonably ascertainable. This includes the patient's behaviour, wishes, feelings, views beliefs and values. Circumstances from the past are to be considered only so far as it is still appropriate to consider them. Paragraph 1 of the Explanatory Notes note that force cannot be used under s 64D to administer treatment if the patient objects to that treatment, but state that:[112]

> 'If the patient does not object to treatment, force is permitted and that may be in cases where, for example, the patient is suffering from tremor and physical force is needed as a practical measure to administer the treatment.'

Adult patients have greater protection than children since it is a condition under s 64D that treatment must not conflict with an advance decision which the person giving the treatment is satisfied is valid and applicable. Equally, for adults, but not for children treatment may not be given if it conflicts with a decision of a donee, a deputy or of the Court of Protection. It is important to remember that the conditions of using s 64D only prohibit the use of force, undefined, whereas s 6 of the MCA 2005 prohibits restraint, which includes the use or threat of physical force, unless the restraint is a proportionate response to the likelihood of the person suffering harm and the seriousness of the harm. So a situation might arise where a patient objects to the treatment, and is told that if he or she does not agree to have it, he or she may be recalled to hospital. No force is used within the meaning of Part 4A to secure compliance, but the threat of forcible recall would amount to restraint under s 6 of the MCA 2005.

---

[111] MCA 2005, s 25.
[112] *Explanatory Notes to the MHA 2007*, para 130.

Emergency treatment, using force if necessary, of adult and child patients

10.61 Force may only be used to give treatment to patients who lack capacity or to children who lack competence against their objections if the emergency conditions in s 64G are met. Section 64G authorises emergency treatment of patients over 16 who are reasonably believed to lack capacity, or children under 16 reasonably believed to lack competence to consent. Treatment is emergency treatment where it is immediately necessary:

(a)   to save the patient's life; or

(b)   to prevent a serious deterioration in the patient's condition and is not irreversible; or

(c)   to prevent serious suffering by the patient and is not irreversible or hazardous; or

(d)   to prevent the patient from behaving violently or being a danger to himself or others, as long as the treatment is the minimum interference necessary, and is neither irreversible nor hazardous.[113]

If the treatment is ECT it may only be given under paras (a) or (b) above, not paras (c) or (d). Irreversible means having unfavourable irreversible physical or psychological consequences, and hazardous means entailing significant physical hazard.[114] Section 64G authorises force to be used, but only where emergency treatment needs to be given to prevent harm to the patient and the use of force is proportionate to the likelihood of the patient's suffering harm and to the seriousness of that harm. It is possible that force could be used to prevent harm to others if harm to the patient could also thereby be prevented. For example if a patient is stopped from verbally abusing others or assaulting them, he or she will not suffer harm from retaliation.

CONCLUSION

10.62 There are two parallel regimes authorising treatment without consent, under the MCA 2005 where the patient lacks capacity and the treatment is necessary in the patient's best interests, or under Parts 4 or 4A of the MHA 1983. Following the MHA 2007 there are now four second opinion procedures under the MHA 1983 – under ss 57, 58, 58A and 64C. Part 4 employs the MHA concept of capacity. Part 4A employs the MCA concept of capacity, but whilst the MCA places limits on the use of 'restraint' (the use or threat of force) under s 6, Part 4A places limits only on the use of force. Each must operate within the requirements of Arts 3 and 8 of the Convention. A

---

[113]   MHA 1983, s 64C(5).
[114]   MHA 1983, s 62(3).

particular issue is the interface between the two statutes. Section 28 only prohibits the use of the MCA decision-making framework where the patient is already subject to Parts 4 or 4A. It does not answer the question whether s 58 or s 58A type treatment for mental disorder may be given under the MCA if the patient is not already subject to the MHA regimes for treatment without consent.

10.63 What would the position be of an informal adult patient who lacks capacity and is deemed to require ECT or anti-psychotic medication? Richard Jones argues that the '1983 Act should be invoked in respect of a mentally incapacitated person who needs to be hospitalised for treatment for mental disorder in two circumstances' (assuming the criteria for compulsion are met):

(1)   where there is a deprivation of liberty; and

(2)   where it is considered that the provisions of a valid and applicable advance decision refusing a particular treatment for the patient's mental disorder should be overridden.[115]

It has been argued elsewhere in this work that:[116]

'if a person lacks capacity and the decision-maker is assuming complete control over treatment to the extent that they are making decisions about the administration of strong psychotropic medication or even ECT to a patient, then that is assuming complete control over treatment and would be a factor tipping the balance firmly towards there being a deprivation of liberty requiring use of the MHA 1983.'

Jones disagrees, contending that:[117]

'As the provision of any medical treatment to a mentally incapacitated patient involves a clinician assuming complete control over that patient's treatment ... the provision of treatments mentioned by Fennell in the absence of other factors confirming that professionals treating and managing the patient exercised complete and effective control over his movements would not lead to a finding that there has been a deprivation of liberty ... a whole range of factors must be taken into account.'

Peter Bartlett agrees with Richard Jones that ECT can be given to an informal patient lacking capacity 'provided that procedures in the MCA 2005 are followed', although this view was expressed before the passage of s 58A.[118] The MCA 2005, ss 5 and 6 do not provide procedures, they provide a defence to proceedings for battery if certain steps have been taken. If ECT is a treatment which can be given under the MCA 2005, it is likely to be deemed a 'serious

---

[115]   RM Jones *Mental Capacity Act Manual* (Sweet and Maxwell, 2nd edn, 2007), p 96.

[116]   P Fennell 'The Mental Capacity Act 2005, the Mental Health Act 1983 and the Common Law' (2005) *Journal of Mental Health Law* 167.

[117]   RM Jones *Mental Capacity Act Manual* (Sweet and Maxwell, 2nd edn, 2007), p 99.

[118]   P Bartlett *Blackstones Guide to the Mental Capacity Act 2005* (OUP, 2005), para 3.43.

treatment' for the purposes of s 37 of the MCA 2005. If there is nobody other than a paid carer to consult in determining what would be in P's best interests, there would be a requirement on the relevant NHS body to appoint and consult an Independent Mental Capacity Advocate ('IMCA') and the submissions made by the IMCA must be taken into account in deciding whether to provide the treatment. Section 37 does not apply to any treatment regulated by Part 4 of the Mental Health Act. Treatment is only regulated by Part 4 if the patient is detained or liable to be detained.

10.64 It is important to bear in mind the statement of the scope of the positive obligation under Art 8, as outlined in *Storck v Germany*:[119]

'The Court ... considers that on account of its obligation to secure to its citizens the right to physical and moral integrity, *the state remained under a duty to exercise supervision and control over private psychiatric institutions.* [emphasis added – The court noted that in the sphere of interferences with a person's physical integrity, German law provided for strong penal sanctions and for liability in tort and went on to say that]. Just as in cases of deprivation of liberty, the Court finds that such retrospective measures alone are not sufficient to provide appropriate protection of the physical integrity of individuals in such a vulnerable position as the applicant. The above findings as to the lack of effective state control over private psychiatric institutions at the relevant time are equally applicable as far as the protection of individuals against infringements of their personal integrity is concerned. The Court therefore concludes that the respondent state failed to comply with its positive obligation to protect the applicant against interferences with her private life as guaranteed by Article 8(1).'

Section 58A provides safeguards in relation to ECT without consent to incapacitated detained patients, and to informal patients who are under 18. In the case of informal child patients the treatment is authorised under parental authority or the MCA, but the s 58A safeguards apply as well. Informal patients who are children will have superior safeguards in relation to ECT compared with their counterparts who are over 18. This may be argued to be a discrimination on grounds of age in the protection of Art 8 rights to physical integrity, contrary to Art 14 of the Convention. It may well also be that to administer ECT without consent to an informal patient who lacks capacity lifts the level of control over treatment and movement above the threshold for deprivation of liberty.

---

[119] *Storck v Germany* (2005) 43 EHRR 96, at para 150.

Chapter 11

CHILDREN

OVERVIEW

11.1 A 'child' is anyone under 18 years old.[1] There is no age limit to the powers of detention or Supervised Community Treatment under the Mental Health Act, although guardianship may not be used where the patient is under 16.[2] Children may be admitted to a psychiatric institution in one of four ways:

(1)   informally with their own consent;

(2)   informally with the consent of a parent or someone with parental responsibility;

(3)   under the compulsory powers in Part 2 or Part 3 of the 1983 Act;

(4)   under s 25 of the Children Act 1989.

Patients detained under the Mental Health Act 1983 have the same rights to review of detention by Mental Health Review Tribunals ('MHRTs') as their adult counterparts (see Chapter 9).

11.2 Treatment of a child patient who is detained under the MHA 1983 is governed by Part 4 of the MHA 1983. Treatment of child community patients who remain in the community is governed by Part 4A. Authority to treat an informal capable child patient is based on the consent of the child her or himself. Authority to treat an informal patient admitted on parental consent who lacks capacity is based either on the MCA 2005 if the child is 16 or 17, or on parental consent if the patient is under 16.

11.3 Section 2(5) of the MCA 2005 provides that no power which a person may possess in relation to a person who lacks capacity or is reasonably believed to lack capacity is exercisable in relation to a person under 16. Neither the power to make an advance decision refusing treatment, nor to grant a lasting power of attorney is exercisable by a person under the age of 18. The *Bournewood* provisions for deprivation of liberty (see paras **6.24–6.76** above) do not apply to people under 18. The effect is that if a 16 or 17-year-old child who

---

[1]   Children Act 1989, s 105(1).
[2]   MHA 1983, s 7(1).

lacks capacity requires admission to a psychiatric hospital in circumstances not amounting to a deprivation of liberty, ss 5 and 6 of the MCA 2005 may be used.

Mental health services for children

11.4   Best Practice Guidance issued by the DfES and DoH states that:[3]

> 'All children and young people, from birth to their eighteenth birthday, who have mental health problems and disorders, should have access to timely, integrated, high quality, multi-disciplinary mental health services to ensure effective assessment, treatment and support, for them and their families.'

Specialist Child and Adolescent Mental Health Services ('CAMHS') are designed to treat children and young people suffering from mental disorder. The Draft Code of Practice emphasises that CAMHS should be fully involved with the care of children and young people from their initial assessment and that the special needs of children and young people must be recognised.[4]

The Mental Health Act 2007

11.5   Section 31 of the MHA 2007 amends the MHA 1983 to introduce new duties in relation to providing suitable accommodation for children, and to amend the existing rules about informal admission of 16 and 17-year-olds to make clear that those with parental responsibility cannot admit the patient informally by parental consent. New s 58A provides additional safeguards in relation to Electro Convulsive Therapy ('ECT') given to children (discussed in full above at paras **10.36–10.40** and **10.62–10.64**), and new ss 64E, 64F and 64G set out the rules for treating child patients in the community.

Human rights

11.6   The UK Government has ratified the UN Convention on the Rights of the Child 1989 ('CRC'), thereby undertaking to respect, protect and promote the rights in the Convention. Article 3 of the CRC states that the best interests of the child shall be the primary consideration in all actions concerning children. Article 12 of the CRC requires states parties to:

> 'assure to the child who is capable of forming his or her own views the right to express those views freely in all matters affecting the child, the views of the child being given due weight in accordance with the age and maturity of the child.'

---

[3]   Department for Education and Department of Health *The Mental Health and Psychological Well-being of Children and Young People* (October 2004, Standard 9).

[4]   Department of Health *Mental Health Act 1983 Draft Revised Code of Practice* (2007), para 39.4. See http://www.dh.gov.uk/en/Consultations.

In *R (on the application of Williamson) v Secretary of State for Education and Employment* Baroness Hale of Richmond said that:[5]

> 'the State is entitled to give children the protection they are given by an international instrument to which the United Kingdom is a party, the United Nations Convention on the Rights of a Child.'

Article 19 of the CRC entitles children to protection from all forms of physical or mental violence, injury or abuse, neglect or negligent treatment, maltreatment or exploitation including sexual abuse. The Art 19 right under the CRC reflects the positive obligation on states under Art 3 of the European Convention on Human Rights to protect all citizens against torture or inhuman or degrading treatment. Article 37(c) of the Convention on the Rights of the Child states that 'every child deprived of his liberty shall be separated from adults unless it is considered in the child's best interests not to do so'. The United Kingdom Government has reserved the right not to comply with Art 37(c):[6]

> 'where at any time there is a lack of suitable accommodation or adequate facilities in any institution where young offenders are detained, or where the mixing of adults and children is mutually beneficial.'

11.7 In *Nielsen v Denmark* the European Court of Human Rights considered the lawfulness of admitting a twelve-and-a-half-year-old for over five months by a decision of his mother who was the sole holder of parental rights. Because he was admitted in this way he had no rights to challenge his detention and claimed breach of Art 5(1) and (4) of the European Convention on Human Rights ('ECHR'). The court held that his hospitalisation did not amount to a deprivation of liberty within Art 5, but was a responsible exercise by the mother of her custodial rights in the interests of the child.[7] Those rights include 'a broad range of parental rights and responsibilities in regard to the care and custody of minor children' and were incorporated in the right to respect for family life in Art 8. The court accepted however that parental rights could not be unlimited and it was incumbent on states to provide safeguards against abuse.

11.8 Article 12 of the Convention on the Rights of the Child requires consideration of children's views in deciding issues affecting them, 'taking into account the age and maturity of the child'. This, coupled with the European Court's 2005 ruling in *Storck v Germany*[8] that there had been breaches of Arts 5 and 8 of the ECHR, suggests that the scope of parental authority is narrower today than it was in *Nielsen*, and is certainly not sufficient to oust the protection of the child's right to liberty under Art 5 and to physical integrity

---

5   [2005] UKHL 15 at [80].
6   RM Jones *Mental Health Act Manual – Supplement to 10th edn* (Sweet and Maxwell, 2007), para 4–284.
7   (1988) 11 EHRR 175, at paras 61, 72, 73.
8   (2005) 43 EHRR 96, ECtHR.

under Art 8. Ms Storck was 15-year-old (almost three years older than Nielsen) when she was admitted at the behest of her father and against her wishes to a private clinic in Germany, where she was detained and forcibly treated. The Court held that States have a positive obligation under Arts 5 and 8 to ensure that there is effective supervision and review of decisions to detain or to treat without consent. In this case parental responsibility and rights comprised in the right to respect for family life under Art 8 did not operate to exclude the protection of the child's right to liberty and physical integrity under Arts 5 and 8. The Court held that states are under an obligation to provide effective supervision and review of deprivations of liberty and interferences with the physical integrity of a young person.

THE CHILD'S RIGHT TO SUITABLE ACCOMMODATION AND CARE

11.9 There was considerable debate during the passage of the MHA 2007 about the practice of placing children on adult psychiatric wards, and the risks of abuse to which they may thereby be exposed, highlighted in the Children's Commissioner's report *Pushed into the Shadows: Young People's Experience of Adult Mental Health Facilities*. This provided evidence from young people's experiences that their health or safety may be seriously compromised by such placements.[9] The Parliamentary Joint Committee on Human Rights considered that the positive obligation under Art 3 was potentially engaged by a placement on an adult ward, if a child is not effectively protected from abuse. The Committee recommended adoption of an amendment to ensure that young people receive age appropriate assessment and placement, but avoids rendering illegal the placement of a child on an adult ward when this is the only way that their needs can be met.[10]

11.10 The Government accepted amendments designed to promote the care of children in age appropriate environments. Section 31 of the MHA 2007 Act:

(a) introduces a new s 131A to the MHA 1983, placing a limited duty on hospital managers to ensure that the hospital environment of a child patient is 'suitable having regard to his age (subject to his needs)';

(b) inserts new subss (1A) and (1B) into s 39 of the MHA 1983 to empower a sentencing court to request information about the availability of accommodation designed to be specially suitable for child patients; and

---

[9] The Children's Commissioner for England (January 2007).
[10] House of Lords, House of Commons Joint Committee on Human Rights *Legislative Scrutiny: Seventh Progress Report: Fifteenth Report of Session 2006–2007* (HL Paper 555, HC Paper 112), para 1.17.

(c) amends s 140 of the MHA 1983 to require relevant health bodies to notify local social services authorities within their area of their arrangements for providing accommodation or facilities designed to be specially suitable for child patients.

These stand alongside the duties to visit and exercise parental responsibility where a child in care is admitted to hospital under s 116 of the MHA 1983, and the duty under ss 85 and 86 of the Children Act 1989 of health bodies and managers of private institutions where a child is accommodated for more than three months to notify the appropriate social services.

The section 131A duty to provide an age suitable environment

11.11 Section 131A will come into force in April 2010. It applies to detained and informal child patients, and requires the managers of a NHS or private hospital to ensure that the patient's environment in the hospital is suitable having regard to his age (subject to his needs). The duty is not absolute, since if the patient's needs for mental health care and treatment cannot be met in an environment which suitable for his age, it will be acceptable for them to be met elsewhere. In deciding how to carry out their duty managers must consult 'a person who appears to them to have knowledge or experience of cases involving patients who have not attained the age of 18 years which makes him suitable to be consulted'. The Draft Code stresses that:[11]

> 'At least one of the people involved in the assessment of a person who is less than 18 years old, ie one of the two medical practitioners or the AMHP should be a clinician specialising in CAMHS. Where this is not possible, a CAMHS clinician should be consulted as soon as possible.'

11.12 This means that at least one of the two doctors or the AMHP involved in any Mental Health Act assessment of a child should be a clinician specialising in CAMHS. Where this is not possible a CAMHS clinician should be consulted as soon as possible. Where possible those responsible for the care and treatment of children should be CAMHS specialists. Where this is not possible, it is good practice for the clinical staff to have access to a CAMHS specialist for advice and consultation. The Draft Code says that:[12]

> 'Children should have appropriate physical facilities; staff with the right training to understand and address their specific needs as children and young people; and a hospital routine that will allow their personal, social and educational development to continue as normally as possible. Hospital managers must ensure that the environment is suitable and in reaching their determination must consult a person they consider to be suitable as experienced in child and adolescent mental health services cases i.e. a Tier 3 or 4 CAMHS specialist.'

---

[11] Department of Health *Mental Health Act 1983 Draft Revised Code of Practice* (2007), para 39.5. See http://www.dh.gov.uk/en/Consultations.

[12] Ibid, para 39.46.

Finally, the Draft Code stresses that:[13]

> 'All children, including 16 or 17-year-old patients who wish to continue their education, should not be denied access to learning merely because they are receiving medical treatment for a mental health condition.'

11.13 The duty is to ensure that the environment is suitable 'having regard to the patient's needs'. There may be circumstances therefore where a child's need to be accommodated in a safe environment will take precedence over their entitlement to a suitable environment. So, if accommodation dedicated to children is not available and a child needs in-patient treatment, the Code advises that:[14]

> 'Discrete accommodation in an adult ward, with facilities, security and staffing appropriate to the needs of the child might provide the most satisfactory solution. Where possible all those involved in the care and treatment of children should be child specialists. They must always be criminal record background (CBR) vetted.'

There is a clear difference between what is acceptable in an emergency and what is acceptable on a long-term basis, and the Code advises that once an emergency subsides, 'a suitable environment would widen to include a place where the patient can mix with individuals of their own age, receive visitors of all ages, and have access to education.' Hospital managers have a duty under s 131A to consider whether a patient should be transferred to more appropriate accommodation and, if so, for this to be arranged as soon as possible.[15]

The section 39 duty to provide information about age suitable hospital provision for child offenders

11.14 Section 39 empowers a criminal court deciding whether to make a hospital order or interim hospital order in respect of any person to request from the relevant PCT or Health Authority information about hospitals in their area where the person could be admitted if an order were to be made. The relevant PCT or Health Authority is either the one for the area where the person resides or last resided or any other PCT or Health Authority that appears to the court to be appropriate. The PCT or Health Authority must comply with the court's request.

11.15 Section 31 adds new subss (1A) and (1B) to s 39. Section 39(1A) extends the s 39 power in the case of children so that it may be exercised where the court is considering remand to hospital for reports (s 35) or treatment (s 36) or committal by the magistrates under s 44. The purpose of this provision is to ensure that courts do not place a child in a prison setting when a suitable hospital bed would be more appropriate.[16] Section 39(1B) specifies that in the

---

[13]   Ibid, para 39.51.
[14]   Ibid, para 39.48.
[15]   Ibid, para 39.49.
[16]   *Explanatory Notes to the Mental Health Act 2007*, para 105.

case of a child, the information which may be requested includes 'in particular, information about the availability of accommodation or facilities designed so as to be specially suitable for patients who have not attained the age of 18 years'.

The section 140 duty on NHS bodies to notify social services about hospital accommodation suitable for children

11.16 Section 140 of the MHA 1983 places a duty on PCTs and Health Authorities to notify the local social services authorities in their area of the hospitals administered by them or otherwise available to them where:[17]

> 'arrangements are from time to time in force—
>
> (a) for the reception of cases of special urgency, and
> (b) for the provision of accommodation or facilities designed so as to be specially suitable for patients who have not attained the age of 18 years.'

The section 116 duty to visit and exercise parental responsibility

11.17 Section 116 of the MHA 1983 places a duty on each local authority, where a child who is in their care under a care order is admitted to a hospital, independent hospital or care home, to arrange for visits to be made to the patient on their behalf. This duty applies whether the hospitalisation 'is for treatment for mental disorder or for any other reason'. The local authority is also required to take such other steps in relation to the patient while they are in the hospital or home, as would be expected to be taken by his parents.

Sections 85 and 86 of the Children Act 1989: the duty to notify social services about child in-patients

11.18 These provisions require that when a child is provided with accommodation for a period of three months by any Health Authority, NHS Trust, local education authority, independent hospital or residential care home, the body or the proprietors of the relevant private hospital or home must notify the appropriate local authority. That local authority is then under a duty to take steps to ensure that the child's welfare is safeguarded.

Section 11 of the Children Act 2004: the duty to safeguard and promote the child's welfare

11.19 All NHS bodies and the services they contract for have a duty under the Children Act 2004, s 11, to carry out their functions having regard to the need to safeguard and promote the welfare of children.[18]

---

17 MHA 1983, s 140, as amended by MHA 2007, s 31(4).
18 HM Government *Statutory guidance on making arrangements to safeguard and promote the*

THE DECISION TO ADMIT A CHILD TO HOSPITAL

11.20 With children, as with other groups of mentally disordered people perceived as vulnerable (such as elderly and learning disabled people) there is often a reluctance to use the compulsory powers in the MHA 1983, justified on the grounds that it will be 'less stigmatising' to rely on informal admission by parental consent or powers under the Children Act 1989.

11.21 A child may consent to treatment if they are 16 or 17 and have capacity,[19] or are under 16 but are *Gillick* competent.[20] As with adults, children may be admitted informally if they have capacity and consent to admission. A difficult question arises over the circumstances in which a child may be admitted informally with consent from someone with parental responsibilities. The Children Act 1989 defines parental responsibility as all the rights, duties, powers, responsibilities and authority which by law a parent of a child has in relation to the child and his property.[21] There are four categories of child patient requiring consideration:

(1)   children aged 16 or 17 with capacity;

(2)   children aged 16 and 17 who lack capacity;

(3)   children under 16 who are '*Gillick* competent';

(4)   children under 16 who are not '*Gillick* competent'.

Each will be discussed in turn.

16 and 17-year-olds with capacity

11.22 Section 8(1) of the Family Law Reform Act 1969 provides that the consent of a young person of 16 years:

> 'to any surgical, medical or dental treatment which, in the absence of consent, would constitute a trespass to his person, [and the consent] shall be as effective as it would be if he were of full age; and where a minor has by virtue of this section given an effective consent to any treatment, it shall not be necessary to obtain any consent for it from his parent or guardian.'

11.23 Section 43 of the MHA 2007 inserts four new subss into s 131 of the MHA 1983 dealing with informal admission of 16 and 17-year-olds. A patient

---

welfare of children under section 11 of the Children Act 2004 (available at http://www. everychildmatters.gov.uk/_files/9204C14C73ACCA279701DDF9731B16F6.pdf).

[19]   Family Law Reform Act 1969, s 8(1): 'the consent of a minor who has attained the age of sixteen … shall be as effective as it would be if he were of full age; and where a minor has … given an effective consent to any treatment it shall not be necessary to obtain any consent for it from his parent or guardian.'

[20]   *Gillick v West Norfolk and Wisbech Area Health Authority* [1986] AC 112, HL.

[21]   Children Act 1989, s 3(1).

aged 16 or 17 who has capacity within the terms of ss 2 and 3 of the MCA 2005 may consent to informal admission even though there may be one or more persons who have parental responsibility for him. In such a case the child should be treated as an informal patient even if a person with parental responsibility is refusing consent.

11.24 Conversely, if the patient has capacity but does not consent, he or she may not be admitted by the consent of anyone with parental responsibility.[22] In *Re W (a minor) (medical treatment)*,[23] W was 16, suffering from anorexia, and subject to a care order. The local authority made an application to the High Court for authority under the inherent jurisdiction to act in the welfare and best interests of a child. Lord Donaldson MR said that s 8 of the Family Law Reform Act 1969 did not empower a child to veto treatment:[24]

> 'No minor of whatever age has power by refusing consent to treatment to override a consent to treatment by someone who has parental responsibility for the minor, and a fortiori a consent by the Court. Nevertheless such a refusal is a very important consideration in making clinical judgments and for parents and the court in deciding whether themselves to give consent. Its importance increases with the age and maturity of the child.'

Although *Re W (a minor) (medical treatment)*[25] may be authority for the proposition that a capable 16 or 17-year-old's decision to consent to or refuse treatment may be over-ridden by a person with parental responsibility, by virtue of ss 131(2)–(5) of the MHA 1983 this does not apply in relation to detention for treatment of mental disorder. If admission to hospital for treatment for mental disorder is necessary in the case of refusal, it will have to be carried out under Part 2 of the MHA 1983, assuming the criteria for detention are met.

11.25 If the primary issue is not the provision of medical treatment for mental disorder but the deprivation of the young person's liberty, it may be appropriate to use s 25 of the Children Act 1989. If a child or young person is seriously mentally ill they may require treatment under the Mental Health Act, whereas if they are behaviourally disturbed their need to be detained to protect them from harm might be more appropriately met within secure accommodation under the Children Act 1989.[26]

16 and 17-year-olds without capacity

11.26 Where a 16 or 17-year-old is regarded as being unable to make a decision for himself in relation to a matter because of an impairment of, or a disturbance in, the functioning of the mind or brain, the provisions of the

---

[22] MHA 1983, s 131(2)–(5), as inserted by MHA 2007, s 43.
[23] [1992] 4 All ER 627, CA.
[24] [1992] 4 All ER 627 at 639–640.
[25] [1992] 4 All ER 627, CA.
[26] Department of Health *Mental Health Act 1983 Draft Revised Code of Practice* (2007), para 39.11. See http://www.dh.gov.uk/en/Consultations.

Mental Capacity Act apply (see paras **6.25–6.34** above and the Mental Capacity Act 2005 Code of Practice). The *Bournewood* provisions for deprivation of liberty do not apply to people under 18, so the choice of powers of detention should deprivation of liberty be needed, is between Part 2 of the MHA or s 25 of the Children Act 1989. If the primary purpose is treatment of the mental disorder, as long as the conditions of detention are met the MHA 1983 should be used (see Chapter 6 above). If the primary purpose is to deprive the child of liberty for their own safety or the safety of others, then s 25 of the Children Act 1989 should be used.

11.27 Section 25 of the Children Act 1989 provides criteria for a child to be placed in secure accommodation, meaning any accommodation used for the restriction of liberty. Local authorities are under a duty to take reasonable steps to avoid a child being placed in secure accommodation.[27] The maximum aggregate period for which a child can be placed in secure accommodation without a court order under s 25 is 72 hours in any 28 days.[28] If a court order is required the grounds in s 25 must be met. They are either:

(a)   the child has a history of absconding and is likely to abscond from any other description of accommodation; and if he absconds he is likely to suffer significant harm; or

(b)   if the child is kept in any other kind of accommodation he is likely to injure himself or other persons.

The maximum permissible period of detention of a child who has been remanded by a criminal court to secure accommodation is the period of the remand. For others it is three months, which may be extended for periods of up to six months at a time.[29] Children detained under the MHA 1983 may be placed in secure accommodation without a court order, as there is already authority to detain them.

16 or 17-year-olds lacking capacity

11.28 Section 2(5) of the Mental Capacity Act 2005 provides that no power which a person may possess in relation to a person who lacks capacity or is reasonably believed to lack capacity is exercisable in relation to a person under 16. This leaves open the possibility that under 16 year olds are entitled to the presumption of capacity in s 1 of the MCA. The *Bournewood* provisions for deprivation of liberty do not apply to people under 18.[30] The effect is that if a 16 or 17-year-old child who lacks capacity requires admission to a psychiatric hospital in circumstances not amounting to a deprivation of liberty, ss 5 and 6 of the MCA 2005 may be used. In such a case the parents would have to be consulted about whether admission is in the child's best interests.

---

[27]   Children Act 1989, Sch 2, para 7(c).
[28]   SI 1991/1505, reg 10.
[29]   SI 1991/1505, regs 11–13.
[30]   Mental Capacity Act 2005, Sch A1, para 13, as inserted by MHA 2007, Sch 7.

11.29 If a 16 or 17-year-old lacks capacity and their primary need is treatment for mental disorder in conditions amounting to a deprivation of liberty, Part 2 of the MHA 1983 should be used to authorise detention. If the primary need is containment for their own safety or that of others, then s 25 of the Children Act 1989 should be used. Section 131(2) and (4) provide that if a patient *who has capacity* within ss 2 and 3 of the MCA 2005 does not consent to arrangements for informal admission, they may not be made or carried out on the basis of the consent of a person who has parental responsibility for him. This does not rule out the possibility that parental responsibilities might encompass the right to admit an incapacitated 16 or 17-year-old informally, even if they object, but the guidance in the Code and the developing case-law on the balance between parental responsibility and the child's right of self-determination (discussed at paras **11.40–11.43** below) suggest that this should occur only in the most exceptional circumstances.

Children under 16 who are *Gillick* competent

11.30 Children under 16 who are capable of consenting to treatment are described as '*Gillick* competent'. It is a matter for the treating doctor to determine whether a child is '*Gillick* competent' in the sense that she/he has the capacity to make the decision to have the proposed treatment and has sufficient maturity and understanding to be capable of making up her or his own mind.[31]

Gillick competence

11.31 In *Re R (a minor)* Lord Donaldson said that what *Gillick* competence involves is a full understanding and appreciation not only of the nature of the proposed treatment, but also of the intended effects of the treatment and its possible side effects, and 'equally important, of the consequences of a failure to treat'.[32]

11.32 Although the test of capacity in ss 2 and 3 of the MCA 2005 does not apply to children under the age of 16, the issue of *Gillick* competence is whether the child has the maturity and understanding to be capable for the purposes of the MCA 2005. Support for the view that *Gillick* competence is to be judged against the adult standard is found in *Re C (Detention: Medical Treatment)*,[33] where Wall J applied the common law test of capacity[34] for adults in the case of a child under 16. In a sense it is misleading to refer to *Gillick* competence, since what a *Gillick* competent child achieves is the competence to make the relevant decision which an adult would have. The difference for children under 16 is that doctors, instead of presuming the patient to be capable as would happen with an adult, must ask themselves whether the child has the maturity and understanding to be competent in

---

[31] *Gillick v West Norfolk and Wisbech Area Health Authority* [1986] AC 112, HL.
[32] [1991] 4 All ER 177 at 187e.
[33] [1997] 2 FLR 180, FD.
[34] *Re MB (an adult: medical treatment)* [1997] 2 FLR 426, CA.

relation to that treatment proposal.[35] The test for competence for adults is whether the adult has sufficient understanding, intelligence and memory to be able to understand a broad terms explanation in simple language of what is proposed, to hold it in their head, and to weigh it in the balance to arrive at a decision. There must be no disturbance or disability of mind or brain which is stopping the person from being able to carry out these tasks, or from believing the relevant treatment information.

11.33 A *Gillick* competent child can consent to informal admission. The Draft Code states that:[36]

> 'For children who are *Gillick* competent the assumption is that they are able to make their own decisions and clinicians are advised not to rely on the consent of a person with parental responsibility. As a result, children who are *Gillick* competent (and have the capacity to make a decision on their health care) should be treated in the same way as adults. To put it simply, their decisions to consent or refuse admission to hospital for treatment or to the treatment itself should not be over-ridden by a person with parental responsibility.'

This strong statement of the rights of *Gillick* competent children has disappeared from the Revised Draft Code, perhaps because it runs counter to the case-law from the 1990s. Although it is clear that a *Gillick* competent child can consent to treatment where there is a doctor willing to offer it, there is a line of Court of Appeal decisions from the 1990s to the effect that even a *Gillick* competent child's refusal can be overridden by the High Court, by those with parental responsibility, or by the local authority if the child is in care.[37] These cases have been described as reflecting 'a retreat from *Gillick*, in that they allow a *Gillick* competent child to consent to treatment but not to refuse it.'[38]

11.34 In *Re R (a minor)* R was under 16 and the issue was whether the court could authorise treatment by antipsychotic medication against her wishes. R was not regarded as being *Gillick* competent, but the Court of appeal held that, even if she had been competent her wishes could have been overridden by the Court or her parents.[39] In *R v Kirklees Metropolitan Borough Council, ex parte C (a minor)* C was not *Gillick* competent. The Court of Appeal held she could be admitted on parental consent, and since C was in care parental consent could be given by the authority in whose care the child is. In this case the council's action was held to be a responsible exercise of parental authority.[40] Whatever the legal position about overriding refusal by a child, refusal by a

---

[35]   P Fennell 'Informal Compulsion: The Informal Treatment of Juveniles at Common Law' (1992) *Journal of Social Welfare and Family Law* 311–333.

[36]   Department of Health *Mental Health Act 1983 Draft Illustrative Code of Practice* (2006), para 35.17.

[37]   See *Re R (a minor)* [1992] Fam 11, CA; *R v Kirklees Metropolitan Borough Council, ex parte C (a minor)* [1993] 2 FLR 187, CA; *Re W (a minor) (medical treatment)* [1992] 4 All ER 627, CA.

[38]   G Douglas 'The Retreat from Gillick' (1992) 55 MLR 569.

[39]   [1992] Fam 11.

[40]   [1993] 2 FLR 187, CA.

Gillick competent child would clearly be a strong countervailing factor in a clinician's decision whether to effect informal admission by parental consent.

11.35 Jones argues that whilst Lord Donaldson's statement in *Re W* 'may be regarded as the authoritative statement of the law on this issue' the child's refusal 'would clearly influence the doctors decision whether to admit him or her informally'[41] by parental or local authority consent. Despite the disappearance from the latest draft of the strong statement of the rights of *Gillick* competent children, that their right to consent to or refuse admission to hospital or treatment should not be overridden by those with parental responsibility, it is submitted that this is correct and that in such cases if the patient is to be detained for treatment the powers under Part 2 of the MHA 1983 should be used.

11.36 Support for this view is found in the decision of the European Court of Human Rights in *Storck v Germany*[42] that parental responsibility does not extinguish the protection of Arts 5 and 8 ECHR, from *R (on the application of Axon) v Secretary of State for Health (Family Planning Association intervening)* where Silber J said:[43]

> 'As a matter of principle, it is difficult to see why a parent should still retain an Article 8 right to parental authority relating to a medical decision where the young person concerned *understands* the advice provided by the medical professional and its implications ...'

and from the Draft Code of Practice on the MHA 1983.

Children under 16 lacking competence

11.37 Where a child is not *Gillick* competent the Draft Code suggests that:[44]

> 'it will usually be possible for a person with parental responsibility to consent to treatment on their behalf. However the Draft also cautions that 'Before relying on parental consent in relation to a child under 16 who is not *Gillick* competent, an assessment should be made of whether the matter is within 'the zone of parental responsibility.'

'The parental zone of responsibility'

11.38 As the Draft Code of Practice Notes:

---

[41]   RM Jones *Mental Health Act Manual* (Sweet and Maxwell, 10th edn, 2006), para 1.1182.
[42]   (2005) 43 EHRR 96, ECtHR.
[43]   [2006] 2 FLR 206, [2006] 2 WLR 1130 at [130]. *Axon* has been described by Taylor as potentially marking a reversal of the retreat from *Gillick*: see Taylor 'Reversing the Retreat from Gillick?' (2007) 17 *Child and Family Law Quarterly* 81–97.
[44]   Department of Health *Mental Health Act 1983 Draft Revised Code of Practice* (2007), para 39.20. See http://www.dh.gov.uk/en/Consultations.

> 'Clinicians will need to determine whether it is appropriate to rely on parental consent. In order for parental consent to be relied upon it should be a decision which comes within the parental zone of responsibility.'

This is not a legal term. The Draft Code says that:[45]

> 'A decision is likely to be within the parental zone of responsibility if it is the sort of decision that a parent would be expected to make, having regard to what is considered to be normal practice in our society having regard to any relevant decisions in relation to Human Rights by the courts.'

Although parental responsibility is a well-known concept, 'the zone' of parental responsibility is not a term used in Family Law. It is intended to assist in identifying the circumstances when parental consent may be relied upon as authority to admit or treat without consent where the patient is under 16, or is 16 or 17 and lacks capacity to consent.

Parental responsibilities

11.39 'Parental responsibilities' is a broad concept consisting of 'a collection of rights and duties that concerns the taking care of the child's person and property'.[46] In domestic legal terms, s 3 of the Children Act 1989 defines 'parental responsibility' as 'all the rights, duties, powers, responsibilities and authority which by law a parent of a child has in relation to the child and his property.' Parental responsibilities include the duty to seek medical assistance for a child under the age of 16. Those with parental responsibilities risk prosecution for child neglect if they do not seek treatment for the child, and it can be established that they knew that medical treatment was required, but decided not to secure it or did not care whether the child needed medical assistance.[47] A prosecution under s 127 of the MHA 1983 for wilful neglect might also be possible. Whilst Art 5 of the UN Convention on the Rights of the Child requires states to respect the responsibilities rights and duties of parents, it also, in Art 12, requires them to assure to the child who is capable of forming his or her own views the right to express those views freely in all matters affecting the child, the views of the child being given due weight in accordance with the age and maturity of the child.

---

[45]   Ibid, para 39.43.
[46]   K Boele-Woelki, F Ferrand, C Gonzalez Beilfuss, M Jantera-Jareborg, N Lowe, D Martiny, W Pintens *Commission on European Family Law Principles of European Family Law Regarding Parental Responsibilities* (Intersentia Antwerpen, 2007), p 14.
[47]   *R v Sheppard* [1981] AC 394, HL.

Balancing children's rights to autonomy and physical integrity and parental responsibilities

11.40 There is a need to achieve a delicate balance between the child's right to autonomy and need for protection. As Boele-Woelki et al put it in their important study *Principles of European Family Law Regarding Parental Responsibilities*:[48]

'Almost every right in the convention includes elements of participation in the decision-making process. The child's autonomy should be respected in accordance with the developing ability and need for the child to act independently.'

They go on to say that: 'Medical treatment for the child is part and parcel of the right and duty to care for the child.' The authors urge a 'careful approach' to resolving:[49]

'the tension between the right and duty of the holders of parental responsibility to take all necessary steps concerning medical treatment in order to safeguard the physical and mental well-being of the child, and ... his or her right of self-determination ... If the child is sufficiently mature, his or her consent should be required.'

11.41 Parental controls are to be exercised for the benefit of the child and they are justified only in so far as they enable the parent to perform his duties towards the child and towards other children in the family.[50] In *Mabon v Mabon*[51] Thorpe LJ referred to the need for judges in deciding whether there was compliance with Art 12 of the Convention on the Rights of the Child:

'correctly to focus on the sufficiency of the child's understanding and, in measuring that sufficiency, reflect the extent to which, in the 21st century, there is a keener appreciation of the autonomy of the child and the child's consequential right to participate in decision-making processes that fundamentally affect his family life.'

11.42 The Draft Code states that the parameters of the zone of parental responsibility will depend on a number of factors, all of which need to be considered by the registered medical practitioner or approved clinician. They are:[52]

---

[48] K Boele-Woelki, F Ferrand, C Gonzalez Beilfuss, M Jantera-Jareborg, N Lowe, D Martiny, W Pintens *Commission on European Family Law Principles of European Family Law Regarding Parental Responsibilities* (Intersentia Antwerpen, 2007), p 39.

[49] Ibid, p 129.

[50] *Gillick v West Norfolk and Wisbech Area Health Authority* [1986] 1 AC 112, per Lord Frazer at 170D.

[51] [2005] 3 WLR 460, CA.

[52] Department of Health *Mental Health Act 1983 Draft Revised Code of Practice* (2007), para 39.44. See http://www.dh.gov.uk/en/Consultations.

'•   the nature and invasiveness of what is to be done to the child (including the extent to which the child's liberty will be curtailed) – the more extreme the intervention, the more likely it will be that it falls outside the zone;
•   whether the child is resisting – treating a child that is resisting needs more justification;
•   general social standards in force at the time as to the sorts of decisions it is acceptable for parents to make – anything that goes beyond the kind of decisions parents routinely make will be more suspect;
•   the age and maturity of the child – the greater this is, the more likely it will be that it should be the child who is taking the decision; and
•   the extent to which a parent's interest may conflict with those of the child – this may suggest the parent will not act in the best interests of the child.'

The Code gives the example that it may be within the zone of parental responsibility for a parent to consent to treatment of a 15-year-old child against his will for an eating disorder (where the nature of the illness makes the child unable to consent for himself). However, if force-feeding was required by means of invasive treatment in the form of a gastric tube, it might be considered that the extremity of the treatment took it outside the kind of treatment to which a parent could give consent. In such a case the child might need to be detained under the MHA 1983 rather than treated as an informal patient.[53] Detaining a patient who requires forcible feeding by naso-gastric tube will not provide extra procedural safeguards, since forcible feeding may be given under s 63 of the MHA 1983 without consent or a second opinion if it is given by or under the authority of the Responsible Clinician or Approved Clinician in charge of treatment.[54] The Parliamentary Joint Committee on Human Rights ('JCHR') considered that, given the potential for forcible feeding to breach Arts 3 and 8 of the ECHR,[55] it should be subject to regulation by statutory second opinion under s 58 of the MHA 1983. The JCHR considered that the positive obligation under Art 8 as elaborated in *Storck v Germany*[56] requires effective supervision and review of decisions to treat against an individual's will, and that the direction of the responsible clinician, even if that person is a medical practitioner, is not sufficient to provide such supervision and review.[57] The idea of the 'zone of parental responsibility' is that parental consent will not provide authority for treatments which are invasive or controversial, because of the need to recognise a mature minor's objection under Art 12 of the CRC, and the positive obligation under Arts 5 and 8 of the ECHR to provide effective supervision and review of decisions to detain and treat without consent.

---

[53]   Ibid, para 39.45.
[54]   *Re C (a minor) (detention for medical treatment)* [1997] 2 FLR 180, FD.
[55]   *Nevmerzhitsky v Ukraine (Application 54825/00)* Judgment of 5 April 2005, ECtHR.
[56]   (2005) 43 EHRR 96, ECtHR.
[57]   House of Lords, House of Commons Joint Committee on Human Rights *Legislative Scrutiny: Seventh Progress Report: Fifteenth Report of Session 2006–2007* (HL Paper 555, HC Paper 112), paras 67–69.

Treatment of children admitted informally by parental consent

11.43 The child's views should be taken into account, even if they are not *Gillick* competent, but how much weight should be attached to them depends on the maturity and understanding of the child. If the decision regarding the treatment of a child (including how the child is to be kept safely in one place) is within the zone of parental responsibility and consent is given by a person with parental responsibility, then the clinician may rely on that consent and treat on that basis as an informal patient. If it is within the zone of parental responsibility, reliance can be placed on the person with parental responsibility to act in the best interests of the child.

11.44 The Draft Code emphasises that those responsible for the care and treatment of the child must be 'clear about who has parental responsibility and always request copies of any court orders for reference on the hospital ward.' These orders may include care orders, residence orders, contact orders, evidence of appointment as the child's guardian, parental responsibility agreements or orders, and any order under wardship.[58]

11.45 Informal admission under parental responsibility does not mean that there is automatic consent to all components of a treatment programme regarded as 'necessary'. The Draft Code emphasises that:[59]

'Consent must be sought for each aspect of the child's care and treatment as it arises, and 'blanket' consent forms should not be used.'

11.46 Treatment which is subject to the s 57 second opinion procedure (psychosurgery and the surgical implantation of hormones to reduce male sex drive) may only be given with the consent of a patient who is capable of understanding the nature purpose and likely effects of the treatment and has consented to it. Under s 58A a child informal patient may only be given ECT when they are not capable of consenting if a SOAD has certified that it is appropriate for the treatment to be given.

11.47 The Draft Code notes that it is possible to treat a child informally on the basis of an order made by the court under its inherent jurisdiction or by way of a specific issue order made under s 8 of the Children Act 1989, but this is not likely to be used 'as there is a statutory alternative of treating under the MHA 1983.'[60] In relation to forcible feeding it may be advisable to seek the authority of a s 8 specific issue order.

11.48 The assistance of the Family Division of the High Court may be needed if a child under 16 lacks *Gillick* competence where no-one with parental

---

[58] Children Act 1989, ss 4 and 8.

[59] Department of Health *Mental Health Act 1983 Draft Revised Code of Practice* (2007), para 39.23. See http://www.dh.gov.uk/en/Consultations.

[60] Ibid, para 39.24.

responsibility can be identified, or where there is doubt as to whether a person with parental responsibility is making treatment decisions in the best interests of the child.

Treatment of 16 or 17-year-olds admitted under the Mental Capacity Act 2005

11.49 If a child aged 16 or 17 lacks capacity and is admitted to hospital in circumstances not amounting to a deprivation of liberty under the MCA 2005, they may be given treatment which is necessary in their best interests for physical or mental disorder under ss 5 and 6 of the MCA 2005. If the treatment is ECT it may only be given with the approval of a Second Opinion Appointed Doctor ('SOAD') under s 58A.

Treatment of patients subject to Part 4 of the Mental Health Act 1983

11.50 If a child patient is liable to be detained and according to s 56 subject to Part 4 (see para **10.12** above) treatment will be authorised by s 63, subject to the safeguards in ss 57, 58 and 58A. Patients may be given emergency treatment subject to s 62. The second opinion safeguards apply. A child patient who lacks capacity may not be given a s 57 treatment. A child patient may not be given ECT if he or she is capable (over 16) or competent (under 16) and refusing it. However, ECT may be given it if a SOAD deems the patient to be incapable of understanding its nature purpose and likely effects, and considers it appropriate for the treatment to be given. Medicines for mental disorder may be given under s 58 without consent whether a child patient is incapable or refusing treatment (see paras **10.13–10.53** above).

Treatment of 16 and 17-year-old community patients under Part 4A

11.51 Supervised Community Treatment ('SCT') may be applied to a patient who is under 18 (see paras **8.17–8.45** above). Treatment in the community without recall to hospital may be administered to a community patient if there is:

(1) authority to give it; and

(2) if it is medicine or ECT for mental disorder, where the certificate requirement is met.

Authority to treat

11.52 There is authority to give treatment if the patient consents. As long as force is not necessary, there is authority to give treatment without consent if:

(1) the patient lacks capacity;

(2) the treatment is 'immediately necessary'; and

(3) it is not in conflict with a valid and applicable advance decision, the decision of a health care attorney, a deputy, or the Court of Protection.

Force may be used to administer treatment if the emergency conditions in s 63G are met.

Scope of Part 4A

11.53 Part 4A applies to 16 or 17-year-olds as if to an adult (see paras **10. 54–10.61** above), and to child community patients under 16 with the substitution of competence for capacity wherever it appears. The principal difference between children under 18 and adults is that treatment in the community may not be given to an incapable adult in a non-emergency situation if it is contrary to a valid and effective advance decision, or is contrary to the decision of a health care attorney, a deputy or the Court Of Protection. Children under 18 may not make an advance decision, nor may they appoint a deputy, so the right to make arrangements in advance is not open to them.

11.54 The difference between 16 and 17-year-olds and children under 16 is that the test of 'competence' rather than 'capacity' applies to their decision-making, although (as suggested at paras **11. 31–11.32** above) in practice there may be no difference between the the two tests.

Treatment of community patients under 16 under Part 4A

11.55 Part 4A makes special provision for 'child community patients' defined as those who are under 16 and have not been recalled to hospital.[61] Section 64E provides that treatment may not be given to a child community patient unless there is authority to give it.

Authority to treat

11.56 There is authority to give treatment to a child community patient under 16 if:

(a) the patient is competent and consents to it being given; or

(b) it is authorised by s 64F (treatment for child patients lacking competence); or

---

[61] MHA 1983, s 64E(1).

(c)   the treatment is emergency treatment under s 64G.[62]

If the treatment is a s 58 or s 58A type treatment (currently medicines or ECT) the certificate requirement must be met unless one of the exceptions applies. These are:

(a)   the treatment is emergency treatment authorised under s 64G; or

(b)   in a case where the patient is competent to consent to the treatment and does consent to it, the treatment is immediately necessary; or

(c)   where the treatment is medicines and one month has not elapsed since the CTO was made.[63]

If none of these exceptions applies the SOAD must have authorised treatment by medication or ECT, and treatment will only be authorised in the circumstances specified by the SOAD.

Treatment without force of child community patients who lack competence

11.57 Section 64F sets out the conditions that must be satisfied before ECT or medicines for mental disorder can be provided to a community patient who is under 16 and who lacks the competence to consent. The treatment cannot be given if force would have to be used to ensure that an objecting patient received the treatment. Force can be used in an emergency if the conditions in s 64G are met. Section 64F authorises the approved clinician in charge of a child community patient's treatment to give or direct the giving of relevant treatment, subject to the following conditions. First, the AC must follow the steps outlined in s 5(1)(a) and (b)(i) of the MCA 2005, namely:

(a)   take reasonable steps to establish whether the patient lacks competence to consent to the treatment; and

(b)   when giving the treatment, must reasonably believe that the patient lacks competence to consent to it.

Second, the AC must have no reason to believe that the patient objects to being given the treatment; or if the AC does have reason to believe that the patient objects, it must not be necessary to use force against the patient in order to give the treatment. Adult patients have greater protection than children since it is a condition under s 64D but not s 64F that treatment must not conflict with an advance decision which the person giving the treatment is satisfied is valid and

---

[62]   MHA 1983, s 64E.
[63]   MHA 1983, s 64E(3)–(4).

applicable. Equally, for adults, but not for children treatment may not be given if it conflicts with a decision of a donee, a deputy or of the Court of Protection.

Emergency treatment, using force if necessary, of child patients

11.58 Force may only be used to give treatment to patients who lack capacity or to children under 16 who lack competence against their objections if the emergency conditions in s 64G are met. Section 64G authorises emergency treatment of patients over 16 who are reasonably believed to lack capacity, or children under 16 reasonably believed to lack competence to consent. Treatment is emergency treatment where it is immediately necessary:

(a)   to save the patient's life; or

(b)   to prevent a serious deterioration in the patient's condition and is not irreversible; or

(c)   to prevent serious suffering by the patient and is not irreversible or hazardous; or

(d)   to prevent the patient from behaving violently or being a danger to himself or others, as long as the treatment is the minimum interference necessary, and is neither irreversible nor hazardous.[64]

If the treatment is ECT it may only be given under paras (a) or (b) above, not paras (c) or (d). Irreversible means having unfavourable irreversible physical or psychological consequences, and hazardous means entailing significant physical hazard.[65] Section 64G authorises force to be used, but only where emergency treatment needs to be given to prevent harm to the patient and the use of force is proportionate to the likelihood of the patient's suffering harm and to the seriousness of that harm.

REVIEWING DETENTION

11.59 If a child patient is admitted informally on their own consent they may seek to leave hospital at anytime subject to the AC's or the nurse's power under s 5 of the MHA 1983 to hold them in hospital. A child patient admitted on parental consent may challenge that decision by invoking the inherent jurisdiction of the High Court on the basis that the intervention is not in their best interests, by seeking a specific issue order under s 8 of the Children Act 1989, or by seeking judicial review on the grounds that their detention infringes a Convention right. A child patient who is detained or subject to SCT

---

[64]   MHA 1983, s 64C(5).
[65]   MHA 1983, s 62(3).

under the MHA 1983 (as amended) has the same rights to seek review of detention or a CTO before a Mental Health Review Tribunal as if they were an adult (see Chapter 9 above).

CONCLUSION

11.60 Admission of children to psychiatric hospital brings difficult ethical and legal issues into play, including the need for a safe and appropriate treatment environment, the need to provide safeguards in relation to controversial treatments, and the tension between the package of powers and rights attached to parental responsibilities, which diminish as the child matures, and the right of the child to self determination. Complexity is added to the law by what has been argued is an artificial distinction between adult capacity and *Gillick* competence.

11.61 As with other aspects of mental health law there is a choice of legal regimes under which admission to hospital may take place. Anthony Harbour has argued that during the 1990s there has been an increase in use of MHA powers to detain children, despite the law's retreat from *Gillick* with statements that parental rights or the court could override the refusal of even a competent child to authorise informal admission at common law. Harbour ascribes this to a number of factors, including a desire to ensure that child patients have rights themselves to challenge detention and compulsory treatment, but perhaps most notably because many specialist child and adolescent units had for the first time obtained registration to allow them to receive patients detained under the MHA 1983.[66] The 1983 Act as amended now provides a complete (and elaborate) statutory framework for treating children whether they are in hospital or the community. There are gaps in the protection afforded to children, and the extent to which the procedural obligation under Art 8 ECHR is met, such as in relation to forcible feeding by naso-gastric tube.

11.62 The Draft Code of Practice introduces the novel concept of the 'zone of parental responsibility' which as we have seen is an attempt to reflect Art 12 of the UN Convention on the Rights of the Child, and the need to provide effective supervision and review of decisions to detain and treat without consent following *Storck v Germany*.[67] The key factors in identifying whether an issue is within 'the zone' are the age and maturity of the child, the nature and invasiveness of the procedure and the extent to which it restricts liberty, whether the child is refusing, and whether the relationship between the parent and the child has broken down and there is concern that the parent may not act in the best interests of the child. In this sense 'the zone' is intended to offer

---

[66] A Harbour 'Young People and Psychiatric Treatment' Paper delivered at the Seminar: 'Children, Mental Health and Human Rights' held at Northumbria University on 22 June 2007.
[67] (2005) 43 EHRR 96, ECtHR.

greater protection for the autonomy rights of the child than the case-law,[68] but it is important to realise that detention under the MHA 1983 will not necessarily bring increased protection for Art 8 rights, as in relation to naso-gastric feeding.

---

[68] *Re R (a minor)* [1992] Fam 11, CA; *R v Kirklees Metropolitan Borough Council, ex parte C (a minor)* [1993] 2 FLR 187, CA; *Re W (a minor)* [1992] 4 All ER 627, CA.

Chapter 12

CRIMINAL OFFENCES AND TRANSFER OF PATIENTS BETWEEN JURISDICTIONS

OVERVIEW

12.1 The positive duty under Art 3 requires states to provide effective protection of vulnerable people against torture or inhuman or degrading treatment.[1] Ill-treatment of mentally disordered people and sexual abuse amount to inhuman and degrading treatment and States have a duty to provide effective protection via the criminal law. The MHA 1983 (as amended) contains a number of offences. Some are designed to protect mentally disordered people against wilful neglect and abuse. Others are designed to protect the integrity of the system, such as the prohibition on forgery of statutory documents or obstruction of people carrying out statutory functions. Yet others are designed to proscribe harbouring or offering assistance to patients who have escaped or absented themselves without leave. Protection of mentally disordered people against inhuman or degrading treatment in the form of sexual abuse is provided under the Sexual Offences Act 2003 where the victim suffers from a mental disorder.

12.2 This chapter also deals with the arrangements in Part 6 of the MHA 1983 for transfer of patients from England and Wales to other jurisdictions and vice versa. These provisions have been substantially amended by the MHA 2007 to provide, inter alia, for the transfer of patients who are subject to CTOs to other jurisdictions. Such transfers have to be in the patient's interests, and since the right to respect for family life is potentially engaged, there should be consultation with the nearest relative unless the patient has objected. Finally, the chapter deals with the provisions of s 86, cross-titled 'Removal of Aliens'.

OFFENCES UNDER THE MENTAL HEALTH ACT 1983

12.3 Part 10 of the MHA 1983 makes provision for a number of criminal offences in connection with the operation of the Act and for the protection of people suffering from mental disorder. The maximum penalty on imprisonment on summary conviction for offences under ss 126, 127 or 128 will increase from six months to one year on the commencement of ss 154 and 282 of the Criminal Justice Act 2003. The offences under Part 9 of the MHA 1983 may be

---

[1]   *A v United Kingdom (human rights: punishment of child) (Application 25599/94)* (1998) 27 EHRR 611, ECtHR.

prosecuted by local authorities, although proceedings under s 127 for ill-treatment or wilful neglect of a patient require the consent of the Director of Public prosecutions. As Jones notes, local authority staff charged with the duty of investigating offences under Part 9 must refer to the relevant provisions of the Police and Criminal Evidence Act 1984 Codes of Practice, and must administer the following caution to a suspect before questioning:[2]

> 'You do not have to say anything. But it may harm your defence if you do not mention when questioned something which you later rely on in court. Anything you do say may be given in evidence.'

Section 126: forgery and false statements

12.4   There are four offences under s 126:

(1)   it is an offence for anyone, without lawful authority or excuse, to have in his custody or control any document which he knows or believes to be false, and which purports to be an application under Part 2, a medical recommendation or other report, or 'any other document required or authorised to be made for any of the purposes of this Act';

(2)   it is an offence for anyone, without lawful authority or excuse, to make, or have in his custody or under his control, any document so closely resembling a document mentioned in (1) above as to be calculated to deceive;

(3)   it is an offence for anyone wilfully to make a false entry or statement in any application, recommendation, report, record or other document required or authorised to be made for any of the purposes of the MHA 1983;

(4)   it is an offence for anyone, with intent to deceive, to make use of any entry or statement in any such document which he knows to be false. This offence is triable either summarily (where a fine or maximum prison term of six months[3] may be imposed) or in the Crown Court (where a fine or maximum prison term of two years may be imposed).

Section 127: ill-treatment of patients

12.5   At common law those who have care or control of mentally disordered patients or are responsible for their treatment owe a duty of care.[4] Section 127 creates two separate offences of ill-treatment or wilful neglect of patients:

---

[2]   Police and Criminal Evidence Act Code of Practice C, para 10.5.
[3]   To be increased to 12 months when the Criminal Justice Act 2003, ss 154 and 282 are introduced.
[4]   *R (on the application of Munjaz) v Mersey Care NHS Trust* [2005] UKHL 58 at [4].

(1)   it is an offence for anyone who is an officer on the staff of or otherwise employed in, or who is one of the managers of, a hospital, independent hospital or care home to ill-treat or wilfully to neglect a patient who is receiving treatment for mental disorder as an in-patient in that hospital or home. This offence also applies to ill-treatment or wilful neglect on the premises of the hospital or home of a person who is receiving treatment there as an out-patient;

(2)   it is an offence for any individual to ill-treat or wilfully to neglect a mentally disordered patient who is for the time being subject to his guardianship under this Act or otherwise in his custody or care (whether by virtue of any legal or moral obligation or otherwise).[5]

To be guilty of an offence under s 127(2) the individual must have the patient in their custody or care by virtue of any legal or moral obligation, so a carer who is looking after a CTO patient could be guilty of either offence by virtue of a moral obligation.

12.6   In *R v Newington*[6] the Court of Appeal advised the Crown Prosecution Service that ill-treatment and wilful neglect are separate offences. Section 139 does not apply to prosecutions brought under this section, so there is no defence of lack of bad faith or negligence.[7] A single act of ill-treatment can be sufficient to constitute an offence under this section.[8] To secure a conviction for ill-treatment the prosecution must prove:

(1)   deliberate conduct by the accused which could properly be described as ill-treatment irrespective of whether it damaged or threatened to damage the patient's health;

(2)   a guilty mind involving either an appreciation by the defendant that s/he was inexcusably ill-treating a patient, or recklessness at to whether she was inexcusably committing acts of ill-treatment;

(3)   that the victim is a mentally disordered person.[9]

Although a local authority may institute proceedings under this section the consent of the Director of Public Prosecutions is required for a prosecution to proceed.[10] This offence is triable either summarily (where a fine or maximum prison term of six months[11] may be imposed) or in the Crown Court (where a

---

[5]   Schedule 5, para 11 of the MHA 2007 repeals s 127(2A) which created the offence of ill-treatment and neglect of a person who is subject to after care under supervision.
[6]   (1990) 91 Cr App R 247, CA.
[7]   MHA 1983, s 139(3).
[8]   *R v Holmes* [1979] Crim LR 52.
[9]   *R v Newington* (1990) 91 Cr App R 247, CA.
[10]   MHA 1983, ss 127(4) and 130.
[11]   To be increased to 12 months when the Criminal Justice Act 2003, ss 154 and 282 are introduced.

fine or maximum prison term of 5 years may be imposed). The maximum Crown Court sentence was increased from two to five years by s 42 of the MHA 2007.

Section 128: assisting patients to absent themselves without leave

12.7   Although it is not an offence for a patient to absent her or himself without leave or escape from legal custody under s 137, it is an offence to assist such a person to do so. It is also an offence knowingly to 'harbour', or assist a patient who has escaped or is absent without leave to avoid being retaken.

12.8   There are four offences under s 128:

(1)   it is an offence to induce or knowingly assist anyone who is liable to be detained, or is subject to guardianship or a CTO to absent himself without leave. This might include assisting someone to absent her or himself from the place where they are required to reside as a condition of guardianship or a CTO;

(2)   it is an offence to induce or knowingly to assist another person to escape from legal custody within the meaning of s 137;

(3)   it is an offence knowingly to harbour a patient who is absent without leave or is otherwise at large and liable to be retaken under the MHA 1983;

(4)   it is an offence knowingly to assist a patient who is absent without leave or is otherwise at large and liable to be retaken with intent to prevent, hinder or interfere with his being taken into custody or returned to the hospital or other place where he ought to be.

The phrase 'other place where he ought to be' is sufficiently wide to cover required places of residence under guardianship or a CTO. The maximum period of imprisonment which may be imposed on summary conviction is six months[12] or two years following conviction on indictment in the Crown Court.

Section 129: Obstruction

12.9   The offence of obstruction under s 129 is committed by any person who, without reasonable cause:

(a)   refuses to allow the inspection of any premises; or

(b)   refuses to allow the visiting, interviewing or examination of any person by a person authorised in that behalf by or under this Act or to give access to any person to a person so authorised; or

---

[12]   To be increased to 12 months when the Criminal Justice Act 2003, ss 154 and 282 are introduced.

(c)   refuses to produce for the inspection of any person so authorised any document or record the production of which is duly required by him; or

(d)   otherwise obstructs any such person in the exercise of his functions.

A separate offence under s 129(2) is committed by anyone who insists on being present when required to withdraw by a person authorised under the Act to interview or examine a person in private.

12.10 The maximum penalty on summary conviction is three months' imprisonment. The Committee of Inquiry into Complaints at Ashworth Hospital 'inclined to the view' that s 129 abrogates the right of silence by making it an 'offence for anyone, without reasonable excuse, to obstruct an authorised investigation'.[13]

OFFENCES UNDER PART 1 OF THE SEXUAL OFFENCES ACT 2003

12.11 Part 1 of the Sexual Offences Act 2003 ('SOA 2003') creates a number of sexual offences against persons with what the cross-headings but not the sections themselves call 'a mental disorder impeding choice'.

Mental disorder impeding choice

12.12 To be guilty the offender must have known or be reasonably be expected to have known that the person has a mental disorder and that because of it or for a reason related to it is likely to be unable to refuse. A person is unable to refuse if:

(a)   he or she lacks the capacity to choose whether to agree to the touching (whether because he or she lacks sufficient understanding of the nature or reasonably foreseeable consequences of what is being done, or for any other reason); or

(b)   he or she is unable to communicate such a choice to the defendant.

Hence a mental disorder impeding choice is a mental disorder which causes the person to lack capacity to choose whether to agree to the touching or to communicate such a choice.

12.13 There are four offences where an ingredient of the offence is that the victim must suffer from a mental disorder impeding choice. Two carry a maximum sentence of 14 years or life imprisonment. They are the offences under ss 30 and 31 of engaging in sexual activity (intentional touching of a

---

[13]   *The Committee of Inquiry into Complaints at Ashworth Hospital*, Cm 2028 (1992), vol 1, chap XIII, para 126.

sexual nature) with a person who is unable to refuse because of, or for a reason related to, mental disorder, or intentionally causing or inciting such a person to engage in sexual activity.

12.14 The maximum sentence for sexual activity or incitement generally on summary conviction is six months,[14] and following conviction on indictment 14 years. The offender is liable, on conviction on indictment, to imprisonment for life if the sexual activity involves penetrative sex with insertion of any part of the offender's body or any other object into the anus or vagina of the victim, or if it involves fellatio by or on either party.

12.15 The other two offences are engaging in sexual activity in the presence of a person with mental disorder impeding choice, and causing a person with a mental disorder impeding choice to watch a sexual act.[15] They carry a maximum sentence of 10 years' imprisonment following conviction on indictment or six months following summary conviction.[16]

12.16 Sections 34–38 of the SOA 2003 create the offences where the victim suffers from mental disorder, but there is no requirement that the mental disorder must impede choice. The offences under ss 34 and 35 carry the same penalties as offences under ss 30 and 31 (see para **12.14** above). They are:

- offering an inducement or making a threat or deception in order to procure sexual activity. Sexual activity must have taken place, and the mentally disordered victim's participation must have been secured by an inducement offered, a threat made or a deception practised by the offender;[17]

- causing a person with a mental disorder to engage in or agree to engage in sexual activity by inducement, threat or deception.

For both offences the offender must have known or be reasonably expected to have known that the victim had a mental disorder.[18]

12.17 The offences under ss 36 and 37 are:

- engaging in sexual activity in the presence, procured by inducement, threat or deception, of a person with a mental disorder;

- causing a person with a mental disorder to watch a sexual act by inducement, threat or deception.

---

[14] To be increased to 12 months on the commencement of ss 154 and 282 of the Criminal Justice Act 2003.
[15] Sexual Offences Act 2007, ss 32–33.
[16] To be increased to 12 months on the commencement of ss 154 and 282 of the Criminal Justice Act 2003.
[17] Sexual Offences Act 2003, s 34.
[18] Sexual Offences Act 2003, s 35.

These offences carry the same maximum penalties as offences under ss 33 and
34 (see para **12.15** above).

Offences by carers

12.18 As Jones notes:[19]

> 'the 2003 Act also introduces a number of specific offences in relation to care
> workers [which] elevate the position of trust and responsibility enjoyed by a care
> worker from a simple aggravating feature of an offence to an offence in its own
> right.'

Sections 38–41 of the SOA 2003 introduce four offences which may be
committed by what the cross heading calls 'care workers', or more accurately
'persons involved in the care of another person in a way which falls within s 42
of that Act'. Section 42 applies to three groups:

(1) anyone whose work in the course of their employment brings or is likely
     to bring them into regular face to face contact with the mentally
     disordered person in a care home, community home, children's home, or
     voluntary home;

(2) anyone whose work in the course of their employment brings or is likely
     to bring them into regular face-to-face contact with a mentally disordered
     person for whom services are provided by a NHS body or an independent
     medical agency, or in an independent clinic or an independent hospital;

(3) anyone who is, whether or not in the course of employment, a provider of
     care, assistance or services to a mentally disordered person in connection
     with their mental disorder, and as such, has had or is likely to have regular
     face-to-face contact with B.

Hence these offences may be committed not only by 'care workers' who provide
care in the course of their employment, but also by unpaid carers, family
members, or friends who provide care, assistance, or services in connection with
the mental disorder.

12.19 With all four offences a defendant can only be found guilty if he or she
knew or ought reasonably to have known that the alleged victim was suffering
from mentally disorder, but once it is proved that the person has a mental
disorder the burden shifts to the defendant to adduce sufficient evidence to '
raise an issue as to whether he knew or could reasonably have been expected to
know it.'[20]

---

[19]   RM Jones *Mental Health Act Manual* (Sweet and Maxwell, 10th edn, 2006), para 1–1149.
[20]   Sexual Offences Act 2003, ss 38(2), 39(2), 40(2) and 41(2).

Engaging in, or causing or inciting, sexual activity with a person with a mental disorder

12.20 Under ss 38 and 39 a carer commits an offence if he or she engages in sexual activity (intentional touching of a sexual nature) with a person whom he or she knew or ought reasonably to have known was suffering from mentally disorder, or causes or incites such activity to take place. The maximum sentence for sexual activity or incitement generally on summary conviction is six months,[21] and following conviction on indictment 10 years. The offender is liable, on conviction on indictment, to imprisonment for up to 14 years if the sexual activity involves penetrative sex with insertion of any part of the offender's body or any other object into the anus or vagina of the victim, or if it involves fellatio by or on either party.

12.21 The offences under ss 40 and 41 are sexual activity in the presence of a person with a mental disorder, and causing a person with a mental disorder to watch a sexual act. Anyone convicted summarily of these offences faces a maximum sentence of six months, or seven years following trial on indictment.

CROSS-BORDER ARRANGEMENTS

12.22 Part 6 of the MHA 1983 deals with the transfer of patients subject to compulsory powers between United Kingdom jurisdictions and the Channel Islands or the Isle of Man, by ensuring that they remain in legal custody whilst in transit and on arrival at their destination are liable to equivalent compulsory powers in the receiving jurisdiction. Part 6 applies to people who are detained (other than those detained under ss 35, 36 or 38), who are conditionally discharged restricted patients, or who are subject to guardianship or to a community treatment order or equivalent. Part 6 also provides, in s 86 for the removal of patients suffering from mental disorder who are neither British citizens nor Commonwealth citizens with the right of abode here to other jurisdictions.

12.23 Section 39 of the MHA 2007 deals with cross-border leave and transfer between jursidictions. Section 39(1) introduces subss (6) and (7) into s 17 of the MHA 1983. These apply to patients from Scotland, Northern Ireland, the Isle of Man and the Channel Islands who are given leave of absence to visit England and Wales and where the clinician has determined that it is necessary in the patient's own interests, or for the protection of others that he or she remain in custody during the leave of absence. Subsections (6) and (7) of s 17 are designed to authorise patients from these jurisdictions who visit England and Wales on escorted leave to be conveyed, kept in custody or detained by their escort while in England and Wales, and re-taken in the event that they escape.

---

[21] To be increased to 12 months on the commencement of ss 154 and 282 of the Criminal Justice Act 2003.

12.24 Section 39(2) of the MHA 2007 gives effect to Sch 5. The amendments in Sch 5 to the MHA 2007 provide for community patients to be transferred between jurisdictions. They also provide for detained patients to be transferred from Scotland to England. The various provisions also specify what date the detention or community compulsion in the receiving jurisdiction is to run from, which is important in terms of the renewal requirement and entitlement to apply for or have a case referred to a MHRT.

Scotland

12.25 Under the MHA 1983 removal of detained (other than those detained under ss 35, 36 or 38) and guardianship patients to Scotland is dealt with by s 80. Schedule, 5 para 2 removes the provision in s 80 for transfer of patients under guardianship in England and Wales to Scotland as Scotland no longer has the equivalent of mental health guardianship. It then introduces four new sections, 80ZA and 80B–80D. The Secretary of State for Health (England) or the National Assembly for Wales may authorise the transfer of a non-restricted patient if it is in the interests of the patient to remove him to Scotland, and that arrangements have been made for admitting him to hospital there. If the patient is subject to restrictions or to a limitation direction the decision-maker is the Minister of Justice. Before transfer takes place the views of the nearest relative should be ascertained and reported to the decision-making authority.

12.26 New s 80ZA empowers the Secretary of State or the Welsh Ministers to authorise the transfer of a community patient to Scotland if a transfer under this section is in the patient's interests; and 'arrangements have been made for dealing with him under enactments in force in Scotland corresponding or similar to those relating to community patients in this Act'. The relevant national authority may not act if the patient has been recalled to hospital.[22]

12.27 Section 80A empowers the Minister of Justice, with the consent of the relevant Scottish Minister, to authorise the transfer of a conditionally discharged restriction order patient to Scotland if it appears to be in the interests of the patient.

12.28 Schedule 5, para 4(1) introduces new ss 80B–80D in relation to Scotland. New s 80B applies to a detained patient who is transferred from Scotland to England or Wales. The date of his hospital admission for renewal purposes will be the date of his arrival at the hospital in England or Wales under the provision in force which most closely corresponds to the Scottish legislation under which the patient was detained.

12.29 New s 80C applies to a patient who is subject to compulsion in the community in Scotland and is transferred to England or Wales. On arrival at the required place of residence in England or Wales, the patient will be treated as if admitted to a hospital in England or Wales on that date under ss 3 or 37

---

22   MHA 1983, s 80ZA(3).

and a CTO had been made discharging him from that hospital. The Explanatory Notes to the MHA 2007 say that:[23]

> 'As soon as practicable after the arrival of a community patient in England and Wales a CTO should be made and deemed to be dated from the day of the patient's arrival. A community patient transferred from Scotland will not be detained in hospital following their transfer prior to becoming a community patient in England and Wales.'

As soon as practicable after the patient's arrival, the RC must specify the conditions that the patient will be subject to under the CTO.

12.30 New s 80D provides for transfer of a conditionally discharged patient from Scotland to England or Wales. On his arrival in England or Wales the patient will be treated as a restricted patient who had been granted a conditional discharge under either s 42 or s 73.

Northern Ireland

12.31 Under the MHA 1983, removal of detained and guardianship patients to Northern Ireland is dealt with by s 81. The Secretary of State for Health (England) or the National Assembly for Wales may authorise the transfer of a non-restricted patient or guardianship if it is in the interests of the patient to remove him to Northern Ireland, and that arrangements have been made for admission to hospital or reception into guardianship there. If the patient is subject to restrictions or to a limitation direction the decision-maker is the Minister of Justice. Before transfer takes place the views of the nearest relative should be ascertained and reported to the decision-making authority. A patient who is transferred to Northern Ireland shall be treated as if on the day of admission he or she had been admitted in pursuance of an application made under the corresponding enactment in Northern Ireland, and the English authority to detain will cease to have effect.

12.32 New s 81ZA applies the removal arrangements to Northern Ireland for detained and guardianship patients and to community patients.[24] No provision is made in the Act for the transfer of community patients from Northern Ireland as there is currently no provision for community patients in Northern Ireland.

12.33 Section 81A empowers the Minister of Justice, with the consent of the Minister exercising corresponding functions in Northern Ireland to arrange for the transfer of responsibility for a conditionally discharged restricted patient, where it appears that to do so would be in the interests of the patient. The patient is treated as if he or she had been conditionally discharged on the date of the transfer and as if subject to a restriction order or restriction direction under the corresponding enactment in force in Northern Ireland. Although

---

[23] *Explanatory Notes to the MHA 2007*, para 164.
[24] Introduced by MHA 2007, Sch 5, para 6.

when the MHA 2007 comes into force all restriction orders will be without limit of time, time limited orders made prior to the 2007 Act, or orders made outside England and Wales having the same effect, expire on the date when they would have expired had the patient not been transferred.

12.34 Section 82 empowers the Department of Health and Social Services for Northern Ireland in Northern Ireland to authorise removal to England or Wales of a patient who is detained (other than under the equivalents of ss 35, 36 or 38) or subject to guardianship under the (Northern Ireland) Order 1986. It must appear to the relevant authority that it is in the interests of the patient to remove him to England and Wales, and that arrangements have been made for the patient's admission to hospital or reception into guardianship. Detention or guardianship under the corresponding provision of the MHA 1983 will commence on the date of admission to hospital or arrival at the required place of residence in England or Wales.

12.35 Section 82A empowers the Minister in Northern Ireland exercising functions corresponding to those of the Minister of Justice, acting with the consent of the Minister of Justice, to authorise the transfer of a conditionally discharged restricted patient subject to the Mental Health (Northern Ireland) Order 1986 if it appears to be in the interests of the patient to do so. The patient is then treated as if he or she had been conditionally discharged under ss 42 or 73 of the MHA 1983 on the date of the transfer. If the patient was in Northern Ireland subject to a time limited restriction order or restriction direction, the English restriction order or direction shall expire on the date when it would have expired had the transfer not been made.

12.36 Schedule 5 also amends s 88 of the MHA 1983, which provides for patients absent from hospitals in England and Wales to be taken into custody and returned to England and Wales, to apply to Northern Ireland only. The Channel Islands and the Isle of Man have powers of their own, which they can use to return patients from England and Wales. In Scotland regulations can be made on such matters under s 309 (patients from other jurisdictions) of the Mental Health (Care and Treatment) (Scotland) Act 2003.

The Channel Islands and the Isle of Man

12.37 Schedule 5 to the MHA 2007 amends the provisions in ss 83 and 85 of the MHA 1983 providing for detained (other than those detained under ss 35, 36 or 38), guardianship and conditionally discharged restricted patients to be transferred from England and Wales to the Channel Islands and the Isle of Man and vice versa. These provisions are similar to those authorising transfer to and from Scotland and Northern Ireland in terms of the criteria (in the patient's interests and arrangements must exist for reception of the patient), and in terms of the 'deeming provisions' whereby detention guardianship and CTOs are deemed to commence on the date of transfer or arrival at the place of residence or receiving hospital.

12.38 New ss 83ZA and 85ZA provide for community patients to be transferred from England and Wales to the Channel Islands and the Isle of Man and vice versa. Section 83ZA applies to community patients s 83 of the MHA 1983 which authorises transfer of guardianship or detained patients to the Channel Islands or the Isle of Man. Section 85ZA authorises transfer from the Channel Islands or the Isle of Man comes into effect only if there are in force in the relevant jurisdiction 'relevant enactments' corresponding or similar to those relating to community patients in this Act. The Explanatory Notes say that:[25]

> 'At present the Channel Islands and the Isle of Man do not have legislation enabling patients to be treated in the community under arrangements similar to Supervised Community Treatment so [these sections] would not, as things stand, have any effect in relation to the Channel Islands or the Isle of Man.'

Curiously, although Northern Ireland also currently has no provision for community patients, the 2007 Act amendments provide only for transfer to Northern Ireland of CTO patients, and no anticipatory provision equivalent to s 85ZA has been introduced.

Removal of aliens

12.39 Section 86 empowers the Secretary of State for Health to issue a warrant authorising removal from the place where he or she is receiving treatment in England and Wales or Northern Ireland of any in-patient detained under an application for admission for treatment, who is neither a British citizen nor a Commonwealth citizen having the right of abode in the United Kingdom. A similar power in relation to patients subject to a hospital order or equivalent is conferred on the Minister of Justice. Whereas previously the section applied only to people with mental illness, it now applies to all mental disorders The conditions for issuing a warrant are that it must appear to the Minister of Justice:

(a)   that proper arrangements have been made for the removal of the patient to a country or territory outside the United Kingdom, the Isle of Man and the Channel Islands and for his care or treatment there; and

(b)   that it is in the interests of the patient to remove her or him.

The Minister may give such directions as he or she thinks fit for the conveyance of the patient to his destination in that country or territory and for his detention in any place or on board any ship or aircraft until his arrival at any specified port or place in any such country or territory.

12.40 The Minister's powers under this section may only be exercised with the approval of a Mental Health Review Tribunal for England, Wales or Northern Ireland. However in *R (on the application of X) v Secretary of State for the*

---

[25]   *Explanatory Notes to the MHA 2007*, para 166.

Home Department the Court of Appeal held that a parallel power existed where the patient had no basis to remain under the Immigration Act 1971. Hence, the Minister of Justice was entitled to remove him using powers under the parallel regime of the Immigration Act and was not confined by the power in s 86 with its requirement for approval by the MHRT. Schiemann LJ said that clearly if the Minister wishes to use Immigration Act powers in relation to a mentally disordered person, the mental disorder would be a factor which he must take into account.[26] The Court of Appeal in *X* held that, whatever power was used, there would be no breach of the prohibition of inhuman or degrading treatment in Art 3 under the principle in *D v United Kingdom*[27] if X was returned to Malta to receive in-patient treatment there.

CONCLUSION

12.41 This outline of the provisions on offences and transfers of patients between jurisdictions completes our consideration of the effects of the MHA 2007 on the MHA 1983. Introduced as an amending Act rather than a complete new Code, the 2007 Act has nevertheless achieved radical reform whilst retaining almost intact the overall framework of the 1983 Act. The offences under the MHA 1983 are virtually untouched by the MHA 2007 with the exception of the increased penalty for ill-treatment or wilful neglect. Reform of the antiquated sexual offences with their unfortunate terminology in relation to mentally disordered people had already been achieved by the Sexual Offences Act 2003.

12.42 The changes in relation to transfers between jurisdictions are significant. The MHA 2007 achieves a complete system of rules for detention and compulsory treatment in the community of adult and child patients. The provisions in relation to transfer replace a somewhat haphazard system with an attempt at a comprehensive code for the transfer in custody of patients subject to compulsion in hospital or the community between all jurisdictions. They create the possibility to move patients in custody from one jurisdiction to another with a seamless transition between the patient being subject to the powers of detention or community compulsion in one country and becoming subject to those in the receiving jurisdiction.

---

[26]   [2000] MHLR 67 at [28].
[27]   (1997) 24 EHRR 423, ECtHR.

Appendix 1

MENTAL HEALTH ACT 1983 (1983 C 20) (AS AMENDED BY THE MENTAL HEALTH ACT 2007)

ARRANGEMENT OF SECTIONS

PART I
APPLICATION OF ACT

PART II
COMPULSORY ADMISSION TO HOSPITAL AND GUARDIANSHIP

Procedure for hospital admission

General provisions as to applications and recommendations

Community Treatment Orders

PART III

PATIENTS CONCERNED IN CRIMINAL PROCEEDINGS OR
UNDER SENTENCE

Remands to hospital

Hospital and guardianship orders

Restriction orders

Hospital and limitation directions

Transfer to hospital of prisoners etc

PART IV
CONSENT TO TREATMENT

PART 4A
TREATMENT OF COMMUNITY PATIENTS NOT RECALLED TO HOSPITAL

PART V
MENTAL HEALTH REVIEW TRIBUNALS

Constitution etc

Applications and references concerning Part II patients

PART VI

REMOVAL AND RETURN OF PATIENTS WITHIN UNITED KINGDOM, ETC

Removal to and from Scotland

Removal to and from Northern Ireland

Removal to and from Channel Islands and Isle of Man

Removal of aliens

PART I
APPLICATION OF ACT

1 Application of Act: 'mental disorder'

(1) The provisions of this Act shall have effect with respect to the reception, care and treatment of mentally disordered patients, the management of their property and other related matters.

(2) In this Act –

'mental disorder' means any disorder or disability of the mind; and
'mentally disordered' shall be construed accordingly;

and other expressions shall have the meanings assigned to them in section 145 below.

(2A) But a person with learning disability shall not be considered by reason of that disability to be –

(a) suffering from mental disorder for the purposes of the provisions mentioned in subsection (2B) below; or

(b)   requiring treatment in hospital for mental disorder for the purposes of
sections 17E and 50 to 53 below,

unless that disability is associated with abnormally aggressive or seriously
irresponsible conduct on his part.

(2B) The provisions are –

(a)   sections 3, 7, 17A, 20 and 20A below;
(b)   sections 35 to 38, 45A, 47, 48 and 51 below; and
(c)   section 72(1)(b) and (c) and (4) below.

(3) Dependence on alcohol or drugs is not considered to be a disorder or
disability of the mind for the purposes of subsection (2) above.

(4) In subsection (2A) above, 'learning disability' means a state of arrested or
incomplete development of the mind which includes significant impairment of
intelligence and social functioning.'

NOTES

Prospective amendments. Definitions in subs (2) prospectively repealed and substituted: MHA 2007,
s 1(1), (2). Subss (2A), (2B) prospectively inserted: MHA 2007, s 2(1), (2). Subs (3) prospectively
substituted: MHA 2007, s 3. Subs (4) prospectively substituted: MHA 2007, s 2(1), (3). For
transitional provisions and savings see MHA 2007, s 53, Sch 10, paras 1, 2.

PART II
COMPULSORY ADMISSION TO HOSPITAL AND GUARDIANSHIP

Procedure for hospital admission

2 Admission for assessment

(1) A patient may be admitted to a hospital and detained there for the period
allowed by subsection (4) below in pursuance of an application (in this Act
referred to as 'an application for admission for assessment') made in
accordance with subsections (2) and (3) below.

(2) An application for admission for assessment may be made in respect of a
patient on the grounds that –

(a)   he is suffering from mental disorder of a nature or degree which
warrants the detention of the patient in a hospital for assessment (or
for assessment followed by medical treatment) for at least a limited
period; and
(b)   he ought to be so detained in the interests of his own health or safety
or with a view to the protection of other persons.

(3) An application for admission for assessment shall be founded on the
written recommendations in the prescribed form of two registered medical
practitioners, including in each case a statement that in the opinion of the
practitioner the conditions set out in subsection (2) above are complied with.

(4) Subject to the provisions of section 29(4) below, a patient admitted to
hospital in pursuance of an application for admission for assessment may be

detained for a period not exceeding 28 days beginning with the day on which he is admitted, but shall not be detained after the expiration of that period unless before it has expired he has become liable to be detained by virtue of a subsequent application, order or direction under the following provisions of this Act.

3 Admission for treatment

(1) A patient may be admitted to a hospital and detained there for the period allowed by the following provisions of this Act in pursuance of an application (in this Act referred to as 'an application for admission for treatment') made in accordance with this section.

(2) An application for admission for treatment may be made in respect of a patient on the grounds that –

(a) he is suffering from mental disorder of a nature or degree which makes it appropriate for him to receive medical treatment in a hospital; and

(b) (*repealed*)

(c) it is necessary for the health or safety of the patient or for the protection of other persons that he should receive such treatment and it cannot be provided unless he is detained under this section; and

(d) appropriate medical treatment is available for him.

(3) An application for admission for treatment shall be founded on the written recommendations in the prescribed form of two registered medical practitioners, including in each case a statement that in the opinion of the practitioner the conditions set out in subsection (2) above are complied with; and each such recommendation shall include –

(a) such particulars as may be prescribed of the grounds for that opinion so far as it relates to the conditions set out in paragraphs (a) and (d) of that subsection; and

(b) a statement of the reasons for that opinion so far as it relates to the conditions set out in paragraph (c) of that subsection, specifying whether other methods of dealing with the patient are available and, if so, why they are not appropriate.

(4) In this Act, references to appropriate medical treatment, in relation to a person suffering from mental disorder, are references to medical treatment which is appropriate in his case, taking into account the nature and degree of the mental disorder and all other circumstances of his case.

NOTES

Prospective amendments. Words in subs (2)(a) prospectively substituted: MHA 2007, s 1(4), Sch 1, Pt 1, paras 1, 2. Subs 2(b) prospectively repealed, subs (2)(d) prospectively inserted and words in subs (3)(a) prospectively substituted: MHA 2007, s 4(1), (2). Subs (4) prospectively inserted: MHA 2007, s 4(3).

4 Admission for assessment in cases of emergency

(1) In any case of urgent necessity, an application for admission for assessment may be made in respect of a patient in accordance with the following provisions of this section, and any application so made is in this Act referred to as 'an emergency application'.

(2) An emergency application may be made either by an approved mental health professional or by the nearest relative of the patient; and every such application shall include a statement that it is of urgent necessity for the patient to be admitted and detained under section 2 above, and that compliance with the provisions of this Part of this Act relating to applications under that section would involve undesirable delay.

(3) An emergency application shall be sufficient in the first instance if founded on one of the medical recommendations required by section 2 above, given, if practicable, by a practitioner who has previous acquaintance with the patient and otherwise complying with the requirements of section 12 below so far as applicable to a single recommendation, and verifying the statement referred to in subsection (2) above.

(4) An emergency application shall cease to have effect on the expiration of a period of 72 hours from the time when the patient is admitted to the hospital unless –

  (a) the second medical recommendation required by section 2 above is given and received by the managers within that period; and
  (b) that recommendation and the recommendation referred to in subsection (3) above together comply with all the requirements of section 12 below (other than the requirement as to the time of signature of the second recommendation).

(5) In relation to an emergency application, section 11 below shall have effect as if in subsection (5) of that section for the words 'the period of 14 days ending with the date of the application' there were substituted the words 'the previous 24 hours'.

NOTES

Prospective amendments. Words in subs (2) prospectively substituted: MHA 2007, s 21, Sch 2, para 2(a).

5 Application in respect of patient already in hospital

(1) An application for the admission of a patient to a hospital may be made under this Part of this Act notwithstanding that the patient is already an in-patient in that hospital or, in the case of an application for admission for treatment, that the patient is for the time being liable to be detained in the hospital in pursuance of an application for admission for assessment; and where an application is so made the patient shall be treated for the purposes of this Part of this Act as if he had been admitted to the hospital at the time when that application was received by the managers.

(2) If, in the case of a patient who is an in-patient in a hospital, it appears to the registered medical practitioner or approved clinician in charge of the treatment of the patient that an application ought to be made under this Part of this Act for the admission of the patient to hospital, he may furnish to the managers a report in writing to that effect; and in any such case the patient may be detained in the hospital for a period of 72 hours from the time when the report is so furnished.

(3) The registered medical practitioner or approved clinician in charge of the treatment of a patient in a hospital may nominate one (but not more than one) person to act for him under subsection (2) above in his absence.

(3A) For the purposes of subsection (3) above –

(a)   the registered medical practitioner may nominate another registered medical practitioner, or an approved clinician, on the staff of the hospital; and

(b)   the approved clinician may nominate another approved clinician, or a registered medical practitioner, on the staff of the hospital.

(4) If, in the case of a patient who is receiving treatment for mental disorder as an in-patient in a hospital, it appears to a nurse of the prescribed class –

(a)   that the patient is suffering from mental disorder to such a degree that it is necessary for his health or safety or for the protection of others for him to be immediately restrained from leaving the hospital; and

(b)   that it is not practicable to secure the immediate attendance of a practitioner or clinician for the purpose of furnishing a report under subsection (2) above,

the nurse may record that fact in writing; and in that event the patient may be detained in the hospital for a period of six hours from the time when that fact is so recorded or until the earlier arrival at the place where the patient is detained of a practitioner or clinician having power to furnish a report under that subsection.

(5) A record made under subsection (4) above shall be delivered by the nurse (or by a person authorised by the nurse in that behalf) to the managers of the hospital as soon as possible after it is made; and where a record is made under that subsection the period mentioned in subsection (2) above shall begin at the time when it is made.

(6) The reference in subsection (1) above to an in-patient does not include an in-patient who is liable to be detained in pursuance of an application under this Part of this Act or a community patient and the references in subsections (2) and (4) above do not include an in-patient who is liable to be detained in a hospital under this Part of this Act or a community patient.

(7) In subsection (4) above 'prescribed' means prescribed by an order made by the Secretary of State.

NOTES

Prospective amendments. Words in subss (2) and (4) prospectively inserted, and subss (3) and (3A) prospectively substituted for current subs (3): MHA 2007, s 9(1), (2). Words in subs (6) prospectively inserted: MHA 2007, s 32(4), Sch 3, paras 1, 2.

Note. Current subs (3) allows nomination only of a person on the staff of the hospital, but see prospectively inserted subs (3A).

6 Effect of application for admission

(1) An application for the admission of a patient to a hospital under this Part of this Act, duly completed in accordance with the provisions of this Part of this Act, shall be sufficient authority for the applicant, or any person authorised by the applicant, to take the patient and convey him to the hospital at any time within the following period, that is to say –

    (a)   in the case of an application other than an emergency application, the period of 14 days beginning with the date on which the patient was last examined by a registered medical practitioner before giving a medical recommendation for the purposes of the application;

    (b)   in the case of an emergency application, the period of 24 hours beginning at the time when the patient was examined by the practitioner giving the medical recommendation which is referred to in section 4(3) above, or at the time when the application is made, whichever is the earlier.

(2) Where a patient is admitted within the said period to the hospital specified in such an application as is mentioned in subsection (1) above, or, being within that hospital, is treated by virtue of section 5 above as if he had been so admitted, the application shall be sufficient authority for the managers to detain the patient in the hospital in accordance with the provisions of this Act.

(3) Any application for the admission of a patient under this Part of this Act which appears to be duly made and to be founded on the necessary medical recommendations may be acted upon without further proof of the signature or qualification of the person by whom the application or any such medical recommendation is made or given or of any matter of fact or opinion stated in it.

(4) Where a patient is admitted to a hospital in pursuance of an application for admission for treatment, any previous application under this Part of this Act by virtue of which he was liable to be detained in a hospital or subject to guardianship shall cease to have effect.

7 Application for guardianship

(1) A patient who has attained the age of 16 years may be received into guardianship, for the period allowed by the following provisions of this Act, in pursuance of an application (in this Act referred to as 'a guardianship application') made in accordance with this section.

(2) A guardianship application may be made in respect of a patient on the grounds that –

(a) he is suffering from mental disorder of a nature or degree which warrants his reception into guardianship under this section; and

(b) it is necessary in the interests of the welfare of the patient or for the protection of other persons that the patient should be so received.

(3) A guardianship application shall be founded on the written recommendations in the prescribed form of two registered medical practitioners, including in each case a statement that in the opinion of the practitioner the conditions set out in subsection (2) above are complied with; and each such recommendation shall include –

(a) such particulars as may be prescribed of the grounds for that opinion so far as it relates to the conditions set out in paragraph (a) of that subsection; and

(b) a statement of the reasons for that opinion so far as it relates to the conditions set out in paragraph (b) of that subsection.

(4) A guardianship application shall state the age of the patient or, if his exact age is not known to the applicant, shall state (if it be the fact) that the patient is believed to have attained the age of 16 years.

(5) The person named as guardian in a guardianship application may be either a local social services authority or any other person (including the applicant himself); but a guardianship application in which a person other than a local social services authority is named as guardian shall be of no effect unless it is accepted on behalf of that person by the local social services authority for the area in which he resides, and shall be accompanied by a statement in writing by that person that he is willing to act as guardian.

NOTES

Prospective amendments. Words in subs (2)(a) prospectively repealed: MHA 2007, ss 1(4), 55, Sch 1, paras 1, 3, Sch 11, Pt 1.

8 Effect of guardianship application, etc

(1) Where a guardianship application, duly made under the provisions of this Part of this Act and forwarded to the local social services authority within the period allowed by subsection (2) below is accepted by that authority, the application shall, subject to regulations made by the Secretary of State, confer on the authority or person named in the application as guardian, to the exclusion of any other person –

(a) the power to require the patient to reside at a place specified by the authority or person named as guardian;

(b) the power to require the patient to attend at places and times so specified for the purpose of medical treatment, occupation, education or training;

(c) the power to require access to the patient to be given, at any place where the patient is residing, to any registered medical practitioner,approved mental health professional or other person so specified.

(2) The period within which a guardianship application is required for the purposes of this section to be forwarded to the local social services authority is the period of 14 days beginning with the date on which the patient was last examined by a registered medical practitioner before giving a medical recommendation for the purposes of the application.

(3) A guardianship application which appears to be duly made and to be founded on the necessary medical recommendations may be acted upon without further proof of the signature or qualification of the person by whom the application or any such medical recommendation is made or given, or of any matter of fact or opinion stated in the application.

(4) If within the period of 14 days beginning with the day on which a guardianship application has been accepted by the local social services authority the application, or any medical recommendation given for the purposes of the application, is found to be in any respect incorrect or defective, the application or recommendation may, within that period and with the consent of that authority, be amended by the person by whom it was signed; and upon such amendment being made the application or recommendation shall have effect and shall be deemed to have had effect as if it had been originally made as so amended.

(5) Where a patient is received into guardianship in pursuance of a guardianship application, any previous application under this Part of this Act by virtue of which he was subject to guardianship or liable to be detained in a hospital shall cease to have effect.

NOTES

Prospective amendments. Words in subs (1)(c) prospectively substituted: MHA 2007, s 21, Sch 2, paras 1, 2(b).

9 Regulations as to guardianship

(1) Subject to the provisions of this Part of this Act, the Secretary of State may make regulations –

(a)   for regulating the exercise by the guardians of patients received into guardianship under this Part of this Act of their powers as such; and

(b)   for imposing on such guardians, and upon local social services authorities in the case of patients under the guardianship of persons other than local social services authorities, such duties as he considers necessary or expedient in the interests of the patients.

(2) Regulations under this section may in particular make provision for requiring the patients to be visited, on such occasions or at such intervals as may be prescribed by the regulations, on behalf of such local social services authorities as may be so prescribed, and shall provide for the appointment, in the case of every patient subject to the guardianship of a person other than a local social services authority, of a registered medical practitioner to act as the nominated medical attendant of the patient.

10 Transfer of guardianship in case of death, incapacity, etc of guardian

(1) If any person (other than a local social services authority) who is the guardian of a patient received into guardianship under this Part of this Act –

    (a)   dies; or

    (b)   gives notice in writing to the local social services authority that he desires to relinquish the functions of guardian,

the guardianship of the patient shall thereupon vest in the local social services authority, but without prejudice to any power to transfer the patient into the guardianship of another person in pursuance of regulations under section 19 below.

(2) If any such person, not having given notice under subsection (1)(b) above, is incapacitated by illness or any other cause from performing the functions of guardian of the patient, those functions may, during his incapacity, be performed on his behalf by the local social services authority or by any other person approved for the purposes by that authority.

(3) If it appears to the county court, upon application made by an approved mental health professional acting on behalf of the local social services authority, that any person other than a local social services authority having the guardianship of a patient received into guardianship under this Part of this Act has performed his functions negligently or in a manner contrary to the interests of the welfare of the patient, the court may order that the guardianship of the patient be transferred to the local social services authority or to any other person approved for the purpose by that authority.

(4) Where the guardianship of a patient is transferred to a local social services authority or other person by or under this section, subsection (2)(c) of section 19 below shall apply as if the patient had been transferred into the guardianship of that authority or person in pursuance of regulations under that section.

(5) In this section 'the local social services authority', in relation to a person (other than a local social services authority) who is the guardian of a patient, means the local social services authority for the area in which that person resides (or resided immediately before his death).

NOTES

Prospective amendments. Words in subs (3) prospectively substituted, and subs (5) prospectively inserted: MHA 2007, s 21, Sch 2, paras 1, 3.

General provisions as to applications and recommendations

11 General provisions as to applications

(1) Subject to the provisions of this section, an application for admission for assessment, an application for admission for treatment and a guardianship application may be made either by the nearest relative of the patient or by an approved mental health professional; and every such application shall specify the qualification of the applicant to make the application.

(1A) No application mentioned in subsection (1) above shall be made by an approved mental health professional if the circumstances are such that there would be a potential conflict of interest for the purposes of regulations under section 12A below.

(2) Every application for admission shall be addressed to the managers of the hospital to which admission is sought and every guardianship application shall be forwarded to the local social services authority named in the application as guardian, or, as the case may be, to the local social services authority for the area in which the person so named resides.

(3) Before or within a reasonable time after an application for the admission of a patient for assessment is made by an approved mental health professional, that professional shall take such steps as are practicable to inform the person (if any) appearing to be the nearest relative of the patient that the application is to be or has been made and of the power of the nearest relative under section 23(2)(a) below.

(4) An approved mental health professional may not make an application for admission for treatment or a guardianship application in respect of a patient in either of the following cases –

(a)   the nearest relative of the patient has notified that professional, or the local social services authority on whose behalf the professional is acting, that he objects to the application being made; or

(b)   that professional has not consulted the person (if any) appearing to be the nearest relative of the patient, but the requirement to consult that person does not apply if it appears to the professional that in the circumstances such consultation is not reasonably practicable or would involve unreasonable delay.

(5) None of the applications mentioned in subsection (1) above shall be made by any person in respect of a patient unless that person has personally seen the patient within the period of 14 days ending with the date of the application. Subsection 6 is deleted. It related to the subcategories of mental disorder and required each medical recommendation to describe the patient as suffering from at least one subcategory of mental disorder in common.

(6) (*repealed*)

(7) Each of the applications mentioned in subsection (1) above shall be sufficient if the recommendations on which it is founded are given either as separate recommendations, each signed by a registered medical practitioner, or as a joint recommendation signed by two such practitioners.

NOTES

Prospective amendments. Words in subss (1) and (3) prospectively substituted, and subs (4) prospectively substituted: MHA 2007, s 21, Sch 2, paras 1, 4. Subs (6) prospectively repealed: MHA 2007, s 55, Sch 11, Pt 1.

12 General provisions as to medical recommendations

(1) The recommendations required for the purposes of an application for the admission of a patient under this Part of this Act or a guardianship application (in this Act referred to as 'medical recommendations') shall be signed on or before the date of the application, and shall be given by practitioners who have personally examined the patient either together or separately, but where they have examined the patient separately not more than five days must have elapsed between the days on which the separate examinations took place.

(2) Of the medical recommendations given for the purposes of any such application, one shall be given by a practitioner approved for the purposes of this section by the Secretary of State as having special experience in the diagnosis or treatment of mental disorder; and unless that practitioner has previous acquaintance with the patient, the other such recommendation shall, if practicable, be given by a registered medical practitioner who has such previous acquaintance.

(2A) A registered medical practitioner who is an approved clinician shall be treated as also approved for the purposes of this section under subsection (2) above as having special experience as mentioned there.

(3) No medical recommendation shall be given for the purposes of an application mentioned in subsection (1) above if the circumstances are such that there would be a potential conflict of interest for the purposes of regulations under section 12A below.

NOTES

Prospective amendments. Words in sub s (1) prospectively inserted: MHA 2007, s 22(1), (3). Subs (2A) prospectively inserted: MHA 2007, s 16. Subs (3) prospectively substituted for current subss (3)–(7): MHA 2007, s 22(1), (4).

12A Conflicts of interest

(1) The appropriate national authority may make regulations as to the circumstances in which there would be a potential conflict of interest such that –

(a)   an approved mental health professional shall not make an application mentioned in section 11(1) above;

(b)   a registered medical practitioner shall not give a recommendation for the purposes of an application mentioned in section 12(1) above.

(2) Regulations under subsection (1) above may make –

(a)   provision for the prohibitions in paragraphs (a) and (b) of that subsection to be subject to specified exceptions;

(b)   different provision for different cases; and

(c)   transitional, consequential, incidental or supplemental provision.

(3) In subsection (1) above, 'the appropriate national authority' means –

(a)   in relation to applications in which admission is sought to a hospital in England or to guardianship applications in respect of which the area of the relevant local social services authority is in England, the Secretary of State;

(b)   in relation to applications in which admission is sought to a hospital in Wales or to guardianship applications in respect of which the area of the relevant local social services authority is in Wales, the Welsh Ministers.

(4) References in this section to the relevant local social services authority, in relation to a guardianship application, are references to the local social services authority named in the application as guardian or (as the case may be) the local social services authority for the area in which the person so named resides.'

NOTES

Prospective amendments. Section prospectively inserted: MHA 2007, s 22(1), (5).

13 Duty of approved mental health professionals to make applications for admission or guardianship

(1) If a local social services authority have reason to think that an application for admission to hospital or a guardianship application may need to be made in respect of a patient within their area, they shall make arrangements for an approved mental health professional to consider the patient's case on their behalf.

(1A) If that professional is –

(a)   satisfied that such an application ought to be made in respect of the patient; and

(b)   of the opinion, having regard to any wishes expressed by relatives of the patient or any other relevant circumstances, that it is necessary or proper for the application to be made by him,

he shall make the application.

(1B) Subsection (1C) below applies where –

(a)   a local social services authority makes arrangements under subsection (1) above in respect of a patient;

(b)   an application for admission for assessment is made under subsection (1A) above in respect of the patient;

(c)   while the patient is liable to be detained in pursuance of that application, the authority have reason to think that an application for admission for treatment may need to be made in respect of the patient; and

(d)   the patient is not within the area of the authority.

(1C) Where this subsection applies, subsection (1) above shall be construed as requiring the authority to make arrangements under that subsection in place of the authority mentioned there.

(2) Before making an application for the admission of a patient to hospital an approved mental health professional shall interview the patient in a suitable manner and satisfy himself that detention in a hospital is in all the circumstances of the case the most appropriate way of providing the care and medical treatment of which the patient stands in need.

(3) An application under subsection (1A) above may be made outside the area of the local social services authority on whose behalf the approved mental health professional is considering the patient's case.

(4) It shall be the duty of a local social services authority, if so required by the nearest relative of a patient residing in their area, make arrangements under subsection (1) above for an approved mental health professional to consider the patient's case with a view to making an application for his admission to hospital; and if in any such case that approved social worker that professional decides not to make an application he shall inform the nearest relative of his reasons in writing.

(5) Nothing in this section shall be construed as authorising or requiring an application to be made by an approved mental health professional in contravention of the provisions of section 11(4) above or of regulations under section 12A above, or as restricting the power of a local social services authority to make arrangements with an approved mental health professional to consider a patient's case or of an approved mental health professional to make any application under this Act.

NOTES

Prospective amendments. Section heading substituted, subss (1)–(1C) substitued for current subs (1), words in subss (2), (4), (5) prospectively substituted, subs (3) prospectively substituted, and words in subs (5) prospectively inserted: MHA 2007, s 21, Sch 2, paras 1, 5. Words in subs (5) prospectively inserted: MHA 2007, s 22(1), (6).

14 Social reports

Where a patient is admitted to a hospital in pursuance of an application (other than an emergency application) made under this Part of this Act by his nearest relative, the managers of the hospital shall as soon as practicable give notice of that fact to the local social services authority for the area in which the patient resided immediately before his admission; and that authority shall as soon as practicable arrange for an approved mental health professional to interview the patient and provide the managers with a report on his social circumstances.

NOTES

Prospective amendments. Words prospectively substituted: MHA 2007, s 21, Sch 2, paras 1, 6.

15 Rectification of applications and recommendations

(1) If within the period of 14 days beginning with the day on which a patient has been admitted to a hospital in pursuance of an application for admission for assessment or for treatment the application, or any medical recommendation given for the purposes of the application, is found to be in any respect incorrect or defective, the application or recommendation may, within that

period and with the consent of the managers of the hospital, be amended by the person by whom it was signed; and upon such amendment being made the application or recommendation shall have effect and shall be deemed to have had effect as if it had been originally made as so amended.

(2) Without prejudice to subsection (1) above, if within the period mentioned in that subsection it appears to the managers of the hospital that one of the two medical recommendations on which an application for the admission of a patient is founded is insufficient to warrant the detention of the patient in pursuance of the application, they may, within that period, give notice in writing to that effect to the applicant; and where any such notice is given in respect of a medical recommendation, that recommendation shall be disregarded, but the application shall be, and shall be deemed always to have been, sufficient if –

   (a)   a fresh medical recommendation complying with the relevant provisions of this Part of this Act (other than the provisions relating to the time of signature and the interval between examinations) is furnished to the managers within that period; and

   (b)   that recommendation, and the other recommendation on which the application is founded, together comply with those provisions.

(3) Where the medical recommendations upon which an application for admission is founded are, taken together, insufficient to warrant the detention of the patient in pursuance of the application, a notice under subsection (2) above may be given in respect of either of those recommendations.

(4) Nothing in this section shall be construed as authorising the giving of notice in respect of an application made as an emergency application, or the detention of a patient admitted in pursuance of such an application, after the period of 72 hours referred to in section 4(4) above, unless the conditions set out in paragraphs (a) and (b) of that section are complied with or would be complied with apart from any error or defect to which this section applies.

NOTES

Prospective amendments. Words in subs (3) prospectively repealed: MHA 2007, s55, Sch 11 Pt 1.

16 ...

(*repealed*)

NOTES

Prospective amendment. Section prospectively repealed: MHA 2007, s 55, Sch 11, Pt 1.

Note. Section 16, which governed reclassification of patients, is repealed consequent upon the abolition of the sub-categories of mental disorder.

17 Leave of absence from hospital

(1) The responsible clinician may grant to any patient who is for the time being liable to be detained in a hospital under this Part of this Act leave to be absent

from the hospital subject to such conditions (if any) as that clinician considers necessary in the interests of the patient or for the protection of other persons.

(2) Leave of absence may be granted to a patient under this section either indefinitely or on specified occasions or for any specified period; and where leave is so granted for a specified period, that period may be extended by further leave granted in the absence of the patient.

(2A) But longer-term leave of absence may not be granted to a patient unless the responsible clinician first considers whether the patient should be dealt with under section 17A instead.

(2B) For these purposes, longer-term leave is granted to a patient if –

(a)   leave of absence is granted to him under this section either indefinitely or for a specified period of more than seven consecutive days; or

(b)   a specified period is extended under this section such that the total period for which leave of absence will have been granted to him under this section exceeds seven consecutive days.

(3) Where it appears to the responsible clinician that it is necessary so to do in the interests of the patient or for the protection of other persons, he may, upon granting leave of absence under this section, direct that the patient remain in custody during his absence; and where leave of absence is so granted the patient may be kept in the custody of any officer on the staff of the hospital, or of any other person authorised in writing by the managers of the hospital or, if the patient is required in accordance with conditions imposed on the grant of leave of absence to reside in another hospital, of any officer on the staff of that other hospital.

(4) In any case where a patient is absent from a hospital in pursuance of leave of absence granted under this section, and it appears to the responsible clinician that it is necessary so to do in the interests of the patient's health or safety or for the protection of other persons, that clinician may, subject to subsection (5) below, by notice in writing given to the patient or to the person for the time being in charge of the patient, revoke the leave of absence and recall the patient to the hospital.

(5) A patient to whom leave of absence is granted under this section shall not be recalled under subsection (4) above after he has ceased to be liable to be detained under this Part of this Act.

(6) Subs (7) below applies to a person who is granted leave: or: virtue of a provision –

(a)   in force in Scotland, Northern Ireland, any of the Channel Islands or the Isle of Man; and

(b)   corresponding to subs (1) above.

(7) For the purpose of giving effect to a direction or condition imposed: virtue of a provision corresponding to subs (3) above, the person may be conveyed to a place in, or kept in custody or detained at a place of safety in, England and Wales: a person authorised in that behalf: the direction or condition.

NOTES

Prospective amendments. Words in subss (1), (3), (4) prospectively substituted: MHA 2007, s 9(1), (3). Subss (2A) and (2B) prospectively inserted: MHA 2007, s 33(1), (2).

Community Treatment Orders

17A Community treatment orders

(1) The responsible clinician may by order in writing discharge a detained patient from hospital subject to his being liable to recall in accordance with section 17E below.

(2) A detained patient is a patient who is liable to be detained in a hospital in pursuance of an application for admission for treatment.

(3) An order under subsection (1) above is referred to in this Act as a 'community treatment order'.

(4) The responsible clinician may not make a community treatment order unless –

    (a)   in his opinion, the relevant criteria are met; and

    (b)   an approved mental health professional states in writing –

        (i)   that he agrees with that opinion; and

        (ii)   that it is appropriate to make the order.

(5) The relevant criteria are –

    (a)   the patient is suffering from mental disorder of a nature or degree which makes it appropriate for him to receive medical treatment;

    (b)   it is necessary for his health or safety or for the protection of other persons that he should receive such treatment;

    (c)   subject to his being liable to be recalled as mentioned in paragraph (d) below, such treatment can be provided without his continuing to be detained in a hospital;

    (d)   it is necessary that the responsible clinician should be able to exercise the power under section 17E(1) below to recall the patient to hospital; and

    (e)   appropriate medical treatment is available for him.

(6) In determining whether the criterion in subsection (5)(d) above is met, the responsible clinician shall, in particular, consider, having regard to the patient's history of mental disorder and any other relevant factors, what risk there would be of a deterioration of the patient's condition if he were not detained in a hospital (as a result, for example, of his refusing or neglecting to receive the medical treatment he requires for his mental disorder).

(7) In this Act –

'community patient' means a patient in respect of whom a community treatment order is in force;

'the community treatment order', in relation to such a patient, means the community treatment order in force in respect of him; and 'the responsible hospital', in relation to such a patient, means the hospital in which he was liable to be detained immediately before the community treatment order was made, subject to section 19A below.

NOTES

Prospective amendments. Section prospectively inserted: MHA 207, s 32(1), (2). For transitional provisions and savings, see MHA 2007, s 53, Sch 10, paras 1, 5.

17B Conditions

(1) A community treatment order shall specify conditions to which the patient is to be subject while the order remains in force.

(2) But, subject to subsection (3) below, the order may specify conditions only if the responsible clinician, with the agreement of the approved mental health professional mentioned in section 17A(4)(b) above, thinks them necessary or appropriate for one or more of the following purposes –

  (a) ensuring that the patient receives medical treatment;
  (b) preventing risk of harm to the patient's health or safety;
  (c) protecting other persons.

(3) The order shall specify –

  (a) a condition that the patient make himself available for examination under section 20A below; and
  (b) a condition that, if it is proposed to give a certificate under Part 4A of this Act in his case, he make himself available for examination so as to enable the certificate to be given.

(4) The responsible clinician may from time to time by order in writing vary the conditions specified in a community treatment order.

(5) He may also suspend any conditions specified in a community treatment order.

(6) If a community patient fails to comply with a condition specified in the community treatment order by virtue of subsection (2) above, that fact may be taken into account for the purposes of exercising the power of recall under section 17E(1) below.

(7) But nothing in this section restricts the exercise of that power to cases where there is such a failure.

NOTES

Prospective amendments. Section prospectively inserted: MHA 207, s 32(1), (2). For transitional provisions and savings, see MHA 2007, s 53, Sch 10, paras 1, 5.

17C Duration of community treatment order

A community treatment order shall remain in force until –

  (a) the period mentioned in section 20A(1) below (as extended under any provision of this Act) expires, but this is subject to sections 21 and 22 below;

(b) the patient is discharged in pursuance of an order under section 23 below or a direction under section 72 below;

(c) the application for admission for treatment in respect of the patient otherwise ceases to have effect; or

(d) the order is revoked under section 17F below, whichever occurs first.

NOTES

Prospective amendments. Section prospectively inserted: MHA 207, s 32(1), (2). For transitional provisions and savings, see MHA 2007, s 53, Sch 10, paras 1, 5.

17D Effect of community treatment order

(1) The application for admission for treatment in respect of a patient shall not cease to have effect by virtue of his becoming a community patient.

(2) But while he remains a community patient –

(a) the authority of the managers to detain him under section 6(2) above in pursuance of that application shall be suspended; and

(b) reference (however expressed) in this or any other Act, or in any subordinate legislation (within the meaning of the Interpretation Act 1978), to patients liable to be detained, or detained, under this Act shall not include him.

(3) And section 20 below shall not apply to him while he remains a community patient.

(4) Accordingly, authority for his detention shall not expire during any period in which that authority is suspended by virtue of subsection (2)(a) above.

NOTES

Prospective amendments. Section prospectively inserted: MHA 207, s 32(1), (2). For transitional provisions and savings, see MHA 2007, s 53, Sch 10, paras 1, 5.

17E Power to recall to hospital

(1) The responsible clinician may recall a community patient to hospital if in his opinion –

(a) the patient requires medical treatment in hospital for his mental disorder; and

(b) there would be a risk of harm to the health or safety of the patient or to other persons if the patient were not recalled to hospital for that purpose.

(2) The responsible clinician may also recall a community patient to hospital if the patient fails to comply with a condition specified under section 17B(3) above.

(3) The hospital to which a patient is recalled need not be the responsible hospital.

(4) Nothing in this section prevents a patient from being recalled to a hospital even though he is already in the hospital at the time when the power of recall is exercised; references to recalling him shall be construed accordingly.

(5) The power of recall under subsections (1) and (2) above shall be exercisable by notice in writing to the patient.

(6) A notice under this section recalling a patient to hospital shall be sufficient authority for the managers of that hospital to detain the patient there in accordance with the provisions of this Act.

NOTES

Prospective amendments. Section prospectively inserted: MHA 207, s 32(1), (2). For transitional provisions and savings, see MHA 2007, s 53, Sch 10, paras 1, 5.

17F Powers in respect of recalled patients

(1) This section applies to a community patient who is detained in a hospital by virtue of a notice recalling him there under section 17E above.

(2) The patient may be transferred to another hospital in such circumstances and subject to such conditions as may be prescribed in regulations made by the Secretary of State (if the hospital in which the patient is detained is in England) or the Welsh Ministers (if that hospital is in Wales).

(3) If he is so transferred to another hospital, he shall be treated for the purposes of this section (and section 17E above) as if the notice under that section were a notice recalling him to that other hospital and as if he had been detained there from the time when his detention in hospital by virtue of the notice first began.

(4) The responsible clinician may by order in writing revoke the community treatment order if –

> (a) in his opinion, the conditions mentioned in section 3(2) above are satisfied in respect of the patient; and
> (b) an approved mental health professional states in writing –
> > (i) that he agrees with that opinion; and
> > (ii) that it is appropriate to revoke the order.

(5) The responsible clinician may at any time release the patient under this section, but not after the community treatment order has been revoked.

(6) If the patient has not been released, nor the community treatment order revoked, by the end of the period of 72 hours, he shall then be released.

(7) But a patient who is released under this section remains subject to the community treatment order.

(8) In this section –

> (a) 'the period of 72 hours' means the period of 72 hours beginning with the time when the patient's detention in hospital by virtue of the notice under section 17E above begins; and

(b) references to being released shall be construed as references to being released from that detention (and accordingly from being recalled to hospital).

NOTES

Prospective amendments. Section prospectively inserted: MHA 207, s 32(1), (2). For transitional provisions and savings, see MHA 2007, s 53, Sch 10, paras 1, 5.

17G Effect of revoking community treatment order

(1) This section applies if a community treatment order is revoked under section 17F above in respect of a patient.

(2) Section 6(2) above shall have effect as if the patient had never been discharged from hospital by virtue of the community treatment order.

(3) The provisions of this or any other Act relating to patients liable to be detained (or detained) in pursuance of an application for admission for treatment shall apply to the patient as they did before the community treatment order was made, unless otherwise provided.

(4) If, when the order is revoked, the patient is being detained in a hospital other than the responsible hospital, the provisions of this Part of this Act shall have effect as if –

(a) the application for admission for treatment in respect of him were an application for admission to that other hospital; and

(b) he had been admitted to that other hospital at the time when he was originally admitted in pursuance of the application.

(5) But, in any case, section 20 below shall have effect as if the patient had been admitted to hospital in pursuance of the application for admission for treatment on the day on which the order is revoked.'

NOTES

Prospective amendments. Section prospectively inserted: MHA 207, s 32(1), (2). For transitional provisions and savings, see MHA 2007, s 53, Sch 10, paras 1, 5.

18 Return and readmission of patients absent without leave

(1) Where a patient who is for the time being liable to be detained under this Part of this Act in a hospital –

(a) absents himself from the hospital without leave granted under section 17 above; or

(b) fails to return to the hospital on any occasion on which, or at the expiration of any period for which, leave of absence was granted to him under that section, or upon being recalled under that section; or

(c) absents himself without permission from any place where he is required to reside in accordance with conditions imposed on the grant of leave of absence under that section,

he may, subject to the provisions of this section, be taken into custody and returned to the hospital or place by any approved mental health professional, by any officer on the staff of the hospital, by any constable, or by any person authorised in writing by the managers of the hospital.

(2) Where the place referred to in paragraph (c) of subsection (1) above is a hospital other than the one in which the patient is for the time being liable to be detained, the references in that subsection to an officer on the staff of the hospital and the managers of the hospital shall respectively include references to an officer on the staff of the first-mentioned hospital and the managers of that hospital.

(2A) Where a community patient is at any time absent from a hospital to which he is recalled under section 17E above, he may, subject to the provisions of this section, be taken into custody and returned to the hospital by any approved mental health professional, by any officer on the staff of the hospital, by any constable, or by any person authorised in writing by the responsible clinician or the managers of the hospital.

(3) Where a patient who is for the time being subject to guardianship under this Part of this Act absents himself without the leave of the guardian from the place at which he is required by the guardian to reside, he may, subject to the provisions of this section, be taken into custody and returned to that place by any officer on the staff of a local social services authority, by any constable, or by any person authorised in writing by the guardian or a local social services authority.

(4) A patient shall not be taken into custody under this section after the later of –

    (a)   the end of the period of six months beginning with the first day of his absence without leave; and

    (b)   the end of the period for which (apart from section 21 below) he is liable to be detained or subject to guardianship or, in the case of a community patient, the community treatment order is in force

and, in determining for the purposes of paragraph (b) above or any other provision of this Act whether a person who is or has been absent without leave is at any time liable to be detained or subject to guardianship, a report furnished under section 20 or 21B below before the first day of his absence without leave shall not be taken to have renewed the authority for his detention or guardianship unless the period of renewal began before that day.

(4A) In determining for the purposes of subsection (4)(b) above or any other provision of this Act whether a person who is or has been absent without leave is at any time liable to be detained or subject to guardianship, a report furnished under section 20 or 21B below before the first day of his absence without leave shall not be taken to have renewed the authority for his detention or guardianship unless the period of renewal began before that day.

(4B) Similarly, in determining for those purposes whether a community treatment order is at any time in force in respect of a person who is or has been absent without leave, a report furnished under section 20A or 21B below before the first day of his absence without leave shall not be taken to have extended the community treatment period unless the extension began before that day.

(5) A patient shall not be taken into custody under this section if the period for which he is liable to be detained is that specified in section 2(4), 4(4) or 5(2) or (4) above and that period has expired.

(6) In this Act 'absent without leave' means absent from any hospital or other place and liable to be taken into custody and returned under this section, and related expressions shall be construed accordingly.

(7) In relation to a patient who has yet to comply with a requirement imposed by virtue of this Act to be in a hospital or place, references in this Act to his liability to be returned to the hospital or place shall include his liability to be taken to that hospital or place; and related expressions shall be construed accordingly.

NOTES

Prospective amendments. Words in subs (1) prospectively substituted: MHA 2007, Sch 2, para 7(a). Subss (2A), (4A), (4B) and (7), and words in subs (4), prospectively inserted: MHA 2007, s 32(4), Sch 3, paras 1, 3(1), (2), (4), (5). Words in subs (4) prospectively repealed: MHA 2007, s 32(4), Sch 3, paras 1, 3(3).

19 Regulations as to transfer of patients

(1) In such circumstances and subject to such conditions as may be prescribed by regulations made by the Secretary of State –

    (a)   a patient who is for the time being liable to be detained in a hospital by virtue of an application under this Part of this Act may be transferred to another hospital or into the guardianship of a local social services authority or of any person approved by such an authority;

    (b)   a patient who is for the time being subject to the guardianship of a local social services authority or other person by virtue of an application under this Part of this Act may be transferred into the guardianship of another local social services authority or person, or be transferred to a hospital.

(2) Where a patient is transferred in pursuance of regulations under this section, the provisions of this Part of this Act (including this subsection) shall apply to him as follows, that is to say –

    (a)   in the case of a patient who is liable to be detained in a hospital by virtue of an application for admission for assessment or for treatment and is transferred to another hospital, as if the application were an application for admission to that other hospital and as if the patient had been admitted to that other hospital at the time when he was originally admitted in pursuance of the application;

    (b)   in the case of a patient who is liable to be detained in a hospital by virtue of such an application and is transferred into guardianship, as if the application were a guardianship application duly accepted at the said time;

(c)   in the case of a patient who is subject to guardianship by virtue of a guardianship application and is transferred into the guardianship of another authority or person, as if the application were for his reception into the guardianship of that authority or person and had been accepted at the time when it was originally accepted;

(d)   in the case of a patient who is subject to guardianship by virtue of a guardianship application and is transferred to a hospital, as if the guardianship application were an application for admission to that hospital for treatment and as if the patient had been admitted to the hospital at the time when the application was originally accepted.

(3) Without prejudice to subsections (1) and (2) above, any patient who is for the time being liable to be detained under this Part of this Act in a hospital vested in the Secretary of State for the purposes of his functions under the National Health Service Act 2006, in a hospital vested in the Welsh Ministers for the purposes of their functions under the National Health Service (Wales) Act 2006, in any accommodation used under either of those Acts, by the managers of such a hospital or in a hospital vested in a National Health Service trust, NHS foundation trust, Local Health Board or Primary Care Trust, may at any time be removed to any other such hospital or accommodation which is managed by the managers of, or is vested in the National Health Service trust, NHS foundation trust, Local Health Board or Primary Care Trust for, the first mentioned hospital; and paragraph (a) of subsection (2) above shall apply in relation to a patient so removed as it applies in relation to a patient transferred in pursuance of regulations made under this section.

(4) Regulations made under this section may make provision for regulating the conveyance to their destination of patients authorised to be transferred or removed in pursuance of the regulations or under subsection (3) above.

19A Regulations as to assignment of responsibility for community patients

(1) Responsibility for a community patient may be assigned to another hospital in such circumstances and subject to such conditions as may be prescribed by regulations made by the Secretary of State (if the responsible hospital is in England) or the Welsh Ministers (if that hospital is in Wales).

(2) If responsibility for a community patient is assigned to another hospital –

(a)   the application for admission for treatment in respect of the patient shall have effect (subject to section 17D above) as if it had always specified that other hospital;

(b)   the patient shall be treated as if he had been admitted to that other hospital at the time when he was originally admitted in pursuance of the application (and as if he had subsequently been discharged under section 17A above from there); and

(c)   that other hospital shall become 'the responsible hospital' in relation to the patient for the purposes of this Act.

NOTES

Prospective amendments. Section prospectively inserted: MHA 2007, s 32(4), Sch 3, paras 1, 4.

Duration of authority and discharge

NOTES

Amendments. Word in cross-heading substituted: MHA 2007, s 32(3).

20 Duration of authority

(1) Subject to the following provisions of this Part of this Act, a patient admitted to hospital in pursuance of an application for admission for treatment, and a patient placed under guardianship in pursuance of a guardianship application, may be detained in a hospital or kept under guardianship for a period not exceeding six months beginning with the day on which he was so admitted, or the day on which the guardianship application was accepted, as the case may be, but shall not be so detained or kept for any longer period unless the authority for his detention or guardianship is renewed under this section.

(2) Authority for the detention or guardianship of a patient may, unless the patient has previously been discharged under section 23 below, be renewed –

    (a)   from the expiration of the period referred to in subsection (1) above, for a further period of six months;

    (b)   from the expiration of any period of renewal under paragraph (a) above, for a further period of one year,

and so on for periods of one year at a time.

(3) Within the period of two months ending on the day on which a patient who is liable to be detained in pursuance of an application for admission for treatment would cease under this section to be so liable in default of the renewal of the authority for his detention, it shall be the duty of the responsible clinician –

    (a)   to examine the patient; and

    (b)   if it appears to him that the conditions set out in subsection (4) below are satisfied, to furnish to the managers of the hospital where the patient is detained a report to that effect in the prescribed form;

and where such a report is furnished in respect of a patient the managers shall, unless they discharge the patient under section 23 below, cause him to be informed.

(4) The conditions referred to in subsection (3) above are that –

    (a)   the patient is suffering from mental disorder of a nature or degree which makes it appropriate for him to receive medical treatment in a hospital; and

    (c)   it is necessary for the health or safety of the patient or for the protection of other persons that he should receive such treatment and that it cannot be provided unless he continues to be detained; and

(d)   appropriate medical treatment is available for him.

(5) Before furnishing a report under subsection (3) above the responsible clinician shall consult one or more other persons who have been professionally concerned with the patient's medical treatment.

(5A) But the responsible clinician may not furnish a report under subsection (3) above unless a person –

(a)   who has been professionally concerned with the patient's medical treatment; but

(b)   who belongs to a profession other than that to which the responsible clinician belongs, states in writing that he agrees that the conditions set out in subsection (4) above are satisfied.'

(6) Within the period of two months ending with the day on which a patient who is subject to guardianship under this Part of this Act would cease under this section to be so liable in default of the renewal of the authority for his guardianship, it shall be the duty of the appropriate practitioner –

(a)   to examine the patient; and

(b)   if it appears to him that the conditions set out in subsection (7) below are satisfied, to furnish to the guardian and, where the guardian is a person other than a local social services authority, to the responsible local social services authority a report to that effect in the prescribed form; and where such a report is furnished in respect of a patient, the local social services authority shall, unless they discharge the patient under section 23 below, cause him to be informed.

(7) The conditions referred to in subsection (6) above are that –

(a)   the patient is suffering from mental disorder of a nature or degree which warrants his reception into guardianship; and

(b)   it is necessary in the interests of the welfare of the patient or for the protection of other persons that the patient should remain under guardianship.

(8) Where a report is duly furnished under subsection (3) or (6) above, the authority for the detention or guardianship of the patient shall be thereby renewed for the period prescribed in that case by subsection (2) above.

NOTES

Prospective amendments. Words in subss (2), (3) and (6) prospectively inserted: MHA 2007, s 32(4), Sch 3, para 5. Words in subss (3), (5) prospectively substituted: MHA 2007, s 9(1), (4)(a). Words in subs (4)(a) and (7)(a) prospectively substituted: MHA 2007, s 1(4), Sch 1, paras 4(a), (b). Subs (4)(b) prospectively repealed: MHA 2007, ss 4(1), (4)(a), 55, Sch 11, Pt 2. Subs (4)(d) and preceding word prospectively inserted: MHA 2007, s 4(1), (4)(b). Words in subs (4) prospectively repealed: MHA 2007, ss 4(1), (4)(c), 55, Sch 11, Pt 2. Subs 5A prospectively inserted: MHA 2007, s 9(1), (4)(b). Words in subs (6) prospectively substituted: MHA 2007, s 9(1), (4)(c). Subs (9) prospectively repealed: MHA 2007, s 55, Sch 11, Pt 1. Subs (10) prospectively repealed: MHA 2007, ss 9(1), (4)(d), 55, Sch 11, Pt 3.

20A Community treatment period

(1) Subject to the provisions of this Part of this Act, a community treatment order shall cease to be in force on expiry of the period of six months beginning with the day on which it was made.

(2) That period is referred to in this Act as 'the community treatment period'.

(3) The community treatment period may, unless the order has previously ceased to be in force, be extended –

    (a)   from its expiration for a period of six months;
    (b)   from the expiration of any period of extension under paragraph (a) above for a further period of one year, and so on for periods of one year at a time.

(4) Within the period of two months ending on the day on which the order would cease to be in force in default of an extension under this section, it shall be the duty of the responsible clinician –

    (a)   to examine the patient; and
    (b)   if it appears to him that the conditions set out in subsection (6) below are satisfied and if a statement under subsection (8) below is made, to furnish to the managers of the responsible hospital a report to that effect in the prescribed form.

(5) Where such a report is furnished in respect of the patient, the managers shall, unless they discharge him under section 23 below, cause him to be informed.

(6) The conditions referred to in subsection (4) above are that –

    (a)   the patient is suffering from mental disorder of a nature or degree which makes it appropriate for him to receive medical treatment;
    (b)   it is necessary for his health or safety or for the protection of other persons that he should receive such treatment;
    (c)   subject to his continuing to be liable to be recalled as mentioned in paragraph (d) below, such treatment can be provided without his being detained in a hospital;
    (d)   it is necessary that the responsible clinician should continue to be able to exercise the power under section 17E(1) above to recall the patient to hospital; and
    (e)   appropriate medical treatment is available for him.

(7) In determining whether the criterion in subsection (6)(d) above is met, the responsible clinician shall, in particular, consider, having regard to the patient's history of mental disorder and any other relevant factors, what risk there would be of a deterioration of the patient's condition if he were to continue not to be detained in a hospital (as a result, for example, of his refusing or neglecting to receive the medical treatment he requires for his mental disorder).

(8) The statement referred to in subsection (4) above is a statement in writing by an approved mental health professional –

(a)   that it appears to him that the conditions set out in subsection (6) above are satisfied; and

(b)   that it is appropriate to extend the community treatment period.

(9) Before furnishing a report under subsection (4) above the responsible clinician shall consult one or more other persons who have been professionally concerned with the patient's medical treatment.

(10) Where a report is duly furnished under subsection (4) above, the community treatment period shall be thereby extended for the period prescribed in that case by subsection (3) above.

NOTES

Prospective amendments. Section prospectively inserted: MHA 2007, s 32(1), (3).

20B   Effect of expiry of community treatment order

(1) A community patient shall be deemed to be discharged absolutely from liability to recall under this Part of this Act, and the application for admission for treatment cease to have effect, on expiry of the community treatment order, if the order has not previously ceased to be in force.

(2) For the purposes of subsection (1) above, a community treatment order expires on expiry of the community treatment period as extended under this Part of this Act, but this is subject to sections 21 and 22 below.

NOTES

Prospective amendments. Section prospectively inserted: MHA 2007, s 32(1), (3).

21   Special provisions as to patients absent without leave

(1) Where a patient is absent without leave –

(a)   on the day on which (apart from this section) he would cease to be liable to be detained or subject to guardianship under this Part of this Act or, in the case of a community patient, the community treatment order would cease to be in force; or

(b)   within the period of one week ending with that day, he shall not cease to be so liable or subject, or the order shall not cease to be in force, until the relevant time.

(2) For the purposes of subsection (1) above the relevant time –

(a)   where the patient is taken into custody under section 18 above, is the end of the period of one week beginning with the day on which he is returned to the hospital or place where he ought to be;

(b)   where the patient returns himself to the hospital or place where he ought to be within the period during which he can be taken into custody under section 18 above, is the end of the period of one week beginning with the day on which he so returns himself; and

(c)   otherwise, is the end of the period during which he can be taken into custody under section 18 above.

(3) Where a patient is absent without leave on the day on which (apart from this section) the managers would be required under section 68 below to refer the patient's case to a Mental Health Review Tribunal, that requirement shall not apply unless and until –

    (a)   the patient is taken into custody under section 18 above and returned to the hospital where he ought to be; or

    (b)   the patient returns himself to the hospital where he ought to be within the period during which he can be taken into custody under section 18 above.

(4) Where a community patient is absent without leave on the day on which (apart from this section) the 72-hour period mentioned in section 17F above would expire, that period shall not expire until the end of the period of 72 hours beginning with the time when –

    (a)   the patient is taken into custody under section 18 above and returned to the hospital where he ought to be; or

    (b)   the patient returns himself to the hospital where he ought to be within the period during which he can be taken into custody under section 18 above.

(5) Any reference in this section, or in sections 21A to 22 below, to the time when a community treatment order would cease, or would have ceased, to be in force shall be construed as a reference to the time when it would cease, or would have ceased, to be in force by reason only of the passage of time.

NOTES

Prospective amendments. Words in subss (1), (4) and (5) prospectively inserted: MHA 2007, s 32(4), Sch 3, paras 1, 6(1)–(3). Subs (3) prospectively inserted: MHA 2007, s 37(1), (2).

21A Patients who are taken into custody or return within 28 days

(1) This section applies where a patient who is absent without leave is taken into custody under section 18 above, or returns himself to the hospital or place where he ought to be, not later than the end of the period of 28 days beginning with the first day of his absence without leave.

(2) Where the period for which the patient is liable to be detained or subject to guardianship is extended by section 21 above, any examination and report to be made and furnished in respect of the patient under section 20(3) or (6) above may be made and furnished within the period as so extended.

(3) Where the authority for the detention or guardianship of the patient is renewed by virtue of subsection (2) above after the day on which (apart from section 21 above) that authority would have expired, the renewal shall take effect as from that day.

(4) In the case of a community patient, where the period for which the community treatment order is in force is extended by section 21 above, any examination and report to be made and furnished in respect of the patient under section 20A(4) above may be made and furnished within the period as so extended.

(5) Where the community treatment period is extended by virtue of subsection (4) above after the day on which (apart from section 21 above) the order would have ceased to be in force, the extension shall take effect as from that day.

NOTES

Prospective amendments. Subss (4), (5) prospectively inserted: MHA 2007, s 32(4), Sch 3, para 7.

21B Patients who are taken into custody or return after more than 28 days

(1) This section applies where a patient who is absent without leave is taken into custody under section 18 above, or returns himself to the hospital or place where he ought to be, later than the end of the period of 28 days beginning with the first day of his absence without leave.

(2) It shall be the duty of the appropriate practitioner, within the period of one week beginning with the day on which the patient is returned or returns himself to the hospital or place where he ought to be (his 'return day') –

(a)   to examine the patient; and
(b)   if it appears to him that the relevant conditions are satisfied, to furnish to the appropriate body a report to that effect in the prescribed form; and where such a report is furnished in respect of the patient the appropriate body shall cause him to be informed.

(3) Where the patient is liable to be detained or is a community patient (as opposed to subject to guardianship) the appropriate practitioner shall, before furnishing a report under subsection (2) above, consult –

(a)   one or more other persons who have been professionally concerned with the patient's medical treatment; and
(b)   approved mental health professional.

(4) Where –

(a)   the patient would (apart from any renewal of the authority for his detention or guardianship on or after his return day) be liable to be detained or subject to guardianship after the end of the period of one week beginning with that day; or
(b)   in the case of a community patient, the community treatment order would (apart from any extension of the community treatment period on or after that day) be in force after the end of that period, he shall cease to be so liable or subject, or the community treatment period shall be deemed to expire, at the end of that period unless a report is duly furnished in respect of him under subsection (2) above.

(4A) If, in the case of a community patient, the community treatment order is revoked under section 17F above during the period of one week beginning with his return day –

(a)   subsections (2) and (4) above shall not apply; and
(b)   any report already furnished in respect of him under subsection (2) above shall be of no effect.

(5) Where the patient would (apart from section 21 above) have ceased to be liable to be detained or subject to guardianship on or before the day on which a report is duly furnished in respect of him under subsection (2) above, the report shall renew the authority for his detention or guardianship for the period prescribed in that case by section 20(2) above.

(6) Where the authority for the detention or guardianship of the patient is renewed by virtue of subsection (5) above –

(a) the renewal shall take effect as from the day on which (apart from section 21 above and that subsection) the authority would have expired; and

(b) if (apart from this paragraph) the renewed authority would expire on or before the day on which the report is furnished, the report shall further renew the authority, as from the day on which it would expire, for the period prescribed in that case by section 20(2) above.

(6A) In the case of a community patient, where the community treatment order would (apart from section 21 above) have ceased to be in force on or before the day on which a report is duly furnished in respect of him under subsection (2) above, the report shall extend the community treatment period for the period prescribed in that case by section 20A(3) above.

(6B) Where the community treatment period is extended by virtue of subsection (6A) above –

(a) the extension shall take effect as from the day on which (apart from section 21 above and that subsection) the order would have ceased to be in force; and

(b) if (apart from this paragraph) the period as so extended would expire on or before the day on which the report is furnished, the report shall further extend that period, as from the day on which it would expire, for the period prescribed in that case by section 20A(3) above.

(7) Where the authority for the detention or guardianship of the patient would expire within the period of two months beginning with the day on which a report is duly furnished in respect of him under subsection (2) above, the report shall, if it so provides, have effect also as a report duly furnished under section 20(3) or (6) above; and the reference in this subsection to authority includes any authority renewed under subsection (5) above by the report.

(7A) In the case of a community patient, where the community treatment order would (taking account of any extension under subsection (6A) above) cease to be in force within the period of two months beginning with the day on which a report is duly furnished in respect of him under subsection (2) above, the report shall, if it so provides, have effect also as a report duly furnished under section 20A(4) above.

(10) In this section –

'the appropriate body' means –

(a) in relation to a patient who is liable to be detained in a hospital, the managers of the hospital;

(b)   in relation to a patient who is subject to guardianship, the responsible local social services authority;

(c)   in relation to a community patient, the managers of the responsible hospital; and

'the relevant conditions' means –

(a)   in relation to a patient who is liable to be detained in a hospital, the conditions set out in subsection (4) of section 20 above;

(b)   in relation to a patient who is subject to guardianship, the conditions set out in subsection (7) of that section;

(c)   in relation to a community patient, the conditions set out in section 20A(6) above.

NOTES

Prospective amendments. Words in subss (2) and (3) substituted: MHA 2007, s 9(1), (5)(a). Words in subss (2), (3) prospectively inserted: MHA 2007, s 32(4), Sch 3, para 8. Words in subs (3)(b) prospectively substituted: MHA 2007, s 21, Sch 2, paras 1, 7(b). Subs (4) prospectively substituted, and subss (4A), 6(A), 6(B) and (7A) prospectively inserted: MHA 2007, s 32(4), Sch 3, paras 8(1), (4)–(7). Subss (8) and (9) prospectively repealed: MHA 2007, s 55, Sch 11, Pt 1. Definition in subs (10) prospectively repealed: MHA 2007, s 9(1), (5)(b), 55, Sch 11, Pt 3. Definitions in subs (10) prospectively substituted: MHA 2007, s 32(4), Sch 3, paras 1, 8(1), (8).

22 Special provisions as to patients sentenced to imprisonment, etc

(1) If –

(a)   a qualifying patient is detained in custody in pursuance of any sentence or order passed or made by a court in the United Kingdom (including an order committing or remanding him in custody); and

(b)   he is so detained for a period exceeding, or for successive periods exceeding in the aggregate, six months, the relevant application shall cease to have effect on expiry of that period.

(2) A patient is a qualifying patient for the purposes of this section if –

(a)   he is liable to be detained by virtue of an application for admission for treatment;

(b)   he is subject to guardianship by virtue of a guardianship application; or

(c)   he is a community patient.

(3) 'The relevant application', in relation to a qualifying patient, means –

(a)   in the case of a patient who is subject to guardianship, the guardianship application in respect of him;

(b)   in any other case, the application for admission for treatment in respect of him.

(4) The remaining subsections of this section shall apply if a qualifying patient is detained in custody as mentioned in subsection (1)(a) above but for a period not exceeding, or for successive periods not exceeding in the aggregate, six months.

(5) If apart from this subsection –

(a) the patient would have ceased to be liable to be detained or subject to guardianship by virtue of the relevant application on or before the day on which he is discharged from custody; or

(b) in the case of a community patient, the community treatment order would have ceased to be in force on or before that day, he shall not cease and shall be deemed not to have ceased to be so liable or subject, or the order shall not cease and shall be deemed not to have ceased to be in force, until the end of that day.

(6) In any case (except as provided in subsection (8) below), sections 18, 21 and 21A above shall apply in relation to the patient as if he had absented himself without leave on that day.

(7) In its application by virtue of subsection (6) above section 18 shall have effect as if –

(a) in subsection (4) for the words from 'later of' to the end there were substituted 'end of the period of 28 days beginning with the first day of his absence without leave'; and

(b) subsections (4A) and (4B) were omitted.

(8) In relation to a community patient who was not recalled to hospital under section 17E above at the time when his detention in custody began –

(a) section 18 above shall not apply; but

(b) sections 21 and 21A above shall apply as if he had absented himself without leave on the day on which he is discharged from custody and had returned himself as provided in those sections on the last day of the period of 28 days beginning with that day.

NOTES

Prospective amendments. Section prospectively substituted: MHA 2007, s 32(4), Sch 3, paras 1, 9.

23 Discharge of patients

(1) Subject to the provisions of this section and section 25 below, a patient who is for the time being liable to be detained or subject to guardianship under this Part of this Act shall cease to be so liable or subject if an order in writing discharging him absolutely from detention or guardianship is made in accordance with this section.

(1A) Subject to the provisions of this section and section 25 below, a community patient shall cease to be liable to recall under this Part of this Act, and the application for admission for treatment cease to have effect, if an order in writing discharging him from such liability is made in accordance with this section.

(1B) An order under subsection (1) or (1A) above shall be referred to in this Act as 'an order for discharge'.

(2) An order for discharge may be made in respect of a patient –

(a) where the patient is liable to be detained in a hospital in pursuance of an application for admission for assessment or for treatment by the responsible clinician, by the managers or by the nearest relative of the patient;

(b) where the patient is subject to guardianship, by the responsible clinician, by the responsible local social services authority or by the nearest relative of the patient;

(c) where the patient is a community patient, by the responsible clinician, by the managers of the responsible hospital or by the nearest relative of the patient.

(3) Where the patient falls within subsection (3A) below, an order for his discharge may, without prejudice to subsection (2) above, be made by the Secretary of State and, if arrangements have been made in respect of the patient under a contract with a National Health Service trust, NHS foundation trust, Local Health Board, Special Health Authority or Primary Care Trust, by that National Health Service trust, NHS foundation trust, Local Health Board, Special Health Authority or Primary Care Trust.

(3A) A patient falls within this subsection if –

(a) he is liable to be detained in a registered establishment in pursuance of an application for admission for assessment or for treatment; or

(b) he is a community patient and the responsible hospital is a registered establishment.

(4) The powers conferred by this section on any authority trust, board (other than an NHS foundation trust),board or body of persons may be exercised subject to subsection (3) below by any three or more members of that authority, trust, board or body authorised by them in that behalf or by three or more members of a committee or subcommittee of that authority, trust, board or body which has been authorised by them in that behalf.

(5) The reference in subsection (4) above to the members of an authority, trust, board or body or the members of a committee or sub-committee of an authority, trust, board or body, –

(a) in the case of a Local Health Board, Special Health Authority or Primary Care Trust or a committee or sub-committee of a Local Health Board, Special Health Authority or Primary Care Trust, is a reference only to the chairman of the authority or trust or board and such members (of the authority, trust, board, committee or sub-committee, as the case may be) as are not also officers of the authority or trust or board within the meaning of the National Health Service Act 2006 or the National Health Service (Wales) Act 2006; and

(b) in the case of a National Health Service trust or a committee or subcommittee of such a trust, is a reference only to the chairman of the trust and such directors or (in the case of a committee or subcommittee) members as are not also employees of the trust.

(6) The powers conferred by this section on any NHS foundation trust may be exercised by any three or more persons authorised by the board of the trust in that behalf each of whom is neither an executive director of the board nor an employee of the trust.

NOTES

Amendment. Words in subs (6) substituted: MHA 2007, s 45(1).

Prospective amendments. Words in subs (1) prospectively substituted, and subss (1A) and (1B) prospectively inserted: MHA 2007, s 32(4), Sch 3, paras 1, 10(1)–(3). Words in subss (2)(a), (b) prospectively substituted: MHA 2007, s 9(1), (6). Subss (2)(c) and (3A) prospectively inserted: MHA 2007, s 32(4), Sch 3, paras 1, 10(1), (4), (6). Words in subs (3) prospectively substituted: s 32(4), Sch 3, paras 10(1), (5)(a), (b).

24 Visiting and examination of patients

(1) For the purpose of advising as to the exercise by the nearest relative of a patient who is liable to be detained or subject to guardianship under this Part of this Act, or who is a community patient, of any power to order his discharge, any registered medical practitioner or approved clinician authorised by or on behalf of the nearest relative of the patient may, at any reasonable time, visit the patient and examine him in private.

(2) Any registered medical practitioner or approved clinician authorised for the purposes of subsection (1) above to visit and examine a patient may require the production of and inspect any records relating to the detention or treatment of the patient in any hospital or to any after-care services provided for the patient under section 117 below.

(3) Where application is made by the Secretary of State or a Local Health Board, Special Health Authority, Primary Care Trust, National Health Service trust or NHS foundation trust to exercise, any power under section 23(3) above to make an order for a patient's discharge, the following persons, that is to say –

(a) any registered medical practitioner or approved clinician authorised by the Secretary of State or, as the case may be, that Local Health Board, Special Health Authority, Primary Care Trust, National Health Service trust or NHS foundation trust; and

(b) any other person (whether a registered medical practitioner or approved clinician or not) authorised under Part II of the Care Standards Act 2000 to inspect the establishment in question;

may at any reasonable time visit the patient and interview him in private.

(4) Any person authorised for the purposes of subsection (3) above to visit a patient may require the production of and inspect any documents constituting or alleged to constitute the authority for the detention of the patient, or (as the case may be) for his liability to recall, under this Part of this Act; and any person so authorised, who is a registered medical practitioner or approved clinician, may examine the patient in private, and may require the production of and inspect any other records relating to the treatment of the patient in the establishment or to any after-care services provided for the patient under section 117 below.

NOTES

Prospective amendments. Words in subs (1) prospectively inserted: MHA 2007, s 32(4), Sch 3, paras 1, 11(2). Words prospectively inserted in subss (1), (2), (3) and (4): MHA 2007, s 9(7). Words in subss (3) and (4) prospectively substituted: MHA 2007, s 32(4), Sch 3, paras 11(1), (3), (4)(b). Words in subs (4) prospectively inserted: MHA 2007, s 32(4), Sch 3, paras 11(1), (4)(a).

25 Restrictions on discharge by nearest relative

(1) An order for the discharge of a patient who is liable to be detained in a hospital shall not be made under section 23 above by his nearest relative except after giving not less than 72 hours' notice in writing to the managers of the hospital; and if, within 72 hours after such notice has been given, the responsible clinician furnishes to the managers a report certifying that in the opinion of that clinician the patient, if discharged, would be likely to act in a manner dangerous to other persons or to himself –

    (a)   any order for the discharge of the patient made by that relative in pursuance of the notice shall be of no effect; and

    (b)   no further order for the discharge of the patient shall be made by that relative during the period of six months beginning with the date of the report.

(1A) Subsection (1) above shall apply to an order for the discharge of a community patient as it applies to an order for the discharge of a patient who is liable to be detained in a hospital, but with the reference to the managers of the hospital being read as a reference to the managers of the responsible hospital.

(2) In any case where a report under subsection (1) above is furnished in respect of a patient who is liable to be detained in pursuance of an application for admission for treatment, or in respect of a community patient, the managers shall cause the nearest relative of the patient to be informed.

NOTES

Prospective amendments. Words in subss (1) and (2) prospectively inserted: MHA 2007, Sch 3 paras 12(1), (2), (4). Subs (1A) prospectively inserted: Sch 3 paras 12(1), (3). Words in subs (1) prospectively substituted: MHA 2007, s 9(1), (8)(a), (b).

Functions of relatives of patients

26 Definition of 'relative' and 'nearest relative'

(1) In this Part of this Act 'relative' means any of the following persons –

    (a)   husband or wife or civil partner;

    (b)   son or daughter;

    (c)   father or mother;

    (d)   brother or sister;

    (e)   grandparent;

    (f)   grandchild;

    (g)   uncle or aunt;

    (h)   nephew or niece.

(2) In deducing relationships for the purposes of this section, any relationship of the half-blood shall be treated as a relationship of the whole blood, and an illegitimate person shall be treated as the legitimate child of

(a)   his mother, and
(b)   if his father has parental responsibility for him within the meaning of section 3 of the Children Act 1989, his father.

(3) In this Part of this Act, subject to the provisions of this section and to the following provisions of this Part of this Act, the 'nearest relative' means the person first described in subsection (1) above who is for the time being surviving, relatives of the whole blood being preferred to relatives of the same description of the half-blood and the elder or eldest of two or more relatives described in any paragraph of that subsection being preferred to the other or others of those relatives, regardless of sex.

(4) Subject to the provisions of this section and to the following provisions of this Part of this Act, where the patient ordinarily resides with or is cared for by one or more of his relatives (or, if he is for the time being an in-patient in a hospital, he last ordinarily resided with or was cared for by one or more of his relatives) his nearest relative shall be determined –

(a)   by giving preference to that relative or those relatives over the other or others; and
(b)   as between two or more such relatives, in accordance with subsection (3) above.

(5) Where the person who, under subsection (3) or (4) above, would be the nearest relative of a patient –

(a)   in the case of a patient ordinarily resident in the United Kingdom, the Channel Islands or the Isle of Man, is not so resident; or
(b)   is the husband or wife or civil partner of the patient, but is permanently separated from the patient, either by agreement or under an order of a court, or has deserted or has been deserted by the patient for a period which has not come to an end; or
(c)   is a person other than the husband, wife, civil partner, father or mother of the patient, and is for the time being under 18 years of age;
(d)   the nearest relative of the patient shall be ascertained as if that person were dead.

(6) In this section 'husband', 'wife' and 'civil partner' include a person who is living with the patient as the patient's husband or wife or as if they were civil partners, as the case may be (or, if the patient is for the time being an in-patient in a hospital, was so living until the patient was admitted), and has been or had been so living for a period of not less than six months; but a person shall not be treated by virtue of this subsection as the nearest relative of a married patient or a patient in a civil partnership unless the husband, wife or civil partner of the patient is disregarded by virtue of paragraph (b) of subsection (5) above.

(7) A person, other than a relative, with whom the patient ordinarily resides (or, if the patient is for the time being an in-patient in a hospital, last ordinarily

resided before he was admitted), and with whom he has or had been ordinarily residing for a period of not less than five years, shall be treated for the purposes of this Part of this Act as if he were a relative but –

(a)   shall be treated for the purposes of subsection (3) above as if mentioned last in subsection (1) above; and

(b)   shall not be treated by virtue of this subsection as the nearest relative of a married patient or a patient in a civil partnership unless the husband, wife or civil partner of the patient is disregarded by virtue of paragraph (b) of subsection (5) above.

NOTES

Amendments. Words in subss (1), (5) inserted: MHA 2007, s 26(1)–(3). Words in subss (6), (7) substituted: MHA 2007, s 26(1), (4), (5).

27 Children and young persons in care

Where –

(a)   a patient who is a child or young person is in the care of a local authority by virtue of a care order within the meaning of the Children Act 1989; or

(b)   the rights and powers of a parent of a patient who is a child or young person are vested in a local authority by virtue of section 16 of the Social Work (Scotland) Act 1968,

the authority shall be deemed to be the nearest relative of the patient in preference to any person except the patient's husband or wife or civil partner (if any).

NOTES

Amendment. Words inserted: MHA 2007, s 26(6).

28 Nearest relative of minor under guardianship, etc

(1) Where –

(a)   a guardian has been appointed for a person who has not attained the age of eighteen years; or

(b)   a residence order (as defined by section 8 of the Children Act 1989) is in force with respect to such a person, the guardian (or guardians, where there is more than one) or the person named in the residence order shall, to the exclusion of any other person, be deemed to be his nearest relative.

(2) Subsection (5) of section 26 above shall apply in relation to a person who is, or who is one of the persons, deemed to be the nearest relative of a patient by virtue of this section as it applies in relation to a person who would be the nearest relative under subsection (3) of that section.

(3) In this section 'guardian' includes a special guardian (within the meaning of the Children Act 1989), but does not include a guardian under this Part of this Act.

(4) In this section 'court' includes a court in Scotland or Northern Ireland, and 'enactment' includes an enactment of the Parliament of Northern Ireland, a Measure of the Northern Ireland Assembly and an Order in Council under Schedule 1 of the Northern Ireland Act 1974.

29 Appointment by court of acting nearest relative

(1) The county court may, upon application made in accordance with the provisions of this section in respect of a patient, by order direct that the functions of the nearest relative of the patient under this Part of this Act and sections 66 and 69 below shall, during the continuance in force of the order, be exercisable by the person specified in the order.

(1A) If the court decides to make an order on an application under subsection (1) above, the following rules have effect for the purposes of specifying a person in the order –

(a) if a person is nominated in the application to act as the patient's nearest relative and that person is, in the opinion of the court, a suitable person to act as such and is willing to do so, the court shall specify that person (or, if there are two or more such persons, such one of them as the court thinks fit);

(b) otherwise, the court shall specify such person as is, in its opinion, a suitable person to act as the patient's nearest relative and is willing to do so.

(2) An order under this section may be made on the application of –

(za) the patient;
(a) any relative of the patient;
(b) any other person with whom the patient is residing (or, if the patient is then an in-patient in a hospital, was last residing before he was admitted); or
(c) approved mental health professional;

(3) An application for an order under this section may be made upon any of the following grounds, that is to say –

(a) that the patient has no nearest relative within the meaning of this Act, or that it is not reasonably practicable to ascertain whether he has such a relative, or who that relative is;

(b) that the nearest relative of the patient is incapable of acting as such by reason of mental disorder or other illness;

(c) that the nearest relative of the patient unreasonably objects to the making of an application for admission for treatment or a guardianship application in respect of the patient; or

(d) that the nearest relative of the patient has exercised without due regard to the welfare of the patient or the interests of the public his power to discharge the patient under this Part of this Act, or is likely to do so; or

(e) that the nearest relative of the patient is otherwise not a suitable person to act as such.

(4) If, immediately before the expiration of the period for which a patient is liable to be detained by virtue of an application for admission for assessment, an application under this section, which is an application made on the ground specified in subsection (3)(c) or (d) above, is pending in respect of the patient, that period shall be extended –

    (a)   in any case, until the application under this section has been finally disposed of; and

    (b)   if an order is made in pursuance of the application under this section, for a further period of seven days;

and for the purposes of this subsection an application under this section shall be deemed to have been finally disposed of at the expiration of the time allowed for appealing from the decision of the court or, if notice of appeal has been given within that time, when the appeal has been heard or withdrawn, and 'pending' shall be construed accordingly.

(5) An order made on the ground specified in subsection (3)(a), (b) or (e) above may specify a period for which it is to continue in force unless previously discharged under section 30 below,

(6) While an order made under this section is in force, the provisions of this Part of this Act (other than this section and section 30 below) and sections 66, 69, 132(4) and 133 below shall apply in relation to the patient as if for any reference to the nearest relative of the patient there were substituted a reference to the person having the functions of that relative and (without prejudice to section 30 below) shall so apply notwithstanding that the person who was the patient's nearest relative when the order was made is no longer his nearest relative; but this subsection shall not apply to section 66 below in the case mentioned in paragraph (h) of subsection (1) of that section.

NOTES

Prospective amendments. Words substituted in subs (1): MHA 2007, s 23(1), (2). Subs (1A) prospectively inserted: MHA 2007, s 23(1), (3). Para prospectively inserted and words prospectively repealed in subs (2): MHA 2007, s 23(1), (4). Words prospectively substituted in subs (2): MHA 2007, s 21, Sch 2, paras 1, 7(c). Word prospectively repealed and para prospectively inserted in subs (3): MHA 2007, s 23(1), (5), Sch 11, Pt 4. Words prospectively repealed in subs (3): MHA 2007, ss 32(4), 55, Sch 3, paras 1, 13, Sch 11, Pt 5. Words prospectively substituted in subs (5): MHA 2007, s 23(1), (6).

30 Discharge and variation of orders under s 29

(1) An order made under section 29 above in respect of a patient may be discharged by the county court upon application made –

    (a)   in any case, by the patient or the person having the functions of the nearest relative of the patient by virtue of the order;

    (b)   where the order was made on the ground specified in paragraph (a) or paragraph (b),(b) or (e) of section 29(3) above, or where the person who was the nearest relative of the patient when the order was made has ceased to be his nearest relative, on the application of the nearest relative of the patient.

(1A) But, in the case of an order made on the ground specified in paragraph (e) of section 29(3) above, an application may not be made under subsection (1)(b) above by the person who was the nearest relative of the patient when the order was made except with leave of the county court.

(2) An order made under section 29 above in respect of a patient may be varied by the county court, on the application of the patient or of the person having the functions of the nearest relative by virtue of the order or on the application of an approved mental health professional, by substituting for the first-mentioned person a local social services authority or any other person who in the opinion of the court is a proper person to exercise those functions, being an authority or person who is willing to do so another person for the person having those functions.

(2A) If the court decides to vary an order on an application under subsection (2) above, the following rules have effect for the purposes of substituting another person –

(a) if a person is nominated in the application to act as the patient's nearest relative and that person is, in the opinion of the court, a suitable person to act as such and is willing to do so, the court shall specify that person (or, if there are two or more such persons, such one of them as the court thinks fit);

(b) otherwise, the court shall specify such person as is, in its opinion, a suitable person to act as the patient's nearest relative and is willing to do so.

(3) If the person having the functions of the nearest relative of a patient by virtue of an order under section 29 above dies –

(a) subsections (1) and (2) above shall apply as if for any reference to that person there were substituted a reference to any relative of the patient, and

(b) until the order is discharged or varied under those provisions the functions of the nearest relative under this Part of this Act and sections 66 and 69 below shall not be exercisable by any person.

(4) An order made on the ground specified in paragraph (c) or (d) of section 29(3) above shall, unless previously discharged under subsection (1) above, cease to have effect as follows –

(a) if –
    (i) on the date of the order the patient was liable to be detained or subject to guardianship by virtue of a relevant application, order or direction; or

    (ii) he becomes so liable or subject within the period of three months beginning with that date; or

    (iii) he was a community patient on the date of the order, it shall cease to have effect when he is discharged under section 23 above or 72 below or the relevant application, order or direction otherwise ceases to have effect (except as a result of his being transferred in pursuance of regulations under section 19 above);

(b)   otherwise, it shall cease to have effect at the end of the period of three months beginning with the date of the order.

(4A) In subsection (4) above, reference to a relevant application, order or direction is to any of the following –

(a)   an application for admission for treatment;
(b)   a guardianship application;
(c)   an order or direction under Part 3 of this Act (other than under section 35, 36 or 38).

(4B) An order made on the ground specified in paragraph (a), (b) or (e) of section 29(3) above shall –

(a)   if a period was specified under section 29(5) above, cease to have effect on expiry of that period, unless previously discharged under subsection (1) above;
(b)   if no such period was specified, remain in force until it is discharged under subsection (1) above.

(5) The discharge or variation under this section of an order made under section 29 above shall not affect the validity of anything previously done in pursuance of the order.

NOTES

Prospective amendments. Words inserted and substituted in subs (1): MHA 2007, s 24(1), (2). Subs (1A) prospectively inserted: MHA 2007, s 24(1), (3). Words prospectively substituted in subs (2): MHA 2007, s 21, Sch 2, paras 1, 7(d). Words prospectively inserted and prospectively substituted in subs (2): MHA 2007, s 24(1), (4). Subs (2A) prospectively inserted: MHA 2007, s 24(1), (5). Words prospectively substituted in subs (4): MHA 2007, s 24(1), (6). Paras prospectively substituted in subs (4), and subs (4A) prospectively inserted: MHA 2007, s 32(4), Sch 3, paras 1, 14(1)–(3). Subs (4B) prospectively inserted: MHA 2007, s 24(1), (7).

Supplemental

31 Procedure on applications to county court

County court rules which relate to applications authorised by this Part of this Act to be made to a county court may make provision –

(a)   for the hearing and determination of such applications otherwise than in open court;
(b)   for the admission on the hearing of such applications of evidence of such descriptions as may be specified in the rules notwithstanding anything to the contrary in any enactment or rule of law relating to the admissibility of evidence;
(c)   for the visiting and interviewing of patients in private by or under the directions of the court.

32 Regulations for purposes of Part II

(1) The Secretary of State may make regulations for prescribing anything which, under this Part of this Act, is required or authorised to be prescribed, and otherwise for carrying this Part of this Act into full effect.

(2) Regulations under this section may in particular make provision –

(a) for prescribing the form of any application, recommendation, report, order, notice or other document to be made or given under this Part of this Act;

(b) for prescribing the manner in which any such application, recommendation, report, order, notice or other document may be proved, and for regulating the service of any such application, report, order or notice;

(c) for requiring such bodies as may be prescribed by the regulations to keep such registers or other records as may be so prescribed in respect of patients liable to be detained or subject to guardianship under this Part of this Act or community patients, and to furnish or make available to those patients, and their relatives, such written statements of their rights and powers under this Act as may be so prescribed;

(d) for the determination in accordance with the regulations of the age of any person whose exact age cannot be ascertained by reference to the registers kept under the Births and Deaths Registration Act 1953; and

(e) for enabling the functions under this Part of this Act of the nearest relative of a patient to be performed, in such circumstances and subject to such conditions (if any) as may be prescribed by the regulations, by any person authorised in that behalf by that relative;

and for the purposes of this Part of this Act any application, report or notice the service of which is regulated under paragraph (b) above shall be deemed to have been received by or furnished to the authority or person to whom it is authorised or required to be furnished, addressed or given if it is duly served in accordance with the regulations.

(3) Without prejudice to subsections (1) and (2) above, but subject to section 23(4) and (6) above, regulations under this section may determine the manner in which functions under this Part of this Act of the managers of hospitals, local social services authorities, Health Authorities, Special Health Authorities, Primary Care Trusts, National Health Service trusts or NHS foundation trusts are to be exercised, and such regulations may in particular specify the circumstances in which, and the conditions subject to which, any such functions may be performed by officers of or other persons acting on behalf of those managers authorities and trusts.

NOTES

Amendment. Words inserted in subs (3): MHA 2007, s 45(2).

Prospective amendments. Words prospectively repealed in subs (2): MHA 2007, s 55, Sch 11, Pt 5. Words prospectively inserted in subs (2): MHA 2007, s 32(4), Sch 3, paras 1, 15.

33 Special provisions as to wards of court

(1) An application for the admission to hospital of a minor who is a ward of court may be made under this Part of this Act with the leave of the court; and section 11(4) above shall not apply in relation to an application so made.

(2) Where a minor who is a ward of court is liable to be detained in a hospital by virtue of an application for admission under this Part of this Act or is a community patient, any power exercisable under this Part of this Act or under section 66 below in relation to the patient by his nearest relative shall be exercisable by or with the leave of the court.

(3) Nothing in this Part of this Act shall be construed as authorising the making of a guardianship application in respect of a minor who is a ward of court, or the transfer into guardianship of any such minor.

(4) Where a community treatment order has been made in respect of a minor who is a ward of court, the provisions of this Part of this Act relating to community treatment orders and community patients have effect in relation to the minor subject to any order which the court makes in the exercise of its wardship jurisdiction; but this does not apply as regards any period when the minor is recalled to hospital under section 17E above.

NOTES

Prospective amendments. Words prospectively inserted in subs (2): s 32(4), Sch 3, paras 1, 16(1), (2). Subs (4) prospectively substituted: MHA 2007, s 32(4), Sch 3, paras 1, 16(1), (3).

34 Interpretation of Part II

(1) In this Part of this Act –

'the appropriate practitioner' means –
  (a)   in the case of a patient who is subject to the guardianship of a person other than a local social services authority, the nominated medical attendant of the patient; and
  (b)   in any other case, the responsible clinician;

'the nominated medical attendant', in relation to a patient who is subject to the guardianship of a person other than a local social services authority, means the person appointed in pursuance of regulations made under section 9(2) above to act as the medical attendant of the patient;
'registered establishment' means an establishment –
  (a)   which would not, apart from subsection (2) below, be a hospital for the purposes of this Part; and
  (b)   in respect of which a person is registered under Part II of the Care Standards Act 2000 as an independent hospital in which treatment or nursing (or both) are provided for persons liable to be detained under this Act;

'the responsible clinician' means –
  (a)   in relation to a patient liable to be detained by virtue of an application for admission for assessment or an application for

admission for treatment, or a community patient, the approved clinician with overall responsibility for the patient's case;

    (b)   in relation to a patient subject to guardianship, the approved clinician authorised by the responsible local social services authority to act (either generally or in any particular case or for any particular purpose) as the responsible clinician;

(2) Except where otherwise expressly provided, this Part of this Act applies in relation to a registered establishment, as it applies in relation to a hospital, and references in this Part of this Act to a hospital, and any reference in this Act to a hospital to which this Part of this Act applies, shall be construed accordingly.

(3) In relation to a patient who is subject to guardianship in pursuance of a guardianship application, any reference in this Part of this Act to the responsible local social services authority is a reference –

    (a)   where the patient is subject to the guardianship of a local social services authority, to that authority;

    (b)   where the patient is subject to the guardianship of a person other than a local social services authority, to the local social services authority for the area in which that person resides.

NOTES

Prospective amendments. Definition prospectively inserted in subs (1): MHA 2007, s 9(1), (9). Definitions and subs (1A) prospectively repealed: MHA 2007, s 55, Sch 11, Pt 5. Definition prospectively substituted: MHA 2007, s 9(1), (10).

PART III
PATIENTS CONCERNED IN CRIMINAL PROCEEDINGS OR UNDER SENTENCE

Remands to hospital

35 Remand to hospital for report on accused's mental condition

(1) Subject to the provisions of this section, the Crown Court or a magistrates' court may remand an accused person to a hospital specified by the court for a report on his mental condition.

(2) For the purposes of this section an accused person is –

    (a)   in relation to the Crown Court, any person who is awaiting trial before the court for an offence punishable with imprisonment or who has been arraigned before the court for such an offence and has not yet been sentenced or otherwise dealt with for the offence on which he has been arraigned;

    (b)   in relation to a magistrates' court, any person who has been convicted by the court of an offence punishable on summary conviction with imprisonment and any person charged with such an offence if the court is satisfied that he did the act or made the omission charged or he has consented to the exercise by the court of the powers conferred by this section.

(3) Subject to subsection (4) below, the powers conferred by this section may be exercised if –

    (a)   the court is satisfied, on the written or oral evidence of a registered medical practitioner, that there is reason to suspect that the accused person is suffering from mental disorder; and

    (b)   the court is of the opinion that it would be impracticable for a report on his mental condition to be made if he were remanded on bail;

but those powers shall not be exercised by the Crown Court in respect of a person who has been convicted before the court if the sentence for the offence of which he has been convicted is fixed by law.

(4) The court shall not remand an accused person to a hospital under this section unless satisfied, on the written or oral evidence of the approved clinician who would be responsible for making the report or of some other person representing the managers of the hospital, that arrangements have been made for his admission to that hospital and for his admission to it within the period of seven days beginning with the date of the remand; and if the court is so satisfied it may, pending his admission, give directions for his conveyance to and detention in a place of safety.

(5) Where a court has remanded an accused person under this section it may further remand him if it appears to the court, on the written or oral evidence of the approved clinician responsible for making the report, that a further remand is necessary for completing the assessment of the accused person's mental condition.

(6) The power of further remanding an accused person under this section may be exercised by the court without his being brought before the court if he is represented by counsel or a solicitor and his counsel or solicitor is given an opportunity of being heard.

(7) An accused person shall not be remanded or further remanded under this section for more than 28 days at a time or for more than 12 weeks in all; and the court may at any time terminate the remand if it appears to the court that it is appropriate to do so.

(8) An accused person remanded to hospital under this section shall be entitled to obtain at his own expense an independent report on his mental condition from a registered medical practitioner or approved clinician chosen by him and to apply to the court on the basis of it for his remand to be terminated under subsection (7) above.

(9) Where an accused person is remanded under this section –

    (a)   a constable or any other person directed to do so by the court shall convey the accused person to the hospital specified by the court within the period mentioned in subsection (4) above; and

    (b)   the managers of the hospital shall admit him within that period and thereafter detain him in accordance with the provisions of this section.

(10) If an accused person absconds from a hospital to which he has been remanded under this section, or while being conveyed to or from that hospital, he may be arrested without warrant by any constable and shall, after being arrested, be brought as soon as practicable before the court that remanded him; and the court may thereupon terminate the remand and deal with him in any way in which it could have dealt with him if he had not been remanded under this section.

NOTES

Prospective amendments. Words prospectively substituted in subs (3)(a): MHA 2007, s 1(4), Sch 1, Pt 1, paras 1, 5. Words prospectively substituted in subss (4), (5): MHA 2007, s 10(1), (2)(a). Words inserted in subs (8): MHA 2007, s 10(1), (2)(b).

36 Remand of accused person to hospital for treatment

(1) Subject to the provisions of this section, the Crown Court may, instead of remanding an accused person in custody, remand him to a hospital specified by the court if satisfied, on the written or oral evidence of two registered medical practitioners, that

    (a)   he is suffering from mental disorder of a nature or degree which makes it appropriate for him to be detained in a hospital for medical treatment; and

    (b)   appropriate medical treatment is available for him.

(2) For the purposes of this section an accused person is any person who is in custody awaiting trial before the Crown Court for an offence punishable with imprisonment (other than an offence the sentence for which is fixed by law) or who at any time before sentence is in custody in the course of a trial before that court for such an offence.

(3) The court shall not remand an accused person under this section to a hospital unless it is satisfied, on the written or oral evidence of the approved clinician who would have overall responsibility for his case or of some other person representing the managers of the hospital, that arrangements have been made for his admission to that hospital and for his admission to it within the period of seven days beginning with the date of the remand; and if the court is so satisfied it may, pending his admission, give directions for his conveyance to and detention in a place of safety.

(4) Where a court has remanded an accused person under this section it may further remand him if it appears to the court, on the written or oral evidence of the responsible clinician, that a further remand is warranted.

(5) The power of further remanding an accused person under this section may be exercised by the court without his being brought before the court if he is represented by counsel or a solicitor and his counsel or solicitor is given an opportunity of being heard.

(6) An accused person shall not be remanded or further remanded under this section for more than 28 days at a time or for more than 12 weeks in all; and the court may at any time terminate the remand if it appears to the court that it is appropriate to do so.

(7) An accused person remanded to hospital under this section shall be entitled to obtain at his own expense an independent report on his mental condition from a registered medical practitioner or approved clinician chosen by him and to apply to the court on the basis of it for his remand to be terminated under subsection (6) above.

(8) Subsections (9) and (10) of section 35 above shall have effect in relation to a remand under this section as they have effect in relation to a remand under that section.

NOTES

Prospective amendments. Subs (1)(a) prospectively substituted: MHA 2007, s 1(4), Sch 1, Pt 1, paras 1, 6. Subs (1)(b) and preceding word prospectively inserted: MHA 2007, s 5(1), (2). Words prospectively substituted in subss (3), (4), and words prospectively inserted in subs (7): MHA 2007, s 10(3)(a)–(c).

Hospital and guardianship orders

37 Powers of courts to order hospital admission or guardianship

(1) Where a person is convicted before the Crown Court of an offence punishable with imprisonment other than an offence the sentence for which is fixed by law, or is convicted by a magistrates' court of an offence punishable on summary conviction with imprisonment, and the conditions mentioned in subsection (2) below are satisfied, the court may by order authorise his admission to and detention in such hospital as may be specified in the order or, as the case may be, place him under the guardianship of a local social services authority or of such other person approved by a local social services authority as may be so specified.

(1A) In the case of an offence the sentence for which would otherwise fall to be imposed –

(a)   under section 51A(2) of the Firearms Act 1968,
(b)   under section 110(2) or 111(2) of the Powers of Criminal Courts (Sentencing) Act 2000
(c)   under any of sections 225 to 228 of the Criminal Justice Act 2003, or
(d)   under section 29(4) or (6) of the Violent Crime Reduction Act 2006 (minimum sentences in certain cases of using someone to mind a weapon),

nothing in those provisions shall prevent a court from making an order under subs (1) above for the admission of the offender to a hospital.

(1B) References in subsection (1A) above to a sentence falling to be imposed under any of the provisions mentioned in that subsection are to be read in accordance with section 305(4) of the Criminal Justice Act 2003.

(2) The conditions referred to in subsection (1) above are that –

    (a)   the court is satisfied, on the written or oral evidence of two registered medical practitioners, that the offender is suffering from mental disorder and that either –

        (i)   the mental disorder from which the offender is suffering is of a nature or degree which makes it appropriate for him to be detained in a hospital for medical treatment and appropriate medical treatment is available for him or

        (ii)   in the case of an offender who has attained the age of 16 years, the mental disorder is of a nature or degree which warrants his reception into guardianship under this Act; and

    (b)   the court is of the opinion, having regard to all the circumstances Including the nature of the offence and the character and antecedents of the offender, and to the other available methods of dealing with him, that the most suitable method of disposing of the case is by means of an order under this section.

(3) Where a person is charged before a magistrates' court with any act or omission as an offence and the court would have power, on convicting him of that offence, to make an order under subsection (1) above in his case as being a person suffering from mental illness or severe mental impairment, then, if the court is satisfied that the accused did the act or made the omission charged, the court may, if it thinks fit, make such an order without convicting him.

(4) An order for the admission of an offender to a hospital (in this Act referred to as 'a hospital order') shall not be made under this section unless the court is satisfied on the written or oral evidence of the approved clinician who would have overall responsibility for his case or of some other person representing the managers of the hospital that arrangements have been made for his admission to that hospital, and for his admission to it within the period of 28 days beginning with the date of the making of such an order; and the court may, pending his admission within that period, give such directions as it thinks fit for his conveyance to and detention in a place of safety.

(5) If within the said period of 28 days it appears to the Secretary of State that by reason of an emergency or other special circumstances it is not practicable for the patient to be received into the hospital specified in the order, he may give directions for the admission of the patient to such other hospital as appears to be appropriate instead of the hospital so specified; and where such directions are given –

    (a)   the Secretary of State shall cause the person having the custody of the patient to be informed, and

    (b)   the hospital order shall have effect as if the hospital specified in the directions were substituted for the hospital specified in the order.

(6) An order placing an offender under the guardianship of a local social services authority or of any other person (in this Act referred to as 'a

guardianship order') shall not be made under this section unless the court is satisfied that that authority or person is willing to receive the offender into guardianship.

(7) A hospital order or guardianship order shall specify the form or forms of mental disorder referred to in subsection (2)(a) above from which, upon the evidence taken into account under that subsection, the offender is found by the court to be suffering; and no such order shall be made unless the offender is described by each of the practitioners whose evidence is taken into account under that subsection as suffering from the same one of those forms of mental disorder, whether or not he is also described by either of them as suffering from another of them.

(8) Where an order is made under this section, the court shall not –

    (a)   pass sentence of imprisonment or impose a fine or make a community order (within the meaning of Part 12 of the Criminal Justice Act 2003) in respect of the offence,

    (b)   if the order under this section is a hospital order, make a referral order (within the meaning of the Powers of Criminal Courts (Sentencing) Act 2000) in respect of the offence, or

    (c)   make in respect of the offender a supervision order (within the meaning of that Act) or an order under section 150 of that Act (binding over of parent or guardian),

but the court may make any other order which it has power to make apart from this section; and for the purposes of this subsection 'sentence of imprisonment' includes any sentence or order for detention.

NOTES

Prospective amendments. Words in subs (2)(a) prospectively substituted: MHA 2007, s 1(4), Sch 1, Pt 1, paras 1, 7(a). Words in subs (2)(a)(i) prospectively substituted: MHA 2007, s 4(1), (5). Words in subs (3) prospectively repealed: MHA 2007, ss 1(4), 55, Sch 1, Pt 1, paras 1, 7(b), Sch 11, Pt 1. Words in subs (4) prospectively substituted: MHA 2007, s 10(1), (4). Subs (7) prospectively repealed: MHA 2007, s 55, Sch 11, Pt 1.

38 Interim hospital orders

(1) Where a person is convicted before the Crown Court of an offence punishable with imprisonment (other than an offence the sentence for which is fixed by law) or is convicted by a magistrates' court of an offence punishable on summary conviction with imprisonment and the court before or by which he is convicted is satisfied, on the written or oral evidence of two registered medical practitioners –

    (a)   that the offender is suffering from mental disorder; and

    (b)   that there is reason to suppose that the mental disorder from which the offender is suffering is such that it may be appropriate for a hospital order to be made in his case,

the court may, before making a hospital order or dealing with him in some other way, make an order (in this Act referred to as 'an interim hospital order') authorising his admission to such hospital as may be specified in the order and his detention there in accordance with this section.

(2) In the case of an offender who is subject to an interim hospital order the court may make a hospital order without his being brought before the court if he is represented by counsel or a solicitor and his counsel or solicitor is given an opportunity of being heard.

(3) At least one of the registered medical practitioners whose evidence is taken into account under subsection (1) above shall be employed at the hospital which is to be specified in the order.

(4) An interim hospital order shall not be made for the admission of an offender to a hospital unless the court is satisfied, on the written or oral evidence of the approved clinician who would have overall responsibility for his case or of some other person representing the managers of the hospital, that arrangements have been made for his admission to that hospital and for his admission to it within the period of 28 days beginning with the date of the order; and if the court is so satisfied the court may, pending his admission, give directions for his conveyance to and detention in a place of safety.

(5) An interim hospital order –

(a) shall be in force for such period, not exceeding 12 weeks, as the court may specify when making the order; but

(b) may be renewed for further periods of not more than 28 days at a time if it appears to the court, on the written or oral evidence of the responsible clinician, that the continuation of the order is warranted;

but no such order shall continue in force for more than twelve months in all and the court shall terminate the order if it makes a hospital order in respect of the offender or decides after considering the written or oral evidence of the responsible clinician, to deal with the offender in some other way.

(6) The power of renewing an interim hospital order may be exercised without the offender being brought before the court if he is represented by counsel or a solicitor and his counsel or solicitor is given an opportunity of being heard.

(7) If an offender absconds from a hospital in which he is detained in pursuance of an interim hospital order, or while being conveyed to or from such a hospital, he may be arrested without warrant by a constable and shall, after being arrested, be brought as soon as practicable before the court that made the order; and the court may thereupon terminate the order and deal with him in any way in which it could have dealt with him if no such order had been made.

NOTES

Prospective amendments. Words in subs (1)(a) prospectively substituted: MHA 2007, s 1(4), Sch 1, Pt 1, paras 1, 8. Words in subss (4), (5) prospectively substituted: MHA 2007, s 10(1), (5)(a), (b).

39 Information as to hospitals

(1) Where a court is minded to make a hospital order or interim hospital order in respect of any person it may request –

    (a)   the Primary Care Trust or Local Health Board for the area in which that person resides or last resided; or

    (b)   the National Assembly for Wales or any other Primary Care Trust or Local Health Board that appears to the court to be appropriate,

to furnish the court with such information as that Primary Care Trust or Local Health Board or National Assembly for Wales have or can reasonably obtain with respect to the hospital or hospitals (if any) in their area or elsewhere at which arrangements could be made for the admission of that person in pursuance of the order, and that Primary Care Trust or Local Health Board or National Assembly for Wales shall comply with any such request.

(1A) In relation to a person who has not attained the age of 18 years, subsection (1) above shall have effect as if the reference to the making of a hospital order included a reference to a remand under section 35 or 36 above or the making of an order under section 44 below.

(1B) Where the person concerned has not attained the age of 18 years, the information which may be requested under subsection (1) above includes, in particular, information about the availability of accommodation or facilities designed so as to be specially suitable for patients who have not attained the age of 18 years.'

(2) (*repealed*)

NOTES

Prospective amendments. Subss (1A), (1B) prospectively inserted: MHA 2007 s 31(1), (2).

39A Information to facilitate guardianship orders

(1) Where a court is minded to make a hospital order or interim hospital order in respect of any offender it may request the local social services authority for the area in which the offender resides or last resided, or any other local social services authority which seems to the court to be appropriate –

    (a)   to inform the court whether it on any person approved by it is willing to receive the offender into guardianship; and

    (b)   if so, to give such information as it reasonably can about how it or the other person could be expected to exercise in relation to the offender the powers conferred by section 40(2) below

and that authority shall comply with any such request.

40 Effect of hospital orders, guardianship orders and interim hospital orders

(1) A hospital order shall be sufficient authority –

(a) for a constable, an approved mental health professional or any other person directed to do so by the court to convey the patient to the hospital specified in the order within a period of 28 days; and

(b) for the managers of the hospital to admit him at any time within that period and thereafter detain him in accordance with the provisions of this Act.

(2) A guardianship order shall confer on the authority or person named in the order as guardian the same powers as a guardianship application made and accepted under Part II of this Act.

(3) Where an interim hospital order is made in respect of an offender –

(a) a constable or any other person directed to do so by the court shall convey the offender to the hospital specified in the order within the period mentioned in section 38(4) above; and

(b) the managers of the hospital shall admit him within that period and thereafter detain him in accordance with the provisions of section 38 above.

(4) A patient who is admitted to a hospital in pursuance of a hospital order, or placed under guardianship by a guardianship order, shall, subject to the provisions of this subsection, be treated for the purposes of the provisions of this Act mentioned in Part I of Schedule 1 to this Act as if he had been so admitted or placed on the date of the order in pursuance of an application for admission for treatment or a guardianship application, as the case may be, duly made under Part II of this Act, but subject to any modifications of those provisions specified in that Part of that Schedule.

(5) Where a patient is admitted to a hospital in pursuance of a hospital order, or placed under guardianship by a guardianship order, any previous application, hospital order or guardianship order by virtue of which he was liable to be detained in a hospital or subject to guardianship shall cease to have effect; but if the first-mentioned order, or the conviction on which it was made, is quashed on appeal, this subsection shall not apply and section 22 above shall have effect as if during any period for which the patient was liable to be detained or subject to guardianship under the order, he had been detained in custody as mentioned in that section.

(6) Where –

(a) a patient admitted to a hospital in pursuance of a hospital order is absent without leave;

(b) a warrant to arrest him has been issued under section 72 of the Criminal Justice Act 1967; and

(c) he is held pursuant to the warrant in any country or territory other than the United Kingdom, any of the Channel Islands and the Isle of Man, he shall be treated as having been taken into custody under section 18 above on first being so held.

NOTES

Prospective amendments. Words in subs (1)(a) prospectively substituted: MHA 2007, s 21, Sch 2, paras 1, 7(e).

Restriction orders

41 Power of higher courts to restrict discharge from hospital

(1) Where a hospital order is made in respect of an offender by the Crown Court, and it appears to the court, having regard to the nature of the offence, the antecedents of the offender and the risk of his committing further offences if set at large, that it is necessary for the protection of the public from serious harm so to do, the court may, subject to the provisions of this section, further order that the offender shall be subject to the special restrictions set out in this section; and an order under this section shall be known as 'a restriction order'.

(2) A restriction order shall not be made in the case of any person unless at least one of the registered medical practitioners whose evidence is taken into account by the court under section 37(2)(a) above has given evidence orally before the court.

(3) The special restrictions applicable to a patient in respect of whom a restriction order is in force are as follows –

    (a)   none of the provisions of Part II of this Act relating to the duration, renewal and expiration of authority for the detention of patients shall apply, and the patient shall continue to be liable to be detained by virtue of the relevant hospital order until he is duly discharged under the said Part II or absolutely discharged under section 42, 73, 74 or 75 below;

    (aa)   none of the provisions of Part II of this Act relating to community treatment orders and community patients shall apply;

    (b)   no application shall be made to a Mental Health Review Tribunal in respect of a patient under section 66 or 69(1) below;

    (c)   the following powers shall be exercisable only with the consent of the Secretary of State, namely –

        (i)   power to grant leave of absence to the patient under section 17 above;

        (ii)   power to transfer the patient in pursuance of regulations under section 19 above or in pursuance of subsection (3) of that section; and

        (iii)   power to order the discharge of the patient under section 23 above; and if leave of absence is granted under the said section 17 power to recall the patient under that section shall vest in the Secretary of State as well as the responsible clinician; and

    (d)   the power of the Secretary of State to recall the patient under the said section 17 and power to take the patient into custody and return him under section 18 above may be exercised at any time; and in relation to any such patient section 40(4) above shall have effect as if it referred to Part II of Schedule 1 to this Act instead of Part I of that Schedule.

(4) A hospital order shall not cease to have effect under section 40(5) above if a restriction order in respect of the patient is in force at the material time.

(5) Where a restriction order in respect of a patient ceases to have effect while the relevant hospital order continues in force, the provisions of section 40 above and Part I of Schedule 1 to this Act shall apply to the patient as if he had been admitted to the hospital in pursuance of a hospital order (without a restriction order) made on the date on which the restriction order ceased to have effect.

(6) While a person is subject to a restriction order the responsible clinician shall at such intervals (not exceeding one year) as the Secretary of State may direct examine and report to the Secretary of State on that person; and every report shall contain such particulars as the Secretary of State may require.

NOTES

Amendments. Words in subs (1) repealed: MHA 2007, ss 40(1), 55, Sch 11, Pt 8. Words in subss (3)(c), (6) substituted: MHA 2007, s 10(1), (6).

Prospective amendments. Words in subs (3)(aa) prospectively substituted: MHA 2007, s 32(4), Sch 3, paras 1, 17.

42 Powers of Secretary of State in respect of patients subject to restriction orders

(1) If the Secretary of State is satisfied that in the case of any patient a restriction order is no longer required for the protection of the public from serious harm, he may direct that the patient cease to be subject to the special restrictions set out in section 41(3) above; and where the Secretary of State so directs, the restriction order shall cease to have effect, and section 41(5) above shall apply accordingly.

(2) At any time while a restriction order is in force in respect of a patient, the Secretary of State may, if he thinks fit, by warrant discharge the patient from hospital, either absolutely or subject to conditions; and where a person is absolutely discharged under this subsection, he shall thereupon cease to be liable to be detained by virtue of the relevant hospital order, and the restriction order shall cease to have effect accordingly.

(3) The Secretary of State may at any time during the continuance in force of a restriction order in respect of a patient who has been conditionally discharged under subsection (2) above by warrant recall the patient to such hospital as may be specified in the warrant.

(4) Where a patient is recalled as mentioned in subsection (3) above –

(a) if the hospital specified in the warrant is not the hospital from which the patient was conditionally discharged, the hospital order and the restriction order shall have effect as if the hospital specified in the warrant were substituted for the hospital specified in the hospital order;

(b) in any case, the patient shall be treated for the purposes of section 18 above as if he had absented himself without leave from the hospital specified in the warrant.

(5) If a restriction order in respect of a patient ceases to have effect after the patient has been conditionally discharged under this section, the patient shall, unless previously recalled under subsection (3) above, be deemed to be absolutely discharged on the date when the order ceases to have effect, and shall cease to be liable to be detained by virtue of the relevant hospital order accordingly.

(6) The Secretary of State may, if satisfied that the attendance at any place in Great Britain of a patient who is subject to a restriction order is desirable in the interests of justice or for the purposes of any public inquiry, direct him to be taken to that place; and where a patient is directed under this subsection to be taken to any place he shall, unless the Secretary of State otherwise directs, be kept in custody while being so taken, while at that place and while being taken back to the hospital in which he is liable to be detained.

NOTES

Amendment. Words in subs (4)(b) repealed: MHA 2007, ss 40(2), 55, Sch 11, Pt 8.

43 Power of magistrates' courts to commit for restriction order

(1) If in the case of a person of or over the age of 14 years who is convicted by a magistrates' court of an offence punishable on summary conviction with imprisonment –

- (a) the conditions which under section 37(1) above are required to be satisfied for the making of a hospital order are satisfied in respect of the offender; but
- (b) it appears to the court, having regard to the nature of the offence, the antecedents of the offender and the risk of his committing further offences if set at large, that if a hospital order is made a restriction order should also be made, the court may, instead of making a hospital order or dealing with him in any other manner, commit him in custody to the Crown Court to be dealt with in respect of the offence.

(2) Where an offender is committed to the Crown Court under this section, the Crown Court shall inquire into the circumstances of the case and may –

- (a) if that court would have power so to do under the foregoing provisions of this Part of this Act upon the conviction of the offender before that court of such an offence as is described in section 37(1) above, make a hospital order in his case, with or without a restriction order;
- (b) if the court does not make such an order, deal with the offender in any other manner in which the magistrates' court might have dealt with him.

(3) The Crown Court shall have the same power to make orders under sections 35, 36 and 38 above in the case of a person committed to the court under this section as the Crown Court has under those sections in the case of an accused person within the meaning of section 35 or 36 above or of a person convicted before that court as mentioned in section 38 above.

(4) The powers of a magistrates' court under section 3 or 3B of the Powers of Criminal Courts (Sentencing) Act 2000 (which enable such a court to commit an offender to the Crown Court where the court is of the opinion, or it appears to the court, as mentioned in the section in question) shall also be exercisable by a magistrates' court where it is of that opinion (or it so appears to it) unless a hospital order is made in the offender's case with a restriction order.

44 Committal to hospital under s 43

(1) Where an offender is committed under section 43(1) above and the magistrates' court by which he is committed is satisfied on written or oral evidence that arrangements have been made for the admission of the offender to a hospital in the event of an order being made under this section, the court may, instead of committing him in custody, by order direct him to be admitted to that hospital, specifying it, and to be detained there until the case is disposed of by the Crown Court, and may give such directions as it thinks fit for his production from the hospital to attend the Crown Court by which his case is to be dealt with.

(2) The evidence required by subsection (1) above shall be given by the approved clinician who would have overall responsibility for the offender's case or by some other person representing the managers of the hospital in question.

(3) The power to give directions under section 37(4) above, section 37(5) above and section 40(1) above shall apply in relation to an order under this section as they apply in relation to a hospital order, but as if references to the period of 28 days mentioned in section 40(1) above were omitted; and subject as aforesaid an order under this section shall, until the offender's case is disposed of by the Crown Court, have the same effect as a hospital order together with a restriction order.

NOTES

Amendment. Words in subs (3) repealed subject to saving: MHA 2007, ss 40(3)(a), 55, Sch 11, Pt 8. For saving see MHA 2007, s 40(7).

Prospective amendment. Words in subs (2) prospectively substituted: MHA 2007, s 10(1), (7).

45 Appeals from magistrates' courts

(1) Where on the trial of an information charging a person with an offence a magistrates' court makes a hospital order or guardianship order in respect of him without convicting him, he shall have the same right of appeal against the order as if it had been made on his conviction; and on any such appeal the Crown Court shall have the same powers as if the appeal had been against both conviction and sentence.

(2) An appeal by a child or young person with respect to whom any such order has been made, whether the appeal is against the order or against the finding upon which the order was made, may be brought by him or by his parent or guardian on his behalf.

Hospital and limitation directions

45A Power of higher courts to direct hospital admission

(1) This section applies where, in the case of a person convicted before the Crown Court of an offence the sentence for which is not fixed by law –

(a)   the conditions mentioned in subsection (2) below are fulfilled; and

(b)   the court considers making a hospital order in respect of him before deciding to impose a sentence of imprisonment ('the relevant sentence') in respect of the offence.

(2) The conditions referred to in subsection (1) above are that the court is satisfied, on the written or oral evidence of two registered medical practitioners –

(a)   that the offender is suffering from mental disorder;

(b)   that the mental disorder from which the offender is suffering is of a nature or degree which makes it appropriate for him to be detained in a hospital for medical treatment; and

(c)   that appropriate medical treatment is available for him.

(3) The court may give both of the following directions, namely –

(a)   a direction that, instead of being removed to and detained in a prison, the offender be removed to and detained in such hospital as may be specified in the direction (in this Act referred to as a 'hospital direction'); and

(b)   a direction that the offender be subject to the special restrictions set out in section 41 above (in this Act referred to as a 'limitation direction').

(4) A hospital direction and a limitation direction shall not be given in relation to an offender unless at least one of the medical practitioners whose evidence is taken into account by the court under subsection (2) above has given evidence orally before the court.

(5) A hospital direction and a limitation direction shall not be given in relation to an offender unless the court is satisfied on the written or oral evidence of the approved clinician who would have overall responsibility for his case, or of some other person representing the managers of the hospital that arrangements have been made –

(a)   for his admission to that hospital; and

(b)   for his admission to it within the period of 28 days beginning with the day of the giving of such directions;

and the court may, pending his admission within that period, give such directions as it thinks fit for his conveyance to and detention in a place of safety.

(6) If within the said period of 28 days it appears to the Secretary of State that by reason of an emergency or other special circumstances it is not practicable for the patient to be received into the hospital specified in the hospital

direction, he may give instructions for the admission of the patient to such other hospital as appears to be appropriate instead of the hospital so specified.

(7) Where such instructions are given –

(a) the Secretary of State shall cause the person having the custody of the patient to be informed, and

(b) the hospital direction shall have effect as if the hospital specified in the instructions were substituted for the hospital specified in the hospital direction.

(8) Section 38(1) and (5) and section 39 above shall have effect as if any reference to the making of a hospital order included a reference to the giving of a hospital direction and a limitation direction.

(9) A hospital direction and a limitation direction given in relation to an offender shall have effect not only as regards the relevant sentence but also (so far as applicable) as regards any other sentence of imprisonment imposed on the same or a previous occasion.

NOTES

Prospective amendments. Words in subs (2)(a) prospectively substituted: MHA, s 1(4), Sch 1, Pt 1, paras 1, 9. Subs (2)(c) prospectively substituted: MHA 2007, s 4(1), (6). Words in subs (5) prospectively substituted: MHA 2007, s 10(1), (8). Subss (10), (11) prospectively repealed: MHA 2007, s 55, Sch 11, Pt 1.

45B Effect of hospital and limitation directions

(1) A hospital direction and a limitation direction shall be sufficient authority –

(a) for a constable or any other person directed to do so by the court to convey the patient to the hospital specified in the hospital direction within a period of 28 days; and

(b) for the managers of the hospital to admit him at any time within that period and thereafter detain him in accordance with the provisions of this Act.

(2) With respect to any person –

(a) a hospital direction shall have effect as a transfer direction; and

(b) a limitation direction shall have effect as a restriction direction.

(3) While a person is subject to a hospital direction and a limitation direction the responsible medical officer responsible clinician shall at such intervals (not exceeding one year) as the Secretary of State may direct examine and report to the Secretary of State on that person; and every report shall contain such particulars as the Secretary of State may require.

NOTES

Prospective amendments. Words in subs (3) prospectively substituted: MHA 2007, s 10(1), (9)(a).

46 ...

(*repealed*)

Transfer to hospital of prisoners etc

47 Removal to hospital of persons serving sentences of imprisonment, etc

(1) If in the case of a person serving a sentence of imprisonment the Secretary of State is satisfied, by reports from at least two registered medical practitioners –

(a)   that the said person is suffering from mental disorder; and

(b)   that the mental disorder from which that person is suffering is of a nature or degree which makes it appropriate for him to be detained in a hospital for medical treatment; and

(c)   that appropriate medical treatment is available for him;

the Secretary of State may, if he is of the opinion having regard to the public interest and all the circumstances that it is expedient so to do, by warrant direct that that person be removed to and detained in such hospital as may be specified in the direction; and a direction under this section shall be known as 'a transfer direction'.

(2) A transfer direction shall cease to have effect at the expiration of the period of 14 days beginning with the date on which it is given unless within that period the person with respect to whom it was given has been received into the hospital specified in the direction.

(3) A transfer direction with respect to any person shall have the same effect as a hospital order made in his case.

(4) (*repealed*)

(5) References in this Part of this Act to a person serving a sentence of imprisonment include references –

(a)   to a person detained in pursuance of any sentence or order for detention made by a court in criminal proceedings or service disciplinary proceedings (other than an order made in consequence of a finding of insanity or unfitness to stand trial or a sentence of service detention within the meaning of the Armed Forces Act 2006);

(b)   to a person committed to custody under section 115(3) of the Magistrates' Courts Act 1980 (which relates to persons who fail to comply with an order to enter into recognisances to keep the peace or be of good behaviour); and

(c)   to a person committed by a court to a prison or other institution to which the Prison Act 1952 applies in default of payment of any sum adjudged to be paid on his conviction.

(6) In subsection (5)(a) 'service disciplinary proceedings' means proceedings in respect of a service offence within the meaning of the Armed Forces Act 2006.

NOTES

Prospective amendments. Words in subs (1)(a) prospectively substituted: MHA 2007, s 1(4), Sch 1, Pt 1, paras 1, 10. Words in subs (1)(b) prospectively repealed, and subs (1)(c) and preceding word prospectively inserted: MHA 2007, s 4(1), (7). Subs (4) prospectively repealed: s 55, Sch 11, Pt 1. Words in subs (5)(a) prospectively inserted and substituted, and subs (6) prospectively inserted: Armed Forces Act 2006, s 378(1), Sch 16, para 97(1)–(3).

48 Removal to hospital of other prisoners

(1) If in the case of a person to whom this section applies the Secretary of State is satisfied by the same reports as are required for the purposes of section 47 above that that person is suffering from mental illness or severe mental impairment of a nature or degree which makes it appropriate for him to be detained in a hospital for medical treatment and that he is in urgent need of such treatment,

    (a)   that person is suffering from mental disorder of a nature or degree which makes it appropriate for him to be detained in hospital for medical treatment; and

    (b)   he is in urgent need of such treatment; and

    (c)   appropriate medical treatment is available for him;

the Secretary of State shall have the same power of giving a transfer direction in respect of him under that section as if he were serving a sentence of imprisonment.

(2) This section applies to the following persons, that is to say –

    (a)   persons detained in a prison or remand centre, not being person serving a sentence of imprisonment or persons falling within the following paragraphs of this subsection;

    (b)   persons remanded in custody by a magistrates' court;

    (c)   civil prisoners, that is to say, persons committed by a court to prison for a limited term, who are not persons falling to be dealt with under section 47 above;

    (d)   persons detained under the Immigration Act 1971 or under section 62 of the Nationality, Immigration and Asylum Act 2002 (detention by Secretary of State).

(3) Subsections (2) and (3) of section 47 above shall apply for the purposes of this section and of any transfer direction given by virtue of this section as they apply for the purposes of that section and of any transfer direction under that section.

NOTES

Prospective amendments. Words in subs (1) prospectively repealed and subs (1)(a), (b) prospectively substituted: MHA 2007, s 1(4), Sch 1, Pt 1, paras 1, 11(a); Subs(1)(c) prospectively inserted: MHA 2007, s 5(1), (3); Words in subs (3) prospectively substituted: s 1(4), Sch 1, Pt 1, paras 1, 11(b).

49 Restriction on discharge of prisoners removed to hospital

(1) Where a transfer direction is given in respect of any person, the Secretary of State, if he thinks fit, may by warrant further direct that that person shall be subject to the special restrictions set out in section 41 above; and where the Secretary of State gives a transfer direction in respect of any such person as is described in paragraph (a) or (b) of section 48(2) above, he shall also give a direction under this section applying those restrictions to him.

(2) A direction under this section shall have the same effect as a restriction order made under section 41 above and shall be known as 'a restriction direction'.

(3) While a person is subject to a restriction direction the responsible clinician shall at such intervals (not exceeding one year) as the Secretary of State may direct examine and report to the Secretary of State on that person; and every report shall contain such particulars as the Secretary of State may require.

NOTES

Prospective amendments. Words in subs (3) prospectively substituted: MHA 2007, s 10(9)(b).

50 Further provisions as to prisoners under sentence

(1) Where a transfer direction and a restriction direction have been given in respect of a person serving a sentence of imprisonment and before his release date the Secretary of State is notified by the responsible clinician, approved clinician or a Mental Health Review Tribunal that that person no longer requires treatment in hospital for mental disorder or that no effective treatment for his disorder can be given in the hospital to which he has been removed, the Secretary of State may –

    (a)   by warrant direct that he be remitted to any prison or other institution in which he might have been detained if he had not been removed to hospital, there to be dealt with as if he had not been so removed; or

    (b)   exercise any power of releasing him on licence or discharging him under supervision which could have been exercisable if he had been remitted to such a prison or institution as aforesaid,

and on his arrival in the prison or other institution or, as the case may be, his release or discharge as aforesaid, the transfer direction and the restriction direction shall cease to have effect.

(2) A restriction direction in the case of a person serving a sentence of imprisonment shall cease to have effect, if it has not previously done so, on his release date.

(3) In this section, references to a person's release date are to the day (if any) on which he would be entitled to be released (whether unconditionally or on licence) from any prison or other institution in which he might have been detained if the transfer direction had not been given; and in determining that day there shall be disregarded –

(a) any powers that would be exercisable by the Parole Board if he were detained in such a prison or other institution, and

(b) any practice of the Secretary of State in relation to the early release under discretionary powers of persons detained in such a prison or other institution.

(4) For the purposes of section 49(2) of the Prison Act 1952 (which provides for discounting from the sentences of certain prisoners periods while they are unlawfully at large) a patient who, having been transferred in pursuance of a transfer direction from any such institution as is referred to in that section, is at large in circumstances in which he is liable to be taken into custody under any provision of this Act, shall be treated as unlawfully at large and absent from that institution.

(5) The preceding provisions of this section shall have effect as if –

(a) the reference in subsection (1) to a transfer direction and a restriction direction having been given in respect of a person serving a sentence of imprisonment included a reference to a hospital direction and a limitation direction having been given in respect of a person sentenced to imprisonment;

(b) the reference in subsection (2) to a restriction direction included a reference to a limitation direction; and

(c) references in subsections (3) and (4) to a transfer direction included references to a hospital direction.

NOTES

Prospective amendments. Words prospectively substituted: MHA 2007, s 11(1), (2)(a).

51 Further provisions as to detained persons

(1) This section has effect where a transfer direction has been given in respect of any such person as is described in paragraph (a) of section 48(2) above and that person is in this section referred to as 'the detainee'.

(2) The transfer direction shall cease to have effect when the detainee's case is disposed of by the court having jurisdiction to try or otherwise deal with him, but without prejudice to any power of that court to make a hospital order or other order under this Part of this Act in his case.

(3) If the Secretary of State is notified by the responsible clinician, any other approved clinician or a Mental Health Review Tribunal at any time before the detainee's case is disposed of by that court –

(a) that the detainee no longer requires treatment in hospital for mental disorder; or

(b) that no effective treatment for his disorder can be given at the hospital to which he has been removed,

the Secretary of State may by warrant direct that he be remitted to any place where he might have been detained if he had not been removed to hospital, there to be dealt with as if he had not been so removed, and on his arrival at the place to which he is so remitted the transfer direction shall cease to have effect.

(4) If (no direction having been given under subsection (3) above) the court having jurisdiction to try or otherwise deal with the detainee is satisfied on the written or oral evidence of the ~~responsible medical officer~~ responsible clinician –

    (a)   that the detainee no longer requires treatment in hospital for mental disorder; or

    (b)   that no effective treatment for his disorder can be given at the hospital to which he has been removed,

the court may order him to be remitted to any such place as is mentioned in subsection (3) above or, subject to section 25 of the Criminal Justice and Public Order Act 1994, released on bail and on his arrival at that place or, as the case may be, his release on bail the transfer direction shall cease to have effect.

(5) If (no direction or order having been given or made under subsection (3) or (4) above) it appears to the court having jurisdiction to try or otherwise deal with the detainee –

    (a)   that it is impracticable or inappropriate to bring the detainee before the court; and

    (b)   that the conditions set out in subsection (6) below are satisfied,

the court may make a hospital order (with or without a restriction order) in his case in his absence and, in the case of a person awaiting trial, without convicting him.

(6) A hospital order may be made in respect of a person under subsection (5) above if the court –

    (a)   is satisfied, on the written or oral evidence of at least two registered medical practitioners, that;

        (i)   the detainee is suffering from mental disorder of a nature or degree which makes it appropriate for the patient to be detained in a hospital for medical treatment; and

        (ii)   appropriate medical treatments is available for him; and

    (b)   is of the opinion, after considering any depositions or other documents required to be sent to the proper officer of the court, that it is proper to make such an order.

(7) Where a person committed to the Crown Court to be dealt with under section 43 above is admitted to a hospital in pursuance of an order under section 44 above, subsections (5) and (6) above shall apply as if he were a person subject to a transfer direction.

NOTES

Prospective amendments. Words in subss (3), (4) prospectively substituted: MHA 2007, s 11(1), (3). Subs (6)(a)(i) prospectively substituted: MHA 2007, s 1(4), Sch 1, Pt 1, paras 1, 12. Subs (6)(a)(ii) and preceding word prospectively inserted: MHA 2007, s 5(1), (4).

52 Further provisions as to persons remanded by magistrates' courts

(1) This section has effect where a transfer direction has been given in respect of any such person as is described in paragraph (b) of section 48(2) above; and that person is in this section referred to as 'the accused'.

(2) Subject to subsection (5) below, the transfer direction shall cease to have effect on the expiration of the period of remand unless the accused is sent in custody to the Crown Court for trial or to be otherwise dealt with.

(3) Subject to subsection (4) below, the power of further remanding the accused under section 128 of the Magistrates' Courts Act 1980 may be exercised by the court without his being brought before the court; and if the court further remands the accused in custody (whether or not he is brought before the court) the period of remand shall, for the purposes of this section, be deemed not to have expired.

(4) The court shall not under subsection (3) above further remand the accused in his absence unless he has appeared before the court within the previous six months.

(5) If the magistrates' court is satisfied, on the written or oral evidence of the responsible clinician –

(a)   that the accused no longer requires treatment in hospital for mental disorder; or

(b)   that no effective treatment for his disorder can be given in the hospital

to which he has been removed, the court may direct that the transfer direction shall cease to have effect notwithstanding that the period of remand has not expired or that the accused is sent to the Crown Court as mentioned in subsection (2) above.

(6) If the accused is sent to the Crown Court as mentioned in subsection (2) above and the transfer direction has not ceased to have effect under subsection (5) above, section 51 above shall apply as if the transfer direction given in his case were a direction given in respect of a person falling within that section.

(7) The magistrates' court may, in the absence of the accused, send him to the Crown Court for trial under section 51 or 51A of the Crime and Disorder Act 1998 if –

(a)   the court is satisfied, on the written or oral evidence of the responsible clinician, that the accused is unfit to take part in the proceedings; and

(b)   the accused is represented by counsel or a solicitor.

NOTES

Prospective amendments. Words in subss (5), (7)(a) prospectively substituted: MHA 2007, s 11(1), (4).

53 Further provisions as to civil prisoners and persons detained under the Immigration Acts

(1) Subject to subsection (2) below, a transfer direction given in respect of any such person as is described in paragraph (c) or (d) of section 48(2) above shall cease to have effect on the expiration of the period during which he would, but for his removal to hospital, be liable to be detained in the place from which he was removed.

(2) Where a transfer direction and a restriction direction have been given in respect of any such person as is mentioned in subsection (1) above, then, if the Secretary of State is notified by the responsible clinician, any other registered medical practitioner any other approved clinician or a Mental Health Review Tribunal at any time before the expiration of the period there mentioned –

(a)   that that person no longer requires treatment in hospital for mental disorder; or

(b)   that no effective treatment for his disorder can be given in the hospital to which he has been removed,

the Secretary of State may by warrant direct that he be remitted to any place where he might have been detained if he had not been removed to hospital, and on his arrival at the place to which he is so remitted the transfer direction and the restriction direction shall cease to have effect.

NOTES

Prospective amendments. Words in subs (2) prospectively substituted: MHA 2007, s 11(1), (5).

Supplemental

54 Requirements as to medical evidence

(1) The registered medical practitioner whose evidence is taken into account under section 35(3)(a) above and at least one of the registered medical practitioners whose evidence is taken into account under sections 36(1), 37(2)(a), 38(1), 45A(2) and 51(6)(a) above and whose reports are taken into account under sections 47(1) and 48(1) above shall be a practitioner approved for the purposes of section 12 above by the Secretary of State as having special experience in the diagnosis or treatment of mental disorder.

(2) For the purposes of any provision of this Part of this Act under which a court may act on the written evidence of any person, a report in writing purporting to be signed by that person may, subject to the provisions of this section, be received in evidence without proof of the following –

(a)   the signature of the person; or

(b)   his having the requisite qualifications or approval or authority or being of the requisite description to give the report.

(2A) But the court may require the signatory of any such report to be called to give oral evidence.

(3) Where, in pursuance of a direction of the court, any such report is tendered in evidence otherwise than by or on behalf of the person who is the subject of the report, then –

(a) if that person is represented by counsel or a solicitor, a copy of the report shall be given to his counsel or solicitor;

(b) if that person is not so represented, the substance of the report shall be disclosed to him or, where he is a child or young person, to his parent or guardian if present in court; and

(c) except where the report relates only to arrangements for his admission to a hospital, that person may require the signatory of the report to be called to give oral evidence, and evidence to rebut the evidence contained in the report may be called by or on behalf of that person.

NOTES

Prospective amendments. Subss (2), (2A) prospectively substituted for existing subs (2): MHA 2007, s 11(1), (6).

54A Reduction of period for making hospital orders

(1) The Secretary of State may by order reduce the length of the periods mentioned in sections 37(4) and (5) and 38(4) above.

(2) An order under subsection (1) above may make such consequential amendments of sections 40(1) and 44(3) above as appear to the Secretary of State to be necessary or expedient.

55 Interpretation of Part III

(1) In this Part of this Act –

'child' and 'young person' have the same meaning as in the Children and Young Persons Act 1933;

'civil prisoner' has the meaning given to it by section 48(2)(c) above;

'guardian', in relation to a child or young person, has the same meaning as in the Children and Young Persons Act 1933;

'place of safety', in relation to a person who is not a child or young person, means any police station, prison or remand centre, or any hospital the managers of which are willing temporarily to receive him, and in relation to a child or young person has the same meaning as in the Children and Young Persons Act 1933;

'responsible clinician', in relation to a person liable to be detained in a hospital within the meaning of Part 2 of this Act, means the approved clinician with overall responsibility for the patient's case.

(2) Any reference in this Part of this Act to an offence punishable on summary conviction with imprisonment shall be construed without regard to any prohibition or restriction imposed by or under any enactment relating to the imprisonment of young offenders.

(3) *(repealed)*

(4) Any reference to a hospital order, a guardianship order or a restriction order in section 40(2), (4) or (5), section 41(3) to (5), or section 42 above or section 69(1) below shall be construed as including a reference to any order or direction under this Part of this Act having the same effect as the firstmentioned order; and the exceptions and modifications set out in Schedule 1 to this Act in respect of the provisions of this Act described in that Schedule accordingly include those which are consequential on the provisions of this subsection.

(5) Section 34(2) above shall apply for the purposes of this Part of this Act as it applies for the purposes of Part II of this Act.

(6) References in this Part of this Act to persons serving a sentence of imprisonment shall be construed in accordance with section 47(5) above.

(7) Section 99 of the Children and Young Persons Act 1933 (which relates to the presumption and determination of age) shall apply for the purposes of this Part of this Act as it applies for the purposes of that Act.

NOTES

Prospective amendments. Definitions in subs (1) prospectively repealed and prospectively substituted: MHA 2007, s 11(1), (7). Subs (3) prospectively repealed: MHA 2007, s 55, Sch 11, Pt 1.

PART IV
CONSENT TO TREATMENT

56 Patients to whom Part 4 applies

(1) Section 57 and, so far as relevant to that section, sections 59 to 62 below apply to any patient.

(2) Subject to that and to subsection (5) below, this Part of this Act applies to a patient only if he falls within subsection (3) or (4) below.

(3) A patient falls within this subsection if he is liable to be detained under this Act but not if –

  (a)   he is so liable by virtue of an emergency application and the second medical recommendation referred to in section 4(4)(a) above has not been given and received;
  (b)   he is so liable by virtue of section 5(2) or (4) or 35 above or section 135 or 136 below or by virtue of a direction for his detention in a place of safety under section 37(4) or 45A(5) above; or
  (c)   he has been conditionally discharged under section 42(2) above or section 73 or 74 below and he is not recalled to hospital.

(4) A patient falls within this subsection if –

  (a)   he is a community patient; and
  (b)   he is recalled to hospital under section 17E above.

(5) Section 58A and, so far as relevant to that section, sections 59 to 62 below also apply to any patient who –

    (a)   does not fall within subsection (3) above;
    (b)   is not a community patient; and
    (c)   has not attained the age of 18 years.

NOTES

Prospective amendment. Section prospectively inserted: MHA 2007 s 34(1), (2)

57 Treatment requiring consent and a second opinion

(1) This section applies to the following forms of medical treatment for mental disorder –

    (a)   any surgical operation for destroying brain tissue or for destroying the functioning of brain tissue; and
    (b)   such other forms of treatment as may be specified for the purposes of this section by regulations made by the Secretary of State.

(2) Subject to section 62 below, a patient shall not be given any form of treatment to which this section applies unless he has consented to it and –

    (a)   a registered medical practitioner appointed for the purposes of this Part of this Act by the Secretary of State (not being the responsible clinician (if there is one) in charge of the treatment in question) and two other persons appointed for the purposes of this paragraph by the Secretary of State (not being registered medical practitioners) have certified in writing that the patient is capable of understanding the nature, purpose and likely effects of the treatment in question and has consented to it; and
    (b)   the registered medical practitioner referred to in paragraph (a) above has certified in writing that it is appropriate for the treatment to be given.

(3) Before giving a certificate under subsection (2)(b) above the registered medical practitioner concerned shall consult two other persons who have been professionally concerned with the patient's medical treatment, but of those persons:

    (a)   one shall be a nurse and the other shall be neither a nurse nor a registered medical practitioner; and –
    (b)   neither shall be the responsible clinician (if there is one) or the person in charge of the treatment in question.

(4) Before making any regulations for the purpose of this section the Secretary of State shall consult such bodies as appear to him to be concerned.

NOTES

Prospective amendments. Words in subs (2)(a) prospectively substituted: MHA 2007, s 12(1), (2)(a). Words in subs (2)(b) prospectively substituted: MHA 2007, s 6(1), (2)(a). Words in subs (3) prospectively substituted: MHA 2007, s 12(1), (2)(b).

Note. Subss 57(2)(a), (3) are prospectively amended to take account of the new responsible clinician status, and the old test in s 57(2)(b) that the treatment 'ought to be given, having regard to the likelihood that it will alleviate or prevent deterioration in the patient's condition' is replaced. The new test that it is 'appropriate for the treatment to be given'.

58 Treatment requiring consent or a second opinion

(1) This section applies to the following forms of medical treatment for mental disorder –

 (a) such forms of treatment as may be specified for the purposes of this section by regulations made by the Secretary of State;

 (b) the administration of medicine to a patient by any means (not being a form of treatment specified under paragraph (a) above or section 57 above or section 58A(1)(b) below) at any time during a period for which he is liable to be detained as a patient to whom this Part of this Act applies if three months or more have elapsed since the first occasion in that period when medicine was administered to him by any means for his mental disorder.

(2) The Secretary of State may by order vary the length of the period mentioned in subsection (1)(b) above.

(3) Subject to section 62 below, a patient shall not be given any form of treatment to which this section applies unless –

 (a) he has consented to that treatment and either the approved clinician in charge of it or a registered medical practitioner appointed for the purposes of this Part of this Act by the Secretary of State has certified in writing that the patient is capable of understanding its nature, purpose and likely effects and has consented to it;

 (b) a registered medical practitioner appointed as aforesaid (not being the responsible clinician or the approved clinician in charge of the treatment in question) has certified in writing that the patient is not capable of understanding the nature, purpose and likely effects of that treatment or 'being so capable' has not consented to it but that it is appropriate for the treatment to be given.

(4) Before giving a certificate under subsection (3)(b) above the registered medical practitioner concerned shall consult two other persons who have been professionally concerned with the patient's medical treatment, and of those persons one shall be a nurse and the other shall be neither a nurse nor a registered medical practitioner nor the responsible clinician.

(5) Before making any regulations for the purposes of this section the Secretary of State shall consult such bodies as appear to him to be concerned.

NOTES

Prospective amendments. Words in subs (1)(b) prospectively inserted: MHA 2007, s 28(1), (2)(a). Words in subs (3)(a) prospectively substituted: MHA 2007, s 12(1), (3)(a)(i). Words in subs (3)(b) prospectively substituted: MHA 2007, s 12(1), (3)(a)(ii). Words in subs (3)(b) prospectively inserted: MHA 2007, s 28(1), (2)(b). Words in subs (3)(b) prospectively substituted: MHA 2007, s 6(1), (2)(b). Words in subs (4) prospectively substituted: MHA 2007, s 12(1), (3)(b).

58A Electro-convulsive therapy, etc

(1) This section applies to the following forms of medical treatment for mental disorder –

(a)   electro-convulsive therapy; and

(b)   such other forms of treatment as may be specified for the purposes of this section by regulations made by the appropriate national authority.

(2) Subject to section 62 below, a patient shall be not be given any form of treatment to which this section applies unless he falls within subsection (3), (4) or (5) below.

(3) A patient falls within this subsection if –

(a)   he has attained the age of 18 years;

(b)   he has consented to the treatment in question; and

(c)   either the approved clinician in charge of it or a registered medical practitioner appointed as mentioned in section 58(3) above has certified in writing that the patient is capable of understanding the nature, purpose and likely effects of the treatment and has consented to it.

(4) A patient falls within this subsection if –

(a)   he has not attained the age of 18 years; but

(b)   he has consented to the treatment in question; and

(c)   a registered medical practitioner appointed as aforesaid (not being the approved clinician in charge of the treatment) has certified in writing –

(i)   that the patient is capable of understanding the nature, purpose and likely effects of the treatment and has consented to it; and

(ii)   that it is appropriate for the treatment to be given.

(5) A patient falls within this subsection if a registered medical practitioner appointed as aforesaid (not being the responsible clinician (if there is one) or the approved clinician in charge of the treatment in question) has certified in writing –

(a)   that the patient is not capable of understanding the nature, purpose and likely effects of the treatment; but

(b)   that it is appropriate for the treatment to be given; and

(c)   that giving him the treatment would not conflict with –

(i)   an advance decision which the registered medical practitioner concerned is satisfied is valid and applicable; or

(ii)   a decision made by a donee or deputy or by the Court of Protection.

(6) Before giving a certificate under subsection (5) above the registered medical practitioner concerned shall consult two other persons who have been professionally concerned with the patient's medical treatment but, of those persons –

(a)   one shall be a nurse and the other shall be neither a nurse nor a registered medical practitioner; and

(b)   neither shall be the responsible clinician (if there is one) or the approved clinician in charge of the treatment in question.

(7) This section shall not by itself confer sufficient authority for a patient who falls within section 56(5) above to be given a form of treatment to which this section applies if he is not capable of understanding the nature, purpose and likely effects of the treatment (and cannot therefore consent to it).

(8) Before making any regulations for the purposes of this section, the appropriate national authority shall consult such bodies as appear to it to be concerned.

(9) In this section –

(a) a reference to an advance decision is to an advance decision (within the meaning of the Mental Capacity Act 2005) made by the patient;

(b) 'valid and applicable', in relation to such a decision, means valid and applicable to the treatment in question in accordance with section 25 of that Act;

(c) a reference to a donee is to a donee of a lasting power of attorney (within the meaning of section 9 of that Act) created by the patient, where the donee is acting within the scope of his authority and in accordance with that Act; and

(d) a reference to a deputy is to a deputy appointed for the patient by the Court of Protection under section 16 of that Act, where the deputy is acting within the scope of his authority and in accordance with that Act.

(10) In this section, 'the appropriate national authority' means –

(a) in a case where the treatment in question would, if given, be given in England, the Secretary of State;

(b) in a case where the treatment in question would, if given, be given in Wales, the Welsh Ministers.

59 Plans of treatment

Any consent or certificate under section 57, 58 or 58A above may relate to a plan of treatment under which the patient is to be given (whether within a specified period or otherwise) one or more of the forms of treatment to which that section applies.

NOTES

Prospective amendments. Words substituted: MHA 2007, s 28(1), (3).

60 Withdrawal of consent

(1) Where the consent of a patient to any treatment has been given for the purposes of section 57, 58 or 58A above, the patient may, subject to section 62 below, at any time before the completion of the treatment withdraw his consent, and those sections shall then apply as if the remainder of the treatment were a separate form of treatment.

(1A) Subsection (1B) below applies where –

(a) the consent of a patient to any treatment has been given for the purposes of section 57, 58 or 58A above; but

(b) before the completion of the treatment, the patient ceases to be capable of understanding its nature, purpose and likely effects.

(1B) The patient shall, subject to section 62 below, be treated as having withdrawn his consent, and those sections shall then apply as if the remainder of the treatment were a separate form of treatment.

(1C) Subsection (1D) below applies where –

(a) a certificate has been given under section 58 or 58A above that a patient is not capable of understanding the nature, purpose and likely effects of the treatment to which the certificate applies; but

(b) before the completion of the treatment, the patient becomes capable of understanding its nature, purpose and likely effects.

(1D) The certificate shall, subject to section 62 below, cease to apply to the treatment and those sections shall then apply as if the remainder of the treatment were a separate form of treatment.

(2) Without prejudice to the application of subsections (1) to (1D) above to any treatment given under the plan of treatment to which a patient has consented, a patient who has consented to such a plan may, subject to section 62 below, at any time withdraw his consent to further treatment, or to further treatment of any description, under the plan.

NOTES

Prospective amendments. Words in subs (1) prospectively substituted: MHA 2007, s 28(1), (4). Subss (1A)–(1D) prospectively inserted: MHA 2007, s 29(1), (2). Words in subs (2) prospectively substituted: MHA 2007, s 29(1), (3).

61 Review of treatment

(1) Where a patient is given treatment in accordance with section 57(2), 58(3)(b) or 58A(4) or (5) above or by virtue of section 62A below in accordance with a Part 4A certificate (within the meaning of that section) a report on the treatment and the patient's condition shall be given by the approved clinician in charge of the treatment to the Secretary of State –

(a) on the next occasion on which the responsible clinician furnishes a report under section 20(3), 20A(4) or 21B(2) above in respect of the patient; and

(b) at any other time if so required by the Secretary of State.

(2) In relation to a patient who is subject to a restriction order, limitation direction or restriction direction subsection (1) above shall have effect as if paragraph (a) required the report to be made –

(a) in the case of treatment in the period of six months beginning with the date of the order or direction, at the end of that period;

(b)   in the case of treatment at any subsequent time, on the next occasion on which the responsible clinician makes a report in respect of the patient under section 41(6), 45B(3) or 49(3) above.

(3) The Secretary of State may at any time give notice to the responsible clinician directing that, subject to section 62 below, a certificate given in respect of a patient under section 57(2), 58(3)(b) or 58A(4) or (5) above shall not apply to treatment given to him after a date specified in the notice and sections 57, 58 and 58A above shall then apply to any such treatment as if that certificate had not been given.

(3A) The notice under subsection (3) above shall be given to the approved clinician in charge of the treatment.

NOTES

Prospective amendments. Words in subs (1) prospectively substituted: MHA 2007, s 28(1), (5)(a). Words in subs (1) prospectively inserted: MHA 2007, s 34(1), (3)(a). Words in subs (1) prospectively substituted: MHA 2007, s 12(1), (4)(a)(i). Words in subs (1) prospectively substituted: MHA 2007, s 12(1), (4)(a)(ii). Words in subs (1)(a) prospectively substituted: MHA 2007, s 34(1), (3)(b). Words in subs (2)(b) prospectively substituted: MHA 2007, s 12(1), (4)(b). Words in subs (3) prospectively repealed: MHA 2007, ss 12(1), (4)(c), 55, Sch 11, Pt 3. Words in subs (3) prospectively substituted: MHA 2007, s 28(1), (5)(b)(i). Words in subs (3) prospectively substituted: MHA 2007, s 28(1), (5)(b)(ii). Subs (3A) prospectively inserted: MHA 2007, s 12(1), (4)(d).

62 Urgent treatment

(1) Sections 57 and 58 above shall not apply to any treatment –

(a)   which is immediately necessary to save the patient's life; or
(b)   which (not being irreversible) is immediately necessary to prevent a serious deterioration of his condition; or
(c)   which (not being irreversible or hazardous) is immediately necessary to alleviate serious suffering by the patient; or
(d)   which (not being irreversible or hazardous) is immediately necessary and represents the minimum interference necessary to prevent the patient from behaving violently or being a danger to himself or to others.

(1A) Section 58A above, in so far as it relates to electro-convulsive therapy by virtue of subsection (1)(a) of that section, shall not apply to any treatment which falls within paragraph (a) or (b) of subsection (1) above.

(1B) Section 58A above, in so far as it relates to a form of treatment specified by virtue of subsection (1)(b) of that section, shall not apply to any treatment which falls within such of paragraphs (a) to (d) of subsection (1) above as may be specified in regulations under that section.

(1C) For the purposes of subsection (1B) above, the regulations –

(a)   may make different provision for different cases (and may, in particular, make different provision for different forms of treatment);
(b)   may make provision which applies subject to specified exceptions; and
(c)   may include transitional, consequential, incidental or supplemental provision.

(2) Sections 60 and 61(3) above shall not preclude the continuation of any treatment or of treatment under any plan pending compliance with section 57, 58 or 58A above if the approved clinician in charge of the treatment considers that the discontinuance of the treatment or of treatment under the plan would cause serious suffering to the patient.

(3) For the purposes of this section treatment is irreversible if it has unfavourable irreversible physical or psychological consequences and hazardous if it entails significant physical hazard.

NOTES

Prospective amendments. Subss (1A)–(1C) prospectively inserted: MHA 2007, s 28(1), (6). Words in subs (2) prospectively substituted: MHA 2007, s 28(1), (7).

62A Treatment on recall of community patient or revocation of order

(1) This section applies where –

    (a)   a community patient is recalled to hospital under section 17E above; or

    (b)   a patient is liable to be detained under this Act following the revocation of a community treatment order under section 17F above in respect of him.

(2) For the purposes of section 58(1)(b) above, the patient is to be treated as if he had remained liable to be detained since the making of the community treatment order.

(3) But section 58 above does not apply to treatment given to the patient if –

    (a)   the certificate requirement is met (within the meaning of section 64C below); or

    (b)   as a result of section 64B(4) or 64E(4) below, the certificate requirement would not apply (were the patient a community patient not recalled to hospital under section 17E above).

(4) In a case where this section applies, the certificate requirement is met only in so far as –

    (a)   the Part 4A certificate expressly provides that it is appropriate for one or more specified forms of treatment to be given to the patient in that case (subject to such conditions as may be specified); or

    (b)   a notice having been given under subsection (4) of section 64H below, treatment is authorised by virtue of subsection (7) of that section.

(5) Subsection (4)(a) above shall not preclude the continuation of any treatment, or of treatment under any plan, pending compliance with section 58 above if the approved clinician in charge of the treatment considers that the discontinuance of the treatment, or of the treatment under the plan, would cause serious suffering to the patient.

(6) In a case where subsection (1)(b) above applies, subsection (3) above only applies pending compliance with section 58 above.

(7) In subsection (4) above –

'Part 4A certificate' has the meaning given in section 64H below; and 'specified', in relation to a Part 4A certificate, means specified in the certificate.

NOTES

Prospective amendments. Section prospectively inserted: MHA 2007, s 34(1), (4).

63 Treatment not requiring consent

The consent of a patient shall not be required for any medical treatment given to him for the mental disorder from which he is suffering, not being a form of treatment to which section 57, 58 or 58A above applies, if the treatment is given by or under the direction of the approved clinician in charge of the treatment.

NOTES

Prospective amendments. Words prospectively substituted: MHA 2007, ss 12(1), (6), 28(1), (8).

64 Supplementary provisions for Part 4

(1) In this Part of this Act 'the responsible clinician' means the approved clinician with overall responsibility for the case of the patient in question and 'hospital' includes a registered establishment.

(1A) References in this Part of this Act to the approved clinician in charge of a patient's treatment shall, where the treatment in question is a form of treatment to which section 57 above applies, be construed as references to the person in charge of the treatment.

(1B) References in this Part of this Act to the approved clinician in charge of a patient's treatment shall, where the treatment in question is a form of treatment to which section 58A above applies and the patient falls within section 56(5) above, be construed as references to the person in charge of the treatment.

(1C) Regulations made by virtue of section 32(2)(d) above apply for the purposes of this Part as they apply for the purposes of Part 2 of this Act.

(2) Any certificate for the purposes of this Part of this Act shall be in such form as may be prescribed by regulations made by the Secretary of State.

(3) For the purposes of this Part of this Act, it is appropriate for treatment to be given to a patient if the treatment is appropriate in his case, taking into account the nature and degree of the mental disorder from which he is suffering and all other circumstances of his case.

NOTES

Prospective amendments. Words in subs (1) prospectively substituted and subs (1A) prospectively inserted: MHA 2007, s 12(1), (7). Subss (1B), (1C) prospectively inserted: MHA 2007, s 28(1), (9). Subs (3) prospectively inserted: MHA 2007, s 6(1), (3).

PART 4A
TREATMENT OF COMMUNITY PATIENTS NOT RECALLED TO HOSPITAL

64A Meaning of 'relevant treatment'

In this Part of this Act 'relevant treatment', in relation to a patient, means medical treatment which –

    (a)   is for the mental disorder from which the patient is suffering; and

    (b)   is not a form of treatment to which section 57 above applies.

NOTES

Prospective amendment. Part prospectively inserted: MHA 2007, s 35(1).

64B Adult community patients

(1) This section applies to the giving of relevant treatment to a community patient who –

    (a)   is not recalled to hospital under section 17E above; and

    (b)   has attained the age of 16 years.

(2) The treatment may not be given to the patient unless –

    (a)   there is authority to give it to him; and

    (b)   if it is section 58 type treatment or section 58A type treatment, the certificate requirement is met.

(3) But the certificate requirement does not apply if –

    (a)   giving the treatment to the patient is authorised in accordance with section 64G below; or

    (b)   the treatment is immediately necessary and –

        (i)   the patient has capacity to consent to it and does consent to it; or

        (ii)   a donee or deputy or the Court of Protection consents to the treatment on the patient's behalf.

(4) Nor does the certificate requirement apply in so far as the administration of medicine to the patient at any time during the period of one month beginning with the day on which the community treatment order is made is section 58 type treatment.

(5) The reference in subsection (4) above to the administration of medicine does not include any form of treatment specified under section 58(1)(a) above.

NOTES

Prospective amendment. Part prospectively inserted: MHA 2007, s 35(1).

64C Section 64B: supplemental

(1) This section has effect for the purposes of section 64B above.

(2) There is authority to give treatment to a patient if –

(a)   he has capacity to consent to it and does consent to it;

(b)   a donee or deputy or the Court of Protection consents to it on his behalf; or

(c)   giving it to him is authorised in accordance with section 64D or 64G below.

(3) Relevant treatment is section 58 type treatment or section 58A type treatment if, at the time when it is given to the patient, section 58 or 58A above (respectively) would have applied to it, had the patient remained liable to be detained at that time (rather than being a community patient).

(4) The certificate requirement is met in respect of treatment to be given to a patient if –

(a)   a registered medical practitioner appointed for the purposes of Part 4 of this Act (not being the responsible clinician or the person in charge of the treatment) has certified in writing that it is appropriate for the treatment to be given or for the treatment to be given subject to such conditions as may be specified in the certificate; and

(b)   if conditions are so specified, the conditions are satisfied.

(5) In a case where the treatment is section 58 type treatment, treatment is immediately necessary if –

(a)   it is immediately necessary to save the patient's life; or

(b)   it is immediately necessary to prevent a serious deterioration of the patient's condition and is not irreversible; or

(c)   it is immediately necessary to alleviate serious suffering by the patient and is not irreversible or hazardous; or

(d)   it is immediately necessary, represents the minimum interference necessary to prevent the patient from behaving violently or being a danger to himself or others and is not irreversible or hazardous.

(6) In a case where the treatment is section 58A type treatment by virtue of subsection (1)(a) of that section, treatment is immediately necessary if it falls within paragraph (a) or (b) of subsection (5) above.

(7) In a case where the treatment is section 58A type treatment by virtue of subsection (1)(b) of that section, treatment is immediately necessary if it falls within such of paragraphs (a) to (d) of subsection (5) above as may be specified in regulations under that section.

(8) For the purposes of subsection (7) above, the regulations –

(a)   may make different provision for different cases (and may, in particular, make different provision for different forms of treatment);

(b)   may make provision which applies subject to specified exceptions; and

(c)   may include transitional, consequential, incidental or supplemental provision.

(9) Subsection (3) of section 62 above applies for the purposes of this section as it applies for the purposes of that section.

NOTES

Prospective amendment. Part prospectively inserted: MHA 2007, s 35(1).

64D Adult community patients lacking capacity

(1) A person is authorised to give relevant treatment to a patient as mentioned in section 64C(2)(c) above if the conditions in subsections (2) to (6) below are met.

(2) The first condition is that, before giving the treatment, the person takes reasonable steps to establish whether the patient lacks capacity to consent to the treatment.

(3) The second condition is that, when giving the treatment, he reasonably believes that the patient lacks capacity to consent to it.

(4) The third condition is that –

    (a)   he has no reason to believe that the patient objects to being given the treatment; or

    (b)   he does have reason to believe that the patient so objects, but it is not necessary to use force against the patient in order to give the treatment.

(5) The fourth condition is that –

    (a)   he is the person in charge of the treatment and an approved clinician; or

    (b)   the treatment is given under the direction of that clinician.

(6) The fifth condition is that giving the treatment does not conflict with –

    (a)   an advance decision which he is satisfied is valid and applicable; or

    (b)   a decision made by a donee or deputy or the Court of Protection.

(7) In this section –

    (a)   reference to an advance decision is to an advance decision (within the meaning of the Mental Capacity Act 2005) made by the patient; and

    (b)   'valid and applicable', in relation to such a decision, means valid and applicable to the treatment in question in accordance with section 25 of that Act.

NOTES

Prospective amendment. Part prospectively inserted: MHA 2007, s 35(1).

64E Child community patients

(1) This section applies to the giving of relevant treatment to a community patient who –

    (a)   is not recalled to hospital under section 17E above; and

    (b)   has not attained the age of 16 years.

(2) The treatment may not be given to the patient unless –

    (a)   there is authority to give it to him; and

(b)   if it is section 58 type treatment or section 58A type treatment, the certificate requirement is met.

(3) But the certificate requirement does not apply if –

(a)   giving the treatment to the patient is authorised in accordance with section 64G below; or

(b)   in a case where the patient is competent to consent to the treatment and does consent to it, the treatment is immediately necessary.

(4) Nor does the certificate requirement apply in so far as the administration of medicine to the patient at any time during the period of one month beginning with the day on which the community treatment order is made is section 58 type treatment.

(5) The reference in subsection (4) above to the administration of medicine does not include any form of treatment specified under section 58(1)(a) above.

(6) For the purposes of subsection (2)(a) above, there is authority to give treatment to a patient if –

(a)   he is competent to consent to it and he does consent to it; or

(b)   giving it to him is authorised in accordance with section 64F or 64G below.

(7) Subsections (3) to (9) of section 64C above have effect for the purposes of this section as they have effect for the purposes of section 64B above.

(8) Regulations made by virtue of section 32(2)(d) above apply for the purposes of this section as they apply for the purposes of Part 2 of this Act.

NOTES

Prospective amendment. Part prospectively inserted: MHA 2007, s 35(1).

64F Child community patients lacking competence

(1) A person is authorised to give relevant treatment to a patient as mentioned in section 64E(6)(b) above if the conditions in subsections (2) to (5) below are met.

(2) The first condition is that, before giving the treatment, the person takes reasonable steps to establish whether the patient is competent to consent to the treatment.

(3) The second condition is that, when giving the treatment, he reasonably believes that the patient is not competent to consent to it.

(4) The third condition is that –

(a)   he has no reason to believe that the patient objects to being given the treatment; or

(b)   he does have reason to believe that the patient so objects, but it is not necessary to use force against the patient in order to give the treatment.

(5) The fourth condition is that –

(a)   he is the person in charge of the treatment and an approved clinician; or

(b)   the treatment is given under the direction of that clinician.

NOTES

Prospective amendment. Part prospectively inserted: MHA 2007, s 35(1).

64G Emergency treatment for patients lacking capacity or competence

(1) A person is also authorised to give relevant treatment to a patient as mentioned in section 64C(2)(c) or 64E(6)(b) above if the conditions in subsections (2) to (4) below are met.

(2) The first condition is that, when giving the treatment, the person reasonably believes that the patient lacks capacity to consent to it or, as the case may be, is not competent to consent to it.

(3) The second condition is that the treatment is immediately necessary.

(4) The third condition is that if it is necessary to use force against the patient in order to give the treatment –

(a)   the treatment needs to be given in order to prevent harm to the patient; and

(b)   the use of such force is a proportionate response to the likelihood of the patient's suffering harm, and to the seriousness of that harm.

(5) Subject to subsections (6) to (8) below, treatment is immediately necessary if –

(a)   it is immediately necessary to save the patient's life; or

(b)   it is immediately necessary to prevent a serious deterioration of the patient's condition and is not irreversible; or

(c)   it is immediately necessary to alleviate serious suffering by the patient and is not irreversible or hazardous; or

(d)   it is immediately necessary, represents the minimum interference necessary to prevent the patient from behaving violently or being a danger to himself or others and is not irreversible or hazardous.

(6) Where the treatment is section 58A type treatment by virtue of subsection (1)(a) of that section, treatment is immediately necessary if it falls within paragraph (a) or (b) of subsection (5) above.

(7) Where the treatment is section 58A type treatment by virtue of subsection (1)(b) of that section, treatment is immediately necessary if it falls within such of paragraphs (a) to (d) of subsection (5) above as may be specified in regulations under section 58A above.

(8) For the purposes of subsection (7) above, the regulations –

(a)   may make different provision for different cases (and may, in particular, make different provision for different forms of treatment);

(b)   may make provision which applies subject to specified exceptions; and

(c)   may include transitional, consequential, incidental or supplemental provision.

(9) Subsection (3) of section 62 above applies for the purposes of this section as it applies for the purposes of that section.

NOTES

Prospective amendment. Part prospectively inserted: MHA 2007, s 35(1).

64H Certificates: supplementary provisions

(1) A certificate under section 64B(2)(b) or 64E(2)(b) above (a 'Part 4A certificate') may relate to a plan of treatment under which the patient is to be given (whether within a specified period or otherwise) one or more forms of section 58 type treatment or section 58A type treatment.

(2) A Part 4A certificate shall be in such form as may be prescribed by regulations made by the appropriate national authority.

(3) Before giving a Part 4A certificate, the registered medical practitioner concerned shall consult two other persons who have been professionally concerned with the patient's medical treatment but, of those persons –

(a)   at least one shall be a person who is not a registered medical practitioner; and
(b)   neither shall be the patient's responsible clinician or the person in charge of the treatment in question.

(4) Where a patient is given treatment in accordance with a Part 4A certificate, a report on the treatment and the patient's condition shall be given by the person in charge of the treatment to the appropriate national authority if required by that authority.

(5) The appropriate national authority may at any time give notice directing that a Part 4A certificate shall not apply to treatment given to a patient after a date specified in the notice, and the relevant section shall then apply to any such treatment as if that certificate had not been given.

(6) The relevant section is –

(a)   if the patient is not recalled to hospital in accordance with section 17E above, section 64B or 64E above;
(b)   if the patient is so recalled or is liable to be detained under this Act following revocation of the community treatment order under section 17F above –
(i)   section 58 above, in the case of section 58 type treatment;
(ii)   section 58A above, in the case of section 58A type treatment; (subject to section 62A(2) above).

(7) The notice under subsection (5) above shall be given to the person in charge of the treatment in question.

(8) Subsection (5) above shall not preclude the continuation of any treatment or of treatment under any plan pending compliance with the relevant section if

the person in charge of the treatment considers that the discontinuance of the treatment or of treatment under the plan would cause serious suffering to the patient.

(9) In this section, 'the appropriate national authority' means –

    (a)   in relation to community patients in respect of whom the responsible hospital is in England, the Secretary of State;

    (b)   in relation to community patients in respect of whom the responsible hospital is in Wales, the Welsh Ministers.

NOTES

Prospective amendment. Part prospectively inserted: MHA 2007, s 35(1).

64I Liability for negligence

Nothing in section 64D, 64F or 64G above excludes a person's civil liability for loss or damage, or his criminal liability, resulting from his negligence in doing anything authorised to be done by that section.

NOTES

Prospective amendment. Part prospectively inserted: MHA 2007, s 35(1).

64J Factors to be considered in determining whether patient objects to treatment

(1) In assessing for the purposes of this Part whether he has reason to believe that a patient objects to treatment, a person shall consider all the circumstances so far as they are reasonably ascertainable, including the patient's behaviour, wishes, feelings, views, beliefs and values.

(2) But circumstances from the past shall be considered only so far as it is still appropriate to consider them.

NOTES

Prospective amendment. Part prospectively inserted: MHA 2007, s 35(1).

64K Interpretation of Part 4A

(1) This Part of this Act is to be construed as follows.

(2) References to a patient who lacks capacity are to a patient who lacks capacity within the meaning of the Mental Capacity Act 2005.

(3) References to a patient who has capacity are to be read accordingly.

(4) References to a donee are to a donee of a lasting power of attorney (within the meaning of section 9 of the Mental Capacity Act 2005) created by the patient, where the donee is acting within the scope of his authority and in accordance with that Act.

(5) References to a deputy are to a deputy appointed for the patient by the Court of Protection under section 16 of the Mental Capacity Act 2005, where the deputy is acting within the scope of his authority and in accordance with that Act.

(6) Reference to the responsible clinician shall be construed as a reference to the responsible clinician within the meaning of Part 2 of this Act.

(7) References to a hospital include a registered establishment.

(8) Section 64(3) above applies for the purposes of this Part of this Act as it applies for the purposes of Part 4 of this Act.

NOTES

Prospective amendment. Part prospectively inserted: MHA 2007, s 35(1).

PART V
MENTAL HEALTH REVIEW TRIBUNALS

Constitution etc

65 Mental Health Review Tribunals

(1) There shall be –

    (a)   a Mental Health Review Tribunal for England; and
    (b)   a Mental Health Review Tribunal for Wales.

(1A) The purpose of the Mental Health Review Tribunals is to deal with applications and references by and in respect of patients under the provisions of this Act.

(2) The provisions of Schedule 2 to this Act shall have effect with respect to the constitution of Mental Health Review Tribunals.

(3) Subject to the provisions of Schedule 2 to this Act, and to rules made by the Lord Chancellor under this Act, the jurisdiction of a Mental Health Review Tribunal may be exercised by any three or more of its members, and references in this Act to a Mental Health Review Tribunal shall be construed accordingly.

(4) The Secretary of State may pay to the members of Mental Health Review Tribunals such remuneration and allowances as he may with the consent of the Treasury determine, and defray the expenses of such tribunals to such amount as he may with the consent of the Treasury determine, and may provide for each such tribunal such officers and servants, and such accommodation, as the tribunal may require.

NOTES

Prospective amendments. Existing subss (1), (1A)–(1C) prospectively substituted by subss (1), (1A): MHA 2007, s 38(1), (2).

Applications and references concerning Part II patients

66 Applications to tribunals

(1) Where –

(a) a patient is admitted to a hospital in pursuance of an application for admission for assessment; or

(b) a patient is admitted to a hospital in pursuance of an application for admission for treatment; or

(c) a patient is received into guardianship in pursuance of a guardianship application; or

(ca) a community treatment order is made in respect of a patient; or

(cb) a community treatment order is revoked under section 17F above in respect of a patient; or

(e) a patient is transferred from guardianship to a hospital in pursuance of regulations made under section 19 above; or

(f) a report is furnished under section 20 above in respect of a patient and the patient is not discharged under section 23 above; or

(fza) a report is furnished under section 20A above in respect of a patient and the patient is not discharged under section 23 above; or

(fa) a report is furnished under subsection (2) of section 21B above in respect of a patient and subsection (5) of that section applies (or subsections (5) and (6)(b) of that section apply) in the case of the report; or

(faa) a report is furnished under subsection (2) of section 21B above in respect of a community patient and subsection (6A) of that section applies (or subsections (6A) and (6B)(b) of that section apply) in the case of the report; or

(g) a report is furnished under section 25 above in respect of a patient who is detained in pursuance of an application for admission for treatment or a community patient; or

(h) an order is made under section 29 above on the ground specified in paragraph (c) or (d) of subsection (3) of that section in respect of a patient who is or subsequently becomes liable to be detained or subject to guardianship under Part II of this Act or who is a community patient,

an application may be made to a Mental Health Review Tribunal within the relevant period –

(i) by the patient (except in the cases mentioned in paragraphs (g) and (h) above, and

(ii) in the cases mentioned in paragraphs (g) and (h) above, by his nearest relative.

(2) In subsection (1) above 'the relevant period' means –

(a) in the case mentioned in paragraph (a) of that subsection, 14 days beginning with the day on which the patient is admitted as so mentioned;

(b)   in the case mentioned in paragraph (b) of that subsection, six months beginning with the day on which the patient is admitted as so mentioned;

(c)   in the case mentioned in paragraph (c) of that subsection, six months beginning with the day on which the application is accepted;

(ca)   in the case mentioned in paragraph (ca) of that subsection, six months beginning with the day on which the community treatment order is made;

(cb)   in the case mentioned in paragraph (cb) of that subsection, six months beginning with the day on which the community treatment order is revoked;

(d)   in the case mentioned in paragraph (g) of that subsection, 28 days beginning with the day on which the applicant is informed that the report has been furnished;

(e)   in the case mentioned in paragraph (e) of that subsection, six months beginning with the day on which the patient is transferred;

(f)   in the case mentioned in paragraph (f) or (fa) of that subsection, the period or periods for which authority for the patient's detention or guardianship is renewed by virtue of the report;

(fza)   in the cases mentioned in paragraphs (fza) and (faa) of that subsection, the period or periods for which the community treatment period is extended by virtue of the report;

(g)   in the case mentioned in paragraph (h) of that subsection, 12 months beginning with the date of the order, and in any subsequent period of 12 months during which the order continues in force.

(2A) Nothing in subsection (1)(b) above entitles a community patient to make an application by virtue of that provision even if he is admitted to a hospital on being recalled there under section 17E above.

(3) Section 32 above shall apply for the purposes of this section as it applies for the purposes of Part II of this Act.

NOTES

Prospective amendments. Subs (1)(ca), (cb) prospectively inserted: MHA 2007, s 32(4), Sch 3, paras 1, 18(1), (2)(a). Subs (1)(d) prospectively repealed: MHA 2007, s 55, Sch 11, Pt 1. Words in subs (1)(f) prospectively inserted: MHA 2007, s 32(4), Sch 3, paras 1, 18(1), (2)(b). Subs (1)(fza) prospectively inserted: MHA 2007, s 32(4), Sch 3, paras 1, 18(1), (2)(c). Subs (1)(faa) prospectively inserted: MHA 2007, s 32(4), Sch 3, paras 1, 18(1), (2)(d). Subs (1)(fb) prospectively repealed: MHA 2007, s 55, Sch 11, Pt 1. Words in subs (1)(g) prospectively inserted: MHA 2007, s 32(4), Sch 3, paras 1, 18(1), (2)(e). Subs (1) paras (ga)–(gc) prospectively repealed: MHA 2007, s 55, Sch 11, Pt 5. Words in subs (1)(h) prospectively inserted: MHA 2007, s 25. Words in subs (1)(i) prospectively inserted: MHA 2007, s 32(4), Sch 3, paras 1, 18(1), (2)(f). Words in subs (1)(i) prospectively repealed: MHA 2007, s 55, Sch 11, Pt 5. Words in subs (2)(c) prospectively substituted: MHA 2007, s 36(1), (3). Subs (2)(ca), (cb) prospectively inserted: MHA 2007, s 32(4), Sch 3, paras 1, 18(1), (3)(a). Words in subs (2)(d) prospectively substituted: MHA 2007, s 1(4), Sch 1, Pt 1, paras 1, 13. Words in subs (2)(d) prospectively repealed: MHA 2007, s 55, Sch 11, Pt 5. Subs (2)(fza) prospectively inserted: MHA 2007, s 32(4), Sch 3, paras 1, 18(1), (3)(b). Subs (2)(fa) prospectively repealed: MHA 2007, s 55, Sch 11, Pt 5. Subs (2A) prospectively inserted: MHA 2007, s 32(4), Sch 3, paras 1, 18(1), (4).

67 References to tribunals by Secretary of State concerning Part II patients

(1) The Secretary of State may, if he thinks fit, at any time refer to a Mental Health Review Tribunal the case of any patient who is liable to be detained or subject to guardianship under Part II of this Act or of any community patient.

(2) For the purpose of furnishing information for the purposes of a reference under subsection (1) above any registered medical practitioner or approved clinician authorised by or on behalf of the patient may, at any reasonable time, visit the patient and examine him in private and require the production of and inspect any records relating to the detention or treatment of the patient in any hospital or to any after-care services provided for the patient under section 117 below.

(3) Section 32 above shall apply for the purposes of this section as it applies for the purposes of Part II of this Act.

NOTES

Prospective amendments. Words in subs (1) prospectively repealed: MHA 2007, s 55, Sch 11, Pt 5. Words in subs (1) prospectively inserted: MHA 2007, s 32(4), Sch 3, paras 1, 19. Words in subs (2) prospectively inserted: MHA 2007, s 13(1), (2)(a).

68 Duty of managers of hospitals to refer cases to tribunal

(1) This section applies in respect of the following patients –

   (a)   a patient who is admitted to a hospital in pursuance of an application for admission for assessment;
   (b)   a patient who is admitted to a hospital in pursuance of an application for admission for treatment;
   (c)   a community patient;
   (d)   a patient whose community treatment order is revoked under section 17F above;
   (e)   a patient who is transferred from guardianship to a hospital in pursuance of regulations made under section 19 above.

(2) On expiry of the period of six months beginning with the applicable day, the managers of the hospital shall refer the patient's case to a Mental Health Review Tribunal.

(3) But they shall not do so if during that period –

   (a)   any right has been exercised by or in respect of the patient by virtue of any of paragraphs (b), (ca), (cb), (e), (g) and (h) of section 66(1) above;
   (b)   a reference has been made in respect of the patient under section 67(1) above, not being a reference made while the patient is or was liable to be detained in pursuance of an application for admission for assessment; or
   (c)   a reference has been made in respect of the patient under subsection (7) below.

(4) A person who applies to a tribunal but subsequently withdraws his application shall be treated for these purposes as not having exercised his right

to apply, and if he withdraws his application on a date after expiry of the period mentioned in subsection (2) above, the managers shall refer the patient's case as soon as possible after that date.

(5) In subsection (2) above, 'the applicable day' means –

(a)   in the case of a patient who is admitted to a hospital in pursuance of an application for admission for assessment, the day on which the patient was so admitted;

(b)   in the case of a patient who is admitted to a hospital in pursuance of an application for admission for treatment –

   (i)   the day on which the patient was so admitted; or
   (ii)   if, when he was so admitted, he was already liable to be detained in pursuance of an application for admission for assessment, the day on which he was originally admitted in pursuance of the application for admission for assessment;

(c)   in the case of a community patient or a patient whose community treatment order is revoked under section 17F above, the day mentioned in sub-paragraph (i) or (ii), as the case may be, of paragraph (b) above;

(d)   in the case of a patient who is transferred from guardianship to a hospital, the day on which he was so transferred.

(6) The managers of the hospital shall also refer the patient's case to a Mental Health Review Tribunal if a period of more than three years (or, if the patient has not attained the age of 18 years, one year) has elapsed since his case was last considered by such a tribunal, whether on his own application or otherwise.

(7) If, in the case of a community patient, the community treatment order is revoked under section 17F above, the managers of the hospital shall also refer the patient's case to a Mental Health Review Tribunal as soon as possible after the order is revoked.

(8) For the purposes of furnishing information for the purposes of a reference under this section, a registered medical practitioner or approved clinician authorised by or on behalf of the patient may at any reasonable time –

(a)   visit and examine the patient in private; and

(b)   require the production of and inspect any records relating to the detention or treatment of the patient in any hospital or any after-care services provided for him under section 117 below.

(9) Reference in this section to the managers of the hospital –

(a)   in relation to a community patient, is to the managers of the responsible hospital;

(b)   in relation to any other patient, is to the managers of the hospital in which he is liable to be detained.

NOTES

Prospective amendment. Section substituted: MHA 2007, s 37(1), (3).

68A Power to reduce periods under section 68

(1) The appropriate national authority may from time to time by order amend subsections (2) or (6) of section 68 above so as to substitute for a period mentioned there such shorter period as is specified in the order.

(2) The order may include such transitional, consequential, incidental or supplemental provision as the appropriate national authority thinks fit.

(3) The order may, in particular, make provision for a case where –

    (a)   a patient in respect of whom subsection (1) of section 68 above applies is, or is about to be, transferred from England to Wales or from Wales to England; and

    (b)   the period by reference to which subsection (2) or (6) of that section operates for the purposes of the patient's case is not the same in one territory as it is in the other.

(4) A patient is transferred from one territory to the other if –

    (a)   he is transferred from a hospital, or from guardianship, in one territory to a hospital in the other in pursuance of regulations made under section 19 above;

    (b)   he is removed under subsection (3) of that section from a hospital or accommodation in one territory to a hospital or accommodation in the other;

    (c)   he is a community patient responsibility for whom is assigned from a hospital in one territory to a hospital in the other in pursuance of regulations made under section 19A above;

    (d)   on the revocation of a community treatment order in respect of him under section 17F above he is detained in a hospital in the territory other than the one in which the responsible hospital was situated; or.

    (e)   he is transferred or removed under section 123 below from a hospital in one territory to a hospital in the other.

(5) Provision made by virtue of subsection (3) above may require or authorise the managers of a hospital determined in accordance with the order to refer the patient's case to a Mental Health Review Tribunal.

(6) In so far as making provision by virtue of subsection (3) above, the order –

    (a)   may make different provision for different cases;

    (b)   may make provision which applies subject to specified exceptions.

(7) Where the appropriate national authority for one territory makes an order under subsection (1) above, the appropriate national authority for the other territory may by order make such provision in consequence of the order as it thinks fit.

(8) An order made under subsection (7) above may, in particular, make provision for a case within subsection (3) above (and subsections (4) to (6) above shall apply accordingly).

(9) In this section, 'the appropriate national authority' means –

(a) in relation to the managers of a hospital in England, the Secretary of State;

(b) in relation to the managers of a hospital in Wales, the Welsh Ministers.

NOTES

Prospective amendment. Section substituted with new s 68 for existing s 68: MHA 2007, s 37(1), (3).

Applications and references concerning Part III patients

69 Applications to tribunals concerning patients subject to hospital and guardianship orders

(1) Without prejudice to any provision of section 66(1) above as applied by section 40(4) above, an application to a Mental Health Review Tribunal may also be made –

(a) in respect of a patient liable to be detained in pursuance of a hospital order or a community patient who was so liable immediately before he became a community patient, by the nearest relative of the patient in any period in which an application may be made by the patient under any such provision as so applied;

(b) in respect of a patient placed under guardianship by a guardianship order –

   (i) by the patient, within the period of six months beginning with the date of the order;

   (ii) by the nearest relative of the patient, within the period of 12 months beginning with the date of the order and in any subsequent period of 12 months.

(2) Where a person detained in a hospital –

(a) is treated as subject to a hospital order, hospital direction or transfer direction by virtue of section 41(5) above, 82(2) or 85(2) below, or article 2(2) of the Mental Health (Care and Treatment) (Scotland) Act 2003 (Consequential Provisions) Order 2005 or section 80B(2), 82(2) or 85(2) below; or

(b) is subject to a direction having the same effect as a hospital order by virtue of section 47(3) or 48(3) above,

then, without prejudice to any provision of Part II of this Act as applied by section 40 above, that person may make an application to a Mental Health Review Tribunal in the period of six months beginning with the date of the order or direction mentioned in paragraph (a) above or, as the case may be, the date of the direction mentioned in paragraph (b) above.

(3) The provisions of section 66 above as applied by section 40(4) above are subject to subsection (4) below.

(4) If the initial detention period has not elapsed when the relevant application period begins, the right of a hospital order patient to make an application by

virtue of paragraph (ca) or (cb) of section 66(1) above shall be exercisable only during whatever remains of the relevant application period after the initial detention period has elapsed.

(5) In subsection (4) above –

(a) 'hospital order patient' means a patient who is subject to a hospital order, excluding a patient of a kind mentioned in paragraph (a) or (b) of subsection (2) above;

(b) 'the initial detention period', in relation to a hospital order patient, means the period of six months beginning with the date of the hospital order; and

(c) 'the relevant application period' means the relevant period mentioned in paragraph (ca) or (cb), as the case may be, of section 66(2) above.

NOTES

Amendments. Words in subs (2) inserted: MHA 2007, s 39(2), Sch 5, Pt 2, para 18(a).

Prospective amendments. Subs (1): para (a) prospectively substituted: MHA 2007, s 32(4), Sch 3, paras 1, 20(a). Words in subs (2)(a) prospectively substituted: MHA 2007, s 39(2), Sch 5, Pt 2, para 18(b). Reference in subs (2)(b) prospectively repealed: MHA 2007, ss 32(4), 55, Sch 3, paras 1, 20(b), Sch 11, Pt 5. Subss (3)–(5): prospectively inserted: MHA 2007, s 32(4), Sch 3, paras 1, 20(c).

70 Applications to tribunals concerning restricted patients

A patient who is a restricted patient within the meaning of section 79 below and is detained in a hospital may apply to a Mental Health Review Tribunal –

(a) in the period between the expiration of six months and the expiration of 12 months beginning with the date of the relevant hospital order, hospital direction or transfer direction; and

(b) in any subsequent period of 12 months.

71 References by Secretary of State concerning restricted patients

(1) The Secretary of State may at any time refer the case of a restricted patient to a Mental Health Review Tribunal.

(2) The Secretary of State shall refer to a Mental Health Review Tribunal the case of any restricted patient detained in a hospital whose case has not been considered by such a tribunal, whether on his own application or otherwise, within the last three years.

(3) The Secretary of State may by order vary the length of the period mentioned in subsection (2) above.

(3A) An order under subsection (3) above may include such transitional, consequential, incidental or supplemental provision as the Secretary of State thinks fit.

(4) Any reference under subsection (1) above in respect of a patient who has been conditionally discharged and not recalled to hospital shall be made to the tribunal for the area in which the patient resides.

NOTES

Prospective amendments. Subs (3A) prospectively inserted: MHA 2007, s 37(1), (4).

Discharge of patients

72 Powers of tribunals

(1) Where application is made to a Mental Health Review Tribunal by or in respect of a patient who is liable to be detained under this Act or is a community patient, the tribunal may in any case direct that the patient be discharged, and –

    (a)   the tribunal shall direct the discharge of a patient liable to be detained under section 2 above if they are not satisfied –

        (i)   that he is then suffering from mental disorder or from mental disorder of a nature or degree which warrants his detention in a hospital for assessment (or for assessment followed by medical treatment) for at least a limited period; or

        (ii)   that his detention as aforesaid is justified in the interests of his own health or safety or with a view to the protection of other persons;

    (b)   the tribunal shall direct the discharge of a patient liable to be detained otherwise than under section 2 above if they are not satisfied –

        (i)   that he is then suffering from mental disorder or from mental disorder of a nature or degree which makes it appropriate for him to be liable to be detained in a hospital for medical treatment; or

        (ii)   that it is necessary for the health of safety of the patient or for the protection of other persons that he should receive such treatment; or

        (iia)   that appropriate medical treatment is available for him; or

        (iii)   in the case of an application by virtue of paragraph (g) of section 66(1) above, that the patient, if released, would be likely to act in a manner dangerous to other persons or to himself.

    (c)   the tribunal shall direct the discharge of a community patient if they are not satisfied –

        (i)   that he is then suffering from a mental disorder or mental disorder of a nature or degree which makes it appropriate for him to receive medical treatment; or

        (ii)   that it is necessary for his health or safety or for the protection of other persons that he should receive such treatment; or

        (iii)   that it is necessary that the responsible clinician should be able to exercise the power under s 17E(1) to recall the patient to hospital; or

        (iv)   that appropriate medical treatment is available for him; or

        (v)   in the case of an application by virtue of paragraph (g) of section 66(1) above, that the patient, if discharged, would be likely to act in a manner dangerous to other persons or to himself.

(1A) In determining whether the criterion in subsection (1)(c)(iii) above is met, the tribunal shall, in particular, consider, having regard to the patient's history of mental disorder and any other relevant factors, what risk there would be of a deterioration of the patient's condition if he were to continue not to be detained in a hospital (as a result, for example, of his refusing or neglecting to receive the medical treatment he requires for his mental disorder.

(2) *(repealed)*

(3) A tribunal may under subsection (1) above direct the discharge of a patient on a future date specified in the direction; and where a tribunal do not direct the discharge of a patient under that subsection the tribunal may –

- (a) with a view to facilitating his discharge on a future date, recommend that he be granted leave of absence or transferred to another hospital or into guardianship; and
- (b) further consider his case in the event of any such recommendation not being complied with.

(3A) Subsection (1) above does not require a tribunal to direct the discharge of a patient just because they think it might be appropriate for the patient to be discharged (subject to the possibility of recall) under a community treatment order; and a tribunal –

- (a) may recommend that the responsible clinician consider whether to make a community treatment order; and
- (b) may (but need not) further consider the patient's case if the responsible clinician does not make an order.

(4) Where application is made to a Mental Health Review Tribunal by or in respect of a patient who is subject to guardianship under this Act, the tribunal may in any case direct that the patient be discharged, and shall so direct if they are satisfied –

- (a) that he is not then suffering from mental disorder; or
- (b) that it is not necessary in the interests of the welfare of the patient, or for the protection of other persons, that the patient should remain under such guardianship.

(5) *(repealed)*

(6) Subsections (1) to (4) above apply in relation to references to a Mental Health Review Tribunal as they apply in relation to applications made to such a tribunal by or in respect of a patient.

(7) Subsection (1) above shall not apply in the case of a restricted patient except as provided in sections 73 and 74 below.

NOTES

Prospective amendments. Words in subs (1) prospectively inserted: MHA 2007, s 32(4), Sch 3, paras 1, 21(1), (2)(a). Words in subs (1)(b)(i) prospectively substituted: MHA 2007, s 1(4), Sch 1, Pt 1, paras 1, 14(a). Para (1)(b)(iia) prospectively inserted: MHA 2007, s 4(1), (8)(a). Para (1)(c) prospectively inserted: MHA 2007, s 32(4), Sch 3, paras 1, 21(1), (2)(b). Subs (1A) prospectively inserted: MHA 2007, s 32(4), Sch 3, paras 1, 21(1), (3). Subs (2) prospectively repealed: MHA 2007, ss 4(1), (8)(b), 55, Sch 11, Pt 2. Subs (3A) prospectively substituted: MHA 2007, s 32(4), Sch 3, paras 1, 21(1), (4). Words in subs (4)(a) prospectively substituted: MHA 2007, s 1(4), Sch 1, Pt 1, paras 1, 14(b). Subs (4A) prospectively repealed: MHA 2007, s 55, Sch 11, Pt 5. Subs (5) prospectively repealed: MHA 2007, s 55, Sch 11, Pt 1. Reference in subs (6) prospectively substituted: MHA 2007, s 1(4), Sch 1, Pt 1, paras 1, 14(c).

73 Power to discharge restricted patients

(1) Where an application to a Mental Health Review Tribunal is made by a restricted patient who is subject to a restriction order, or where the case of such a patient is referred to such a tribunal, the tribunal shall direct the absolute discharge of the patient if –

  (a) the tribunal are not satisfied as to the matters mentioned in paragraph (b)(i), (ii) or (iia) of section 72(1) above;
  (b) the tribunal are satisfied that it is not appropriate for the patient to remain liable to be recalled to hospital for further treatment.

(2) Where in the case of any such patient as is mentioned in subsection (1) above –

  (a) paragraph (a) of that subsection applies; but
  (b) paragraph (b) of that subsection does not apply, the tribunal shall direct the conditional discharge of the patient.

(3) Where a patient is absolutely discharged under this section he shall thereupon cease to be liable to be detained by virtue of the relevant hospital order, and the restriction order shall cease to have effect accordingly.

(4) Where a patient is conditionally discharged under this section –

  (a) he may be recalled by the Secretary of State under subsection (3) of section 42 above as if he had been conditionally discharged under subsection (2) of that section; and
  (b) the patient shall comply with such conditions (if any) as may be imposed at the time of discharge by the tribunal or at any subsequent time by the Secretary of State.

(5) The Secretary of State may from time to time vary any condition imposed (whether by the tribunal or by him) under subsection (4) above.

(6) Where a restriction order in respect of a patient ceases to have effect after he has been conditionally discharged under this section the patient shall, unless previously recalled, be deemed to be absolutely discharged on the date when the order ceases to have effect and shall cease to be liable to be detained by virtue of the relevant hospital order.

(7) A tribunal may defer a direction for the conditional discharge of a patient until such arrangements as appear to the tribunal to be necessary for that purpose have been made to their satisfaction; and where by virtue of any such deferment no direction has been given on an application or reference before the time when the patient's case comes before the tribunal on a subsequent application or reference, the previous application or reference shall be treated as one on which no direction under this section can be given.

(8) This section is without prejudice to section 42 above.

NOTES

Prospective amendments. Words in subs (1)(a) prospectively substituted: MHA 2007, s 4(1), (9).

74 Restricted patients subject to restriction directions

(1) Where an application to a Mental Health Review Tribunal is made by a restricted patient who is subject to a limitation direction or restriction direction, or where the case of such a patient is referred to such a tribunal the tribunal –

(a) shall notify the Secretary of State whether, in their opinion, the patient would, if subject to a restriction order, be entitled to be absolutely or conditionally discharged under section 73 above; and

(b) if they notify him that the patient would be entitled to be conditionally discharged, may recommend that in the event of his not being discharged under this section he should continue to be detained in hospital.

(2) If in the case of a patient not falling within subsection (4) below –

(a) the tribunal notify the Secretary of State that the patient would be entitled to be absolutely or conditionally discharged; and

(b) within the period of 90 days beginning with the date of that notification the Secretary of State gives notice to the tribunal that the patient may be so discharged,

the tribunal shall direct the absolute or, as the case may be, the conditional discharge of the patient.

(3) Where a patient continues to be liable to be detained in a hospital at the end of the period referred to in subsection (2)(b) above because the Secretary of State has not given the notice there mentioned, the managers of the hospital shall, unless the tribunal have made a recommendation under subsection (1)(b) above, transfer the patient to a prison or other institution in which he might have been detained if he had not been removed to hospital, there to be dealt with as if he had not been so removed.

(4) If, in the case of a patient who is subject to a transfer direction under section 48 above, the tribunal notify the Secretary of State that the patient would be entitled to be absolutely or conditionally discharged, the Secretary of State shall, unless the tribunal have made a recommendation under subsection (1)(b) above, by warrant direct that the patient be remitted to a prison or other institution in which he might have been detained if he had not been removed to hospital, there to be dealt with as if he had not been so removed.

(5) Where a patient is transferred or remitted under subsection (3) or (4) above the relevant hospital direction and the limitation direction or, as the case may be, the relevant transfer direction and the restriction direction shall cease to have effect on his arrival in the prison or other institution.

(5A) Where the tribunal have made a recommendation under subsection (1)(b) above in the case of a patient who is subject to a restriction direction or a limitation direction –

    (a)   the fact that the restriction direction or limitation direction remains in force does not prevent the making of any application or reference to the Parole Board by or in respect of him or the exercise by him of any power to require the Secretary of State to refer his case to the Parole Board, and

    (b)   if the Parole Board make a direction or recommendation by virtue of which the patient would become entitled to be released (whether unconditionally or on licence) from any prison or other institution in which he might have been detained if he had not been removed to hospital, the restriction direction or limitation direction shall cease to have effect at the time when he would become entitled to be so released.

(6) Subsections (3) to (8) of section 73 above shall have effect in relation to this section as they have effect in relation to that section, taking references to the relevant hospital order and the restriction order as references to the hospital direction and the limitation direction or, as the case may be, to the transfer direction and the restriction direction.

(7) This section is without prejudice to sections 50 to 53 above in their application to patients who are not discharged under this section.

75 Applications and references concerning conditionally discharged restricted patients

(1) Where a restricted patient has been conditionally discharged under section 42(2), 73 or 74 above and is subsequently recalled to hospital –

    (a)   the Secretary of State shall, within one month of the day on which the patient returns or is returned to hospital, refer his case to a Mental Health Review Tribunal; and

    (b)   section 70 above shall apply to the patient as if the relevant hospital order, hospital direction or transfer direction had been made on that day.

(2) Where a restricted patient has been conditionally discharged as aforesaid but has not been recalled to hospital he may apply to a Mental Health Review Tribunal –

    (a)   in the period between the expiration of 12 months and the expiration of two years beginning with the date on which he was conditionally discharged; and

    (b)   in any subsequent period of two years.

(3) Sections 73 and 74 above shall not apply to an application under subsection (2) above but on any such application the tribunal may –

(a) vary any condition to which the patient is subject in connection with his discharge or impose any condition which might have been imposed in connection therewith; or

(b) direct that the restriction order, limitation direction or restriction direction to which he is subject shall cease to have effect;

and if the tribunal give a direction under paragraph (b) above the patient shall cease to be liable to be detained by virtue of the relevant hospital order, hospital direction or transfer direction.

NOTES

Amendments. Words in subs (3)(b) prospectively inserted: MHA 2007, s 41(a), (b).

General

76 Visiting and examination of patients

(1) For the purpose of advising whether an application to a Mental Health Review Tribunal should be made by or in respect of a patient who is liable to be detained or subject to guardianship under Part II of this Act or a community patient, or of furnishing information as to the condition of a patient for the purposes of such an application, any registered medical practitioner or approved clinician authorised by or on behalf of the patient or other person who is entitled to make or has made the application –

(a) may at any reasonable time visit the patient and examine him in private, and

(b) may require the production of and inspect any records relating to the detention or treatment of the patient in any hospital or to any after-care services provided for the patient under section 117 below.

(2) Section 32 above shall apply for the purposes of this section as it applies for the purposes of Part II of this Act.

NOTES

Prospective amendments. Words in subs (1) prospectively repealed: MHA 2007, s 55, Sch 11, Pt 5. Words in subs (1) prospectively inserted: MHA 2007, s 32(4), Sch 3, paras 1, 22. Words in subs (1) prospetively inserted: MHA 2007, s 13(1), (2)(b).

77 General provisions concerning tribunal applications

(1) No application shall be made to a Mental Health Review Tribunal by or in respect of a patient except in such cases and at such times as are expressly provided by this Act.

(2) Where under this Act any person is authorised to make an application to a Mental Health Review Tribunal within a specified period, not more than one such application shall be made by that person within that period but for that purpose there shall be disregarded any application which is withdrawn in accordance with rules made under section 78 below.

(3) Subject to subsection (4) below an application to a Mental Health Review Tribunal authorised to be made by or in respect of a patient under this Act shall be made by notice in writing addressed

(a) in the case of a patient who is liable to be detained in a hospital, to the tribunal for the area in which that hospital is situated;

(b) in the case of a community patient, to the tribunal for the area in which the responsible hospital is situated;

(c) in the case of a patient subject to guardianship, to the tribunal for the area in which the patient is residing.

(4) Any application under section 75(2) above shall be made to the tribunal for the area in which the patient resides.

NOTES

Prospective amendments. Subs (3)(a)–(c) substituted for existing words: MHA 2007, s 32(4), Sch 3, paras 1, 23.

78 Procedure of tribunals

(1) The Lord Chancellor may make rules with respect to the making of applications to Mental Health Review Tribunals and with respect to the proceedings of such tribunals and matters incidental to or consequential on such proceedings.

(2) Rules made under this section may in particular make provision –

(a) for enabling a tribunal, or the President of a tribunal, to postpone the consideration of any application by or in respect of a patient, or of any such application of any specified class, until the expiration of such period (not exceeding 12 months) as may be specified in the rules from the date on which an application by or in respect of the same patient was last considered and determined by that or the other tribunal under this Act;

(b) for the transfer of proceedings from one tribunal to the other in any case where, after the making of the application, the patient is removed out of the area of the tribunal to which it was made;

(c) for restricting the persons qualified to serve as members of a tribunal for the consideration of any application, or of an application of any specified class;

(d) for enabling a tribunal to dispose of an application without a formal hearing where such a hearing is not requested by the applicant or it appears to the tribunal that such a hearing would be detrimental to the health of the patient;

(e) for enabling a tribunal to exclude members of the public, or any specified class of members of the public, from any proceedings of the tribunal, or to prohibit the publication of reports of any such proceedings or the names of any persons concerned in such proceedings;

(f) for regulating the circumstances in which, and the persons by whom, applicants and patients in respect of whom applications are made to a tribunal may, if not desiring to conduct their own case, be represented for the purposes of those applications;

(g) for regulating the methods by which information relevant to an application may be obtained by or furnished to the tribunal, and in particular for authorising the members of a tribunal, or any one or more of them, to visit and interview in private any patient by or in respect of whom an application has been made;

(h) for making available to any applicant, and to any patient in respect of whom an application is made to a tribunal, copies of any documents obtained by or furnished to the tribunal in connection with the application, and a statement of the substance of any oral information so obtained or furnished except where the tribunal considers it undesirable in the interests of the patient or for other special reasons;

(i) for requiring a tribunal, if so requested in accordance with the rules, to furnish such statements of the reasons for any decision given by the tribunal as may be prescribed by the rules, subject to any provision made by the rules for withholding such a statement from a patient or any other person in cases where the tribunal considers that furnishing it would be undesirable in the interests of the patient or for other special reasons;

(j) for conferring on the tribunals such ancillary powers as the Lord Chancellor thinks necessary for the purposes of the exercise of their functions under this Act;

(k) for enabling any functions of a tribunal which relate to matters preliminary or incidental to an application to be performed by the President of the tribunal.

(3) Subsections (1) and (2) above apply in relation to references to Mental Health Review Tribunals as they apply in relation to applications to such tribunals by or in respect of patients.

(4) Rules under this section may make provision as to the procedure to be adopted in cases concerning restricted patients and, in particular –

(a) for restricting the persons qualified to serve as president of a tribunal for the consideration of an application or reference relating to a restricted patient;

(b) for the transfer of proceedings from one tribunal to the other in any case where, after the making of a reference or application in accordance with section 71(4) or 77(4) above, the patient ceases to reside in the area of the tribunal to which the reference or application was made.

(5) Rules under this section may be so framed as to apply to all applications or references or to applications or references of any specified class and may make different provision in relation to different cases.

(6) Any functions conferred on the President of a Mental Health Review Tribunal by rules under this section may be exercised by another member of that tribunal appointed by him for the purpose.

(7) A Mental Health Review Tribunal may pay allowances in respect of travelling expenses, subsistence and loss of earnings to any person attending the tribunal as an applicant or witness, to the patient who is the subject of the proceedings if he attends otherwise than as the applicant or a witness and to any person (other than counsel or a solicitor) who attends as the representative of an applicant.

(8) A Mental Health Review Tribunal may, and if so required by the High Court shall, state in the form of a special case for determination by the High Court any question of law which may arise before them.

(9) Part I of the Arbitration Act 1996 shall not apply to any proceedings before a Mental Health Review Tribunal except so far as any provisions of that Act may be applied, with or without modifications, by rules made under this section.

NOTES

Prospective amendments. Words in subs (2)(a) prospectively substituted: MHA 2007, s 38(1), (3)(a), (b). Words in subs (2)(b) prospectively substituted: MHA 2007, s 38(1), (3)(c). Words in subs (2)(k) prospectively substituted: MHA 2007, s 38(1), (3)(a). Words in subs (4)(a) prospectively substituted: MHA 2007, s 38(1), (3)(d). Words in subs (4)(b) prospectively substituted: MHA 2007, s 38(1), (3)(c). Words in subs (6) prospectively substituted: MHA 2007, s 38(1), (3)(a). Words in subs (6) prospectively repealed: MHA 2007, ss 38(1), (3)(e), 55, Sch 11, Pt 6.

79 Interpretation of Part V

(1) In this Part of this Act 'restricted patient' means a patient who is subject to a restriction order, limitation direction or restriction direction and this Part of this Act shall, subject to the provisions of this section, have effect in relation to any person who –

    (a)   is treated by virtue of any enactment as subject to a hospital order and a restriction order; or

    (b)   (*repealed*)

    (c)   is treated as subject to a hospital order and a restriction order, or to a hospital direction and a limitation direction, or to a transfer direction and a restriction direction, by virtue of any provision of Part 6 of this Act (except section 80D(3), 82A(2) or 85A(2) below),

as it has effect in relation to a restricted patient.

(2) Subject to the following provisions of this section, in this Part of this Act 'the relevant hospital order', 'the relevant hospital direction' and 'the relevant transfer direction', in relation to a restricted patient, mean the hospital order, the hospital direction or transfer direction by virtue of which he is liable to be detained in a hospital.

(3) In the case of a person within paragraph (a) of subsection (1) above, references in this Part of this Act to the relevant hospital order or restriction order shall be construed as references to the direction referred to in that paragraph.

(4) In the case of a person within paragraph (b) of subsection (1) above, references in this Part of this Act to the relevant hospital order or restriction order shall be construed as references to the order under the provisions mentioned in that paragraph.

(5) In the case of a person within paragraph (c) of subsection (1) above, references in this Part of this Act to the relevant hospital order, the relevant hospital direction, the relevant transfer direction, the restriction order, limitation direction or the restriction direction or to a transfer direction under section 48 above shall be construed as references to the hospital order, hospital direction, transfer direction, restriction order, limitation direction, restriction direction or transfer direction under that section to which that person is treated as subject by virtue of the provisions mentioned in that paragraph.

(5A) Section 75 above shall, subject to the modifications in subsection (5C) below, have effect in relation to a qualifying patient as it has effect in relation to a restricted patient who is conditionally discharged under section 42(2), 73 or 74 above.

(5B) A patient is a qualifying patient if he is treated by virtue of section 80D(3), 82A(2) or 85A(2) below as if he had been conditionally discharged and were subject to a hospital order and a restriction order, or to a hospital direction and a limitation direction, or to a transfer direction and a restriction direction.

(5C) The modifications mentioned in subsection (5A) above are –

   (a) references to the relevant hospital order, hospital direction or transfer direction, or to the restriction order, limitation direction or restriction direction to which the patient is subject, shall be construed as references to the hospital order, hospital direction or transfer direction, or restriction order, limitation direction or restriction direction, to which the patient is treated as subject by virtue of section 80D(3), 82A(2) or 85A(2) below; and
   (b) the reference to the date on which the patient was conditionally discharged shall be construed as a reference to the date on which he was treated as conditionally discharged by virtue of a provision mentioned in paragraph (a) above.

(6) In this Part of this Act, unless the context otherwise requires, 'hospital' means a hospital, and 'the responsible clinician' means the responsible clinician within the meaning of Part II of this Act.

(7) For the purposes of this Part of this Act –

   (a) the area of the Mental Health Review Tribunal for England is England; and
   (b) the area of the Mental Health Review Tribunal for Wales is Wales.

NOTES

Amendments. Subs (1)(c) substituted: MHA 2007, s 39(2), Sch 5, Pt 2, para 19(1), (2). Words in subs (5) inserted: MHA 2007, s 39(2), Sch 5, Pt 2, para 19(1), (3)(a)–(d). Subss (5A)–(5C) inserted: MHA 2007, s 39(2), Sch 5, Pt 2, para 19(1), (4).

Prospective amendments. Words in subs (6) prospectively substituted: MHA 2007, s 13(1), (3). Subs (7) prospectively substituted: MHA 2007, s 38(1), (4).

PART VI
REMOVAL AND RETURN OF PATIENTS WITHIN UNITED KINGDOM, ETC

Removal to and from Scotland

80 Removal of patients to Scotland

(1) If it appears to the Secretary of State, in the case of a patient who is for the time being liable to be detained under this Act (otherwise than by virtue of section 35, 36 or 38 above), that it is in the interests of the patient to remove him to Scotland, and that arrangements have been made for admitting him to a hospital or, where he is not to be admitted to a hospital, for his detention in hospital to be authorised by virtue of the Mental Health (Care and Treatment) (Scotland) Act 2003 or the Criminal Procedure (Scotland) Act 1995 the Secretary of State may authorise his removal to Scotland and may give any necessary directions for his conveyance to his destination.

(2)–(6) (*repealed in relation to England and Wales*)

(7) In this section 'hospital' has the same meaning as in the Mental Health (Care and Treatment) (Scotland) Act 2003.

(8) Reference in this section to a patient's detention in hospital being authorised by virtue of the Mental Health (Care and Treatment) (Scotland) Act 2003 or the Criminal Procedure (Scotland) Act 1995 shall be read as including reference to a patient in respect of whom a certificate under one of the provisions listed in section 290(7)(a) of the Act of 2003 is in operation.

NOTES

Prospective amendments. Preceding cross-heading prospectively substituted: MHA 2007, s 39(2), Sch 5, Pt 1, paras 1, 2. Words in subs (1) prospectively repealed: MHA 2007, ss 39(2), 55, Sch 5, Pt 1, paras 1, 2, Sch 11, Pt 7.

80ZA Transfer of responsibility for community patients to Scotland

(1) If it appears to the appropriate national authority, in the case of a community patient, that the conditions mentioned in subsection (2) below are met, the authority may authorise the transfer of responsibility for him to Scotland.

(2) The conditions are –

   (a) a transfer under this section is in the patient's interests; and
   (b) arrangements have been made for dealing with him under enactments in force in Scotland corresponding or similar to those relating to community patients in this Act.

(3) The appropriate national authority may not act under subsection (1) above while the patient is recalled to hospital under section 17E above.

(4) In this section, 'the appropriate national authority' means –

    (a)   in relation to a community patient in respect of whom the responsible hospital is in England, the Secretary of State;

    (b)   in relation to a community patient in respect of whom the responsible hospital is in Wales, the Welsh Ministers.

NOTES

Prospective amendments. Section prospectively inserted: MHA 2007, s 39(2), Sch 5, Pt 1, paras 1, 3.

80A Transfer of responsibility for conditionally discharged patients to Scotland

(1) If it appears to the Secretary of State, in the case of a patient who –

    (a)   is subject to a restriction order under section 41 above; and

    (b)   has been conditionally discharged under section 42 or 73 above,

that a transfer under this section would be in the interests of the patient, the Secretary of State may, with the consent of the Minister exercising corresponding functions in Scotland, transfer responsibility for the patient to that Minister.

80B Removal of detained patients from Scotland

(1) This section applies to a patient if –

    (a)   he is removed to England and Wales under regulations made under section 290(1)(a) of the Mental Health (Care and Treatment) (Scotland) Act 2003 ('the 2003 Act');

    (b)   immediately before his removal, his detention in hospital was authorised by virtue of that Act or the Criminal Procedure (Scotland) Act 1995; and

    (c)   on his removal, he is admitted to a hospital in England or Wales.

(2) He shall be treated as if, on the date of his admission to the hospital, he had been so admitted in pursuance of an application made, or an order or direction made or given, on that date under the enactment in force in England and Wales which most closely corresponds to the enactment by virtue of which his detention in hospital was authorised immediately before his removal.

(3) If, immediately before his removal, he was subject to a measure under any enactment in force in Scotland restricting his discharge, he shall be treated as if he were subject to an order or direction under the enactment in force in England and Wales which most closely corresponds to that enactment.

(4) If, immediately before his removal, the patient was liable to be detained under the 2003 Act by virtue of a transfer for treatment direction, given while he was serving a sentence of imprisonment (within the meaning of section 136(9) of that Act) imposed by a court in Scotland, he shall be treated as if the sentence had been imposed by a court in England and Wales.

(5) If, immediately before his removal, the patient was subject to a hospital direction or transfer for treatment direction, the restriction direction to which

he is subject by virtue of subsection (3) above shall expire on the date on which that hospital direction or transfer for treatment direction (as the case may be) would have expired if he had not been so removed.

(6) If, immediately before his removal, the patient was liable to be detained under the 2003 Act by virtue of a hospital direction, he shall be treated as if any sentence of imprisonment passed at the time when that hospital direction was made had been imposed by a court in England and Wales.

(7) Any directions given by the Scottish Ministers under regulations made under section 290 of the 2003 Act as to the removal of a patient to which this section applies shall have effect as if they were given under this Act.

(8) Subsection (8) of section 80 above applies to a reference in this section as it applies to one in that section.

(9) In this section –

'hospital direction' means a direction made under section 59A of the Criminal Procedure (Scotland) Act 1995; and 'transfer for treatment direction' has the meaning given by section 136 of the 2003 Act.

NOTES

Prospective amendments. Section prospectively inserted: MHA 2007, s 39(2), Sch 5, Pt 1, paras 1, 4.

80C Removal of patients subject to compulsion in the community from Scotland

(1) This section applies to a patient if –

  (a) he is subject to an enactment in force in Scotland by virtue of which regulations under section 289(1) of the Mental Health (Care and Treatment) (Scotland) Act 2003 apply to him; and

  (b) he is removed to England and Wales under those regulations.

(2) He shall be treated as if on the date of his arrive at the place where he is reside in England or Wales –

  (a) he had been admitted to a hospital in England or Wales in pursuance of an application or order made on that date under the; and

  (b) a community treatment order had then been made discharging him from the hospital.

(3) For these purposes –

  (a) if the enactment to which the patient was subject in Scotland was an enactment contained in the Mental Health (Care and Treatment) (Scotland) Act 2003, the corresponding enactment is section 3 of this Act;

  (b) if the enactment to which he was subject in Scotland was an enactment contained in the Criminal Procedure (Scotland) Act 1995, the corresponding enactment is section 37 of this Act.

(4) 'The responsible hospital', in the case of a patient in respect of whom a community treatment order is in force by virtue of subsection (2) above, means

the hospital to which he is treated as having been admitted by virtue of that subsection, subject to section 19A above.

(5) As soon as practicable after the patient's arrival at the place where he is to reside in England or Wales, the responsible clinician shall specify the conditions to which he is to be subject for the purposes of section 17B(1) above, and the conditions shall be deemed to be specified in the community treatment order.

(6) But the responsible clinician may only specify conditions under subsection (5) above which an approved mental health professional agrees should be specified.

NOTES

Prospective amendments. Section prospectively inserted: MHA 2007, s 39(2), Sch 5, Pt 1, paras 1, 4.

80D Transfer of conditionally discharged patients from Scotland

(1) This section applies to a patient who is subject to –

(a) a restriction order under section 59 of the Criminal Procedure (Scotland) Act 1995; and

(b) a conditional discharge under section 193(7) of the Mental Health (Care and Treatment) (Scotland) Act 2003 ('the 2003 Act').

(2) A transfer of the patient to England and Wales under regulations made under section 290 of the 2003 Act shall have effect only if the Secretary of State has consented to the transfer.

(3) If a transfer under those regulations has effect, the patient shall be treated as if –

(a) on the date of the transfer he had been conditionally discharged under section 42 or 73 above; and

(b) he were subject to a hospital order under section 37 above and a restriction order under section 41 above.

(4) If the restriction order to which the patient was subject immediately before the transfer was of limited duration, the restriction order to which he is subject by virtue of subsection (3) above shall expire on the date on which the first-mentioned order would have expired if the transfer had not been made.

NOTES

Prospective amendments. Section prospectively inserted: MHA 2007, s 39(2), Sch 5, Pt 1, paras 1, 4.

Removal to and from Northern Ireland

81 Removal of patients to Northern Ireland

(1) If it appears to the Secretary of State, in the case of a patient who is for the time being liable to be detained or subject to guardianship under this Act (otherwise than by virtue of section 35, 36 or 38 above), that it is in the interests of the patient to remove him to Northern Ireland, and that arrangements have been made for admitting him to a hospital or, as the case may be, for receiving

him into guardianship there, the Secretary of State may authorise his removal to Northern Ireland and may give any necessary directions for his conveyance to his destination.

(2) Subject to the provisions of subsections (4) and (5) below, where a patient liable to be detained under this Act by virtue of an application, order or direction under any enactment in force in England and Wales is removed under this section and admitted to a hospital in Northern Ireland, he shall be treated as if on the date of his admission he had been so admitted in pursuance of an application made, or an order or direction made or given, on that date under the corresponding enactment in force in Northern Ireland, and, where he is subject to a hospital order and a restriction order or a transfer direction and a restriction direction under any enactment in this Act, as if he were subject to a hospital order and a restriction order or a transfer direction and a restriction direction under the corresponding enactment in force in Northern Ireland.

(3) Where a patient subject to guardianship under this Act by virtue of an application, order or direction under any enactment in force in England and Wales is removed under this section and received into guardianship in Northern Ireland, he shall be treated as if on the date on which he arrives at the place where he is to reside he had been so received in pursuance of an application, order or direction under the corresponding enactment in force in Northern Ireland, and as if the application had been accepted or, as the case may be, the order or direction had been made or given on that date.

(4) Where a person removed under this section was immediately before his removal liable to be detained by virtue of an application for admission for assessment under this Act, he shall, on his admission to a hospital in Northern Ireland, be treated as if he had been admitted to the hospital in pursuance of an application for assessment under Article 4 of the Mental Health (Northern Ireland) Order 1986 made on the date of his admission.

(5) Where a person removed under this section was immediately before his removal liable to be detained by virtue of an application for admission for treatment under this Act, he shall, on his admission to a hospital in Northern Ireland, be treated as if he were detained for treatment under Part II of the Mental Health (Northern Ireland) Order 1986 by virtue of a report under Article 12(1) of that Order made on the date of his admission.

(6) Where a patient removed under this section was immediately before his removal liable to be detained under this Act by virtue of a transfer direction given while he was serving a sentence of imprisonment (within the meaning of section 47(5) above) imposed by a court in England and Wales, he shall be treated as if the sentence had been imposed by a court in Northern Ireland.

(7) Where a person removed under this section was immediately before his removal subject to a restriction direction of limited duration, the restriction direction to which he is subject by virtue of subsection (2) above shall expire on the date on which the first-mentioned restriction order or restricted direction would have expired if he had not been so removed.

(8) In this section 'hospital' has the same meaning as in the (Northern Ireland) Order 1986.

NOTES

Amendment. Words in subs (7) repealed: MHA 2007, ss 40(4), 55, Sch 11, Pt 8.

Prospective amendment. Words in subs (2) prospectively substituted: MHA 2007, s 39(2), Sch 5, Pt 1, paras 1, 5.

81ZA Removal of community patients to Northern Ireland

(1) Section 81 above shall apply in the case of a community patient as it applies in the case of a patient who is for the time being liable to be detained under this Act, as if the community patient were so liable.

(2) Any reference in that section to the application, order or direction by virtue of which a patient is liable to be detained under this Act shall be construed, for these purposes, as a reference to the application, order or direction under this Act in respect of the patient.

NOTES

Prospective amendment. Section prospectively inserted: MHA 2007, s 39(2), Sch 5, Pt 1, paras 1, 6.

81A Transfer of responsibility for patients to Northern Ireland

(1) If it appears to the Secretary of State, in the case of a patient who –

    (a)   is subject to a hospital order under section 37 above and a restriction order under section 41 above or to a transfer direction under section 47 above and a restriction direction under section 49 above; and

    (b)   has been conditionally discharged under section 42 or 73 above, that a transfer under this section would be in the interests of the patient, the Secretary of State may, with the consent of the Minister exercising corresponding functions in Northern Ireland, transfer responsibility for the patient to that Minister.

(2) Where responsibility for such a patient is transferred under this section, the patient shall be treated –

    (a)   as if on the date of the transfer he had been conditionally discharged under the corresponding enactment in force in Northern Ireland; and

    (b)   as if he were subject to a restriction order or restriction direction a hospital order and a restriction order, or to a transfer direction and a restriction direction, under the corresponding enactment in force in Northern Ireland.

(3) Where a patient responsibility for whom is transferred under this section was immediately before the transfer subject to a restriction direction of limited duration, the restriction direction to which he is subject by virtue of subsection (2) above shall expire on the date on which the first-mentioned order or direction would have expired if the transfer had not been made.

NOTES

Amendments. Subs (1)(a) and words in subs (2)(b) substituted: MHA 2007, s 39(2), Sch 5, Pt 1, paras 1, 7(1)–(3). Words in subs (3) repealed: MHA 2007, ss 40(5)(a), (b), 55, Sch 11, Pt 8.

Note. In subs (3) the words 'restriction order or' are repealed because, when the 2007 Act comes into force, all restriction orders will be without limit of time, but the provision does apply to time limited restriction orders made prior to the 2007 Act coming into force as well as to orders made outside England and Wales, which have the effect of a time limited restriction order.

82 Removal to England and Wales of patients from Northern Ireland

(1) If it appears to the responsible authority, in the case of a patient who is for the time being liable to be detained or subject to guardianship under the (Northern Ireland) Order 1986 (otherwise than by virtue of Article 42, 43 or 45 of that Order), that it is in the interests of the patient to remove him to England and Wales, and that arrangements have been made for admitting him to a hospital or, as the case may be, for receiving him into guardianship there, the responsible authority may authorise his removal to England and Wales and may give any necessary directions for his conveyance to his destination.

(2) Subject to the provisions of subsections (4) and (4A) below, where a patient who is liable to be detained under the Mental Health (Northern Ireland) Order 1986 by virtue of an application, order or direction under any enactment in force in Northern Ireland is removed under this section and admitted to a hospital in England and Wales, he shall be treated as if on the date of his admission he had been so admitted in pursuance of an application made, or an order or direction made or given, on that date under the corresponding enactment in force in England and Wales and, where he is subject to a hospital order and a restriction order or a transfer direction and a restriction direction under any enactment in that Order, as if he were subject to a hospital order and a restriction order or a transfer direction and a restriction direction under the corresponding enactment in force in England and Wales.

(3) Where a patient subject to guardianship under the Mental Health (Northern Ireland) Order 1986 by virtue of an application, order or direction under any enactment in force in Northern Ireland is removed under this section and received into guardianship in England and Wales, he shall be treated as if on the date on which he arrives at the place where he is to reside he had been so received in pursuance of an application, order or direction under the corresponding enactment in force in England and Wales and as if the application had been accepted or, as the case may be, the order or direction had been made or given on that date.

(4) Where a person removed under this section was immediately before his removal liable to be detained for treatment by virtue of a report under Article 12(1) or 13 of the Mental Health (Northern Ireland) Order 1986, he shall be treated, on his admission to a hospital in England and Wales, as if he had been admitted to the hospital in pursuance of an application for admission for treatment made on the date of his admission.

(4A) Where a person removed under this section was immediately before his removal liable to be detained by virtue of an application for assessment under

Article 4 of the Mental Health (Northern Ireland) Order 1986, he shall be treated, on his admission to a hospital in England and Wales, as if he had been admitted to the hospital in pursuance of an application for admission for assessment made on the date of his admission.

(5) Where a patient removed under this section was immediately before his removal liable to be detained under the Mental Health (Northern Ireland) Order 1986 by virtue of a transfer direction given while he was serving a sentence of imprisonment (within the meaning of Article 53(5) of that Order) imposed by a court in Northern Ireland, he shall be treated as if the sentence had been imposed by a court in England and Wales.

(6) Where a person removed under this section was immediately before his removal subject to a restriction order or restriction direction of limited duration, the restriction order or restriction direction to which he is subject by virtue of subsection (2) above shall expire on the date on which the first-mentioned restriction order or restriction direction would have expired if he had not been so removed.

(7) In this section 'the responsible authority' means the Department of Health and Social Services for Northern Ireland or, in relation to a patient who is subject to a restriction order or restriction direction, the Secretary of State.

NOTES

Amendment. Words in subs (2) substituted: MHA 2007, s 39(2), Sch 5, Pt 1, paras 1, 8.

82A Transfer of responsibility for conditionally discharged patients to England and Wales from Northern Ireland

(1) If it appears to the relevant Minister, in the case of a patient who –

  (a) is subject to a restriction order or restriction direction under Article 47(1) or 55(1) of the Mental Health (Northern Ireland) Order 1986; and
  (b) has been conditionally discharged under Article 48(2) or 78(2) of that Order,

that a transfer under this section would be in the interests of the patient, that Minister may, with the consent of the Secretary of State, transfer responsibility for the patient to the Secretary of State.

(2) Where responsibility for such a patient is transferred under this section, the patient shall be treated –

  (a) as if on the date of the transfer he had been conditionally discharged under section 42 or 73 above; and
  (b) as if he were subject to a hospital order under section 37 above and a restriction order under section 41 above or to a transfer direction under section 47 above and a restriction direction under section 49 above.

(3) Where a patient responsibility for whom is transferred under this section was immediately before the transfer subject to a restriction order or restriction

direction of limited duration, the restriction order or restriction direction to which he is subject by virtue of subsection (2) above shall expire on the date on which the first-mentioned order or direction would have expired if the transfer had not been made.

(4) In this section 'the relevant Minister' means the Minister exercising in Northern Ireland functions corresponding to those of the Secretary of State.

NOTES

Prospective amendments. Section heading and subs (2)(b) substituted: MHA 2007, s 39(2), Sch 5, Pt 1, paras 1, 9.

Removal to and from Channel Islands and Isle of Man

83 Removal of patients to Channel Islands or Isle of Man

If it appears to the Secretary of State, in the case of a patient who is for the time being liable to be detained or subject to guardianship under this Act (otherwise than by virtue of section 35, 36 or 38 above), that it is in the interests of the patient to remove him to any of the Channel Islands or to the Isle of Man, and that arrangements have been made for admitting him to a hospital or, as the case may be, for receiving him into guardianship there, the Secretary of State may authorise his removal to the island in question and may give any necessary directions for his conveyance to his destination.

83ZA Removal or transfer of community patients to Channel Islands or Isle of Man

(1) Section 83 above shall apply in the case of a community patient as it applies in the case of a patient who is for the time being liable to be detained under this Act, as if the community patient were so liable.

(2) But if there are in force in any of the Channel Islands or the Isle of Man enactments ('relevant enactments') corresponding or similar to those relating to community patients in this Act –

    (a)   subsection (1) above shall not apply as regards that island; and
    (b)   subsections (3) to (6) below shall apply instead.

(3) If it appears to the appropriate national authority, in the case of a community patient, that the conditions mentioned in subsection (4) below are met, the authority may authorise the transfer of responsibility for him to the island in question.

(4) The conditions are –

    (a)   a transfer under subsection (3) above is in the patient's interests; and
    (b)   arrangements have been made for dealing with him under the relevant enactments.

(5) But the authority may not act under subsection (3) above while the patient is recalled to hospital under section 17E above.

(6) In this section, 'the appropriate national authority' means –

(a)   in relation to a community patient in respect of whom the responsible hospital is in England, the Secretary of State;

(b)   in relation to a community patient in respect of whom the responsible hospital is in Wales, the Welsh Ministers.

NOTES

Prospective amendments. Section prospectively inserted: MHA 2007, s 39(2), Sch 5, Pt 1, paras 1, 10.

83A Transfer of responsibility for conditionally discharged patients to Channel Islands or Isle of Man

If it appears to the Secretary of State, in the case of a patient who –

(a)   is subject to a restriction order or restriction direction under section 41 or 49 above; and

(b)   has been conditionally discharged under section 42 or 73 above, that a transfer under this section would be in the interests of the patient, the Secretary of State may, with the consent of the authority exercising corresponding functions in any of the Channel Islands or in the Isle of Man, transfer responsibility for the patient to that authority.

84 Removal to England and Wales of offenders found insane in Channel Islands and Isle of Man

(1) The Secretary of State may by warrant direct that any offender found by a court in any of the Channel Islands or in the Isle of Man to be insane or to have been insane at the time of the alleged offence, and ordered to be detained during Her Majesty's pleasure, be removed to a hospital in England and Wales.

(2) A patient removed under subsection (1) above shall, on his reception into the hospital in England and Wales, be treated as if he were subject to a hospital order together with a restriction order.

(3) The Secretary of State may by warrant direct that any patient removed under this section from any of the Channel Islands or from the Isle of Man be returned to the island from which he was so removed, there to be dealt with according to law in all respects as if he had not been removed under this section.

NOTES

Amendment. Words in subs (2) repealed: MHA 2007, ss 40(3)(b), 55, Sch 11, Pt 8.

85 Patients removed from Channel Islands or Isle of Man

(1) This section applies to any patient who is removed to England and Wales from any of the Channel Islands or the Isle of Man under a provision corresponding to section 83 above and who immediately before his removal was liable to be detained or subject to guardianship in the island in question under a provision corresponding to an enactment contained in this Act (other than section 35, 36 or 38 above).

(2) Where the patient is admitted to a hospital in England and Wales he shall be treated as if on the date of his admission he had been so admitted in pursuance of an application made, or an order or direction made or given, on that date under the corresponding enactment contained in this Act and, where he is subject to an order or direction restricting his discharge, as if he were subject to a restriction order or restriction direction to a hospital order and a restriction order or to a hospital direction and a limitation direction or to a transfer direction and a restriction direction.

(3) Where the patient is received into guardianship in England and Wales, he shall be treated as if on the date on which he arrives at the place where he is to reside he had been so received in pursuance of an application, order or direction under the corresponding enactment contained in this Act and as if the application had been accepted or, as the case may be, the order or direction had been made or given on that date.

(4) Where the patient was immediately before his removal liable to be detained by virtue of a transfer direction given while he was serving a sentence of imprisonment imposed by a court in the island in question, he shall be treated as if the sentence had been imposed by a court in England and Wales.

(5) Where the patient was immediately before his removal subject to an order or direction restricting his discharge, being an order or direction of limited duration, the restriction order or restriction direction to which he is subject by virtue of subsection (2) above shall expire on the date on which the first-mentioned order or direction would have expired if he had not been removed.

(6) While being conveyed to the hospital referred to in subsection (2) or, as the case may be, the place referred to in subsection (3) above, the patient shall be deemed to be in legal custody, and section 138 below shall apply to him as if he were in legal custody by virtue of section 137 below.

(7) In the case of a patient removed from the Isle of Man the reference in subsection (4) above to a person serving a sentence of imprisonment includes a reference to a person detained as mentioned in section 60(6)(a) of the Mental Health Act 1974 (an Act of Tynwald).

NOTES

Amendment. Words in subs (2) substituted: MHA 2007, s 39(2), Sch 5, Pt 1, paras 1, 11.

85ZA Responsibility for community patients transferred from Channel Islands or Isle of Man

(1) This section shall have effect if there are in force in any of the Channel Islands or the Isle of Man enactments ('relevant enactments') corresponding or similar to those relating to community patients in this Act.

(2) If responsibility for a patient is transferred to England or Wales under a provision corresponding to section 83ZA(3) above, he shall be treated as if on the date of his arrival at the place where he is to reside in England or Wales –

(a) he had been admitted to the hospital in pursuance of an application made, or an order or direction made or given, on that date under the enactment in force in England and Wales which most closely corresponds to the relevant enactments; and

(b) a community treatment order had then been made discharging him from the hospital.

(3) 'The responsible hospital', in his case, means the hospital to which he is treated as having been admitted by virtue of subsection (2), subject to section 19A above.

(4) As soon as practicable after the patient's arrival at the place where he is to reside in England or Wales, the responsible clinician shall specify the conditions to which he is to be subject for the purposes of section 17B(1) above, and the conditions shall be deemed to be specified in the community treatment order.

(5) But the responsible clinician may only specify conditions under subsection (4) above which an approved mental health professional agrees should be specified.

NOTES

Prospective amendment. Section prospectively inserted: MHA 2007, s 39(2), Sch 5, Pt 1, paras 1, 12.

85A Responsibility for conditionally discharged patients transferred from Channel Islands or Isle of Man

(1) This section applies to any patient responsibility for whom is transferred to the Secretary of State by the authority exercising corresponding functions in any of the Channel Islands or the Isle of Man under a provision corresponding to section 83A above.

(2) The patient shall be treated –

(a) as if on the date of the transfer he had been conditionally discharged under section 42 or 73 above; and

(b) as if he were subject to a hospital order under section 37 above and a restriction order under section 41 above, or to a hospital direction and a limitation direction under section 45A above, or to a transfer direction under section 47 above and a restriction direction under section 49 above.

(3) Where the patient was immediately before the transfer subject to an order or direction restricting his discharge, being an order or direction of limited duration, the restriction order, limitation direction or restriction direction to which he is subject by virtue of subsection (2) above shall expire on the date on which the first-mentioned order or direction would have expired if the transfer had not been made.

NOTES

Amendments. Section heading substituted: MHA 2007, s 39(2), Sch 5, para 12. Subs (2)(b) substituted: MHA 2007, s 39(2), Sch 5, Pt 1, paras 1, 13(1), (2). Words in subs (3) inserted: MHA 2007, s 39(1), Sch 5, Pt 1, paras 1, 13(1), (3).

Removal of aliens

86 Removal of alien patients

(1) This section applies to any patient who is neither a British citizen nor a Commonwealth citizen having the right of abode in the United Kingdom by virtue of section 2(1)(b) of the Immigration Act 1971, being a patient who is receiving treatment for mental disorder as an in-patient in a hospital in England and Wales or a hospital within the meaning of the Mental Health (Northern Ireland) Order 1986 and is detained pursuant to –

    (a)   an application for admission for treatment or a report under Article 12(1) or 13 of that Order;

    (b)   a hospital order under section 37 above or Article 44 of that Order; or

    (c)   an order or direction under this Act (other than under section 35, 36 or 38 above) or under that Order (other than under Article 42, 43 or 45 of that Order) having the same effect as such a hospital order.

(2) If it appears to the Secretary of State that proper arrangements have been made for the removal of a patient to whom this section applies to a country or territory outside the United Kingdom, the Isle of Man and the Channel Islands and for his care or treatment there and that it is in the interests of the patient to remove him, the Secretary of State may, subject to subsection (3) below –

    (a)   by warrant authorise the removal of the patient from the place where he is receiving treatment as mentioned in subsection (1) above, and

    (b)   give such directions as the Secretary of State thinks fit for the conveyance of the patient to his destination in that country or territory and for his detention in any place or on board any ship or aircraft until his arrival at any specified port or place in any such country or territory.

(3) The Secretary of State shall not exercise his powers under subsection (2) above in the case of any patient except with the approval of a Mental Health Review Tribunal or, as the case may be, of the Mental Health Review Tribunal for Northern Ireland.

(4) In relation to a patient receiving treatment in a hospital within the meaning of the Mental Health (Northern Ireland) Order 1986, the reference in subsection (1) above to mental disorder shall be construed in accordance with that Order.

NOTES

Prospective amendments. Words in subs (1) prospectively substituted and subs (4) prospectively inserted: MHA 2007, s 1(4), Sch 1, Pt 1, paras 1, 15(1)–(3).

Return of patients absent without leave

87 Patients absent from hospitals in Northern Ireland

(1) Any person who –

(a) under Article 29 or 132 of the Mental Health (Northern Ireland) Order 1986 (which provide, respectively, for the retaking of patients absent without leave and for the retaking of patients escaping from custody); or

(b) under the said Article 29 as applied by Article 31 of the said Order (which makes special provision as to persons sentenced to imprisonment);

may be taken into custody in Northern Ireland, may be taken into custody in, and returned to Northern Ireland from, England and Wales by an approved mental health professional, by any constable or by any person authorised by or by virtue of the said Order to take him into custody.

(2) This section does not apply to any person who is subject to guardianship.

NOTES

Prospective amendments. Words in subs (1) prospectively substituted: MHA 2007, s 21, Sch 2, paras 1, 7(f).

88 Patients absent from hospitals in England and Wales

(1) Subject to the provisions of this section, any person who, under section 18 above or section 138 below or under the said section 18 as applied by section 22 above, may be taken into custody in England and Wales may be taken into custody in, and returned to England and Wales from, Northern Ireland.

(2) For the purposes of the enactments referred to in subsection (1) above in their application by virtue of this section, the expression 'constable' includes an officer or constable of the Police Service of Northern Ireland.

(3) For the purposes of the said enactments in their application by virtue of this section, any reference to an approved mental health professional shall be construed as including a reference –

(a) (*repealed*)

(b) to any approved social worker within the meaning of the Mental Health (Northern Ireland) Order 1986.

(4) This section does not apply to any person who is subject to guardianship.

NOTES

Prospective amendments. Words in subs (1) prospectively substituted: MHA 2007, s 39(2), Sch 5, Pt 1, paras 1, 14(1), (2). Subs (2) prospectively substituted: MHA 2007, s 39(2), Sch 5, Pt 1, paras 1, 14(1), (3). Words in subs (3) prospectively repealed: MHA 2007, ss 39(2), 55, Sch 5, Pt 1, paras 1, 14(1), (4)(a), Sch 11, Pt 7. Words in subs (3) prospectively substituted: MHA 2007, s 21, Sch 2, paras 1, 7(g). Subs (3)(a) repealed: MHA 2007, ss 39(2), 55, Sch 5, Pt 1, paras 1, 14(1), (4)(b), Sch 11, Pt 7.

89 Patients absent from hospitals in the Channel Islands or Isle of Man

(1) Any person who under any provision corresponding to section 18 above or 138 below may be taken into custody in any of the Channel Islands or the Isle

of Man may be taken into custody in, and returned to the island in question from, England and Wales by an approved mental health professional or a constable.

(2) This section does not apply to any person who is subject to guardianship.

NOTES

Prospective amendments. Words in subs (1) prospectively substituted: MHA 2007, s 21, Sch 2, paras 1, 7(h).

General

90 Regulations for purposes of Part VI

Section 32 above shall have effect as if references in that section to Part II of this Act included references to this Part of this Act, so far as this Part of this Act applies to patients removed to England and Wales or for whom responsibility is transferred to England and Wales.

NOTES

Prospective amendments. Words prospectively substituted: MHA 2007, s 39(2), Sch 5, Pt 1, paras 1, 15.

91 General provisions as to patients removed from England and Wales

(1) Subject to subsection (2) below, where a patient liable to be detained or subject to guardianship by virtue of an application, order or direction under Part II or III of this Act (other than section 35, 36 or 38 above) is removed from England and Wales in pursuance of arrangements under this Part of this Act, the application, order or direction shall cease to have effect when he is duly received into a hospital or other institution, or placed under guardianship or, where he is not received into a hospital but his detention in hospital is authorised by virtue of the Mental Health (Care and Treatment) (Scotland) Act 2003 or the Criminal Procedure (Scotland) Act 1995, in pursuance of those arrangements.

(2) Where the Secretary of State exercises his powers under section 86(2) above in respect of a patient who is detained pursuant to a hospital order under section 37 above and in respect of whom a restriction order is in force, those orders shall continue in force so as to apply to the patient if he returns to England and Wales.

(2A) Where responsibility for a community patient is transferred to a jurisdiction outside England and Wales (or such a patient is removed outside England and Wales) in pursuance of arrangements under this Part of this Act, the application, order or direction mentioned in subsection (1) above in force in respect of him shall cease to have effect on the date on which responsibility is so transferred (or he is so removed) in pursuance of those arrangements.

(3) Reference in this section to a patient's detention in hospital being authorised by virtue of the Mental Health (Care and Treatment) (Scotland) Act 2003 or the Criminal Procedure (Scotland) Act 1995 shall be read as

including references to a patient in respect of whom a certificate under one of the provisions listed in section 290(7)(a) of the Act of 2003 is in operation.

NOTES

Amendment. Words in subs (2) repealed: MHA 2007, ss 40(6), 55, Sch 11, Pt 8.

Prospective amendment. Subs (2A) prospectively inserted: MHA 2007, s 39(2), Sch 5, Pt 1, paras 1, 16.

92 Interpretation of Part VI

(1) References in this Part of this Act to a hospital, being a hospital in England and Wales, shall be construed as references to a hospital within the meaning of Part II of this Act.

(1A) References in this Part of this Act to the responsible clinician shall be construed as references to the responsible clinician within the meaning of Part 2 of this Act.

(2) Where a patient is treated by virtue of this Part of this Act as if he had been removed to a hospital in England and Wales in pursuance of a direction under Part III of this Act, that direction shall be deemed to have been given on the date of his reception into the hospital.

(4) Sections 80 to 85A above shall have effect as if –

    (a)   any hospital direction under section 45A above were a transfer direction under section 47 above; and

    (b)   any limitation direction under section 45A above were a restriction direction under section 49 above.

(5) Sections 80(5), 81(6) and 85(4) above shall have effect as if any reference to a transfer direction given while a patient was serving a sentence of imprisonment imposed by a court included a reference to a hospital direction given by a court after imposing a sentence of imprisonment on a patient.

NOTES

Prospective amendments. Subs (1A) prospectively inserted: MHA 2007, s 39(2), Sch 5, Pt 1, paras 1, 17. Subs (3) repealed: MHA 2007, s 55, Sch 11, Pt 1.

PART VII
(REPEALED)

PART VIII
MISCELLANEOUS FUNCTIONS OF LOCAL AUTHORITIES AND THE SECRETARY OF STATE

Approved mental health professionals

114 Approval by local social services authority

(1) A local social services authority may approve a person to act as an approved mental health professional for the purposes of this Act.

(2) But a local social services authority may not approve a registered medical practitioner to act as an approved mental health professional.

(3) Before approving a person under subsection (1) above, a local social services authority shall be satisfied that he has appropriate competence in dealing with persons who are suffering from mental disorder.

(4) The appropriate national authority may by regulations make provision in connection with the giving of approvals under subsection (1) above.

(5) The provision which may be made by regulations under subsection (4) above includes, in particular, provision as to –

  (a)   the period for which approvals under subsection (1) above have effect;
  (b)   the courses to be undertaken by persons before such approvals are to be given and during the period for which such approvals have effect;
  (c)   the conditions subject to which such approvals are to be given; and
  (d)   the factors to be taken into account in determining whether persons have appropriate competence as mentioned in subsection (3) above.

(6) Provision made by virtue of subsection (5)(b) above may relate to courses approved or provided by such person as may be specified in the regulations (as well as to courses approved under section 114A below).

(7) An approval by virtue of subsection (6) above may be in respect of a course in general or in respect of a course in relation to a particular person.

(8) The power to make regulations under subsection (4) above includes power to make different provision for different cases or areas.

(9) In this section 'the appropriate national authority' means –

  (a)   in relation to persons who are or wish to become approved to act as approved mental health professionals by a local social services authority whose area is in England, the Secretary of State;
  (b)   in relation to persons who are or wish to become approved to act as approved mental health professionals by a local social services authority whose area is in Wales, the Welsh Ministers.

(10) In this Act 'approved mental health professional' means –

  (a)   in relation to acting on behalf of a local social services authority whose area is in England, a person approved under subsection (1) above by any local social services authority whose area is in England, and
  (b)   in relation to acting on behalf of a local social services authority whose area is in Wales, a person approved under that subsection by any local social services authority whose area is in Wales.'

NOTES

Prospective amendments. Section and preceding cross-heading prospectively substituted: MHA 2007, s 18.

114A Approval of courses etc for approved mental health professionals

(1) The relevant Council may, in accordance with rules made by it, approve courses for persons who are or wish to become approved mental health professionals.

(2) For that purpose –

(a) subsections (2) to (4)(a) and (7) of section 63 of the Care Standards Act 2000 apply as they apply to approvals given, rules made and courses approved under that section; and

(b) sections 66 and 71 of that Act apply accordingly.

(3) In subsection (1), 'the relevant Council' means –

(a) in relation to persons who are or wish to become approved to act as approved mental health professionals by a local social services authority whose area is in England, the General Social Care Council;

(b) in relation to persons who are or wish to become approved to act as approved mental health professionals by a local social services authority whose area is in Wales, the Care Council for Wales.

(4) The functions of an approved mental health professional shall not be considered to be relevant social work for the purposes of Part 4 of the Care Standards Act 2000.

(5) The General Social Care Council and the Care Council for Wales may also carry out, or assist other persons in carrying out, research into matters relevant to training for approved mental health professionals.

NOTES

Amendment. Section inserted: MHA 2007, s 19.

115 Powers of entry and inspection

(1) An approved mental health professional may at all reasonable times enter and inspect any premises (other than a hospital) in which a mentally disordered patient is living, if he has reasonable cause to believe that the patient is not under proper care.

(2) The power under subsection (1) above shall be exercisable only after the professional has produced, if asked to do so, some duly authenticated document showing that he is an approved mental health professional.

NOTES

Prospective amendment. Section prospectively substituted: MHA 2007, s 21, Sch 2, paras 1, 8.

Visiting patients

116 Welfare of certain hospital patients

(1) Where a patient to whom this section applies is admitted to a hospital, independent hospital or care home in England and Wales (whether for treatment for mental disorder or for any other reason) then, without prejudice

to their duties in relation to the patient apart from the provisions of this section, the authority shall arrange for visits to be made to him on behalf of the authority, and shall take such other steps in relation to the patient while in the hospital, independent hospital or care home as would be expected to be taken by his parents.

(2) This section applies to –

   (a)   a child or young person –
      (i)   who is in the care of a local authority by virtue of a care order within the meaning of the Children Act 1989, or
      (ii)   in respect of whom the rights and powers of a parent are vested in a local authority by virtue of section 16 of the Social Work (Scotland) Act 1968;
   (b)   a person who is subject to the guardianship of a local social services authority under the provisions of this Act; or
   (c)   a person the functions of whose nearest relative under this Act are for the time being transferred to a local social services authority.

After-care

117 After-care

(1) This section applies to persons who are detained under section 3 above, or admitted to a hospital in pursuance of a hospital order made under section 37 above, or transferred to a hospital in pursuance of a hospital direction made under section 45A above or a transfer direction made under section 47 or 48 above, and then cease to be detained and (whether or not immediately after so ceasing) leave hospital.

(2) It shall be the duty of the Primary Care Trust or Local Health Board and of the local social services authority to provide, in co-operation with relevant voluntary agencies, after-care services for any person to whom this section applies until such time as the Primary Care Trust or Local Health Board and the local social services authority are satisfied that the person concerned is no longer in need of such services; but they shall not be so satisfied in the case of a community patient while he remains such a patient.

(2B) Section 32 above shall apply for the purposes of this section as it applies for the purposes of Part II of this Act.

(2A) *(repealed)*

(3) In this section 'the Primary Care Trust or Local Health Board' means the Primary Care Trust or Local Health Board, and 'the local social services authority' means the local social services authority, for the area in which the person concerned is resident or to which he is sent on discharge by the hospital in which he was detained.

NOTES

Prospective amendments. Words in subs (2) prospectively substituted: MHA 2007, s 32(4), Sch 3, paras 1, 24. Subs (2A) prospectively repealed: MHA 2007, s 55, Sch 11, Pt 5.

Note. Existing subs (2A) provides that: '(2A) It shall be the duty of the Primary Care Trust or Local Health Board to secure that at all times while a patient is subject to after-care under supervision – (a) a person who is a registered medical practitioner approved for the purposes of section 12 above by the Secretary of State as having special experience in the diagnosis or treatment of mental disorder is in charge of the medical treatment provided for the patient as part of the after-care services provided for him under this section; and (b) a person professionally concerned with any of the after-care services so provided is supervising him with a view to securing that he receives the after-care services so provided.'

Functions of the Secretary of State

118 Code of practice

(1) The Secretary of State shall prepare, and from time to time revise, a code of practice –

(a) for the guidance of registered medical practitioners, approved clinicians, managers and staff of hospitals, independent hospitals and care homes and approved mental health professionals in relation to the admission of patients to hospitals and registered establishments under this Act and to guardianship and community patients under this Act; and

(b) for the guidance of registered medical practitioners and members of other professions in relation to the medical treatment of patients suffering from mental disorder.

(2) The code shall, in particular, specify forms of medical treatment in addition to any specified by regulations made for the purposes of section 57 above which in the opinion of the Secretary of State give rise to special concern and which should accordingly not be given by a registered medical practitioner unless the patient has consented to the treatment (or to a plan of treatment including that treatment) and a certificate in writing as to the matters mentioned in subsection (2)(a) and (b) of that section has been given by another registered medical practitioner, being a practitioner appointed for the purposes of this section by the Secretary of State.

(2A) The code shall include a statement of the principles which the Secretary of State thinks should inform decisions under this Act.

(2B) In preparing the statement of principles the Secretary of State shall, in particular, ensure that each of the following matters is addressed –

(a) respect for patients' past and present wishes and feelings,

(b) respect for diversity generally including, in particular, diversity of religion, culture and sexual orientation (within the meaning of section 35 of the Equality Act 2006),

(c) minimising restrictions on liberty,

(d) involvement of patients in planning, developing and delivering care and treatment appropriate to them,

(e) avoidance of unlawful discrimination,

(f) effectiveness of treatment,

(g) views of carers and other interested parties,

(h)   patient wellbeing and safety, and
(i)   public safety.

(2C) The Secretary of State shall also have regard to the desirability of ensuring –

(a)   the efficient use of resources, and
(b)   the equitable distribution of services.

(2D) In performing functions under this Act persons mentioned in subsection (1)(a) or (b) shall have regard to the code.'

(3) Before preparing the code or making any alteration in it the Secretary of State shall consult such bodies as appear to him to be concerned.

(4) The Secretary of State shall lay copies of the code and of any alteration in the code before Parliament; and if either House of Parliament passes a resolution requiring the code or any alteration in it to be withdrawn the Secretary of State shall withdraw the code or alteration and, where he withdraws the code, shall prepare a code in substitution for the one which is withdrawn.

(5) No resolution shall be passed by either House of Parliament under subsection (4) above in respect of a code or alteration after the expiration of the period of 40 days beginning with the day on which a copy of the code or alteration was laid before that House; but for the purposes of this subsection no account shall be taken of any time during which Parliament is dissolved or prorogued or during which both Houses are adjourned for more than four days.

(6) The Secretary of State shall publish the code as for the time being in force.

NOTES

Prospective amendments. Words in subs (1) prospectively inserted: MHA 2007, s 14(1), (2). Words in subs (1)(a) prospectively substituted: MHA 2007, s 21, Sch 2, paras 1, 9. Words in subs (1)(a) prospectively substituted: MHA 2007, s 32(4), Sch 3, paras 1, 25. Subss (2A)–(2D) prospectively inserted: MHA 2007, s 8.

119 Practitioners approved for Part IV and s 118

(1) The Secretary of State may make such provision as he may with the approval of the Treasury determine for the payment of remuneration, allowances, pensions or gratuities to or in respect of registered medical practitioners appointed by him for the purposes of Part IV of this Act and section 118 above and to or in respect of other persons appointed for the purposes of section 57(2)(a) above.

(2) A registered medical practitioner or other person appointed by the Secretary of State for the purposes of the provisions mentioned in subsection (1) above may, for the purpose of exercising his functions under those provisions or under Part 4A of this Act, at any reasonable time –

(a)   visit and interview and, in the case of a registered medical practitioner, examine in private any patient detained in a hospital or registered establishment or any community patient in a hospital or establishment of any description or (if access is granted) other place; and

(b) require the production of and inspect any records relating to the treatment of the patient there.

(3) In this section, 'establishment of any description' shall be construed in accordance with section 4(8) of the Care Standards Act 2000.

NOTES

Prospective amendments. Words in subs (2) prospectively inserted: MHA 2007, s 35(2)(a)(i). Words in subs (2)(a) prospectively substituted: MHA 2007, s 35(2)(a)(ii). Words in subs (2)(b) prospectively substituted: MHA 2007, s 35(2)(a)(iii). Words in subs (3) prospectively inserted: MHA 2007, s 35(2)(b).

120 General protection of detained patients

(1) The Secretary of State shall keep under review the exercise of the powers and the discharge of the duties conferred or imposed by this Act so far as relating to the detention of patients or to patients liable to be detained under this Act or to community patients and shall make arrangements for persons authorised by him in that behalf –

(a) to visit and interview in private patients detained under this Act in hospitals and registered establishments and community patients in hospitals and establishments of any description and (if access is granted) other places; and

(b) to investigate –

    (i) any complaint made by a person in respect of a matter that occurred while he was detained under this Act in, or recalled under section 17E above to, a hospital or registered establishment and which he considers has not been satisfactorily dealt with by the managers of that hospital or registered establishment; and

    (ii) any other complaint as to the exercise of the powers or the discharge of the duties conferred or imposed by this Act in respect of a person who is or has been so detained or is or has been a community patient.

(2) The arrangements made under this section in respect of the investigation of complaints may exclude matters from investigation in specified circumstances and shall not require any person exercising functions under the arrangements to undertake or continue with any investigation where he does not consider it appropriate to do so.

(3) Where any such complaint as is mentioned in subsection (1)(b)(ii) above is made by a Member of Parliament and investigated under the arrangements made under this section the results of the investigation shall be reported to him.

(4) For the purpose of any such review as is mentioned in subsection (1) above or of carrying out his functions under arrangements made under this section any person authorised in that behalf by the Secretary of State may at any reasonable time –

(a) visit and interview and, if he is a registered medical practitioner or approved clinician, examine in private any patient in a hospital or establishment of any description; and

(b) require the production of and inspect any records relating to the detention or treatment of any person who is or has been detained in a registered establishment under this Act or who is or has been a community patient.

(5) (*repealed*)

(6) The Secretary of State may make such provision as he may with the approval of the Treasury determine for the payment of remuneration, allowances, pensions or gratuities to or in respect of persons exercising functions in relation to any such review as is mentioned in subsection (1) above or functions under arrangements made under this section.

(7) The powers and duties referred to in subsection (1) above do not include any power or duty conferred or imposed by Part VII of this Act.

(8) In this section, 'establishment of any description' has the same meaning as in section 119 above.

NOTES

Prospective amendments. Words in subs (1) prospectively inserted: MHA 2007, s 32(4), Sch 3, paras 1, 26(1), (2)(a). Words in subs (1)(a) prospectively inserted: MHA 2007, s 32(4), Sch 3, paras 1, 26(1), (2)(b). Words in subs (1)(b)(i) prospectively inserted: MHA 2007, s 32(4), Sch 3, paras 1, 26(1), (2)(c)(i). Words in subs (1)(b)(ii) prospectively inserted: MHA 2007, s 32(4), Sch 3, paras 1, 26(1), (2)(c)(ii). Words in subs (4) prospectively inserted: MHA 2007, s 14(1), (3)(a). Words in subs (4)(a) prospectively substituted: MHA 2007, s 32(4), Sch 3, paras 1, 26(1), (3)(a). Words in subs (4)(b) prospectively substituted: MHA 2007, s 32(4), Sch 3, paras 1, 26(1), (3)(b). Subs (8) prospectively inserted: MHA 2007, s 32(4), Sch 3, paras 1, 26(1), (4).

121 Mental Health Act Commission

(1) Without prejudice to section 273(1) of the National Health Service Act 2006, or section 204(1) of the National Health Service (Wales) Act 2006 (power to vary or revoke orders or directions) there shall continue to be a Special Health Authority known as the Mental Health Act Commission established under section 11 of that Act.

(2) Without prejudice to the generality of his powers under section 13 of that Act, the Secretary of State shall direct the Commission to perform on his behalf –

(a) the function of appointing registered medical practitioners for the purposes of Part IV of this Act and section 118 above and of appointing other persons for the purposes of section 57(2)(a) above; and

(b) the functions of the Secretary of State under sections 61, 64H(5) and 120(1) and (4) above.

(3) The registered medical practitioners and other persons appointed for the purposes mentioned in subsection (2)(a) above may include members of the Commission.

(4) The Secretary of State may, at the request of or after consultation with the Commission and after consulting such other bodies as appear to him to be concerned, direct the Commission to keep under review the care and treatment, or any aspect of the care and treatment, in hospitals, independent hospitals and care homes of patients who are neither liable to be detained under this Act nor community patients.

(5) For the purpose of any such review as is mentioned in subsection (4) above any person authorised in that behalf by the Commission may at any reasonable time –

(a) visit and interview and, if he is a registered medical practitioner or approved clinician, examine in private any patient in an independent hospital or a care home; and

(b) require the production of and inspect any records relating to the treatment of any person who is or has been a patient in an independent hospital or a care home.

(6) The Secretary of State may make such provision as he may with the approval of the Treasury determine for the payment of remuneration, allowances, pensions or gratuities to or in respect of persons exercising functions in relation to any such review as is mentioned in subsection (4) above.

(7) The Commission shall review any decision to withhold a postal packet (or anything contained in it) under subsection (1)(b) or (2) of section 134 below if any application in that behalf is made –

(a) in a case under subsection (1)(b), by the patient; or

(b) in a case under subsection (2), either by the patient or by the person by whom the postal packet was sent; and any such application shall be made within six months of the receipt by the applicant of the notice referred to in subsection (6) of that section.

(8) On an application under subsection (7) above the Commission may direct that the postal packet which is the subject of the application (or anything contained in it) shall not be withheld and the managers in question shall comply with any such direction.

(9) The Secretary of State may by regulations make provision with respect to the making and determination of applications under subsection (7) above, including provision for the production to the Commission of any postal packet which is the subject of such an application.

(10) The Commission shall in the second year after its establishment and subsequently in every second year publish a report on its activities; and copies of every such report shall be sent by the Commission to the Secretary of State who shall lay a copy before each House of Parliament.

(11) Paragraph 2 of Schedule 6 to the National Health Service Act 2006, and paragraph 2 of Schedule 5 to the National Health Service (Wales) Act 2006 (pay and allowances for chairmen and members of Special Health Authorities) shall have effect in relation to the Mental Health Act Commission as if

references in sub-paragraphs (1) and (2) to the chairman included references to any member and as if the reference to a member in sub-paragraph (4) included a reference to the chairman.

NOTES

Prospective amendments. Reference in subs (2)(b) prospectively inserted: MHA 2007, s 35(3). Words in subs (4) prospectively substituted: MHA 2007, s 32(4), Sch 3, paras 1, 27. Words in subs (5)(a) prospectively inserted: MHA 2007, s 14(1), (3)(b).

122 Provision of pocket money for in-patients in hospital

(1) The Secretary of State may pay to persons who are receiving treatment as inpatients (whether liable to be detained or not) in hospitals wholly or mainly used for the treatment of persons suffering from mental disorder, such amounts as he thinks fit in respect of their occasional personal expenses where it appears to him that they would otherwise be without resources to meet those expenses.

(2) For the purposes of the National Health Service Act 2006 and the National Health Service (Wales) Act 2006, the making of payments under this section to persons for whom hospital services are provided under either of those Acts shall be treated as included among those services.

123 Transfers to and from special hospitals

(1) Without prejudice to any other provisions of this Act with respect to the transfer of patients, any patient who is for the time being liable to be detained under this Act (other than under section 35, 36 or 38 above) in a hospital at which high security psychiatric services are provided may, upon the directions of the Secretary of State, at any time be removed into any other hospital at which those services are provided.

(2) Without prejudice to any such provision, the Secretary of State may give directions for the transfer of any patient who is for the time being liable to be so detained into a hospital at which those services are not provided.

(3) Subsections (2) and (4) of section 19 above shall apply in relation to the transfer or removal of a patient under this section as they apply in relation to the transfer or removal of a patient from one hospital to another under that section.

124 ...

(repealed)

125 ...

(repealed)

PART IX
OFFENCES

126 Forgery, false statements, etc

(1) Any person who without lawful authority or excuse has in his custody or under his control any document to which this subsection applies, which is, and which he knows or believes to be, false within the meaning of Part I of the Forgery and Counterfeiting Act 1981, shall be guilty of an offence.

(2) Any person who without lawful authority or excuse makes, or has in his custody or under his control, any document so closely resembling a document to which subsection (1) above applies as to be calculated to deceive shall be guilty of an offence.

(3) The documents to which subsection (1) above applies are any documents purporting to be –

    (a)   an application under Part II of this Act;

    (b)   a medical or other recommendation or report under this Act; and

    (c)   any other document required or authorised to be made for any of the purposes of this Act.

(4) Any person who –

    (a)   wilfully makes a false entry or statement in any application, recommendation, report, record or other document required or authorised to be made for any of the purposes of this Act; or

    (b)   with intent to deceive, makes use of any such entry or statement which he knows to be false, shall be guilty of an offence.

(5) Any person guilty of an offence under this section shall be liable –

    (a)   on summary conviction, to imprisonment for a term not exceeding six months or to a fine not exceeding the statutory maximum, or to both;

    (b)   on conviction on indictment, to imprisonment for a term not exceeding two years or to a fine of any amount, or to both.

127 Ill-treatment of patients

(1) It shall be an offence for any person who is an officer on the staff of or otherwise employed in, or who is one of the managers of, a hospital, independent hospital or care home –

    (a)   to ill-treat or wilfully to neglect a patient for the time being receiving treatment for mental disorder as an in-patient in that hospital or home; or

    (b)   to ill-treat or wilfully to neglect, on the premises of which the hospital or home forms part, a patient for the time being receiving such treatment there as an out-patient.

(2) It shall be an offence for any individual to ill-treat or wilfully to neglect a mentally disordered patient who is for the time being subject to his

guardianship under this Act or otherwise in his custody or care (whether by virtue of any legal or moral obligation or otherwise).

(2A) (*repealed*)

(3) Any person guilty of an offence under this section shall be liable –

    (a)   on summary conviction, to imprisonment for a term not exceeding six months or to a fine not exceeding the statutory maximum, or to both;

    (b)   on conviction on indictment, to imprisonment for a term not exceeding five years or to a fine of any amount, or to both.

(4) No proceedings shall be instituted for an offence under this section except by or with the consent of the Director of Public Prosecutions.

NOTES

Amendment. Words in subs (3)(b) substituted: MHA 2007, s 42.

Prospective amendment. Subs (2A) (which relates to after care under supervision) prospectively repealed: MHA 2007, s 55, Sch 11, Pt 5.

128 Assisting patients to absent themselves without leave, etc

(1) Where any person induces or knowingly assists another person who is liable to be detained in a hospital within the meaning of Part II of this Act or is subject to guardianship under this Act or is a community patient to absent himself without leave he shall be guilty of an offence.

(2) Where any person induces or knowingly assists another person who is in legal custody by virtue of section 137 below to escape from such custody he shall be guilty of an offence.

(3) Where any person knowingly harbours a patient who is absent without leave or is otherwise at large and liable to be retaken under this Act or gives him any assistance with intent to prevent, hinder or interfere with his being taken into custody or returned to the hospital or other place where he ought to be he shall be guilty of an offence.

(4) Any person guilty of an offence under this section shall be liable –

    (a)   on summary conviction, to imprisonment for a term not exceeding six months or to a fine not exceeding the statutory maximum, or to both;

    (b)   on conviction on indictment, to imprisonment for a term not exceeding two years or to a fine of any amount, or to both.

NOTES

Prospective amendments. Words in subs (1) prospectively inserted: MHA 2007, s 32(4), Sch 3, paras 1, 28.

129 Obstruction

(1) Any person who without reasonable cause –

    (a)   refuses to allow the inspection of any premises; or

(b) refuses to allow the visiting, interviewing or examination of any person by a person authorised in that behalf by or under this Act or to give access to any person to a person so authorised; or

(c) refuses to produce for the inspection of any person so authorised any document or record the production of which is duly required by him; or

(d) otherwise obstructs any such person in the exercise of his functions,

shall be guilty of an offence.

(2) Without prejudice to the generality of subsection (1) above, any person who insists on being present when required to withdraw by a person authorised by or under this Act to interview or examine a person in private shall be guilty of an offence.

(3) Any person guilty of an offence under this section shall be liable on summary conviction to imprisonment for a term not exceeding three months or to a fine not exceeding level 4 on the standard scale or to both.

130 Prosecutions by local authorities

A local social services authority may institute proceedings for any offence under this Part of this Act, but without prejudice to any provision of this Part of this Act requiring the consent of the Director of Public Prosecutions for the institution of such proceedings.

PART X
MISCELLANEOUS AND SUPPLEMENTARY

Miscellaneous provisions

130A Independent mental health advocates

(1) The appropriate national authority shall make such arrangements as it considers reasonable to enable persons ('independent mental health advocates') to be available to help qualifying patients.

(2) The appropriate national authority may by regulations make provision as to the appointment of persons as independent mental health advocates.

(3) The regulations may, in particular, provide –

(a) that a person may act as an independent mental health advocate only in such circumstances, or only subject to such conditions, as may be specified in the regulations;

(b) for the appointment of a person as an independent mental health advocate to be subject to approval in accordance with the regulations.

(4) In making arrangements under this section, the appropriate national authority shall have regard to the principle that any help available to a patient under the arrangements should, so far as practicable, be provided by a person who is independent of any person who is professionally concerned with the patient's medical treatment.

(5) For the purposes of subsection (4) above, a person is not to be regarded as professionally concerned with a patient's medical treatment merely because he is representing him in accordance with arrangements –

(a)　under section 35 of the Mental Capacity Act 2005; or
(b)　of a description specified in regulations under this section.

(6) Arrangements under this section may include provision for payments to be made to, or in relation to, persons carrying out functions in accordance with the arrangements.

(7) Regulations under this section –

(a)　may make different provision for different cases;
(b)　may make provision which applies subject to specified exceptions;
(c)　may include transitional, consequential, incidental or supplemental provision.

NOTES

Prospective amendments. Section prospectively inserted: MHA 2007, s 30(1), (2).

130B Arrangements under section 130A

(1) The help available to a qualifying patient under arrangements under section 130A above shall include help in obtaining information about and understanding –

(a)　the provisions of this Act by virtue of which he is a qualifying patient;
(b)　any conditions or restrictions to which he is subject by virtue of this Act;
(c)　what (if any) medical treatment is given to him or is proposed or discussed in his case;
(d)　why it is given, proposed or discussed;
(e)　the authority under which it is, or would be, given; and
(f)　the requirements of this Act which apply, or would apply, in connection with the giving of the treatment to him.

(2) The help available under the arrangements to a qualifying patient shall also include –

(a)　help in obtaining information about and understanding any rights which may be exercised under this Act by or in relation to him; and
(b)　help (by way of representation or otherwise) in exercising those rights.

(3) For the purpose of providing help to a patient in accordance with the arrangements, an independent mental health advocate may –

(a)　visit and interview the patient in private;
(b)　visit and interview any person who is professionally concerned with his medical treatment;
(c)　require the production of and inspect any records relating to his detention or treatment in any hospital or registered establishment or to any after-care services provided for him under section 117 above;

(d) require the production of and inspect any records of, or held by, a local social services authority which relate to him.

(4) But an independent mental health advocate is not entitled to the production of, or to inspect, records in reliance on subsection (3)(c) or(d) above unless –

(a) in a case where the patient has capacity or is competent to consent, he does consent; or

(b) in any other case, the production or inspection would not conflict with a decision made by a donee or deputy or the Court of Protection and the person holding the records, having regard to such matters as may be prescribed in regulations under section 130A above, considers that –

    (i) the records may be relevant to the help to be provided by the advocate; and

    (ii) the production or inspection is appropriate.

(5) For the purpose of providing help to a patient in accordance with the arrangements, an independent mental health advocate shall comply with any reasonable request made to him by any of the following for him to visit and interview the patient –

(a) the person (if any) appearing to the advocate to be the patient's nearest relative;

(b) the responsible clinician for the purposes of this Act;

(c) an approved mental health professional.

(6) But nothing in this Act prevents the patient from declining to be provided with help under the arrangements.

(7) In subsection (4) above –

(a) the reference to a patient who has capacity is to be read in accordance with the Mental Capacity Act 2005;

(b) the reference to a donee is to a donee of a lasting power of attorney (within the meaning of section 9 of that Act) created by the patient, where the donee is acting within the scope of his authority and in accordance with that Act;

(c) the reference to a deputy is to a deputy appointed for the patient by the Court of Protection under section 16 of that Act, where the deputy is acting within the scope of his authority and in accordance with that Act.

NOTES

Prospective amendments. Section prospectively inserted: MHA 2007, s 30(1), (2).

130C Section 130A: supplemental

(1) This section applies for the purposes of section 130A above.

(2) A patient is a qualifying patient if he is –

(a) liable to be detained under this Act (otherwise than by virtue of section 4 or 5(2) or (4) above or section 135 or 136 below);

(b) subject to guardianship under this Act; or

(c) a community patient.

(3) A patient is also a qualifying patient if –

(a) not being a qualifying patient falling within subsection (2) above, he discusses with a registered medical practitioner or approved clinician the possibility of being given a form of treatment to which section 57 above applies; or

(b) not having attained the age of 18 years and not being a qualifying patient falling within subsection (2) above, he discusses with a registered medical practitioner or approved clinician the possibility of being given a form of treatment to which section 58A above applies.

(4) Where a patient who is a qualifying patient falling within subsection (3) above is informed that the treatment concerned is proposed in his case, he remains a qualifying patient falling within that subsection until –

(a) the proposal is withdrawn; or

(b) the treatment is completed or discontinued.

(5) References to the appropriate national authority are –

(a) in relation to a qualifying patient in England, to the Secretary of State;

(b) in relation to a qualifying patient in Wales, to the Welsh Ministers.

(6) For the purposes of subsection (5) above –

(a) a qualifying patient falling within subsection (2)(a) above is to be regarded as being in the territory in which the hospital or registered establishment in which he is liable to be detained is situated;

(b) a qualifying patient falling within subsection (2)(b) above is to be regarded as being in the territory in which the area of the responsible local social services authority within the meaning of section 34(3) above is situated;

(c) a qualifying patient falling within subsection (2)(c) above is to be regarded as being in the territory in which the responsible hospital is situated;

(d) a qualifying patient falling within subsection (3) above is to be regarded as being in the territory determined in accordance with arrangements made for the purposes of this paragraph, and published, by the Secretary of State and the Welsh Ministers.

NOTES

Prospective amendments. Section prospectively inserted: MHA 2007, s 30(1), (2).

130D Duty to give information about independent mental health advocates

(1) The responsible person in relation to a qualifying patient (within the meaning given by section 130C above) shall take such steps as are practicable to ensure that the patient understands –

(a)   that help is available to him from an independent mental health advocate; and

(b)   how he can obtain that help.

(2) In subsection (1) above, 'the responsible person' means –

(a)   in relation to a qualifying patient falling within section 130C(2)(a) above (other than one also falling within paragraph (b) below), the managers of the hospital or registered establishment in which he is liable to be detained;

(b)   in relation to a qualifying patient falling within section 130C(2)(a) above and conditionally discharged by virtue of section 42(2), 73 or 74 above, the responsible clinician;

(c)   in relation to a qualifying patient falling within section 130C(2)(b) above, the responsible local social services authority within the meaning of section 34(3) above;

(d)   in relation to a qualifying patient falling within section 130C(2)(c) above, the managers of the responsible hospital;

(e)   in relation to a qualifying patient falling within section 130C(3) above, the registered medical practitioner or approved clinician with whom the patient first discusses the possibility of being given the treatment concerned.

(3) The steps to be taken under subsection (1) above shall be taken –

(a)   where the responsible person falls within subsection (2)(a) above, as soon as practicable after the patient becomes liable to be detained;

(b)   where the responsible person falls within subsection (2)(b) above, as soon as practicable after the conditional discharge;

(c)   where the responsible person falls within subsection (2)(c) above, as soon as practicable after the patient becomes subject to guardianship;

(d)   where the responsible person falls within subsection (2)(d) above, as soon as practicable after the patient becomes a community patient;

(e)   where the responsible person falls within subsection (2)(e) above, while the discussion with the patient is taking place or as soon as practicable thereafter.

(4) The steps to be taken under subsection (1) above shall include giving the requisite information both orally and in writing.

(5) The responsible person in relation to a qualifying patient falling within section 130C(2) above (other than a patient liable to be detained by virtue of Part 3 of this Act) shall, except where the patient otherwise requests, take such steps as are practicable to furnish the person (if any) appearing to the responsible person to be the patient's nearest relative with a copy of any information given to the patient in writing under subsection (1) above.

(6) The steps to be taken under subsection (5) above shall be taken when the information concerned is given to the patient or within a reasonable time thereafter.'

Prospective amendments. Section prospectively inserted: MHA 2007, s 30(1), (2).

131 Informal admission of patients

(1) Nothing in this Act shall be construed as preventing a patient who requires treatment for mental disorder from being admitted to any hospital or registered establishment in pursuance of arrangements made in that behalf and without any application, order or direction rendering him liable to be detained under this Act, or from remaining in any hospital or registered establishment in pursuance of such arrangements after he has ceased to be so liable to be detained.

(2) Subsections (3) and (4) below apply in the case of a patient aged 16 or 17 years who has capacity to consent to the making of such arrangements as are mentioned in subsection (1) above.

(3) If the patient consents to the making of the arrangements, they may be made, carried out and determined on the basis of that consent even though there are one or more persons who have parental responsibility for him.

(4) If the patient does not consent to the making of the arrangements, they may not be made, carried out or determined on the basis of the consent of a person who has parental responsibility for him.

(5) In this section –

  (a) the reference to a patient who has capacity is to be read in accordance with the Mental Capacity Act 2005; and
  (b) 'parental responsibility' has the same meaning as in the Children Act 1989.'

NOTES

Prospective amendment. Subs (2) prospectively substituted by subss (2)–(5): MHA 2007, s 43, with effect from 1 January 2008.

131A Accommodation, etc for children

(1) This section applies in respect of any patient who has not attained the age of 18 years and who –

  (a) is liable to be detained in a hospital under this Act; or
  (b) is admitted to, or remains in, a hospital in pursuance of such arrangements as are mentioned in section 131(1) above.

(2) The managers of the hospital shall ensure that the patient's environment in the hospital is suitable having regard to his age (subject to his needs).

(3) For the purpose of deciding how to fulfil the duty under subsection (2) above, the managers shall consult a person who appears to them to have knowledge or experience of cases involving patients who have not attained the age of 18 years which makes him suitable to be consulted.

(4) In this section, 'hospital' includes a registered establishment.'

NOTES

Prospective amendment. Section prospectively inserted: MHA 2007, s 31(1), (3).

132 Duty of managers of hospitals to give information to detained patients

(1) The managers of a hospital or registered establishment in which a patient is detained under this Act shall take such steps as are practicable to ensure that the patient understands –

    (a)   under which of the provisions of this Act he is for the time being detained and the effect of that provision; and

    (b)   what rights of applying to a Mental Health Review Tribunal are available to him in respect of his detention under that provision;

and those steps shall be taken as soon as practicable after the commencement of the patient's detention under the provision in question.

(2) The managers of a hospital or registered establishment in which a patient is detained as aforesaid shall also take such steps as are practicable to ensure that the patient understands the effect, so far as relevant in his case, of sections 23, 25, 56 to 64, 66(1)(g), 118 and 120 above and section 134 below; and those steps shall be taken as soon as practicable after the commencement of the patient's detention in the hospital or establishment.

(3) The steps to be taken under subsections (1) and (2) above shall include giving the requisite information both orally and in writing.

(4) The managers of a hospital or registered establishment in which a patient is detained as aforesaid shall, except where the patient otherwise requests, take such steps as are practicable to furnish the person (if any) appearing to them to be his nearest relative with a copy of any information given to him in writing under subsections (1) and (2) above; and those steps shall be taken when the information is given to the patient or within a reasonable time thereafter.

NOTES

Prospective amendments. Words in subs (2) prospectively substituted: MHA 2007, s 32(4), Sch 3, paras 1, 29.

132A Duty of managers of hospitals to give information to community patients

(1) The managers of the responsible hospital shall take such steps as are practicable to ensure that a community patient understands –

    (a)   the effect of the provisions of this Act applying to community patients; and

    (b)   what rights of applying to a Mental Health Review Tribunal are available to him in that capacity;

and those steps shall be taken as soon as practicable after the patient becomes a community patient.

(2) The steps to be taken under subsection (1) above shall include giving the requisite information both orally and in writing.

(3) The managers of the responsible hospital shall, except where the community patient otherwise requests, take such steps as are practicable to furnish the person (if any) appearing to them to be his nearest relative with a copy of any information given to him in writing under subsection (1) above; and those steps shall be taken when the information is given to the patient or within a reasonable time thereafter.

NOTES

Prospective amendments. Section prospectively inserted: MHA 2007, s 32(4), Sch 3, paras 1, 30.

133 Duty of managers of hospitals to inform nearest relatives of discharge

(1) Where a patient liable to be detained under this Act in a hospital or registered establishment is to be discharged otherwise than by virtue of an order for discharge made by his nearest relative, the managers of the hospital or registered establishment shall, subject to subsection (2) below, take such steps as are practicable to inform the person (if any) appearing to them to be the nearest relative of the patient; and that information shall, if practicable, be given at least seven days before the date of discharge.

(1A) The reference in subsection (1) above to a patient who is to be discharged includes a patient who is to be discharged from hospital under section 17A above.

(1B) Subsection (1) above shall also apply in a case where a community patient is discharged under section 23 or 72 above (otherwise than by virtue of an order for discharge made by his nearest relative), but with the reference in that subsection to the managers of the hospital or registered establishment being read as a reference to the managers of the responsible hospital.

(2) Subsection (1) above shall not apply if the patient or his nearest relative has requested that information about the patient's discharge should not be given under this section.

NOTES

Prospective amendments. Subss (1A), (1B) prospectively inserted: MHA 2007, s 32(4), Sch 3, paras 1, 31.

134 Correspondence of patients

(1) A postal packet addressed to any person by a patient detained in a hospital under this Act and delivered by the patient for dispatch may be withheld from the postal operator concerned –

    (a)   if that person has requested that communications addressed to him by the patient should be withheld; or

    (b)   subject to subsection (3) below, if the hospital is one at which high security psychiatric services are provided and the managers of the hospital consider that the postal packet is likely –

        (i)   to cause distress to the person to whom it is addressed or to any other person (not being a person on the staff of the hospital); or

        (ii)   to cause danger to any person;

and any request for the purposes of paragraph (a) above shall be made by a notice in writing given to the managers of the hospital, the approved clinician with overall responsibility for the patient's case or the Secretary of State.

(2) Subject to subsection (3) below, a postal packet addressed to a patient detained under this Act in a hospital at which high security psychiatric services are provided may be withheld from the patient if, in the opinion of the managers of the hospital, it is necessary to do so in the interests of the safety of the patient or for the protection of other persons.

(3) Subsections (1)(b) and (2) above do not apply to any postal packet addressed by a patient to, or sent to a patient by or on behalf of –

(a)　any Minister of the Crown or the Scottish Ministers or Member of either House of Parliament or member of the Scottish Parliament or of the Northern Ireland Assembly;

(b)　any judge or officer of the Court of Protection, any of the Court of Protection Visitors or any person asked by that Court for a report under section 49 of the Mental Capacity Act 2005 concerning the patient;

(c)　the Parliamentary Commissioner for Administration, the Scottish Public Services Ombudsman, the Public Services Ombudsman for Wales, the Health Service Commissioner for England or a Local Commissioner within the meaning of Part III of the Local Government Act 1974;

(d)　a Mental Health Review Tribunal;

(e)　a Strategic Health Authority, Local Health Board, Special Health Authority or Primary Care Trust, a local social services authority, a Community Health Council, a Patients' Forum or a local probation board established under section 4 of the Criminal Justice and Court Services Act 2000;

(ea)　a provider of a patient advocacy and liaison service for the assistance of patients at the hospital and their families and carers;

(eb)　a provider of independent advocacy services for the patient;

(f)　the managers of the hospital in which the patient is detained;

(g)　any legally qualified person instructed by the patient to act as his legal adviser; or

(h)　the European Commission of Human Rights or the European Court of Human Rights.

(3A) In subsection (3) above –

(a)　'patient advocacy and liaison service' means a service of a description prescribed by regulations made by the Secretary of State, and

(b)　'independent advocacy services' means services provided under –

(i)　arrangements under section 130A above;

(ii)　arrangements under section 248 of the National Health Service Act 2006 or section 187 of the National Health Service (Wales) Act 2006; or

(iii)　arrangements of a description prescribed as mentioned in paragraph (a) above.

(4) The managers of a hospital may inspect and open any postal packet for the purposes of determining –

    (a)   whether it is one to which subsection (1) or (2) applies, and

    (b)   in the case of a postal packet to which subsection (1) or (2) above applies, whether or not it should be withheld under that subsection; and the power to withhold a postal packet under either of those subsections includes power to withhold anything contained in it.

(5) Where a postal packet or anything contained in it is withheld under subsection (1) or (2) above the managers of the hospital shall record that fact in writing.

(6) Where a postal packet or anything contained in it is withheld under subsection (1)(b) or (2) above the managers of the hospital shall within seven days give notice of that fact to the patient and, in the case of a packet withheld under subsection (2) above, to the person (if known) by whom the postal packet was sent; and any such notice shall be given in writing and shall contain a statement of the effect of section 121(7) and (8) above.

(7) The functions of the managers of a hospital under this section shall be discharged on their behalf by a person on the staff of the hospital appointed by them for that purpose and different persons may be appointed to discharge different functions.

(8) The Secretary of State may make regulations with respect to the exercise of the powers conferred by this section.

(9) In this section 'hospital' has the same meaning as in Part II of this Act and 'postal operator' and 'postal packet' have the same meaning as in the Postal Services Act 2000.

NOTES

Prospective amendments. Words in subs (1) prospectively substituted: MHA 2007, s 14(1), (4). Subs (3A)(b) prospectively substituted: MHA 2007, s 30(1), (3).

135 Warrant to search for and remove patients

(1) If it appears to a justice of the peace, on information on oath laid by an approved mental health professional, that there is reasonable cause to suspect that a person believed to be suffering from mental disorder –

    (a)   has been, or is being, ill-treated, neglected or kept otherwise than under proper control, in any place within the jurisdiction of the justice, or

    (b)   being unable to care for himself, is living alone in any such place, the justice may issue a warrant authorising any constable to enter, if need be by force, any premises specified in the warrant in which that person is believed to be, and, if thought fit, to remove him to a place of safety with a view to the making of an application in respect of him under Part II of this Act, or of other arrangements for his treatment or care.

(2) If it appears to a justice of the peace, on information on oath laid by any constable or other person who is authorised by or under this Act or under article 8 of the Mental Health (Care and Treatment) (Scotland) Act 2003 (Consequential Provisions) Order 2005 to take a patient to any place, or to take into custody or retake a patient who is liable under this Act or under the said article 8 to be so taken or retaken –

    (a)   that there is reasonable cause to believe that the patient is to be found on premises within the jurisdiction of the justice; and

    (b)   that admission to the premises has been refused or that a refusal of such admission is apprehended, the justice may issue a warrant authorising any constable to enter the premises, if need be by force, and remove the patient.

(3) A patient who is removed to a place of safety in the execution of a warrant issued under this section may be detained there for a period not exceeding 72 hours.

(3A) A constable, an approved mental health professional or a person authorised by either of them for the purposes of this subsection may, before the end of the period of 72 hours mentioned in subsection (3) above, take a person detained in a place of safety under that subsection to one or more other places of safety.

(3B) A person taken to a place of safety under subsection (3A) above may be detained there for a period ending no later than the end of the period of 72 hours mentioned in subsection (3) above.

(4) In the execution of a warrant issued under subsection (1) above, a constable shall be accompanied by an approved mental health professional and by a registered medical practitioner, and in the execution of a warrant issued under subsection (2) above a constable may be accompanied –

    (a)   by a registered medical practitioner;

    (b)   by any person authorised by or under this Act or under article 8 of the Mental Health (Care and Treatment) (Scotland) Act 2003 (Consequential Provisions) Order 2005 to take or retake the patient.

(5) It shall not be necessary in any information or warrant under subsection (1) above to name the patient concerned.

(6) In this section 'place of safety' means residential accommodation provided by a local social services authority under Part III of the National Assistance Act 1948, a hospital as defined by this Act, a police station, an independent hospital or care home for mentally disordered persons or any other suitable place the occupier of which is willing temporarily to receive the patient.

NOTES

Prospective amendments. Words in subss (1) and (4) prospectively substituted: MHA 2007, s 21, Sch 2, paras 1, 10(a). Subss (3A), (3B) prospectively inserted: MHA 2007, s 44(1), (2).

136 Mentally disordered persons found in public places

(1) If a constable finds in a place to which the public have access a person who appears to him to be suffering from mental disorder and to be in immediate need of care or control, the constable may, if he thinks it necessary to do so in the interests of that person or for the protection of other persons, remove that person to a place of safety within the meaning of section 135 above.

(2) A person removed to a place of safety under this section may be detained there for a period not exceeding 72 hours for the purpose of enabling him to be examined by a registered medical practitioner and to be interviewed by an approved mental health professional and of making any necessary arrangements for his treatment or care.

(3) A constable, an approved mental health professional or a person authorised by either of them for the purposes of this subsection may, before the end of the period of 72 hours mentioned in subsection (2) above, take a person detained in a place of safety under that subsection to one or more other places of safety.

(4) A person taken to a place of a safety under subsection (3) above may be detained there for a purpose mentioned in subsection (2) above for a period ending no later than the end of the period of 72 hours mentioned in that subsection.

NOTES

Prospective amendments. Words in subs (2) prospectively substituted: MHA 2007, s 21, Sch 2, paras 1, 10(b). Subss (3), (4) prospectively inserted: MHA 2007, s 44(1), (3).

137 Provisions as to custody, conveyance and detention

(1) Any person required or authorised by or by virtue of this Act to be conveyed to any place or to be kept in custody or detained in a place of safety or at any place to which he is taken under section 42(6) above shall, while being so conveyed, detained or kept, as the case may be, be deemed to be in legal custody.

(2) A constable or any other person required or authorised by or by virtue of this Act to take any person into custody, or to convey or detain any person shall, for the purposes of taking him into custody or conveying or detaining him, have all the powers, authorities, protection and privileges which a constable has within the area for which he acts as constable.

(3) In this section 'convey' includes any other expression denoting removal from one place to another.

138 Retaking of patients escaping from custody

(1) If any person who is in legal custody by virtue of section 137 above escapes, he may, subject to the provisions of this section, be retaken –

  (a) in any case, by the person who had his custody immediately before the escape, or by any constable or approved mental health professional;

(b) if at the time of the escape he was liable to be detained in a hospital within the meaning of Part II of this Act, or subject to guardianship under this Act, or a community patient who was recalled to hospital under section 17E above, by any other person who could take him into custody under section 18 above if he had absented himself without leave.

(2) A person to whom paragraph (b) of subsection (1) above applies shall not be retaken under this section after the expiration of the period within which he could be retaken under section 18 above if he had absented himself without leave on the day of the escape unless he is subject to a restriction order under Part III of this Act or an order or direction having the same effect as such an order; and subsection (4) of the said section 18 shall apply with the necessary modifications accordingly.

(3) A person who escapes while being taken to or detained in a place of safety under section 135 or 136 above shall not be retaken under this section after the expiration of the period of 72 hours beginning with the time when he escapes or the period during which he is liable to be so detained, whichever expires first.

(4) This section, so far as it relates to the escape of a person liable to be detained in a hospital within the meaning of Part II of this Act, shall apply in relation to a person who escapes –

(a) while being taken to or from such a hospital in pursuance of regulations under section 19 above, or of any order, direction or authorisation under Part III or VI of this Act (other than under section 35, 36, 38, 53, 83 or 85) or under section 123 above; or

(b) while being taken to or detained in a place of safety in pursuance of an order under Part III of this Act (other than under section 35, 36 or 38 above) pending his admission to such a hospital, as if he were liable to be detained in that hospital and, if he had not previously been received in that hospital, as if he had been so received.

(5) In computing for the purposes of the power to give directions under section 37(4) above and for the purposes of sections 37(5) and 40(1) above the period of 28 days mentioned in those sections, no account shall be taken of any time during which the patient is at large and liable to be retaken by virtue of this section.

(6) Section 21 above shall, with any necessary modifications, apply in relation to a patient who is at large and liable to be retaken by virtue of this section as it applies in relation to a patient who is absent without leave and references in that section to section 18 above shall be construed accordingly.

NOTES

Prospective amendments. Words in subs (1)(a) prospectively substituted: MHA 2007, s 21, Sch 2, paras 1, 10(c). Words in subs (1)(b) prospectively inserted: MHA 2007, s 32(4), Sch 3, paras 1, 32.

139 Protection for acts done in pursuance of this Act

(1) No person shall be liable, whether on the ground of want of jurisdiction or on any other ground, to any civil or criminal proceedings to which he would have been liable apart from this section in respect of any act purporting to be done in pursuance of this Act or any regulations or rules made under this Act, unless the act was done in bad faith or without reasonable care.

(2) No civil proceedings shall be brought against any person in any court in respect of any such act without the leave of the High Court; and no criminal proceedings shall be brought against any person in any court in respect of any such act except by or with the consent of the Director of Public Prosecutions.

(3) This section does not apply to proceedings for an offence under this Act, being proceedings which, under any other provision of this Act, can be instituted only by or with the consent of the Director of Public Prosecutions.

(4) This section does not apply to proceedings against the Secretary of State or against a Strategic Health Authority, Local Health Board, Special Health Authority or Primary Care Trust or against a National Health Service trust established under the National Health Service Act 2006 or the National Health Service (Wales) Act 2006 or NHS foundation trust.

(5) In relation to Northern Ireland the reference in this section to the Director of Public Prosecutions shall be construed as a reference to the Director of Public Prosecutions for Northern Ireland.

140 Notification of hospitals having arrangements for special cases

It shall be the duty of every Primary Care Trust and of every Local Health Board to give notice to every local social services authority for an area wholly or partly comprised within the area of the Primary Care Trust or Local Health Board specifying the hospital or hospitals administered by or otherwise available to the Primary Care Trust or Local Health Board in which arrangements are from time to time in force –

   (a)   for the reception of patients in cases of special urgency;
   (b)   for the provision of accommodation or facilities designed so as to be specially suitable for patients who have not attained the age of 18 years.'

NOTES

Prospective amendments. Section heading prospectively substituted, and paras (a), (b) substituted for existing words: MHA 2007, s 31(1), (4).

141 Members of Parliament suffering from mental illness

(1) Where a member of the House of Commons is authorised to be detained under a relevant enactment on the ground (however formulated) that he is suffering from mental disorder, it shall be the duty of the court, authority or person on whose order or application, and of any registered medical practitioner upon whose recommendation or certificate, the detention was authorised, and of the person in charge of the hospital or other place in which

the member is authorised to be detained, to notify the Speaker of the House of Commons that the detention has been authorised.

(2) Where the Speaker receives a notification under subsection (1) above, or is notified by two members of the House of Commons that they are credibly informed that such an authorisation has been given, the Speaker shall cause the member to whom the notification relates to be visited and examined by two registered medical practitioners appointed in accordance with subsection (3) below.

(3) The registered medical practitioners to be appointed for the purposes of subsection (2) above shall be appointed by the President of the Royal College of Psychiatrists and shall be practitioners appearing to the President to have special experience in the diagnosis or treatment of mental disorders.

(4) The registered medical practitioners appointed in accordance with subsection (3) above shall report to the Speaker whether the member is suffering from mental disorder and is authorised to be detained under a relevant enactment as such.

(5) If the report is to the effect that the member is suffering from mental disorder and authorised to be detained as aforesaid, the Speaker shall at the expiration of six months from the date of the report, if the House is then sitting, and otherwise as soon as may be after the House next sits, again cause the member to be visited and examined by two such registered medical practitioners as aforesaid, and the registered medical practitioners shall report as aforesaid.

(6) If the second report is that the member is suffering from mental disorder and authorised to be detained as mentioned in subsection (4) above, the Speaker shall forthwith lay both reports before the House of Commons, and thereupon the seat of the member shall become vacant.

(6A) For the purposes of this section, the following are relevant enactments –

   (a)   this Act;
   (b)   the Criminal Procedure (Scotland) Act 1995 and the Mental Health (Care and Treatment) (Scotland) Act 2003 ('the Scottish enactments'); and
   (c)   the Mental Health (Northern Ireland) Order 1986 ('the 1986 Order').

(6B) In relation to an authorisation for detention under the Scottish enactments or the 1986 Order, the references in this section to mental disorder shall be construed in accordance with those enactments or that Order (as the case may be).

(6C) References in this section to a member who is authorised to be detained shall not include a member who is a community patient (whether or not he is recalled to hospital under section 17E above).

(7) Any sums required for the payment of fees and expenses to registered medical practitioners acting in relation to a member of the House of Commons under this section shall be defrayed out of moneys provided by Parliament.

(8) This section also has effect in relation to members of the Scottish Parliament but as if –

(a)　any references to the House of Commons or the Speaker were references to the Scottish Parliament or (as the case may be) the Presiding Officer, and

(b)　subsection (7) were omitted.

(9) This section also has effect in relation to members of the National Assembly for Wales but as if –

(a)　references to the House of Commons were to the Assembly and references to the Speaker were to the presiding officer, and

(b)　in subsection (7), for 'defrayed out of moneys provided by Parliament' there were substituted 'paid by the National Assembly for Wales Commission'.

(10)　This section also has effect in relation to members of the Northern Ireland Assembly but as if –

(a)　references to the House of Commons were to the Assembly and references to the Speaker were to the Presiding Officer; and

(b)　in subsection (7), for 'provided by Parliament' there were substituted 'appropriated by Act of the Assembly'.

NOTES

Prospective amendments. Words in subs (1) prospectively inserted and substituted: MHA 2007, s 1(4), Sch 1, Pt 1, paras 1, 16(1), (2). Words in subs (4) prospectively substituted and inserted: MHA 2007, s 1(4), Sch 1, Pt 1, paras 1, 16(1), (3). Words in subs (5) prospectively substituted: MHA 2007, s 1(4), Sch 1, Pt 1, paras 1, 16(1), (4). Words in subs (6) prospectively substituted: MHA 2007, s 1(4), Sch 1, Pt 1, paras 1, 16(1), (4). Subss (6A), (6B) prospectively inserted: MHA 2007, s 1(4), Sch 1, Pt 1, paras 1, 16(1), (5). Subs (6C) prospectively inserted: MHA 2007, s 32(4), Sch 3, paras 1, 33.

142 ...

(*repealed*)

142A　Regulations as to approvals in relation to England and Wales

The Secretary of State jointly with the Welsh Ministers may by regulations make provision as to the circumstances in which –

(a)　a practitioner approved for the purposes of section 12 above, or

(b)　a person approved to act as an approved clinician for the purposes of this Act, approved in relation to England is to be treated, by virtue of his approval, as approved in relation to Wales too, and vice versa.

NOTES

Prospective amendment. Section prospectively inserted: MHA 2007, s 17.

142B Delegation of powers of managers of NHS foundation trusts

(1) The constitution of an NHS foundation trust may not provide for a function under this Act to be delegated otherwise than in accordance with provision made by or under this Act.

(2) Paragraph 15(3) of Schedule 7 to the National Health Service Act 2006 (which provides that the powers of a public benefit corporation may be delegated to a committee of directors or to an executive director) shall have effect subject to this section.

NOTES

Prospective amendments. Section prospectively inserted: MHA 2007, s 45(3).

Supplemental

143 General provisions as to regulations, orders and rules

(1) Any power of the Secretary of State or the Lord Chancellor to make regulations, orders or rules under this Act shall be exercisable by statutory instrument.

(2) Any Order in Council under this Act or any order made by the Secretary of State under section 54A or 68A(7) or 65 above and any statutory instrument containing regulations made by the Secretary of State, or rules made, under this Act shall be subject to annulment in pursuance of a resolution of either House of Parliament.

(3) No order shall be made by the Secretary of State under section 45A(10), 68(4) 68A(1) or 71(3) above unless a draft of it has been approved by a resolution of each House of Parliament.

(3A) Subsections (3B) to (3D) apply where power to make regulations or an order under this Act is conferred on the Welsh Ministers (other than by or by virtue of the Government of Wales Act 2006).

(3B) Any power of the Welsh Ministers to make regulations or an order shall be exercisable by statutory instrument.

(3C) Any statutory instrument containing regulations made by the Welsh Ministers, or an order under section 68A(7) above, made by the Welsh Ministers shall be subject to annulment in pursuance of a resolution of the National Assembly for Wales.

(3D) No order shall be made under section 68A(1) above by the Welsh Ministers unless a draft of it has been approved by a resolution of the National Assembly for Wales.

(3E) In this section –

    (a)   references to the Secretary of State include the Secretary of State and the Welsh Ministers acting jointly; and

    (b)   references to the Welsh Ministers include the Welsh Ministers and the Secretary of State acting jointly.

(4) This section does not apply to rules which are, by virtue of section 108 of this Act, to be made in accordance with Part 1 of Schedule 1 to the Constitutional Reform Act 2005.

NOTES

Prospective amendments. Words in subs (2) prospectively inserted: MHA 2007, s 37(1), (5)(a). Words in subs (2) prospectively repealed: MHA 2007, s 55, Sch 11, Pt 6. Words in subs (2) prospectively substituted: MHA 2007, s 47(1), (2). Words in subs (3) prospectively inserted: MHA 2007, s 37(1), (5)(b)(i). Reference in subs (3) prospectively substituted: MHA 2007, s 37(1), (5)(b)(ii). Subss (3A)–(3E) prospectively inserted: MHA 2007, s 47(1), (3).

144 Power to amend local Acts

Her Majesty may by Order in Council repeal or amend any local enactment so far as appears to Her Majesty to be necessary in consequence of this Act.

145 Interpretation

(1) In this Act, unless the context otherwise requires –

'absent without leave' has the meaning given to it by section 18 above and related expressions (including expressions relating to a patient's liability to be returned to a hospital or other place) shall be construed accordingly;

'application for admission for assessment' has the meaning given in section 2 above;

'application for admission for treatment' has the meaning given in section 3 above;

'approved clinician' means a person approved by the Secretary of State (in relation to England) or by the Welsh Ministers (in relation to Wales) to act as an approved clinician for the purposes of this Act;

'approved mental health professional' has the meaning given in section 114 above;

'care home' has the same meaning as in the Care Standards Act 2000;

'community patient' has the meaning given in section 17A above;

'community treatment order' and 'the community treatment order' have the meanings given in section 17A above;

'the community treatment period' has the meaning given in section 20A above;

(*repealed*)

'high security psychiatric services' has the same meaning as in section 4 of the National Health Service Act 2006 or section 4 of the National Health Service (Wales) Act 2006;

'hospital' means –

(a) any health service hospital within the meaning of the National Health Service Act 2006 or the National Health Service (Wales) Act 2006; and

(b) any accommodation provided by a local authority and used as a hospital by or on behalf of the Secretary of State under that Act; and

(c)   any hospital as defined by section 206 of the National Health Service (Wales) Act 2006 which is vested in a Local Health Board;

'hospital within the meaning of Part II of this Act' has the meaning given in section 34 above;

'hospital direction' has the meaning given in section 45A(3)(a) above;

'hospital order' and 'guardianship order' have the meanings respectively given in section 37 above;

'independent hospital' has the same meaning as in the Care Standards Act 2000;

'interim hospital order' has the meaning given in section 38 above;

'limitation direction' has the meaning given in section 45A(3)(b) above;

'Local Health Board' means a Local Health Board established under section 11 of the National Health Services (Wales) Act 2006;

'local social services authority' means a council which is a local authority for the purpose of the Local Authority Social Services Act 1970;

'the managers' means –

(a)   in relation to a hospital vested in the Secretary of State for the purposes of his functions under the National Health Service Act 2006, or in the Welsh Ministers for the purposes of their functions under the National Health Service (Wales) Act 2006, and in relation to any accommodation provided by a local authority and used as a hospital by or on behalf of the Secretary of State under the National Health Service Act 2006, or of the Welsh Ministers under the National Health Service (Wales) Act 2006, the Primary Care Trust, Strategic Health Authority, Local Health Board or Special Health Authority responsible for the administration of the hospital;

(bb) in relation to a hospital vested in a Primary Care Trust or a National Health Service trust, the trust;

(bc) in relation to a hospital vested in an NHS foundation trust, the trust;

(bd) in relation to a hospital vested in a Local Health Board, the Board;

(c)   in relation to a registered establishment, the person or persons registered in respect of the establishment;

and in this definition 'hospital' means a hospital within the meaning of Part II of this Act;

'medical treatment' includes nursing, and also includes psychological intervention and specialist mental health habilitation, rehabilitation and Care (but see also subsection (4) below);

'mental disorder' has the meaning given in section 1 above (subject to sections 86(4) and 141(6B));

'nearest relative', in relation to a patient, has the meaning given in Part II of this Act;

'patient' means a person suffering or appearing to be suffering from mental disorder;

'Primary Care Trust' means a Primary Care Trust established under section 18 of the National Health Service Act 2006;

'registered establishment' has the meaning given in section 34 above;

'the responsible hospital' has the meaning given in section 17A above;

'restriction direction' has the meaning given to it by section 49 above;

'restriction order' has the meaning given to it by section 41 above;

'Special Health Authority' means a Special Health Authority established under section 28 of the National Health Service Act 2006, or section 22 of the National Health Service (Wales) Act 2006;

'Strategic Health Authority' means a Strategic Health Authority established under section 13 of the National Health Service Act 2006;

'transfer direction' has the meaning given to it by section 47 above.

(1AA) Where high security psychiatric services and other services are provided at a hospital, the part of the hospital at which high security psychiatric services are provided and the other part shall be treated as separate hospitals for the purposes of this Act.

(1AB) References in this Act to appropriate medical treatment shall be construed in accordance with section 3(4) above.

(1AC) References in this Act to an approved mental health professional shall be construed as references to an approved mental health professional acting on behalf of a local social services authority, unless the context otherwise requires.

(3) In relation to a person who is liable to be detained or subject to guardianship or a community patient by virtue of an order or direction under Part III of this Act (other than under section 35, 36 or 38), any reference in this Act to any enactment contained in Part II of this Act or in section 66 or 67 above shall be construed as a reference to that enactment as it applies to that person by virtue of Part III of this Act.

(4) Any reference in this Act to medical treatment, in relation to mental disorder, shall be construed as a reference to medical treatment the purpose of which is to alleviate, or prevent a worsening of, the disorder or one or more of its symptoms or manifestations.

NOTES

Amendments. Para (c) and preceding word inserted in definition 'hospital' in subs (1): MHA 2007, s 46(1), (3)(a). Para (bd) inserted in definition 'the managers' in subs (1): MHA 2007, s 46(1), (3)(b).

Prospective amendments. Words in definition 'absent without leave' in subs (1) prospectively inserted: MHA 2007, s 32(4), Sch 3, paras 1, 34(1), (2). Definition 'approved clinician' in subs (1) prospectively inserted: MHA 2007, s 14(1), (5). Definition 'approved mental health professional' in subs (1) prospectively substituted for definition 'approved social worker': MHA 2007, s 21, Sch 2, paras 1, 11(1), (2). Definition 'community patient' in subs (1) prospectively inserted: MHA 2007, s 32(4), Sch 3, paras 1, 34(1), (3). Definitions 'community treatment order' and 'the community treatment order" prospectively inserted: MHA 2007, s 32(4), Sch 3, paras 1, 34(1), (3). Definition 'the community treatment period' in subs (1) prospectively inserted: MHA 2007, s 32(4), Sch 3, paras 1, 34(1), (3). Words in definition 'medical treatment' in subs (1) prospectively substituted: MHA 2007, s 7(1), (2). Definition 'mental disorder' in subs (1) prospectively substituted for definitions 'mental disorder', 'severe mental impairment', 'mental impairment' and 'psychopathic disorder': MHA 2007, s 1(4), Sch 1, Pt 1, paras 1, 17. Definition 'the responsible after-care bodies' in subs (1) prospectively repealed: MHA 2007, s 55, Sch 11, Pt 5. Definition 'the responsible hospital' in subs (1) prospectively inserted: MHA 2007, s 32(4), Sch 3, paras 1, 34(1), (3). Definition 'supervision application' in subs (1) prospectively repealed: MHA 2007, s 55, Sch 11, Pt 5. Subs (1AB) prospectively inserted: MHA 2007, s 4(1), (10). Subs (1AC) prospectively inserted: MHA 2007, s 21, Sch 2, paras 1, 11(1), (3). Subs (1A) prospectively repealed: MHA 2007, s 55, Sch 11, Pt 5. Words in subs (3) prospectively inserted: MHA 2007, s 32(4), Sch 3, paras 1, 34(1), (4). Subs (4) prospectively inserted: MHA 2007, s 7(1), (3).

146 Application to Scotland

Sections 42(6), 80, 116, 122, 137, 139(1), 141, 142, 143 (so far as applicable to any Order in Council extending to Scotland) and 144 above shall extend to Scotland together with any amendment or repeal by this Act of or any provision of Schedule 5 to this Act relating to any enactment which so extends; but, except as aforesaid and except so far as it relates to the interpretation or commencement of the said provisions, this Act shall not extend to Scotland.

NOTES

Prospective amendments. Words prospectively repealed in relation to England and Wales: MHA 2007, ss 32(4), 39(2), 55, Sch 3, paras 1, 35, Sch 5, Pt 2, para 20, Sch 11, Pts 5, 7.

147 Application to Northern Ireland

Sections 81, 82, 86, 87, 88 (and so far as applied by that section sections 18, 22 and 138), section 128 (except so far as it relates to patients subject to guardianship), 137, 139, 141, 142, 143 (so far as applicable to any Order in Council extending to Northern Ireland) and 144 above shall extend to Northern Ireland together with any amendment or repeal by this Act of or any provision of Schedule 5 to this Act relating to any enactment which so extends; but except as aforesaid and except so far as it relates to the interpretation or commencement of the said provisions, this Act shall not extend to Northern Ireland.

148 Consequential and transitional provisions and repeals

(1) Schedule 4 (consequential amendments) and Schedule 5 (transitional and saving provisions) to this Act shall have effect but without prejudice to the operation of sections 15 to 17 of the Interpretation Act 1978 (which relate to the effect of repeals).

(2) Where any amendment in Schedule 4 to this Act affects an enactment amended by the Mental Health (Amendment) Act 1982 the amendment in Schedule 4 shall come into force immediately after the provision of the Act of 1982 amending that enactment.

(3) The enactments specified in Schedule 6 to this Act are hereby repealed to the extent mentioned in the third column of that Schedule.

149 Short title, commencement and application to Scilly Isles

(1) This Act may be cited as the Mental Health Act 1983.

(2) Subject to subsection (3) below and Schedule 5 to this Act, this Act shall come into force on 30th September 1983.

(3) (*repealed*)

(4) Section 130(4) of the National Health Service Act 1977 (which provides for the extension of that Act to the Isles of Scilly) shall have effect as if the references to that Act included references to this Act.

****

SCHEDULE 1
Application of Certain Provisions to Patients Subject to Hospital and Guardianship Orders

Sections 40(4), 41(3), (5), 55(4)

PART I
PATIENTS NOT SUBJECT TO SPECIAL RESTRICTIONS

1

Sections 9, 10, 17 to 17C, 17E, 17F, 20A, 21 to 21B, 24(3) and (4), 26 to 28, 31, 32, 34, 67 and 76 shall apply in relation to the patient without modification.

2

Sections 17D, 17G, 18 to 20, 20B, 22, 23, 66 and 68 shall apply in relation to the patient with the modifications specified in paragraphs 2A to 10 below.

2A

In section 17D(2)(a) for the reference to section 6(2) above there shall be substituted a reference to section 40(1)(b) below.

2B

In section 17G –

(a) in subsection (2) for the reference to section 6(2) above there shall be substituted a reference to section 40(1)(b) below;

(b) in subsection (4) for paragraphs (a) and (b) there shall be substituted the words 'the order or direction under Part 3 of this Act in respect of him were an order or direction for his admission or removal to that other hospital'; and

(c) in subsection (5) for the words from 'the patient' to the end there shall be substituted the words 'the date of the relevant order or direction under Part 3 of this Act were the date on which the community treatment order is revoked'.

3

(*repealed*)

4

In section 18 subsection (5) shall be omitted.

5

In section 19(2) for the words from 'as follows' to the end of the subsection there shall be substituted the words 'as if the order or direction under Part III of this Act by virtue of which he was liable to be detained or subject to guardianship before being transferred were an order or direction for his admission or removal to the hospital to which he is transferred, or placing him under the guardianship of the authority or person into whose guardianship he is transferred, as the case may be'.

5A

In section 19A(2), paragraph (b) shall be omitted.

6

In section 20 –

(a)   in subsection (1) for the words from 'day on which he was' to 'as the case may be' there shall be substituted the words 'date of the relevant order or direction under Part III of this Act';

(b)   (*repealed*)

6A

In section 20B(1), for the reference to the application for admission for treatment there shall be substituted a reference to the order or direction under Part 3 of this Act by virtue of which the patient is liable to be detained.

7

In section 22 for references to an application for admission or a guardianship application there shall be substituted references to the order or direction under Part III of thisAct by virtue of which the patient is liable to be detained or subject to guardianship.

8

In section 23(2) –

(a)   in paragraph (a) the words 'for assessment or' shall be omitted; and

(b)   in paragraphs (a) to (c) the references to the nearest relative shall be omitted.

8A

(*repealed*)

9

In section 66 –

(a)   in subsection (1), paragraphs (a), (b), (c), (g) and (h), the words in parenthesis in paragraph (i) and paragraph (ii) shall be omitted; and

(b)   in subsection (2), paragraphs (a), (b), (c) and (g), and in paragraph (d) ', (g)', shall be omitted.

10

In section 68 –

(a)   in subsection (1) paragraph (a) shall be omitted; and(b) subsections (2) to (5) shall apply if the patient falls within paragraph (e) of subsection (1), but not otherwise.

NOTES

Prospective amendments: Words prospectively substituted: Mental Health Act 2007, s 32(4), Sch 3, paras 1, 36(1), (2). Definitions in para 1 prospectively repealed and subsequent reference prospectively substituted, MHA 2007, s 55, Sch 11, Pt 1, Para 2 reference prospectively repealed and subsequent words substituted MHA 2007, s 32(4), Sch 3, paras 1, 36(1), (3) (a) (b), s 37(1), (6) (a) (i); paras (2A), (2B) prospectively inserted by MHA 2007, s 32(4), Sch 3, paras 1, 36(1), (4). Para 3 prospectively repealed by MHA 2007, s 55, Sch 11, Pt 1, para (5A) prospectively inserted by MHA 2007, s 32(4), Sch 3, paras 1, 36(1), (5), para 6 words prospectively repealed and subsequent words substituted by MHA 2007, s 53, Sch 3, paras 1, 2; para (6A), prospectively inserted by MHA 2007, s 32(4), Sch 3, paras 1, 36(1), (6); para (8) words prospectively repealed and subsequent words substituted by MHA 2007, s 32(4), Sch 3, paras 1, 36(1), (7); para (8A) prospectively repealed: MHA 2007, s 55, Sch 11, Pt 5; para (10) prospectively inserted by MHA 2007, s 37 (1), (6) (b).

PART II
PATIENTS SUBJECT TO SPECIAL RESTRICTIONS

1

Sections 24(3) and (4), 32 and 76 shall apply in relation to the patient without modification.

2

Sections 17, 18, 19, 22, 23 and 34 shall apply in relation to the patient with the modifications specified in paragraphs 3 to 8 below.

3

In section 17 –

(a)   in subsection (1) after the word 'may' there shall be inserted the words 'with the consent of the Secretary of State';

(aa) subsections (2A) and (2B) shall be omitted;

(b)   in subsection (4) after the words 'the responsible clinician' and after the words 'that clinician' there shall be inserted the words 'or the Secretary of State'; and

(c) in subsection (5) after the word 'recalled' there shall be inserted the words 'by the responsible clinician', and for the words from 'he has ceased' to the end of the subsection there shall be substituted the words 'the expiration of the period of twelve months beginning with the first day of his absence on leave'.

4

In section 18 there shall be omitted –

(a) in subsection (1) the words 'subject to the provisions of this section'; and
(b) subsections (3), (4) and (5).

5

In section 19 –

(a) in subsection (1) after the word 'may' in paragraph (a) there shall be inserted the words 'with the consent of the Secretary of State', and the words from 'or into' to the end of the subsection shall be omitted; ...
(b) in subsection (2) for the words from 'as follows' to the end of the subsection there shall be substituted the words 'as if the order or direction under Part III of this Act by virtue of which he was liable to be detained before being transferred were an order or direction for his admission or removal to the hospital to which he is transferred'; and
(c) in subsection (3) after the words 'may at any time' there shall be inserted the words ', with the consent of the Secretary of State,'.

6

In section 22, subsections (1) and (5) shall not apply.

7

In section 23 –

(a) in subsection (1) references to guardianship shall be omitted and after the word 'made' there shall be inserted the words 'with the consent of the Secretary of State and'; and
(b) in subsection (2) –
(i) in paragraph (a) to the words 'for assessment or' and 'or by the nearest relative of the patient' shall be omitted; and
(ii) paragraph (b) shall be omitted.

8

In section 34, in subsection (1) the definition of 'the nominated medical attendant' and subsection (3) shall be omitted.

NOTES

Prospective amendments. Words in para 2 prospectively repealed and subsequent words substituted by MHA 2007, s 32(4). Sch 3, paras 1, 37(1), (2), para 3, sub-para (aa) prospectively inserted by

MHA 2007, s 33 (1), (3), para 3 words repealed and subsequent words substituted by MHA 2007, s 11 (1), (8) (a), (b); para 6 prospectively substituted by MHA 2007, s 32(4), Sch 3, paras 1, 37 (1), (3).

SCHEDULE 2
Mental Health Review Tribunals

Section 65(2)

1

Each of the Mental Health Review Tribunals shall consist of –

    (a)   a number of persons (referred to in this Schedule as 'the legal members') appointed by the Lord Chancellor and having such legal experience as the Lord Chancellor considers suitable;

    (b)   a number of persons (referred to in this Schedule as 'the medical members') being registered medical practitioners appointed by the Lord Chancellor ...; and

    (c)   a number of persons appointed by the Lord Chancellor ... and having such experience in administration, such knowledge of social services or such other qualifications or experience as the Lord Chancellor considers suitable.

1A

As part of the selection process for an appointment under paragraph 1(b) or (c) the Judicial Appointments Commission shall consult the Secretary of State.

2

Subject to paragraph 2A below the members of Mental Health Review Tribunals shall hold and vacate office under the terms of the instrument under which they are appointed, but may resign office by notice in writing to the Lord Chancellor; and any such member who ceases to hold office shall be eligible for re-appointment.

2A

A member of a Mental Health Review Tribunal shall vacate office on the day on which he attains the age of 70 years; but this paragraph is subject to section 26(4) to (6) of the Judicial Pensions and Retirement Act 1993 (power to authorise continuance in office up to the age of 75 years).

3

(1) The Lord Chancellor shall appoint one of the legal members of the Mental Health Review Tribunal for England to be the President of that tribunal.

(2) The Lord Chancellor shall appoint one of the legal members of the Mental Health Review Tribunal for Wales to be the President of that tribunal.

4

Subject to rules made by the Lord Chancellor under section 78(2)(c) above, the members who are to constitute a Mental Health Review Tribunal for the purposes of any proceedings or class or group of proceedings under this Act shall be appointed by the President of the tribunal or by another member of the tribunal appointed for the purpose by the President; and of the members so appointed –

(a) one or more shall be appointed from the legal members;

(b) one or more shall be appointed from the medical members; and

(c) one or more shall be appointed from the members who are neither legal nor medical members.

5

A member of a Mental Health Review Tribunal for one area may be appointed under paragraph 4 above as one of the persons to constitute a Mental Health Review Tribunal for the other area for the purposes of any proceedings or class or group of proceedings; and for the purposes of this Act, a person so appointed shall, in relation to the proceedings for which he was appointed, be deemed to be a member of that other tribunal.

6

Subject to any rules made by the Lord Chancellor under section 78(4)(a) above, where the President of the tribunal is included among the persons appointed under paragraph 4 above, he shall be chairman of the tribunal; and in any other case the chairman of the tribunal shall be such one of the members so appointed (being one of the legal members) as the President may nominate.

NOTES

Prospective amendments. Para 3 prospectively substituted: MHA 2007, s 38 (1), (5), (6); para 4 words prospectively repealed and subsequent words substituted: MHA 2007, s 38 (1), (5), (7) (a); para 5 words prospectively repealed and subsequent words substituted: MHA 2007, s 38 (1), (5), (8) (a); para 6 words prospectively repealed and subsequent words substituted: MHA 2007, s 38 (1), (5), (9) (a), (b).

SCHEDULE 3
(repealed)

SCHEDULE 4
Consequential Amendments

Section 148

(repealed)

SCHEDULE 5
Transitional and Saving Provisions

Section 148

1

Where any period of time specified in an enactment repealed by this Act is current at the commencement of this Act, this Act shall have effect as if the corresponding provision of this Act had been in force when that period began to run.

2

Nothing in this Act shall affect the interpretation of any provision of the Mental Health Act 1959 which is not repealed by this Act and accordingly sections 1 and 145(1) of this Act shall apply to any such provision as if it were contained in this Act.

3

Where, apart from this paragraph, anything done under or for the purposes of any enactment which is repealed by this Act would cease to have effect by virtue of that repeal it shall have effect as if it had been done under or for the purposes of the corresponding provision of this Act.

4

(*repealed*)

5

(*repealed*)

6

This Act shall apply in relation to any authority for the detention or guardianship of a person who was liable to be detained or subject to guardianship under the Mental Health Act 1959 immediately before 30th September 1983 as if the provisions of this Act which derive from provisions amended by sections 1 or 2 of the Mental Health (Amendment) Act 1982 and the amendments in Schedule 3 to that Act which are consequential on those sections were included in this Act in the form the provisions from which they derive would take if those amendments were disregarded but this provision shall not apply to any renewal of that authority on or after that date.

7

(*repealed*)

8

(*repealed*)

9

(1) (*repealed*)

(2) Section 20(2) of this Act shall have effect in relation to any authority renewed before 1st October 1983 with the substitution for the words 'six months' of the words 'one year' and for the words 'one year' in both places they occur of the words 'two years'.

(3) (*repealed*)

10

(*repealed*)

11

(*repealed*)

12

(*repealed*)

13

(*repealed*)

14

(*repealed*)

15

The provisions of this Act which derive from sections 24 to 27 of the Mental Health (Amendment) Act 1982 shall have effect in relation to a transfer direction given before 30th September 1983 as well as in relation to one given later, but where, apart from this paragraph, a transfer direction given before 30th September 1983 would by virtue of the words in section 50(3) of this Act which are derived from section 24(3) of the Mental Health (Amendment) Act 1982 have ceased to have effect before that date it shall cease to have effect on that date.

16

The words in section 42(1) of this Act which derive from the amendment of section 66(1) of the Mental Health Act 1959 by section 28(1) of the Mental Health (Amendment) Act 1982 and the provisions of this Act which derive from section 28(3) of and Schedule 1 to that Act have effect in relation to a restriction order or, as the case may be, a restriction direction made or given before 30th September 1983 as well as in relation to one made or given later, but –

    (a)   any reference to a tribunal under section 66(6) of the said Act of 1959 in respect of a patient shall be treated for the purposes of subsections

(1) and (2) of section 77 of this Act in their application to sections 70 and 75(2) of this Act as an application made by him; and

(b)   sections 71(5) and 75(1)(a) of this Act do not apply where the period in question has expired before 30th September 1983.

17

Section 91(2) of this Act shall not apply in relation to a patient removed from England and Wales before 30th September 1983.

18

(*repealed*)

19

(*repealed*)

20

The repeal by the Mental Health (Amendment) Act 1982 of section 77 of the Mental Health Act 1959 does not affect subsection (4) of that section in its application to a transfer direction given before 30th September 1983, but after the coming into force of this Act that subsection shall have effect for that purpose as if for the references to subsection (6) of section 60, Part IV of that Act and the provisions of that Act there were substituted respectively references to section 37(8), Part II and the provisions of this Act.

21

Any direction to which section 71(4) of the Mental Health Act 1959 applied immediately before the commencement of this Act shall have the same effect as a hospital order together with a restriction order, made without limitation of time.

22

(*repealed*)

23

For any reference in any enactment, instrument, deed or other document to a receiver under Part VIII of the Mental Health Act 1959 there shall be substituted a reference to a receiver under Part VII of this Act.

24

Nothing in this Act shall affect the operation of the proviso to section 107(5) of the Mental Health Act 1959 in relation to a charge created before the commencement of this Act under that section.

25

Nothing in this Act shall affect the operation of subsection (6) of section 112 of the Mental Health Act 1959 in relation to a charge created before the commencement of this Act by virtue of subsection (5) of that section.

26

(*repealed*)

27

Nothing in this Act shall affect the operation of section 116 of the Mental Health Act 1959 in relation to orders made, directions or authorities given or other instruments issued before the commencement of this Act.

28

References to applications, recommendations, reports and other documents in section 126 of this Act shall include those to which section 125 of the Mental Health Act 1959 applied immediately before the commencement of this Act and references in section 139 of this Act to the Acts to which that section applies shall include those to which section 141 of the said Act of 1959 applied at that time.

29

The repeal by the Mental Health Act 1959 of the Mental Treatment Act 1930 shall not affect any amendment effected by section 20 of that Act in any enactment not repealed by the said Act of 1959.

30

The repeal by the Mental Health Act 1959 of the provisions of the Lunacy Act 1890 and of the Mental Deficiency Act 1913 relating to the superannuation of officers or employees shall not affect any arrangements for the payment of allowances or other benefits made in accordance with those provisions and in force on 1st November 1960.

31

(1) Any patient who immediately before the commencement of this Act was liable to be detained in a hospital or subject to guardianship by virtue of paragraph 9 of Schedule 6 to the Mental Health Act 1959 shall unless previously discharged continue to be so liable for the remainder of the period of his treatment current on 1st November 1960.

(2) The patient may before the expiration of the period of treatment referred to in sub-paragraph (1) above apply to a Mental Health Review Tribunal.

32

Any patient who immediately before the commencement of this Act was liable to be detained or subject to guardianship by virtue of an authority which had been renewed under paragraph 11 of Schedule 6 to the Mental Health Act 1959 shall unless previously discharged continue to be so liable during the period for which that authority was so renewed.

33

(1)   This paragraph applies to patients who at the commencement of this Act are liable to be detained or subject to guardianship by virtue of paragraph 31 or 32 above.

(2)   Authority for the detention or guardianship of the patient may on the expiration of the relevant period, unless the patient has previously been discharged, be renewed for a further period of two years.

(3)   Sections 20(3) to (10) and 66(1)(f) of this Act shall apply in relation to the renewal of authority for the detention or guardianship of a patient under this paragraph as they apply in relation to the renewal of authority for the detention or guardianship of the patient under section 20(2).

(4)   In this paragraph 'the relevant period' means –

    (a)   in relation to a patient liable to be detained or subject to guardianship by virtue of the said paragraph 31, the period of his treatment referred to in that paragraph;

    (b)   in relation to a patient detained by virtue of the said paragraph 32, the period for which authority for the detention or guardianship of the patient has been renewed under paragraph 11 of Schedule 6 to the 1959 Act;

    (c)   in relation to a patient the authority for whose detention or guardianship has previously been renewed under this paragraph, the latest period for which it has been so renewed.

34

(1)   Any patient who is liable to be detained in a hospital or subject to guardianship by virtue of paragraph 31 above shall (subject to the exceptions and modifications specified in the following provisions of this paragraph) be treated as if he had been admitted to the hospital in pursuance of an application for admission for treatment under Part II of this Act or had been received into guardianship in pursuance of a guardianship application under the said Part II and had been so admitted or received as a patient suffering from the form or forms of mental disorder recorded under paragraph 7 of Schedule 6 to the Mental Health Act 1959 or, if a different form or forms have been specified in a report under section 38 of that Act as applied by that paragraph, the form or forms so specified.

(2)   Section 20 of this Act shall not apply in relation to the patient, but the provisions of paragraph 33 above shall apply instead.

(3)   Any patient to whom paragraph 9(3) of Schedule 6 to the Mental Health Act 1959 applied at the commencement of this Act who fell within paragraph (b) of that paragraph shall cease to be liable to be detained on attaining the age of 25 years unless, during the period of two months ending on the date when he attains that age, the responsible medical officer records his opinion under the following provisions of this Schedule that the patient is unfit for discharge.

(4)   If the patient was immediately before 1st November 1960 liable to be detained by virtue of section 6, 8(1) or 9 of the Mental Deficiency Act 1913, the power of discharging him under section 23 of this Act shall not be exercisable by his nearest relative, but his nearest relative may make one application in respect of him to a Mental Health Review Tribunal in any period of 12 months.

35

(1)   The responsible medical officer may record for the purposes of paragraph 34(3) above his opinion that a patient detained in a hospital is unfit for discharge if it appears to the responsible medical officer –

(a)   that if that patient were released from the hospital he would be likely to act in a manner dangerous to other persons or to himself, or would be likely to resort to criminal activities; or

(b)   that that patient is incapable of caring for himself and that there is no suitable hospital or other establishment into which he can be admitted and where he would be likely to remain voluntarily;

and where the responsible medical officer records his opinion as aforesaid he shall also record the grounds for his opinion.

(2)   Where the responsible medical officer records his opinion under this paragraph in respect of a patient, the managers of the hospital or other persons in charge of the establishment where he is for the time being detained or liable to be detained shall cause the patient to be informed, and the patient may, at any time before the expiration of the period of 28 days beginning with the date on which he is so informed, apply to a Mental Health Review Tribunal.

(3)   On any application under sub-paragraph (2) above the tribunal shall, if satisfied that none of the conditions set out in paragraphs (a) and (b) of sub-paragraph (1) above are fulfilled, direct that the patient be discharged, and subsection (1) of section 72 of this Act shall have effect in relation to the application as if paragraph (b) of that subsection were omitted.

36

Any person who immediately before the commencement of this Act was deemed to have been named as the guardian of any patient under paragraph 14 of Schedule 6 to the Mental Health Act 1959 shall be deemed for the purposes of this Act to have been named as the guardian of the patient in an application for his reception into guardianship under Part II of this Act accepted on that person's behalf by the relevant local authority.

37

(1) This paragraph applies to patients who immediately before the commencement of this Act were transferred patients within the meaning of paragraph 15 of Schedule 6 to the Mental Health Act 1959.

(2) A transferred patient who immediately before the commencement of this Act was by virtue of sub-paragraph (2) of that paragraph treated for the purposes of that Act as if he were liable to be detained in a hospital in pursuance of a direction under section 71 of that Act shall be treated as if he were so liable in pursuance of a hospital order together with a restriction order, made without limitation of time.

(3) A transferred patient who immediately before the commencement of this Act was by virtue of sub-paragraph (3) of that paragraph treated for the purposes of that Act as if he were liable to be detained in a hospital by virtue of a transfer direction under section 72 of that Act and as if a direction restricting his discharge had been given under section 74 of that Act shall be treated as if he were so liable by virtue of a transfer direction under section 47 of this Act and as if a restriction direction had been given under section 49 of this Act.

(4) Section 84 of this Act shall apply to a transferred patient who was treated by virtue of sub-paragraph (5) of that paragraph immediately before the commencement of this Act as if he had been removed to a hospital under section 89 of that Act as if he had been so removed under the said section 84.

(5) Any person to whom sub-paragraph (6) of that paragraph applied immediately before the commencement of this Act shall be treated for the purposes of this Act as if he were liable to be detained in a hospital in pursuance of a transfer direction given under section 48 of this Act and as if a restriction direction had been given under section 49 of this Act.

38

Any patient who immediately before the commencement of this Act was treated by virtue of sub-paragraph (1) of paragraph 16 of Schedule 6 to the Mental Health Act 1959 as if he had been conditionally discharged under section 66 of that Act shall be treated as if he had been conditionally discharged under section 42 of this Act and any such direction as is mentioned in paragraph (b) of that sub-paragraph shall be treated as if it had been given under the said section 42.

39

(*repealed*)

40

A person who immediately before the commencement of this Act was detained by virtue of paragraph 19 of Schedule 6 to the Mental Health Act 1959 may continue to be detained until the expiration of the period of his treatment current on 1st November 1960 or until he becomes liable to be detained or subject to guardianship under this Act, whichever occurs first, and may be so detained in any place in which he might have been detained under that paragraph.

41

Any opinion recorded by the responsible medical officer under the foregoing provisions of this Schedule shall be recorded in such form as may be prescribed by regulations made by the Secretary of State.

42

(1)   In the foregoing provisions of this Schedule –

(a)   references to the period of treatment of a patient that was current on 1st November 1960 are to the period for which he would have been liable to be detained or subject to guardianship by virtue of any enactment repealed or excluded by the Mental Health Act 1959, or any enactment repealed or replaced by any such enactment as aforesaid, being a period which began but did not expire before that date; and

(b)   'the responsible medical officer' means –

(i)   in relation to a patient subject to guardianship, the medical officer authorised by the local social services authority to act (either generally or in any particular case or for any particular purpose) as the responsible medical officer;

(ii)   in relation to any other class of patient, the registered medical practitioner in charge of the treatment of the patient.

(2)   Subsection (2) of section 34 of this Act shall apply for the purposes of the foregoing provisions of this Schedule as it applies for the purposes of Part II of this Act.

(3)   The sentence or other period of detention of a person who was liable to be detained or subject to guardianship immediately before 1st November 1960 by virtue of an order under section 9 of the Mental Deficiency Act 1913 shall be treated for the purposes of the foregoing provisions of this Schedule as expiring at the end of the period for which that person would have been liable to be detained in a prison or other institution if the order had not been made.

(4)   For the purposes of the foregoing provisions of this Schedule, an order sending a person to an institution or placing a person under guardianship made before 9th March 1956 on a petition presented under the Mental Deficiency Act 1913 shall be deemed to be valid if it was so deemed immediately before the commencement of this Act by virtue of section 148(2) of the Mental Health Act 1959.

43

(*repealed*)

44

(*repealed*)

45

(*repealed*)

46

(*repealed*)

NOTES

Prospective amendments. Words prospectively repealed, MHA 2007, s 55, Sch 11, Pt 1.

****

Appendix 2

DOMESTIC VIOLENCE, CRIME AND VICTIMS ACT 2004 (2004 C 28) (AS AMENDED BY THE MENTAL HEALTH ACT 2007)

ARRANGEMENT OF SECTIONS

PART 3
VICTIMS ETC

Chapter 2
Representations and information

Hospital orders

****

PART 3
VICTIMS ETC

****

Chapter 2
Representations and information

****

Hospital orders

36 Victims' rights: preliminary

(1) This section applies if the conditions in subsections (2) and (3) are met.

(2) The first condition is that one of these applies in respect of a person ('the patient') charged with a sexual or violent offence –

- (a)   the patient is convicted of the offence;
- (b)   a verdict is returned that the patient is not guilty of the offence by reason of insanity;
- (c)   a finding is made –
    - (i)   under section 4 of the Criminal Procedure (Insanity) Act 1964 that the patient is under a disability, and
    - (ii)   under section 4A of that Act that he did the act or made the omission charged against him as the offence.

(3) The second condition is that a hospital order, whether with or without a restriction order, is made in respect of the patient by a court dealing with him for the offence.

(4) The local probation board for the area in which the determination mentioned in subsection (2)(a), (b) or (c) is made must take all reasonable steps to ascertain whether a person who appears to the board to be the victim of the offence or to act for the victim of the offence wishes –

- (a)   to make representations about the matters specified in subsection (5);
- (b)   to receive the information specified in subsection (6).

(5) The matters are –

- (a)   whether the patient should be subject to any conditions in the event of his discharge from hospital while a restriction order is in force in respect of him;
- (b)   if so, what conditions;
- (c)   what conditions he should be subject to in the event of his discharge from hospital under a community treatment order.

(6) The information is information about any conditions to which the patient is to be subject in the event of his discharge from hospital.

NOTES

Prospective amendments. Words in subs (3) prospectively substituted: MHA 2007, s 48, Sch 6, paras 1, 2(1), (2). Words in subs (5)(a) prospectively inserted: MHA 2007, s 48, Sch 6, paras 1, 2(1), (3)(a). Para (c) prospectively inserted in subs (5): MHA 2007, s 48, Sch 6, paras 1, 2(1), (3)(b).

36A Supplemental provision for case where no restriction order made

(1) This section applies if, in a case where section 36 applies, the hospital order in respect of the patient was made without a restriction order.

(2) Subsection (3) applies if a person who appears to the local probation board mentioned in section 36(4) to be the victim of the offence or to act for the victim of the offence, when his wishes are ascertained under section 36(4), expresses a wish –

  (a)   to make representations about a matter specified in section 36(5), or
  (b)   to receive the information specified in section 36(6).

(3) The local probation board must –

  (a)   notify the managers of the hospital in which the patient is detained of that person's wish and of that person's name and address, and
  (b)   notify that person of the name and address of the hospital.

(4) Subsection (5) applies if a person who appears to the local probation board mentioned in section 36(4) to be the victim of the offence or to act for the victim of the offence, subsequently to his wishes being ascertained under section 36(4), expresses a wish to do something specified in subsection (2)(a) or (b).

(5) The local probation board mentioned in section 36(4) must take all reasonable steps –

  (a)   to ascertain whether the hospital order made in respect of the patient continues in force and whether a community treatment order is in force in respect of him, and
  (b)   if the board ascertains that the hospital order does continue in force –
      (i)   to notify the managers of the relevant hospital of that person's wish, and
      (ii)   to notify that person of the name and address of the hospital.

(6) The relevant hospital is –

  (a)   the hospital in which the patient is detained, or
  (b)   if a community treatment order is in force in respect of the patient, the responsible hospital.

NOTES

Prospective amendment. Section prospectively inserted: MHA 2007, s 48, Sch 6, paras 1, 3.

37 Representations where restriction order made

(1) This section applies if, in a case where section 36 applies, the hospital order in respect of the patient was made with a restriction order.

(2) If –

  (a)   a person makes representations about a matter specified in section 36(5) to the local probation board mentioned in section 36(4) or the relevant local probation board, and

(b)   it appears to the relevant local probation board that the person is the victim of the offence or acts for the victim of the offence,

the relevant local probation board must forward the representations to the persons responsible for determining the matter.

(3) The duty in subsection (2) applies only while the restriction order made in respect of the patient is in force.

(4) The Secretary of State must inform the relevant local probation board if he is considering –

(a)   whether to give a direction in respect of the patient under section 42(1) of the Mental Health Act 1983 (directions lifting restrictions),

(b)   whether to discharge the patient under section 42(2) of that Act, either absolutely or subject to conditions, or

(c)   if the patient has been discharged subject to conditions, whether to vary the conditions.

(5) A Mental Health Review Tribunal must inform the relevant local probation board if –

(a)   an application is made to the tribunal by the patient under section 69, 70 or 75 of the Mental Health Act 1983 (applications concerning restricted patients), or

(b)   the Secretary of State refers the patient's case to the tribunal under section 71 of that Act (references concerning restricted patients).

(6) Subsection (7) applies if –

(a)   the relevant local probation board receives information under subsection (4) or (5), and

(b)   a person who appears to the relevant local probation board to be the victim of the offence or to act for the victim of the offence –

(i)   when his wishes were ascertained under section 36(4), expressed a wish to make representations about a matter specified in section 36(5), or

(ii) has made representations about such a matter to the relevant local probation board or the local probation board mentioned in section 36(4).

(7) The relevant local probation board must provide the information to the person.

(8) The relevant local probation board is –

(a)   if the patient is to be discharged subject to a condition that he reside in a particular area, the local probation board for the area;

(b)   in any other case, the local probation board for the area in which the hospital in which the patient is detained is situated.

NOTES

Prospective amendments. Section heading prospectively substituted: MHA 2007, s 48, Sch 6, paras 1, 4. Words in subs (1) prospectively substituted: MHA 2007, s 48, Sch 6, paras 1, 4.

37A Representations where restriction order not made

(1) This section applies if, in a case where section 36 applies, the hospital order in respect of the patient was made without a restriction order.

(2) Subsection (3) applies if –

    (a)   a person makes representations about a matter specified in section 36(5) to the managers of the relevant hospital, and

    (b)   it appears to the managers that the person is the victim of the offence or acts for the victim of the offence.

(3) The managers must forward the representations to the persons responsible for determining the matter.

(4) The responsible clinician must inform the managers of the relevant hospital if he is considering making –

    (a)   an order for discharge in respect of the patient under section 23(2) of the Mental Health Act 1983,

    (b)   a community treatment order in respect of the patient, or

    (c)   an order under section 17B(4) of the Mental Health Act 1983 to vary the conditions specified in a community treatment order in force in respect of the patient.

(5) Any person who has the power to make an order for discharge in respect of the patient under section 23(3) of the Mental Health Act 1983 must inform the managers of the relevant hospital if he is considering making that order.

(6) A Mental Health Review Tribunal must inform the managers of the relevant hospital if –

    (a)   an application is made to the tribunal under section 66 or 69 of the Mental Health Act 1983, or

    (b)   the patient's case is referred to the tribunal under section 67 of that Act.

(7) Subsection (8) applies if –

    (a)   the managers of the relevant hospital receive information under subsection (4), (5) or (6), and

    (b)   a person who appears to the managers to be the victim of the offence or to act for the victim of the offence –

        (i)   when his wishes were ascertained under section 36(4), expressed a wish to make representations about a matter specified in section 36(5), or

        (ii)   has made representations about such a matter to the managers of the hospital in which the patient was, at the time in question, detained.

(8) The managers of the relevant hospital must provide the information to the person.

(9) The relevant hospital has the meaning given in section 36A(6).

NOTES

Prospective amendment. Section prospectively inserted: MHA 2007, s 48, Sch 6, paras 1, 5.

38 Information where restriction order made

(1) This section applies if, in a case where section 36 applies, the hospital order in respect of the patient was made with a restriction order.

(2) Subsection (3) applies if a person who appears to the relevant local probation board to be the victim of the offence or to act for the victim of the offence –

    (a)   when his wishes were ascertained under section 36(4), expressed a wish to receive the information specified in section 36(6), or

    (b)   has subsequently informed the relevant local probation board that he wishes to receive that information.

(3) The relevant local probation board must take all reasonable steps –

    (a)   to inform that person whether or not the patient is to be subject to any conditions in the event of his discharge;

    (b)   if he is, to provide that person with details of any conditions which relate to contact with the victim or his family;

    (c)   if the restriction order in respect of the patient is to cease to have effect, to notify that person of the date on which it is to cease to have effect;

    (d)   to provide that person with such other information as the board considers appropriate in all the circumstances of the case.

(4) The Secretary of State must inform the relevant local probation board –

    (a)   whether the patient is to be discharged;

    (b)   if he is, whether he is to be discharged absolutely or subject to conditions;

    (c)   if he is to be discharged subject to conditions, what the conditions are to be;

    (d)   if he has been discharged subject to conditions –

        (i)   of any variation of the conditions by the Secretary of State;

        (ii)   of any recall to hospital under section 42(3) of the Mental Health Act 1983;

    (e)   if the restriction order is to cease to have effect by virtue of action to be taken by the Secretary of State, of the date on which the restriction order is to cease to have effect.

(5) Subsections (6) and (7) apply (instead of subsection (4)) if –

    (a)   an application is made to a Mental Health Review Tribunal by the patient under section 69, 70 or 75 of the Mental Health Act 1983 (applications concerning restricted patients), or

    (b)   the Secretary of State refers the patient's case to a Mental Health Review Tribunal under section 71 of that Act (references concerning restricted patients).

(6) The tribunal must inform the relevant local probation board –

    (a)   of the matters specified in subsection (4)(a) to (c);

    (b)   if the patient has been discharged subject to conditions, of any variation of the conditions by the tribunal;

    (c)   if the restriction order is to cease to have effect by virtue of action to be taken by the tribunal, of the date on which the restriction order is to cease to have effect.

(7) The Secretary of State must inform the relevant local probation board of the matters specified in subsection (4)(d) and (e).

(8) The duties in subsections (3) to (7) apply only while the restriction order is in force.

(9) The relevant local probation board has the meaning given in section 37(8).

NOTES

Prospective amendments. Section heading prospectively substituted: MHA 2007, s 48, Sch 6, paras 1, 6. Words in subs (1) prospectively substituted: MHA 2007, s 48, Sch 6, paras 1, 6.

38A Information where restriction order not made

(1) This section applies if, in a case where section 36 applies, the hospital order in respect of the patient was made without a restriction order.

(2) The responsible clinician must inform the managers of the relevant hospital –

    (a)   whether he is to make an order for discharge in respect of the patient under section 23(2) of the Mental Health Act 1983;

    (b)   whether he is to make a community treatment order in respect of the patient;

    (c)   if a community treatment order is to be made in respect of the patient, what conditions are to be specified in the order;

    (d)   if a community treatment order is in force in respect of the patient, of any variation to be made under section 17B(4) of the Mental Health Act 1983 of the conditions specified in the order;

    (e)   if a community treatment order in respect of the patient is to cease to be in force, of the date on which it is to cease to be in force;

    (f)   if, following the examination of the patient under section 20 of the Mental Health Act 1983, it does not appear to the responsible clinician that the conditions set out in subsection (4) of that section are satisfied, of the date on which the authority for the patient's detention is to expire.

(3) Any person who has the power to make an order for discharge in respect of the patient under section 23(3) of the Mental Health Act 1983 must inform the managers of the relevant hospital if he is to make that order.

(4) Subsection (5) applies if –

    (a)   an application is made to a Mental Health Review Tribunal under section 66 or 69 of the Mental Health Act 1983,

(b) the patient's case is referred to a Mental Health Review Tribunal under section 67 of that Act, or

(c) the managers of the relevant hospital refer the patient's case to a Mental Health Review Tribunal under section 68 of that Act.

(5) The tribunal must inform the managers of the relevant hospital if it directs that the patient is to be discharged.

(6) Subsection (7) applies if a person who appears to the managers of the relevant hospital to be the victim of the offence or to act for the victim of the offence –

(a) when his wishes were ascertained under section 36(4), expressed a wish to receive the information specified in section 36(6), or

(b) has subsequently informed the managers of the relevant hospital that he wishes to receive that information.

(7) The managers of the relevant hospital order must take all reasonable steps –

(a) to inform that person whether the patient is to be discharged under section 23 or 72 of the Mental Health Act 1983;

(b) to inform that person whether a community treatment order is to be made in respect of the patient;

(c) if a community treatment order is to be made in respect of the patient and is to specify conditions which relate to contact with the victim or his family, to provide that person with details of those conditions;

(d) if a community treatment order is in force in respect of the patient and the conditions specified in the order are to be varied under section 17B(4) of the Mental Health Act 1983, to provide that person with details of any variation which relates to contact with the victim or his family;

(e) if a community treatment order in respect of the patient is to cease to be in force, to inform that person of the date on which it is to cease to be in force;

(f) if, following the examination of the patient under section 20 of the Mental Health Act 1983, the authority for the patient's detention is not to be renewed, to inform that person of the date on which the authority is to expire;

(g) to provide that person with such other information as the managers of the relevant hospital consider appropriate in all the circumstances of the case.

(8) The relevant hospital has the meaning given by section 36A(6).

NOTES

Prospective amendment. Section prospectively inserted: MHA 2007, s 48, Sch 6, paras 1, 7.

38B Removal of restriction

(1) This section applies if, in a case where section 36 applies –

(a)   the hospital order in respect of the patient was made with a restriction order, and

(b)   the restriction order ceases to have effect while the hospital order continues in force.

(2) Subsection (3) applies if a person who appears to the relevant local probation board to be the victim of the offence or to act for the victim of the offence –

(a)   when his wishes were ascertained under section 36(4), expressed a wish to make representations about a matter specified in section 36(5) or to receive the information specified in section 36(6), or

(b)   has subsequently informed the relevant local probation board that he wishes to make representations about such a matter or to receive that information.

(3) The relevant local probation board must take all reasonable steps –

(a)   to notify the managers of the relevant hospital of an address at which that person may be contacted;

(b)   to notify that person of the name and address of the hospital.

(4) While the hospital order continues in force, the patient is to be regarded as a patient in respect of whom a hospital order was made without a restriction order; and sections 37A and 38A are to apply in relation to him accordingly.

(5) The relevant hospital has the meaning given in section 36A(6).

(6) The relevant local probation board has the meaning given in section 37(8).

NOTES

Prospective amendment. Section prospectively inserted: MHA 2007, s 48, Sch 6, paras 1, 7.

Hospital directions

39 Victims' rights: preliminary

(1) This section applies if –

(a)   a person ('the offender') is convicted of a sexual or violent offence,

(b)   a relevant sentence is imposed on him in respect of the offence, and

(c)   a hospital direction and a limitation direction are given in relation to him by a court dealing with him for the offence.

(2) The local probation board for the area in which the hospital direction is given must take all reasonable steps to ascertain whether a person who appears to the board to be the victim of the offence or to act for the victim of the offence wishes –

(a)   to make representations about the matters specified in subsection (3);

(b)   to receive the information specified in subsection (4).

(3) The matters are –

(a)   whether the offender should, in the event of his discharge from hospital while he is subject to a limitation direction, be subject to any conditions and, if so, what conditions;

(aa) what conditions he should be subject to in the event of his discharge from hospital under a community treatment order;

(b)   whether the offender should, in the event of his release from hospital, be subject to any licence conditions or supervision requirements and, if so, what licence conditions or supervision requirements;

(c)   if the offender is transferred to a prison or other institution in which he might have been detained if he had not been removed to hospital, whether he should, in the event of his release from prison or another such institution, be subject to any licence conditions or supervision requirements and, if so, what licence conditions or supervision requirements.

(4) The information is –

(a)   information about any conditions to which the offender is to be subject in the event of his discharge;

(b)   information about any licence conditions or supervision requirements to which the offender is to be subject in the event of his release.

NOTES

Prospective amendments. Words in subs (3)(a) prospectively inserted: MHA 2007, s 48, Sch 6, paras 1, 8(a). Para (aa) in subs (3) prospectively inserted: MHA 2007, s 48, Sch 6, paras 1, 8(b).

40 Representations

(1) This section applies if section 39 applies.

(2) If –

(a)   a person makes representations about a matter specified in section 39(3) to the local probation board mentioned in section 39(2) or the relevant local probation board, and

(b)   it appears to the relevant local probation board that the person is the victim of the offence or acts for the victim of the offence,

the relevant local probation board must forward the representations to the persons responsible for determining the matter.

(3) If the representations are about a matter specified in section 39(3)(a), the duty in subsection (2) applies only while the limitation direction given in relation to the offender is in force.

(4) The Secretary of State must inform the relevant local probation board if he is considering –

(a)   whether to give a direction in respect of the offender under section 42(1) of the Mental Health Act 1983 (directions lifting restrictions),

(b)   whether to discharge the offender under section 42(2) of that Act, either absolutely or subject to conditions, or

(c) if the offender has been discharged subject to conditions, whether to vary the conditions.

(5) A Mental Health Review Tribunal must inform the relevant local probation board if –

(a) an application is made to the tribunal by the offender under section 69, 70 or 75 of the Mental Health Act 1983 (applications concerning restricted patients), or

(b) the Secretary of State refers the offender's case to the tribunal under section 71 of that Act (references concerning restricted patients).

(6) Subsection (7) applies if –

(a) the relevant local probation board receives information under subsection (4) or (5), and

(b) a person who appears to the relevant local probation board to be the victim of the offence or to act for the victim of the offence –

    (i) when his wishes were ascertained under section 39(2), expressed a wish to make representations about a matter specified in section 39(3)(a), or

    (ii) has made representations about such a matter to the relevant local probation board or the local probation board mentioned in section 39(2).

(7) The relevant local probation board must provide the information to the person.

(8) The relevant local probation board is –

(a) if the offender is to be discharged from hospital subject to a condition that he reside in a particular area, the local probation board for the area;

(b) if the offender is to be supervised on release by an officer of a local probation board, that local probation board;

(c) in any other case, the local probation board for the area in which the hospital, prison or other place in which the offender is detained is situated.

41 Information

(1) This section applies if section 39 applies.

(2) Subsection (3) applies if a person who appears to the relevant local probation board to be the victim of the offence or to act for the victim of the offence –

(a) when his wishes were ascertained under section 39(2), expressed a wish to receive the information specified in section 39(4), or

(b) has subsequently informed the relevant local probation board that he wishes to receive that information.

(3) The relevant local probation board must take all reasonable steps –

(a)   to inform that person whether or not the offender is to be subject to any conditions in the event of his discharge;

(b)   if he is, to provide that person with details of any conditions which relate to contact with the victim or his family;

(c)   if the limitation direction in respect of the offender is to cease to have effect, to notify that person of the date on which it is to cease to have effect;

(d)   to inform that person whether or not the offender is to be subject to any licence conditions or supervision requirements in the event of his release;

(e)   if he is, to provide that person with details of any licence conditions or supervision requirements which relate to contact with the victim or his family;

(f)   to provide that person with such other information as the board considers appropriate in all the circumstances of the case.

(4) The Secretary of State must inform the relevant local probation board –

(a)   whether the offender is to be discharged;

(b)   if he is, whether he is to be discharged absolutely or subject to conditions;

(c)   if he is to be discharged subject to conditions, what the conditions are to be;

(d)   if he has been discharged subject to conditions –
      (i)   of any variation of the conditions by the Secretary of State;
      (ii)   of any recall to hospital under section 42(3) of the Mental Health Act 1983;

(e)   if the limitation direction is to cease to have effect by virtue of action to be taken by the Secretary of State, of the date on which the limitation direction is to cease to have effect.

(5) Subsections (6) and (7) apply (instead of subsection (4)) if –

(a)   an application is made to a Mental Health Review Tribunal by the offender under section 69, 70 or 75 of the Mental Health Act 1983 (applications concerning restricted patients), or

(b)   the Secretary of State refers the offender's case to a Mental Health Review Tribunal under section 71 of that Act (references concerning restricted patients).

(6) The tribunal must inform the relevant local probation board –

(a)   of the matters specified in subsection (4)(a) to (c);

(b)   if the offender has been discharged subject to conditions, of any variation of the conditions by the tribunal;

(c)   if the limitation direction is to cease to have effect by virtue of action to be taken by the tribunal, of the date on which the limitation direction is to cease to have effect.

(7) The Secretary of State must inform the relevant local probation board of the matters specified in subsection (4)(d) and (e).

(8) The duties in subsections (3)(a) to (c) and (4) to (7) apply only while the limitation direction is in force.

(9) The relevant local probation board has the meaning given in section 40(8).

41A Removal of restriction

(1) This section applies if, in a case where section 39 applies –

(a) the limitation direction in respect of the offender ceases to be in force, and

(b) he is treated for the purposes of the Mental Health Act 1983 as a patient in respect of whom a hospital order has effect.

(2) Subsection (3) applies if a person who appears to the relevant local probation board to be the victim of the offence or to act for the victim of the offence –

(a) when his wishes were ascertained under section 39(2), expressed a wish to make representations about a matter specified in section 39(3) or to receive the information specified in section 39(4), or

(b) has subsequently informed the relevant local probation board that he wishes to make representations about such a matter or to receive that information.

(3) The relevant local probation board must take all reasonable steps –

(a) to notify the managers of the relevant hospital of an address at which that person may be contacted;

(b) to notify that person of the address of the hospital.

(4) The offender is to be regarded as a patient in respect of whom a hospital order was made without a restriction order; and sections 37A and 38A are to apply in relation to him accordingly.

(5) The relevant hospital has the meaning given in section 36A(6).

(6) The relevant local probation board has the meaning given in section 40(8).

NOTES

Prospective amendment. Section prospectively inserted: MHA 2007, s 48, Sch 6, paras 1, 9.

Transfer directions

42 Victims' rights: preliminary

(1) This section applies if –

(a) a person ('the offender') is convicted of a sexual or violent offence,

(b) a relevant sentence is imposed on him in respect of the offence, and

(c) while the offender is serving the sentence, the Secretary of State gives a transfer direction in respect of the offender (whether or not he also gives a restriction direction in respect of the offender).

(2) The local probation board for the area in which the hospital specified in the transfer direction is situated must take all reasonable steps to ascertain whether a person who appears to the board to be the victim of the offence or to act for the victim of the offence wishes –

(a)   to make representations about the matters specified in subsection (3);
(b)   to receive the information specified in subsection (4).

(3) The matters are –

(a)   whether the offender should be subject to any conditions in the event of his discharge from hospital at a time when a restriction direction is in force in respect of him;
(b)   if so, what conditions;
(c)   what conditions he should be subject to in the event of his discharge from hospital under a community treatment order.

(4) The information is information about any conditions to which the offender is to be subject in the event of his discharge from hospital.

NOTES

Prospective amendments. Words in subs (1)(c) prospectively substituted: MHA 2007, s 48, Sch 6, paras 1, 10(1), (2). Words in subs (3)(a) prospectively inserted: MHA 2007, s 48, Sch 6, paras 1, 10(1), (3)(a). Para (c) in subs (3) prospectively inserted: MHA 2007, s 48, Sch 6, paras 1, 10(1), (3)(b).

42A   Supplemental provision for case where no restriction direction given

(1) This section applies if, in a case where section 42 applies, the transfer direction in respect of the patient was given without a restriction direction.

(2) Subsection (3) applies if a person who appears to the local probation board mentioned in section 42(2) to be the victim of the offence or to act for the victim of the offence, when his wishes are ascertained under section 42(2), expresses a wish –

(a)   to make representations about a matter specified in section 42(3), or
(b)   to receive the information specified in section 42(4).

(3) The local probation board must –

(a)   notify the managers of the hospital in which the patient is detained of that person's wish and of that person's name and address, and
(b)   notify that person of the name and address of the hospital.

(4) Subsection (5) applies if a person who appears to the local probation board mentioned in section 42(2) to be the victim of the offence or to act for the victim of the offence, subsequently to his wishes being ascertained under section 42(2), expressed a wish to do something specified in subsection (2)(a) or (b).

(5) The local probation board mentioned in section 42(2) must take all reasonable steps –

(a) to ascertain whether the transfer direction given in respect of the patient continues in force and whether a community treatment order is in force in respect of him, and

(b) if the board ascertains that the transfer direction does continue in force –

 (i) to notify the managers of the relevant hospital of that person's wish, and

 (ii) to notify that person of the name and address of the hospital.

(6) The relevant hospital has the meaning given in section 36A(6).

NOTES

Prospective amendment. Section prospectively inserted: MHA 2007, s 48, Sch 6, paras 1, 11.

43 Representations where restriction direction made

(1) This section applies if, in a case where section 42 applies, the transfer direction in respect of the patient was given with a restriction direction.

(2) If –

(a) a person makes representations about a matter specified in section 42(3) to the local probation board mentioned in section 42(2) or the relevant local probation board, and

(b) it appears to the relevant local probation board that the person is the victim of the offence or acts for the victim of the offence,

the relevant local probation board must forward the representations to the persons responsible for determining the matter.

(3) The duty in subsection (2) applies only while the restriction direction given in respect of the offender is in force.

(4) The Secretary of State must inform the relevant local probation board if he is considering –

(a) whether to give a direction in respect of the offender under section 42(1) of the Mental Health Act 1983 (directions lifting restrictions),

(b) whether to discharge the offender under section 42(2) of that Act, either absolutely or subject to conditions, or

(c) if the offender has been discharged subject to conditions, whether to vary the conditions.

(5) A Mental Health Review Tribunal must inform the relevant local probation board if –

(a) an application is made to the tribunal by the offender under section 69, 70 or 75 of the Mental Health Act 1983 (applications concerning restricted patients), or

(b) the Secretary of State refers the offender's case to the tribunal under section 71 of that Act (references concerning restricted patients).

(6) Subsection (7) applies if –

(a)   the relevant local probation board receives information under subsection (4) or (5), and

(b)   a person who appears to the relevant local probation board to be the victim of the offence or to act for the victim of the offence –

   (i)   when his wishes were ascertained under section 42(2), expressed a wish to make representations about a matter specified in section 42(3), or

   (ii)   has made representations about such a matter to the relevant local probation board or the local probation board mentioned in section 42(2).

(7) The relevant local probation board must provide the information to the person.

(8) The relevant local probation board is –

(a)   if the offender is to be discharged subject to a condition that he reside in a particular area, the local probation board for the area;

(b)   in any other case, the local probation board for the area in which the hospital in which the offender is detained is situated.

NOTES

Prospective amendments. Section heading prospectively substituted: MHA 2007, s 48, Sch 6, paras 1, 12. Words in subs (1) prospectively substituted: MHA 2007, s 48, Sch 6, paras 1, 12.

43A   Representations where restriction direction not given

(1) This section applies if, in a case where section 42 applies, the transfer direction in respect of the patient was given without a restriction direction.

(2) Subsection (3) applies if –

(a)   a person makes representations about a matter specified in section 42(3) to the managers of the relevant hospital, and

(b)   it appears to the managers that the person is the victim of the offence or acts for the victim of the offence.

(3) The managers must forward the representations to the persons responsible for determining the matter.

(4) The responsible clinician must inform the managers of the relevant hospital if he is considering making –

(a)   an order for discharge in respect of the patient under section 23(2) of the Mental Health Act 1983,

(b)   a community treatment order in respect of him, or

(c)   an order under section 17B(4) of the Mental Health Act 1983 to vary the conditions specified in a community treatment order in force in respect of the patient.

(5) Any person who has power to make an order for discharge in respect of the patient under section 23(3) of the Mental Health Act 1983 must inform the managers of the relevant hospital if he is considering making that order.

(6) A Mental Health Review Tribunal must inform the managers of the relevant hospital if –

    (a)   an application is made to the tribunal under section 66 or 69 of the Mental Health Act 1983, or

    (b)   the patient's case is referred to the tribunal under section 67 of that Act.

(7) Subsection (8) applies if –

    (a)   the managers of the relevant hospital receive information under subsection (4), (5) or (6), and

    (b)   a person who appears to the managers to be the victim of the offence or to act for the victim of the offence –

        (i)   when his wishes were ascertained under section 42(2), expressed a wish to make representations about a matter specified in section 42(3), or

        (ii)   has made representations about such a matter to the managers of the hospital in which the patient was, at the time in question, detained.

(8) The managers of the relevant hospital must provide the information to the person.

(9) The relevant hospital has the meaning given in section 36A(6).

NOTES

Prospective amendment. Section prospectively inserted: MHA 2007, s 48, Sch 6, paras 1, 13.

44 Information where restriction direction made

(1) This section applies if, in a case where section 42 applies, the transfer direction in respect of the patient was given with a restriction direction.

(2) Subsection (3) applies if a person who appears to the relevant local probation board to be the victim of the offence or to act for the victim of the offence –

    (a)   when his wishes were ascertained under section 42(2), expressed a wish to receive the information specified in section 42(4), or

    (b)   has subsequently informed the relevant local probation board that he wishes to receive that information.

(3) The relevant local probation board must take all reasonable steps –

    (a)   to inform that person whether or not the offender is to be subject to any conditions in the event of his discharge;

    (b)   if he is, to provide that person with details of any conditions which relate to contact with the victim or his family;

    (c)   if the restriction direction in respect of the offender is to cease to have effect, to notify that person of the date on which it is to cease to have effect;

(d)   to provide that person with such other information as the board considers appropriate in all the circumstances of the case.

(4) The Secretary of State must inform the relevant local probation board –

(a)   whether the offender is to be discharged;

(b)   if he is, whether he is to be discharged absolutely or subject to conditions;

(c)   if he is to be discharged subject to conditions, what the conditions are to be;

(d)   if he has been discharged subject to conditions –

    (i)   of any variation of the conditions by the Secretary of State;

    (ii)   of any recall to hospital under section 42(3) of the Mental Health Act 1983;

(e)   if the restriction direction is to cease to have effect by virtue of action to be taken by the Secretary of State, of the date on which the restriction direction is to cease to have effect.

(5) Subsections (6) and (7) apply (instead of subsection (4)) if –

(a)   an application is made to a Mental Health Review Tribunal by the offender under section 69, 70 or 75 of the Mental Health Act 1983 (applications concerning restricted patients), or

(b)   the Secretary of State refers the offender's case to a Mental Health Review Tribunal under section 71 of that Act (references concerning restricted patients).

(6) The tribunal must inform the relevant local probation board –

(a)   of the matters specified in subsection (4)(a) to (c);

(b)   if the offender has been discharged subject to conditions, of any variation of the conditions by the tribunal;

(c)   if the restriction direction is to cease to have effect by virtue of action to be taken by the tribunal, of the date on which the restriction direction is to cease to have effect.

(7) The Secretary of State must inform the relevant local probation board of the matters specified in subsection (4)(d) and (e).

(8) The duties in subsections (3) to (7) apply only while the restriction direction is in force.

(9) The relevant local probation board has the meaning given in section 43(8).

NOTES

Prospective amendments. Section heading prospectively substituted: MHA 2007, s 48, Sch 6, paras 1, 14. Words in subs (1) prospectively substituted: MHA 2007, s 48, Sch 6, paras 1, 14.

44A Information where restriction direction not given

(1) This section applies if, in a case where section 42 applies, the transfer direction in respect of the patient was given without a restriction direction.

(2) The responsible clinician must inform the managers of the relevant hospital –

(a) whether he is to make an order for discharge in respect of the patient under section 23(2) of the Mental Health Act 1983;

(b) whether he is to make a community treatment order in respect of the patient;

(c) if a community treatment order is to be made in respect of the patient, what conditions are to be specified in the order;

(d) if a community treatment order is in force in respect of the patient, of any variation to be made under section 17B(4) of the Mental Health Act 1983 of the conditions specified in the order;

(e) if a community treatment order in respect of the patient is to cease to be in force, of the date on which it is to cease to be in force;

(f) if, following the examination of the patient under section 20 of the Mental Health Act 1983, it does not appear to the responsible clinician that the conditions set out in subsection (4) of that section are satisfied, of the date on which the authority for the patient's detention is to expire.

(3) Any person who has power to make an order for discharge in respect of the patient under section 23(3) of the Mental Health Act 1983 must inform the managers of the relevant hospital if he is to make that order.

(4) Subsection (5) applies if –

(a) an application is made to a Mental Health Review Tribunal under section 66 or 69 of the Mental Health Act 1983,

(b) the patient's case is referred to a Mental Health Review Tribunal under section 67 of that Act, or

(c) the managers of the relevant hospital refer the patient's case to a Mental Health Review Tribunal under section 68 of that Act.

(5) The tribunal must inform the managers of the relevant hospital if it directs that the patient be discharged.

(6) Subsection (7) applies if a person who appears to the managers of the relevant hospital to be the victim of the offence or to act for the victim of the offence –

(a) when his wishes were ascertained under section 42(2), expressed a wish to receive the information specified in section 42(4), or

(b) has subsequently informed the managers of the relevant hospital that he wishes to receive that information.

(7) The managers of the relevant hospital order must take all reasonable steps –

(a) to inform that person whether the patient is to be discharged under section 23 or 72 of the Mental Health Act 1983;

(b) to inform that person whether a community treatment order is to be made in respect of the patient;

(c)   if a community treatment order is to be made in respect of the patient and is to specify conditions which relate to contact with the victim or his family, to provide that person with details of those conditions;

(d)   if a community treatment order is in force in respect of the patient and the conditions specified in the order are to be varied under section 17B(4) of the Mental Health Act 1983, to provide that person with details of any variation which relates to contact with the victim or his family;

(e)   if a community treatment order in respect of the patient is to cease to be in force, to inform that person of the date on which it is to cease to be in force;

(f)   if, following the examination of the patient under section 20 of the Mental Health Act 1983, the authority for the patient's detention is not to be renewed, to inform that person of the date on which the authority is to expire;

(g)   to provide that person with such other information as the managers of the relevant hospital consider appropriate in all the circumstances of the case.

(8) The relevant hospital has the meaning given by section 36A(6).

NOTES

Prospective amendment. Section prospectively inserted: MHA 2007, s 48, Sch 6, paras 1, 15.

44B Removal of restriction

(1) This section applies if, in a case where section 42 applies –

(a)   the transfer direction in respect of the patient was given with a restriction direction, and

(b)   the restriction direction ceases to be in force while the transfer direction continues in force.

(2) Subsection (3) applies if a person who appears to the relevant local probation board to be the victim of the offence or to act for the victim of the offence –

(a)   when his wishes were ascertained under section 42(2), expressed a wish to make representations about a matter specified in section 42(3) or to receive the information specified in section 42(4), or

(b)   has subsequently informed the relevant local probation board that he wishes to make representations about such a matter or to receive that information.

(3) The relevant local probation board must take all reasonable steps –

(a)   to notify the managers of the relevant hospital of an address at which that person may be contacted;

(b)   to notify that person of the name and address of the hospital.

(4) While the transfer direction continues in force, the patient is to be regarded as a patient in respect of whom a transfer direction was given without a restriction direction; and sections 43A and 44A are to apply in relation to him accordingly.

(5) The relevant hospital has the meaning given in section 36A(6).

(6) The relevant local probation board has the meaning given in section 43(8).

NOTES

Prospective amendment. Section prospectively inserted: MHA 2007, s 48, Sch 6, paras 1, 15.

Interpretation

45 Interpretation: sections 35 to 44B

(1) In sections 35 to 44B –

'community treatment order' has the meaning given in section 17A of the Mental Health Act 1983;

'court' does not include a court-martial or the Courts-Martial Appeal Court;

'hospital direction' has the meaning given in section 45A(3)(a) of the Mental Health Act 1983;

'hospital order' has the meaning given in section 37(4) of that Act;

'licence condition' means a condition in a licence;

'limitation direction' has the meaning given in section 45A(3)(b) of the Mental Health Act 1983;

'local probation board' means a local probation board established under section 4 of the Criminal Justice and Court Services Act 2000;

'the managers' has the meaning given in section 145 of the Mental Health Act 1983;

'relevant sentence' means any of these –

(a) a sentence of imprisonment for a term of 12 months or more;

(b) a sentence of detention during Her Majesty's pleasure;

(c) a sentence of detention for a period of 12 months or more under section 91 of the Powers of Criminal Courts (Sentencing) Act 2000 (offenders under 18 convicted of certain serious offences);

(d) a detention and training order for a term of 12 months or more;

'responsible clinician' means the responsible clinician for the purposes of Part 3 of the Mental Health Act 1983;

'responsible hospital' has the meaning given in section 17A of the Mental Health Act 1983;

'restriction direction' has the meaning given in section 49(2) of the Mental Health Act 1983;

'restriction order' has the meaning given in section 41(1) of that Act;

'supervision requirements' means requirements specified in a notice under section 103(6) of the Powers of Criminal Courts (Sentencing) Act 2000;

'transfer direction' has the meaning given in section 47(1) of the Mental Health Act 1983.

(2) For the purposes of sections 35 to 44B, an offence is a sexual or violent offence if it is any of these –

(a)   murder or an offence specified in Schedule 15 to the Criminal Justice Act 2003;

(b)   an offence in respect of which the patient or offender is subject to the notification requirements of Part 2 of the Sexual Offences Act 2003);

(c)   an offence against a child within the meaning of Part 2 of the Criminal Justice and Court Services Act 2000.

(3) A reference in sections 35 to 44B to a place in which a person is detained includes a reference to a place in which he is liable to be detained under the Mental Health Act 1983.

(4) For the purposes of section 32(3) of that Act (regulations as to delegation of managers' functions, etc) as applied by Parts 1 and 2 of Schedule 1 to that Act, a function conferred on the managers of a hospital under sections 35 to 44B of this Act is to be treated as a function of theirs under Part 3 of that Act.

NOTES

Prospective amendments. Section heading prospectively substituted: MHA 2007, s 48, Sch 6, paras 1, 16(1). Reference in subs (1) prospectively substituted: MHA 2007, s 48, Sch 6, paras 1, 16(1), (2)(a). Definition 'community treatment order' in subs (1) prospectively inserted: MHA 2007, s 48, Sch 6, paras 1, 16(1), (2)(b). Definition 'the managers' in subs (1) prospectively inserted: MHA 2007, s 48, Sch 6, paras 1, 16(1), (2)(b). Definition 'responsible clinician' in subs (1) prospectively inserted: MHA 2007, s 48, Sch 6, paras 1, 16(1), (2)(b). Definition 'responsible hospital' in subs (1) prospectively inserted: MHA 2007, s 48, Sch 6, paras 1, 16(1), (2)(b). Reference in subs (2) prospectively substituted: MHA 2007, s 48, Sch 6, paras 1, 16(1), (3). Subss (3), (4) prospectively inserted: MHA 2007, s 48, Sch 6, paras 1, 16(1), (4).

Note. Definition 'court' in subs (1) prospectively amended: Armed Forces Act 2006, s 378(1), Sch 16, para 239.

****

Appendix 3

MENTAL HEALTH ACT 2007 (2007 C 12) (REMAINING PROVISIONS)

ARRANGEMENT OF SECTIONS

PART 1
AMENDMENTS TO MENTAL HEALTH ACT 1983

Chapter 2
Professional Roles

Approved Mental Health Professionals

Chapter 3
Safeguards for Patients

Consent to Treatment

Chapter 4
Supervised Community Treatment

PART 2
AMENDMENTS TO OTHER ACTS

Chapter 1
Amendments to Domestic Violence, Crime and Victims Act 2004

Chapter 2
Amendments to Mental Capacity Act 2005

PART 3
GENERAL

PART 1
AMENDMENTS TO MENTAL HEALTH ACT 1983

****

Chapter 2
Professional Roles

****

Approved Mental Health Professionals

20 Amendment to section 62 of Care Standards Act 2000

In section 62 of the Care Standards Act 2000 (c 14) (codes of practice), after
subsection (1) insert –

> '(1A) The codes may also lay down standards of conduct and practice
> expected of social workers when carrying out the functions of an
> approved mental health professional (as defined in section 114 of the
> Mental Health Act 1983).'

Chapter 3
Safeguards for Patients

****

Consent to Treatment

28 Section 27: supplemental

...

(10) In section 28 of the Mental Capacity Act 2005 (c 9) (Mental Health Act matters), after subsection (1) insert –

'(1A) Subsection (1) does not apply in relation to any form of treatment to which section 58A of that Act (electro-convulsive therapy, etc) applies if the patient comes within subsection (7) of that section (informal patient under 18 who cannot give consent).'.

****

Chapter 4
Supervised Community Treatment

****

35 Authority to treat

…

(4) The Mental Capacity Act 2005 (c 9) is amended as follows.

(5) In section 28 (Mental Health Act matters), after subsection (1A) (inserted by

section 28 of this Act) insert –

'(1B) Section 5 does not apply to an act to which section 64B of the Mental Health Act applies (treatment of community patients not recalled to hospital).'

PART 2
AMENDMENTS TO OTHER ACTS

Chapter 1
Amendments to Domestic Violence, Crime and Victims Act 2004

48 Victims' rights

Schedule 6 (which makes amendments to Chapter 2 of Part 3 of the Domestic Violence, Crime and Victims Act 2004 (c 28)) has effect.

Chapter 2
Amendments to Mental Capacity Act 2005

49 Independent mental capacity advocacy service: exceptions

For section 40 of the Mental Capacity Act 2005 (c 9) (independent mental capacity advocacy service: exceptions) substitute –

'40 Exceptions

The duty imposed by section 37(3), 38(3) or (4) or 39(4) or (5) does not apply where there is –

(a) a person nominated by P (in whatever manner) as a person to be consulted on matters to which that duty relates,

(b) a donee of a lasting power of attorney created by P who is authorised to make decisions in relation to those matters, or

(c) a deputy appointed by the court for P with power to make decisions in relation to those matters.'

50 Mental Capacity Act 2005: deprivation of liberty

(1) The Mental Capacity Act 2005 (c 9) is amended as follows.

(2) After section 4 insert –

'4A Restriction on deprivation of liberty

(1) This Act does not authorise any person ('D') to deprive any other person ('P') of his liberty.

(2) But that is subject to –

(a) the following provisions of this section, and
(b) section 4B.

(3) D may deprive P of his liberty if, by doing so, D is giving effect to a relevant decision of the court.

(4) A relevant decision of the court is a decision made by an order under section 16(2)(a) in relation to a matter concerning P's personal welfare.

(5) D may deprive P of his liberty if the deprivation is authorised by Schedule A1 (hospital and care home residents: deprivation of liberty).

4B Deprivation of liberty necessary for life-sustaining treatment etc

(1) If the following conditions are met, D is authorised to deprive P of his liberty while a decision as respects any relevant issue is sought from the court.

(2) The first condition is that there is a question about whether D is authorised to deprive P of his liberty under section 4A.

(3) The second condition is that the deprivation of liberty –

(a) is wholly or partly for the purpose of –
   (i)   giving P life-sustaining treatment, or
   (ii) doing any vital act, or
(b) consists wholly or partly of –
   (i)   giving P life-sustaining treatment, or
   (ii) doing any vital act.

(4) The third condition is that the deprivation of liberty is necessary in order to –

(a) give the life-sustaining treatment, or
(b) do the vital act.

(5) A vital act is any act which the person doing it reasonably believes to be necessary to prevent a serious deterioration in P's condition.'

(3) After section 16 insert –

'16A Section 16 powers: Mental Health Act patients etc

(1) If a person is ineligible to be deprived of liberty by this Act, the court may not include in a welfare order provision which authorises the person to be deprived of his liberty.

(2) If –

   (a)   a welfare order includes provision which authorises a person to be deprived of his liberty, and

   (b)   that person becomes ineligible to be deprived of liberty by this Act,

the provision ceases to have effect for as long as the person remains ineligible.

(3) Nothing in subsection (2) affects the power of the court under section 16(7) to vary or discharge the welfare order.

(4) For the purposes of this section –

   (a)   Schedule 1A applies for determining whether or not P is ineligible to be deprived of liberty by this Act;

   (b)   'welfare order' means an order under section 16(2)(a).'

(4) Omit the following provisions (which make specific provision about deprivation of liberty) –

   (a)   section 6(5);

   (b)   section 11(6);

   (c)   section 20(13).

(5) Schedule 7 (which inserts the new Schedule A1 into the Mental Capacity Act 2005 (c 9)) has effect.

(6) Schedule 8 (which inserts the new Schedule 1A into the Mental Capacity Act 2005) has effect.

(7) Schedule 9 (which makes other amendments to the Mental Capacity Act 2005 and to other Acts) has effect.

(8) In subsection (9) –

'GOWA 1998' means the Government of Wales Act 1998 (c 38);
'GOWA 2006' means the Government of Wales Act 2006 (c 32);
'initial period' has the same meaning as in Schedule 11 to GOWA 2006.

(9) If this Act is passed after the end of the initial period, the functions conferred on the National Assembly for Wales by virtue of any provision of this Part of this Act are to be treated for the purposes of Schedule 11 to GOWA 2006 as if they –

(a) had been conferred on the Assembly constituted by GOWA 1998 by an Act passed before the end of the initial period, and

(b) were exercisable by that Assembly immediately before the end of the initial period.

(10) If any function of making subordinate legislation conferred by virtue of any provision of this Part of this Act is transferred to the Welsh Ministers (whether by virtue of subsection (9) or otherwise) –

(a) paragraphs 34 and 35 of Schedule 11 to the Government of Wales Act 2006 do not apply; and

(b) subsections (11) and (12) apply instead.

(11) If a relevant statutory instrument contains regulations under paragraph 42(2)(b), 129, 162 or 163 of Schedule A1 to the Mental Capacity Act 2005 (whether or not it also contains other regulations), the instrument may not be made unless a draft has been laid before and approved by resolution of the National Assembly for Wales.

(12) Subject to that, a relevant statutory instrument is subject to annulment in pursuance of a resolution of the National Assembly for Wales.

(13) In subsections (11) and (12) 'relevant statutory instrument' means a statutory instrument containing subordinate legislation made in exercise of a function transferred as mentioned in subsection (10).

51 Amendment to section 20(11) of Mental Capacity Act 2005

In section 20 of the Mental Capacity Act 2005 (c 9) (restrictions on deputies), in subsection (11)(a), for 'or' substitute 'and'.

PART 3
GENERAL

52 Meaning of '1983 Act'

In this Act 'the 1983 Act' means the Mental Health Act 1983 (c 20).

53 Transitional provisions and savings

Schedule 10 (which contains transitional provisions and savings) has effect.

54 Consequential provisions

(1) The Secretary of State may by order made by statutory instrument make supplementary, incidental or consequential provision for the purposes of, in consequence of, or for giving full effect to a provision of this Act.

(2) An order under subsection (1) may, in particular –

(a) amend or repeal any provision of an Act passed before, or in the same Session as, this Act;

(b) amend or revoke any provision of subordinate legislation made before the passing of this Act;

(c) include transitional or saving provision in connection with the coming into force of provision made by the order.

(3) In relation to provision which deals with matters with respect to which functions are exercisable by the Welsh Ministers –

(a) the power under subsection (1) is exercisable by the Secretary of State only with agreement of the Welsh Ministers, and

(b) the power under that subsection is also exercisable by the Welsh Ministers except that provision may not be made by virtue of subsection (2)(a).

(4) The amendments that may be made by virtue of subsection (2) are in addition to those made by or by virtue of any other provision of this Act.

(5) A statutory instrument containing an order under subsection (1) which makes provision by virtue of subsection (2)(a) may not be made unless a draft of the instrument has been laid before and approved by a resolution of each House of Parliament.

(6) A statutory instrument containing any other order under subsection (1) made by the Secretary of State is subject to annulment in pursuance of a resolution of either House of Parliament.

(7) A statutory instrument containing an order under subsection (1) made by the Welsh Ministers is subject to annulment in pursuance of a resolution of the National Assembly for Wales.

(8) In subsection (2), 'subordinate legislation' has the same meaning as in the Interpretation Act 1978 (c 30).

55 Repeals and revocations

The enactments mentioned in Schedule 11 are repealed or revoked to the extent specified.

56 Commencement

(1) This Act (other than sections 51 to 53 (and Schedule 10), this section and sections 57 to 59) comes into force in accordance with provision made by the Secretary of State by order made by statutory instrument.

(2) In relation to provision which deals with matters with respect to which functions are exercisable by the Welsh Ministers, the power under subsection (1) is exercisable only with their agreement.

(3) Section 51 comes into force in accordance with provision made by the Lord Chancellor by order made by statutory instrument.

(4) An order under this section may –

(a) make different provision for different purposes (including different provision for different areas and different provision for different descriptions of patient);

(b) include transitional or saving provision.

(5) The provision which may be made by virtue of subsection (4)(b) includes provision modifying the application of a provision of this Act pending the commencement of a provision of another enactment.

(6) A statutory instrument containing an order under this section which makes provision by virtue of subsection (4)(b) (including provision within section 57) is subject to annulment in pursuance of a resolution of either House of Parliament.

57 Commencement of section 36

(1) An order under section 56 providing for the commencement of section 36 may, in particular, provide –

- (a) for that section not to apply to or affect a patient who is subject to after-care under supervision immediately before that commencement, and
- (b) for the patient to cease to be subject to after-care under supervision, and for his case to be dealt with, in accordance with provision made by the order.

(2) The order may require –

- (a) a Primary Care Trust or Local Health Board to secure that the patient is examined by a registered medical practitioner of a description specified in the order;
- (b) the registered medical practitioner to examine the patient with a view to making a decision about his case by reference to criteria specified in the order.

(3) The order may require the registered medical practitioner, having complied with provision made by virtue of subsection (2)(b) –

- (a) to discharge the patient,
- (b) to recommend that he be detained in hospital,
- (c) to recommend that he be received into guardianship, or
- (d) to make a community treatment order in respect of him.

(4) The order may, in respect of a recommendation made by virtue of subsection (3)(b) or (c) –

- (a) provide that the recommendation is to be made to a local social services authority determined in accordance with the order;
- (b) provide that the recommendation is to be made in accordance with any other requirements specified in the order;
- (c) require the local social services authority determined in accordance with paragraph (a), in response to the recommendation, to make arrangements for an approved mental health professional to consider the patient's case on their behalf.

(5) The order may provide that a registered medical practitioner shall not make a community treatment order in respect of a patient unless an approved mental health professional states in writing –

(a) that he agrees with the decision made by the practitioner about the patient's case, and

(b) that it is appropriate to make the order.

(6) An order requiring a registered medical practitioner to make a community treatment order in respect of a patient shall include provision about –

(a) the effect of the community treatment order (in particular, replacing after-care under supervision with a contingent requirement to attend, and be detained at, a hospital), and

(b) the effect of its revocation (including, in particular, provision for detention under section 3 of the 1983 Act).

(7) The order may modify a provision of the 1983 Act in its application in relation to a patient who is subject to after-care under supervision immediately before the commencement of section 36.

(8) Provision made by virtue of subsection (7) may, in particular –

(a) modify any of sections 25A to 25J of the 1983 Act in their application in relation to a patient for so long as he is, by virtue of subsection (1)(a), subject to after-care under supervision after the commencement of section 36;

(b) modify any of sections 17A to 17G, 20A and 20B of that Act (inserted by section 32 of this Act) in their application in relation to a patient in respect of whom a community treatment order is made by virtue of subsection (3)(d).

(9) A reference in this section to section 36 includes the amendments and repeals in Schedules 3 and 11 consequential on that section.

(10) An expression used in this section and in the 1983 Act has the same meaning in this section as it has in that Act.

58 Extent

(1) The provisions of this Act which amend other enactments have the same extent as the enactments which they amend.

(2) But subsection (1) is subject to –

(a) paragraph 35 of Schedule 3,

(b) paragraphs 3, 4 and 20 of Schedule 5, and

(c) paragraph 12 of Schedule 9.

(3) Section 54 extends to the United Kingdom.

59 Short title

This Act may be cited as the Mental Health Act 2007.

SCHEDULE 4
Supervised community treatment: amendments to other Acts

Section 32

Administration of Justice Act 1960

1

After section 5 of the Administration of Justice Act 1960 (c 65) insert –

'5A Power to order continuation of community treatment order

(1) Where the defendant in any proceedings from which an appeal lies under section 1 of this Act would, but for the decision of the court below, be liable to recall, and immediately after that decision the prosecutor is granted, or gives notice that he intends to apply for, leave to appeal, the court may make an order under this section.

(2) For the purposes of this section, a person is liable to recall if he is subject to a community treatment order (within the meaning of the Mental Health Act 1983) and, when that order was made, he was liable to be detained in pursuance of an order or direction under Part 3 of that Act.

(3) An order under this section is an order providing for the continuation of the community treatment order and the order or direction under Part 3 of that Act so long as any appeal under section 1 of this Act is pending.

(4) Where the court makes an order under this section, the provisions of the Mental Health Act 1983 with respect to persons liable to recall (including provisions as to the extension of the community treatment period, the removal or discharge of community patients, the revocation of community treatment orders and the re-detention of patients following revocation) shall apply accordingly.

(5) An order under this section shall (unless the appeal has previously been disposed of) cease to have effect at the expiration of the period for which the defendant would, but for the decision of the court below, have been –

    (a)   liable to recall; or

    (b)   where the community treatment order is revoked, liable to be detained in pursuance of the order or direction under Part 3 of the Mental Health Act 1983.

(6) Where the court below has power to make an order under this section, and either no such order is made or the defendant is discharged by virtue of subsection (4) or (5) of this section before the appeal is disposed of, the defendant shall not be liable to be again detained as the result of the decision of the Supreme Court on the appeal.'

Criminal Appeal Act 1968

2

(1) The Criminal Appeal Act 1968 (c 19) is amended as follows.

(2) In section 8 (supplementary provisions as to retrial), after subsection (3A) insert –

> **'(3B) If the person ordered to be retried –**
>
> > (a)   was liable to be detained in pursuance of an order or direction under Part 3 of the Mental Health Act 1983;
> >
> > (b)   was then made subject to a community treatment order (within the meaning of that Act); and
> >
> > (c)   was subject to that community treatment order immediately before the determination of his appeal,
>
> the order or direction under Part 3 of that Act and the community treatment order shall continue in force pending the retrial as if the appeal had not been allowed, and any order made by the Court of Appeal under this section for his release on bail shall have effect subject to the community treatment order.'

(3) After section 37 insert –

> **'37A Continuation of community treatment order on appeal by the Crown**
>
> (1) The following provisions apply where, immediately after a decision of the Court of Appeal from which an appeal lies to the Supreme Court, the prosecutor is granted, or gives notice that he intends to apply for, leave to appeal.
>
> (2) If, but for the decision of the Court of Appeal, the defendant would be liable to recall, the Court of Appeal may make an order under this section.
>
> (3) For the purposes of this section, a person is liable to recall if he is subject to a community treatment order (within the meaning of the Mental Health Act 1983) and, when that order was made, he was liable to be detained in pursuance of an order or direction under Part 3 of that Act.
>
> (4) An order under this section is an order providing for the continuation of the community treatment order and the order or direction under Part 3 of that Act so long as an appeal to the Supreme Court is pending.
>
> (5) Where an order is made under this section the provisions of the Mental Health Act 1983 with respect to persons liable to recall (including provisions as to the extension of the community treatment period, the removal or discharge of community patients, the revocation of community treatment orders and the re-detention of patients following revocation) shall apply accordingly.

(6) An order under this section shall (unless the appeal has previously been disposed of) cease to have effect at the expiration of the period for which the defendant would, but for the decision of the Court of Appeal, have been –

(a) liable to recall; or

(b) where the community treatment order is revoked, liable to be detained in pursuance of the order or direction under Part 3 of the Mental Health Act 1983.

(7) Where the Court of Appeal have power to make an order under this section, and either no such order is made or the defendant is discharged, by virtue of subsection (5) or (6) of this section, before the appeal is disposed of, the defendant shall not be liable to be again detained as the result of the decision of the Supreme Court on the appeal.'

Courts-Martial (Appeals) Act 1968

3

(1) The Courts-Martial (Appeals) Act 1968 (c 20) is amended as follows.

(2) In section 20 (implementation of authority for retrial etc), after subsection (4) insert –

'(4A) Where retrial is authorised in the case of a person who –

(a) was liable to be detained in pursuance of an order or direction under Part 3 of the Mental Health Act 1983;

(b) was then made subject to a community treatment order (within the meaning of that Act); and

(c) was subject to that community treatment order immediately before the date of the authorisation,

the order or direction under Part 3 of that Act and the community treatment order shall continue in force until the relevant time (as defined in subsection (3A)) as if his conviction had not been quashed.

(4B) An order under subsection (1E)(a) is of no effect in relation to a person for so long as he is subject to a community treatment order.'

(3) In section 43 (detention of accused), after subsection (3) insert –

'(3A) The relevant provisions of the Mental Health Act 1983 with respect to community treatment orders (within the meaning of that Act) shall also apply for the purposes of subsection (3).'

(4) After that section insert –

'43A Continuation of community treatment order

(1) The Appeal Court may make an order under this section where –

(a) but for the decision of the Appeal Court, the accused would be liable to recall; and

(b)   immediately after that decision, the Director of Service Prosecutions is granted leave to appeal or gives notice that he intends to apply for leave to appeal.

(2) For the purposes of this section, a person is liable to recall if he is subject to a community treatment order (within the meaning of the Mental Health Act 1983) and, when that order was made, he was liable to be detained in pursuance of an order or direction under Part 3 of that Act.

(3) An order under this section is an order providing for the continuation of the community treatment order and the order or direction under Part 3 of that Act so long as any appeal to the Supreme Court is pending.

(4) Where the Appeal Court makes an order under this section, the relevant provisions of the Mental Health Act 1983 with respect to persons liable to recall (including provisions as to the extension of the community treatment period, the removal or discharge of community patients, the revocation of community treatment orders and the re-detention of patients following revocation) shall apply accordingly.

(5) An order under this section shall (unless the appeal has been previously disposed of) cease to have effect at the end of the period for which the accused would, but for the decision of the Appeal Court, have been –

(a)   liable to recall; or

(b)   where the community treatment order is revoked, liable to be detained in pursuance of the order or direction under Part 3 of the Mental Health Act 1983.

(6) Where the Appeal Court has power to make an order under this section and either no such order is made or the accused is discharged by virtue of subsection (4) or (5) above before the appeal is disposed of, the accused shall not be liable to be again detained as a result of the decision of the Supreme Court on the appeal.'

Juries Act 1974

4

In Schedule 1 to the Juries Act 1974 (c 23) (mentally disordered persons and persons disqualified from serving), at the end of paragraph 2 insert 'or subject to a community treatment order under section 17A of that Act'.

SCHEDULE 6
Victims' rights

Section 48

Introduction

1

Chapter 2 of Part 3 of the Domestic Violence, Crime and Victims Act 2004 (c 28) (provision of information to victims of restricted patients under the 1983 Act, etc) is amended as set out in this Schedule.

Hospital orders (with or without restriction orders)

2

(1) Section 36 (victims' rights: preliminary) is amended as follows.

(2) In subsection (3), for 'with a restriction order' substitute ', whether with or without a restriction order,'.

(3) In subsection (5) –

    (a)   in paragraph (a), after 'discharge from hospital' insert 'while a restriction order is in force in respect of him', and

    (b)   after paragraph (b) insert ';

        '(c)   what conditions he should be subject to in the event of his discharge from hospital under a community treatment order'.

3

After section 36 insert –

    '36A Supplemental provision for case where no restriction order made

    (1) This section applies if, in a case where section 36 applies, the hospital order in respect of the patient was made without a restriction order.

    (2) Subsection (3) applies if a person who appears to the local probation board mentioned in section 36(4) to be the victim of the offence or to act for the victim of the offence, when his wishes are ascertained under section 36(4), expresses a wish –

        (a)   to make representations about a matter specified in section 36(5), or

        (b)   to receive the information specified in section 36(6).

    (3) The local probation board must –

        (a)   notify the managers of the hospital in which the patient is detained of that person's wish and of that person's name and address, and

        (b)   notify that person of the name and address of the hospital.

(4) Subsection (5) applies if a person who appears to the local probation board mentioned in section 36(4) to be the victim of the offence or to act for the victim of the offence, subsequently to his wishes being ascertained under section 36(4), expresses a wish to do something specified in subsection (2)(a) or (b).

(5) The local probation board mentioned in section 36(4) must take all reasonable steps –

  (a)   to ascertain whether the hospital order made in respect of the patient continues in force and whether a community treatment order is in force in respect of him, and
  (b)   if the board ascertains that the hospital order does continue in force –
      (i)   to notify the managers of the relevant hospital of that person's wish, and
      (ii) to notify that person of the name and address of the hospital.

(6) The relevant hospital is –

  (a)   the hospital in which the patient is detained, or
  (b)   if a community treatment order is in force in respect of the patient, the responsible hospital.'

4

In section 37 (the title to which becomes 'Representations where restriction order made'), in subsection (1), for 'if section 36 applies' substitute 'if, in a case where section 36 applies, the hospital order in respect of the patient was made with a restriction order'.

5

After section 37 insert –

'37A   Representations where restriction order not made

(1) This section applies if, in a case where section 36 applies, the hospital order in respect of the patient was made without a restriction order.

(2) Subsection (3) applies if –

  (a)   a person makes representations about a matter specified in section 36(5) to the managers of the relevant hospital, and
  (b)   it appears to the managers that the person is the victim of the offence or acts for the victim of the offence.

(3) The managers must forward the representations to the persons responsible for determining the matter.

(4) The responsible clinician must inform the managers of the relevant hospital if he is considering making –

(a)   an order for discharge in respect of the patient under
      section 23(2) of the Mental Health Act 1983,

(b)   a community treatment order in respect of the patient, or

(c)   an order under section 17B(4) of the Mental Health Act 1983 to
      vary the conditions specified in a community treatment order in
      force in respect of the patient.

(5) Any person who has the power to make an order for discharge in
respect of the patient under section 23(3) of the Mental Health Act 1983
must inform the managers of the relevant hospital if he is considering
making that order.

(6) A Mental Health Review Tribunal must inform the managers of the
relevant hospital if –

(a)   an application is made to the tribunal under section 66 or 69 of
      the Mental Health Act 1983, or

(b)   the patient's case is referred to the tribunal under section 67 of
      that Act.

(7) Subsection (8) applies if –

(a)   the managers of the relevant hospital receive information under
      subsection (4), (5) or (6), and

(b)   a person who appears to the managers to be the victim of the
      offence or to act for the victim of the offence –

      (i)   when his wishes were ascertained under section 36(4),
            expressed a wish to make representations about a matter
            specified in section 36(5), or

      (ii) has made representations about such a matter to the
            managers of the hospital in which the patient was, at the
            time in question, detained.

(8) The managers of the relevant hospital must provide the information
to the person.

(9) The relevant hospital has the meaning given in section 36A(6).'

6

In section 38 (the title to which becomes 'Information where restriction order
made'), in subsection (1) for 'if section 36 applies' substitute 'if, in a case where
section 36 applies, the hospital order in respect of the patient was made with a
restriction order'.

7

After section 38 insert –

'38A Information where restriction order not made

(1) This section applies if, in a case where section 36 applies, the hospital
order in respect of the patient was made without a restriction order.

(2) The responsible clinician must inform the managers of the relevant hospital –

(a) whether he is to make an order for discharge in respect of the patient under section 23(2) of the Mental Health Act 1983;

(b) whether he is to make a community treatment order in respect of the patient;

(c) if a community treatment order is to be made in respect of the patient, what conditions are to be specified in the order;

(d) if a community treatment order is in force in respect of the patient, of any variation to be made under section 17B(4) of the Mental Health Act 1983 of the conditions specified in the order;

(e) if a community treatment order in respect of the patient is to cease to be in force, of the date on which it is to cease to be in force;

(f) if, following the examination of the patient under section 20 of the Mental Health Act 1983, it does not appear to the responsible clinician that the conditions set out in subsection (4) of that section are satisfied, of the date on which the authority for the patient's detention is to expire.

(3) Any person who has the power to make an order for discharge in respect of the patient under section 23(3) of the Mental Health Act 1983 must inform the managers of the relevant hospital if he is to make that order.

(4) Subsection (5) applies if –

(a) an application is made to a Mental Health Review Tribunal under section 66 or 69 of the Mental Health Act 1983,

(b) the patient's case is referred to a Mental Health Review Tribunal under section 67 of that Act, or

(c) the managers of the relevant hospital refer the patient's case to a Mental Health Review Tribunal under section 68 of that Act.

(5) The tribunal must inform the managers of the relevant hospital if it directs that the patient is to be discharged.

(6) Subsection (7) applies if a person who appears to the managers of the relevant hospital to be the victim of the offence or to act for the victim of the offence –

(a) when his wishes were ascertained under section 36(4), expressed a wish to receive the information specified in section 36(6), or

(b) has subsequently informed the managers of the relevant hospital that he wishes to receive that information.

(7) The managers of the relevant hospital order must take all reasonable steps –

(a) to inform that person whether the patient is to be discharged under section 23 or 72 of the Mental Health Act 1983;

(b)   to inform that person whether a community treatment order is to be made in respect of the patient;

(c)   if a community treatment order is to be made in respect of the patient and is to specify conditions which relate to contact with the victim or his family, to provide that person with details of those conditions;

(d)   if a community treatment order is in force in respect of the patient and the conditions specified in the order are to be varied under section 17B(4) of the Mental Health Act 1983, to provide that person with details of any variation which relates to contact with the victim or his family;

(e)   if a community treatment order in respect of the patient is to cease to be in force, to inform that person of the date on which it is to cease to be in force;

(f)   if, following the examination of the patient under section 20 of the Mental Health Act 1983, the authority for the patient's detention is not to be renewed, to inform that person of the date on which the authority is to expire;

(g)   to provide that person with such other information as the managers of the relevant hospital consider appropriate in all the circumstances of the case.

(8) The relevant hospital has the meaning given by section 36A(6).

38B Removal of restriction

(1) This section applies if, in a case where section 36 applies –

(a)   the hospital order in respect of the patient was made with a restriction order, and

(b)   the restriction order ceases to have effect while the hospital order continues in force.

(2) Subsection (3) applies if a person who appears to the relevant local probation board to be the victim of the offence or to act for the victim of the offence –

(a)   when his wishes were ascertained under section 36(4), expressed a wish to make representations about a matter specified in section 36(5) or to receive the information specified in section 36(6), or

(b)   has subsequently informed the relevant local probation board that he wishes to make representations about such a matter or to receive that information.

(3) The relevant local probation board must take all reasonable steps –

(a)   to notify the managers of the relevant hospital of an address at which that person may be contacted;

(b)   to notify that person of the name and address of the hospital.

(4) While the hospital order continues in force, the patient is to be regarded as a patient in respect of whom a hospital order was made without a restriction order; and sections 37A and 38A are to apply in relation to him accordingly.

(5) The relevant hospital has the meaning given in section 36A(6).

(6) The relevant local probation board has the meaning given in section 37(8).'

Hospital directions and limitation directions

8

In section 39 (victims' rights: preliminary), in subsection (3) –

(a)   in paragraph (a), after 'discharge from hospital' insert 'while he is subject to a limitation direction', and

(b)   after that paragraph insert –

'(aa) what conditions he should be subject to in the event of his discharge from hospital under a community treatment order;'.

9

After section 41 insert –

'41A Removal of restriction

(1) This section applies if, in a case where section 39 applies –

(a)   the limitation direction in respect of the offender ceases to be in force, and

(b)   he is treated for the purposes of the Mental Health Act 1983 as a patient in respect of whom a hospital order has effect.

(2) Subsection (3) applies if a person who appears to the relevant local probation board to be the victim of the offence or to act for the victim of the offence –

(a)   when his wishes were ascertained under section 39(2), expressed a wish to make representations about a matter specified in section 39(3) or to receive the information specified in section 39(4), or

(b)   has subsequently informed the relevant local probation board that he wishes to make representations about such a matter or to receive that information.

(3) The relevant local probation board must take all reasonable steps –

(a)   to notify the managers of the relevant hospital of an address at which that person may be contacted;

(b)   to notify that person of the address of the hospital.

(4) The offender is to be regarded as a patient in respect of whom a hospital order was made without a restriction order; and sections 37A and 38A are to apply in relation to him accordingly.

(5) The relevant hospital has the meaning given in section 36A(6).

(6) The relevant local probation board has the meaning given in section 40(8).'

Transfer directions (with or without restriction directions)

10

(1) Section 42 (victims' rights: preliminary) is amended as follows.

(2) In subsection (1)(c), for 'and a restriction direction in respect of him' substitute 'in respect of the offender (whether or not he also gives a restriction direction in respect of the offender)'.

(3) In subsection (3) –

    (a)   in paragraph (a), after 'discharge from hospital' insert 'at a time when a restriction direction is in force in respect of him', and

    (b)   after paragraph (b) insert ';

        '(c)   what conditions he should be subject to in the event of his discharge from hospital under a community treatment order'.

11

After section 42 insert –

'42A Supplemental provision for case where no restriction direction given

(1) This section applies if, in a case where section 42 applies, the transfer direction in respect of the patient was given without a restriction direction.

(2) Subsection (3) applies if a person who appears to the local probation board mentioned in section 42(2) to be the victim of the offence or to act for the victim of the offence, when his wishes are ascertained under section 42(2), expresses a wish –

    (a)   to make representations about a matter specified in section 42(3), or

    (b)   to receive the information specified in section 42(4).

(3) The local probation board must –

    (a)   notify the managers of the hospital in which the patient is detained of that person's wish and of that person's name and address, and

    (b)   notify that person of the name and address of the hospital.

(4) Subsection (5) applies if a person who appears to the local probation board mentioned in section 42(2) to be the victim of the offence or to act

for the victim of the offence, subsequently to his wishes being ascertained under section 42(2), expressed a wish to do something specified in subsection (2)(a) or (b).

(5) The local probation board mentioned in section 42(2) must take all reasonable steps –

(a)   to ascertain whether the transfer direction given in respect of the patient continues in force and whether a community treatment order is in force in respect of him, and

(b)   if the board ascertains that the transfer direction does continue in force –

(i)   to notify the managers of the relevant hospital of that person's wish, and

(ii)   to notify that person of the name and address of the hospital.

(6) The relevant hospital has the meaning given in section 36A(6).'

12

In section 43 (the title to which becomes 'Representations where restriction direction made'), in subsection (1), for 'if section 42 applies' substitute 'if, in a case where section 42 applies, the transfer direction in respect of the patient was given with a restriction direction'.

13

After section 43 insert –

'43A   Representations where restriction direction not given

(1) This section applies if, in a case where section 42 applies, the transfer direction in respect of the patient was given without a restriction direction.

(2) Subsection (3) applies if –

(a)   a person makes representations about a matter specified in section 42(3) to the managers of the relevant hospital, and

(b)   it appears to the managers that the person is the victim of the offence or acts for the victim of the offence.

(3) The managers must forward the representations to the persons responsible for determining the matter.

(4) The responsible clinician must inform the managers of the relevant hospital if he is considering making –

(a)   an order for discharge in respect of the patient under section 23(2) of the Mental Health Act 1983,

(b)   a community treatment order in respect of him, or

(c)   an order under section 17B(4) of the Mental Health Act 1983 to vary the conditions specified in a community treatment order in force in respect of the patient.

(5) Any person who has power to make an order for discharge in respect of the patient under section 23(3) of the Mental Health Act 1983 must inform the managers of the relevant hospital if he is considering making that order.

(6) A Mental Health Review Tribunal must inform the managers of the relevant hospital if –

(a)   an application is made to the tribunal under section 66 or 69 of the Mental Health Act 1983, or
(b)   the patient's case is referred to the tribunal under section 67 of that Act.

(7) Subsection (8) applies if –

(a)   the managers of the relevant hospital receive information under subsection (4), (5) or (6), and
(b)   a person who appears to the managers to be the victim of the offence or to act for the victim of the offence –
    (i)   when his wishes were ascertained under section 42(2), expressed a wish to make representations about a matter specified in section 42(3), or
    (ii)   has made representations about such a matter to the managers of the hospital in which the patient was, at the time in question, detained.

(8) The managers of the relevant hospital must provide the information to the person.

(9) The relevant hospital has the meaning given in section 36A(6).'

14

In section 44 (the title to which becomes 'Information where restriction direction made'), in subsection (1), for 'if section 42 applies' substitute 'if, in a case where section 42 applies, the transfer direction in respect of the patient was given with a restriction direction'.

15

After section 44 insert –

'44A Information where restriction direction not given

(1) This section applies if, in a case where section 42 applies, the transfer direction in respect of the patient was given without a restriction direction.

(2) The responsible clinician must inform the managers of the relevant hospital –

(a) whether he is to make an order for discharge in respect of the patient under section 23(2) of the Mental Health Act 1983;

(b) whether he is to make a community treatment order in respect of the patient;

(c) if a community treatment order is to be made in respect of the patient, what conditions are to be specified in the order;

(d) if a community treatment order is in force in respect of the patient, of any variation to be made under section 17B(4) of the Mental Health Act 1983 of the conditions specified in the order;

(e) if a community treatment order in respect of the patient is to cease to be in force, of the date on which it is to cease to be in force;

(f) if, following the examination of the patient under section 20 of the Mental Health Act 1983, it does not appear to the responsible clinician that the conditions set out in subsection (4) of that section are satisfied, of the date on which the authority for the patient's detention is to expire.

(3) Any person who has power to make an order for discharge in respect of the patient under section 23(3) of the Mental Health Act 1983 must inform the managers of the relevant hospital if he is to make that order.

(4) Subsection (5) applies if –

(a) an application is made to a Mental Health Review Tribunal under section 66 or 69 of the Mental Health Act 1983,

(b) the patient's case is referred to a Mental Health Review Tribunal under section 67 of that Act, or

(c) the managers of the relevant hospital refer the patient's case to a Mental Health Review Tribunal under section 68 of that Act.

(5) The tribunal must inform the managers of the relevant hospital if it directs that the patient be discharged.

(6) Subsection (7) applies if a person who appears to the managers of the relevant hospital to be the victim of the offence or to act for the victim of the offence –

(a) when his wishes were ascertained under section 42(2), expressed a wish to receive the information specified in section 42(4), or

(b) has subsequently informed the managers of the relevant hospital that he wishes to receive that information.

(7) The managers of the relevant hospital order must take all reasonable steps –

(a) to inform that person whether the patient is to be discharged under section 23 or 72 of the Mental Health Act 1983;

(b) to inform that person whether a community treatment order is to be made in respect of the patient;

(c)   if a community treatment order is to be made in respect of the patient and is to specify conditions which relate to contact with the victim or his family, to provide that person with details of those conditions;

(d)   if a community treatment order is in force in respect of the patient and the conditions specified in the order are to be varied under section 17B(4) of the Mental Health Act 1983, to provide that person with details of any variation which relates to contact with the victim or his family;

(e)   if a community treatment order in respect of the patient is to cease to be in force, to inform that person of the date on which it is to cease to be in force;

(f)   if, following the examination of the patient under section 20 of the Mental Health Act 1983, the authority for the patient's detention is not to be renewed, to inform that person of the date on which the authority is to expire;

(g)   to provide that person with such other information as the managers of the relevant hospital consider appropriate in all the circumstances of the case.

(8) The relevant hospital has the meaning given by section 36A(6).

44B Removal of restriction

(1) This section applies if, in a case where section 42 applies –

(a)   the transfer direction in respect of the patient was given with a restriction direction, and

(b)   the restriction direction ceases to be in force while the transfer direction continues in force.

(2) Subsection (3) applies if a person who appears to the relevant local probation board to be the victim of the offence or to act for the victim of the offence –

(a)   when his wishes were ascertained under section 42(2), expressed a wish to make representations about a matter specified in section 42(3) or to receive the information specified in section 42(4), or

(b)   has subsequently informed the relevant local probation board that he wishes to make representations about such a matter or to receive that information.

(3) The relevant local probation board must take all reasonable steps –

(a)   to notify the managers of the relevant hospital of an address at which that person may be contacted;

(b)   to notify that person of the name and address of the hospital.

(4) While the transfer direction continues in force, the patient is to be regarded as a patient in respect of whom a transfer direction was given without a restriction direction; and sections 43A and 44A are to apply in relation to him accordingly.

(5) The relevant hospital has the meaning given in section 36A(6).

(6) The relevant local probation board has the meaning given in section 43(8).'

Interpretation

16

(1) Section 45 (the title to which becomes 'Interpretation: sections 35 to 44B') is amended as follows.

(2) In subsection (1) –

    (a)   for '44' substitute '44B', and
    (b)   at the appropriate places insert –

        "community treatment order' has the meaning given in section 17A of the Mental Health Act 1983;',
        "the managers' has the meaning given in section 145 of the Mental Health Act 1983;',
        "responsible clinician' means the responsible clinician for the purposes of Part 3 of the Mental Health Act 1983;', and
        "responsible hospital' has the meaning given in section 17A of the Mental Health Act 1983;'.

(3) In subsection (2), for '44' substitute '44B'.

(4) After subsection (2) insert –

'(3) A reference in sections 35 to 44B to a place in which a person is detained includes a reference to a place in which he is liable to be detained under the Mental Health Act 1983.

(4) For the purposes of section 32(3) of that Act (regulations as to delegation of managers' functions, etc) as applied by Parts 1 and 2 of Schedule 1 to that Act, a function conferred on the managers of a hospital under sections 35 to 44B of this Act is to be treated as a function of theirs under Part 3 of that Act.'

SCHEDULE 7
Mental Capacity Act 2005: new Schedule A1

Section 50

Before Schedule 1 to the Mental Capacity Act 2005 (c 9) insert –

'SCHEDULE A1
Hospital and care home residents: deprivation of liberty

PART 1
AUTHORISATION TO DEPRIVE RESIDENTS OF LIBERTY ETC

Application of Part

1

(1) This Part applies if the following conditions are met.

(2) The first condition is that a person ('P') is detained in a hospital or care home – for the purpose of being given care or treatment – in circumstances which amount to deprivation of the person's liberty.

(3) The second condition is that a standard or urgent authorisation is in force.

(4) The third condition is that the standard or urgent authorisation relates –

  (a)   to P, and
  (b)   to the hospital or care home in which P is detained.

Authorisation to deprive P of liberty

2

The managing authority of the hospital or care home may deprive P of his liberty by detaining him as mentioned in paragraph 1(2).

No liability for acts done for purpose of depriving P of liberty

3

(1) This paragraph applies to any act which a person ('D') does for the purpose of detaining P as mentioned in paragraph 1(2).

(2) D does not incur any liability in relation to the act that he would not have incurred if P –

  (a)   had had capacity to consent in relation to D's doing the act, and
  (b)   had consented to D's doing the act.

No protection for negligent acts etc

4

(1) Paragraphs 2 and 3 do not exclude a person's civil liability for loss or damage, or his criminal liability, resulting from his negligence in doing any thing.

(2) Paragraphs 2 and 3 do not authorise a person to do anything otherwise than for the purpose of the standard or urgent authorisation that is in force.

(3) In a case where a standard authorisation is in force, paragraphs 2 and 3 do not authorise a person to do anything which does not comply with the conditions (if any) included in the authorisation.

PART 2
INTERPRETATION: MAIN TERMS

Introduction

5

This Part applies for the purposes of this Schedule.

Detained resident

6

'Detained resident' means a person detained in a hospital or care home – for the purpose of being given care or treatment – in circumstances which amount to deprivation of the person's liberty.

Relevant person etc

7

In relation to a person who is, or is to be, a detained resident –

'relevant person' means the person in question;
'relevant hospital or care home' means the hospital or care home in question;
'relevant care or treatment' means the care or treatment in question.

Authorisations

8

'Standard authorisation' means an authorisation given under Part 4.

9

'Urgent authorisation' means an authorisation given under Part 5.

10

'Authorisation under this Schedule' means either of the following –

(a) a standard authorisation;
(b) an urgent authorisation.

11

(1) The purpose of a standard authorisation is the purpose which is stated in the authorisation in accordance with paragraph 55(1)(d).

(2) The purpose of an urgent authorisation is the purpose which is stated in the authorisation in accordance with paragraph 80(d).

PART 3
THE QUALIFYING REQUIREMENTS

The qualifying requirements

12

(1) These are the qualifying requirements referred to in this Schedule –

    (a)   the age requirement;
    (b)   the mental health requirement;
    (c)   the mental capacity requirement;
    (d)   the best interests requirement;
    (e)   the eligibility requirement;
    (f)   the no refusals requirement.

(2) Any question of whether a person who is, or is to be, a detained resident meets the qualifying requirements is to be determined in accordance with this Part.

(3) In a case where –

    (a)   the question of whether a person meets a particular qualifying requirement arises in relation to the giving of a standard authorisation, and
    (b)   any circumstances relevant to determining that question are expected to change between the time when the determination is made and the time when the authorisation is expected to come into force,

those circumstances are to be taken into account as they are expected to be at the later time.

The age requirement

13

The relevant person meets the age requirement if he has reached 18.

The mental health requirement

14

(1) The relevant person meets the mental health requirement if he is suffering from mental disorder (within the meaning of the Mental Health Act, but disregarding any exclusion for persons with learning disability).

(2) An exclusion for persons with learning disability is any provision of the Mental Health Act which provides for a person with learning disability not to be regarded as suffering from mental disorder for one or more purposes of that Act.

The mental capacity requirement

15

The relevant person meets the mental capacity requirement if he lacks capacity in relation to the question whether or not he should be accommodated in the relevant hospital or care home for the purpose of being given the relevant care or treatment.

The best interests requirement

16

(1) The relevant person meets the best interests requirement if all of the following conditions are met.

(2) The first condition is that the relevant person is, or is to be, a detained resident.

(3) The second condition is that it is in the best interests of the relevant person for him to be a detained resident.

(4) The third condition is that, in order to prevent harm to the relevant person, it is necessary for him to be a detained resident.

(5) The fourth condition is that it is a proportionate response to –

    (a)   the likelihood of the relevant person suffering harm, and
    (b)   the seriousness of that harm,

for him to be a detained resident.

The eligibility requirement

17

(1) The relevant person meets the eligibility requirement unless he is ineligible to be deprived of liberty by this Act.

(2) Schedule 1A applies for the purpose of determining whether or not P is ineligible to be deprived of liberty by this Act.

The no refusals requirement

18

The relevant person meets the no refusals requirement unless there is a refusal within the meaning of paragraph 19 or 20.

19

(1) There is a refusal if these conditions are met –

(a)   the relevant person has made an advance decision;
(b)   the advance decision is valid;
(c)   the advance decision is applicable to some or all of the relevant treatment.

(2) Expressions used in this paragraph and any of sections 24, 25 or 26 have the same meaning in this paragraph as in that section.

20

(1) There is a refusal if it would be in conflict with a valid decision of a donee or deputy for the relevant person to be accommodated in the relevant hospital or care home for the purpose of receiving some or all of the relevant care or treatment –

(a)   in circumstances which amount to deprivation of the person's liberty, or
(b)   at all.

(2) A donee is a donee of a lasting power of attorney granted by the relevant person.

(3) A decision of a donee or deputy is valid if it is made –

(a)   within the scope of his authority as donee or deputy, and
(b)   in accordance with Part 1 of this Act.

PART 4
STANDARD AUTHORISATIONS

Supervisory body to give authorisation

21

Only the supervisory body may give a standard authorisation.

22

The supervisory body may not give a standard authorisation unless –

(a)   the managing authority of the relevant hospital or care home have requested it, or

(b) paragraph 71 applies (right of third party to require consideration of whether authorisation needed).

23

The managing authority may not make a request for a standard authorisation unless –

(a) they are required to do so by paragraph 24 (as read with paragraphs 27 to 29),

(b) they are required to do so by paragraph 25 (as read with paragraph 28), or

(c) they are permitted to do so by paragraph 30.

Duty to request authorisation: basic cases

24

(1) The managing authority must request a standard authorisation in any of the following cases.

(2) The first case is where it appears to the managing authority that the relevant person –

(a) is not yet accommodated in the relevant hospital or care home,

(b) is likely – at some time within the next 28 days – to be a detained resident in the relevant hospital or care home, and

(c) is likely –
   (i) at that time, or
   (ii) at some later time within the next 28 days,
to meet all of the qualifying requirements.

(3) The second case is where it appears to the managing authority that the relevant person –

(a) is already accommodated in the relevant hospital or care home,

(b) is likely – at some time within the next 28 days – to be a detained resident in the relevant hospital or care home, and

(c) is likely –
   (i) at that time, or
   (ii) at some later time within the next 28 days,
to meet all of the qualifying requirements.

(4) The third case is where it appears to the managing authority that the relevant person –

(a) is a detained resident in the relevant hospital or care home, and

(b) meets all of the qualifying requirements, or is likely to do so at some time within the next 28 days.

(5) This paragraph is subject to paragraphs 27 to 29.

Duty to request authorisation: change in place of detention

25

(1) The relevant managing authority must request a standard authorisation if it appears to them that these conditions are met.

(2) The first condition is that a standard authorisation –

    (a)   has been given, and
    (b)   has not ceased to be in force.

(3) The second condition is that there is, or is to be, a change in the place of detention.

(4) This paragraph is subject to paragraph 28.

26

(1) This paragraph applies for the purposes of paragraph 25.

(2) There is a change in the place of detention if the relevant person –

    (a)   ceases to be a detained resident in the stated hospital or care home, and
    (b)   becomes a detained resident in a different hospital or care home ('the new hospital or care home').

(3) The stated hospital or care home is the hospital or care home to which the standard authorisation relates.

(4) The relevant managing authority are the managing authority of the new hospital or care home.

Other authority for detention: request for authorisation

27

(1) This paragraph applies if, by virtue of section 4A(3), a decision of the court authorises the relevant person to be a detained resident.

(2) Paragraph 24 does not require a request for a standard authorisation to be made in relation to that detention unless these conditions are met.

(3) The first condition is that the standard authorisation would be in force at a time immediately after the expiry of the other authority.

(4) The second condition is that the standard authorisation would not be in force at any time on or before the expiry of the other authority.

(5) The third condition is that it would, in the managing authority's view, be unreasonable to delay making the request until a time nearer the expiry of the other authority.

(6) In this paragraph –

    (a)   the other authority is –

(i) the decision mentioned in sub-paragraph (1), or
(ii) any further decision of the court which, by virtue of section 4A(3), authorises, or is expected to authorise, the relevant person to be a detained resident;

(b) the expiry of the other authority is the time when the other authority is expected to cease to authorise the relevant person to be a detained resident.

Request refused: no further request unless change of circumstances

28

(1) This paragraph applies if –

(a) a managing authority request a standard authorisation under paragraph 24 or 25, and
(b) the supervisory body are prohibited by paragraph 50(2) from giving the authorisation.

(2) Paragraph 24 or 25 does not require that managing authority to make a new request for a standard authorisation unless it appears to the managing authority that –

(a) there has been a change in the relevant person's case, and
(b) because of that change, the supervisory body are likely to give a standard authorisation if requested.

Authorisation given: request for further authorisation

29

(1) This paragraph applies if a standard authorisation –

(a) has been given in relation to the detention of the relevant person, and
(b) that authorisation ('the existing authorisation') has not ceased to be in force.

(2) Paragraph 24 does not require a new request for a standard authorisation ('the new authorisation') to be made unless these conditions are met.

(3) The first condition is that the new authorisation would be in force at a time immediately after the expiry of the existing authorisation.

(4) The second condition is that the new authorisation would not be in force at any time on or before the expiry of the existing authorisation.

(5) The third condition is that it would, in the managing authority's view, be unreasonable to delay making the request until a time nearer the expiry of the existing authorisation.

(6) The expiry of the existing authorisation is the time when it is expected to cease to be in force.

Power to request authorisation

30

(1) This paragraph applies if –

    (a)   a standard authorisation has been given in relation to the detention of the relevant person,

    (b)   that authorisation ('the existing authorisation') has not ceased to be in force,

    (c)   the requirement under paragraph 24 to make a request for a new standard authorisation does not apply, because of paragraph 29, and

    (d)   a review of the existing authorisation has been requested, or is being carried out, in accordance with Part 8.

(2) The managing authority may request a new standard authorisation which would be in force on or before the expiry of the existing authorisation; but only if it would also be in force immediately after that expiry.

(3) The expiry of the existing authorisation is the time when it is expected to cease to be in force.

(4) Further provision relating to cases where a request is made under this paragraph can be found in –

    (a)   paragraph 62 (effect of decision about request), and

    (b)   paragraph 124 (effect of request on Part 8 review).

Information included in request

31

A request for a standard authorisation must include the information (if any) required by regulations.

Records of requests

32

(1) The managing authority of a hospital or care home must keep a written record of –

    (a)   each request that they make for a standard authorisation, and

    (b)   the reasons for making each request.

(2) A supervisory body must keep a written record of each request for a standard authorisation that is made to them.

Relevant person must be assessed

33

(1) This paragraph applies if the supervisory body are requested to give a standard authorisation.

(2) The supervisory body must secure that all of these assessments are carried out in relation to the relevant person –

    (a)   an age assessment;
    (b)   a mental health assessment;
    (c)   a mental capacity assessment;
    (d)   a best interests assessment;
    (e)   an eligibility assessment;
    (f)   a no refusals assessment.

(3) The person who carries out any such assessment is referred to as the assessor.

(4) Regulations may be made about the period (or periods) within which assessors must carry out assessments.

(5) This paragraph is subject to paragraphs 49 and 133.

Age assessment

34

An age assessment is an assessment of whether the relevant person meets the age requirement.

Mental health assessment

35

A mental health assessment is an assessment of whether the relevant person meets the mental health requirement.

36

When carrying out a mental health assessment, the assessor must also –

    (a)   consider how (if at all) the relevant person's mental health is likely to be affected by his being a detained resident, and
    (b)   notify the best interests assessor of his conclusions.

Mental capacity assessment

37

A mental capacity assessment is an assessment of whether the relevant person meets the mental capacity requirement.

Best interests assessment

38

A best interests assessment is an assessment of whether the relevant person meets the best interests requirement.

39

(1) In carrying out a best interests assessment, the assessor must comply with the duties in sub-paragraphs (2) and (3).

(2) The assessor must consult the managing authority of the relevant hospital or care home.

(3) The assessor must have regard to all of the following –

   (a)   the conclusions which the mental health assessor has notified to the best interests assessor in accordance with paragraph 36(b);
   (b)   any relevant needs assessment;
   (c)   any relevant care plan.

(4) A relevant needs assessment is an assessment of the relevant person's needs which –

   (a)   was carried out in connection with the relevant person being accommodated in the relevant hospital or care home, and
   (b)   was carried out by or on behalf of –
      (i)   the managing authority of the relevant hospital or care home, or
      (ii)   the supervisory body.

(5) A relevant care plan is a care plan which –

   (a)   sets out how the relevant person's needs are to be met whilst he is accommodated in the relevant hospital or care home, and
   (b)   was drawn up by or on behalf of –
      (i)   the managing authority of the relevant hospital or care home, or
      (ii)   the supervisory body.

(6) The managing authority must give the assessor a copy of –

   (a)   any relevant needs assessment carried out by them or on their behalf, or
   (b)   any relevant care plan drawn up by them or on their behalf.

(7) The supervisory body must give the assessor a copy of –

   (a)   any relevant needs assessment carried out by them or on their behalf, or
   (b)   any relevant care plan drawn up by them or on their behalf.

(8) The duties in sub-paragraphs (2) and (3) do not affect any other duty to consult or to take the views of others into account.

40

(1) This paragraph applies whatever conclusion the best interests assessment comes to.

(2) The assessor must state in the best interests assessment the name and address of every interested person whom he has consulted in carrying out the assessment.

41

Paragraphs 42 and 43 apply if the best interests assessment comes to the conclusion that the relevant person meets the best interests requirement.

42

(1) The assessor must state in the assessment the maximum authorisation period.

(2) The maximum authorisation period is the shorter of these periods –

(a) the period which, in the assessor's opinion, would be the appropriate maximum period for the relevant person to be a detained resident under the standard authorisation that has been requested;

(b) 1 year, or such shorter period as may be prescribed in regulations.

(3) Regulations under sub-paragraph (2)(b) –

(a) need not provide for a shorter period to apply in relation to all standard authorisations;

(b) may provide for different periods to apply in relation to different kinds of standard authorisations.

(4) Before making regulations under sub-paragraph (2)(b) the Secretary of State must consult all of the following –

(a) each body required by regulations under paragraph 162 to monitor and report on the operation of this Schedule in relation to England;

(b) such other persons as the Secretary of State considers it appropriate to consult.

(5) Before making regulations under sub-paragraph (2)(b) the National Assembly for Wales must consult all of the following –

(a) each person or body directed under paragraph 163(2) to carry out any function of the Assembly of monitoring and reporting on the operation of this Schedule in relation to Wales;

(b) such other persons as the Assembly considers it appropriate to consult.

43

The assessor may include in the assessment recommendations about conditions to which the standard authorisation is, or is not, to be subject in accordance with paragraph 53.

44

(1) This paragraph applies if the best interests assessment comes to the conclusion that the relevant person does not meet the best interests requirement.

(2) If, on the basis of the information taken into account in carrying out the assessment, it appears to the assessor that there is an unauthorised deprivation of liberty, he must include a statement to that effect in the assessment.

(3) There is an unauthorised deprivation of liberty if the managing authority of the relevant hospital or care home are already depriving the relevant person of his liberty without authority of the kind mentioned in section 4A.

45

The duties with which the best interests assessor must comply are subject to the provision included in appointment regulations under Part 10 (in particular, provision made under paragraph 146).

Eligibility assessment

46

An eligibility assessment is an assessment of whether the relevant person meets the eligibility requirement.

47

(1) Regulations may –

    (a) require an eligibility assessor to request a best interests assessor to provide relevant eligibility information, and

    (b) require the best interests assessor, if such a request is made, to provide such relevant eligibility information as he may have.

(2) In this paragraph –

    'best interests assessor' means any person who is carrying out, or has carried out, a best interests assessment in relation to the relevant person;

    'eligibility assessor' means a person carrying out an eligibility assessment in relation to the relevant person;

'relevant eligibility information' is information relevant to assessing whether or not the relevant person is ineligible by virtue of paragraph 5 of Schedule 1A.

No refusals assessment

48

A no refusals assessment is an assessment of whether the relevant person meets the no refusals requirement.

Equivalent assessment already carried out

49

(1) The supervisory body are not required by paragraph 33 to secure that a particular kind of assessment ('the required assessment') is carried out in relation to the relevant person if the following conditions are met.

(2) The first condition is that the supervisory body have a written copy of an assessment of the relevant person ('the existing assessment') that has already been carried out.

(3) The second condition is that the existing assessment complies with all requirements under this Schedule with which the required assessment would have to comply (if it were carried out).

(4) The third condition is that the existing assessment was carried out within the previous 12 months; but this condition need not be met if the required assessment is an age assessment.

(5) The fourth condition is that the supervisory body are satisfied that there is no reason why the existing assessment may no longer be accurate.

(6) If the required assessment is a best interests assessment, in satisfying themselves as mentioned in sub-paragraph (5), the supervisory body must take into account any information given, or submissions made, by –

(a)   the relevant person's representative,
(b)   any section 39C IMCA, or
(c)   any section 39D IMCA.

(7) It does not matter whether the existing assessment was carried out in connection with a request for a standard authorisation or for some other purpose.

(8) If, because of this paragraph, the supervisory body are not required by paragraph 33 to secure that the required assessment is carried out, the existing assessment is to be treated for the purposes of this Schedule –

(a)   as an assessment of the same kind as the required assessment, and
(b)   as having been carried out under paragraph 33 in connection with the request for the standard authorisation.

Duty to give authorisation

50

(1) The supervisory body must give a standard authorisation if –

(a)   all assessments are positive, and

(b)   the supervisory body have written copies of all those assessments.

(2) The supervisory body must not give a standard authorisation except in accordance with sub-paragraph (1).

(3) All assessments are positive if each assessment carried out under paragraph 33 has come to the conclusion that the relevant person meets the qualifying requirement to which the assessment relates.

Terms of authorisation

51

(1) If the supervisory body are required to give a standard authorisation, they must decide the period during which the authorisation is to be in force.

(2) That period must not exceed the maximum authorisation period stated in the best interests assessment.

52

A standard authorisation may provide for the authorisation to come into force at a time after it is given.

53

(1) A standard authorisation may be given subject to conditions.

(2) Before deciding whether to give the authorisation subject to conditions, the supervisory body must have regard to any recommendations in the best interests assessment about such conditions.

(3) The managing authority of the relevant hospital or care home must ensure that any conditions are complied with.

Form of authorisation

54

A standard authorisation must be in writing.

55

(1) A standard authorisation must state the following things –

(a)   the name of the relevant person;

(b) the name of the relevant hospital or care home;

(c) the period during which the authorisation is to be in force;

(d) the purpose for which the authorisation is given;

(e) any conditions subject to which the authorisation is given;

(f) the reason why each qualifying requirement is met.

(2) The statement of the reason why the eligibility requirement is met must be framed by reference to the cases in the table in paragraph 2 of Schedule 1A.

56

(1) If the name of the relevant hospital or care home changes, the standard authorisation is to be read as if it stated the current name of the hospital or care home.

(2) But sub-paragraph (1) is subject to any provision relating to the change of name which is made in any enactment or in any instrument made under an enactment.

Duty to give information about decision

57

(1) This paragraph applies if –

(a) a request is made for a standard authorisation, and

(b) the supervisory body are required by paragraph 50(1) to give the standard authorisation.

(2) The supervisory body must give a copy of the authorisation to each of the following –

(a) the relevant person's representative;

(b) the managing authority of the relevant hospital or care home;

(c) the relevant person;

(d) any section 39A IMCA;

(e) every interested person consulted by the best interests assessor.

(3) The supervisory body must comply with this paragraph as soon as practicable after they give the standard authorisation.

58

(1) This paragraph applies if –

(a) a request is made for a standard authorisation, and

(b) the supervisory body are prohibited by paragraph 50(2) from giving the standard authorisation.

(2) The supervisory body must give notice, stating that they are prohibited from giving the authorisation, to each of the following –

(a) the managing authority of the relevant hospital or care home;

    (b)   the relevant person;

    (c)   any section 39A IMCA;

    (d)   every interested person consulted by the best interests assessor.

(3) The supervisory body must comply with this paragraph as soon as practicable after it becomes apparent to them that they are prohibited from giving the authorisation.

Duty to give information about effect of authorisation

59

(1) This paragraph applies if a standard authorisation is given.

(2) The managing authority of the relevant hospital or care home must take such steps as are practicable to ensure that the relevant person understands all of the following –

    (a)   the effect of the authorisation;

    (b)   the right to make an application to the court to exercise its jurisdiction under section 21A;

    (c)   the right under Part 8 to request a review;

    (d)   the right to have a section 39D IMCA appointed;

    (e)   how to have a section 39D IMCA appointed.

(3) Those steps must be taken as soon as is practicable after the authorisation is given.

(4) Those steps must include the giving of appropriate information both orally and in writing.

(5) Any written information given to the relevant person must also be given by the managing authority to the relevant person's representative.

(6) They must give the information to the representative as soon as is practicable after it is given to the relevant person.

(7) Sub-paragraph (8) applies if the managing authority is notified that a section 39D IMCA has been appointed.

(8) As soon as is practicable after being notified, the managing authority must give the section 39D IMCA a copy of the written information given in accordance with sub-paragraph (4).

Records of authorisations

60

A supervisory body must keep a written record of all of the following information –

    (a)   the standard authorisations that they have given;

    (b)   the requests for standard authorisations in response to which they have not given an authorisation;

(c)   in relation to each standard authorisation given: the matters stated in the authorisation in accordance with paragraph 55.

Variation of an authorisation

61

(1) A standard authorisation may not be varied except in accordance with Part 7 or 8.

(2) This paragraph does not affect the powers of the Court of Protection or of any other court.

Effect of decision about request made under paragraph 25 or 30

62

(1) This paragraph applies where the managing authority request a new standard authorisation under either of the following –

(a)   paragraph 25 (change in place of detention);
(b)   paragraph 30 (existing authorisation subject to review).

(2) If the supervisory body are required by paragraph 50(1) to give the new authorisation, the existing authorisation terminates at the time when the new authorisation comes into force.

(3) If the supervisory body are prohibited by paragraph 50(2) from giving the new authorisation, there is no effect on the existing authorisation's continuation in force.

When an authorisation is in force

63

(1) A standard authorisation comes into force when it is given.

(2) But if the authorisation provides for it to come into force at a later time, it comes into force at that time.

64

(1) A standard authorisation ceases to be in force at the end of the period stated in the authorisation in accordance with paragraph 55(1)(c).

(2) But if the authorisation terminates before then in accordance with paragraph 62(2) or any other provision of this Schedule, it ceases to be in force when the termination takes effect.

(3) This paragraph does not affect the powers of the Court of Protection or of any other court.

65

(1) This paragraph applies if a standard authorisation ceases to be in force.

(2) The supervisory body must give notice that the authorisation has ceased to be in force.

(3) The supervisory body must give that notice to all of the following –

    (a)   the managing authority of the relevant hospital or care home;
    (b)   the relevant person;
    (c)   the relevant person's representative;
    (d)   every interested person consulted by the best interests assessor.

(4) The supervisory body must give that notice as soon as practicable after the authorisation ceases to be in force.

When a request for a standard authorisation is 'disposed of'

66

A request for a standard authorisation is to be regarded for the purposes of this Schedule as disposed of if the supervisory body have given –

    (a)   a copy of the authorisation in accordance with paragraph 57, or
    (b)   notice in accordance with paragraph 58.

Right of third party to require consideration of whether authorisation needed

67

For the purposes of paragraphs 68 to 73 there is an unauthorised deprivation of liberty if –

    (a)   a person is already a detained resident in a hospital or care home, and
    (b)   the detention of the person is not authorised as mentioned in section 4A.

68

(1) If the following conditions are met, an eligible person may request the supervisory body to decide whether or not there is an unauthorised deprivation of liberty.

(2) The first condition is that the eligible person has notified the managing authority of the relevant hospital or care home that it appears to the eligible person that there is an unauthorised deprivation of liberty.

(3) The second condition is that the eligible person has asked the managing authority to request a standard authorisation in relation to the detention of the relevant person.

(4) The third condition is that the managing authority has not requested a standard authorisation within a reasonable period after the eligible person asks it to do so.

(5) In this paragraph 'eligible person' means any person other than the managing authority of the relevant hospital or care home.

69

(1) This paragraph applies if an eligible person requests the supervisory body to decide whether or not there is an unauthorised deprivation of liberty.

(2) The supervisory body must select and appoint a person to carry out an assessment of whether or not the relevant person is a detained resident.

(3) But the supervisory body need not select and appoint a person to carry out such an assessment in either of these cases.

(4) The first case is where it appears to the supervisory body that the request by the eligible person is frivolous or vexatious.

(5) The second case is where it appears to the supervisory body that –

(a)   the question of whether or not there is an unauthorised deprivation of liberty has already been decided, and
(b)   since that decision, there has been no change of circumstances which would merit the question being decided again.

(6) The supervisory body must not select and appoint a person to carry out an assessment under this paragraph unless it appears to the supervisory body that the person would be –

(a)   suitable to carry out a best interests assessment (if one were obtained in connection with a request for a standard authorisation relating to the relevant person), and
(b)   eligible to carry out such a best interests assessment.

(7) The supervisory body must notify the persons specified in sub-paragraph (8) –

(a)   that the supervisory body have been requested to decide whether or not there is an unauthorised deprivation of liberty;
(b)   of their decision whether or not to select and appoint a person to carry out an assessment under this paragraph;
(c)   if their decision is to select and appoint a person, of the person appointed.

(8) The persons referred to in sub-paragraph (7) are –

(a)   the eligible person who made the request under paragraph 68;
(b)   the person to whom the request relates;
(c)   the managing authority of the relevant hospital or care home;
(d)   any section 39A IMCA.

70

(1) Regulations may be made about the period within which an assessment under paragraph 69 must be carried out.

(2) Regulations made under paragraph 129(3) apply in relation to the selection and appointment of a person under paragraph 69 as they apply to the selection of a person under paragraph 129 to carry out a best interests assessment.

(3) The following provisions apply to an assessment under paragraph 69 as they apply to an assessment carried out in connection with a request for a standard authorisation –

(a)   paragraph 131 (examination and copying of records);
(b)   paragraph 132 (representations);
(c)   paragraphs 134 and 135(1) and (2) (duty to keep records and give copies).

(4) The copies of the assessment which the supervisory body are required to give under paragraph 135(2) must be given as soon as practicable after the supervisory body are themselves given a copy of the assessment.

71

(1) This paragraph applies if –

(a)   the supervisory body obtain an assessment under paragraph 69,
(b)   the assessment comes to the conclusion that the relevant person is a detained resident, and
(c)   it appears to the supervisory body that the detention of the person is not authorised as mentioned in section 4A.

(2) This Schedule (including Part 5) applies as if the managing authority of the relevant hospital or care home had, in accordance with Part 4, requested the supervisory body to give a standard authorisation in relation to the relevant person.

(3) The managing authority of the relevant hospital or care home must supply the supervisory body with the information (if any) which the managing authority would, by virtue of paragraph 31, have had to include in a request for a standard authorisation.

(4) The supervisory body must notify the persons specified in paragraph 69(8) –

(a)   of the outcome of the assessment obtained under paragraph 69, and
(b)   that this Schedule applies as mentioned in sub-paragraph (2).

72

(1) This paragraph applies if –

    (a)   the supervisory body obtain an assessment under paragraph 69, and

    (b)   the assessment comes to the conclusion that the relevant person is not a detained resident.

(2) The supervisory body must notify the persons specified in paragraph 69(8) of the outcome of the assessment.

73

(1) This paragraph applies if –

    (a)   the supervisory body obtain an assessment under paragraph 69,

    (b)   the assessment comes to the conclusion that the relevant person is a detained resident, and

    (c)   it appears to the supervisory body that the detention of the person is authorised as mentioned in section 4A.

(2) The supervisory body must notify the persons specified in paragraph 69(8) –

    (a)   of the outcome of the assessment, and

    (b)   that it appears to the supervisory body that the detention is authorised.

PART 5
URGENT AUTHORISATIONS

Managing authority to give authorisation

74

Only the managing authority of the relevant hospital or care home may give an urgent authorisation.

75

The managing authority may give an urgent authorisation only if they are required to do so by paragraph 76 (as read with paragraph 77).

Duty to give authorisation

76

(1) The managing authority must give an urgent authorisation in either of the following cases.

(2) The first case is where –

    (a)   the managing authority are required to make a request under paragraph 24 or 25 for a standard authorisation, and

(b) they believe that the need for the relevant person to be a detained resident is so urgent that it is appropriate for the detention to begin before they make the request.

(3) The second case is where –

(a) the managing authority have made a request under paragraph 24 or 25 for a standard authorisation, and

(b) they believe that the need for the relevant person to be a detained resident is so urgent that it is appropriate for the detention to begin before the request is disposed of.

(4) References in this paragraph to the detention of the relevant person are references to the detention to which paragraph 24 or 25 relates.

(5) This paragraph is subject to paragraph 77.

77

(1) This paragraph applies where the managing authority have given an urgent authorisation ('the original authorisation') in connection with a case where a person is, or is to be, a detained resident ('the existing detention').

(2) No new urgent authorisation is to be given under paragraph 76 in connection with the existing detention.

(3) But the managing authority may request the supervisory body to extend the duration of the original authorisation.

(4) Only one request under sub-paragraph (3) may be made in relation to the original authorisation.

(5) Paragraphs 84 to 86 apply to any request made under sub-paragraph (3).

Terms of authorisation

78

(1) If the managing authority decide to give an urgent authorisation, they must decide the period during which the authorisation is to be in force.

(2) That period must not exceed 7 days.

Form of authorisation

79

An urgent authorisation must be in writing.

80

An urgent authorisation must state the following things –

(a) the name of the relevant person;
(b) the name of the relevant hospital or care home;
(c) the period during which the authorisation is to be in force;
(d) the purpose for which the authorisation is given.

81

(1) If the name of the relevant hospital or care home changes, the urgent authorisation is to be read as if it stated the current name of the hospital or care home.

(2) But sub-paragraph (1) is subject to any provision relating to the change of name which is made in any enactment or in any instrument made under an enactment.

Duty to keep records and give copies

82

(1) This paragraph applies if an urgent authorisation is given.

(2) The managing authority must keep a written record of why they have given the urgent authorisation.

(3) As soon as practicable after giving the authorisation, the managing authority must give a copy of the authorisation to all of the following –

(a) the relevant person;
(b) any section 39A IMCA.

Duty to give information about authorisation

83

(1) This paragraph applies if an urgent authorisation is given.

(2) The managing authority of the relevant hospital or care home must take such steps as are practicable to ensure that the relevant person understands all of the following –

(a) the effect of the authorisation;
(b) the right to make an application to the court to exercise its jurisdiction under section 21A.
(3) Those steps must be taken as soon as is practicable after the authorisation is given.

(4) Those steps must include the giving of appropriate information both orally and in writing.

Request for extension of duration

84

(1) This paragraph applies if the managing authority make a request under paragraph 77 for the supervisory body to extend the duration of the original authorisation.

(2) The managing authority must keep a written record of why they have made the request.

(3) The managing authority must give the relevant person notice that they have made the request.

(4) The supervisory body may extend the duration of the original authorisation if it appears to them that –

    (a)   the managing authority have made the required request for a standard authorisation,

    (b)   there are exceptional reasons why it has not yet been possible for that request to be disposed of, and

    (c)   it is essential for the existing detention to continue until the request is disposed of.

(5) The supervisory body must keep a written record that the request has been made to them.

(6) In this paragraph and paragraphs 85 and 86 –

    (a)   'original authorisation' and 'existing detention' have the same meaning as in paragraph 77;

    (b)   the required request for a standard authorisation is the request that is referred to in paragraph 76(2) or (3).

85

(1) This paragraph applies if, under paragraph 84, the supervisory body decide to extend the duration of the original authorisation.

(2) The supervisory body must decide the period of the extension.

(3) That period must not exceed 7 days.

(4) The supervisory body must give the managing authority notice stating the period of the extension.

(5) The managing authority must then vary the original authorisation so that it states the extended duration.

(6) Paragraphs 82(3) and 83 apply (with the necessary modifications) to the variation of the original authorisation as they apply to the giving of an urgent authorisation.

(7) The supervisory body must keep a written record of –

    (a)   the outcome of the request, and

(b)   the period of the extension.

86

(1) This paragraph applies if, under paragraph 84, the supervisory body decide not to extend the duration of the original authorisation.

(2) The supervisory body must give the managing authority notice stating –

(a)   the decision, and
(b)   their reasons for making it.

(3) The managing authority must give a copy of that notice to all of the following –

(a)   the relevant person;
(b)   any section 39A IMCA.

(4) The supervisory body must keep a written record of the outcome of the request.

No variation

87

(1) An urgent authorisation may not be varied except in accordance with paragraph 85.

(2) This paragraph does not affect the powers of the Court of Protection or of any other court.

When an authorisation is in force

88

An urgent authorisation comes into force when it is given.

89

(1) An urgent authorisation ceases to be in force at the end of the period stated in the authorisation in accordance with paragraph 80(c) (subject to any variation in accordance with paragraph 85).

(2) But if the required request is disposed of before the end of that period, the urgent authorisation ceases to be in force as follows.

(3) If the supervisory body are required by paragraph 50(1) to give the requested authorisation, the urgent authorisation ceases to be in force when the requested authorisation comes into force.

(4) If the supervisory body are prohibited by paragraph 50(2) from giving the requested authorisation, the urgent authorisation ceases to be in force when the managing authority receive notice under paragraph 58.

(5) In this paragraph –

'required request' means the request referred to in paragraph 76(2) or (3);

'requested authorisation' means the standard authorisation to which the required request relates.

(6) This paragraph does not affect the powers of the Court of Protection or of any other court.

90

(1) This paragraph applies if an urgent authorisation ceases to be in force.

(2) The supervisory body must give notice that the authorisation has ceased to be in force.

(3) The supervisory body must give that notice to all of the following –

(a) the relevant person;
(b) any section 39A IMCA.

(4) The supervisory body must give that notice as soon as practicable after the authorisation ceases to be in force.

PART 6
ELIGIBILITY REQUIREMENT NOT MET: SUSPENSION OF STANDARD AUTHORISATION

91

(1) This Part applies if the following conditions are met.

(2) The first condition is that a standard authorisation –

(a) has been given, and
(b) has not ceased to be in force.

(3) The second condition is that the managing authority of the relevant hospital or care home are satisfied that the relevant person has ceased to meet the eligibility requirement.

(4) But this Part does not apply if the relevant person is ineligible by virtue of paragraph 5 of Schedule 1A (in which case see Part 8).

92

The managing authority of the relevant hospital or care home must give the supervisory body notice that the relevant person has ceased to meet the eligibility requirement.

93

(1) This paragraph applies if the managing authority give the supervisory body notice under paragraph 92.

(2) The standard authorisation is suspended from the time when the notice is given.

(3) The supervisory body must give notice that the standard authorisation has been suspended to the following persons –

    (a)   the relevant person;

    (b)   the relevant person's representative;

    (c)   the managing authority of the relevant hospital or care home.

94

(1) This paragraph applies if, whilst the standard authorisation is suspended, the managing authority are satisfied that the relevant person meets the eligibility requirement again.

(2) The managing authority must give the supervisory body notice that the relevant person meets the eligibility requirement again.

95

(1) This paragraph applies if the managing authority give the supervisory body notice under paragraph 94.

(2) The standard authorisation ceases to be suspended from the time when the notice is given.

(3) The supervisory body must give notice that the standard authorisation has ceased to be suspended to the following persons –

    (a)   the relevant person;

    (b)   the relevant person's representative;

    (c)   any section 39D IMCA;

    (d)   the managing authority of the relevant hospital or care home.

(4) The supervisory body must give notice under this paragraph as soon as practicable after they are given notice under paragraph 94.

96

(1) This paragraph applies if no notice is given under paragraph 94 before the end of the relevant 28 day period.

(2) The standard authorisation ceases to have effect at the end of the relevant 28 day period.

(3) The relevant 28 day period is the period of 28 days beginning with the day on which the standard authorisation is suspended under paragraph 93.

97

The effect of suspending the standard authorisation is that Part 1 ceases to apply for as long as the authorisation is suspended.

PART 7
STANDARD AUTHORISATIONS: CHANGE IN SUPERVISORY RESPONSIBILITY

Application of this Part

98

(1) This Part applies if these conditions are met.

(2) The first condition is that a standard authorisation –

    (a)   has been given, and
    (b)   has not ceased to be in force.

(3) The second condition is that there is a change in supervisory responsibility.

(4) The third condition is that there is not a change in the place of detention (within the meaning of paragraph 25).

99

For the purposes of this Part there is a change in supervisory responsibility if –

    (a)   one body ('the old supervisory body') have ceased to be supervisory body in relation to the standard authorisation, and
    (b)   a different body ('the new supervisory body') have become supervisory body in relation to the standard authorisation.

Effect of change in supervisory responsibility

100

(1) The new supervisory body becomes the supervisory body in relation to the authorisation.

(2) Anything done by or in relation to the old supervisory body in connection with the authorisation has effect, so far as is necessary for continuing its effect after the change, as if done by or in relation to the new supervisory body.

(3) Anything which relates to the authorisation and which is in the process of being done by or in relation to the old supervisory body at the time of the change may be continued by or in relation to the new supervisory body.

(4) But –

(a) the old supervisory body do not, by virtue of this paragraph, cease to be liable for anything done by them in connection with the authorisation before the change; and

(b) the new supervisory body do not, by virtue of this paragraph, become liable for any such thing.

PART 8
STANDARD AUTHORISATIONS: REVIEW

Application of this Part

101

(1) This Part applies if a standard authorisation –

(a) has been given, and
(b) has not ceased to be in force.

(2) Paragraphs 102 to 122 are subject to paragraphs 123 to 125.

Review by supervisory body

102

(1) The supervisory body may at any time carry out a review of the standard authorisation in accordance with this Part.

(2) The supervisory body must carry out such a review if they are requested to do so by an eligible person.

(3) Each of the following is an eligible person –

(a) the relevant person;
(b) the relevant person's representative;
(c) the managing authority of the relevant hospital or care home.

Request for review

103

(1) An eligible person may, at any time, request the supervisory body to carry out a review of the standard authorisation in accordance with this Part.

(2) The managing authority of the relevant hospital or care home must make such a request if one or more of the qualifying requirements appear to them to be reviewable.

Grounds for review

104

(1) Paragraphs 105 to 107 set out the grounds on which the qualifying requirements are reviewable.

(2) A qualifying requirement is not reviewable on any other ground.

Non-qualification ground

105

(1) Any of the following qualifying requirements is reviewable on the ground that the relevant person does not meet the requirement –

    (a)   the age requirement;
    (b)   the mental health requirement;
    (c)   the mental capacity requirement;
    (d)   the best interests requirement;
    (e)   the no refusals requirement.

(2) The eligibility requirement is reviewable on the ground that the relevant person is ineligible by virtue of paragraph 5 of Schedule 1A.

(3) The ground in sub-paragraph (1) and the ground in sub-paragraph (2) are referred to as the non-qualification ground.

Change of reason ground

106

(1) Any of the following qualifying requirements is reviewable on the ground set out in sub-paragraph (2) –

    (a)   the mental health requirement;
    (b)   the mental capacity requirement;
    (c)   the best interests requirement;
    (d)   the eligibility requirement;
    (e)   the no refusals requirement.

(2) The ground is that the reason why the relevant person meets the requirement is not the reason stated in the standard authorisation.

(3) This ground is referred to as the change of reason ground.

Variation of conditions ground

107

(1) The best interests requirement is reviewable on the ground that –

    (a)   there has been a change in the relevant person's case, and

(b)   because of that change, it would be appropriate to vary the conditions to which the standard authorisation is subject.

(2) This ground is referred to as the variation of conditions ground.

(3) A reference to varying the conditions to which the standard authorisation is subject is a reference to –

(a)   amendment of an existing condition,
(b)   omission of an existing condition, or
(c)   inclusion of a new condition (whether or not there are already any existing conditions).

Notice that review to be carried out

108

(1) If the supervisory body are to carry out a review of the standard authorisation, they must give notice of the review to the following persons –

(a)   the relevant person;
(b)   the relevant person's representative;
(c)   the managing authority of the relevant hospital or care home.

(2) The supervisory body must give the notice –

(a)   before they begin the review, or
(b)   if that is not practicable, as soon as practicable after they have begun it.

(3) This paragraph does not require the supervisory body to give notice to any person who has requested the review.

Starting a review

109

To start a review of the standard authorisation, the supervisory body must decide which, if any, of the qualifying requirements appear to be reviewable.

No reviewable qualifying requirements

110

(1) This paragraph applies if no qualifying requirements appear to be reviewable.

(2) This Part does not require the supervisory body to take any action in respect of the standard authorisation.

One or more reviewable qualifying requirements

111

(1) This paragraph applies if one or more qualifying requirements appear to be reviewable.

(2) The supervisory body must secure that a separate review assessment is carried out in relation to each qualifying requirement which appears to be reviewable.

(3) But sub-paragraph (2) does not require the supervisory body to secure that a best interests review assessment is carried out in a case where the best interests requirement appears to the supervisory body to be non-assessable.

(4) The best interests requirement is non-assessable if –

    (a)   the requirement is reviewable only on the variation of conditions ground, and

    (b)   the change in the relevant person's case is not significant.

(5) In making any decision whether the change in the relevant person's case is significant, regard must be had to –

    (a)   the nature of the change, and

    (b)   the period that the change is likely to last for.

Review assessments

112

(1) A review assessment is an assessment of whether the relevant person meets a qualifying requirement.

(2) In relation to a review assessment –

    (a)   a negative conclusion is a conclusion that the relevant person does not meet the qualifying requirement to which the assessment relates;

    (b)   a positive conclusion is a conclusion that the relevant person meets the qualifying requirement to which the assessment relates.

(3) An age review assessment is a review assessment carried out in relation to the age requirement.

(4) A mental health review assessment is a review assessment carried out in relation to the mental health requirement.

(5) A mental capacity review assessment is a review assessment carried out in relation to the mental capacity requirement.

(6) A best interests review assessment is a review assessment carried out in relation to the best interests requirement.

(7) An eligibility review assessment is a review assessment carried out in relation to the eligibility requirement.

(8) A no refusals review assessment is a review assessment carried out in relation to the no refusals requirement.

113

(1) In carrying out a review assessment, the assessor must comply with any duties which would be imposed upon him under Part 4 if the assessment were being carried out in connection with a request for a standard authorisation.

(2) But in the case of a best interests review assessment, paragraphs 43 and 44 do not apply.

(3) Instead of what is required by paragraph 43, the best interests review assessment must include recommendations about whether – and, if so, how – it would be appropriate to vary the conditions to which the standard authorisation is subject.

Best interests requirement reviewable but non-assessable

114

(1) This paragraph applies in a case where –

(a)   the best interests requirement appears to be reviewable, but
(b)   in accordance with paragraph 111(3), the supervisory body are not required to secure that a best interests review assessment is carried out.

(2) The supervisory body may vary the conditions to which the standard authorisation is subject in such ways (if any) as the supervisory body think are appropriate in the circumstances.

Best interests review assessment positive

115

(1) This paragraph applies in a case where –

(a)   a best interests review assessment is carried out, and
(b)   the assessment comes to a positive conclusion.

(2) The supervisory body must decide the following questions –

(a)   whether or not the best interests requirement is reviewable on the change of reason ground;
(b)   whether or not the best interests requirement is reviewable on the variation of conditions ground;
(c)   if so, whether or not the change in the person's case is significant.

(3) If the supervisory body decide that the best interests requirement is reviewable on the change of reason ground, they must vary the standard authorisation so that it states the reason why the relevant person now meets that requirement.

(4) If the supervisory body decide that –

(a)   the best interests requirement is reviewable on the variation of conditions ground, and

(b)   the change in the relevant person's case is not significant,

they may vary the conditions to which the standard authorisation is subject in such ways (if any) as they think are appropriate in the circumstances.

(5) If the supervisory body decide that –

(a)   the best interests requirement is reviewable on the variation of conditions ground, and

(b)   the change in the relevant person's case is significant,

they must vary the conditions to which the standard authorisation is subject in such ways as they think are appropriate in the circumstances.

(6) If the supervisory body decide that the best interests requirement is not reviewable on –

(a)   the change of reason ground, or

(b)   the variation of conditions ground,

this Part does not require the supervisory body to take any action in respect of the standard authorisation so far as the best interests requirement relates to it.

Mental health, mental capacity, eligibility or no refusals review assessment positive

116

(1) This paragraph applies if the following conditions are met.

(2) The first condition is that one or more of the following are carried out –

(a)   a mental health review assessment;

(b)   a mental capacity review assessment;

(c)   an eligibility review assessment;

(d)   a no refusals review assessment.

(3) The second condition is that each assessment carried out comes to a positive conclusion.

(4) The supervisory body must decide whether or not each of the assessed qualifying requirements is reviewable on the change of reason ground.

(5) If the supervisory body decide that any of the assessed qualifying requirements is reviewable on the change of reason ground, they must vary the standard authorisation so that it states the reason why the relevant person now meets the requirement or requirements in question.

(6) If the supervisory body decide that none of the assessed qualifying requirements are reviewable on the change of reason ground, this Part does not require the supervisory body to take any action in respect of the standard authorisation so far as those requirements relate to it.

(7) An assessed qualifying requirement is a qualifying requirement in relation to which a review assessment is carried out.

One or more review assessments negative

117

(1) This paragraph applies if one or more of the review assessments carried out comes to a negative conclusion.

(2) The supervisory body must terminate the standard authorisation with immediate effect.

Completion of a review

118

(1) The review of the standard authorisation is complete in any of the following cases.

(2) The first case is where paragraph 110 applies.

(3) The second case is where –

  (a) paragraph 111 applies, and
  (b) paragraph 117 requires the supervisory body to terminate the standard authorisation.

(4) In such a case, the supervisory body need not comply with any of the other provisions of paragraphs 114 to 116 which would be applicable to the review (were it not for this sub-paragraph).

(5) The third case is where –

  (a) paragraph 111 applies,
  (b) paragraph 117 does not require the supervisory body to terminate the standard authorisation, and
  (c) the supervisory body comply with all of the provisions of paragraphs 114 to 116 (so far as they are applicable to the review).

Variations under this Part

119

Any variation of the standard authorisation made under this Part must be in writing.

Notice of outcome of review

120

(1) When the review of the standard authorisation is complete, the supervisory body must give notice to all of the following –

    (a)   the managing authority of the relevant hospital or care home;
    (b)   the relevant person;
    (c)   the relevant person's representative;
    (d)   any section 39D IMCA.

(2) That notice must state –

    (a)   the outcome of the review, and
    (b)   what variation (if any) has been made to the authorisation under this Part.

Records

121

A supervisory body must keep a written record of the following information –

    (a)   each request for a review that is made to them;
    (b)   the outcome of each request;
    (c)   each review which they carry out;
    (d)   the outcome of each review which they carry out;
    (e)   any variation of an authorisation made in consequence of a review.

Relationship between review and suspension under Part 6

122

(1) This paragraph applies if a standard authorisation is suspended in accordance with Part 6.

(2) No review may be requested under this Part whilst the standard authorisation is suspended.

(3) If a review has already been requested, or is being carried out, when the standard authorisation is suspended, no steps are to be taken in connection with that review whilst the authorisation is suspended.

Relationship between review and request for new authorisation

123

(1) This paragraph applies if, in accordance with paragraph 24 (as read with paragraph 29), the managing authority of the relevant hospital or care home make a request for a new standard authorisation which would be in force after the expiry of the existing authorisation.

(2) No review may be requested under this Part until the request for the new standard authorisation has been disposed of.

(3) If a review has already been requested, or is being carried out, when the new standard authorisation is requested, no steps are to be taken in connection with that review until the request for the new standard authorisation has been disposed of.

124

(1) This paragraph applies if –

    (a)   a review under this Part has been requested, or is being carried out, and

    (b)   the managing authority of the relevant hospital or care home make a request under paragraph 30 for a new standard authorisation which would be in force on or before, and after, the expiry of the existing authorisation.

(2) No steps are to be taken in connection with the review under this Part until the request for the new standard authorisation has been disposed of.

125

In paragraphs 123 and 124 –

    (a)   the existing authorisation is the authorisation referred to in paragraph 101;

    (b)   the expiry of the existing authorisation is the time when it is expected to cease to be in force.

PART 9
ASSESSMENTS UNDER THIS SCHEDULE

Introduction

126

This Part contains provision about assessments under this Schedule.

127

An assessment under this Schedule is either of the following –

(a)   an assessment carried out in connection with a request for a standard authorisation under Part 4;

(b)   a review assessment carried out in connection with a review of a standard authorisation under Part 8.

128

In this Part, in relation to an assessment under this Schedule –

'assessor' means the person carrying out the assessment;
'relevant procedure' means –

(a)   the request for the standard authorisation, or

(b)   the review of the standard authorisation;

'supervisory body' means the supervisory body responsible for securing that the assessment is carried out.

Supervisory body to select assessor

129

(1) It is for the supervisory body to select a person to carry out an assessment under this Schedule.

(2) The supervisory body must not select a person to carry out an assessment unless the person –

(a)   appears to the supervisory body to be suitable to carry out the assessment (having regard, in particular, to the type of assessment and the person to be assessed), and

(b)   is eligible to carry out the assessment.

(3) Regulations may make provision about the selection, and eligibility, of persons to carry out assessments under this Schedule.

(4) Sub-paragraphs (5) and (6) apply if two or more assessments are to be obtained for the purposes of the relevant procedure.

(5) In a case where the assessments to be obtained include a mental health assessment and a best interests assessment, the supervisory body must not select the same person to carry out both assessments.

(6) Except as prohibited by sub-paragraph (5), the supervisory body may select the same person to carry out any number of the assessments which the person appears to be suitable, and is eligible, to carry out.

130

(1) This paragraph applies to regulations under paragraph 129(3).

(2) The regulations may make provision relating to a person's –

(a)   qualifications,

(b)   skills,

(c)   training,

(d)   experience,
(e)   relationship to, or connection with, the relevant person or any other person,
(f)   involvement in the care or treatment of the relevant person,
(g)   connection with the supervisory body, or
(h)   connection with the relevant hospital or care home, or with any other establishment or undertaking.

(3) The provision that the regulations may make in relation to a person's training may provide for particular training to be specified by the appropriate authority otherwise than in the regulations.

(4) In sub-paragraph (3) the 'appropriate authority' means –

(a)   in relation to England: the Secretary of State;
(b)   in relation to Wales: the National Assembly for Wales.

(5) The regulations may make provision requiring a person to be insured in respect of liabilities that may arise in connection with the carrying out of an assessment.

(6) In relation to cases where two or more assessments are to be obtained for the purposes of the relevant procedure, the regulations may limit the number, kind or combination of assessments which a particular person is eligible to carry out.

(7) Sub-paragraphs (2) to (6) do not limit the generality of the provision that may be made in the regulations.

Examination and copying of records

131

An assessor may, at all reasonable times, examine and take copies of –

(a)   any health record,
(b)   any record of, or held by, a local authority and compiled in accordance with a social services function, and
(c)   any record held by a person registered under Part 2 of the Care Standards Act 2000,

which the assessor considers may be relevant to the assessment which is being carried out.

Representations

132

In carrying out an assessment under this Schedule, the assessor must take into account any information given, or submissions made, by any of the following –

(a)   the relevant person's representative;
(b)   any section 39A IMCA;

    (c)   any section 39C IMCA;

    (d)   any section 39D IMCA.

Assessments to stop if any comes to negative conclusion

133

(1) This paragraph applies if an assessment under this Schedule comes to the conclusion that the relevant person does not meet one of the qualifying requirements.

(2) This Schedule does not require the supervisory body to secure that any other assessments under this Schedule are carried out in relation to the relevant procedure.

(3) The supervisory body must give notice to any assessor who is carrying out another assessment in connection with the relevant procedure that they are to cease carrying out that assessment.

(4) If an assessor receives such notice, this Schedule does not require the assessor to continue carrying out that assessment.

Duty to keep records and give copies

134

(1) This paragraph applies if an assessor has carried out an assessment under this Schedule (whatever conclusions the assessment has come to).

(2) The assessor must keep a written record of the assessment.

(3) As soon as practicable after carrying out the assessment, the assessor must give copies of the assessment to the supervisory body.

135

(1) This paragraph applies to the supervisory body if they are given a copy of an assessment under this Schedule.

(2) The supervisory body must give copies of the assessment to all of the following –

    (a)   the managing authority of the relevant hospital or care home;

    (b)   the relevant person;

    (c)   any section 39A IMCA;

    (d)   the relevant person's representative.

(3) If –

    (a)   the assessment is obtained in relation to a request for a standard authorisation, and

    (b)   the supervisory body are required by paragraph 50(1) to give the standard authorisation, the supervisory body must give the copies of the assessment when they give copies of the authorisation in accordance with paragraph 57.

(4) If –

    (a)   the assessment is obtained in relation to a request for a standard authorisation, and

    (b)   the supervisory body are prohibited by paragraph 50(2) from giving the standard authorisation,

the supervisory body must give the copies of the assessment when they give notice in accordance with paragraph 58.

(5) If the assessment is obtained in connection with the review of a standard authorisation, the supervisory body must give the copies of the assessment when they give notice in accordance with paragraph 120.

136

(1) This paragraph applies to the supervisory body if –

    (a)   they are given a copy of a best interests assessment, and

    (b)   the assessment includes, in accordance with paragraph 44(2), a statement that it appears to the assessor that there is an unauthorised deprivation of liberty.

(2) The supervisory body must notify all of the persons listed in sub-paragraph (3) that the assessment includes such a statement.

(3) Those persons are –

    (a)   the managing authority of the relevant hospital or care home;

    (b)   the relevant person;

    (c)   any section 39A IMCA;

    (d)   any interested person consulted by the best interests assessor.

(4) The supervisory body must comply with this paragraph when (or at some time before) they comply with paragraph 135.

PART 10
RELEVANT PERSON'S REPRESENTATIVE

The representative

137

In this Schedule the relevant person's representative is the person appointed as such in accordance with this Part.

138

(1) Regulations may make provision about the selection and appointment of representatives.

(2) In this Part such regulations are referred to as 'appointment regulations'.

Supervisory body to appoint representative

139

(1) The supervisory body must appoint a person to be the relevant person's representative as soon as practicable after a standard authorisation is given.

(2) The supervisory body must appoint a person to be the relevant person's representative if a vacancy arises whilst a standard authorisation is in force.

(3) Where a vacancy arises, the appointment under sub-paragraph (2) is to be made as soon as practicable after the supervisory body becomes aware of the vacancy.

140

(1) The selection of a person for appointment under paragraph 139 must not be made unless it appears to the person making the selection that the prospective representative would, if appointed –

- (a) maintain contact with the relevant person,
- (b) represent the relevant person in matters relating to or connected with this Schedule, and
- (c) support the relevant person in matters relating to or connected with this Schedule.

141

(1) Any appointment of a representative for a relevant person is in addition to, and does not affect, any appointment of a donee or deputy.

(2) The functions of any representative are in addition to, and do not affect –

- (a) the authority of any donee,
- (b) the powers of any deputy, or
- (c) any powers of the court.

Appointment regulations

142

Appointment regulations may provide that the procedure for appointing a representative may begin at any time after a request for a standard authorisation is made (including a time before the request has been disposed of).

143

(1) Appointment regulations may make provision about who is to select a person for appointment as a representative.

(2) But regulations under this paragraph may only provide for the following to make a selection –

    (a)   the relevant person, if he has capacity in relation to the question of which person should be his representative;

    (b)   a donee of a lasting power of attorney granted by the relevant person, if it is within the scope of his authority to select a person;

    (c)   a deputy, if it is within the scope of his authority to select a person;

    (d)   a best interests assessor;

    (e)   the supervisory body.

(3) Regulations under this paragraph may provide that a selection by the relevant person, a donee or a deputy is subject to approval by a best interests assessor or the supervisory body.

(4) Regulations under this paragraph may provide that, if more than one selection is necessary in connection with the appointment of a particular representative –

    (a)   the same person may make more than one selection;

    (b)   different persons may make different selections.

(5) For the purposes of this paragraph a best interests assessor is a person carrying out a best interests assessment in connection with the standard authorisation in question (including the giving of that authorisation).

144

(1) Appointment regulations may make provision about who may, or may not, be –

    (a)   selected for appointment as a representative, or

    (b)   appointed as a representative.

(2) Regulations under this paragraph may relate to any of the following matters –

    (a)   a person's age;

    (b)   a person's suitability;

    (c)   a person's independence;

    (d)   a person's willingness;

    (e)   a person's qualifications.

145

Appointment regulations may make provision about the formalities of appointing a person as a representative.

146

In a case where a best interests assessor is to select a person to be appointed as a representative, appointment regulations may provide for the variation of the assessor's duties in relation to the assessment which he is carrying out.

Monitoring of representatives

147

Regulations may make provision requiring the managing authority of the relevant hospital or care home to –

    (a)   monitor, and
    (b)   report to the supervisory body on,

the extent to which a representative is maintaining contact with the relevant person.

Termination

148

Regulations may make provision about the circumstances in which the appointment of a person as the relevant person's representative ends or may be ended.

149

Regulations may make provision about the formalities of ending the appointment of a person as a representative.

Suspension of representative's functions

150

(1) Regulations may make provision about the circumstances in which functions exercisable by, or in relation to, the relevant person's representative (whether under this Schedule or not) may be –

    (a)   suspended, and
    (b)   if suspended, revived.

(2) The regulations may make provision about the formalities for giving effect to the suspension or revival of a function.

(3) The regulations may make provision about the effect of the suspension or revival of a function.

Payment of representative

151

Regulations may make provision for payments to be made to, or in relation to, persons exercising functions as the relevant person's representative.

Regulations under this Part

152

The provisions of this Part which specify provision that may be made in regulations under this Part do not affect the generality of the power to make such regulations.

Effect of appointment of section 39C IMCA

153

Paragraphs 159 and 160 make provision about the exercise of functions by, or towards, the relevant person's representative during periods when –

(a) no person is appointed as the relevant person's representative, but
(b) a person is appointed as a section 39C IMCA.

PART 11
IMCAS

Application of Part

154

This Part applies for the purposes of this Schedule.

The IMCAs

155

A section 39A IMCA is an independent mental capacity advocate appointed under section 39A.

156

A section 39C IMCA is an independent mental capacity advocate appointed under section 39C.

157

A section 39D IMCA is an independent mental capacity advocate appointed under section 39D.

158

An IMCA is a section 39A IMCA or a section 39C IMCA or a section 39D IMCA.

Section 39C IMCA: functions

159

(1) This paragraph applies if, and for as long as, there is a section 39C IMCA.

(2) In the application of the relevant provisions, references to the relevant person's representative are to be read as references to the section 39C IMCA.

(3) But sub-paragraph (2) does not apply to any function under the relevant provisions for as long as the function is suspended in accordance with provision made under Part 10.

(4) In this paragraph and paragraph 160 the relevant provisions are –

    (a)   paragraph 102(3)(b) (request for review under Part 8);
    (b)   paragraph 108(1)(b) (notice of review under Part 8);
    (c)   paragraph 120(1)(c) (notice of outcome of review under Part 8).

160

(1) This paragraph applies if –

    (a)   a person is appointed as the relevant person's representative, and
    (b)   a person accordingly ceases to hold an appointment as a section 39C IMCA.

(2) Where a function under a relevant provision has been exercised by, or towards, the section 39C IMCA, there is no requirement for that function to be exercised again by, or towards, the relevant person's representative.

Section 39A IMCA: restriction of functions

161

(1) This paragraph applies if –

    (a)   there is a section 39A IMCA, and
    (b)   a person is appointed under Part 10 to be the relevant person's representative (whether or not that person, or any person subsequently appointed, is currently the relevant person's representative).

(2) The duties imposed on, and the powers exercisable by, the section 39A IMCA do not apply.

(3) The duties imposed on, and the powers exercisable by, any other person do not apply, so far as they fall to be performed or exercised towards the section 39A IMCA.

(4) But sub-paragraph (2) does not apply to any power of challenge exercisable by the section 39A IMCA.

(5) And sub-paragraph (3) does not apply to any duty or power of any other person so far as it relates to any power of challenge exercisable by the section 39A IMCA.

(6) Before exercising any power of challenge, the section 39A IMCA must take the views of the relevant person's representative into account.

(7) A power of challenge is a power to make an application to the court to exercise its jurisdiction under section 21A in connection with the giving of the standard authorisation.

PART 12
MISCELLANEOUS

Monitoring of operation of Schedule

162

(1) Regulations may make provision for, and in connection with, requiring one or more prescribed bodies to monitor, and report on, the operation of this Schedule in relation to England.

(2) The regulations may, in particular, give a prescribed body authority to do one or more of the following things –

    (a)   to visit hospitals and care homes;

    (b)   to visit and interview persons accommodated in hospitals and care homes;

    (c)   to require the production of, and to inspect, records relating to the care or treatment of persons.

(3) 'Prescribed' means prescribed in regulations under this paragraph.

163

(1) Regulations may make provision for, and in connection with, enabling the National Assembly for Wales to monitor, and report on, the operation of this Schedule in relation to Wales.

(2) The National Assembly may direct one or more persons or bodies to carry out the Assembly's functions under regulations under this paragraph.

Disclosure of information

164

(1) Regulations may require either or both of the following to disclose prescribed information to prescribed bodies –

(a)   supervisory bodies;
(b)   managing authorities of hospitals or care homes.

(2) 'Prescribed' means prescribed in regulations under this paragraph.

(3) Regulations under this paragraph may only prescribe information relating to matters with which this Schedule is concerned.

Directions by National Assembly in relation to supervisory functions

165

(1) The National Assembly for Wales may direct a Local Health Board to exercise in relation to its area any supervisory functions which are specified in the direction.

(2) Directions under this paragraph must not preclude the National Assembly from exercising the functions specified in the directions.

(3) In this paragraph 'supervisory functions' means functions which the National Assembly have as supervisory body, so far as they are exercisable in relation to hospitals (whether NHS or independent hospitals, and whether in Wales or England).

166

(1) This paragraph applies where, under paragraph 165, a Local Health Board ('the specified LHB') is directed to exercise supervisory functions ('delegated functions').

(2) The National Assembly for Wales may give directions to the specified LHB about the Board's exercise of delegated functions.

(3) The National Assembly may give directions for any delegated functions to be exercised, on behalf of the specified LHB, by a committee, sub-committee or officer of that Board.

(4) The National Assembly may give directions providing for any delegated functions to be exercised by the specified LHB jointly with one or more other Local Health Boards.

(5) Where, under sub-paragraph (4), delegated functions are exercisable jointly, the National Assembly may give directions providing for the functions to be exercised, on behalf of the Local Health Boards in question, by a joint committee or joint sub-committee.

167

(1) Directions under paragraph 165 must be given in regulations.

(2) Directions under paragraph 166 may be given –

    (a)   in regulations, or

    (b)   by instrument in writing.

168

The power under paragraph 165 or paragraph 166 to give directions includes power to vary or revoke directions given under that paragraph.

Notices

169

Any notice under this Schedule must be in writing.

Regulations

170

(1) This paragraph applies to all regulations under this Schedule, except regulations under paragraph 162, 163, 167 or 183.

(2) It is for the Secretary of State to make such regulations in relation to authorisations under this Schedule which relate to hospitals and care homes situated in England.

(3) It is for the National Assembly for Wales to make such regulations in relation to authorisations under this Schedule which relate to hospitals and care homes situated in Wales.

171

It is for the Secretary of State to make regulations under paragraph 162.

172

It is for the National Assembly for Wales to make regulations under paragraph 163 or 167.

173

(1) This paragraph applies to regulations under paragraph 183.

(2) It is for the Secretary of State to make such regulations in relation to cases where a question as to the ordinary residence of a person is to be determined by the Secretary of State.

(3) It is for the National Assembly for Wales to make such regulations in relation to cases where a question as to the ordinary residence of a person is to be determined by the National Assembly.

PART 13
INTERPRETATION

Introduction

174

This Part applies for the purposes of this Schedule.

Hospitals and their managing authorities

175

(1) 'Hospital' means –

    (a)   an NHS hospital, or
    (b)   an independent hospital.

(2) 'NHS hospital' means –

    (a)   a health service hospital as defined by section 275 of the National Health Service Act 2006 or section 206 of the National Health Service (Wales) Act 2006, or
    (b)   a hospital as defined by section 206 of the National Health Service (Wales) Act 2006 vested in a Local Health Board.

(3) 'Independent hospital' means a hospital as defined by section 2 of the Care Standards Act 2000 which is not an NHS hospital.

176

(1) 'Managing authority', in relation to an NHS hospital, means –

    (a)   if the hospital –
        (i)   is vested in the appropriate national authority for the purposes of its functions under the National Health Service Act 2006 or of the National Health Service (Wales) Act 2006, or
        (ii)   consists of any accommodation provided by a local authority and used as a hospital by or on behalf of the appropriate national authority under either of those Acts,
   the Primary Care Trust, Strategic Health Authority, Local Health Board or Special Health Authority responsible for the administration of the hospital;
    (b)   if the hospital is vested in a Primary Care Trust, National Health Service trust or NHS foundation trust, that trust;
    (c)   if the hospital is vested in a Local Health Board, that Board.

(2) For this purpose the appropriate national authority is –

    (a)   in relation to England: the Secretary of State;
    (b)   in relation to Wales: the National Assembly for Wales;

(c)   in relation to England and Wales: the Secretary of State and the National Assembly acting jointly.

177

'Managing authority', in relation to an independent hospital, means the person registered, or required to be registered, under Part 2 of the Care Standards Act 2000 in respect of the hospital.

Care homes and their managing authorities

178

'Care home' has the meaning given by section 3 of the Care Standards Act 2000.

179

'Managing authority', in relation to a care home, means the person registered, or required to be registered, under Part 2 of the Care Standards Act 2000 in respect of the care home.

Supervisory bodies: hospitals

180

(1) The identity of the supervisory body is determined under this paragraph in cases where the relevant hospital is situated in England.

(2) If a Primary Care Trust commissions the relevant care or treatment, that Trust is the supervisory body.

(3) If the National Assembly for Wales or a Local Health Board commission the relevant care or treatment, the National Assembly are the supervisory body.

(4) In any other case, the supervisory body are the Primary Care Trust for the area in which the relevant hospital is situated.

(5) If a hospital is situated in the areas of two (or more) Primary Care Trusts, it is to be regarded for the purposes of sub-paragraph (4) as situated in whichever of the areas the greater (or greatest) part of the hospital is situated.

181

(1) The identity of the supervisory body is determined under this paragraph in cases where the relevant hospital is situated in Wales.

(2) The National Assembly for Wales are the supervisory body.

(3) But if a Primary Care Trust commissions the relevant care or treatment, that Trust is the supervisory body.

Supervisory bodies: care homes

182

(1) The identity of the supervisory body is determined under this paragraph in cases where the relevant care home is situated in England or in Wales.

(2) The supervisory body are the local authority for the area in which the relevant person is ordinarily resident.

(3) But if the relevant person is not ordinarily resident in the area of a local authority, the supervisory body are the local authority for the area in which the care home is situated.

(4) In relation to England 'local authority' means –

    (a)   the council of a county;
    (b)   the council of a district for which there is no county council;
    (c)   the council of a London borough;
    (d)   the Common Council of the City of London;
    (e)   the Council of the Isles of Scilly.

(5) In relation to Wales 'local authority' means the council of a county or county borough.

(6) If a care home is situated in the areas of two (or more) local authorities, it is to be regarded for the purposes of sub-paragraph (3) as situated in whichever of the areas the greater (or greatest) part of the care home is situated.

183

(1) Subsections (5) and (6) of section 24 of the National Assistance Act 1948 (deemed place of ordinary residence) apply to any determination of where a person is ordinarily resident for the purposes of paragraph 182 as those subsections apply to such a determination for the purposes specified in those subsections.

(2) In the application of section 24(6) of the 1948 Act by virtue of subsection (1), section 24(6) is to be read as if it referred to a hospital vested in a Local Health Board as well as to hospitals vested in the Secretary of State and the other bodies mentioned in section 24(6).

(3) Any question arising as to the ordinary residence of a person is to be determined by the Secretary of State or by the National Assembly for Wales.

(4) The Secretary of State and the National Assembly must make and publish arrangements for determining which cases are to be dealt with by the Secretary of State and which are to be dealt with by the National Assembly.

(5) Those arrangements may include provision for the Secretary of State and the National Assembly to agree, in relation to any question that has arisen, which of them is to deal with the case.

(6) Regulations may make provision about arrangements that are to have effect before, upon, or after the determination of any question as to the ordinary residence of a person.

(7) The regulations may, in particular, authorise or require a local authority to do any or all of the following things –

>   (a)   to act as supervisory body even though it may wish to dispute that it is the supervisory body;
>   (b)   to become the supervisory body in place of another local authority;
>   (c)   to recover from another local authority expenditure incurred in exercising functions as the supervisory body.

Same body managing authority and supervisory body

184

(1) This paragraph applies if, in connection with a particular person's detention as a resident in a hospital or care home, the same body are both –

>   (a)   the managing authority of the relevant hospital or care home, and
>   (b)   the supervisory body.

(2) The fact that a single body are acting in both capacities does not prevent the body from carrying out functions under this Schedule in each capacity.

(3) But, in such a case, this Schedule has effect subject to any modifications contained in regulations that may be made for this purpose.

Interested persons

185

Each of the following is an interested person –

>   (a)   the relevant person's spouse or civil partner;
>   (b)   where the relevant person and another person of the opposite sex are not married to each other but are living together as husband and wife: the other person;
>   (c)   where the relevant person and another person of the same sex are not civil partners of each other but are living together as if they were civil partners: the other person;
>   (d)   the relevant person's children and step-children;
>   (e)   the relevant person's parents and step-parents;

(f)   the relevant person's brothers and sisters, half-brothers and half-sisters, and stepbrothers and stepsisters;

(g)   the relevant person's grandparents;

(h)   a deputy appointed for the relevant person by the court;

(i)   a donee of a lasting power of attorney granted by the relevant person.

186

(1) An interested person consulted by the best interests assessor is any person whose name is stated in the relevant best interests assessment in accordance with paragraph 40 (interested persons whom the assessor consulted in carrying out the assessment).

(2) The relevant best interests assessment is the most recent best interests assessment carried out in connection with the standard authorisation in question (whether the assessment was carried out under Part 4 or Part 8).

187

Where this Schedule imposes on a person a duty towards an interested person, the duty does not apply if the person on whom the duty is imposed –

(a)   is not aware of the interested person's identity or of a way of contacting him, and

(b)   cannot reasonably ascertain it.

188

The following table contains an index of provisions defining or otherwise explaining expressions used in this Schedule –

age assessment	paragraph 34
age requirement	paragraph 13
age review assessment	paragraph 112(3)
appointment regulations	paragraph 138
assessment under this Schedule	paragraph 127
assessor (except in Part 8)	paragraph 33
assessor (in Part 8)	paragraphs 33 and 128
authorisation under this Schedule	paragraph 10
best interests (determination of) section 4	
best interests assessment	paragraph 38
best interests requirement	paragraph 16
best interests review assessment	paragraph 112(6)
care home	paragraph 178

SCHEDULE 8
Mental Capacity Act 2005: new Schedule 1A

Section 50

After Schedule 1 to the Mental Capacity Act 2005 (c 9) insert –

'SCHEDULE 1A
Persons ineligible to be deprived of liberty by this Act

PART 1
INELIGIBLE PERSONS

Application

1

This Schedule applies for the purposes of –

(a)   section 16A, and
(b)   paragraph 17 of Schedule A1.

Determining ineligibility

2

A person ('P') is ineligible to be deprived of liberty by this Act ('ineligible') if –

(a)   P falls within one of the cases set out in the second column of the following table, and
(b)   the corresponding entry in the third column of the table –or the provision, or one of the provisions, referred to in that entry – provides that he is ineligible.

	Status of P	*Determination of ineligibility*
Case A	P is – (a) subject to the hospital treatment regime, and (b) detained in a hospital under that regime.	P is ineligible.
Case B	P is – (a) subject to the hospital treatment regime, but (b) not detained in a hospital under that regime.	See paragraphs 3 and 4.

Case C	P is subject to the community treatment regime.	See paragraphs 3 and 4.
Case D	P is subject to the guardianship regime.	See paragraphs 3 and 5.
Case E	P is – (a) within the scope of the Mental Health Act, but (b) not subject to any of the mental health regimes.	See paragraph 5.

Authorised course of action not in accordance with regime

3

(1) This paragraph applies in cases B, C and D in the table in paragraph 2.

(2) P is ineligible if the authorised course of action is not in accordance with a requirement which the relevant regime imposes.

(3) That includes any requirement as to where P is, or is not, to reside.

(4) The relevant regime is the mental health regime to which P is subject.

Treatment for mental disorder in a hospital

4

(1) This paragraph applies in cases B and C in the table in paragraph 2.

(2) P is ineligible if the relevant care or treatment consists in whole or in part of medical treatment for mental disorder in a hospital.

P objects to being a mental health patient etc

5

(1) This paragraph applies in cases D and E in the table in paragraph 2.

(2) P is ineligible if the following conditions are met.

(3) The first condition is that the relevant instrument authorises P to be a mental health patient.

(4) The second condition is that P objects –

    (a)   to being a mental health patient, or
    (b)   to being given some or all of the mental health treatment.

(5) The third condition is that a donee or deputy has not made a valid decision to consent to each matter to which P objects.

(6) In determining whether or not P objects to something, regard must be had to all the circumstances (so far as they are reasonably ascertainable), including the following –

    (a)   P's behaviour;

    (b)   P's wishes and feelings;

    (c)   P's views, beliefs and values.

(7) But regard is to be had to circumstances from the past only so far as it is still appropriate to have regard to them.

PART 2
INTERPRETATION

Application

6

This Part applies for the purposes of this Schedule.

Mental health regimes

7

The mental health regimes are –

    (a)   the hospital treatment regime,

    (b)   the community treatment regime, and

    (c)   the guardianship regime.

Hospital treatment regime

8

(1) P is subject to the hospital treatment regime if he is subject to –

    (a)   a hospital treatment obligation under the relevant enactment, or

    (b)   an obligation under another England and Wales enactment which has the same effect as a hospital treatment obligation.

(2) But where P is subject to any such obligation, he is to be regarded as not subject to the hospital treatment regime during any period when he is subject to the community treatment regime.

(3) A hospital treatment obligation is an application, order or direction of a kind listed in the first column of the following table.

(4) In relation to a hospital treatment obligation, the relevant enactment is the enactment in the Mental Health Act which is referred to in the corresponding entry in the second column of the following table.

Hospital treatment obligation	Relevant enactment
Application for admission for assessment	Section 2
Application for admission for assessment	Section 4
Application for admission for treatment	Section 3
Order for remand to hospital	Section 35
Order for remand to hospital	Section 36
Hospital order	Section 37
Interim hospital order	Section 38
Order for detention in hospital	Section 44
Hospital direction	Section 45A
Transfer direction	Section 47
Transfer direction	Section 48
Hospital order	Section 51

Community treatment regime

9

P is subject to the community treatment regime if he is subject to –

    (a)   a community treatment order under section 17A of the Mental Health Act, or

    (b)   an obligation under another England and Wales enactment which has the same effect as a community treatment order.

Guardianship regime

10

P is subject to the guardianship regime if he is subject to –

    (a)   a guardianship application under section 7 of the Mental Health Act,

    (b)   a guardianship order under section 37 of the Mental Health Act, or

    (c)   an obligation under another England and Wales enactment which has the same effect as a guardianship application or guardianship order.

England and Wales enactments

11

(1) An England and Wales enactment is an enactment which extends to England and Wales (whether or not it also extends elsewhere).

(2) It does not matter if the enactment is in the Mental Health Act or not.

P within scope of Mental Health Act

12

(1) P is within the scope of the Mental Health Act if –

    (a)   an application in respect of P could be made under section 2 or 3 of the Mental Health Act, and

    (b)   P could be detained in a hospital in pursuance of such an application, were one made.

(2) The following provisions of this paragraph apply when determining whether an application in respect of P could be made under section 2 or 3 of the Mental Health Act.

(3) If the grounds in section 2(2) of the Mental Health Act are met in P's case, it is to be assumed that the recommendations referred to in section 2(3) of that Act have been given.

(4) If the grounds in section 3(2) of the Mental Health Act are met in P's case, it is to be assumed that the recommendations referred to in section 3(3) of that Act have been given.

(5) In determining whether the ground in section 3(2)(c) of the Mental Health Act is met in P's case, it is to be assumed that the treatment referred to in section 3(2)(c) cannot be provided under this Act.

Authorised course of action, relevant care or treatment & relevant instrument

13

In a case where this Schedule applies for the purposes of section 16A –

    'authorised course of action' means any course of action amounting to deprivation of liberty which the order under section 16(2)(a) authorises;

    'relevant care or treatment' means any care or treatment which –

        (a)   comprises, or forms part of, the authorised course of action, or

        (b)   is to be given in connection with the authorised course of action;

    'relevant instrument' means the order under section 16(2)(a).

14

In a case where this Schedule applies for the purposes of paragraph 17 of Schedule A1 –

'authorised course of action' means the accommodation of the relevant person in the relevant hospital or care home for the purpose of being given the relevant care or treatment;
'relevant care or treatment' has the same meaning as in Schedule A1;
'relevant instrument' means the standard authorisation under Schedule A1.

15

(1) This paragraph applies where the question whether a person is ineligible to be deprived of liberty by this Act is relevant to either of these decisions –

(a) whether or not to include particular provision ('the proposed provision') in an order under section 16(2)(a);
(b) whether or not to give a standard authorisation under Schedule A1.

(2) A reference in this Schedule to the authorised course of action or the relevant care or treatment is to be read as a reference to that thing as it would be if –

(a) the proposed provision were included in the order, or
(b) the standard authorisation were given.

(3) A reference in this Schedule to the relevant instrument is to be read as follows –

(a) where the relevant instrument is an order under section 16(2)(a): as a reference to the order as it would be if the proposed provision were included in it;
(b) where the relevant instrument is a standard authorisation: as a reference to the standard authorisation as it would be if it were given.

Expressions used in paragraph 5

16

(1) These expressions have the meanings given –

'donee' means a donee of a lasting power of attorney granted by P;
'mental health patient' means a person accommodated in a hospital for the purpose of being given medical treatment for mental disorder;
'mental health treatment' means the medical treatment for mental disorder referred to in the definition of 'mental health patient'.

(2) A decision of a donee or deputy is valid if it is made –

(a)   within the scope of his authority as donee or deputy, and

(b)   in accordance with Part 1 of this Act.

Expressions with same meaning as in Mental Health Act

17

(1) 'Hospital' has the same meaning as in Part 2 of the Mental Health Act.

(2) 'Medical treatment' has the same meaning as in the Mental Health Act.

(3) 'Mental disorder' has the same meaning as in Schedule A1 (see paragraph 14).'.

SCHEDULE 9

Amendments relating to new section 4A of, & Schedule A1 to, Mental Capacity Act 2005

Section 50

PART 1

OTHER AMENDMENTS TO MENTAL CAPACITY ACT 2005

Introduction

1

The Mental Capacity Act 2005 (c 9) is amended as set out in this Part of this Schedule.

New section 21A

2

After section 21 insert –

'Powers of the court in relation to Schedule A1

21A Powers of court in relation to Schedule A1

(1) This section applies if either of the following has been given under Schedule A1 –

(a)   a standard authorisation;

(b)   an urgent authorisation.

(2) Where a standard authorisation has been given, the court may determine any question relating to any of the following matters –

(a)   whether the relevant person meets one or more of the qualifying requirements;

(b)   the period during which the standard authorisation is to be in force;

(c)   the purpose for which the standard authorisation is given;

(d)   the conditions subject to which the standard authorisation is given.

(3) If the court determines any question under subsection (2), the court may make an order –

(a)   varying or terminating the standard authorisation, or

(b)   directing the supervisory body to vary or terminate the standard authorisation.

(4) Where an urgent authorisation has been given, the court may determine any question relating to any of the following matters –

(a)   whether the urgent authorisation should have been given;

(b)   the period during which the urgent authorisation is to be in force;

(c)   the purpose for which the urgent authorisation is given.

(5) Where the court determines any question under subsection (4), the court may make an order –

(a)   varying or terminating the urgent authorisation, or

(b)   directing the managing authority of the relevant hospital or care home to vary or terminate the urgent authorisation.

(6) Where the court makes an order under subsection (3) or (5), the court may make an order about a person's liability for any act done in connection with the standard or urgent authorisation before its variation or termination.

(7) An order under subsection (6) may, in particular, exclude a person from liability.'

Section 35: Appointment of independent mental capacity advocates

3

In section 35, in subsection (1) after 'relate' insert 'or persons who fall within section 39A, 39C or 39D'.

Section 38: IMCAs and provision of accommodation by NHS body

4

(1) Section 38 is amended as follows.

(2) After subsection (2) insert –

'(2A) And this section does not apply if –

(a)   an independent mental capacity advocate must be appointed under section 39A or 39C (whether or not by the NHS body) to represent P, and

(b)   the hospital or care home in which P is to be accommodated under the arrangements referred to in this section is the relevant hospital or care home under the authorisation referred to in that section.'

(3) After subsection (9) insert –

'(10) For the purposes of subsection (1), a person appointed under Part 10 of Schedule A1 to be P's representative is not, by virtue of that appointment, engaged in providing care or treatment for P in a professional capacity or for remuneration.'

Section 39: IMCAs and provision of accommodation by local authority

5

(1) Section 39 is amended as follows.

(2) After subsection (3) insert –

'(3A) And this section does not apply if –

(a)   an independent mental capacity advocate must be appointed under section 39A or 39C (whether or not by the local authority) to represent P, and
(b)   the place in which P is to be accommodated under the arrangements referred to in this section is the relevant hospital or care home under the authorisation referred to in that section.'

(3) After subsection (6) insert –

'(7) For the purposes of subsection (1), a person appointed under Part 10 of Schedule A1 to be P's representative is not, by virtue of that appointment, engaged in providing care or treatment for P in a professional capacity or for remuneration.'

New section 39A

6

After section 39 insert –

'39A Person becomes subject to Schedule A1

(1) This section applies if –

(a)   a person ('P') becomes subject to Schedule A1, and
(b)   the managing authority of the relevant hospital or care home are satisfied that there is no person, other than one engaged in providing care or treatment for P in a professional capacity or for remuneration, whom it would be appropriate to consult in determining what would be in P's best interests.

(2) The managing authority must notify the supervisory body that this section applies.

(3) The supervisory body must instruct an independent mental capacity advocate to represent P.

(4) Schedule A1 makes provision about the role of an independent mental capacity advocate appointed under this section.

(5) This section is subject to paragraph 161 of Schedule A1.

(6) For the purposes of subsection (1), a person appointed under Part 10 of Schedule A1 to be P's representative is not, by virtue of that appointment, engaged in providing care or treatment for P in a professional capacity or for remuneration.

39B Section 39A: supplementary provision

(1) This section applies for the purposes of section 39A.

(2) P becomes subject to Schedule A1 in any of the following cases.

(3) The first case is where an urgent authorisation is given in relation to P under paragraph 76(2) of Schedule A1 (urgent authorisation given before request made for standard authorisation).

(4) The second case is where the following conditions are met.

(5) The first condition is that a request is made under Schedule A1 for a standard authorisation to be given in relation to P ('the requested authorisation').

(6) The second condition is that no urgent authorisation was given under paragraph 76(2) of Schedule A1 before that request was made.

(7) The third condition is that the requested authorisation will not be in force on or before, or immediately after, the expiry of an existing standard authorisation.

(8) The expiry of a standard authorisation is the date when the authorisation is expected to cease to be in force.

(9) The third case is where, under paragraph 69 of Schedule A1, the supervisory body select a person to carry out an assessment of whether or not the relevant person is a detained resident.

39C Person unrepresented whilst subject to Schedule A1

(1) This section applies if –

  (a)   an authorisation under Schedule A1 is in force in relation to a person ('P'),
  (b)   the appointment of a person as P's representative ends in accordance with regulations made under Part 10 of Schedule A1, and
  (c)   the managing authority of the relevant hospital or care home are satisfied that there is no person, other than one engaged in providing care or treatment for P in a professional capacity or for

remuneration, whom it would be appropriate to consult in determining what would be in P's best interests.

(2) The managing authority must notify the supervisory body that this section applies.

(3) The supervisory body must instruct an independent mental capacity advocate to represent P.

(4) Paragraph 159 of Schedule A1 makes provision about the role of an independent mental capacity advocate appointed under this section.

(5) The appointment of an independent mental capacity advocate under this section ends when a new appointment of a person as P's representative is made in accordance with Part 10 of Schedule A1.

(6) For the purposes of subsection (1), a person appointed under Part 10 of Schedule A1 to be P's representative is not, by virtue of that appointment, engaged in providing care or treatment for P in a professional capacity or for remuneration.

39D Person subject to Schedule A1 without paid representative

(1) This section applies if –

   (a)   an authorisation under Schedule A1 is in force in relation to a person ('P'),

   (b)   P has a representative ('R') appointed under Part 10 of Schedule A1, and

   (c)   R is not being paid under regulations under Part 10 of Schedule A1 for acting as P's representative.

(2) The supervisory body must instruct an independent mental capacity advocate to represent P in any of the following cases.

(3) The first case is where P makes a request to the supervisory body to instruct an advocate.

(4) The second case is where R makes a request to the supervisory body to instruct an advocate.

(5) The third case is where the supervisory body have reason to believe one or more of the following –

   (a)   that, without the help of an advocate, P and R would be unable to exercise one or both of the relevant rights;

   (b)   that P and R have each failed to exercise a relevant right when it would have been reasonable to exercise it;

   (c)   that P and R are each unlikely to exercise a relevant right when it would be reasonable to exercise it.

(6) The duty in subsection (2) is subject to section 39E.

(7) If an advocate is appointed under this section, the advocate is, in particular, to take such steps as are practicable to help P and R to understand the following matters –

    (a)   the effect of the authorisation;
    (b)   the purpose of the authorisation;
    (c)   the duration of the authorisation;
    (d)   any conditions to which the authorisation is subject;
    (e)   the reasons why each assessor who carried out an assessment in connection with the request for the authorisation, or in connection with a review of the authorisation, decided that P met the qualifying requirement in question;
    (f)   the relevant rights;
    (g)   how to exercise the relevant rights.

(8) The advocate is, in particular, to take such steps as are practicable to help P or R –

    (a)   to exercise the right to apply to court, if it appears to the advocate that P or R wishes to exercise that right, or
    (b)   to exercise the right of review, if it appears to the advocate that P or R wishes to exercise that right.

(9) If the advocate helps P or R to exercise the right of review –

    (a)   the advocate may make submissions to the supervisory body on the question of whether a qualifying requirement is reviewable;
    (b)   the advocate may give information, or make submissions, to any assessor carrying out a review assessment.

(10) In this section –

'relevant rights' means –

    (a)   the right to apply to court, and
    (b)   the right of review;

'right to apply to court' means the right to make an application to the court to exercise its jurisdiction under section 21A;
'right of review' means the right under Part 8 of Schedule A1 to request a review.

39E Limitation on duty to instruct advocate under section 39D

(1) This section applies if an advocate is already representing P in accordance with an instruction under section 39D.

(2) Section 39D(2) does not require another advocate to be instructed, unless the following conditions are met.

(3) The first condition is that the existing advocate was instructed –

    (a)   because of a request by R, or
    (b)   because the supervisory body had reason to believe one or more of the things in section 39D(5).

(4) The second condition is that the other advocate would be instructed because of a request by P.'

Section 40: Exceptions to duty to appoint IMCAs

7

(1) Section 40 (as substituted by section 49 of this Act) is amended as follows.

(2) The provision of section 40 becomes subsection (1) of section 40.

(3) In subsection (1) for 'or 39(4) or (5)' substitute ', 39(4) or (5), 39A(3), 39C(3) or 39D(2)'.

(4) After subsection (1) insert –

'(2) A person appointed under Part 10 of Schedule A1 to be P's representative is not, by virtue of that appointment, a person nominated by P as a person to be consulted in matters to which a duty mentioned in subsection (1) relates.'

Section 42: Codes of practice

8

(1) Section 42 is amended as follows.

(2) In subsection (1), after paragraph (f) insert –

'(fa) for the guidance of persons exercising functions under Schedule A1,
(fb) for the guidance of representatives appointed under Part 10 of Schedule A1,'.

(3) In subsection (4), after paragraph (d) insert –

'(da) in the exercise of functions under Schedule A1,
(db) as a representative appointed under Part 10 of Schedule A1,'.

Section 50: Application to the Court of Protection

9

In section 50, after subsection (1) insert –

'(1A) Nor is permission required for an application to the court under section 21A by the relevant person's representative.'

Section 64: Interpretation

10

(1) Section 64 is amended as follows.

(2) In subsection (1), insert at the appropriate place –

"authorisation under Schedule A1' means either –

(a)   a standard authorisation under that Schedule, or

(b)   an urgent authorisation under that Schedule.'

(3) In subsection (1), in the definition of 'local authority' after "local authority" insert ', except in Schedule A1,'.

(4) After subsection (4) insert –

'(5) In this Act, references to deprivation of a person's liberty have the same meaning as in Article 5(1) of the Human Rights Convention.

(6) For the purposes of such references, it does not matter whether a person is deprived of his liberty by a public authority or not.'

Section 65: Rules, regulations and orders

11

(1) Section 65 is amended as follows.

(2) After subsection (4) insert –

'(4A) Subsection (2) does not apply to a statutory instrument containing regulations made by the Secretary of State under Schedule A1.

(4B) If such a statutory instrument contains regulations under paragraph 42(2)(b), 129, 162 or 164 of Schedule A1 (whether or not it also contains other regulations), the instrument may not be made unless a draft has been laid before and approved by resolution of each House of Parliament.

(4C) Subject to that, such a statutory instrument is subject to annulment in pursuance of a resolution of either House of Parliament.'

PART 2
AMENDMENTS TO OTHER ACTS

National Assistance Act 1948 (c 29)

12

(1) Section 47 of the National Assistance Act 1948 (removal to suitable premises of persons in need of care and attention) is amended as follows.

(2) After subsection (1) insert –

'(1A) But this section does not apply to a person ('P') in either of the following cases.

(1B) The first case is where an order of the Court of Protection authorises the managing authority of a hospital or care home (within the meaning of Schedule A1 to the Mental Capacity Act 2005) to provide P with proper care and attention.

(1C) The second case is where –

    (a)   an authorisation under Schedule A1 to the Mental Capacity Act 2005 is in force, or

    (b)   the managing authority of a hospital or care home are under a duty under paragraph 24 of that Schedule to request a standard authorisation, and

P is, or would be, the relevant person in relation to the authorisation.'

(3) This paragraph does not extend to Scotland.

Local Authority Social Services Act 1970 (c 42)

13

(1) Schedule 1 to the Local Authority Social Services Act 1970 (Social Services functions of local authorities) is amended as follows.

(2) In the entry relating to the Mental Capacity Act 2005 (c 9), insert the following entries at the appropriate places –

'Section 39A	Instructing independent mental capacity advocate when giving an urgent authorisation, or making a request for a standard authorisation, under Schedule A1 to the Act.'
'Section 39C	Instructing independent mental capacity advocate when no representative for relevant person under Part 10 of Schedule A1 to the Act.'
'Section 39D	Instructing independent mental capacity advocate when representative for relevant person under Part 10 of Schedule A1 to the Act is not being paid.'
'Schedule A1	Any functions.'

SCHEDULE 10
Transitional provisions and savings

Section 53

Interpretation

1

(1) This Schedule is to be read as follows.

(2) Reference to an enactment is to an enactment contained in this Act, unless otherwise stated.

(3) Reference to an enactment contained in the 1983 Act includes reference to that enactment as applied by section 40(4) of that Act (patients concerned in criminal proceedings or under sentence).

Authority to detain etc

2

(1) The provisions mentioned in sub-paragraph (4) do not affect –

    (a)   the authority for the detention or guardianship of a person who is liable to be detained or subject to guardianship under the 1983 Act immediately before the date on which those provisions come into force,

    (b)   the 1983 Act in relation to any application, order or direction for admission or removal to a hospital, or any guardianship application or order, made under that Act before that date or the exercise, before that date, of any power to remand,

    (c)   the power to make on or after that date an application for the admission of a person to a hospital, or a guardianship application, where all the recommendations on which the application is to be founded are signed before that date, or

    (d)   the authority for the detention or guardianship of a person in pursuance of such an application.

(2) But those provisions do apply to the following events occurring on or after that date –

    (a)   any renewal of the authority for the person's detention or guardianship,

    (b)   any consideration of his case by a Mental Health Review Tribunal, and

    (c)   any decision about the exercise of any power to discharge him from detention or guardianship.

(3) Sub-paragraph (2)(b) is subject to paragraph 4.

(4) The provisions are –

    (a)   section 1 and Schedule 1 (removal of categories of mental disorder),

    (b)   section 2 (special provision for persons with learning disability),

    (c)   section 3 (exclusions),

    (d)   section 4 (replacement of 'treatability' and 'care' tests with appropriate treatment test),

    (e)   section 5 (addition of appropriate treatment test),

    (f)   section 7 (definition of 'medical treatment'), and

    (g)   the repeals in Schedule 11 which are consequential on any of those sections or that Schedule.

Consent to treatment

3

(1) The amendments made by section 6 (appropriate treatment test in Part 4 of the 1983 Act) do not affect the application of a certificate under section 57(2)(b) or 58(3)(b) of the 1983 Act given before the date on which the amendments come into force.

(2) The amendments made by sections 27 and 28 (electro-convulsive therapy, etc) do not affect the application of a certificate under subsection (3) of section 58 of the 1983 Act which –

    (a)   relates to electro-convulsive therapy (by virtue of regulations under subsection (1)(a) of that section), and

    (b)   is given before the date on which those amendments come into force.

(3) But any certificate under section 58(3)(b) of the 1983 Act that the patient has not consented to electro-convulsive therapy ceases to apply when those amendments come into force.

Reclassification of patients

4

The amendment made by paragraph 13 of Schedule 1 and the repeal in Schedule 11 of section 66(1)(d) and (fb) of the 1983 Act (which concern a patient's right to apply to a Mental Health Review Tribunal following a report about the form of his mental disorder) do not affect any right to apply in consequence of a report furnished before the date on which the amendment and repeal come into force.

Supervised community treatment

5

Section 32 and the amendments and repeals in Schedules 3 and 11 which are consequential on that section apply to a patient who is liable to be detained under the 1983 Act immediately before the date on which that section and those amendments and repeals come into force, as they apply to a patient who becomes so liable on or after that date.

Nearest relative

6

(1) Subsections (2), (3) and (4)(b) of section 23 (extension of power to appoint acting nearest relative) do not apply to the making of an order under section 29 of the 1983 Act on or after the date on which those provisions come into force, if the application for the order was made before that date.

(2) Subsections (6) and (7) of section 24 (duration of orders appointing nearest relative) do not affect –

    (a)   any order made under section 29 of the 1983 Act before the date on which those subsections come into force, or

    (b)   any order made under that section on or after that date if the application for it was made before that date.

(3) But subsections (2)(a), (4) and (5) of section 24 (applications for discharge and variation) do apply in relation to an order mentioned in sub-paragraph (2)(a) or (b).

(4) Section 25 (restriction of nearest relative's right to apply to tribunal) does not apply in relation to an order mentioned in sub-paragraph (2)(a) or (b).

7

(1) If, by virtue of section 26 (civil partners) coming into force, a person ceases to be a patient's nearest relative, this does not affect –

(a) any application to a Mental Health Review Tribunal under the 1983 Act made by that person, but not determined or withdrawn, before the date on which that section comes into force,

(b) any notice under section 25 of that Act given by that person before that date, or

(c) any application to a county court under section 30(1) of that Act made by that person, but not determined or withdrawn, before that date.

(2) But section 26 does apply to the determination on or after that date of any application under section 29 or 30 of the 1983 Act made before that date.

Independent mental health advocates

8

(1) Section 30 –

(a) applies to a patient who is liable to be detained under the 1983 Act immediately before the commencement date as it applies to a patient who becomes so liable on or after that date;

(b) applies to a patient who is subject to guardianship under that Act immediately before the commencement date as it applies to a patient who becomes so subject on or after that date;

(c) applies to a patient who is a community patient under that Act immediately before the commencement date as it applies to a patient who becomes a community patient on or after that date.

(2) For the purposes of the provisions inserted by that section, a patient is to be treated as a qualifying patient within section 130C(3) of the 1983 Act if –

(a) not being a formal patient, he discussed before the commencement date with a registered medical practitioner or approved clinician the possibility of being given a form of treatment to which section 57 of that Act applies, and

(b) sub-paragraph (4) or (5) applies in relation to him.

(3) A patient is also to be treated for those purposes as a qualifying patient within section 130C(3) of the 1983 Act if –

(a) not having attained the age of 18 years and not being a formal patient, he discussed before the commencement date with a registered medical practitioner or approved clinician the possibility of being given a form of treatment to which section 58A of that Act applies, and

(b) sub-paragraph (4) or (5) applies in relation to him.

(4) This sub-paragraph applies in relation to the patient if, immediately before the commencement date, he has yet to be informed whether or not the treatment is proposed in his case.

(5) This sub-paragraph applies in relation to the patient if, immediately before the commencement date –

(a) he has been informed that the treatment is proposed in his case,
(b) the proposal has not been withdrawn, and
(c) the treatment has not been completed or discontinued.

(6) A qualifying patient in relation to whom sub-paragraph (4) applies and who is informed on or after the commencement date that the treatment is proposed in his case, or in relation to whom sub-paragraph (5) applies, remains a qualifying patient until –

(a) the proposal is withdrawn, or
(b) the treatment is completed or discontinued.

(7) In relation to a patient who is a qualifying patient within section 130C(3) of the 1983 Act by virtue of this paragraph, the responsible person under section 130D of that Act is to be the person with overall responsibility for the patient's case (and subsection (2)(e) of that section is to be read accordingly).

(8) Sub-paragraph (9) applies in relation to a patient –

(a) who is a qualifying patient within section 130C(2) of the 1983 Act by virtue of being a formal patient immediately before the commencement date, or
(b) who is a qualifying patient within section 130C(3) of that Act by virtue of this paragraph.

(9) The steps to be taken under subsection (1) of section 130D of that Act are to be taken on, or as soon as practicable after, the commencement date (and subsection (3) of that section is to be read accordingly).

(10) In this paragraph –

'approved clinician' has the same meaning as in the 1983 Act,
'the commencement date' means the date on which section 30 comes into force, and
'formal patient' means a patient who is –
(a) liable to be detained under the 1983 Act (otherwise than by virtue of section 4, 5(2) or (4), 135 or 136 of that Act),
(b) subject to guardianship under that Act, or
(c) a community patient under that Act.

Applications and references to Mental Health Review Tribunal

9

(1) The amendments made by section 37 apply in relation to a patient who is liable to be detained under the 1983 Act immediately before the date on which the amendments come into force as they apply in relation to one who becomes so liable on or after that date.

(2) The repeal in paragraph 20(b) of Schedule 3 of the reference in section 69(2)(b) of the 1983 Act to section 45B(2) of that Act (which concerns the right of a patient subject to a hospital direction to apply to a Mental Health Review Tribunal in the period of six months beginning with the date of the direction) does not affect any right to apply by virtue of a hospital direction dated before the date on which the repeal comes into force.

SCHEDULE 11
Repeals and revocations

Section 55

PART 1
REMOVAL OF CATEGORIES OF MENTAL DISORDER

Reference	*Extent of repeal or revocation*
Juries Act 1974 (c 23)	In Schedule 1, paragraph 4(1).
Mental Health Act 1983 (c 20)	In section 1(2), the definitions of –
	(a) 'severe mental impairment' and 'severely mentally impaired',
	(b) 'mental impairment' and 'mentally impaired', and
	(c) 'psychopathic disorder'.
	In section 7(2)(a), the words ', being mental illness, severe mental impairment, psychopathic disorder or mental impairment and his mental disorder is'.
	Section 11(6).
	In section 15(3), the words from '; but this subsection' to the end.
	Section 16.
	Section 20(9).
	Section 21B(8) and (9).
	In section 37 –

Reference	Extent of repeal or revocation
	(a) in subsection (3), the words 'as being a person suffering from mental illness or severe mental impairment', and
	(b) subsection (7).
	In section 45A, subsections (10) and (11).
	Section 47(4).
	Section 55(3).
	In section 66(1), paragraphs (d) and (fb) (and the word 'or' at the end of those paragraphs).
	Section 72(5).
	Section 92(3).
	In Part 1 of Schedule 1 –
	(a) in paragraph 2, the word '16,',
	(b) paragraph 3, and
	(c) in paragraph 6, paragraph (b) (and the word 'and' immediately preceding it).
	In Schedule 5 –
	(a) in paragraph 37(5), the words from ', and he shall be so treated' to the end, and
	(b) paragraph 39.
Mental Health (Patients in the Community) Act 1995 (c 52)	In Schedule 1, paragraph 10(4).
Mental Capacity Act 2005 (c 9)	In Schedule 4, in paragraph 23(1), the words '(within the meaning of the Mental Health Act)'.
Mental Health (Care and Treatment) (Scotland) Act 2003 (Consequential Provisions) Order 2005 (S.I. 2005/2078)	In Schedule 1, paragraph 2(8).

PART 2
REPLACEMENT OF 'TREATABILITY' AND 'CARE' TESTS

Reference	*Extent of repeal or revocation*

Mental Health Act 1983 (c 20)	In section 3(2), paragraph (b) (and the word 'and' at the end of that paragraph).
	
	In section 20(4) –
	
	  (a) paragraph (b) (and the word 'and' at the end of that paragraph), and
	
	  (b) the words from 'but, in the case of mental illness' to the end.
	
	Section 72(2).

Reference	*Extent of repeal or revocation*

Mental Health Act 1983 (c 20)	In section 3(2), paragraph (b) (and the word 'and' at the end of that paragraph).
	
	In section 20(4) –
	
	  (a) paragraph (b) (and the word 'and' at the end of that paragraph), and
	
	  (b) the words from 'but, in the case of mental illness' to the end.
	
	Section 72(2).

PART 3
APPROVED CLINICIANS AND RESPONSIBLE CLINICIANS

Reference	*Extent of repeal or revocation*
Mental Health Act 1983 (c 20)	Section 20(10). In section 21B(10), the definition of 'appropriate medical officer'. In section 61(3), the words 'to the responsible medical officer'.
Health and Social Care (Community Health and Standards) Act 2003 (c 43)	In Schedule 4, paragraph 51.
Civil Partnership Act 2004 (c 33)	In Schedule 27, paragraph 86(a).

Reference	Extent of repeal or revocation
National Health Service (Consequential Provisions) Act 2006 (c 43)	In Schedule 1, paragraph 63.

PART 4
SAFEGUARDS FOR PATIENTS

Reference	Extent of repeal or revocation
Mental Health Act 1983	In section 29 – (a) in subsection (2), the words from 'but in relation to' to the end, and (b) in subsection (3), the word 'or' at the end of paragraph (c).

PART 5
SUPERVISED COMMUNITY TREATMENT

Reference	Extent of repeal or revocation
Mental Health Act 1983	In section 18(4), the words from 'and, in determining' to the end. Sections 25A to 25J. In section 29(3)(d), the words 'from hospital or guardianship'. In section 32(2)(c), the words 'or to after-care under supervision'. In section 34 – (a) in subsection (1), the definitions of 'the community responsible medical officer' and 'the supervisor', and (b) subsection (1A). In section 66(1) – (a) paragraphs (ga), (gb) and (gc) (and the word 'or' at the end of each of those paragraphs), and (b) in sub-paragraph (i), the words from 'or, in the cases' to the end. In section 66(2) –

Reference	*Extent of repeal or revocation*
	(a) in paragraph (d), the words 'and (gb)', and
	(b) paragraph (fa).
	In section 67(1), the words 'or to after-care under supervision'.
	In section 69(2)(b), the words '45B(2), 46(3),'.
	Section 72(4A).
	In section 76(1), the words from 'or to after-care' to 'leaves hospital)'.
	Section 117(2A).
	Section 127(2A).
	In section 145 –
	(a) in subsection (1), the definitions of 'the responsible after-care bodies' and 'supervision application', and
	(b) subsection (1A).
	In section 146, the words from '128' to 'guardianship)'.
	In Part 1 of Schedule 1 –
	(a) in paragraph 2, the words ', 25A, 25B', and
	(b) paragraph 8A.
Mental Health (Patients in the Community) Act 1995 (c 52)	Section 1(1).
	In Schedule 1 –
	(a) in paragraph 2, paragraph (c) (and the word 'and' immediately preceding it),
	(b) in paragraph 11, paragraph (a) (and the word 'and' at the end of that paragraph), and
	(c) paragraphs 3, 4, 6, 7, 8(2), 10(1) to (3), 12, 13, 18 and 20.
Crime (Sentences) Act 1997 (c 43)	In Schedule 4, paragraph 12(8).
National Health Service Reform and Health Care Professions Act 2002 (c 17)	In Schedule 2, paragraphs 43 to 45.

Reference	Extent of repeal or revocation
Civil Partnership Act 2004 (c 33)	In Schedule 27, in paragraph 86, paragraph (b) (and the word 'and' immediately preceding it).

PART 6
ORGANISATION OF TRIBUNALS

Reference	Extent of repeal or revocation
Mental Health Act 1983 (c 20)	In section 78(6), the words ', if for any reason he is unable to act,'.
	In section 143(2), the words 'or 65'.
	In paragraph 4 of Schedule 2, the words ', if for any reason he is unable to act,'.
Health Authorities Act 1995 (c 17)	In Schedule 1, paragraph 107(13).

PART 7
CROSS-BORDER ARRANGEMENTS

Reference	Extent of repeal or revocation
Mental Health Act 1983	In section 80(1), the words 'or subject to guardianship' and the words 'or, as the case may be, for receiving him into guardianship'.
	In section 88(3) –
	(a) the words 'to Scotland or Northern Ireland',
	(b) paragraph (a), and
	(c) in paragraph (b), the words 'in Northern Ireland,'.
	In section 146, the words from '88' to '138)'.
Mental Health (Care and Treatment) (Scotland) Act 2003 (Consequential Provisions) Order 2005 (S.I. 2005/2078)	Articles 1(5), 2 and 3.
In Schedule 1, paragraph 2(5).	In Schedule 1, paragraph 2(5).

PART 8
RESTRICTED PATIENTS

Reference	Extent of repeal or revocation
Colonial Prisoners Removal Act 1884 (c 31)	In section 10(3)(a), the words ', made without limitation of time'.
Mental Health Act 1983	In section 41(1), the words ', either without limit of time or during such period as may be specified in the order'.
	In section 42(4)(b), the words from ', and, if the restriction order was made for a specified period,' to the end.
	In section 44(3), the words ', made without limitation of time'.
	In section 81(7), the words 'restriction order or' in each place,
	In section 81A(3) – (a) the words 'restriction order or' in each place, and (b) the words 'order or'.
	In section 84(2), the words ', made without limitation of time'.
	In section 91(2), the words 'at any time before the end of the period for which those orders would have continued in force'.

PART 9
MISCELLANEOUS

Reference	Extent of repeal or revocation
Children Act 1989 (c 41)	In Schedule 13, paragraph 48(5).

PART 10
DEPRIVATION OF LIBERTY

Reference	Extent of repeal or revocation
Mental Capacity Act 2005 (c 9)	Section 6(5). Section 11(6). Section 20(13).

INDEX

References are to paragraph numbers.